# HUMAN DEVELOPMENT

## Traditional and Contemporary Theories

## Doris Bergen

PEARSON

Prentice Hall

Upper Saddle River, New Jersey 07458

Library of Congress Cataloging-in-Publication Data

Bergen, Doris.
    Human development : traditional and contemporary theories / by Doris Bergen.
        p. cm.
    ISBN 0-13-134397-1
    1.   Developmental psychology.    I   Title.
    BF713.B462 2007
        155—dc22

                                                            2006102007

**Executive Editor:** Jeff Marshall
**Editor-in-Chief:** Leah Jewell
**Project Manager (Editorial):** LeeAnn Doherty
**Editorial Assistant:** Jennifer Puma
**Marketing Manager:** Jeanette Moyer
**Marketing Assistant:** Laura Kennedy
**Assistant Managing Editor (Production):**
    Maureen Richardson
**Production Liaison:** Nicole Girrbach/Kathy Sleys
**Production Editor:** Patty Donovan—Laserwords/Pine
    Tree
**Permissions Researcher:** Kathleen Karcher

**Manufacturing Buyer:** Sherry Lewis
**Interior Design:** Laserwords/Pine Tree
**Art Director:** Jayne Conte
**Cover Design:** Bruce Kenselaar
**Cover Illustration/Photo:** Getty Images Inc.—Stone
    Allstock
**Photo Researcher:** Beaura (Kathy) Ringrose
**Image Permission Coordinator:** Robert Farrell
**Composition:** Laserwords/Pine Tree
**Full-Service Project Management:** Patty Donovan,
    Pine Tree Composition
**Printer/Binder:** R.R. Donelley & Sons

Pearson Education Ltd., London
Pearson Education Singapore, Pte. Ltd.
Pearson Education, Canada, Ltd.
Pearson Education–Japan
Pearson Education Australia PTY, Ltd.

Pearson Education North Asia Ltd.
Pearson Educación de Mexico, S.A. de C.V.
Pearson Education Malaysia, Pte. Ltd.
Pearson Education, Upper Saddle River, New Jersey

10 9 8 7 6 5 4 3 2 1
ISBN-13: 978-0-13-134397-9
ISBN-10:    0-13-134397-1

This book is dedicated to my husband, children, grandchildren, parents, other family members, friends, colleagues, and students of preschool to university ages, all of whom have made me ponder both the glorious achievements and the complex challenges inherent in human developmental change.

# Contents

## 8. Theories With Major Emphasis on Sociomoral and Gender Role Development    144

## 9. Further Theoretical Perspectives on Sociomoral and Gender Role Development    160

# Preface

## Rationale for the Approach

Although this book will do many of the things that most books on human development theories do—present ideas of individual theorists, evaluate these theoretical ideas, and provide conceptual schema for comparing these ideas—it is designed to achieve *six* additional objectives. The *first* is to emphasize the major developmental domain focus of each theorist or theoretical school and compare their ideas with those of other theorists whose focus is similar. It will also show the linkages between earlier theories and newer, less well-developed theories and proto-theories to demonstrate how some theories have had great influence on other theorists and/or have changed over time as newer and older ideas are revised and integrated. For example, personality/social/emotional development has been a focus of many theoretical ideas, and contemporary theoretical ideas emphasizing contextual, ecological, and system factors have roots in early person/environment approaches. The *second* objective is to provide life span theoretical perspectives in a systematic manner by including summaries of the theoretical work of such theorists. The *third* objective is to include relevant theoretical views of women whose work has sometimes been overlooked in theoretical texts and to incorporate ideas of theory-builders from a range of world cultures and ethnic backgrounds by including their views and research findings when applicable. Only recently has the work of female theorists and theorists from other cultures gained greater notice; at the time of their work Western male theorists' prominence often overshadowed other perspectives. The *fourth* objective is to make students aware of how recent nonlinear dynamical systems theory is beginning to influence human development theory. This perspective may strongly alter the course of future developmental theory-building. The *fifth* objective is to provide opportunities for student applications of concepts from various theoretical views to problems of practice by including relevant research and practice applications, case study examples, and outlines of basic developmental knowledge. The *sixth* objective is to introduce students to some theoretical "voices" by including original writings for further reading and study. The *overall goal* of the book is to help students in education, special education, family studies, social work, counseling, nursing, school psychology, developmental psychology, or other disciplines acquire a personally relevant understanding of the theories and to gain a meaningful and deep understanding of theoretical ideas that will be useful for them in the practice of their professional lives.

## Organization of the Book

The book is organized differently from other books on human development theories in that, after a general introduction defining and categorizing theories, addressing historical/cultural influences on theory development, and discussing basic research approaches and practical applications (chapters 1 and 2), it focuses most chapters on theories that are especially relevant for understanding specific developmental areas.

Although many theorists touch on numerous developmental domains, their major contributions have often been in one or two areas of focus. For example, theories such as Freud's and Erikson's have been especially informative about personality and social–emotional development. Piaget and Vygotsky have primarily focused on cognitive developmental issues, Chomsky on language development, and Kohlberg on sociomoral and gender role development. The theoretical ideas of others, such as Bowlby, Case, and Damon, have been influenced by these ideas, and they have expanded theoretical perspectives within the same developmental domains. Chapters 3 and 4 focus on personality and social–emotional theoretical domains; chapters 6 and 7 present cognitive and language perspectives; chapters 8 and 9 address sociomoral and gender role issues; and chapter 11 considers physical–motor and perceptual development, as well as newer neuropsychological and behavioral genetics perspectives. Chapter 12 addresses theoretical ideas that view development as a systemic process, and it includes ecological, bioecological, developmental psychobiological, and nonlinear dynamical systems perspectives. Interspersed are two life span chapters, chapter 5 and chapter 10, which describe similar theoretical issues from the perspectives of life span development theorists. The emerging theoretical ideas may have the potential to integrate all developmental domains and eventually lead to an integrated "grand" theory of human development.

## Special Features

Each of the sections focusing on a particular area of development is accompanied by a brief overview of the major "milestone" developmental changes that occur over the life span in that domain. Chapters also are accompanied by references to a set of original writings of the major theorists discussed in that section. The purpose of the inclusion of these writings is to give students the "flavor" of the theorists' perspective expressed in his/her own words. Some of these selected writings are provided in a later section of the text, so that instructors can focus in depth on certain theoretical writings and/or individual students can delve more deeply into the work of those theorists of special interest to them.

## Acknowledgments

The manuscript preparation was greatly aided by Rebecca Yang, who researched source materials and permission addresses, reviewed chapter references, located and formatted figures, compiled records, and provided encouragement when needed. Assistance related to permission seeking and indexing was provided by Emily Beattie and Caren Oyor. My thanks also go to the graduate students in my human development theory classes, who over the past few years gave me honest feedback and useful ideas for content and activities relevant to this manuscript preparation. The contribution of all these persons is greatly appreciated.

I would also like to thank the reviewers whose valuable input helped shape this text: Judith A. Schwartz, University of Missouri-Columbia; Amy Hackney, Georgia Southern University; Connor Walters, Illinois State University; Dianne Draper, Iowa State University; Suzanne Gaskins, Northeastern Illinois University; Michael A. Vandehey, Midwestern State University; Teresa K. DeBacker, University of Oklahoma; Steven Pulos, University of Northern Colorado; Michael E. McCarty, Texas Tech University.

# Defining and Categorizing Theories and Exploring their Historical Roots

One of the most pervasive characteristics of humans is their need to explain what, how, when, where, and especially why life events occur. This need to understand the meaning of their experiences ranges from simple attempts at explanations of ordinary personal life events (e.g., Why did that happen to me? Why did he/she do that?) to elaborate explanations of how life originated and how the universe began (e.g., evolution, relativity, string theory). Not surprisingly, questions of what, how, when, where, and why human development occurs have been the focus of many theories. In earliest times these theories were derived primarily from religious or mystical narratives. For example, most, if not all, cultures have "creation stories," rules for child rearing, and ceremonial markers for certain periods of development, such as puberty, all of which are derived from the culture's "theories" about human development. As scientific inquiry techniques have become pervasive in recent centuries, the search for explanations of human development have been primarily scientifically based and supported by various types of empirical evidence. The questions that both traditional scientific theories and emerging contemporary theories attempt to answer, however, continue to be similar to those asked in earliest times:

- What are the major types of human developmental change?
- How do various factors (biological, environmental) influence developmental change?

- When do human developmental changes occur (sequence and timing)?
- Where in the organism do the processes of change manifest themselves (structures)?
- Why do these developmental changes occur (processes, functions)?

An underlying purpose of scientifically based theory is to guide the collection of empirical evidence that can lead to predictions and thus demonstrate the *validity* (accurate representation) of the theory. Another reason for interest in theories, of course, is to give guidance to those who wish to influence human developmental change, such as parents, educators, counselors, psychologists, medical personnel, and policy makers. Theories derived from various sources have been *useful* (effective in practice) to these groups even before the scientific criteria of empirical validation was expected. For present-day theories, however, both of these questions are important for determining the value of a theory:

- What types of empirical evidence have been obtained to support the validity of the major theoretical constructs and enable predictions or probabilities to be accurately made?
- What useful guidance for solving practical problems of child rearing, education, clinical intervention, and health promotion does the theory provide to promote optimum development (as defined by the particular culture)?

To determine the potential usefulness of theories and to compare scientifically based traditional and contemporary human development theories, it is first necessary to know the definition of a scientific theory, the strengths of scientific theories, and the limitations of theories (these are described in chapter 2). It is also helpful to understand the roots from which present developmental theory grew and to have a categorization scheme to help in organizing theoretical ideas. This chapter provides the historical background and a framework for categorization of specific theories of human development.

# Understanding Theoretical Perspectives

## *Defining Theory*

Although all of us have "naive" theories (Baldwin, 1968) that may explain everyday events and changes in human lives, scientifically based theories have characteristics that make them especially useful. The definition of scientific theory stated by Hall and Lindzey (1957, 1970) is still accurate. They defined scientific theory as:

> A set of relevant assumptions systematically related to each other, together with empirical definitions.

The words in this statement all have importance in establishing the credibility of a theory, as follows:

- A set: a group of ideas
- Relevant assumptions: based on beliefs about a phenomenon

- Systematically related to each other: that are connected in an organized way
- With empirical definitions: having explicit terms that are required to understand the theoretical concepts

Within this broader definition, Ausubel, Sullivan, and Ives (1980) have stated the definition of theories of *child* development, as follows:

> A developmental theory is concerned with the nature and regulation of human structural, functional, and behavioral change over time.

The words in this definition are also especially important:

- Nature: the qualities
- Regulation: the process parameters of these qualities
- Structural: the physical characteristics of the organism
- Functional: the biological and psychological processes occurring within the organism
- Behavioral: the human actions that accompany structural and functional phenomena
- Change: the processes of differentiation and organization
- Over time: throughout the developing years

This definition stresses that "change over time" is a major emphasis of developmental theory building. That is, a central question is how children's development occurs over periods of months and years and, most importantly, what factors (structural or functional) affect that development. The life span perspective on human development is congruent with that definition; however, as Goulet and Baltes (1970) state, it also is

> concerned with the description and explication of ontogenetic (age-related) behavioral change from birth to death; that is, throughout the life span.

In evaluating human development theories, it is important to consider how well each theory meets the criteria of these definitions, what types of empirical evidence support the particular theoretical constructs (credibility and external validity), and how useful the theory is in answering the questions posed earlier.

## Present-Day Theoretical Views of Nature/Nurture Interactions

Most theories of human development take a position on a core assumption about the developmental process: the amount of emphasis the theory places on nature or nurture as influential in development. During the 20th century, there was great debate over whether development was primarily governed by nature (i.e., genetics, maturation of biological structures) or nurture (i.e., child-rearing methods, cultural values, planned learning experiences, unplanned life events). Present-day theorists usually embrace some type of interactionist perspective; that is, theorists do not usually assert that one of these factors is the only explanatory dimension. For example, although theorists studying genetic influences focus on "nature," they have noted that results of their twin studies show about 40% to

50% of development can be attributed to genetics (Plomin, 1986, 1994). Thus, they acknowledge the importance of the shared and unique environments of individuals with similar genetic makeup (Scarr, 1992). Similarly, theorists who focus on social, historical, and culturally related ecological factors also acknowledge that biology and genetics are interacting factors within these contexts (Bronfenbrenner, 2005; Vygotsky, 1978). With the advent of research techniques that can more carefully measure neurological and genetic factors, these dimensions are being studied further, and there is some recurrence of debate about the extent of influence held by genetic and maturational factors (i.e., "wired-in") as compared to brain/environment interaction factors (i.e., "pluripotentiality"), especially in areas such as language development (e.g., Bates, 2005; Pinker, 2002). Although early theorists made assumptions about the original moral nature of humankind—innately evil, good, or neutral—theorists of today rarely address this question. In their writings, however, it seems evident that scientifically based theorists do not hold to the "innate evil" perspective. This view is still prevalent is some theories of religious origin, however.

## Historical Roots of Human Development Theories

Although a few Western philosophers such as Plato and Aristotle (see Friedlander, 1973; Ostwald, 1962) and Eastern philosophers such as Confucius (see Chan, 1963) addressed issues related to children's development and education, in general children were not the focus of developmental attention during much of historical time. This assumption is based on reviews of written records, however, and because through much of history there were few such records, it is possible that children's development was a concern in preliterate cultures. According to Eiss (1994), at least in Western society, "For hundreds of years, children were viewed as miniature adults, whose sole purpose was to become big adults as quickly as possible. Since childhood did not exist . . . there was no promotion of a child's perspective . . . (p. 1). This may be at least partly a result of the generally short life span of the times (about 30 to 40 years), which made childhood short (about to age 7). Usually children were in the workforce by age 8, and marriages occurred for girls shortly after puberty (about age 12). In the late 16th century the idea of children's need for special training because they were "born in sin" gained prominence, and in the 17th century, ideas for educating children became more prominent (Eiss, 1994). The themes expressed by early writers on developmental issues still carry some influence even to the present day.

### Early Philosophical Theories

Although the Greek philosophers, Plato and Aristotle, focused their writing on broader issues, both did address the child's nature and need for education. Plato was concerned with the development of the mind, and he posited three stages of mind development: appetites, spirit, and soul. Appetites composed the initial mind of the child, and thus nurturing of spirit and soul were needed. Although Plato believed that nature played a big role in this development, he also thought that the innate ideas of the mind could be developed further by playful training (Paidia). In his book of *Laws* (Laws, 643bc) Plato asserted, "The correct way to bring up and educate a child is to use his playtime to imbue his soul with the greatest possible devotion to the occupation in which he will have to excel when he matures" (referenced in Morris, 1998). Plato also posited different stages of adult life up to the age of 30 to 35 and suggested that if these stages were accomplished, the individuals could become scientists and politicians in later life (Groffmann, 1970). Plato believed that the sum of all formative influences (Paideia) allowed the adult to reach excellence, "the ultimate end of a human life for all the classical philosophers" (Morris, 1998, p. 110). Aristotle introduced the concept of development, especially as it related to species development (Morris, 1998). He posited three age levels of human development, each of which was 7 years long. These "break points" are not so different from those marked by later-day theorists: age 7, age 14, and age 21. Spiritual and philosophical advice from early Eastern philosophers also focused greatly on training children to think and feel appropriately. For example, Confucius stressed the duties children had to family and ultimately to society, and he outlined the careful training required for a child to develop well, which meant becoming a respectful and ethically responsible member of the family, community, and state (Chan, 1963).

### Western Theories of the 17th and 18th Centuries

As the Puritan view of "original sin" was emphasized during the late 16th century, the development of children's character became a focus in both England and the American colonies. Religious leaders such as John Calvin and St. Aquinas both had stated that infants were born in sin, and thus children's early experiences were vital for curbing behaviors related to their initially sinful nature. Parents and other adults were expected to lead children away from their innately evil ways, including being ready to avoid spoiling the child by sparing the rod. Although this view was harsh, it "was the first to separate the child's world from that of the adult and take on the task of helping children get safely through it" although the educational result was ". . . that children should be taught what to think, not how to think . . ." (Eiss, 1994, p. 5).

During the 17th and 18th centuries, when this Puritan view was influential, other theoretical views were being promoted in Europe. John Amos Comenius, an educator from Czechoslovakia, wrote two books outlining a view of education that suggested children be given interesting and age-appropriate materials to help them learn. Comenius's books (1632, 1657), one of which was illustrated with pictures, were translated into 40 languages. In England, John Locke (1693) also attacked the idea of children's innate evil by asserting that they were really born as *tabula rasa* (blank slates) and should be taught through play rather than fear, which would promote their rational and individual needs. It represented a "neoclassic" view that logic and reason were humans' highest ability. His view of child rearing was that children's abilities could be formed by positive experiences and training directed by adults.

In France, Jean Jacques Rousseau (1762) also attacked the harsh Puritan view; however, his view was derived from a "romanticism" perspective. He stated that children were born innately good and should be kept uncorrupted from the experiences of the civilized world. Thus, he stressed giving children the freedom to develop in their own natural ways. His view was that the adult did not need to lead the child in the right way but should merely provide assistance to the child in his search for knowledge (his view focused on boys). Adults who followed Rousseau's suggestions attempted to follow the child's natural interests, but many took this to extremes, centering efforts on finding instructive value in every activity of their "little angels."

According to Eiss (1994), each of these theoretical perspectives has continued to influence later psychological theories of child development: (a) children as little adults, needing only to gain practical knowledge; (b) children as innately evil and vulnerable, needing adult efforts to drive out evil; (c) children as blank slates, needing adult efforts to drive them in the right direction; and (d) children as pure and uncorrupted, needing adult accompaniment in their search for knowledge.

During this same time period (1835–1883), there was a beginning interest in the subject of aging and the first scientific writings on the relation of age to such factors as creativity, sound perception, and individual differences in aging were published (Charles, 1970).

## Western Theoretical Educational Ideas of the Late 19th to Early 20th Centuries

In the late 19th century, a number of European theorists who were concerned with children's education stressed a view that held both nature and nurture aspects. Most prominent in these times were Johann Pestalozzi (1894), Friedrich Froebel (1887), and Maria Montessori (1914), all of whom drew on Rousseau's view of children's natural goodness and innate motivation toward their own development. These theorists suggested ways children's natural inclinations for play and activity could be channeled into developmental progress. Pestalozzi (1894) designed a system of educational practice to carry out Rousseau's views of education. He advocated giving children opportunities to pursue their own ideas in active ways and recommended that teachers should do direct observation and reflect on those observations to enhance children's development. Pestalozzi's views subsequently influenced both Froebel and Montessori, as well as Horace Mann (1868), who brought these educational ideas to the United States. Froebel (1887), the father of the kindergarten movement, advocated giving "gifts" to children to extend their natural play activities and designed "occupations" (i.e., modes, sequence, and order of presentation) to further certain developmental goals (see Ransbury, 1991). Montessori developed Children's Houses that were initially focused on "raw and unkempt children" (1972, p. 38) but later extended to many settings. They were founded on a set of "scientific principles" related to allowing children's free expression within a highly ordered environment. The purpose of this environment was to assist children in gaining independence; this required providing educational activities that were initially close to their existing abilities and providing ordered/sequenced materials that would enhance those abilities over time (Montessori, 1914/1965).

The perspectives of these theorists were especially influential in educational practice related to young children, and remnants of their views are still evident in present-day kindergartens, preschools, and Montessori schools, as well as in the "developmentally appropriate practice" orientation of many early childhood educators. These educationally oriented theorists were especially concerned about improving educational practice to foster the positive developmental trajectory of children from "at-risk" situations (e.g., poverty, disabilities); however, other early theorists showed little interest in these issues.

Theorists who created the field of developmental psychology were interested in understanding "universal" developmental issues rather than in finding solutions related to improving individual developmental differences or solving problems of educational practice.

### Western Psychological Theories of the Early 20th Century

At the beginning of the 20th century, the emerging field of psychology had some proponents who were beginning to apply psychological principles to children's development, and one of the most prominent early theorists was G. Stanley Hall (1920, 1924), who promoted child development as a separate field worthy of study in the United States. Hall identified adolescence as a particular developmental period and characterized it as a time of "storm and stress." He accepted the concepts of Darwinian theory, which became popular at that time, and saw children's development as a replication of the stages of evolution. He was particularly interested in children's play as evidence of this "theory of recapitulation" because he thought play demonstrated "the motor habits and spirit of the past persisting in the present" (Spodek & Saracho, 1998, p. 10). Although the theory of recapitulation is not generally accepted today, Hall's emphasis on knowing the developmental changes that occur throughout childhood and adolescence was influential in promoting the field of "child study." When he was 78, Hall also published a book about his own aging process (1923). During this period, Sigmund Freud (1936, 1938) was also beginning his writing on developmental issues, and he was invited by Dr. Hall to present his views in the United States.

Other U.S. theorists who were active in the field of child development theory during the early 20th century were John Dewey (1910, 1916), Arnold Gesell (1925), and Myrtle McGraw (1935). Dewey, who was influenced both by Darwinian theory and the work of Hall, was the leader of the functional school of psychology and believed that development resulted from the interaction of an active organism with the environment. He wrote seminal books on the theory of knowledge and on applications of this theory to educational practice. In his work on the role of education in a democracy, he drew on Rousseau's views that native structures and functions, social influences, and direct action on the environment are all essential for optimum child development (Dewey, 1916). Gesell, in his laboratory at Yale University, gave children various tasks that enabled him to observe their development in four areas: motor, adaptive (cognitive), language, and personal–social. He initially studied infancy but because of his interest in the longitudinal nature of development, his studies eventually included the study of developmental change through adolescence. With his research team, which included Louise Bates Ames and Frances Ilg, he described the sequences of development through age 16 in all four of the domains he defined. McGraw primarily studied how maturational and environmental factors influenced the physical–motor development of a set of twins. She had an ongoing professional relationship with

Dewey whose theories of inquiry informed and were informed by McGraw's research (Dalton, 1996). Dewey's interest was in problem solving and judgment; however, he believed these were grounded in motor development and found McGraw's research useful in his theoretical work.

Another perspective was promoted by Edward Thorndike (1914), who conducted research demonstrating the "law of effect," which posits behavior changes based on contingent consequences. He is considered the founder of the field of educational psychology. Another theorist of this time, John Watson (1914), applied principles from this new field of scientific study, behaviorism (i.e., learning theory) in experimental research. He asserted that learning occurs through the use of external reinforcements and that children's developmental change can be explained using behaviorist principles. A famous quote of Watson's about being able to use behaviorist principles to make any child into any type of adult exemplifies the extreme of this theoretical position.

Theorists who were educated in Europe and the Soviet Union were also active during the early to mid-20th century, but much of their work was not translated until the latter part of the century. These include the early writings of Piaget (1924, 1936) and Vygotsky (1963). One European-trained theorist who immigrated to the United States was Kurt Lewin (1931, 1936). He was influential in promoting the view that development can only be understood as a function of the person/environment interaction, and he is also recognized as the founder of the field of social psychology. Many of the themes addressed by these early theorists have counterparts in present-day society, and echos of their ideas can be found in major developmental theories, as well as in the contemporary theories discussed later.

## The Rise of Learning Theory

The perspective that gained increasing prominence in 20th-century U.S. psychology was one that stressed the environmental aspects of development rather than innate good or bad character. Building on the early scientific ideas of Locke, the experiments of Russian scientist Pavlov, and the work of American theorist John Watson, learning theory was promoted strongly by B. F. Skinner (1945a, 1945b, 1974), who viewed human development as a product of environmental experiences (nurture) and posited that developmental change was really a result of cumulative learning experiences promoted by external reinforcement. He believed that humans learned in exactly the same way as other animals; that is, reinforcements provided by the environment shape existing behaviors and result in learning. Thus, the cumulative effects of learning account for stable behavior changes. Although Skinner discussed some developmental issues within that framework when his own children were young (Skinner, 1945b), he did not really provide a theory of human development because his theoretical framework did not include the assumptions of developmental theory. That is, he was not interested in the internal structures and functions related to developmental change or in studying qualitative changes in such structures and function; rather, he saw all development as the result of additive learning experiences. He viewed visible behavior change due to reinforcing conditions as the only important element to consider.

Using Skinner's theory of learning as a springboard, however, a number of researchers and theorists did extend his perspective into issues related to children's longer term development. For example, Sidney Bijou and Donald Baer (1978) applied behaviorist learning principles to the study of young children's behavior and identified associations between existing responses and new consequences. They did not attempt to look at universal stage changes but rather at individuals' changes related to specific reinforcing conditions. They saw development as a result of a cumulative interaction history and did not see it as related necessarily to an individual's age level. They attempted to explain all developmental changes as changes in behavior, even those related to "complex interactions," such as self-management, decision making, and emotional control. Also, Kendler and Kendler (1962) studied children's concept learning using principles of behaviorism and found differences between how young children learned concepts (each as separate perceptions) as compared to older children (verbally mediated associations among perceptual features).

Alfred Bandura initially incorporated a number of behavioral terms into his social learning theory (1977), although his later work stressed internal and developmental aspects (i. e., social cognitive theory, 1986). Behaviorist learning theory influence has continued to be evident in the work of information processing theorists, in particular those studying the development of specific abilities, such as memory or problem solving (e.g., Kail & Bisanz, 1992; Siegler, 1983). The most prominent present-day uses of the theoretical ideas of Skinner, however, focus on behavioral interventions designed to make changes in learning specific to verbal, reading, and math skills and to help children with special needs such as autism learn appropriate behavior. Built on the work of Bijou and colleagues (1964, 1971), the method is now called Applied Behavior Analysis—ABA. Although there are undoubtedly many developmental implications of this work, the major recent emphasis of most learning theory proponents has been on more immediate changes in behavior rather than in charting developmental trends over longer time periods. Thus, with the exception of Bijou's continuing interest in developmental issues, in particular, ones focused on exceptional children (1971), learning theory has taken a different path than developmental theory in both its goals of research and methodological practices. However, the roots of information processing theory, which has had a strong impact on developmental theory, reside in this tradition.

## Categorizing Theories Based on Philosophical Assumptions and Perspectives

Sometimes the plethora of theories seems overwhelming, and consequently various writers have attempted to categorize them, using factors such as their relative emphasis on nature or nurture, holistic or reductionist perspective, and experimental or clinical research methods. Because the phenomena of interest are very complex, intentional theory builders usually attack their developmental questions from some accessible approach, and these approaches are often derived from what has been called the "worldview" of the theorist. Writers of theoretical texts often use an organizing schema to describe these worldviews. For example, Goldhaber (2000) and Thomas (2005) have used as their categorical base the writings of Stephen Pepper (1945), who divided traditional theories of all types (not just those of human development) into four categories. They use three of Pepper's terms: (a) mechanistic, (b) organismic, and (c) contextual, each of which has a concrete image as a metaphor for that worldview: (a) the machine, (b) the living organism, and (c) the historical act. Another categorization scheme has been provided by Robbie Case (1999), who categorized these three perspectives as (a) empiricist, (b) rationalist, and (c) sociohistorical. Case discussed these perspectives in relation to cognitive and language theories; however, they can also be applied to theories focused on other domains (e.g., social-emotional), and they are discussed further here as one way to categorize theoretical ideas. More recently, a distinction has been made between linear and nonlinear theories in a number of scientific disciplines (e.g., physics), and this distinction has also been a useful categorization mechanism for developmental theory.

Case characterized the *empiricist* perspective as viewing knowledge as "acquired by a process in which the sensory organs first detect stimuli in the external world and the mind then detects the customary patterns or conjunctions in these stimuli" (1999, pp. 23–24). These theorists are concerned with observing processes of stimuli discrimination, encoding, association, and transfer. The *rationalist* perspective asserts that knowledge "is acquired by a process in which the human mind imposes order on the data that the senses provide; the mind does not merely detect order in these data" and thus, there are "foundational concepts with which children come equipped at birth" (Case, 1999, p. 26). These theorists are concerned with observing the changes in these foundational concepts with age. In regard to the sociohistorical perspective, Case stated that these theorists see knowledge having "its primary origin in the social and material history of the culture of which the subject is a part and in the tools, concepts, and symbol systems that the culture has developed for interacting with its environment" (1999, pp. 28). Theorists with this view analyze how the social and physical aspects of human cultures affect development of succeeding generations of children. See Table 1.1 for Case's comparisons of these perspectives.

Both empiricist and rationalist theoretical perspectives can also be categorized as *linear* theories, that is, having a perspective focused on predicting developmental directional progress toward higher levels, whereas sociohistorical, bioecological, and dynamical system theories can be thought of as *nonlinear,* that is, having multiple perspectives focused on examining probabilities resulting from the interaction of many levels of factors. Empiricist and rationalist theories have tended to focus on explanations of developmental phenomena that can be applied universally across all cultures, while sociohistorical and ecological theories attach much importance to the phenomena that result in culture-specific developmental change. Whereas nonlinear dynamical system theories are derived from the empiricist tradition of the "hard" sciences, their methods of empirical study appear to incorporate both universal and nonuniversal elements. They characterize human development phenomena as forms of complex dynamical

**Table 1.1**   Comparison of Three Views of Knowledge

| Psychological Constitutes | Empiricist | Rationalist | Sociohistorical |
|---|---|---|---|
| Knowledge | Repertoire of patterns or problems that an individual has learned to detect and operations that one can execute on them. | Structure created by the human mind and evaluated according to rational criteria, such as coherence, consistence, and parsimony. | Creation of a social group as it engages in its daily interaction and praxis and both adapts to and transforms the environment around it. |
| Learning | Process that generates knowledge; begins when one is exposed to a new pattern or problem and continues as one learns to respond to that pattern and generalize one's response to other contexts. | Process that takes place when the mind applies an existing structure to new experience to understand it. | Process of being initiated into the life of a group, so that one can assume a role in its daily praxis. |
| Development | Cumulative learning. | Long-term, transformational change that takes place in the structures into which new experience is assimilated. | The emergence and training of the symbolic and tool-using capacities that make social initiation possible. |
| Intelligence | Individual trait that sets a limit on the maximum rate at which cumulative learning takes place. | Adaptive capability that all children possess to apply and modify their existing cognitive structures; this capability grows with age (and is transformed) | Distributed across a group and intimately tied to the tools, artifacts, and symbolic systems that the group develops. |
| Motivation | Internal state that is subject to external influence and that affects the deployment of attention. | Natural tendencies that draw human beings of all ages toward epistemic activity. | Identification: i.e., the natural tendency of the young to see themselves as being like their elders and to look forward to the day when they assume their elders' role. |
| Education | Process by which the external conditions that affect children's learning and motivation are carefully arranged and sequenced so that socially desirable goals, may be achieved. | Child centered process: involves the provision of an environment that stimulates children's natural curiosity and constructive activity and promotes active reflection on the results of that activity. | Process by which a community takes charge of its young and moves them from a peripheral to a central role in its daily practices. |

*Source:* Reprinted from *Comparison of Three Views of Knowledge from Conceptual Development in the Child and in the Field: A Personal View of the Piagetian Legacy* (p. 31), by R. Case, 1999, in E. K. Scholnick, K. Nelson, S. A. Gelman & P. H. Miller (eds), *Conceptual Development: Piaget's Legacy.* Mahwah, NJ: Lawrence Erlbaum Associates.

organization that can be studied with the methods similar to those used to understand complex phenomena in the physical world (e.g., epidemics, weather).

## Linear Theories

The most prominent human development theories historically have been the linear theories—ones that try to identify specific universal sources of developmental change from which direct predictions can be made. These theories are often described as having a "modern" perspective, which emphasizes progress and reason, universals, family, and maternal love as primary and children as in need of guidance to develop well.

*Empiricist* theories explain human development and test the theoretical assumptions using methods that are similar to the way scientific and technological problems have been studied in other fields. That is, human individuals are seen as composed of discrete pieces (reductions) that can be understood through analysis of the same laws of science that apply to mechanical objects. Development is seen as additive; there are no global stages or qualitative changes, just quantitative change, which may lead to functional change. This continuity of development may result in new behaviors but the changes are due to the compilation of many small linear changes, which makes prediction possible if all the "pieces" can be identified. This perspective is sometimes called a "reductionist" theoretical view because it assumes that identifying all the discrete pieces of behaviors (the variables) will enable understanding of the whole (i.e., human development) to be accomplished. In this view, individuals are more often seen as passive receptors of experiences or limited by genetic qualities with development occurring because environmental stimuli act on them. Case (1999) stated that this theoretical perspective sees knowledge as being a repertoire of patterns that individuals learn and operate on and that this learning is cumulative. This perspective has been especially prominent in the work of early "learning" theorists such as Thorndike (1914) and Watson (1914); the most prominent present-day empiricists working on theory building are behavioral genetic researchers, such as Plomin (1986) and Scarr (1992), and information processing/cognitive science theorists, such as Siegler (1988) and Kail (1979). Of course, an extreme of this position can be seen in the present-day work of scientists who are designing robots that can perform "human" tasks like recognizing people and understanding language commands. They attempt to isolate the specific components of these tasks and to program the robots to perform such behaviors (Coles, 2004). Their goal is to replicate human behavior through analysis of the set of components composing such human abilities. As noted earlier, nonlinear dynamical systems theories also used empiricist methods, but instead of trying to predict with linear assumptions, they view human development as a nonlinear phenomenon. Empiricist theory has been especially prominent in the United States.

*Rationalist* theories have arisen from a different set of assumptions and are typically categorized as holistic, having a "growth" perspective drawn from biological and botanical models. These theorists hold that the whole of human development is more than just its parts, and moreover, newer advanced forms emerge from old forms (e.g., they are epigenetic). Theorists with this perspective focus on qualitative changes in structures and resulting functional changes. They observe both continuities and discontinuities of development and note stages or levels that are qualitatively different than those of earlier developmental periods. Because of these emerging and perhaps multiple change processes, prediction is less clear, but it still has a linear quality because the assumption is that growth to higher level forms of development will occur; that is, there is a point to which ideal development is aimed. Individuals are seen as active in their own developmental progress rather than being passive receptors. Case (1999) indicated that knowledge from this perspective is seen as created by the human mind, and learning takes place when cognitive structures are applied to experiences. Thus it is not just a cumulative process but rather a transformational process. The theorists who most prominently portray this perspective are the "stage" theorists such as Freud (1938), Erikson (1963), and Piaget (1936), who represent a view more commonly seen in Europe. Theorists from the United States with primarily rationalist views include evolutionary theorists and those concerned with personality and social–emotional development (e.g., Greenspan, 1989), metacognition and theory of mind (e.g., Flavell, 1977), and sociomoral development issues (e.g., Damon, 1988). These theorists often use clinical or natural observation methods to study developmental phenomena, but they may also use experimental designs that they interpret through a rationalist perspective.

## Nonlinear Theories

Although the two perspectives described earlier have been the most prominent in human development theory building, other theorists, especially those from "postmodern" perspectives, have stressed dynamical systemic interactions that question the linearity and universal quality of developmental change processes. Postmodern perspectives focus more on systems change, cultural consciousness, diversity of family structures, and an emphasis on child competence rather than incompetence. Perspectives of this type have been labeled sociohistorical, ecological, bioecological, or contextual. New perspectives that are nonlinear include neuropsychological, developmental psychobiological, and dynamical systems theory.

*Sociohistorical* theories, drawing on the earlier work of Kurt Lewin (1931, 1936), focus on environmental influences that may differentiate developmental patterns, and they emphasize culturally diverse rather than universal patterns of development. These theorists believe that human development always reflects the many-layered environmental and sociohistorical perspective of the theorist. Because they think the best way to study development is from within the culture of the individuals, their explanations are "situated" within contexts and thus cannot be universally applied. Rather than being able to predict based on identifying all the separate variables that might affect development (reductionist) or based on knowledge of an unfolding ideal process (epigenetic), these theorists see development as more open ended, with no rigid direction, pattern, or limit. This postmodern view embraces an underlying belief in a moral/ethical imperative of political liberation. Case (1999) explained that knowledge from this perspective is a creation of a social group and that learning is a process of being initiated into the group; thus, development is a process of social initiation. Theorists who have been characterized with this perspective include Vygotsky (1978) and those who study "situated" development, such as Rogoff (1993). Bronfenbrenner's (2005) bioecological theory also draws on this perspective.

In the past 50 years, a number of theorists have focused primarily on developmental change in adulthood. They have promoted the assumption that developmental change occurs at all periods of life, rather than being "completed" by the end of adolescence, and that the sociohistorical environment greatly influences the variability seen in adult development. Life span theorists stress the view that development is an open process with many possible outcomes, that it is "situated" within sociohistorical contexts, and that it is not always progressive but is successive–change does occur but not always toward more positive results (e.g., Neugarten, 1996). This view personifies many life span theorists such as Elder (1974) and Schaie (2005), as well as theorists who write from postmodern theoretical positions, such as feminist theorists (e.g., Bem, 1993). Chapters 5 and 10 will address life span theoretical perspectives.

*Systems* theories are newer approaches to the study of human development, and these have been generated by concepts drawn from the knowledge base of a number of other scientific fields, in particular those of neuroscience and physics. Many of these theorists draw on recent brain research that examines how various structures and functions of the brain develop and are related to perceptual, cognitive, and social–emotional development. They believe that future theorizing will incorporate neurobiological information to enhance the explanatory power of developmental theory (see Segalowitz, 1994). Some present-day theorists are incorporating nonlinear dynamical systems concepts derived from theoretical work in physics, economics, and meteorology into their explanations of human development processes (Vanderven, 1998; Waldrop, 1992). They are positing that human development can be explained as a type of dynamical system, which has characteristics of complexity, plasticity, self-organization, recursive nested features at all levels, and a probabilistic rather than a predictive perspective (Thelen & Smith, 1994). Although the final form of these theories is unknown at this time, they seem to hold the possibility of integrating features of many traditional theoretical perspectives. Most of this theoretical work can be characterized as proto-theory rather than fully developed theory, but these viewpoints have been made explicit by a number of theorists (e.g., Thelen, 2003) and are also being incorporated in views of neo-Piagetian theorists such as Fischer (Fischer & Rose, 1998). Box 1.1 describes some of the characteristics of nonlinear dynamical systems (sometimes called complexity or chaos theory) that are being explored by these theorists.

Although all the conceptual schema outlined earlier can be useful in understanding some of the major assumptions of certain sets of theories, it is also the case that there is overlap in these perspectives and that many contemporary theorists do not fit neatly into one of these categories. In particular, theorists drawing on bioecological, neuropsychological, nonlinear dynamical systems, and cognitive science approaches are more eclectic in their orientation, and they may draw on empiricist, rationalist, and sociohistorical assumptions in their theoretical explanations. Thus, more inclusive theoretical models may be on the horizon. A summary of these four theoretical perspectives is in Box 1.2.

# Box 1.1
# Characteristics of Complexity/Chaos Theory

- *Recursion.* Information from a system is led back on itself, thereby changing the nature of the system and affecting the initial condition. Often recursion effects are responsible for unanticipated or paradoxical outcomes.

- *Entrainment.* Two or more systems join to become a larger, synchronous system, effecting the synchronization of two or more rhythmic systems into a single pulse (Nachmanovitch, 1990, p. 99). Entrainment thus embraces a combinatory notion; that separate entities become juxtaposed or connected in ways that form new combinations and coherent patterns.

- *Disequilibrium.* A system that is in a state capable of change.

- *Weak chaos.* A small amount of chaos that may be introduced into a system to keep it dynamic.

- *Bifurcation.* A transformation can influence a system to re-organize or enter into a completely different, new state; a bifurcation may result in surprise, due to the rapidity and nature of the change.

- *Self-organization.* Characteristic of a complex adaptive system; the spontaneous reemergence of a turbulent, disequilibrious system into patterned, computational behavior that is purposeful.

- *Fractal.* Self-similarity, in which iteration reproduces the a self-similar pattern at different levels of scale, over and over.

- *Attractor.* A system that may appear to exist in apparent disorder may continue to refer, in its evolution, toward a certain "attracted" behavior or state of being.

- *Sensitive dependence on initial conditions.* A very small input into a system may yield widely disparate results, in both form and quantity.

- *Entropy.* "The inexorable tendency of the universe, and any isolated system within it, to slide toward a state of increasing disorder" (Glaick, 1987, p. 257).

- *Dissipative system.* An open, bounded system whose energy is given off to, or dissipated to, its surrounds; as contrasted to a rightly bounded "conservative system" (Goerner, 1994).

- *Determinism.* This refers to the paradoxical act that language makes it possible to describe and prescribe the parameters and behavior of a system although it is not possible to linearly predict the form of its evolution over time.

- *Phase portrait.* Phase portraits or "phase space portraits" are the geometrical, topological representations of the dynamics of a system that enable the "mapping of possible states (the) system can go through" (Goerner, 1994, p. 206)

- *Fuzzy logic.* Reasoning with non-absolute or dichotomous quantities or concepts (Koska, 1993); relates to the mental processes that enable human beings to understand chaos.

*Source: Characteristics of Complexity/Chaos Theory from Play, Proteus and Paradox: Education for a Chaotic and Supersymmetric World* (p. 122) by K. VenderVen (p. 122), 1998, in D. P. Fromberg and D. Bergen (eds.), *Play from Brith to Twelve and Beyond: Contexts, Perspectives, and Meanings.* Copyright © 1998. Reproduced by permission of Routledge/Taylor & Francis Group, LLC.

# Box 1.2
# Categorizing Theories

### *Linear: Empiricist*

The most prominent present day theorist are behavioral genetic researchers and information processing theorists.

This theoretical perspective sees knowledge as being a repertoire of patterns that individuals learn and operate upon and that this learning is cumulative

Development is seen as additive; there are no global stages or qualitative changes, just quantitative change, which may lead to functional change.

This perspective is sometimes called a "reductionist" theoretical view since it assumes that identifying all the discrete pieces of behaviors (the variables) will enable understanding of the whole (i.e., human development) to be accomplished.

Individuals are more often seen as passive receptors of experiences or limited by genetic qualities with development occurring because environmental stimuli act upon them.

These theorists use experimental or quasi-experimental designs or correlational methods that attempt to find relationships among variables.

### *Linear: Rationalist*

These theories are typically categorized as holistic, having a "growth"perspective drawn from biological and botanical models. They hold that human development is more than just its parts and that newer advanced forms emerge from old forms (e.g., they are epigenetic).

Theorists with this perspective focus on qualitative changes in structures and resulting functional changes. They observe both continuities and discontinuities of development; and note stages or levels that are qualitatively different than those of earlier developmental periods.

The assumption is that growth to higher level forms of development will occur; that is, there is a point to which ideal development is aimed. Individuals are seen as active in their own developmental progress rather than being passive receptors.

Knowledge from this perspective is seen as created by the human mind and learning takes place when cognitive structures are applied to experiences. Thus it not just a cumulative process but rather a transformational process.

The theorists who most prominently portray this perspective are the "stage" theorists and many cognitive scientists.

Theorists operating from this perspective often use clinical observation, interviews; and natural observational techniques.

### *Nonlinear: Sociohistorical*

These theorists focus on environmental influences that may differentiate developmental patterns, and they emphasize culturally diverse rather than universal patterns of development.

*(continued)*

These theorists think the best way to study development is from within the culture of the individuals, their explanations are "situated" within contexts and thus, cannot be universally applied.

Rather than being able to predict based on identifying all the separate variables that might affect development or based on knowledge of an unfolding ideal process, these theorists see development as more open-ended, with no rigid direction, pattern, or limit.

Knowledge from this perspective is a creation of a social group and learning is a process of being initiated into the group; thus, development is a process of social initiation.

Theorists who have been characterized as embracing this view are Soviet, life-span, and ecological theorists.

The methods used to study development involve consideration of the total context and its interaction with the individuals of that culture.

### Nonlinear: Dynamical Systems

This theoretical view has been generated by concepts drawn from the knowledge-base of a number of other scientific fields, in particular those of neuroscience and physics.

Many of these theorists draw on recent brain research that examines how various structures and functions of the brain develop and are related to perceptual, cognitive, and social-emotional development.

These theorists incorporate concepts of complexity, plasticity, self-organization, and recursive nested features at all levels.

Most of this theoretical work can be characterized as proto-theory rather than fully developed theory.

These theorists think that chaotic complex systems such as human beings have the ability to self-organize into purposeful behaviors and believe that sensitive dependence on initial conditions, in which a small input in a system may yield disparate results, can explain developmental change.

The research methods of these theorists involve collecting minute process data (microgenesis) and using computers to map the developmental change process.

## Summary

This chapter has discussed human development theoretical perspectives, provided an overview of historical roots of developmental theory, and given a categorization scheme for comparing these perspectives. Because theory can provide the impetus for research and guidelines for practice, the importance of understanding the major theories of human development is evident. Early theoretical ideas have certainly resulted in child-rearing and education actions.

However, with the exception of the education theorists and ABA practitioners, most human development theorists have been minimally concerned with applying their theories to practical developmental problems. They often leave that aspect to proponents of their theory. More recently, with greater emphasis on trying to solve developmental problems such as autism or learning disabilities, and with more precise knowledge of the brain's activity and development, a number of theoretical perspectives are being more strongly applied to problems of practice. Although the ideas of some early theorists who spoke to aspects of human development are not of major influence today, themes from their views still can be found in many present-day theories, as well as in applications of theory to practice. The first case problem requires consideration of the enduring evidence of early theoretical perspectives and their potential relationship to current practice.

## Case 1. Teacher New and Psychologist Old

Teacher New wants to do as much as possible to foster the optimum development of the children in the first grade and has asked Psychologist Old for advice. Tell what advice Psychologist Old might give if the psychologist holds a theory that is congruent with that of:

Locke

Rousseau

Calvin

Comenius, Pestalozzi, Froebel, or Montessori

Watson or Skinner

Now suggest what theorists from each of the knowledge perspectives might say about Teacher New's question. Use the information from Box 1.2 to inform your views.

## Readings

Maria Montessori, *Freedom to Develop; Nature in Education*, pp. 247–254.

B. F. Skinner, *Baby in a Box*, pp. 255–260.

## Suggested Readings

F. Froebel, (1887) *The Education of Man.* NY: Application Century.

M. Montessori, (1972). *The discovery of the child* (6th ed., pp. 61–75).

*Source:* Copyright © 1978 Ashleigh Brilliant. Reprinted by permission.

# Applying Human Development Theories in Research and Practice

Human development theories can be judged on many dimensions, but the criteria of empirically demonstrated credibility/external validity and of practical usefulness are the two of most importance. Many authors have discussed what makes a theory empirically valid and practically useful (e.g., Ausubel, Sullivan, & Ives, 1980; Goldhaber, 2000; Thomas, 2005). Although no theory completely meets these criteria, the eight characteristics listed in Box 2.1 are often included in the criteria for judging the credibility/external validity and usefulness of a particular theory. The potential limitations of theories are also described.

Theories that have been sustained over long periods of time have met many of these criteria, but each has some particular strengths and weaknesses. Contemporary theoretical perspectives are providing additional insights; however, their empirical validity and practical usefulness will also be evaluated over time in relation to these criteria. Because theories are the product of human thought and experience, every theory has limitations, and students of theories often find this frustrating because they would prefer to find one theory that is best for answering all their questions. However, when studying theories, the goal should not be to pick one "favorite" to use exclusively but rather to know a sufficient number of scientifically based theories well enough to find explanatory power for understanding, predicting, and solving a wide range of specific human development

# Box 2.1
# Positive Qualities and Limitations of Theories

### Strengths

- They are testable and stimulate further research that may verify or falsify theory explanations.

- They often appear to be relatively accurate portrayals of human developmental phenomena.

- They are internally consistent—the parts of the theory "fit" together.

- They are economical, using only the minimum number of concepts to explain sufficiently.

- They provide definitions of concepts, simplifying complex phenomena and focusing attention on important aspects.

- They provide models (or frameworks, lenses, maps) through which phenomenon can be viewed.

- They enable predictions to be made using the theoretical concepts.

- They encourage problem solving and result in actions based on predicted changes.

### Limitations

- The testable nature of theories depends on the scientific tools available for testing and therefore some theories may not be falsifiable until greater precision in scientific research methods is obtained.

- The accuracy of their reflections of human developmental phenomena depends on the scientific tools available for studying the phenomena at the time the theory is proposed.

- Although theories vary in their internal consistency, even those that are most consistent may still have unexplained "outliers" that do not fit the organizational pattern of the theory well.

- Some important human development aspects may not be addressed. Usually theorists focus on those phenomena of greatest interest to them and do not explain other phenomena.

- There is tension between the density and abstractness of definitions and the ability to understand the theory. If it is difficult to understand definitions, the theory may be inaccessible to practitioners.

- Although theoretical models focus attention, they may limit what phenomena are observed and may result in relevant data inconsistent with the model being unnoticed or discounted.

- Although attempts at prediction vary with theorists, even for theories with good predictive capability, the variability of individuals and cultural factors can make them inaccurate or inconsistent in prediction; thus, probability rather than predictability is often the standard.

- If predictions cannot be made accurately, then the problem-solving capacity of a theory may be greatly diminished, and the usefulness to practitioners may be limited.

problems. The qualities of theories that are especially important for evaluating their credibility/external validity and usefulness include the following.

- They are testable and stimulate further research that may verify or falsify theory explanations.
- They are internally consistent—the parts of the theory "fit" together.
- They enable predictions to be made using the theoretical concepts.
- They encourage problem solving and result in actions based on predicted changes.

In comparison to what Baldwin (1964) called "naive theory," which is not tested empirically, these qualities enable researchers to test the various theoretical ideas, and they help practitioners to observe the effects of interventions based on the theory. As noted earlier, the two questions of greatest importance to professionals in evaluating intentionally designed scientific theories are

- What types of empirical evidence have been obtained to support the credibility/external validity of the major theoretical constructs and enable predictions or probabilities to be accurately made?
- What useful guidance for solving practical problems of child rearing, education, clinical intervention, and health promotion does the theory provide to promote optimum development (as defined by the particular culture)?

The information in this book provides only a starting point for helping readers create a personally relevant theoretical perspective because each reader brings to the content a set of genetic, neuronal, personality, social, emotional, physical motor, perceptual, cognitive, language, sociomoral, and gender role identity qualities that have already been in dynamic interaction within themselves and with their environment for many years. As readers study these theories, critique their relevance, question their assumptions, select important ideas, and either accept or discard their principles, they should be able to create a personally relevant worldview congruent with their own developmental level. Given the basic assumption of this field, however, it is expected that the perspective readers obtain from this text will continue to develop, change with further experience, and be continually reorganized over their remaining life span. This chapter will outline theory-driven research methods and practical application ideas so that the critical evaluation of the validity and usefulness of theories discussed in later chapters can be promoted. First, however, a brief review of "naive theory" is given to show the contrast between these commonsense explanations of development and the intentional theories that can be evaluated through testing their theoretical constructs.

## Features of Naive Theory

It is not surprising that naive theory (often called common sense) has been used in an informal way to explain human development because everyone has experiences related to raising, teaching, or supervising children and/or youth, interacting and predicting behaviors of family members of varied ages, and/or trying to influence the behaviors of their usual social groups. Although evident in the thinking of most people, naive theory is not systematically designed and thus does not meet many of the criteria of intentionally designed theory. Although it is often used to predict developmental change and to attempt to solve developmental problems, it does not meet the criteria of scientific theories outlined earlier due to flaws in attribution of cause. The explanations of causes for developmental changes are reduced to a small number of factors, and then all behavior is interpreted in terms of these causes (Heider, 1958). It is characterized by the assumption that the truth is self-evident; therefore, no scientific data need to be used to verify these theoretical beliefs. Such theories rely heavily on internally attributed concepts such as ability, effort, motivation, and conscience and on externally attributed concepts such as task difficulty, environmental prescriptions, and opportunities, as well as role expectations. For example, a child's developmental difficulty may be attributed to reasons such as, "She doesn't have the ability"or "If she just made an effort she could do that," without attempts to gain empirical evidence to support these claims. In contrast to scientific theory, naive theory also makes room for supernatural intervention and indeterminate factors such as "luck" as explanatory concepts.

Baldwin (1968) mentioned a number of flaws in naive theory; for example, it usually depends on subjective experience, often attributes explanations to one cause, and gives explanations after rather than before the event (predicts backward). Some ideas studied empirically by scientists have been derived from commonsense beliefs, and a few such explanations of development have received support in experimental studies of intentional theory builders. For example, motivational attributions related to task difficulty and effort have been found to affect performance (Dweck, 1975). Even concepts that have not received empirical support sometimes linger on, however, as everyday explanations of human development changes. Remnants of these views are evident in educational, legal, religious, and child-rearing practices of many cultures. Although each culture has a set of commonsense "truths" that are part of their naive theory, these truths may differ greatly across cultures. For example, in American culture, environment (i.e., a difficult task) is seen to be a strong influential factor, whereas in Asia internal motivation and effort (i.e., try harder) are used more as explanations of achievements. Until those ideas are systematically tested through intentional theoretical research perspectives, however, they will not become prominent as valid theoretical constructs.

## Cross-Cultural Theoretical Perspectives

Developmental theories that have been influential in child rearing and education in non-Western cultures have often been derived from philosophical or religious perspectives rather than from psychological study. They may also have been communicated through oral tradition rather than explained in written essays or psychological texts. In many cultures individual development has not been the subject of study until recently, perhaps because traditionally concern for the group rather than individuals was often emphasized. For example, Confucian principles were very prominent in China until the Communist revolution, when

Mao Zedong emphasized changing education to meet different goals, which required the people "to part with their Confucian past" (Lo, 1987, p. 33). Communist educational values stressed having children learn to "love the collective" and to "love labor." Children were expected to "develop morally, intellectually, and physically, and to acquire social consciousness and culture" (Stevenson, Lee, & Stigler, 1981, p. 2). The underlying Confucian values (as well as Communist values) continue to be evident in current education, however. Burton (1986) reviewed the values promoted for children in primary school education in China and reported that these included expecting children to learn to work harmoniously with other people, be unselfish, be concerned with group welfare, maintain good health, respect adults, respect manual labor, and meet one's obligations. Although at various periods before and after Mao's reign Chinese child-rearing and educational practice have drawn on Russian, Japanese, and Western theorists (see Spodek, 1989), these views have always been adapted to include values related to group harmony. Thus, underlying cultural values have remained a strong force in child rearing and education.

Cross-cultural analyses of permitted behaviors for boys and girls in various other world cultures have also shown differences in child-rearing and educational patterns (e.g., Whiting & Edwards, 1973) and studies of ethnic minority groups within a larger culture, such as Mexican Americans (Gump, Baker, & Roll, 2000), Appalachians (Marger & Obermiller, 1982), and African Americans (Wilson, 1989) suggest that their values and practices may differ, with subsequent variations in developmental consequences. For example, an extended family model may be more normative in African-American homes, with grandparents and other relatives more involved in raising the children of young parents (Wilson, 1989). Although the theories of people from varied cultures are used in practice, with only a few exceptions these groups have not had scientific psychological theories, and until recently, there have not been many intentional human development theory builders from these groups. Thus, these theoretical perspectives have more in common with naive theory because they have not usually been "testable" by the research methods used to validate scientific theories.

# Research Methods Used to Test Scientific Theory

A problem often encountered in evaluating whether a scientific theory meets the criteria of having valid research evidence is that theorists who hold different perspectives may question the generalizations related to evidence provided by other theorists who use research methodology that is not derived from the same set of assumptions. Thus, a review of the research methods usually judged appropriate by each theoretical perspective is warranted.

## Empiricist Research Methods

Because these theorists view knowledge as "acquired by a process in which the sensory organs first detect stimuli in the external world and the mind then detects the customary patterns or conjunctions in these stimuli" (Case, 1999, pp. 23–24), they follow accepted empirical (i.e., modern scientific) research paradigms. The research is designed to control for causal factors that may interfere with the variables being studied by using some type of experimental design. It tests theory-generated hypotheses by identifying variables of interest, randomly selecting experimental and control groups, and collecting data from those groups after some intervention or experimental task related to predictions generated by the theory. In addition to "true" experimental designs, variations of this method are also acceptable, such as studies using quasi-experimental designs that do not have random selection or have natural world interventions rather than laboratory interventions. Other research methods based on assumptions of this theoretical perspective are single-subject functional assessment designs, self-report surveys using rating scales, observation and coding of behaviors that have been operationally defined, and detection of relationships among multiple sets of controlled variables. More recent empirical research has also used microgenetic methods, which involve collecting many successive samples of a particular behavioral process, such as problem solving (e.g., Siegler, 1997). The results of empirical research are usually analyzed with statistical procedures designed to give a probability estimate of whether the results show a "true" difference rather than a "chance" difference between groups or relationships among variables. These results are then discussed in relation to the theoretical constructs being tested.

A typical early example of this approach were the studies of Kendler and Kendler (1962), who conducted a series of laboratory experiments that presented children with stimuli that varied on some dimension, such as shape or color, and provided a small reinforcement if they selected the correct stimuli. They found that young children were less successful that older children and concluded that children younger than age 5 considered the qualities of each object separately, whereas older children could build a set of associations between similar objects and thus respond more quickly to get the reinforcement. Their conclusion was that verbally mediated learning had occurred by the later age; that is, the children had used their increasing verbal ability to build up associational patterns. This research was interpreted as giving evidence in support of a learning theory view of development, which stressed associations rather than development of a stagelike central conceptual structure. The early research of Bandura (Bandura, Ross, & Ross, 1963) provided an example of empirically testing a feature of his social learning theory. The researchers had some children view models who hit an inflated toy; others did not view the violent model. These researchers found that children exposed to models who exhibited violence were more likely to demonstrate similar behavior, in comparison to the control subjects who did not see violent models. Thus, they concluded that the children learned to act violently through observation of models, which was one of the constructs of Bandura's theory.

More recently, information processing and cognitive scientist theorists (e.g., Gopnik & Wellman, 1994; Kail, 1979; Meltzoff & Moore, 1999; Siegler, 1988) have examined specific developmental issues using empirical methods. For example, much of the infant cognition research that has been done in the past decades has involved presenting infants with various stimuli and observing attentional and physiological changes under the various stimuli conditions. Meltzoff and Moore (1994, 1999) have concluded that even young infants can imitate novel behaviors and can replicate the behaviors after a short time period; thus, they posit a "representational" quality existing in infant thought. Similarly, in a study of infant memory, Rovee-Collier (1997) found that 4-month-old infants could remember to kick their feet to make an object move when they were placed back in a crib where they had previously activated the object's movement, demonstrating that memory for events in specific settings exists at an early age. Both of these studies called into question previous theoretical assumptions about infant incompetence. The vast majority of developmental studies of particular domains such as memory, problem solving, perception, and theory of mind have used versions of this research model. Although the methodology has been greatly expanded and many types of sophisticated analysis of extensive data sets are now performed, the basic assumption behind this perspective is that the appropriate way to test the constructs of a theory is by reducing the data to a set of hypothesized specific variables and trying to understand the impact of each of these variables in demonstrating predicted developmental changes. Much of the research published in U.S. professional journals is based on the research methods sanctioned by empiricists.

### Rationalist Research Methods

Although these theorists are also looking at universals of development, the research methods used in theory development and validation, although also rigorous, have primarily been observational or clinical in nature. These theorists are less interested in statistically analyzing specific sets of variables and more interested in giving detailed descriptions of complex behaviors, thoughts, or feelings of their subjects. Because their theories posit the development of internal structures and discontinuity of structural change, they often try to explore the responses of children of different age levels to questions about which they hypothesize. Depending on results, they propose stage-related qualitative changes that support their theoretical constructs. They use many observational and interview techniques ranging from open-ended, anthropological descriptions to precisely structured clinical observations. Typically the number of subjects studied is small, partly because the assumption is that the developmental issues they study are universal and partly because a very detailed description is made of the subjects' responses. Because rationalist theorists see knowledge development as "a process in which the human mind imposes order on the data that the senses provide . . . [and believe that there are] . . . foundational concepts with which children come equipped at birth" (Case, 1999, p. 26), their research is designed to uncover these conceptual structures that children possess and to understand the nature of the changes in structure and function. Research studies congruent with assumptions from the rationalist view typically do not include detailed statistical analysis, but may be primarily descriptive in nature, with the use of conversational examples, charts, and case studies to report the results.

Piaget's studies (e.g., 1945, 1954, 1965, 1976, 1978) from which his theoretical views were drawn are typical of this approach. One type of data he collected was gained through natural observation of infants' play behaviors, preschool children's language, and elementary-age boys' play with marbles. He then gave examples of his observations that informed and supported his theoretical ideas. Much of his later research presented ambiguous cognitive problems to children within a structured clinical setting, and the data collected probed their reasons for answering the problems as they did. Criticism of his theory has come from some empiricists, who questioned his research methods, and many empirical studies were undertaken by other scientists to test his theoretical ideas.

Other theorists who come from a rationalist perspective, such as Kohlberg, Damon, Turiel, and Chess and Thomas, have undertaken observational and interview studies to test the predictions of their theoretical views. For example, Kohlberg (1970) probed the reasoning of children's answers to moral dilemmas and posited stages of moral development. His approach has been used across cultures to test whether the stages he identified are reflected cross-culturally (Snarey, 1985), and findings show both support and nonsupport for some of his stage constructs. Damon (1988) and Turiel (1983) have used similar approaches to test Kohlberg's theory and to expand the theory to determine children's understanding of social conventional dilemmas as well as moral dilemmas. Some rationalist theorists draw on clinical work with adult patients who retrospectively discuss developmental issues (e.g., Erikson, 1963; Freud, 1936). Freud's theory has been criticized by empiricists because its constructs were based primarily on adult clinical reports of childhood experiences and thus were "untestable" by empirical methods. Chess and Thomas (1990) collected their data through parent interviews over many years to develop the constructs of their theory of temperament, and Ainsworth derived some empirical methods to test the constructs of Bowlby's theory of attachment (Ainsworth, 1979).

Because the empiricist tradition is so pervasive in the scientific community in the United States, many results reported in studies by rationalist theories have been retested by researchers using methods of empiricism. In particular, the constructs of Piaget's theory have been rigorously tested by neo-Piagetians. For example, Case (1991) replicated many of Piaget's studies and has results that support some but not all of the constructs. Using very precise methodological procedures, he concluded that the global stages Piaget described have a number of substages as well. Other cognitive researchers, such as Flavell (1992) and Bruner (1973), have also tested aspects of Piagetian theory. For example, Flavell and others used observational and clinical methods to study children's perspective taking (i.e., false belief) and other aspects of "theory of mind" by giving children private information and then asking them to tell the thoughts and perspectives of others who had different information than that given to the children. Bruner also studied many aspects of thought, language, and cultural influences with procedures based on rationalist perspectives.

### Sociohistorical Research Methods

Both of the previous research methods have been criticized by theorists from this perspective because they often fail to take into account the cultural, social, and historical factors that may be influencing developmental change. For example,

Bronfenbrenner (1979) has criticized the experimental approach as too narrow and unnatural and the clinical approach as too subjective and inferential. Because they view the origin of development "in the social and material history of the culture of which the subject is a part and in the tools, concepts, and symbol systems that the culture has developed for interacting with its environment" (Case, 1999, p. 28), theorists from this approach only predict within these contexts. Their research relies on rich descriptions of the ecological factors that interact with the subjects' individual developmental trajectories. They also believe that they cannot divorce their own influence from that of the setting and thus they value "participant observation" and other qualitative approaches, such as case studies using "thick descriptions." They attempt to provide "triangulation" to support the generalizability of their results by collecting similar types of information from numerous data sources.

An example of an early sociohistorical approach is research done by Luria (1979), a colleague of Vygotsky, who studied the thinking patterns of children in remote villages in Russia and determined that their cognitive development was delayed in comparison to that of children in other parts of Russia. He attributed this to their lack of formal education, and because formal learning is viewed as necessary for cognitive development in Vygotskian theory, he saw these results as a confirmation of this theoretical construct. A study by Ogbu (2003) of the achievement orientation of African-American high school students in an upper-socioeconomic community is a recent example of the sociohistorical research approach. He analyzed many features of the students' environment, including parental behavior and their "theories of success," the varied aspects of the school culture, and the general societal messages being given to these youth, and he examined how each influenced their achievement. His research supported one aspect of his theoretical view, which assigns importance to cultural "success theories" that may underlie beliefs and influence behavior.

Life span theorists conduct many studies from this research perspective. For example, Elder's longitudinal study (1974) of adults growing up during a period of depression and war shows "situated" effects on their later thinking and behavior. Typically, to support their theoretical constructs, life span theorists explore many personal, social, cultural, and historic aspects of a developmental issue. They interpret many of their results as giving support for the contextual influences that affect adult developmental variability. Because the sociohistorical perspective is related to a postmodern view of knowledge, it is not usually accepted as a valid method of theory testing by empiricists. However, it has gained increasing acceptance, and many ecologically based studies are now being analyzed in ways that allow empirically based predictions by compiling the "weights" of influence of various ecological factors.

### *Neuropsychological, Developmental Psychobiological, and Dynamical Systems Research Methods*

Research methods used by these theorists may incorporate methodology from all these other approaches. However, it often uses data derived from microgenesis (i.e., the dynamic display of processes; Catan, 1986). Microgenesis involves collection of multiple samples of an ongoing process, and the results are displayed in graphs or other visual displays usually generated by computers. This research method is not new, as it was initially advocated by Werner (1957) and used by Vygotsky (1978) to describe certain processes in his theory. However, recent technological advances have made it a more accessible model for collecting and analyzing research data. Recently, Siegler (1997) and Fischer and colleagues (Fischer & Pipp, 1984; Fischer, Bullock, Rotenberg, & Raya, 1993) have advocated this approach for studying specific skill development in children. In current dynamical systems research, analysis methods derived from neuroscience and physics are also being incorporated into human development research. The computer is an essential component because analysis of the researchers' data often involves computer simulations, brain scans, and other methods dependent on recent technological advances. For example, Panksepp (1989, 1998a) has studied the activity of brain emotional centers in animals and in humans and has examined how the development of higher brain centers affects emotional regulation. Now that computer technologies have the ability to transform extensive data points into patterns, this procedure can be very instructive for mapping developmental trends. The work of Thelen (Thelen & Smith, 1994) exemplifies this approach. In Thelen's studies of infants' walking behavior, she collected numerous data points and then developed computer generated *mappings* showing what factors needed to be present for walking to occur. She used these results to support her view that development can be explained as congruent with concepts from nonlinear dynamical systems theory. With the advent of technological advances in data analysis, many sets of developmental data that have been collected in the past may be reanalyzed using these techniques to show the dynamical systems involved in human development changes.

## Using Research Evidence to Evaluate Theoretical Perspectives

Because the ability to evaluate theories by examining supporting and nonsupporting research evidence is so important, each subsequent chapter gives a brief evaluation of how well proponents of those theories have provided this evidence. It is important to keep in mind that evidence presented from one knowledge schema will not always be accepted by proponents of another; however, if the research is rigorously done and reflects the theorists' view of knowledge, this is usually considered sufficient to provide support for the constructs that have been tested. Readers should maintain an evaluative perspective as they consider the various theories presented in subsequent chapters. Box 2.2 has suggestions for some informal research ideas that students can use to collect observational/interview/behavior data as they read about each set of theories. They can then compare their evidence to the constructs of theorists discussed in the relevant chapters. Because these "practice" exercises are not carefully designed research studies, however, they cannot be used to either confirm or disconfirm the theoretical constructs that are informally tested.

# Box 2.2
# Practicing Testing of Theoretical Concepts

1.  Observe, using a running record, a four to six-person family (may be two or three generations) at a family event lasting at least 1 hour (e.g., dinner time, game playing, birthday party, other family gathering). Each group member should observe a different family. Later, individually interview 2 to 4 members of the family, asking them a set of at least six questions that probe their developmental crises stages. If there are children younger than 3, interview a parent about that child. Be sure to record specific examples of behaviors that may be related to stage crises. After the sets of data are reviewed by the group, compile your information using a content analysis approach, with examples to support your conclusion. Compare the results to Erikson's theory and Marcia's research, indicating whether your data support the constructs of the theory. Then select either Bowlby–Ainsworth, Thomas and Chess, Greenspan, or Bandura and compare the results to that theory. Tell which theory best explains the family interactions and would be likely to predict the future development of the family members.

2.  Investigate, using clinical observation, the preoperational, concrete operational, and/or formal operational thinking of children of differing ages. Select at least four of the tasks of Piaget (e.g., conservation of liquid, seriation, space), spending at least 1 hour on the observation, with each child individually doing the tasks. Each group member should interview two children of the same age, but group members should select different age children to interview. After each child gives each answer, ask them questions to probe why they answered as they did. When sets of data are reviewed by the group, compile the information using percentages and charts and compare results to Piaget's theory, indicating whether your data support the constructs of the theory. Then use Case's or Fischer's alternative theoretical ideas (neo-Piagetian) or a cognitive science theoretical approach (e.g., Kail, Flavell, Siegler) to see if those ideas explain the results also (or instead of). Tell whether Piagetian theory held true for your subjects, whether a neo-Piagetian or cognitive science approach gives a better explanation, and which approach would be likely to predict best the future development of the children.

3.  Select an academic skill that is typically learned in a higher grade and, using clinical observation, try to scaffold the learning of children (preferably from different cultural backgrounds) who are in a lower grade (e.g., pick a 3rd grade skill to teach to 2nd graders.) Use the concepts of Vygotsky's theory to decide what zone level you should use to start the scaffolding and spend at least 1 hour with the children, working with each child separately. After observing how the children have performed, interview them with at least four additional questions to probe what they really understand about the concept. After the sets of data are reviewed by the group, compile your information using either a content analysis or percentages and charts, and compare your results to Vygotsky's theory, indicating whether your data support the constructs of the theory. Then select either a Piagetian, neo-Piagetian, information processing, or cognitive science theorist (e.g, Piaget, Case, Fischer, Kail, Siegler, Flavell, Gopnik) to see if his/her ideas also explain the results. Tell which theory gives a better explanation and which approach would be likely to predict best the future development of the children.

*(continued)*

4. Using informal and clinical observation for at least 1 hour, collect a language corpus from children in the age range of 18 months to 4 years. Collect the language in two situations, one with an adult and the other either with child alone at play or playing with a peer. Each child should be observed separately by a group member. After observing, interview each child's parent, asking at least six questions about the child's language development, first words, understanding of commands, ability to request needs through language. Using psycholinguistic information about language development (phonetic awareness, syntax, semantics, pragmatics), code the language samples. After the sets of data are reviewed by the group, compile your information using percentages, charts, and language examples. Compare your results to psycholinguistic theory (e.g., Chomsky, Nelson, Tomasello) to see if his/her theory explains the children's language development. Then, select either a sociohistorical (Vygotsky), constructivist (Piaget), behaviorist (Skinner), evolutionary (Pinker), or biological (Lenneberg) theoretical alternate perspective and tell how this view would explain results. Indicate whether psycholinguistic theory held true for your subjects, or whether the other selected approach gives a better explanation, and which approach would be likely to predict best the future development of the children.

5. Using clinical observation, present two moral dilemmas and two social convention dilemmas to children of at least two different ages. Working with each child separately, ask them to discuss the dilemmas, giving you their answers and then telling why they answered as they did. Record their reasons. Then bring the children together and ask all the children to consider and discuss the dilemmas again together (hopefully they will have had somewhat different answers), and record whether any of the children change their answers after hearing the reasons of the other children. After the sets of data are reviewed by the group, compile your information using a scoring method like Kohlberg's and Turiel's and compare your results to the theories of Kohlberg and Turiel, indicating whether your data support the constructs of these two theories. Then compare the results to the views of Damon, Eisenberg, and/or Gilligan, and tell which theory gives a better explanation and which approach would be likely to predict best the future development of the children.

6. Observe the same child (age 3 to 15) in three different settings (e.g., home, classroom, playground, church, setting with friends), using a running record, event sample, or time sample method. Keep track of a set of specific behaviors that are of interest to you (e.g., social interactions, learning styles, temperament, language abilities) and record the setting variables that occur, as well as antecedent and consequent events. Total observation should be about 2½ hours (in 30- to 60-minute segments), with all group members observing the same child at different times and in different settings. (You may all observe together in all settings, if group wishes to do so.) After your observation is concluded, interview your subject or subject's parents and ask at least six questions that probe ecological effects on development. After the sets of data are reviewed by the group, compile your information as appropriate for your method and then compare the results to Bronfenbrenner's theory, indicating whether your data support the constructs of the theory. Then compare your results using Bandura's, Erikson's, Fischer's, Vygotsky's, Rogoff's, or Ogbu's theoretical view. Tell which better explains the development of this child and which approach would be likely to predict best the future development of the child.

*(continued)*

7.  Observe, using a running account or a time sample, the children in different families (one family for each group member) as they watch 2 hours of television and/or video that they have chosen. Record both the children's language comments/responses and their behaviors as they watch. Also analyze the program content for the following: adult interaction styles modeled, social/antisocial behaviors modeled, language usage of characters, and gender identity roles displayed. Be sure to record specific examples of violent and gender sterotypic themes in the programs. Then interview the children and at least one of their parents individually, asking at least six questions about the models seen and the social behaviors exhibited by the children after seeing these programs regularly. After the sets of data are reviewed by the group, compile your information as appropriate for your method and compare the results to Bandura's theory, indicating whether your data support the constructs of the theory. Then select either Freud, Bem, Kohlberg, Bronfenbrenner, Damon, or Eisenberg and compare the results to that theoretical view. Tell which better explains the development of these children and which approach would be likely to predict best the future development of the children.

8.  Conduct a 1- to 1½-hour interview with an adult between the ages of 35 and 75, asking detailed questions about their socioemotional, cognitive, language, sociomoral, gender identity, physical, and health conditions over the course of their life span (from childhood to present age). Each group member should select a different individual. Record examples they give that support their viewpoints. Then, using a content analysis approach, identify themes related to the life span theorists' perspectives. Select three of the following theorists who have addressed aspects of life span development: Neugarten, Baltes, Schaie, Labouvie-Vief, Elder, Erikson, Freud, or Bandura, Compare the results to these three theoretical perspectives, and tell which aspects of their theories best explain the developmental progress of each individual interviewed and why. Report which theoretical perspectives would be most likely to predict the future development of these individuals

NOTE: To do observations of human subjects you must also ask their permission and have them sign a permission form for themselves or for their child. The permission form should explain your observation purpose, assure them that they will not be identified by name in your report of findings, and let them know that the observation is a learning experience for you, not research that will be published.

## Putting Theoretical Perspectives into Practice

Often readers of a text on human development theory view the concepts of various theoretical perspectives as information to be remembered long enough to enable them to perform well on a test, but they do not see that information as meaningfully useful for their professional practice. One purpose of this text is to help readers gain sufficient understanding of theoretical constructs and the empirical data supporting those constructs to be able to select useful strategies that will assist them in solving developmental problems they encounter in their professional practice. Whatever one's professional field, a personally defined theoretical perspective must be gained that will be useful in analyzing developmental problems, planning strategies to further developmental goals, and designing methods to test whether such strategies have been fruitful (Paul & Elder, 2003). In addition to being useful in professional practice, such knowledge should contribute guidance for one's personal life as well. Although this goal of incorporating theoretical ideas into everyday practice seems to be straightforward, it is not easily achieved for many reasons. Two of those reason are as follows.

- Although students read and use ideas in their courses, they may not really think those ideas through and internalize their foundational meanings. That is, they may not think critically about the discipline that they are studying (see Paul & Elder, 2003; www.criticalthinking.org).

- Theoretical ideas are often presented out of the context of practical use, and therefore it may be difficult for students to make connections between these constructs and their potential use in practice.

For students to gain a deep understanding of the theoretical perspectives included in this text, these two problems must be addressed. Therefore, a brief discussion of how to study a discipline is warranted, and some suggestions for applying theoretical constructs to practice are needed.

To reach the goal of really understanding the discipline of human development, according to the writers of *How to Study and Learn a Discipline* (Paul & Elder, 2003), the key is to learn to think within the logic of the discipline, which requires the use of "activated knowledge." Rather than learning "inert information" (memorized but not understood) or "activated ignorance" (taking in incorrect information and then using it), it is important to be able to explain the basic ideas and the underlying system of ideas, to define the important terminology in one's own words, to be able to adopt the point of view of the theorist and to think within the theory's logic, to compare these ideas to competing systems of ideas, to raise vital questions, and to relate these ideas to significant professional problems. Table 2.1 provides a set of questions that students can use to be sure they are using activated knowledge.

To reach the goal of having the ability to apply theoretical knowledge to "real-world" problems requires practicing this skill in many ways. To assist in

---

**Table 2.1**  Activated Knowledge Questions

Can I explain the underlying system of ideas that defines this theory?

Can I explain the most basic ideas in it to someone who doesn't understand it?

Could I write a glossary of its most basic vocabulary?

Do I understand the extent to which the theory involves a great deal or very little expert disagreement?

Have I written out the basic logic of the theory?

Can I compare and contrast the logic of the theory with that of other theories?

To what extent can I relate the subject to significant problems in the world?

To what extent has thinking in this field helped me to become more intellectually autonomous?

---

*Source:* Reprinted from *Activated Knowledge Questions [for Human Development Theories]*. From *How to Study and Learn a Discipline Using Critical Thinking Concepts and Tools* (p. 47) by R. Paul and L. Elder, 2003.

this goal, each chapter gives suggestions concerning the practical applications of the theories discussed. In addition, case examples that require putting on the theoretical "glasses" of different theorists are included, as are suggestions for collecting observational data related to various developmental domains and analyzing the data through two or more theoretical perspectives. "Activated knowledge" is essential for practical problem solving, and the first step in fostering this is by "finding the problem" (Dewey, 1910/1997). As information about theory is presented, therefore, students can seek problem examples in their everyday lives that might be explained through various theoretical frameworks. The more they attempt to apply theory to practice, the greater will be their skill in using these theoretical ideas to solve the human development problems they encounter.

## Summary

This chapter has discussed the research methods used by developmental theorists following varied conceptualizations of knowledge attainment and stressed the importance of evaluating theories on the basis of the evidence they provide that supports the theoretical constructs. Because there are differing view of appropriate research methods, however, testability of each theoretical explanation relies on acceptance of the perspective taken by the theorist. The importance of working actively to understand theoretical ideas and to make them personally and professionally relevant has also been stressed. The following case can be used to test understanding of some of the concepts discussed in this chapter.

## Case 2. The Collaborative Research Team

The researchers at Inquiry University are designing a research study for which they hope to get a major federal grant. The team originally consisted of Dr. Empiricist, Dr. Rationalist, and Dr. Sociohistorical, but recently a new researcher, Dr. Dynamical, has just joined the group. They are gathered to discuss a research design for a study of the motor development of toddlers. Their research questions are centered on whether and how toddlers' developing motor skills might influence their language vocabulary development and their social skill development. Think about the various views of knowledge these researchers may hold and what research evidence they would want to find to support their theoretical view. Then answer the following questions.

What factors might each of them think are most important to include in the research design?

How might Dr. Empiricist's and Dr. Rationalist's research designs differ?

What would be some of the concerns of Dr. Sociohistorical and Dr. Dynamical when they evaluate the designs of the other two researchers?

Where would be the team's points of agreement and of disagreement?

Could they get together to submit a design that had components that would satisfy all of them?

(You can use the ideas in Figure 1.3 to help you answer these questions.)

## Readings

K. W. Fischer and S. P. Rose, *Rulers, Models, and Nonlinear Dynamics*, pp. 261–264.

J. U. Ogbu, *Origins of Human Competence*, pp. 265–281.

## Suggested Readings

Bandura, A., Ross, D., & Ross, S. A. (1963) Imitation of film-mediated aggressive models. *Journal of Abnormal and Social Psychology, 66,* 3–9, 11.

Fischer, K. W. & Rose. S. P. (1999). Rulers, models, and nonlinear dynamics: Measurement and method in developmental research. In G. Savelsbergh, H. vander Maas, & P. van Geart (Eds.). *Nonlinear developmental processes* (pp. 197–201). Amsterdam: Royal Netherlands Academy of Arts and Sciences.

Ogbu, J. U. (1981). Origins of human competence: A cultural-ecological perspective. *Child Development, 52,* 413–423; 425–429.

Piaget, J. (1978). Dominoes. In J. Piaget, *Success and understanding* (pp. 13–26). Cambridge, MA: Harvard University Press.

*Source:* Hi & Lois © King Features Syndicate.

# Theories with Major Emphasis on Personality and Social–Emotional Development

One area of great interest to theorists of human development has been that of social and emotional development, perhaps because developmental achievements in these domains often have been used to predict how children become successful adults, as defined by their culture and historical time period. These theorists attempt to explain universals of development, but they often also characterize individual difference aspects. Thus, at times their theories have been called "personality" theories because they explain "a relatively stable pattern of behaving, feeling, and thinking that distinguishes one person from another" (Davis & Pallidino, 2003, p. 459). This chapter focuses on two of the most prominent theorists who were concerned with the development of personality and social/emotional health—Sigmund Freud and Erik Erikson. Although their theories have implications for other developmental areas, their primary focus was on explaining social and emotional developmental stages and the personality dimensions that may be formed by experiences encountered in each stage. The chapter includes information on psychodynamic theorists, as well as an evaluation and critique of psychodynamic theory in relation to the criteria for judging theory testability and usefulness in practice.

# Freud's Theory of Psychosexual Development

Sigmund Freud (1856–1939) was particularly interested in the scientific explanation of human behavior, which became a popular area of study after Darwin's evolutionary theory was published. He lived most of his life in Vienna, leaving only when the Nazis invaded and threatened the life of Jewish citizens, and spent his final year in England. Freud was one of the first theorists who thought that the causes of human behavior could be discovered by scientific methods, and he used the methods that were available in his time to investigate underlying developmental causes of adult mental health issues (1936, 1938, 1962). In his medical training he studied with some of the greatest scientists of that era, such as physiologist Ernest von Bruke and neurologist Jean-Martin Charcot (see Thornton, 2005), and he collaborated with them on some of his early work. For example, he tried (and subsequently rejected) hypnotism, which was advocated by Charcot. Freud was greatly influenced when he was developing his theory by Joseph Breuer's work (see Stein, 1991) about trauma in childhood having a debilitating effect on adult functioning. He and Breuer proposed that these past traumatic experiences highly influenced personality development and thought that it was essential to uncover the traumatic occurrences to resolve adult personality issues. In Freud's clinical work he encountered some patients with emotional problems that may have been related to the actual trauma of sexual abuse; however, given the Victorian mores at that time, this was not an acceptable condition for him to report. He may have reinterpreted such patient reports to be sexual fantasy and desire rather than to be actual abuse. Breuer eventually objected to Freud's stress on the sexual aspects of personality development, and so their collaboration was ended.

## Basic Constructs of Freud's Theory

Because Freud was certain that causes for unhealthy personalities could be found and that they were not explained by conscious thought, he postulated that there must be an unconscious element to the mind that influences the expression of instincts or drives, which were the energizing and motivating forces in humans (1936, 1938, 1962). He proposed that unconscious processes underlie conscious processes, and these unconscious needs and wishes influence feelings and social behaviors. He conceived the conscious mind as only the tip of the "iceberg," with the unconscious comprising most of the mind. He also proposed a preconscious area between these two, which is able to bring some hidden thoughts and feelings to a conscious level.

Freud identified two forces of energy, which he called Eros (the life instinct), which included self-preserving and erotic impulses, and Thanatos (the death instinct), which included self-destruction, aggression, and cruelty. Because he accepted Helmholtz's view (see Bierhalter, 1993) that energy is never lost but just transformed, Freud thought that human energy was never reduced; it just appeared in different forms. The Eros energy, *libido,* was labeled sexual energy by Freud, but the term *sexual* has a broader meaning than "genital"; he explained that the "sexual life comprises the function of obtaining pleasure from any zones of the body" (1938, p. 4). Freud hypothesized that from birth, humans try to meet their needs for bodily pleasure, but when this attempt is thwarted, it causes psychological conflict. Those needs could be transformed into Thanatos energy (e.g., aggression) or could continue to cause conflicts because the Eros energy needs were still dominant. He proposed that children go through a series of conflicts when their Eros and Thanatos needs and the demands of the environment are incongruent. Therefore, major childhood trauma such as abuse or loss of parental care could affect the resolution of these conflicts and have lasting effects on later development.

Freud was particularly concerned with learning how unhealthy personalities develop, and he hypothesized that every child goes through a series of psychosexual conflicts. He thought that each age period has a different conflict issue, and if the conflict is not resolved appropriately, the person becomes fixated at that stage, resulting in the use of ineffective defense mechanisms and exhibition of pathological behaviors. The major concepts of his theory are derived from these assumptions (1938).

Freud believed in an epigenetic principle of growth; that is, development of the personality is biologically based and governed by a preset plan. This is the "nature" element of Freud's theory. As the child develops, three components of the personality are activated. The earliest is the *id*, which is governed by the Pleasure Principle that drives infants toward gaining their basic needs and wishes. The second, the *ego*, develops over the first years of life and is governed by the Reality Principle, which controls the basic needs and wishes in response to environmental demands. Finally, at about age 4 or 5, the *superego*, which is formed by guilt/shame over inappropriate desires related to the parents, is where conscience and morality develop. Note that Freud's three mental areas parallel Plato's view of the tripartite mind (appetite, spirit, soul). When the needs of the Id are not met or able to be regulated appropriately by the Reality Principle or when the demands of the Superego are unreasonable or difficult to perform, the Ego creates defense mechanisms to explain and control the Id's desires and the Superego's demands. Although everyone uses some defense mechanisms, they are the major coping mechanism of the unhealthy personality, and they do not result in effective resolution of problems. For example, Freud saw the defense mechanism of *repression* as being used to move traumatic experiences from conscious awareness to the unconscious. The experiences are not then accessible for rational thought, but they still affect the personality and behavior of the individual, usually in an unhealthy way. Freud explained that repression was a force in "infantile amnesia," the inability of most people to recall events from the first few years of life. (Later information processing theorists would explain this phenomena as due to the inability of infants to code memories in ways that make them easy to recall.) Table 3.1 shows some of the defense mechanisms Freud identified and gives examples of how they might be used.

Although the use of joking is not technically called a defense mechanism, Freud discussed how the use of joking revealed unconscious wishes and thoughts by allowing expression of hostile or sexually oriented thoughts and feelings (1960). That is, although joking often expresses negative feelings, it does so in a way that is usually still acceptable in society, allowing those thoughts to be ex-

**Table 3.1**   Defense Mechanism Examples

| Reason Given | Defense Mechanism |
| --- | --- |
| I'm sorry I'm late but the traffic was just dreadful (really started too late to get to appointment on time). | Rationalization: Giving a false but potentially plausible reason to justify behavior |
| The police said that I hit the other car but I don't remember anything about the accident. | Repression: Burying frightening or unpleasant thoughts in the unconscious mind |
| Telling spouse: This is a horrible dinner; can't you cook anything right! (after having being reprimanded by boss at the office). | Displacement: Redirecting unpleasant emotions to a substitute target from the one who was the source of the emotion |
| After that embarrassment happened in class, I just went home, curled up on my bed, and hugged my old teddy bear. | Regression: Reverting to immature behavior that was outgrown at an earlier age |
| The group hasn't been at all nice and cooperative with me (when person did not treat others well or cooperate). | Projection: Attributing one's own thoughts or feelings on to other persons |
| I never miss the Red Sox games and I wear their cap and t-shirt everywhere (when person is non-athletic). | Identification: Supporting one's self esteem by forming an imaginary (or real) bond with someone or some admirable group |
| I always hug and kiss my sister-in-law Jane when I see her (even though the person dislikes Jane). | Reaction formation: Behaving in the opposite way from how a person feels |
| I used to hit people all the time when I was a kid; now I am a Karate instructor. | Sublimation: Hiding true feelings that are not appropriate by doing something that allows them to be expressed appropriately |

pressed rather than repressed. Freud saw humor as a developmental phenomenon that began as part of play (joy in mastery), but then advanced to a stage of jesting (nonsense and teasing) and finally to joking (deliberate use of riddles and jokes to convey meanings). He saw joking as having two elements: tendacious (hurtful), which involved release of libidinal drives, and nontendacious, which was the cognitive element of joking. He identified the "comic" as being similar to playful childhood expressions and reserved the word *humor* for attempts to cope with negative emotions, that is, to defend against difficult situations without being overwhelmed by unpleasant emotion (Martin, 1998).

### Phases of Psychosexual Development

Freud outlined five "phases" of psychosexual development, each of which has a conflict between instinctual desires (Id) and the need to meet the realities of the environment (Ego). In the third phase, the conflict also includes the demands of the Superego. He saw the environment (nurture) as important for determining how conflicts are resolved. Although the phases are described as distinct, he cautioned that the first three phases do not succeed each other "in a clear-cut fashion: one of them may appear in addition to another, they may overlap one another, they may be present simultaneously" (1938, p. 6).

- The first of these is the Oral phase (ages 0 to 1), in which bodily pleasure is primarily derived from the mouth (sucking). Conflict occurs if the parent is ineffective or erratic in satisfying this need, and conflict is intensified when weaning from breast (or bottle) occurs. It is resolved by the infant gaining satisfaction with a wider range of eating methods, occasional thumb sucking, oral exploration of objects, and use of other exploration means to gain pleasure. If an adult still derives most pleasure from oral activities (e.g., excessive eating, drinking, smoking), Freud would say that this phase was not resolved healthily.

- Freud called ages 1 to 3 the Anal phase, in which pleasure is derived from the anus (control of defecating). The conflict usually occurs with toilet training; contrary to adult views, most infants do not find their fecal matter unpleasant. In this phase, aggressive impulses are higher. This conflict is resolved by infants gaining pleasure in the control of body functions and leads to their learning both to give and receive. If an adult is grasping, miserly, and selfish; profligate and wasteful; or overly aggressive, Freud would say the phase was not resolved healthily.

- The ages 3 to 6 period, which Freud called the Phallic phase, has been the one most often questioned by other theorists. His initial explanations were shocking to the general public as well. He observed that during this age period children most often gain pleasure from touching their genitals (masturbating). Most theorists do agree that this is the age period when gender identity is formed, and because the genitals are the indicator of sex, they are the focus of attention. Freud thought that in developing a stable gender identity, boys may go through a period of castration anxiety, and girls may have a period of penis envy as they learn to understand the differences in male and female sexual organs. Freud elaborated on the conflict of this stage by stating that boys desire their mothers and see their fathers as rivals for their mother's affection (Oedipus complex), but the conflict is resolved by eventual identification with the same-sex parent (the father). He later explained a relatively similar process for girls, that is, first seeing the mother as a rival but then gaining identification with the mother (Electra complex). The process was seen as more complex for boys because the mother is usually the primary caregiver for both boys and girls. If adults are not clear about their gender identity or have other sexual problems, Freud would say the stage was not resolved healthily. Freud also posited that the Superego is developed during this period due to children's guilt over their unconscious desires, resulting in this harsh "overseer" that expects acceptance of the moral values of the identified parent and adherence to strict morality. Thus, another unhealthy result of the Phallic phase would be to find adults with a lack of moral values, especially in regard to guilt for wrongdoing or, conversely, adults who are so consumed by guilt that functioning is impaired. Freud saw guilt as a major force in morality, which is probably another indication of the values of the early 20th century.

- Although Freud identified a Latency phase (ages 6 to 12), he did not see an erotic focus during this age period, and because there were no psychosexual conflicts, he did not elaborate on this stage. He saw it as a time for acceptance of reality principle rules (Ego development), expanding nonsexual social interactions/friendships, and gaining ability to focus on school learning.

- Puberty (age 12+) was seen by Freud as the final phase of psychosexual development, and it results in the ability to have adult sexual intimacy. He called this the Genital phase, which presumably is resolved by finding a sexual partner. His description of this time period was also not as highly developed, although the period between puberty and gaining a sexual partner might extend over many years.

If adult sexual behavior was aberrant from the norms of society, however, Freud did not attribute the reasons for adult sexual problems to these later phases of development. Rather, he believed the crucial psychosexual conflicts occurred in the first three phases, and events from those times were the causes of unhealthy personality development. (Due to infantile amnesia, he thought these events are often inaccessible to the person without therapeutic intervention.) To treat adults who had unresolved conflicts at these stages, Freud probed their unconscious minds through dream recall and free association of words. He founded the clinical method of psychoanalysis as a means of investigating the unconscious feelings and beliefs that had been initiated in early childhood.

### Theoretical Influence

Freud wrote numerous books and gave many lectures explaining his theoretical ideas. These ideas drew a group of other "disciples," and the "psychodynamic school" became a major force in personality theory. It included Alfred Adler; Carl Jung; Freud's daughter, Anna Freud; Karen Horney; and Melanie Klein. Some of these followers initially studied his principles but then went on to revise and develop their own theories, taking some aspects of Freudian theory and discarding others. Although Adler and Jung both took different theoretical paths, Adler focusing on "individual psychology" (1927) and Jung on "collective unconscious" (1917), the psychodynamic school was a dominant force during much of the early and mid 20th century. Horney (1937) and Klein (1949) both expanded the theory in varied directions. Many aspects of Freud's ideas were also embraced by G. Stanley Hall and other theorists in the United States.

Freud's youngest daughter, Anna, carried on the psychoanalytic tradition in Great Britain and created a method of therapy for young children involving their play (A. Freud, 1946; A. Freud & Burlingham, 1943). She thought that children also need to explore their unconscious minds and be helped by therapists to resolve their conflicts, but because they are usually unable to discuss their dreams or use language to free-associate ideas, she used their play (primarily pretense) to enable them to gain access to their unconscious conflicts. By observing children's play, the psychoanalytical therapist can bring to the surface the unconscious concerns of the children. Anna Freud initiated her work with children who had experienced the trauma of World War II, many of whom were separated from parents and sent to the country during the war. The Anna Freud Institute in Great Britain is her legacy. Play therapy methods continue to be considered especially useful for children who have experienced physical and/or sexual abuse or who have suffered other extreme trauma because their trauma can disrupt the naturally healthy uses of play in childhood (A. Freud, 1946, 1989; A. Freud & Burlingham, 1943).

### Critique of Freud's Theory

Although Freud was one of the first to believe that science should be the means for studying human development, his theory has been judged harshly because it does not meet the test of falsifiability. That is, using the techniques of 20th-century science, his theory cannot be objectively studied so that its constructs can be supported or discounted with empirical evidence. Testability, one of the major criteria for valid theory, is difficult because his theory is "circular" in that it has an answer for findings that do not support the theory by maintaining that these contrary results can still be explained as part of the theory. For example, early conflicts over toilet training might result in an adult who is miserly or profligate, and conflicts over superego development might make an adult lack appropriate guilt over wrongdoing or be filled with neurotic guilt. Also, it has a flaw of naive theory in that it "predicts backward," assigning causality after rather than before events. The inconsistency of Freud's analytical and research methods have also been criticized (see Roazen, 1975). Freud's emphasis on sexuality development as the root of personality was difficult for many to accept, even for some of his followers, and his focus primarily on male development in the Oedipal phase has been interpreted as denigrating female development. His views of women's sexual development and of "unhealthy" adult sexuality have been questioned and rejected by both feminist and gay theorists (e.g., Birns & Sternglanz, 1983). Although Freud saw his theory has having universal applicability, it was really "situated" within the patriarchal authoritarian culture of Victorian society, and thus the adult problems of harsh repression and immobilizing guilt that he suggested arose from conflictual early childhood experiences may not be applicable to child-rearing issues of today when other child-rearing techniques are more prevalent.

With the advent of neuroscience and dynamic systems theories, however, some researchers are taking a new look at a few of Freud's ideas. For example, although his characterization of how the human mind deals with emotions is not technically accurate, neuropsychological findings of the influence of certain limbic system structures (e.g., the amygdala) on emotional expression and the neuronal connections of such structures to the frontal lobe's interpretation of traumatic experiences are causing some theorists to look again at the connection between "unconscious" and "conscious" thought (Segalowitz, 1994). Freud's views of the complexity of mental development and on the effects of emotions and desires on thinking processes may gain additional support as in-depth study of the brain continues.

In regard to the "usefulness" criteria, Sigmund Freud's ideas were very powerful influences on mental health and developmental practice during much of the 20th century. Freud's treatment method, psychoanalysis, has continued to be a recognized therapy approach, although it has also changed over time as the types of emotional problems have changed. His theoretical constructs were judged to be very useful in practice for child rearing during the mid 20th century and were the basis for many parental advice books published at that time (e.g., Fraiberg, 1968). Important practical effects of his theory were that parents were made aware of the possible negative long-term results of harsh authoritarian child-rearing practices, and they gained insights into ways to address issues of conflict that children and parents often must address, such as toilet training. Present-day child-rearing practices that permit children's expression of feelings and use authoritative or permissive approaches rather than authoritarian ones owe much of their basis to Freud's views. Recently, evidence of Freud's practical effect in another field has emerged. His ideas apparently influenced the emerging field of public relations because his nephew, Edward Bernays, learned of Freud's concept of the unconscious and the power of "pleasure principle" wishes, and he related them to ways to influence public opinion (Bernays, 1923; Spiegel, 2005). Bernays's use of Freud's ideas had a great impact on advertising methods and public relations efforts; that is, they are often designed to appeal to unconscious wishes (i.e., to "id" desires). Freud was not pleased with this use of his ideas, however.

Interestingly, much of the terminology that Freud invented to describe human development has become part of the common everyday language, and most users of those terms do not even realize that were initially defined by Freud. For example, people use terms such as *regression, repression,* and *projection* in describing their social or emotional actions, characterize children's development using terms such as *ego* and *psychic energy,* and acknowledge the existence of "unconscious" wishes that may be expressed in dreaming. They "free-associate" ideas and make "Freudian slips" (verbal mistakes that are expressions of the unconscious mind's feelings), and they value the use of play therapy to help children who have experienced trauma. In the late 20th century, Freud's theory played a minor role in most child development books and was relegated to a few pages of historical discussion in many general psychology texts. However, his ideas are still influential to some extent, and in certain fields, such as personality theory, they are still taught in detail. Psychoanalytic training still requires a medical degree, and psychiatrists use therapeutic techniques that involve discussions of patients' wishes and dreams, although they also use medications that were unavailable in Freud's time. The school of psychodynamic theory has continued to develop in various ways, in particular focusing more on the development of the ego, and it has influenced the work of John Bowlby, Stanley Greenspan, and Stella Chase and Alexander Thomas, who are discussed in chapter 4. Erik Erikson's theory also has primary roots in Freud's theoretical perspective.

# Erikson's Theory of Psychosocial Development

One theorist from the psychodynamic tradition whose work is considered currently important in explaining human development is Erik Erikson (1902–1994). Erikson also was born in Europe, but he lived most of his adult life in the United States, immigrating before World War II. Although he never received a college degree, he studied psychoanalysis and taught in one of Anna Freud's schools in Vienna before developing his own theory of human development.

## Basic Concepts of Erikson's Theory

Erikson's theory draws on many of Freud's concepts; however, his emphasis is on explaining how healthy personalities develop rather than focusing on unhealthy developmental processes. In defining healthy personality, he accepted the same

time phases of importance that Freud outlined, but he reformulated the early conflicts identified by Freud. He focused on the growth-promoting crises of each period and discussed how these crises can be well resolved to promote psychosocial
development. That is, he outlined how social interactions at each age period may
affect psychological identity—the Ego dimension of Freud's theory. Although
Erikson continued to stress the epigentic unfolding (nature) aspects of personality
(from the rationalist tradition), he put more emphasis on how social factors
throughout life influenced developmental trajectories (nurture). Erikson was one
of the first theorists to hypothesize about life span development by extending the
ego identity crisis periods throughout the life span and defining how healthy resolution of crises in each age period could occur. He identified eight crisis periods
and explained the major social–emotional task of each period. He stressed that
these crisis periods are not mutually exclusive and unchangeable; rather, an important aspect of these crises is that a social–emotional issue that may be primary
at one age can recur again at another crisis stage if events at that time period require a reworking of that issue (Erikson, 1963, 1968).

Perhaps because of the influence of Anna Freud, Erikson was especially interested in how play influenced development, primarily in childhood, but also in
its transformations into the ritual play of later life, and he emphasized the importance of play as a factor in development at all ages (1972, 1977). He wrote extensively about how children use their play (primarily pretense) to gain feelings of
power over their lives and control over their emotions. He also saw emotional
growth as occurring in every period, even in the final phases of life. He agreed
with Freud that if a particular crisis is not successfully resolved, it can affect later
outcomes. However, he thought the issues that were important in that stage
could still be addressed and be resolved successfully at a later age/stage, particularly with the help of psychoanalysis.

### Crises Periods in Psychosocial Development

Erikson's theory might be termed a "growth-oriented" one that focuses on
human strength rather than human vulnerability. Each of the eight periods of
psychosocial development he outlined has two possible outcome extremes, with
healthy personality development being situated at the "optimistic" ego strength
end of the continuum (1963, 1968). Healthy resolution of each crisis, however,
may include social–emotional factors related to the other end of the continuum so
that the monitoring and evaluating experiences will be realistic.

- The first stage, Trust versus Mistrust, occupies the same time period as
  Freud's Oral phase, birth to 1 year. According to Erikson, infants learn to
  trust if their care is consistent, warm, and supportive. Through that type of
  care, trust in the people in the environment develops, and this trust then extends to trust in a ordered world that can be explored safely. The crisis is
  successfully resolved if infants approach the world with trusting attitudes
  and gain expectations that the people in that world can be relied on. This
  trusting attitude will then extend throughout life and make them open to experiences and able to give and receive love and care. Erikson said that the

basic strength gained in this period is *hope*. The crisis is not well resolved if infant care is inconsistent, harsh, unreliable, and abusive or cold, making infants unable to trust in the world. In situations of abuse and/or neglect or in care settings where the caregivers are emotionally uninvolved or unstable, the infant is likely to become mistrusting rather than trusting. Erikson believed that such infants approach others with unclear expectations or show a sense of fear in most situations because they have not learned to trust. Children who have had this experience are often seen to be constantly monitoring their environment, and they often respond to care attempts with rejection or uncaring attitudes. If a strong sense of mistrust persists throughout life, they may have anxieties and insecurities, and they may withdraw from experiences because they mistrust the world. Of course, all infants need to have some inconsistent experiences and at times need to wait to have their needs met; otherwise, they would have an unrealistic view of the world. Such experiences help infants to distinguish between environments in which trust is correctly warranted and ones in which some initial testing (i.e., mistrust) of the situation may be appropriate. Healthy adults are primarily trusting individuals, but not so trusting that they misread the environmental signals that tell them when some mistrust is warranted.

- Erikson transformed Freud's second phase, Anal (ages 1 to 3), into Autonomy versus Shame and Doubt. He still saw this as the age when children learn to control their bodily functions such as walking alone, eating by themselves, and being toilet trained, but he also stressed their interest in being more independent and making choices about what they want to eat or wear or do. Words such as "mine" and phrases such as "Do it myself!" are common in their vocabulary during this age period. The psychosocial environment is important because it can be encouraging of their attempts at autonomy or can restrict or denigrate those attempts. Often parents who controlled everything in their infant's life find it difficult to allow autonomous behavior in their toddlers. The crisis is successfully resolved if children become confident about their abilities and secure about their choices. If children have been criticized and their attempts at autonomy ridiculed or overcontrolled, they may feel inadequate, overdependent, and doubtful of their abilities, which will make them have a sense of shame & doubt about their capabilities. According to Erikson, healthy adults enjoy autonomy and have an accurate appraisal of their abilities. They have a "can do it" attitude and will make the effort to be successful. They a have a sense of dignity and a sense of justice. The basic strength gained in this period is *will* (e.g., determination). Adults who have not resolved this crisis are unsure of themselves and dependent on others' evaluation of their worth, and they may harbor shame about their attempts to be autonomous and doubts about their ability to choose their life paths.

- Having resolved those crises successfully prepares the child for the next stage, which, although it includes the same age period (ages 3 to 6) as Freud's Phallic phase, focuses on the crisis of Initiative versus Guilt. Although Erikson acknowledged the need for children of this age to identify with the same-sex parent and the possibility of rivalry leading to castration fears, he did not really emphasize the processes discussed by Freud. Instead, he focused on the assertiveness of children of this age and their planning of activities, initiation of social interactions, and involvement in creating games and other play activities. This period enables children to take leadership and make decisions and to cooperate in play. Erikson (1963) stated about this period that "the 'Oedipal' stage results not only in the oppressive establishment of a moral sense restricting the horizon of the permissible; it also sets the direction toward the possible and the tangible, which permits the dreams of early childhood to be attached to the goals of an active adult life" (p. 20). Erikson has written extensively about the importance of pretend play during this period for children's social and emotional development. He viewed pretense as the vehicle through which the child can be empowered. In the "real" world, children are still weak and small but in the "pretense" world, they are all powerful. By taking on the role of a super character (Spiderman) or an adult who is powerful in their lives (the doctor), children can experience the leadership and power position of those individuals. If they have gained this ability to take initiative during this period of life, adults are able to assume roles of power and leadership and to imagine great possibilities. The strength developed in this period is *purpose*. The imposing of guilt because the grand plans may be squelched by adult criticism and control or the taking on of roles that are beyond the child's capacities, resulting in a loss of initiative, are unresolved results of this age period. Adults who have not had the opportunity in childhood to "think big" and act powerful may be more hesitant about taking leadership roles and more trapped in guilt for imagining they can succeed.

- Erikson did not see the Latency (ages 6 to 12) period as a time when no major conflicts are occurring. Instead he saw this also as a crisis period, Industry versus Inferiority, in which children learn to produce good work that gains them satisfaction. This is the age period where children learn to be industrious and to know that this industry will result in achievements that will be valued by teachers and parents. Erikson believed that children learn the fundamentals of technology and adjust themselves to the "tool world." Children who are encouraged for their initiative and efforts will gain a view of themselves as able and effective at completing projects, seeing tasks through to completion, and reaching a standard of excellence. The basic strength gained in this period is *competence*. However, a sense of inadequacy and inferiority can ensue if children do not have the tools they need to be competent, if their efforts are not encouraged, or if they are denigrated. Already at this age some children may feel that their industry will not result in good effects, and they become hesitant to try to achieve. They may dismiss their work as not good enough, give up easily, or refuse to make an effort at all. The successful resolution of this crisis is, of course, adults who tackle hard problems, take pride in their accomplishments, and show industry in achieving goals. The adult who does not have these qualities, according to Erikson, has not successfully resolved the Industry versus Inferiority crisis.

- The crisis that Erikson has written extensively about is that of adolescence, the phase Freud named as the time of sexual maturity without elaborating on its consequences. Throughout all his crises, Erikson emphasized the importance of ego development and identity; however, at the adolescent age, he believed that Identity versus Role Confusion is the primary crisis. At this point in life, all the earlier crises periods are revisited, and adolescents may have to revisit conflicts from earlier life periods and resolve them. Erikson thought that the task for this period was to develop an ego identity that integrated all the earlier identifications, creating a continuity with the adolescents' present struggle to meet the challenge of gaining occupational identity. The basic strength gained in this period is *fidelity*, that is, being "true to the self." He defined role confusion as the trying on of many identities, often "overidentifying" with media figures and other unrealistic role models. In his book *Identity, Youth, and Crisis* (1968), he discussed how various socialization factors can influence identity development, and he pointed out that this process may be even harder for adolescents from diverse backgrounds, in which social and cultural forces may give varying messages that affect identity. His initial explanation of the female identity crisis was influenced by the view that "biology is destiny" for females; thus, he felt that female identity was related to intimacy—finding a mate—and so their identity search was often held in abeyance until they found a relationship. In his later writings he moderated this viewpoint. The successful resolution of the adolescent crisis, according to Erikson is for young people to have a strong ego identity (sense of self) that will enable them to accept their abilities and uniqueness and also to have goals for change and further growth. An unsuccessful resolution would make them lack direction, feel unproductive, and be unsure of their own strengths. Although this crisis period is the prime one for developing identity, Erikson believed that there are other crises throughout life when identity will again be examined, but that these reexaminations will lead to further growth.

- The young adulthood crisis, Intimacy versus Isolation, covers a wide age period, depending on the life circumstances of young people. Erikson believed that having a strong identity would make young adults ready for intimacy, which requires sharing and committing to another in partnership. Although the major focus of intimacy is on having a mature sexual relationship, it is also necessary for deep friendship, affiliations with groups, and other interpersonal relationships. In Erikson's view, having a clear sense of one's identity is important before sharing oneself intimately with others. He thought that it is more possible to face the fear of ego loss when one becomes intimate with another if a strong identity is already achieved. A poor resolution of this crisis is in never being able to share one's self with another, resulting in isolation. The person who has not resolved ego identity issues may be afraid to become intimate because of fear of losing identity in the relationship experience. They may be likely to see others as dangerous and thus be exclusive, prejudiced, competitive, and territorial. On the other hand, the person with a strong sense of intimacy will have the basic strength of *love*, which enables them to be intimate with others and finally extend that love to a broad circle of humanity.

• Thus, in middle adulthood, presumably after having successfully resolved both identity and intimacy crises, Erikson proposed the crisis of Generativity versus Stagnation. Although much more emphasis has been placed on Erikson's earlier and later crises, he believed that this period is one of the most important because it is related to higher human concerns of learning, teaching, and building for the future. The crisis in this period is whether the individual will have concern for helping and guiding the next generation, through parenting, teaching, leading organizations, and developing projects that promote future generative institutions. If generativity is not developed, adults may focus only on their own needs and become "self-indulgent," which leads to stagnation and personal impoverishment. Erikson said that the mere fact of becoming a parent does not necessarily make a person generative; rather it is the concern for helping younger individuals develop well that marks the generative person. People who are not parents but who form or strengthen organizations that are concerned about the young have been successful in this crisis; they show the basic strength of *care*. The development of generativity is essential in Erikson's view for meeting the crisis of old age effectively.

• In old age the crisis of Ego Integrity versus Despair can only be resolved successfully if the individual has successfully traversed the earlier crises because it is in this eighth stage that people see their life efforts as having had meaning and value. The crisis consists of being able to accept one's own life cycle and the fact of its final end. Individuals who fear death have not resolved this final crisis. To resolve the crisis, many people find order and meaning in their life's work, in religion, politics, the arts and sciences, or other broader world experiences. Thus they gain the basic strength of *wisdom*, in which emotional integration and a sense of completion reside. If they have successfully resolved the earlier crises and can see the entire cycle of life from its earliest stage, the combination of hope and wisdom should enable them to have faith. Erikson connected the last integrity stage with the earliest trust stage by concluding that if older people have enough integrity not to fear their death, this will enable children to feel confident and fearless in facing life's challenges. Erikson and his wife lived to an old age themselves, and they collaborated on writing more about the final stages of life during those years. He continued to be active as a writer and speaker throughout his own integrity crisis period and emphasized how early play experiences can affect the rituals that enhance the meaning of life at later stages (Erikson, 1977).

Table 3.2 shows how Erikson characterized his model of crisis periods and the strengths that should come from each of them.

**Table 3.2**  Epigenetic Scheme of Psychosocial Development

| | 1 | 2 | 3 | 4 | 5 | 6 | 7 | 8 |
|---|---|---|---|---|---|---|---|---|
| I<br>Infancy | Trust vs. mistrust | | | | Unipolarity vs. premature self-differentiation | | | |
| II<br>Early Childhood | | Autonomy vs. shame, doubt | | | Bipolarity vs. autism | | | |
| III<br>Play Age | | | Initiative vs. guilt | | Play identification vs. (Oedipal) fantasy identities | | | |
| IV<br>School Age | | | | Industry vs. inferiority | Work identification vs. identity foreclosure | | | |
| V<br>Adolescence | Time perspective vs. time diffusion | Self-certainty vs. identity consciousness | Role experimentation vs. negative identity | Anticipation of achievement vs. work paralysis | Identity vs. identity diffusion | Sexual identity vs. bisexual diffusion | Leadership polarization vs. authority diffusion | Ideological polarization vs. diffusion of ideals |
| VI<br>Young Adult | | | | | Solidarity vs. social isolation | Intimacy vs. isolation | | |
| VII<br>Adulthood | | | | | | | Generativity vs. self-absorption | |
| VIII<br>Mature Age | | | | | | | | Integrity vs. disgust, despair |

*Source:* Reproduced from *Epigenetic Scheme of Psychosocial Development from Identity and the Life Cycle* by Erik H. Eirkson. Copyright © 1980 by W. W. Norton & Company, Inc. Copyright © 1959 by International Universities Press, Inc. Used by permission of W. W. Norton & Company, Inc.

## Theoretical Influence

Erikson's theory has continued to be taught in human development classes; however, often the depth of discussion is very superficial. That is, the list of crisis stages may be taught but not the underlying theoretical principles that Erikson discussed. Four particular aspects of his developmental crisis schema have been very influential in regard to research and practice, however, perhaps because they are areas that were not emphasized in Freudian theory. The first is Erikson's focus on ego development, especially in his emphasis on ego identity development during adolescence, which has generated research and provided an impetus for much discussion of the construct of identity development. The second is his emphasis on social–emotional life span development, which has promoted much greater interest in the study of this development during later life crisis stages. His rich descriptions of development after the childhood years, partly derived from biographical work on Luther (Erikson, 1958) and Ghandi (Erikson, 1969) has greatly enriched human development theory. Life span theorists have supported and extended Erikson's life span crises stages, and his later work expanding on the last stage of life has influenced gerontological studies. A third area of influence has been on studies of infant personality and social–emotional development issues, which are a focus of many contemporary theorists. Finally, Erikson's emphasis on play as an important window into young children's development has been of value to early childhood specialists and to psychotherapists. One reason that Erikson's theory has continued to be discussed and expanded may be because it seems to be "intuitively" correct to most people.

## Critique of Erikson's Theory

Although many aspects of Erikson's theory have not been tested empirically, the theory appears to be somewhat more testable than Freud's. Especially in the area of identity development, some studies have at least partially supported his theoretical constructs. For example, a study by Marcia (1966) tested Erikson's identity development construct, and he found that among college-age males, identity development took four forms: identity achievement (Erikson's healthy resolution of the crisis), identity moratorium (crisis in process: searching for options but not decided), identity foreclosure (no crisis: option selected without a search; following parental or "expected" career path), and identity diffusion (no crisis: no urgency in searching for identity). The numbers of males in each category were relatively similar. Thus, Erikson's view that forming an ego identity is crucial for healthy personality development in adolescence was partially supported. Because he emphasized the social nature of development, he would probably agree that changing social conditions may have influenced how and when this crisis is resolved. It is certainly the case that adolescents do "try on" many identities, but because of changing social conditions, they may now do that for a longer period of time without it having unhealthy consequences. Marcia's fourfold model of identity development is shown in Table 3.3.

Other aspects of his theory have received criticism. His characterization of female identity and intimacy development has been critiqued by feminist theo-

**Table 3.3**   Criteria for Identity Statuses

| Position on Occupation and Ideology | Identity Status | | | |
|---|---|---|---|---|
| | Identity Achievement | Foreclosure | Identity Diffusion | Moratorium |
| Crisis | present | absent | present or absent | in crisis |
| Commitment | present | present | absent | present but vague |

*Source:* Reprinted from *Criteria for the identity statuses.* From *Identity in Adolescence* (p. 159) by J. E. Marcia, 1980 in J. Adelson (ed.) *Handbook of Adolescent Psychology.* New York: John Wiley & Sons.

rists because he proposed biological rather than social reasons for female identity development (e.g., Gilligan, 1982). Erikson's descriptions of life span crisis periods may also have been more accurate at the time he wrote than they are presently, because they also were "situated" in that context. For example, his descriptions of identity development written in the 1960s may have been accurate for the time, but changing social norms have made his views on the timing crises for occupational identity not as valid for many groups in Western society. For adolescent males, the urge to find their life work is now less intense because the period of time allowed for occupational identity to be formed has increased through the college years into the mid 20s for a large proportion of the population. If Erikson were developing his theory now, he might address the adolescent and the "youth" crises somewhat differently. The period now being suggested as Youth encompasses the 20s, which, when Erikson wrote, were considered the time for taking on adult responsibilities of job, marriage, and family. Similarly, his views on female identity development might be revised and expressed differently in present times because females' role options have expanded, and the search for an intimate relationship may no longer be as intense for them during the adolescent age period. Thus, what Erikson saw as the undesirable state of role confusion may now be closer to the norm for adolescents, at least in Western societies.

Erikson's discussion of the two final periods of life may also need a revision to account for the longer life span of individuals in present society. At age 60, individuals may still be facing issues of Generativity, especially if marriage age was later than in the past and if their health is good; the issues of Integrity may again need to be addressed at early retirement. Life span theorists have begun to explore all these issues in more depth, and with their sociohistorical perspective, they may be more able to explain the variability in human life span social–emotional and personality development as each historical era affects that development.

In regard to the practical usefulness of his views, there has been great interest in his descriptions of the early childhood crises periods, descriptions of his crises are often discussed in practical advice books for parents, and advice related to his earliest stages has been expanded (e.g., Brazelton, 1974). In particular, his emphasis on the initial stage of trust/mistrust has been emphasized in addressing issues of abuse and neglect, and family therapists have drawn on life span crises descriptions in their work with family members. He has also influenced psychoanalytic practice, especially because of his emphasis on the importance of the development of ego identity.

## Summary

The study of personality, social, and emotional development was a focus of major work during the 20th century, in particular from the rationalist perspective of Freud and Erikson. Both of these theories have received criticism because of their apparent gender bias (against females) and their lack of empirical research evidence in support of their ideas. However, they have also been fruitful theories, not only as influences in the past, but also as catalysts for other research and theory. As neuropsychological and ecological research methods are further developed, theoretical concepts from these theories may received further testing and be reevaluated in the light of new research evidence. The following case may assist in translating these theoretical perspectives into practice.

## Case 3. The Standard Family

The Standard family is gathered at the old homestead of Grandma Mildred Standard on the occasion of her 80th birthday. Present at the event is her oldest son, Bill (age 60), and his wife, Ann (age 61). Their daughter, Madge (age 30), and her husband, Bob (age 35), are there with baby Peter (9 months) and daughter Julie (age 8). Madge's unmarried brother, John (age 24), has just arrived. Grandma's daughter, Janet (age 42), and her husband, Henry (age 48), have brought their children, Donnie (age 2), Jason (age 5), Holly (age 12), Alan (age 16), and Brad (age 20). Mildred also invited Howard (age 72), Mildred's deceased husband's brother, to the celebration, and he has brought his new wife, Sally (age 50). Sally's daughter, Sue (age 33), came with Howard and Sally.

First, draw a diagram of the family system connecting the members of the Standard family and then categorize the psychosocial crises level of each family member according to Erikson's theory of psychosocial development. Think about the basic strengths to be gained in each crisis period. Then imagine that during the year following Mildred's birthday some of these events occur in the family. How might dealing with each event affect resolution of the social–emotional crises facing the family member who is at that stage, and how might the crisis of this individual affect crisis resolutions of various family members who are at other stages?

| | |
|---|---|
| Janet and Henry divorce. | Jason starts kindergarten. |
| Brad graduates from college. | Grandma Mildred has an operation. |
| Madge get a full-time job. | Bill is forced to take early retirement. |
| Alan flunks chemistry. | Peter starts walking and talking. |
| Holly grows 3 inches taller. | Donnie is diagnosed with autism. |
| Julie wins a swimming contest. | Bob gets a promotion. |
| Howard gets Alzheimer's disease. | Sue starts dating John. |

Looking at the younger family members through Freud's eyes, imagine how the psychosexual phase of those children might be affected by some of these family events. What might Freud say would be adult consequences for these children if the conflicts they face are not resolved?

Think about what situated effect these events might have had if they had occurred in the Ramirez family or the Chu family (with culture-appropriate given names). Would the effects have been similar, weaker, stronger?

What if the Standard family had been living in 1930? Would the effects have been similar, weaker, or stronger?

## Readings

E. H. Erikson, *Adolescence*, pp. 282–285.

S. Freud, *Jokes and the Unconscious*, pp. 286–292.

## Suggested Readings

Erikson, E. H. (1968). Adolescence. *Identity, youth, and crisis* (pp. 128–135). New York: Norton.

Erikson, E. H. (1977). The toy stage. *Toys and reason* (pp. 29–39). Toronto: G. J. McLeod Limited.

Freud, A. (1989). Child analysis as the study of mental growth (normal and abnormal). In S. I. Greenspan & G. H. Pollock (Eds.), *The course of life: Vol. 1. Infancy* (pp. 8–14.) Madison, CT: International Universities Press.

Freud, S. (1960). *Jokes and their relation to the unconscious*. London: Routledge & Kegan Paul.

*Source:* Brilliant Enterprises.

# Further Theoretical Perspectives on Personality and Social–Emotional Development

The ideas of Freud and Erikson, which were predominant influences on personality/social–emotional development theory during the mid 20th century, also affected the work of a number of theorists whose influence has been prominent in the late 20th and early 21st centuries. They are Bowlby and Ainsworth, Greenspan, and Chess and Thomas. The major focus of this group of theorists has been on children's personality and social–emotional development during their first two years of life, especially on how interactions of parents and children affect early development. They each incorporated some aspects of the psychodynamic perspective in their theories, but they also rejected some of its basic concepts and drew on other theoretical perspectives. However, all of them did continue the holistic, growth-oriented emphasis of the rationalist tradition. Because these theorists focused more narrowly on particular issues in personality and social–emotional development (attachment, emotional organization, temperament), their ideas may be more accurately described as theoretical perspectives that enrich the rationalist tradition rather than "full-blown"or "grand" theories (a term that has been applied to those of Freud and Erikson; see Deissner & Tiegs, 2001).

Social–emotional development in interaction with cognition has been of interest to Alfred Bandura, a theorist whose roots are in the empiricist perspective. His social cognitive theory grew from and still retains some of the perspective of social learning that he emphasized in his early work, but recently he has focused on internal processes related to development of self-efficacy. Other "self" theorists have also looked at developmental aspects of self-development, using a range of empirical approaches. This theoretical work has grown into a richly described developmental perspective specific to self-development issues. This chapter describes the perspectives of this group of theorists.

## Bowlby's (and Ainsworth's) Theory of Attachment

John Bowlby (1907–1990) was trained as a child psychiatrist at Cambridge University and worked with troubled children as a clinician. From his experiences, he began to believe that psychoanalysis put too much emphasis on children's fantasy life and not enough on the actual separation or other traumatic experiences they had in their family life. In an early study (Bowlby, 1944), he found that a high proportion of juvenile thieves had "affectionless" characters, which he thought was due to their histories of maternal deprivation and separation. Through direct observation of children rather than clinical interviews, he investigated actual patterns of family interaction because he thought these held the key to pathological development. With James Robertson, he looked at the emotional behaviors of hospitalized young children who were separated from their mothers (see Bowlby & Ainsworth, 1965). He described three stages children went through during the separation: protest, related to separation anxiety; despair, related to grief and mourning; and detachment/denial, related to defense of self. Robertson made a movie using a time-sampling technique to observe how one 2-year-old child reacted over time to this separation (Robertson & Robertson, 1953). This powerful film changed hospital practices throughout the world (often hospitals now allow parents to stay with their children). This study of how young children dealt with separation played an important role in the development of Bowlby's attachment theory.

His budding theoretical view was also supported by his work with children made homeless in the post–WW II period, as was his study with the ethologist Robert Hinde (1982). Bowlby thought that ethology (i.e., derived from evolutionary theory) might help him gain a deeper understanding of the effects of separation and deprivation on young children because it focuses on the adaptive nature of behaviors that have been important in the survival of the human species and thus have been selected for reproduction over centuries. Bowlby (1982, 1989) connected this strong need of young children for attachment to their mothers to the ethological idea that certain behaviors have evolved as survival mechanisms. That is, infants' welfare really depends on their ability to attach to caregivers and to engage caregivers in reciprocal attachment. This explained for him why the child's need for attachment was so essential and the child's grief when separated from the attachment figure was so intense. Bowlby questioned a number of psychoanalytical concepts, especially Anna Freud's view that infants cannot show grief and mourning because their ego development is not yet strong. He believed that grief and mourning occur when children's attachment behaviors are activated by a need for the parent, but the parent continues to be unavailable. He observed that separation anxiety cannot be terminated unless reunion is restored; although some coping strategies to deal with separation are used by children, these often lead to attachment problems. In addition to drawing on ethology, Bowlby also thought that these processes could be informed by systems theory. He saw the dynamical systemic interaction as an important part of attachment development.

Although Bowlby developed the major themes of the theory, his colleague Mary Ainsworth (1913–1999) actually elaborated on the theory by carrying out research that identified various types of attachment and discussed their consequences for children. Ainsworth received her doctoral degree in psychology at the University of Toronto. In her doctoral work she had studied the idea of "security" development proposed by her adviser, Blatz. She came to England with her husband and obtained a position working with Bowlby, and her ideas contributed to Bowlby's theorizing. In particular, the aspect of a "secure base" of attachment, from which children's exploration can occur, is one of her theoretical contributions (see Bowlby, 1988). During most of their professional lives, Ainsworth and Bowlby continued their collegial interaction, with Ainsworth reviewing his manuscripts and with Bowlby using results of her research to inform his ideas.

## Basic Constructs and Stages of Bowlby's/Ainsworth's Theory

Bowlby wrote a number of books on the attachment process and how it is affected by separation and loss (1982). He also discussed how attachment develops over the first two years of life. He posited four stages of attachment development, which included

- Preattachment (birth to 6 weeks): In this period the infant is helpless but has characteristics (appearance, behaviors) that cause the mother to respond quickly and consistently to infant needs. The responsiveness of the mother (or other caregiver) is crucial during this period.

- Attachment in the making (6 weeks to 8 months): During this period the infant begins to respond to the actions of the mother (or other caregiver) and begins to trust that his/her needs will be met by the responsive person. The infant's responsiveness then creates a circle of interaction that encourages more responsiveness from the caregiver and causes attachment to grow between them.

- Clear-cut attachment (6 months to 24 months): The attachment of the infant to the mother (or other caregiver) is clear in infant behaviors such as proximity seeking, distress when separated, and language that prompts closeness. Both child and caregiver seem "tuned in" to each other's actions. The child uses the adult as a "secure base" by ranging further from the adult to explore new settings while at the same time keeping eye contact and using verbal means to maintain sporadic contact with the attachment figure. The adult encourages exploration but sets limits that assure the child of adult care and concern.

- Reciprocal relationship (18 months to 24 months): If the attachment process has proceeded well, by this age the child shows autonomy and a strong self-assurance in exploring his/her world. The child is confident that the attachment figure will help if needed, maintain interaction, and monitor situations. In new or strange situations, however, the child and adult will connect more closely in a pattern of reciprocity.

The overlapping of times in the stages accounts for infant variability, but according to Bowlby the sequence is a stable one. Note that Erikson's terminology of trust and autonomy are used in Bowlby's descriptions. A major result of the attachment sequence is that the infant develops an "internal working model" that has "generalized attachment representations" (Bowlby, 1988), which involve a set of expectations about social–emotional interactions with others, in particular with others to whom the person becomes attached. This model becomes part of children's personality, and it extends into their expectations of social interactions with other people throughout life. If attachment develops appropriately, individuals can then become attached to others and can also risk exploring further in their world; that is, the "secure base" provides the support for greater and greater extensions into the world. Caregivers carry their own "internal working model" from their childhood experience, and that can influence the interactions they have with the children they care for. Bowlby and Ainsworth outlined major problematic factors, such as repeated abandonment or threats of abandonment of the parent, rejection by parent, or illness or death of a parent or sibling, especially if the child feels responsible (but, of course, is not), which are likely to affect attachment development (Bowly & Ainsworth, 1965).

To obtain a clear way of measuring aspects of attachment, Ainsworth studied attachment behaviors in children in Africa and then in the United States at the University of Baltimore and the University of Virginia. She devised a "strange situation" experiment in which parents of young children were asked to leave them alone in a room with strangers and then return shortly. Ainsworth observed the types of responses the children exhibited when the parent was gone and on the parent's return. By recording the behaviors of the child when the parent was absent and counting the squares of floor distance the child maintained on the parent's return, Ainsworth (1979) measured a number of child actions related to attachment. She studied their proximity and contact seeking, contact maintaining, resistance to contact, avoidance of contact, distance of interactions, and visual search for absent figures.

After conducting her research, Ainsworth concluded that there were a number of major patterns of attachment. About 65% of the children showed themselves to be securely attached by reestablishing contact when the parent returned. Some children (about 20%) showed insecure-avoidant attachment behavior by staying away from the parent and not reestablishing contact, and some showed insecure-resistant attachment behavior (about 13%) by protesting and lashing out at the parent on the adult's return. The rest of the children were judged "unclassifiable." In later studies with other samples, another category, disordered attachment, was named, occurring in children with disabilities such as severe emotional problems (Main & Solomon, 1990).

From longitudinal studies, the following age differences were found in attachment-related behaviors:

- At age 2 a securely attached child will actively seek contact and comfort on the return of the caregiver, but by 6 years of age the secure child is relaxed, and although the child will initiate interaction with the attachment figure, the child is not highly dependent on it. The child will range far but comes back or verbally interacts to reconnect with that person often.

- At age 2 the avoidant child is unresponsive when the caregiver is present, does not show distress when the caregiver leaves, and avoids or is slow to greet the caregiver on return. The avoidant child of age 6 keeps a distance from the attachment figure and focuses on toys or other activities without maintaining intermittent contact with that person.

- At age 2 the resistant child seeks closeness when the caregiver is present but is angry and resistive when that person returns and is difficult to comfort. The resistant child at age 6 may show exaggerated intimacy but also expresses periodic fear, avoidance, hostility, or sadness.

- The 2-year-old disordered child at reunion is dazed, confused, and shows contradictory and bizarre patterns of behavior, and the disordered child at age 6 is either overly cheerful and active or controlling and rejecting, with patterns of behavior that are still bizarre and contradictory.

### Theoretical Influence and Critique

One of the strengths of attachment theory is that its major theoretical constructs have been testable, and results have generally supported the constructs. Ainsworth's method of measuring the strength and quality of attachment has been of major interest to researchers and to early childhood educators, and her categorization scheme for measuring attachment has been adopted by many other researchers. Although her initial studies were of mother–infant attachment, her later studies and those of others investigated multiple attachments to both mother and father, to grandparents, and to other caregivers, and longitudinal results were undertaken to see age differences in attachment (see Goldberg, Muir, & Kerr, 1995).

Bowlby and Ainsworth also conducted research on attachment behaviors with children from various caregiving backgrounds (Ainsworth & Bowlby, 1991; Bowlby & Ainsworth, 1965). The study results have supported the view that maltreatment, lack of interaction, or bizarre interaction patterns are related to insecure attachment (avoidant, resistant, or disordered). Other factors hypothesized to affect attachment development have been suggested and researched, including not having a consistent caregiver (caregiver deprivation), insensitivity of caregiver to infant needs and lack of synchrony responses (caregiver quality), irritability or nonresponsiveness of infant (infant temperament or disability), and disfunctional expectations of caregivers derived from their own early experiences (poor caregiver internal working model) (Bowlby, 1988). Attachment stability, once established, can still be affected by life changes, such as illness or death of caregiver, hospitalization of child, or other separation experiences.

Cultural difference effects on attachment development have also been studied, because the family's perceptions of life-threatening events affect caregiving and subsequent attachment (Gonzalez-Mena, 2005). If threats are not perceived as imminent, then children may sleep in a separate room, be encouraged to be independent, and have permission to go farther from their "secure base." In areas where life is perceived as very threatening, the child may be kept always near the parent, have on-demand feeding and sleeping patterns, and rarely be allowed to leave the "secure base." That is, if there is perception in a culture that life-threatening events may occur, caregiving behaviors may be more intense and long lasting. These findings support Bowlby's initial view that attachment is an evolutionary adaptive mechanism (Ainsworth & Bowlby, 1991). The amount of time the child spends alone, the number of adults who have close interactions, and the use of alternate caregivers (e.g., child care) may have an effect on the number of people to whom a child attaches. If children have well-established major attachment relationships, having multiple caregivers usually results in their having multiple attachment figures.

A major research consequence of Bowlby's and Ainsworth's work has been the movement to learn more about attachment disorders among children who have had instability in early care, lack of opportunity to form attachments, or bizarre early experiences that did not enable them to go through the expected stages of attachment. Other researchers have extended Ainsworth's attachment studies to later age levels to see if attachment level predicts later interpersonal difficulties (Doyle, 2000). Those researchers who have studied attachment in older children, adolescents, and adults have not usually used Ainsworth's observational method of categorizing attachment but rather have used clinical reports, interviews, and self-reports or other types of ratings. Many of these researchers are American scholars (e.g., Bretherton & Waters, 1985) and have emphasized not only Bowlby's ethological perspective but also his earlier psychoanalytical perspective related to "object relations."

In regard to the usefulness of the theory, attachment theory is one of the major theories discussed in infant development courses and in practical advice to parent books at the present time. It has also been the basis of much advice to child caregivers, because the theory stresses the importance of the consistent presence of such caregivers if multiple attachments to other than parents are to be established (Bergen, Reid, & Torelli, 2001). Clinicians have also used the Bowlby and Ainsworth theory extensively to investigate "attachment disorders" in children. Some of these children are reported to seem overly friendly and outgoing on initial contact, but their social contacts are superficial. If they are adopted after age 2, they may fail to form an attachment to the family or they may show apparent premature attachment after only a brief period. Children with attachment disorders may also appear to lack empathy and trust in social relationships. Reports of therapeutic efforts to remediate attachment disorders have indicated mixed success (Cassidy & Shaver, 1999). In sum, the theory has shown robustness both in its testability, with numerous empirical research studies supporting its major constructs, and it has been judged useful for parental child rearing, child caregiving, and clinical practice, although its scope is narrow. It continues to be the subject of research and practical intervention.

# Greenspan's Theory of Emotional Development

Stanley Greenspan (1941–) is a prominent psychiatrist, theorist, and teacher, who received his medical degree from Yale University. He has drawn on psychoanalytic theory (particularly ego identity psychology), attachment theory, and brain development research in developing his own theory of early emotional development. Ego psychology posits that the ego has the capacity to organize, integrate, differentiate, elaborate, and transform experience. Greenspan's early theoretical work focused on describing how infants organize their experiences through the interplay of those experiences with the processes of maturation of the central nervous system (Greenspan, 1989, 1992).

## *Basic Constructs and Stages of Greenspan's Theory*

Greenspan assumes that the capacity to organize experiences is present early in life, but initially that organization is emotion based rather than cognition based. Emotions are a type of personal cognition, and infants organize differently at different stages of ego development. The emotion-generating centers (e.g., limbic system) of the brain mature earlier than the frontal lobe; therefore, although emotions are evident, interpreting the meaning of emotions relies on maturation of cortical areas. With maturation of the brain this capacity progresses to higher levels of organization, thus enabling cognitive processes to become organized.

Greenspan (Greenspan & Breslau-Lewis, 1999; Greenspan & Greenspan, 1985) stated that emotional organization is primary in infancy, and it is acquired through relationships with those who care for the child. These relationships are essentially developed in playful interactions; thus, social play is the vehicle for promoting emotional organization. The types of experiences that occur at each organizational level must be age appropriate; have range, depth, and stability; and be personally unique. Because cognitive organization is drawn from emotional organization, Greenspan believes that it is essential that emotional organization be developed during the first years of life (Greenspan & Benderly, 1997). He has outlined the stages of emotional development, with six milestones, and explained how these can be fostered (Greenspan, 1990; Greenspan & Greenspan, 1985).

- *Engagement:* Begins about 3 weeks until 8 months, in which infants learn to share attention, relate to others with warmth, positive emotion, and expectation of pleasant interactions, and trust that they are secure. This phase has two milestones: self-regulation and intimacy

- *Two-way Communication:* Between 6 months and 18 months, in which infants learn to signal needs and intentions, comprehend others' intentions, communicate information (motorically and verbally), make assumptions about safety, and have reciprocal interactions. This phase has the milestone of two-way communication

- *Shared Meanings:* Between 18 months and 36 months, in which children learn to relate their behaviors, sensations, and gestures to the world of ideas, engage in pretend play, intentionally use language to communicate, and begin to understand cognitive concepts. This phase has two milestones: complex communication and emotional ideas

- *Emotional Thinking:* 3 to 6 years old, in which children can organize experiences and ideas, make connections among ideas, begin reality testing, gain a sense of themselves and their emotions, see themselves in space and time, and develop categories of experience. This phase has the final milestone: emotional thinking

### Theoretical Influence and Critique

Because of his focus on clinical practice, Greenspan believes that many children do not develop the emotional organization that is the essential basis for cognitive development. Thus, he has been particularly concerned with the usefulness aspect of his theory, designing practical methods for helping parents and teachers facilitate children's emotional development during the infant/toddler/preschool years. He has been active in initiating therapy for children who have regulatory disorders, often called pervasive developmental disorder (PDD), autistic spectrum disorders, multisystem developmental disorders, or disorders of regulation (DeGangi, Breinbauer, Roosevelt, Porges & Greenspan, 2000). For children who have what he believes to be poor emotional organization, he has designed a therapeutic approach, Developmental Individual Difference Relationship Model/Floor Time (similar to adult/child playtime), and he trains parents and teachers in the use of Floor Time techniques (Greenspan 1990; Hanna, Wilford, Benham, & Carter, 1990). He recommends intensive, relationship-based therapy that first assesses through sessions of observing child–caregiver interaction and then designs specific play interactions using the Floor Time process. He has classified regulatory disorders into five patterns: hypersensitive/fearful, hypersensitive/defiant, hyporeactive/pain insensitive, self-absorbed/underreactive, and poor motor planning/inattentive. These conditions can be mild or intense, with PDD children at the intense side of the continuum. Although many strategies are used in floor time, the basic strategy is to have the adult enter into the child's activities, following the child's lead, and creating a warm affective interaction. After mutual, shared engagement is established, the adult elaborates and draws the child into more complex interactions. The purpose of the interactions is to foster children's emotional organization through "opening and closing circles of communication."

With his wife and colleagues, Greenspan has also written numerous books of parental advice on how to foster children's emotional development and has made films describing the therapeutic methods derived from his theory (Greenspan & Greenspan, 1985; Greenspan & Breslau-Lewis, 1999). The American Academy of Pediatrics' guidelines for well-baby exams include suggestions for the developmental examination based on Greenspan's theory and research. He was one of the founders of the Zero to Three Foundation and served as president in its founding years. Although his theoretical writing is deep and extensive, his concern with practice has involved him, with his staff, in yearly in-depth workshops to train practitioners in his methods.

In regard to testability of the theory, the results are still being evaluated through research studies that examine clinical therapeutic and floor time interventions. At present, the research findings are mixed, but because of the many current proponents of Greenspan's approach to therapeutic practice, there is likely to be an extensive research base at some future time. Whether it will provide strong support for Greenspan's intervention approaches is presently unknown. The research methods combine empiricist and rationalist approaches, and thus there may still be controversy over Greenspan's reported theory confirmation. Greenspan's emotional development theory-based approach to helping children diagnosed with autism or PDD is in contrast to behaviorally designed approaches that rely on reinforcements, such as Lovaas (2002). Although Greenspan's emphasis on emotions as the key to cognition draws on current brain research and is thus potentially testable through neurological means, it is also firmly rooted in the rationalist perspective. He believes that the epigenetic process of emotional organization must occur first before cognitive organization can be fully functioning.

## Thomas and Chess's Temperament Theory

Another approach that drew on aspects of earlier personality theory and descriptive child development research was that of Alexander Thomas (1914–2003) and Stella Chess (1914–). Thomas and Chess were a married team of pediatric psychiatrists who were also professors at the Medical School of New York University. They reacted to the view that was pervasive at the time of their training, which claimed that the environment, primarily the child's mother, was responsible for all the child's behavioral or emotional problems. They believed that the "individual difference" component of personality and social–emotional development had been minimized in many theoretical accounts. Although they did not discount the importance of environmental experiences, they were particularly interested in learning more about what infants and children may bring to social and emotional interactions as a result of their initial temperament, which they defined as "individuality of behavioral responsiveness." Thus, they designed the New York Longitudinal Study (Thomas, Chess, Birch, Hertzig, & Korn 1963; Thomas, Chess, & Birch, 1970; Chess & Thomas, 1990). This study began when the infants were 3 months old with the intensive interviewing of parents, and the study continued over a period of 30 years. In 2- to 4-hour interviews conducted often during the first 2 years of the child's life, they asked the parents extensive questions that referred to their children's "concrete objective behaviors rather than to complex motives and other subjective states" (Thomas et al., 1963, p. 24). Some of the questions changed over time as different developmental issues emerged. Chess was the primary observer and describer of the data, and Thomas took the lead in organizing, generalizing, and synthesizing the results. They had three major questions of interest:

1. Is it possible to find a set of consistent dimensions of temperament by which very young children can be categorized on the basis of their individual behavior responsiveness?

2. How do children with varied temperaments fare in interaction with parents; that is, what is their "goodness of fit" with the childrearing environment?

3. Is temperament a stable characteristic over the life span?

### Basic Concepts of Chess and Thomas's Theory

After collecting an extensive body of data, when the children were two-years-old, Thomas and Chess and their colleagues, Herbert Birch and Margaret Hertzig, used data from 80 of them to categorize a set of dimensions that seemed to express individual behavioral responsiveness differences. The nine dimensions are as follows:

- Level and extent of motor activity
- Regularity of basic functions
- Withdrawal or acceptance of new stimuli
- Adaptability to environmental changes
- Sensitivity level to stimuli
- Energy intensity of responses
- General mood or disposition
- Distractibility potential
- Attention span and persistence in activity

Then, using constellations of these characteristics, they found three major temperament types in the 141 children they studied. (They were able to keep 133 of the subjects in the study over the 30-year period!) The greatest proportion of children (40%) were labeled "Easy." They were generally positive in mood, regular in functions, adaptable, and only moderately intense in reactions, and they had approachable responses to new situations. A smaller proportion (10%) were labeled "Difficult" children. These children were often negative in mood, irregular in sleeping and eating patterns, slow to adapt, and very intense in reactions to stimuli, and they tended to withdraw in new situations. Interestingly a larger proportion (15%) were labeled "Slow to Warm Up" because although they had low activity levels and low intensity of reactions, they were very slow to adapt and likely to withdraw in new situations. The other 35% of children had a variety of characteristics but did not fit into any of these three patterns of temperament. Thus, Thomas and Chess concluded that their first question—Can temperament be evaluated at an early age?—was answered primarily positively. Table 4.1 shows the characteristics of the initial group of children in regard to the dimensions of temperament identified by Chess and Thomas.

The longitudinal results of the temperament studies have been particularly important in regard to the second question of Thomas and Chess: How well does the "goodness of fit" between child temperament and the caregiving and later school environment predict long-term effects of temperament on development? Their initial hypothesis that difficult children would be most likely to have problematic development was only partially supported. They stated, "Our findings and those of others have made it clear that no temperamental attribute confers immunity to behavior disorders. Neither does one exist that makes such disorders inevitable. The issue is always decided by the process of interaction between child and environment, in which each actively influences the other" (Chess &

**Table 4.1**  Temperament Characteristics of Children in Original Sample

Distribution of the number of children in period I with preponderant scores in each of the ratings in the nine categories. The total number of children observed is eighty

| Activity | | Rhythmicity | | Adaptability | |
|---|---|---|---|---|---|
| high . . . . . . . . . 35 | | regular . . . . . . . 65 | | adaptive . . . . . 70 | |
| moderate . . . . . 28 | | variable . . . . . . 2 | | variable . . . . . . 0 | |
| low . . . . . . . . . . 7 | | irregular . . . . . 9 | | nonadaptive . . 8 | |
| total | 70* | | 76 | | 78 |

| Approach | | Threshold | | Intensity | |
|---|---|---|---|---|---|
| approach . . . . . 66 | | high . . . . . . . . . 13 | | intense . . . . . . . 18 | |
| variable . . . . . . 0 | | moderate . . . . . 17 | | variable . . . . . . 0 | |
| withdrawal . . . 11 | | low . . . . . . . . . . 46 | | mild . . . . . . . . . 57 | |
| total | 77 | | 76 | | 75 |

| Mood | | Distractibility | | Persistence | |
|---|---|---|---|---|---|
| positive . . . . . . 55 | | yes . . . . . . . . . . 51 | | yes . . . . . . . . . . 64 | |
| variable . . . . . . 0 | | variable . . . . . . 0 | | variable . . . . . . 1 | |
| negative . . . . . 17 | | no . . . . . . . . . . . 17 | | no . . . . . . . . . . . 5 | |
| total | 72 | | 68 | | 70 |

*A number of children's scores were evenly divided between two or more of the ratings in a category. These "ties" are not included in the table.

*Source:* Reprinted from *Distribution of the number of children in period/with preponderant scores in each of the ratings in the nine categories.* From *Behavioral Individuality in Early Childhood* (p. 58). © 1954 by A. Thomas, S. Chess, H. G. Birch, M. E. Hertzig & S. Korn. New York. New York University Press.

Thomas, 1990, p. 185). In their writings, they cited many instances of temperament/environment "fits" and "misfits."

Thomas and Chess clearly illustrated the nature/nurture interaction perspective and have used both the holistic element of a rationalist approach and the objective study of variables approach drawn from empiricist research. In the conclusion of their 1963 book (Thomas et al., 1963, p. 81), they indicated that five factors may be responsible for individual differences, including

1. Genetic familial
2. Prenatal influences
3. Paranatal influences
4. Early life experiences
5. Any combination of the preceding four possibilities

They stated then, ". . . no firm ground exists for preferring any of the factors listed to any other" (1963, p. 81). Later, they emphasized this interactive dynamic and concluded that, in answer to their third question, temperament is a relatively stable characteristic, "although not immutable." They asserted that even in adult-hood "the temperamental component in an adult's behavior is often relatively easy to identify" (Chess & Thomas, 1990, p. 192).

### Theoretical Influence and Critique

Chess and Thomas were committed to validating their theoretical ideas through carefully detailed and extensive longitudinal research, using methodology congruent with the rationalist perspective. Because of the long-term evidence they collected, they were able to make some predictions about temperamental effects, although their results also support the "situated" perspective of development. Cross-cultural studies have also tested their constructs, and the temperament categories seems to hold up, although what may seem to be a difficult temperament in one setting may actually be a positive survival mechanism in another more unstable setting (deVries, 1984). The study of temperament influence continues to be undertaken.

In regard to the usefulness of their theory, Thomas and Chess were strong advocates for teacher consideration of children's temperament within school settings, because they believed that temperamental traits affect how children approach learning tasks and how they interact with others. Therefore, they suggested that it is important for teachers to know children's temperamental style as well as their learning abilities because that style will affect how well they can take advantage of the learning opportunities (Thomas et al., 1970). By providing an empirically tested model for child psychiatry, they also helped to shape present-day clinical practice. Their categories of temperament and discussion of goodness of fit have been valued and used by early childhood and special educators, and they also wrote advice-to-parent books (Chess, Thomas, & Birch, 1972). With the assistance and advice of Thomas and Chess, psychologist William Carey developed the *Carey Scales of Temperament* (Carey & McDevitt, 1978, 1994), which enables temperament to be evaluated reliably on the relevant dimensions without using an extensive interview approach, and this instrument is widely used today. Thomas and Chess did not consider their work as a separate and fully developed theory, however, but rather saw it as an additional component of psychiatric theory. They stressed that the value of their work was in promoting the consideration of temperament characteristics and environmental dynamics as a means for understanding children's behavioral and learning problems. They were successful in making a case for consideration of temperament, and their work has been influential in improving the effectiveness of therapeutic and educational practice.

## Bandura's Social–Cognitive/Self-Efficacy Theory

Albert Bandura (1925–) has always been interested in explaining social–emotional dimensions of human experience. He received his doctorate in psychology from the University of Iowa and is a professor at Stanford University. Although he was educated during the period when behaviorism was the major theoretical orientation, and thus used some behaviorist terms in his writing, he asserts that he was mislabeled as a behaviorist by other writers. In a recent interview, he says, "In the early writings I acknowledged the phenomena encompassed under the labels of conditioning and reinforcement. But what text writers and those relying on secondary sources were missing is that I conceptualized these phenomena as operating through cognitive processes" (Pajeres, 2002, p. 1). His theoretical explanations have continued to evolve over the course of his long career, moving from an emphasis on social learning to social cognitive theory and in particular to its role in influencing "human agency." An empiricist perspective on these phenomena has been evident in much of his work, although in his writings regarding the development of self-efficacy, he described processes that appear to be influenced by aspects of rationalist, sociohistorical, and dynamical systems theory as well.

## Basic Constructs of Bandura's Theory

Bandura's initial developmental interest was in finding an explanation for aggressive behavior because he did not agree with Freud's explanation that aggressive energy is lessened through vicarious aggressive experiences. He also questioned Skinner's explanation of learning because he did not think it explained how novel or complex behaviors were learned. In an early study with Richard Walters (Bandura & Walters, 1959), he looked at aggressive and nonaggressive adolescents and concluded that the adolescents imitated behaviors of family models. Thus, he identified the role of observational learning from models as a major factor in social–emotional development. Models influence children's development in a number of ways: by teaching novel behaviors, encouraging or discouraging expression of various behaviors, and eliciting similar but not identical behaviors. In his and Walter's book on social learning (Bandura & Walters, 1963), they described studies of aggressive behavior in children who observed models who were and were not aggressive toward an inflated Bobo doll. These studies, conducted with colleagues (Bandura, Ross, & Ross, 1963), concluded that children who observed aggressive conditions, whether with live models, films of models, or cartoon characters, exhibited more aggression than controls who did not see such models. Bandura concluded that "vicarious reinforcement" and observational learning were strong influences on children's social–emotional development.

As he analyzed these studies and thought about why some social behaviors were learned and performed more readily than others, and why many persisted even if vicarious reinforcement was not evident, he decided that a major element influencing learning was the way they were interpreted by individuals. Thus, he proposed the model of "reciprocal determinism." He identified three aspects that influenced the social learning process: the person, the person's behavior, and the environment (Bandura, 1986). (This was a major step away from the behaviorist view that there is no need to hypothesize an internal component—that environment and behavior explained everything.) In Bandura's model, the person is the "information processing" element, and as the environment gives information (or response consequences), the way each individual processes the information influences whether there will be a change in the person's behavior. Bandura (1986) proposed four processes that affect how the person might interpret environmental events.

- *Attention:* How well the person attends to the observed information/behavior and to the characteristics of the model. If little attention is paid to the event, then it will not be incorporated into the person's behavior. If cursory attention is paid, then it may be incorporated incompletely or incorrectly.

- *Retention:* How well the person encodes and retains the information/behavior in memory. If the person is ineffective in encoding the event and/or in retrieving it from memory, then it will not be learned well enough to be incorporated into the person's behavior. That is, it may have been stored in an inaccessible manner.

- *Motor Reproduction:* How capable the person is in recalling the action information and motorically reproducing the behavior. If the person is not motorically capable of reproducing the event (too young, too old, too weak), then it may be incorporated only partially and/or incorrectly, or it may be learned, but the person will be unable to reproduce the behavior (or may reproduce at a later time if motor skills become greater).

- *Motivation:* How much the person values the information/behavior and is affected by the reinforcement sources. If the person does not believe that there are relevant response consequences, even if the event is incorporated into the behavior repertoire, it will not be acted on. It may appear not to have been learned, even if attention, retention, and motor reproduction skills are all effectively present.

Thus, Bandura indicated that the process of learning is much more complicated that a simple reinforcement paradigm would suggest because the person (an internal cognitive component) determines what social learning actually occurs and what is demonstrated in behavior. At the time he proposed the reciprocal determinism model, Bandura also relabeled his theoretical terminology. Instead of being called a social "learning" theory, he now calls it a social "cognitive" theory. He increasingly has emphasized the person's ability to self-direct and to use forethought, to symbolize and use vicarious experience, and to self-regulate and self-reflect. The four aspects of social cognition are shown in Table 4.2

Social–cognitive theory is rooted in a view of human agency; that is, all persons are agents who are proactively engaged in their own development. They possess self-beliefs that affect their thinking, feelings, and actions, and these "personal competency" beliefs are derived from how individuals interpret their own performance. Bandura termed this belief system "self-efficacy" and differentiated it from the term "self-concept," which Bandura sees as a global belief about one's self. Self-efficacy is specific to human agency and contains the types of actions, skills, and competencies for which the person feels efficacious. Bandura also differentiates self-efficacy from the term "self-esteem," which Bandura says is belief about how one is valued by others. The way individuals interpret their own performances influence their self-beliefs about their efficacy, which then inform and alter their subsequent performances. According to Bandura (1997), beliefs about one's self-efficacy affect what choices people make about future actions, the amount of effort they expend on certain activities, their perseverance against obstacles, and their resilience when initially unsuccessful.

**Table 4.2** Subprocesses Governing Observational Learning

| Attentional Processes | Retention Processes | Production Processes | Motivational Processes |
|---|---|---|---|
| Modeled Events<br>Salience<br>Affective Valence<br>Complexity<br>Prevalence<br>Functional Value | Symbolic Coding<br>Cognitive Organization<br>Cognitive Rehearsal<br>Enactive Rehearsal | Cognitive Representation<br>Observation of Enactments<br>Feedback Information<br>Conception Matching | External Incentives<br>Sensory<br>Tangible<br>Social<br>Control<br>Vicarious Incentives<br>Self-Incentives<br>Tangible<br>Self-Evaluative |
| Observer Attributes →<br>Perceptual Capabilities<br>Perceptual Set<br>Cognitive Capabilities<br>Arousal Level<br>Acquired Preferences | Observer Attributes →<br>Cognitive Skills<br>Cognitive Structures | Observer Attributes →<br>Physical Capabilities<br>Component Subskills | Observer Attributes →<br>Incentive Preferences<br>Social Comparative Biases<br>Internal Standards |

Modeled Events ——→ (left of table)  Matching Pattern ——→ (right of table)

*Source: Subprocessing Governing Observational Learning* from A. Bandura, *Social Cognitive Theory* (p. 16), 1989 in R. Vasta (ed.), *Annals of Child Development*, 6. Copyright © 1989 by JAI Press.

Because people exist in social environments, they also can experience "collective agency." They can hold common beliefs about their efficacy and work together with others to achieve goals.

### Developmental Change Processes in Bandura's Theory of Human Agency

In his 1997 work, Bandura explained developmental changes in human agency and perceived self-efficacy across the life span. He believes that certain competencies are required for successful functioning at different times in development but that developmental change is not identical for all individuals. People vary in how successful they are in managing their life challenges, and a major reason is the types of beliefs they hold about how much they can affect their lives by their own actions. He states that people's self-efficacy beliefs ". . . are an influential personal resource as they negotiate their lives through the life cycle. Social cognitive theory analyzes developmental changes in perceived self-efficacy in terms of evolvement of human agency across the life span" (1997, p. 162). Bandura outlined this process, which includes both internal and environmental components, as follows.

- Origins of a Sense of Personal Agency: Through observation and experiencing the results of their own actions, infants gradually gain self-recognition and "learn they can make things happen" (p. 164). Their actions produce effects and help them understand causation, which develops a sense of personal agency. They learn that if they behave in certain ways, certain things happen (recognition that actions produce outcomes) and finally realize that the actions are caused by themselves (recognition that they are the agent of those actions). As they act and the people around them refer to them and treat them as distinct persons, they gain ability to use a self-referent label (me, mine) at about 18 months, and they describe themselves as the agent by about 20 months. The responsiveness of caregivers (i.e., parents) plays a role in helping young children exercise personal control. By responding to communication and creating opportunities for children to have efficacious actions, they help them to feel mastery, which then affects their self-beliefs. Initial efficacy experiences are centered in the family, and thus family differences (e.g., models, responsiveness) can affect children's self-efficacy beliefs.

- Developing Self-Appraisal Skills: Young children can improve their self-appraisal skills, and they begin to judge their own efficacy in relation to certain actions. Self-appraisals are fostered by two types of experience: direct experiences and social comparison (monitoring performance in comparison to others). Children also receive direct instruction about the effectiveness of their own actions and the appropriateness of their social comparisons. They constantly observe their own actions and the actions of others. Because of immature self-evaluation skills, they may try actions that they are not yet capable of performing well, and this may undermine their developing sense of self-efficacy.

- Broadening and Validating Self-Efficacy: As children move into the broader community, the role of peers becomes increasingly important. Competent age-mate peers provide models of efficacious styles and social comparisons of self-efficacy. Usually children choose peers who have similar interests and values, and these affiliations affect the direction of efficacy development, whereas personal efficacy influences the choices of peer activities. Children who judge themselves as having low efficacy may exhibit social withdrawal. On the other hand, they may gain a high sense of efficacy for behaviors that are socially alienating (e.g., bullying). Although such personal efficacy for coercive styles of behavior may permit control over peers, it is estranging over the life span. During this age period, the school functions as a major force in promoting (or not promoting) children's self-efficacy. In particular, certain aspects of self-efficacy, such as self-regulation, self-directedness, and self-instructional capacity, can be fostered in school settings. According to Bandura, certain school practices such as "lock-step sequences of instruction," "sorting students," and emphasis on "social-comparative appraisals rather than self-appraisals" can lower many children's sense of self-efficacy. Bandura believes that well-structured cooperative activities can create collective agency during this age period.

- Self-Efficacy in Transition: Adolescence is another period where self-efficacy development can be affected by many factors. The mastery of many new skills are required, more responsibility must be assumed, and decisions that will affect their life course may be made. Bandura believes that many theories overpredict adverse consequences during this period of life, and he stresses rather the way that self-efficacy beliefs can be "enablement factors" to help adolescents meet the transitions they must encounter. Their beliefs about their self-efficacy in social and academic situations also affect their emotional development. One aspect that must be managed is sexuality. The ability to self-regulate is especially important as a means for making this transitional period a positive experience. This is a crucial factor in management of other high-risk experiences as well. Self-appraisal and self-regulatory skills are also important for vocational and higher education successful experiences.

- Career Development and Family Roles: There are a number of ways efficacy beliefs affect these areas of experience. For career development, individuals' beliefs about how well they should prepare, their efforts to find opportunities for education and employment, and their effort and persistence in performing employment responsibilities are all related to their efficacy beliefs. Similarly, in taking on responsibilities such as marriage and parenthood, these beliefs are also important. A strong sense of self-efficacy positively affects the emotional well-being of parents of children with special needs as well. Obviously, when problems occur (loss of employment, divorce) self-efficacy beliefs are strongly challenged. Perceived self-efficacy usually drops during periods of transition.

- Midlife and Later Life Changes: Although there is little research on self-efficacy at these age periods, Bandura stated that there may be a need to "restructure" goals and deal with self-doubts about the meaning and direction of one's life, especially during the middle and later years. However, "opportunities for further self-development always exist" (1997, p. 197). A reappraisal of self-efficacy does occur with advancing age, which is not surprising because many of the efficacious behaviors that composed the person's self-efficacy are reduced or lost. Cognitive, memory, and physical/health decrease, and a major issue may be the perceived loss of control over one's life. Bandura stated, "A key issue in this expanded perspective is how the elderly maintain a sense of personal agency and exercise it in ways that give meaning and purpose to their lives (1997, p. 205).

Bandura (1997) also addressed the issue of collective efficacy, which results from having many individuals who believe that they can affect events by their action. He defined collective efficacy as the shared belief that group members have about their capabilities to work together to organize and act on plans of action that will achieve their "levels of attainments" (p. 478). When a group acts together and can coordinate the interactions of the group members, the result can be greater than the actions of each individual's separate acts.

### Theoretical Influence and Critique

Overall, Bandura has contributed extensively to the social learning, social cognitive, personality, and social–emotional theoretical literature. Many research studies have supported his constructs related to observational learning and influence of models. For example, the composition of youth gangs has been shown to exemplify these constructs, as has research on effects of violent media and gender identity stereotypes (Anderson & Bushman, 2001; Schunk, 1987). Although experimental methods have been effective in testing these aspects of his theory, other methodologies such as self-ratings and interviews have been used to test his later theoretical constructs. There are presently few studies to validate "reciprocal determinism" or chart the development of self-efficacy. However, Bandura and colleagues have conducted multiple studies that support the underlying concept of self-efficacy (see Bandura, 1997).

There has also been longitudinal research on "resiliency," which involves the ability to appraise life events to withstand adverse circumstances. Resilient children are adept at finding ways to promote their self-efficacy despite less than ideal circumstances. Studies show that they usually have at least one stable, caring adult in their lives, as well (Werner, 1992). Bandura also cited studies showing that perceived efficacy to manage sexual experiences decreases unprotected sexual activity and drug and alcohol use in adolescence (Kasen, Vaughan, & Walter, 1992), and perceived parenting efficacy plays a role in successful adaptation to parenthood (Hetherington & Blechman, 1996). Bandura has been active in testing his theoretical ideas through research, and it is likely that his self-efficacy development schema may be further validated as this research is conducted by his students and colleagues.

In regard to the usefulness of the theory for practice, Bandura's constructs about observational learning and importance of models have been prominent in advice for both child rearing and education. His early theories are discussed in most developmental texts, but there has been less attention paid to his self-efficacy work. These constructs have not always been distinguished from other "self" theoretical work (e.g., self-concept, self-perception, self-esteem). Bandura has written extensively about self-efficacy development in relation to cognitive, health, clinical, athletic, and organizational functioning, and his views have begun to influence these fields. He laments that many school practices are not conducive to self-efficacy development, however. Because his self-efficacy constructs are more recently proposed, it is not yet possible to determine what long-term influence they may have on the solving of practical problems in home, school, and society. In the latter part of the 20th century promotion of good "self" constructs was prominent in educational texts and school policy, but in the present era of emphasis on academic performance, social–emotional development is not a strong focus in schools.

## Other Views of Self-Development

Bandura's interest in self-efficacy development is only one of the conceptualizations of the "self" that has been studied recently. One perspective on the self was initially proposed by James (1892), who saw two aspects: the self as actor (I) and the self as object of one's own knowledge (me). Baldwin (1897) viewed the self as bipolar, with one's own self at one pole and the other person(s) at the opposite pole. That is, social interaction and the reflected appraisals of other people form the self (Cooley, 1902). Ego identity development has been one aspect of self-development (Erikson, 1968), and other self dimensions have also been identified. For example, Coopersmith (1967) studied self-esteem, which is a personal judgment of worthiness, and Harter (1983) has focused on self-perception, which includes aspects of self-esteem and self-efficacy. Most of these theorists have not explored self-development across the life span, however, but instead have studied cross-cultural and gender issues in similar age cohorts.

## Trends in Personality and Social–Emotional Development and Themes That May Be Useful for Professional Practice

From the many studies of personality and social/emotional development, a set of commonly accepted timelines for the "range of normality" in development of these domains have been identified. Table 4.3 shows these "typical" developmental achievements. Also, although not all the constructs of the theories discussed in

---

**Table 4.3**  Trends in Personality and Social-Emotional Development
(Ages Are Approximate)

| | |
|---|---|
| Birth to Age 3 | -Basic emotions of interest, surprise, anger, sadness, disgust, joy evident in first year |
| | -Smile appears; social smile by 4-6 mo. |
| | -Clear-cut attachment achieved |
| | -Demonstrates temperament differences |
| | -Self-awareness emerges by 6-8 mo |
| | -Social referencing with attachment figures by 6-12 mo. |
| | -Self-recognition by 12-18 mo. |
| | -Emotions of guilt, shame, pride (self-conscious emotions) by 12-18 mo. |
| | -Initial self-control in compliance to commands by 12-18 mo. |
| | -Joins in pretend play by 12-18 mo. |
| | -Shows empathy but help is related to self-comforting by 18-24 mo. |
| | -Forms play friendships for brief periods by 18-24 mo. |
| | -Shows prosocial behaviors by 18-36 mo. |
| | -Expresses strong feelings through emotional outbursts at 24-36 mo.; gains gradual control. |
| | -Has adequate social play skills by 36 mo. |
| | -Has brief friendships based on play by 36 mo. |
| Ages 3-6 | -Gains understanding of own feelings and those of others and can express them by age 3-5 |
| | -Can describe concrete observable characteristics of self by age 4-5 |
| | -Self-regulation increases but interacts with temperament by age 3-5 |
| | -Has competent social play skills in pretense and simple games with rules by age 4-5 |
| | -Shows prosocial and altruistic behaviors in personal situations by age 4-6 |
| | -Develops strong friendships through play by age 4-6 |

**Table 4.3** (*continued*)

| | |
|---|---|
| Ages 6-12 | -Judges self through social comparison by age 6-8 |
| | -Has perspective taking from other's view point by age 5-7 |
| | -Has friendship groups and individual friendships |
| | -Peer acceptance may vary by child |
| | -May describe self in all or none way |
| | -Emotional control continues to develop |
| | -Concern for others fluctuates with concerns for self |
| Ages 12-20 | -Uses self transformation to fit with desired social groups |
| | -Takes social role models from media and other venues than family |
| | -Search for identity may involve trying on many roles |
| | -Social interest in dating, gaining more intimate friendships; may be intense but brief |
| | -Sexual experimentation by some |
| | -May be engaged by social causes |
| | -Emotions may be nearer surface; imaginary audience affects performance |
| Ages 20-40 | -May have self image as adult or as youth during 20's (a committed worker or postponed responsibilities) |
| | -Experiences emotions of passion, intimacy, commitment |
| | -Early attachment may affect attachment commitments |
| | -May choose mate similar to self |
| | -Marriage patterns may differ: egalitarian or traditional |
| | -Parenthood brings emotional satisfactions but also stress |
| Ages 40-60 | -May encounter transition stress |
| | -Initial awareness of mortality and emphasis on staying healthy |
| | -May have stability in work life or make changes |
| | -Retirement planning begins |
| Ages 60-80 | -Emotional transitions from work life |
| | -New emotional experiences in life changes (volunteering, travel) |
| | -Coming to terms with own mortality and death of loved ones |
| | -Self-image is usually younger than actual age |
| | -May have life theme of legacy to others |
| Ages 80-100 | -Great variation; may be social or isolated |
| | -Personality characteristics become more "like self" |
| | -Emotional evaluation of life; goal integrity |

## Box 4.1
## Theoretically-Derived Themes That May Be Useful For Professional Practice

- The environment provided during the earliest years of life must include consistent care, warm and encouraging emotional interactions, and provision of a range of social experiences if the social and emotional development of the human child is to prosper.
- Young children's ability to develop trust and a strong emotional attachment will have lasting effects on their later development.
- A child may develop multiple attachments in addition to a primary attachment, and these can influence the child's "internal working model" and ability to "close the circle of communication" in social-emotional interactions.
- Each child's development will be different as a result of temperament and other genetic variation, and the "goodness of fit" of the child with environmental experiences will affect how well these temperament differences lead to healthy personality development.
- Cognition is not a separate ability that is devoid of emotional content; rather emotion and cognition are closely connected, and emotion has influence on many cognitive processes, such as memory, self-regulation, and planning.
- Because play and humor assist in coping with social and emotional issues, pretend play in particular provides a means for children to feel powerful and in control over their lives, and the ability to use humor as an acceptable coping strategy can also assist healthy development.
- The development of a sense of human agency (i.e., self-efficacy) is fostered by child active involvement in successful experiences, it continues to develop throughout life, and the life course is greatly influenced by the individual's sense of agency
- Supportive socially interactive intervention and scaffolding for children with social-emotional delays is useful, especially during the early years when brain development has greatest plasticity.

chapters 3 and 4 have been validated by extensive evidence, a few general themes can be derived from this set of theories that may be useful for practice. These are provided in Box 4.1.

## Summary

Some of the theories discussed in this chapter have extended ideas drawn from the theories of Freud and Erikson, while adding new dimensions from other theoretical perspectives. Similarly, although learning theory provided a base for the social learning perspective of Bandura, he has emphasized the internal aspects of human agency in his later work. Although not all these theorists have addressed life span development, the increased emphasis on longitudinal studies have provided a useful perspective. At the present time, these theories are being tested through a variety of research designs, and they are also providing the impetus for numerous intervention programs. Their usefulness, especially in relation to early intervention, appears to be strong, but whether they will all stand the test of time remains to be evaluated. The following case examines how theorists from these differing perspectives might analyze and recommend actions in an early intervention problem.

## Case 4. The Service Family

The Service family adopted Hong from an Asian orphanage when she was about 15 months old. Hong had been in a home care program for the first 8 months of her life and then was placed in the orphanage when the home caregiver could not continue. When the family first saw Hong, she toddled quickly over to them wearing a big smile, and as Mr. Service held out his arms, Hong ran right into them. Even though she spoke no English at that time, she seemed to communicate her wishes easily with gestures and before long she was repeating English words. Hong's transition into the extended family was relatively easy; she "took" to both sets of grandparents and interacted well with her little cousins. The Services enrolled her in a 2-day-a-week preschool at age 2½, and her transition there was also smooth. She showed an outgoing, friendly manner, and by the time she started kindergarten she was an accomplished English speaker with good emerging literacy skills. When Hong was 4½, her parents brought Li into the family. Li had been placed in the Chinese orphanage when she was 5 days old. Initially Li seemed very cautious when the Services approached her. She did not seem terribly upset, however, so they thought she would make a good adjustment. As the first weeks went by, Li seemed to adapt, but her affect toward the Services was very cool. She did seem to enjoy being with her sister, and Hong could engage her in play and get her to show a smile. Li seemed to need a long time before she would let any relatives near her. She usually hid her face in her arms if someone new approached her. She would not engage in new activities until her parents or sister showed her what to do. When the Services put her in preschool, she did not cry, but she only rarely participated in the play, and this concerned the teachers. Li's language skills did not progress well either—at age 4 she was still using a mix of single English words and gestures, and she often did not try to initiate communication. By kindergarten age, she did have basic communication skills, but she had an extremely difficult transition to kindergarten, and the teacher told the Services that Li might have a learning disability.

> To what would Bowlby and Ainsworth be likely to attribute the differences in Hong's and Li's behavior? What advice about Li might they give to the parents and the teacher?
>
> Would Thomas and Chess have an alternate explanation? What would they advise parents and teachers in regard to Hong? To Li?

How would Greenspan evaluate the situation, and what would he suggest to help Li be more connected and comfortable?

What would the perspective of Bandura contribute to the analysis of the situation, and what would he suggest as strategies to use to help both Li and Hong develop well?

Would any of these theorists think that Li's problem was a learning disability?

## Readings

A. Bandura, *Theoretical Perspectives*, pp. 293–307.

S. I. Greenspan, *How Emotional Development Relates to Learning*, pp. 308–311.

## Suggested Readings

Ainsworth, M. D. S., & Bowlby, J. (1991). An ethological approach to personality development. *American Psychologist, 46,* 333–341.

Bandura, A. (1997). Theoretical perspectives. *Self-efficacy: The exercise of control* (pp. 1–15). New York: W. H. Freeman.

Thomas, A., Chess, S., & Birch, H. G. (1970). The origin of personality. *Scientific American, 223,* 102, 104–109.

*Source:* Ziggy © 1972 Ziggy and Friends, Inc. Reprinted with permission of Universal Press Syndicate.

# CHAPTER 5

# Life Span Theoretical Perspectives on Personality and Social–Emotional Developmental Change

As noted in chapter 1, the study of developmental change during childhood and adolescence became important at the turn of the 20th century and has subsequently provided a plethora of theoretical perspectives and accompanying research evidence. The emphasis on these age periods has been so great that it sometimes has fostered an assumption that, by age 18 or 21, human development was essentially "finished." As noted earlier, this may be due to a number of factors. Interestingly, there was some focus on studying developmental aging issues during the late 19th and early 20th centuries (Charles, 1970; Groffmann, 1970). At the time of his writing in 1970, when a life span perspective began to be more prominent, Charles commented that in the past study had been ". . . with little exception . . . of concern with children by one group, and of concern with old people by another group. Where are the psychologists who are concerned with the whole of life?" (p. 48). During the mid 20th century, a number of theorists put forth ideas about the study of developmental change across the life span, and this perspective on human development began to receive increasing attention. Goulet and Baltes (1970), in the book in which the writings of Charles and Groffmann appear, stated that the life span perspective "is concerned with the description and explication of ontogenetic (age-related) behavioral change from birth to death," and they suggested such changes focus on ". . . the entire age span, whereas the focus of conventional developmental psychology has emphasized the first two decades . . ." (p. 12).

The proponents of a life span perspective define development somewhat differently than do theorists who focus on the birth to adolescent age period because those theorists emphasize improvement of skills and growth toward higher levels of functioning, whereas life span theorists chart developmental changes that may or may not be toward higher levels of ability. Often studies of aging have focused on the loss of powers. For example, the pioneer of child study, G. Stanley Hall, also pioneered study of aging changes when he wrote his book about the aging process in his own life (1923). Hall's book focused on the medical and physiological (primarily deteriorating) changes that he noted as he aged. Almost incidentally, a major impetus for study of life span changes and an important body of life span research came from longitudinal studies begun in the mid 20th century. Although the researchers studied child populations initially, they continued to follow the subjects through adulthood (e.g., Baltes & Schaie, 1973; Schaie, 2005), finding many interesting life span developmental issues to address as their subjects aged. This chapter discusses the general approach of life span theorists and describes the work of some who spoke to issues of personality and social/emotional development.

## Assumptions of Life Span Development Perspectives

According to Baltes, Reese, and Nesselroade (1977), life span perspectives represent an approach to the study of human development rather than focusing on a particular theoretical orientation. A number of assumptions are generally accepted as a part of this perspective, as follows:

- The developmental trajectories of individuals (and cohorts of individuals) have both stability and variability. Both intraindividual (development within particular individuals) and interindividual (developmental differences across individuals) changes are of interest.

- Qualitative and quantitative changes in behavior can occur at any point in the life span.

- Changes may be gradual or abrupt and result in positive or negative outcomes.

- Numerous factors determine intraindividual and interindividual changes; the determinants are pluralistic.

- The resources of individuals have an impact on their life span development. Personal resources include biological factors, such as health, physical abilities, and physical appearance; psychological factors, such as cognitive abilities, accumulated knowledge, self-efficacy, and emotional maturity; and social factors, such as personal support systems, cultural values, prior experiences, and socioeconomic status (including income and education).

- To understand developmental change requires conceptualizing and describing the changes in environmental contexts that may influence individual change. That is, the interaction of personal resources and environmental contexts must both be studied to understand life span development.

Baltes et al. (1977) suggest that there are three types of contextual influences: normative, graded, and nonnormative. These are often called life "events," and the sequence of these events is called the "life course." The life course is a descriptive term and involves examining the progressive temporal sequence of the lives over a span of years. This perspective involves looking at the complexities of life, not at only one domain, to examine integrations of domains and how these evolve over time. That is why a sociohistorical (or ecological/contextual) approach is usually used. A normative event is one that is expected by most people, and a nonnormative event is an unusual occurrence. They can be classified by the dimensions of timing, duration, sequencing, and specificity.

Normative life events can be congruent or incongruent, with either personal or societal time expectations. For example, having children is considered a normative life event, but having a child at age 15 or at age 45 would be "off-time," whereas having a child at age 25 would be "on-time." The duration of an event may have three phases: anticipation of the event, the event itself, and postevent influences. Events of long duration such as a war or depression will have a major influence on the life course, whereas events of short duration may have a strong or weak effect, depending on whether they are normative or nonnormative events. For example, a nonnormative event such as winning a lottery, even though of short duration, may have a major influence on the life course. Normative events usually have an acceptable sequence to them. In present society, completing one's education usually comes before getting married or getting a responsible work position. Individuals who gain significant employment before completing education (e.g., a child actor) are considered out of the norm. Getting married and having children and then going to college at age 50 is also considered nonnormative in sequencing. As these examples illustrate, however, normative expectations do differ in various cultures and change more rapidly in some cultures than in others. Nonnormative events usually have specificity; that is, they are unique to individuals, although they may not be unique to families. For example, becoming an elephant trainer is nonnormative, unless one grows up in a circus family. Routine events may also be nonnormative on one or more of the dimensions of timing, duration, or sequencing. An individual may start college at age 14 (timing), get married and divorced in 6 months (duration), or be a successful musician at age 30 and go back to college get a music degree at age 60 (sequencing). All these would be normative events that had nonnormative dimensions.

Although theories focused on infants and young children posit many universals in the timing of developmental changes and empirical evidence supports this view, longitudinal studies typically report much more variability in the lives of their subjects as they encounter a wide range of experiences during their adult lives. For example, the variability in infants' age of sitting up, walking, understanding language, gaining concepts like object permanence, and forming attachments to caregivers is confined to a relatively short time period (thus often prompting a theoretical emphasis on maturational factors). Even across cultural groups, infant development is very similar, whereas developmental changes in adults may cover short or long time periods and have very different results because adults' experiences with wide-ranging social–cultural factors and individual life activities extensively influence the timing and nature of their developmental change. Thus, life span theorists usually stress a sociohistorical perspective because of the need for theoretical explanations that predict the increasing variability of the developmental changes that occur over the life span. They often address issues of personality change and social–emotional development during adulthood in different cohorts of individuals who have experienced varied sets of experiences affected by historical events such as wars or economic changes.

## Charting the Personality and Social–Emotional Life Course

Although life span theorists have studied a variety of developmental change domains in each study, many of them have made particular contributions to knowledge about the personality and social–emotional changes that may occur over the life span. Chapters 3 and 4 have already discussed two views of life span personality and social–emotional development—one outlined by Erikson and another by Bandura. Although the data Erikson used to develop his life span theory came primarily from clinical and literary sources, his attention to life span development is congruent with the concerns of many life span researchers and theorists, who studied the changing social–emotional aspects of identity development in adulthood. Erikson was particularly interested in how resolution of earlier crises stages influenced the last stage of life, integrity versus despair. Bandura, using results from empiricist, rationalist, and sociohistorical research conducted by himself as well as others, has described how issues of self-efficacy development change over time and are affected by personal and professional life contexts, such as business, sports, and health-related events. He found that an important developmental issue for the old age period is how to maintain a sense of personal agency at that time by finding ways to continue to exercise it in meaningful contexts and activities. Chess and Thomas also followed their subjects for many years to evaluate how their early temperament identification was manifested in adulthood. Although Bowlby and Ainsworth focused on early development of attachment, the effects of attachment differences on adult ability to form romantic and other attachment relationships has also been studied by life span theorists. Freud, of course, was also very interested in the influences of early development on adult personality problems, although his work "predicted backward." Another group of theorists interested in life span perspectives have been behavioral genetics researchers (e.g., Plomin, 1986), who have been especially interested in the effects of genes on development. They have typically used an empiricist perspective to conduct studies comparing the development of genetically identical twins to that of fraternal twins and other siblings. Most of these studies follow the subjects longitudinally and try to identify the proportion of the personality that can be attributed to genetic factors and the proportion that is likely to be due to environmental experiences. However, the main concern of life span theorists has been to chart the life course of adult life and the developmental changes that occur in that time period. In addition to Erikson, other theorists have identified typical stages in adult personality, social, and/or emotional life.

## Levinson's Seasons of Life

Using an interview technique Daniel Levinson (1986) examined the life course changes, first of men and then of women, calling them "seasons." Levinson attempted to examine the life cycle (i.e., the underlying order) that might be manifest in various seasons of life. He rejected the idea that there were only three segments of life: childhood/adolescence, adulthood, and old age. In analyzing the data from his study of professional men, he divided adulthood into smaller periods than those defined by other theorists such as Erikson and described transition periods between each of the seasons he described. He labeled the period from birth to about age 22 as Preadulthood but identified an Early Adult Transition period at the end of that era (ages 17 to 22). During this transition, the individual modifies relationships with parents and enters into the adult world. Rather than seeing this as a "finish" to development, as is often assumed by child psychology theorists, Levinson saw this as just providing the basis for the adult life.

Adulthood begins with a season called Entry Life Structure (ages 22 to 28), which is a period of health and energy but also stress related to many decisions to be made that will structure the mode for adult living. At the Age 30 Transition (ages 28 to 30), there is an opportunity to reassess and redesign for the next life period. The Culminating Life Structure (ages 33 to 40) period involves living out the life plans that were designed earlier, but there is usually a Midlife Transition (ages 40 to 45), which involves a reassessment and preparation to enter the next phase. The later life seasons, Entry Life Structure (ages 45 to 50), Age 50 Transition (ages 50 to 55), Culminating Life Structure (ages 55 to 60), and Late Adult Transition (ages 60 to 65), have similar reassessments, plans, and accomplishments. Levinson believed that the same sequence holds for men and women and for people of different cultures, classes, and time periods; however, he admits that there are wide variations in what people do within these sequences. Many other theorists have seen the life seasons of females as being much more varied than those of males, and as people live longer the timing of these seasons may be extended or rearranged for both men and women. His work was important, however, in giving more detail and precision to transition periods and especially to pointing out that development continues throughout the life span.

## Gould's Personality Development Stages

Roger Gould (1975, 1978) also studied adult life personality development, studying both patients who came to him for therapy and a sample of nonpatients in the age range of 16 to 50. He identified seven age-graded groups, each of which seemed to have different major life themes. He concluded that rather than personality being a stable characteristic, it continues to develop throughout life, at least into the fifth decade. Through interviews and surveys, he and his colleagues identified the early themes expressed by interviewees. The youngest age group was grappling with the issue of escape from the dominance of parents, but those who were a little older had established friends as substitutes for family ties and began to see themselves as becoming competent in the real world. During their

30s, his participants became more questioning of their goals, and their self-reflectiveness increased. Their marriages and children were a major focus, and they often had greater financial goals. Gould found that the 40s were a more unstable and uncomfortable time, with decreased marital satisfaction. Subjects in their 40s had "quiet urgency" about reaching their life goals. They also had some regrets about what they had done in the past. By age 50, individuals saw themselves as stable personalities, coming to terms with time, with increasing health concerns and feelings that there was not as much time to achieve their goals. Gould did not conduct interviews with people older than 50; thus, he did not define any other themes. However, he found that by age 50, his subjects were beginning to acknowledge death as a potential presence in their lives. Since Gould's studies, which were conducted in the latter part of the 20th century when old age was thought to be age 60 to 65, the life span age period has been extended. Thus, subjects in their 50s today might have somewhat different perspectives. Whether a new sample would express the same themes but extend them to later ages or have different themes is a question of interest. Gould provided a valuable service, however, because he was one of the first to see adult development as an ongoing process, rather than having development considered essentially over by early adulthood. He believed that his research promoted adults' thinking about their own development, and he recommended that they confront their developmental issues to have a more successful later life period.

## Schaie's View of Midlife Transitions or Crises

Life span theorists have differing views about whether adult changes during the midlife years can be characterized as crisis periods or merely as periods of transition. Crisis implies a more abrupt and salient change period than does transition, which suggests that change may occur over a longer period and not be as intense. Schaie and Willis (1991), in a review of numerous studies, explained the differing views on two grounds. First, some studies have looked at developmental change in people involved in therapy, while others have used a more "normal" population. Second, some studies use in-depth interviews, while others ask respondents to answer self-report surveys or rating scales. Clinical studies typically involve lengthy narratives that tend to emphasize crisis periods, *but* when other types of measures are used, adults usually report more gradual transitions. Of course, there may also be true differences between the experiences of these groups; that is, they may have dissimilar methods of dealing with biological and sociohistorical influences. The majority of these studies have been cross-sectional rather than longitudinal, so it will be difficult to resolve this question until long-term observations of the same groups can be done.

## Valliant's Study of Adult Development and Aging

George Valliant (1977, 2002) has been involved (with other scientists) through most of his career in following three cohorts of people. The Harvard Cohort initially consisted of a group of freshmen men (268) who were followed from 1938 to 1999. The Inner City Cohort initially had 456 men, half of whom had juvenile delinquency records and half of whom did not, and they were followed from 1939 to 2000. The Terman Cohort consisted of 90 women from the 682 gifted children sample who were followed from 1922 to 1987. These groups were interviewed every 2 to 4 years during those time periods; thus, an extensive data set has been collected. Valliant has examined many factors, including their health-related behaviors, genetic relationships, general lifestyle, and social–emotional maturation. His final sample totaled 826 individuals. Valliant was particularly interested in following their development in relation to Erikson's psychosocial stages; however, he added two additional stages to those of Erikson. Calling them "adult life tasks," he charted them as follows:

- *Achieving Identity:* The task is to master separation from childhood and dependence on the family of origin, that is, "knowing where one's family values end and one's own values begin" (Valliant, 2002, p. 46). Some individuals, even at age 50, had not achieved this, and it prevented them from committing themselves to work, friends, or other relationships.

- *Career Consolidation:* The task requires assuming a social identity in the work world (includes employment and/or work at home). Some individuals never developed the "contentment, compensation, competence, and commitment" (p. 47) to achieve this stage. (Valliant's added stage)

- *Generativity:* This task involves guidance of the next generation, which requires giving of self. It includes both caring for others and building community, and those adults in their 70s from all three cohorts who were most joyful had mastered this stage.

- *Keeper of the Meaning:* The task is conservation and preservation of the "collective products of mankind" (p. 48). It involves having concerns outside one's own social radius, guiding groups, speaking out for others, and preserving cultural achievements. It can occur earlier but is usually seen in later life. (Valliants' added stage)

- *Integrity:* The task is accepting one's life and life cycle and having a spiritual sense. This task is accomplished in later life.

The sequential mastery of these tasks by most people was documented in Valliant's longitudinal study; however, he found some people master the tasks in a different order. He commented, "One life stage is not better or more virtuous than another. Adult development is neither a footrace nor a moral imperative. It is a road map to help us make sense of where we and where our neighbors might be located" (2002, p. 50).

Valliant found that individuals who had stable personalities and positive outlooks generally lived longer, and that many variables often thought to predict long life did not do so. For example, in his older group, variables that did not predict longevity included ancestral longevity, cholesterol levels, stress levels, parental characteristics, childhood temperament, and ease in social relationships, although some of these were important at earlier age levels. The seven predictors of healthy aging were never smoking or stopping at a young age, absence of alcohol abuse, healthy weight, exercise of some type, a stable marriage, number of years of education, and an adaptive coping style. Valliant concluded that persons likely to be "happy-well" instead of "sad-sick" at age 80 were more likely to have had healthy lifestyles and satisfying social relationships. Moreover, they tended to have a "mature adaptive style," which included the ability to cope effectively with life changes. He indicated that those who were social isolates tended to die younger and that this factor was more important than social class or intellectual ability. The protective factors he outlined include having a future orientation, a capacity for gratitude and forgiveness, an ability to love and forgive, and a desire to do things (i.e., to play) with other people. In old age, "subjective good health" is more important than "objective good health." Valliant commented, "It is all right to be ill as long as you do not feel sick" (2002, p. 13).

## Measuring Adult Psychological Well-Being

Although many life span theorists have been concerned about the topic of aging well, they often define "well-being" differently, using a range of terminology and theoretical perspectives. According to Carol Ryff (1995), these perspectives have not influenced empirical research because the concept of well-being lacked operational definitions and measures. Often the quality of life in adults has been studied descriptively by asking people about their level of happiness rather than measuring their positive functioning. Ryff designed a model that integrates many theoretical perspectives into a number of "core dimensions" and then asked young, middle-aged, and old-aged adults to rate themselves on each of the dimensions that she had identified. Figure 5.1 gives these dimensions and shows the theoretical concepts from which they were derived.

Ryff and her colleagues found differences in the patterns of the dimensions of well-being in the various age groups. For example, in one study she found that reported dimensions showed environmental mastery and autonomy increased from young adulthood to midlife, personal growth and purpose decreased in later life, and positive relations with others and self-acceptance were stable across the age groups. Later studies with larger national samples showed relatively similar results. In general, women have rated themselves higher on positive relationships and personal growth, whereas the rest of the dimensions have not shown differences. A cross-cultural study with South Korean subjects demonstrated some differences in self-presentation because these subjects rated themselves less high on positive qualities than did U.S. subjects. The Korean subjects rated themselves highest on positive relations with others and lowest on self-acceptance and personal growth; thus, they defined their well-being as more related to the well-being of others. This finding is similar to findings in cross-cultural studies of Asian and Western school-age children's ratings on self-concept scales (e.g., Wang & Ren, 2004). Ryff concluded that how life experiences are interpreted plays an important role in the variations reported in human well-being. She recommends longitudinal study using these core dimensions to gain insight into how life experiences and their interpretation influence psychological well-being in age, gender, and cultural groups.

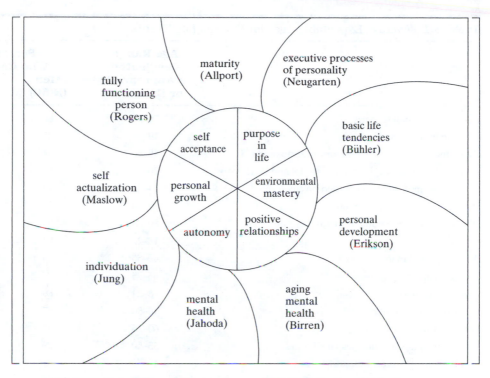

**Figure 5.1**  Core Dimensions of Well Being and Their Psychological Roots

*Source: Core Dimensions of Well-Being and Their Psychological Roots* from *Psychological Well-Being in Adult Life* (p. 100), C. D. Ryff, 1995. *Current Directions in Psychological Science*, 4 (4). Copyright © 1995 by American Psychological Society.

## Neugarten's Views on Personality and Patterns of Aging

An interesting perspective on life span developmental change in the social–emotional domain is that of Bernice Neugarten (1916–2001), who studied life span issues extensively in the mid to late 20th century. Neugarten (1964, 1968) was particularly interested in social and emotional development during middle and late adulthood, especially related to issues of women's life span development. For example, she looked at whether timing of menopause, children's departure for college, and other such life events precipitated crises for women. She reported that within a particular society, individuals develop a concept of the "normal, expectable life cycle," in which they anticipate what will be happening at various points in that cycle. She stated that if events occur at these times (when expected), they do not precipitate major life crises, but instead are viewed as normal turning points, which may involve some changes in identity or self-concept but do not cause crises. When the timing is off—for example, if children don't leave home when expected to do so or if there is a forced retirement before the usual age—it is more likely to result in a crisis period. She commented, "Even death is a normal

**Table 5.1**  Average Expectable Ages for Various Life Events

|  | Age Range Designated as Appropriate or Expected | Percent Who Concur Men (N-50) | Women (N-43) |
|---|---|---|---|
| Best age for a man to marry | 20–25 | 80 | 90 |
| Best age for a woman to marry | 19–24 | 85 | 90 |
| When most people should become grandparents | 45–50 | 84 | 79 |
| Best age for most people to finish school and go to work | 20–22 | 86 | 82 |
| When most men should be settled on a career | 24–26 | 74 | 64 |
| When most men hold their top jobs | 45–50 | 71 | 58 |
| When most people should be ready to retire | 60–85 | 83 | 86 |
| A young man | 18–22 | 84 | 83 |
| A middle-aged man | 40–50 | 86 | 75 |
| An old man | 65–75 | 75 | 57 |
| A young woman | 18–24 | 89 | 88 |
| A middle aged woman | 40–50 | 87 | 77 |
| An old woman | 60–75 | 83 | 87 |
| When a man has the most responsibilities | 35–50 | 79 | 75 |
| When a man accomplishes most | 40–50 | 82 | 71 |
| The prime of life for a man | 35–50 | 86 | 80 |
| When a woman has the most responsibilities | 25–40 | 93 | 91 |
| When a woman accomplishes the most | 30–45 | 94 | 92 |
| A good-looking woman | 20–35 | 92 | 82 |

*Note:* Reprinted from *Average Expectable Ages for Various Life Events* from Neugarten, B. L., Moore, J. C., "Age Norms, Age Constraints, and Adults Socialization." *American Journal of Sociology,* 70:6 (1965), pp. 710–717.

and expectable event for the old. Death is tragic only when it occurs at too young an age" (Neugarten, 1996, p. 117). Table 5.1 shows the typical life span ages that respondents agreed were expectable during the latter 20th century. Many of those expected ages have changed since that time, but some are still the norm.

Neugarten noted that age norms and expectations reflect socially defined times, and thus in periods of rapid social change these norms change. That is, this occurs when the boundaries between life periods become more blurred, when age group definitions change, and when major life event timing changes. Then there are "new inconsistencies in what is considered age-appropriate behavior" (Neugarten, 1996, p. 72).

In Western society, a number of such changes are occurring at the present time. For example, puberty is now starting earlier, a period of "youth" seems to be interposed between adolescence and adulthood, and people are living much longer than in the past. Preparation for entering the workforce requires more years of education, the typical age of marriage and child rearing is somewhat later, marriage is less common, and divorce with multiple marriages is a more common life event. All these sociohistorical dimensions will affect social–emotional development throughout the life span. This same phenomena applies to other cultures that have had differences in timing, duration, and sequencing of normative events and that may even have different normative and nonnormative categories. For example, age of marriage, number of children, employment outside the home, and educational expectations for women vary across many cultures. In addition to cultural expectations, the historical events of the broader society also can have great effects on personality and social–emotional development. The influence of these factors has been studied through cohort perspectives.

## Elder's Study of Cohort Effects on Personality and Social–Emotional Development

The effects of the timing of historical events on social and emotional development throughout the life span has been of particular interest to life span theorist Glen Elder (1934–), who has studied how such development has been affected by life experience differences in various cohorts of individuals. From his theoretical perspective, social–emotional development is highly affected by the timing of historical events and thus may create unique characteristics in individuals born at particular time periods. Elder studied these dimensions in a cohort of people growing up during the depression (Elder, 1974, 1994), and he found that this group, who were in their elementary-age years at the time of the depression, took on "adult" roles earlier to help with the family income and learned coping strategies that fostered human agency. Elder followed the cohort longitudinally and found that World War II affected them fairly positively because they were at high school graduation age when that occurred, and thus the timing was "appropriate" for them to be in the armed services. They later also benefitted from the G.I. bill for college and in general had stable careers. Elder subsequently compared the effects of these historical events on individuals from two other longitudinal data sets (Terman's study of gifted children and the Berkeley Guidance study of young children).

Terman's sample was older at the time these events occurred, and the war, in particular, caused an interruption in their "life course" because they already had jobs and families, whereas the Berkeley study sample was very young at the time of the depression, and they experienced the deprivation but not the ability to contribute to the family income; thus, they had somewhat lower self-confidence as a group. Elder also studied the effects of the Chinese cultural revolution on the cohort of young people who were living at that time (Elder & Rockwell, 1979), and he examined how the concept of adolescence has been affected by sociohistorical events (Elder, 1980). In regard to personality and social/emotional development, therefore, Elder makes the case that the sociohistorical factors present during people's lives are very influential in affecting the life themes that are important to them, their views of the choices available to them, and their beliefs in their ability to affect life conditions (1994, 1999). However, he also pointed out that predicting a life course is not clear-cut, because it is also "... the story of how many women and men successfully overcame disadvantage in their lives" (1999, p. 79). This view relates to Bandura's discussion of the importance of human agency development and to Neugarten's evidence that the "normative" timing of life events affects developmental change. Elder's perspective has also been influential on ecological theorists such as Bronfenbrenner, who followed Elder's challenge to study human development as it is "embedded in the life course and historical time" (1999, p. 79).

## Life Span Views on Attachment Development

As indicated earlier, the attachment issues discussed by Bowlby and Ainsworth have also been of interest to life span researchers. As Lerner and Ryff pointed out (1978), "One of the least debated components of the attachment concept is that an attachment endures over time" (pp. 21–22). Therefore, most life span theorists would agree with their view that this phenomena needs to be studied across the life span, although most researchers have found that the particular behaviors that define attachment are not the same for younger and older age levels. For example, one way young children demonstrate attachment is through proximity seeking behavior but at later ages this might be demonstrated by distal behaviors, such as verbal (calling, talking) and visual (looking, searching, taking pictures) contact. In today's society, attachment might thus be shown by adolescents or adults in frequent initiation of phone conversations, text messaging, or e-mailing photographs to attachment figures. The life span contribution to attachment theory thus involves extending it to find a frame of reference that describes attachment behaviors that are appropriate to each life stage. Issues such as the directions and extensiveness of change, as well as cultural differences, are beginning to be studied. Also, the relationships between early attachment to parents and ability to form friendships and dating/marriage attachments have been of interest to life span theorists.

The theoretical rationale for the stability of attachment behaviors is drawn from Bowlby's internal working model concept. The model adopted by the child incorporates the attachment figures' behavior into the child's own self-identity. According to Belsky and Cassidy (1994), "working models become so deeply ingrained that they influence feelings, thought and behaviour unconsciously and automatically" (p. 379). One method for assessing adolescent and adult working models involves clinical interviews (Main & Goldwyn, 1984). This method has shown correspondences between early attachment status and later internal working models. For example, a number of self-report instruments have also been used, especially in regard to determining whether early internal working models influence adult romantic relationships (Collins & Read, 1990). In a longitudinal study, Collins and Sroufe (1999) found that the quality of attachment in infancy, of caregiver–child interaction at age 13, and of adolescent peer relationships were all related. They suggested that the capacity for intimacy in romantic relationships is also affected by these earlier attachment indicators. Other life span theorists have begun to investigate how adults in midlife deal with their ambivalence in attachment to parental figures when these parents are in need of later life care (Lang, 2004), and how types of attachment affect adult romantic relationships (Maio, Fincham, Regalia, & Paleari, 2004). At this time, there are still many questions to be answered regarding the longitudinal effects of early attachment status, but it is definitely an area of interest in life span study

## Cultural Influences on Social Relationship Development

Most of the early studies of development over the life span focused on majority segments of the population, especially in regard to cultural, racial, and ethnic backgrounds. However, more recently there has been an emphasis on studying these developmental domains in U.S. minority populations. For example, McAdoo (1999) has examined how the family structures and stress levels of African Americans may affect adolescent and adult development, especially in upwardly mobile families. According to McAdoo, African-American families have often had wide support networks (both kin and "fictive" kin) that have enabled them to cope with environmental stress more effectively; that is, the support network has been "stress absorbing." She interviewed the members of high-achieving middle-class families to gain insight into how they coped with economic, race prejudice, and other stresses as they encountered change in their life situations. Those from intact families who were continuing their upward mobility through a number of generations reported the lowest stress levels, whereas those whose children had not obtained the same or higher levels of economic success as their parents reported more stress. This was also true of the one-parent families studied (about one third of the sample), and they were most likely to rely on their kin support network. She found that most African-American families preferred to rely on family rather than agency support systems. She stated, "These ethnic cultural patterns were not eliminated when the families became mobile, but contributed to the maintenance of achievements" (Mc Adoo, 1999, p. 487). The emotional support and help gained from this network were "crucial stress absorbing approaches for the families studied" (p. 487). John Ogbu had written earlier about the differences in child-rearing patterns of African Americans in low socioeconomic areas, which could be partially explained by the "theories of success" that adults in that group embraced (Ogbu, 1981). He noted that parents were equally concerned about their children but did not hold the same definitions of successful lives as parents who lived in other environments; thus, their behavioral and academic achievement expectations differed.

Another area in which cross-cultural study has provided insights is in parent–child play interactions, which are hypothesized by many theorists to structure later social–emotional development. The socialization process used by parents may differ due to parental beliefs about appropriate developmental outcomes. For example, study of parent–child play among mothers and fathers in urban families in India has shown that the "rough-and-tumble" play typically reported between fathers and young children in Western cultures is rarely evident (Roopnarine, Hooper, Ahmeduzzaman, & Pollack, 1993). Father–child play in this culture is very similar to mother–child play, and the emphasis in play is on pleasure not on learning. Indian infants are also held by many family members, as well as by nonfamily members, and the authors concluded that their practices are "functionally appropriate for the India culture subsample assessed" (p. 301). In a study comparing U.S. and Mexican mothers and siblings, Farver (1993) found that although Mexican mothers are very involved with infants, siblings are the primary play partners rather than parents. This is in contrast to many U.S. studies showing that mothers engage in much pretend play with their young children. In this study the Mexican siblings were more similar to the U.S. mothers in play interactions with young children than were the two sets of mothers. In Mexican culture, due to the higher birthrate and size of families, siblings are often responsible for child care and, thus, may provide the socialization experiences that their younger siblings need. Although these examples are not longitudinal, they do illustrate how the inclusion of sociohistorical and cultural contexts in the analysis of developmental change can give insight into developmental variability across the life span.

Effects of culture have also been of interest in the study of romantic and sexual experiences of adolescence. In particular there have been many changes in contemporary social norms regarding these domains, and those changes have often been in conflict with more traditional cultural practices, particularly of certain ethnic, racial, or religious groups (Coates, 1999). For example, African-American young people from low socioeconomic communities sometimes embrace "oppositional cultural norms" (Ogbu, 1994) that challenge general societal norms regarding sexuality and commitment relationships. Also, in the broader contemporary society, changing attitudes toward adolescent involvement in romantic and/or sexual behavior and expectations about timing and exclusiveness of this behavior have resulted in wide variations in adolescent and young adult views and practices regarding commitment, love, and sexual experiences (Graber, Britto, & Brooks-Gunn, 1999). This is another area in need of long-term cohort study to determine how changing social norms influence the timing and character of romantic and sexual relationships among adolescents and young adults.

### Theoretical Influence and Critique

The life span theoretical perspective has really redefined the field because it has provided insight into developmental change as an ongoing process throughout life. It has also promoted awareness of the variations in development that occur as environments and life experiences vary and has drawn attention to the complexity of interactions among these factors. Many researchers are presently testing basic concepts of life span perspectives, but often this research is fragmented and specific to settings. As new research builds on past research, the life course of individuals from many cultural backgrounds and time periods will be described. Then some common themes that can lead to a more integrated theory of life span development may be fostered. It is certainly the case that life span theorists have already demonstrated that human development is not completed by age 21.

## Summary

During the life span, from infancy to old age, there will be many periods of developmental change, precipitated by biological changes, environmental crisis periods, and nature/nurture interactions that will affect later development, depending on how they are resolved, and sensitivity to these change periods as typical in the course of development will facilitate successful resolution.

## Case 5. The Standard Family Revisited

Review the events that might have occurred in the Standard family during the past year (Case 3) and plot out the life course timing of the adolescent, young adult, middle adult, and older adult members of the family, assuming the life conditions listed with that case had occurred. Some of these events were normative and some nonnormative. Also, even the normative events may have differed in timing, duration, sequence, or specificity. Make a chart that categorizes these individual events as normative or nonnormative and then predict how the timing, duration, sequence, or specificity may have affected the individual involved and the family.

Who are the family members who had age-relevant and age-irrelevant life courses?

Which events might Neugarten think were not "expectable," and what consequences might they have for the personality and social–emotional development of those individuals?

Assume the sociohistorical times are current ones. How would historical events that happened 5 years ago have affected the members of the family?

Assume that in the next year, the following events will occur and analyze their influence similarly to the earlier analysis.

| | |
|---|---|
| John moves to London. | Janet gets accepted to medical school. |
| Brad decides to become a priest. | Sue gets a new job in California. |
| Madge is pregnant. | Alan breaks his leg. |
| Grandma Mildred buys a motorcycle. | Henry is diagnosed with cancer. |
| Howard and Sally get married. | Holly joins the ice hockey team. |
| Bill and Ann take a world tour for 4 months. | Bob's National Guard Unit is sent overseas. |

## Readings

G. Elder, *The Depression Experiences in Life Patterns*, pp. 312–319.

Erik Erikson, *Reflections on the Last Stage—and the First*, pp. 320–325.

## Suggested Readings

Elder, G. (1974). Children of the great depression. In G. Elder, *Children of the great depression:* Social change in life experience (pp. 271–283). Chicago: University of Chicago Press.

Erikson, E. H. (1984). Reflections on the last stage—and the first. *Psychoanalytic Study of the Child, 39,* 155–165.

Neugarten, B. L. (1996). Continuities and discontinuities of psychological issues into adult life. In B. L. Neugarten, *The meanings of age: Selected papers of Bernice L. Neugarten* (pp. 88–95). Chicago: University of Chicago Press.

Schaie, K. W., & Willis, S. L. (1991). Midlife: A transition or a crisis? In K. W. Shaie & S. L. Willis, *Adult development and aging* (3rd ed, pp. 69–74). New York: Harper Collins.

*Source:* © United King Features Syndicate, Inc.

# Theories With Major Emphasis on Cognitive and Language Development

Cognitive and language development have been of great interest to many developmental theorists, including ones from every perspective on knowledge development. Foremost among the rationalists is Piaget, who with his colleagues presented a theory of knowledge construction that described the development of logical thought from infancy through adolescence. He also addressed the role of language and play in thought development. Another theorist who explained cognition and language relationships and their development as a coconstructive process is Vygotsky, who emphasized the socio-historic factors influencing that development. He agreed with Piaget on the important roles children's language and play have on thought development, but his interpretation of the reasons for their importance differed. Although both Piaget and Vygotsky saw language as having a strong interface with cognition, the development of language has also been addressed from other perspectives. Theories of language development have been proposed by linguists, behaviorists, ethologists, and constructivists, and they often disagree on questions of the underlying processes of language development (nature or nurture), its universal aspects, and the particular linguistic features of interest. This chapter primarily describes the cognitive and language theories of Piaget and his colleagues (Geneva school) and

Vygotsky and his colleagues (Soviet school), but it also gives an overview of some other theoretical views of language development.

# Piaget's Genetic Epistemological Theory of Development

Jean Piaget (1896–1980) was a native of Switzerland and was educated in the natural sciences at the University of Neuchatel. He was interested in science from an early age, becoming an expert on mollusks in adolescence. He studied psychoanalysis at the University of Zurich and spent a year in France working on standardization of an intelligence test, based on the initial work of Binet and Simon. He was especially interested in the wrong answers that children gave and began some experiments on the development of thought processes at that time, using a clinical interview approach loosely based on psychiatric interviewing techniques. He then taught at the Institut J. J. Rousseau in Geneva and began studying the reasoning and language of children (1924, 1926). He married a student coworker, Valentine Chatenay, and they had three children, who also became the focus of his intense observation and study (1936, 1945). During his long career, he worked primarily in Geneva, collaborating with a number of people but especially with Barbel Inhelder. His student Hermina Sinclair-De Zwart also was active in interpreting his work (Piaget & Inhelder,1969; Piaget, Inhelder, & Sinclair-De Zwart, 1973). Much of his research was conducted during World War II and the period leading up to it, and thus it did not reach American audiences until after that war was over, when it was then published in English. Piaget created and was director of the International Center for Genetic Epistemology from 1955 until his death, and he started the School of Sciences at the University of Geneva. He was also active in UNESCO, serving as a Swiss delegate. He is the author of over 50 books and 100 articles, some of which were written with colleagues. He is considered one of the most influential developmental theorists of the 20th century, as founder of the "Geneva school" of psychology.

## Basic Constructs of Piaget's Theory

According to Case (1999), Piaget based some of his ideas on those of Baldwin, who had written about "genetic epistemology," which is the study of how knowledge (i.e., intelligence) develops (Baldwin, 1894/1968). Piaget drew on a number of hypotheses Baldwin had suggested and systematically studied them, with the major question that guided Piaget's research and theoretical explanations being this: How does knowledge grow; that is, how is intelligence created? From his extensive clinical studies, he derived this answer: Knowledge development is a progressive construction of logical structures, each of which leads to higher and more powerful adult structures. His early studies convinced him that children's thinking is qualitatively different from that of adults. He reported that it progresses through four stages, which he termed sensorimotor, preoperational, concrete operational, and formal operational. His later studies focused more on the functions of thought rather than its structures and on specific cognitive abilities such as memory; he saw functions as invariant across life, whereas structures varied as knowledge developed.

### Functional Invariants of Knowledge Construction

According to Piaget, knowledge construction is neither the gaining of a copy of the external world given to the child nor a reflection of preformed mental structures (1924, 1954). Rather it is built over time through the dynamic process of active engagement with the environment. It occurs through the exploration of the objects (and later, the ideas) in the environment; using existing *schema* (organized action and mental connections). In infants, these are action schema (sensorimotor skills); in older children, these develop into cognitive schema. Construction of knowledge is a biologically based process, necessary for human survival. Piaget stated that the functional invariants that are essential for knowledge construction are the following.

- *Organization* is the internal component of knowledge. It proceeds through two types of hereditary factors: biological structures and biologically based functions. The knowledge construction processes (functions) are the same throughout life, but the mental organization of knowledge (structures) change over time. Children's interactions with the environment influence how the structures of knowledge are organized. Thus, knowledge develops through the interaction between biological maturation and environmental experiences.

- *Adaptation* is the change in behavior or thought that makes evident the organization that has occurred. Thus, knowledge (i.e., intelligence) is an adaptation, not a fixed condition. Organization and adaptation are furthered by two processes:
  - *Assimilation* occurs when a new object (or idea) is incorporated into an existing schema. For example, an action schema that infants have is sucking, and when they are introduced to a bottle rather than the breast, they assimilate the sucking of the bottle nipple to their existing schema. They have not needed to reorganize their schema.
  - *Accommodation* occurs when an existing schema cannot incorporate the new object (or idea) but must be changed to accommodate the new. Thus, existing schema must be reorganized or new schema created. For example, when infants are introduced to a cup, they first try to use their sucking schema, but when that proves unsuccessful, they must accommodate by revising that schema to include a different action that is similar to sucking but not the same. When this accommodation has occurred, infants have demonstrated adaptation.

- *Equilibration* is the dynamic interplay between assimilation and accommodation, which drives the adaptation process. When equilibrium occurs, there is a balance between the structures of the mind and environmental experiences. When they are out of balance, then adaptation must be sought through assimilating new knowledge to existing schema or through accommodating schema to incorporate the new knowledge. There are periods when assimilation dominates, when accommodation dominates, and when equilibrium is evident, and these correspond to stages of cognitive development. As children's knowledge is constructed, the equilibrium period is evident when a new stage is consistently observed.

- *Horizontal Decalage* (disparity in levels of logical reasoning for different tasks) occurs because equilibrium may not be reached across all knowledge domains at the same time.
- *Vertical Decalage* (thinking processes from lower stages that reoccur at higher stages) is evidence of invariant aspects of knowledge construction

### Sources of Knowledge

According to Piaget (1936), knowledge is constructed from three sources, all of which are facilitated through the equilibration process. These sources are (a) interaction with the physical world (*physical knowledge*), (b) comparisons of relationships among objects/ideas (*logicomathematical knowledge*), and (c) knowledge that must be transmitted by other humans (*social arbitrary knowledge*). Physical knowledge involves learning the properties of various objects and their actions in space and time. For example, a ball has a certain shape, and two of its actions are rolling and bouncing. Children can gain this knowledge just by being active in the physical world. That is, the source of knowledge is in the objects themselves and arises from the child's interactions with them. Logicomathematical knowledge involves comparing the relationships among objects (and later, ideas), and this knowledge can be learned by comparing and experimenting with these relationships. For example, sizes (big/small), shapes (round/square), and space (high/low) concepts are learned by comparisons of objects and categorizing with labels. That is, the source of logicomathematical knowledge is in the individual's categorizing and comparing the characteristics of objects (and later ideas), using numeration, seriation, classification, and other internal mental processes.

Some knowledge cannot be learned by the individual alone but must be transmitted by people in the culture. For example, correct language names for objects and ideas, proper manners, important dates, and similar culturally defined facts must be transmitted by other people to the child. This source of knowledge is in the society, and because it is arbitrary (i.e., cannot be uncovered through use of logical thought), it must be transmitted directly from others. (This type of knowledge was made explicit by Sinclair-De Zwart, from her readings of Piaget's work.) Piaget was especially concerned about the misteaching of logicomathematical knowledge as though it is social arbitrary knowledge, that is, by having adults "give/teach" logicomathematical concepts to be memorized rather than providing children with experiences that allow them to construct such concepts themselves.

### Structures of Knowledge at Four Stages

Piaget's studies led him to define four stages through which he said knowledge construction progressed, and he described these stages extensively in his early studies (e.g., 1924,1936, 1945), in his exploration of children's knowledge of number, space, time, seriation, and other basic concepts (e.g., 1954, 1968, 1969), and in his later studies of memory development, procedural knowledge, and problem-solving strategies (e.g., 1976, 1978; Piaget, Inhelder, & Sinclair-De Zwart, 1973). Although he named the age periods for each, these are approximate. The stages and the characteristics Piaget described are as follows.

*Sensorimotor Stage (birth to age 2):* During this period infants use their senses and their motor abilities to gain knowledge. There are six stages during this period:

- *Reflexive actions (Stage 1: birth to 6 weeks):* Infants use primarily reflexive actions such as sucking to interact with the environment. These reflex schemes are used indiscriminately, but are evidence of children's early need to act on their environment
- *Primary Circular Reactions (Stage 2: 1 to 4, 5 months):* These are primarily reflexive actions that infants repeat over and over, such as thumb sucking. Infants typically have only a few action schema that they use repeatedly (e.g., mouthing every object—balls, spoons, fingers, toys).
- *Secondary Circular Reactions (Stage 3: 4 to 10 months):* Infants act on the objects in the environment to get responses, such as squeezing a toy to get a noise. They have more varied action schema but still use the actions indiscriminately (e.g., shaking both a rattle and a ball). They may search for an object if it is partially visible.
- *Coordination of Secondary Schemes (Stage 4: 8 to 12 months):* By this age infants can coordinate a number of schemes to reach a goal. For example, if an object is out of reach (a ball), they may use another object to attempt to pull it closer (the blanket the ball is resting on). Thus, they can use means (an action) to reach an end (goal). They also begin to anticipate events and begin to show object permanence, which is a clear indication of differentiating self from objects. They are then able to look for an object that has been hidden because they can "hold it in mind."
- *Tertiary Circular Reactions (Stage 5: 12 to 18 months):* Toddlers act on objects to get a response and then continue to elaborate the action to get different responses, such as using a stick first to hit a drum, then a block, then the table, and then hitting the same objects with another toy. They have a range of actions that may be differentiated in relation to physical characteristics of the objects (e.g., shaking a rattle, hitting a drum, rubbing a soft object against their face). They use "means/ends" strategies, acting to see the effects by trial and error.
- *Invention of New Means by Mental Combinations (Stage 6: 18 to 24 months):* Toddlers can symbolize mentally, using language, pretend play, deferred imitation, and mental combinations to solve problems, such as opening a door to drive a toy car through or finding a cup to feed a doll. Their action schema are differentiated in relation to their increased social knowledge (e.g., making a doll "walk" and a car "drive" with accompanying appropriate noises). The appearance of language and pretend play are strong indicators of the ability to engage in symbolic thought. These abilities signal the end of the sensorimotor period because they demonstrate the beginnings of symbolic representation.

*Preoperational Stage (2 to 7 years):* Although children of this age can use mental representations to manipulate symbols, a number of characteristics of young children's thinking prevent it from being logical thought (mental operations).

- *Unidimensional (Centration):* In solving a problem, children will focus on one characteristic but not take into account related characteristics. For example, they will look at height and not at width, so can't compare tall and narrow with short and wide.
- *Perceptual Orientation:* They are more likely to accept what they see rather than using logical thought. For example, they do not appear surprised when they see a yellow ball being put into a tube and a green ball coming out the other end; this "magic" is accepted matter-of-factly.
- *Irreversibility:* They have difficulty mentally reversing an action. They don't mentally "undo" an action.
- *Animism:* They have difficulty distinguishing between living and nonliving things. If it moves or acts it may be judged to be alive (e.g., clouds).
- *Egocentrism:* They are not able to see objects from another's visual perspective; they think their perceptual view is the same as that of a person standing on the opposite side of an object. In language development, egocentric speech (a narrative that accompanies a child's actions rather than a true communication attempt) is a prominent part of children's early speech, and socialized speech becomes greater as children mature. They also think others have the same beliefs they have (i.e., no "theory of mind") and they may give explanations that leave out important details another person needs to know. They may be upset when they are not understood, even though they haven't stated their wishes clearly. (Note: Egocentric does not mean selfish (egotistical); it is a characteristic of thought not of social–emotional actions).

*Concrete Operations Stage (7 to 11):* Children of these ages can use logical mental operations to solve problems. Not only can they use symbols, they can also manipulate symbols logically. However, they do this only in concrete situations, not abstractly.

- *Decentration:* They can consider more than one characteristic of an object or event when making decisions. For example, they can see that quantity may be the same in two containers if one is taller but narrower than the other.
- *Conservation:* They understand that a quantity remains the same even if its appearance changes, as long as nothing has been added or taken away. There are many conservation tasks that children understand over this age period. Conservation of discontinuous quantity or number (pennies), continuous quantity (water), mass, area, and length are usually seen about ages 6 to 7, but conservation of weight and of volume are not usually observed until age 10 or 11. See Figure 6.1 for examples of conservation tasks.
- *Reversibility:* They understand that logical actions may be reversed. For example, in a conservation task, if no water is taken away but just poured

| Type of Conservation | Initial Presentation | Manipulation | Preoperational Child's Answer |
|---|---|---|---|
| Number | 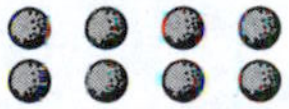 Two identical rows of objects are shown to the child, who agrees they have the same number. |  One row is lengthened and the child is asked whether one row now has more objects. | Yes, the longer row. |
| Matter |  Two identical balls of clay are shown to the child. The child agrees that they are equal. |  The experimenter changes the shape of one of the balls and asks the child whether they still contain equal amounts of clay. | No, the longer one has more. |
| Length |  Two sticks are aligned in front of the child. The child agrees that they are the same length. |  The experimenter moves one stick to the right, then asks the child if they are equal in length. | No, the one on the top is longer. |
| Volume | 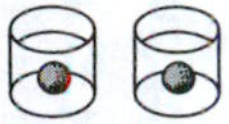 Two balls are placed in two identical glasses, with an equal amount of water. The child sees the balls displace equal amounts of water. | 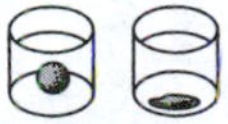 The experimenter changes the shape of one of the balls and asks the child if it still will displace the same amount of water. | No, the longer one on the right displaces more. |
| Area | 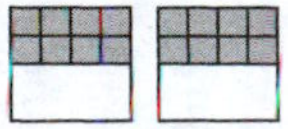 Two identical sheets of cardboard have wooden blocks placed on them in identical positions. The child agrees that the same amount of space is left on each piece of cardboard. | 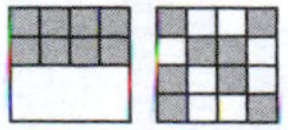 The experimenter scatters the blocks on one piece of cardboard and then asks the child if one of the cardboard pieces has more space covered. | Yes, the one on the right has more space covered up. |

**Figure 6.1**  Conservation Tasks and Sample Answers

*Source:* Reprinted from *Conservation Tasks and Sample Answers from Children*, 8th ed. (p. 309) by J. W. Santrock, 2004. New York: McGraw-Hill. Copyright © 2004 by The McGraw-Hill Companies.

into a different-size container, the action can be reversed to demonstrate it is still the same amount. Reversibility is necessary for mathematical thinking (e.g., number sets such as 2 + 1 = 3; 3 − 2 = 1).

- *Seriation:* They can order objects according to length, width, and other dimensions. This ability is also necessary for mathematical thinking, (e.g., ordering and counting ordered sets).
- *Classification:* They can categorize according to more than one dimension (e.g., color and size) and can begin to do hierarchical classification or class inclusion (e.g., category of birds includes robins, pigeons). Unidimensional and hierarchical classification is also necessary for mathematical thinking (e.g., shapes, matrices, transitivity).

*Formal Operations (12 to adult):* By this age they can apply logical mental operations to abstract problems. This is a primary mode of thinking in adolescence. Although adults have the capability of formal operational reasoning, they do not necessarily use such reasoning in all areas of life, but use it primarily in "scientific" or logical reasoning situations.

- *Hypothetical Reasoning:* They can think of many possible solutions to problems and test each of these systematically. This reasoning does not have to be related to actual facts or ideas. For example, they can explore questions such as, What if coal were black, the world were flat, or people were 10 feet tall?
- *Propositional Reasoning:* They can use properties of logical reasoning to solve abstract problems. For example, they can use proportional reasoning $(X/Y)$ and transitivity $(X<Y<Z)$ to solve abstract problems.
- *Reflective Thinking:* If they reason incorrectly, they can become aware of inconsistencies and mistakes in reasoning and use mental checks and balances to rethink problems and change their answers.
- *Complex Planning:* They can establish long-range goals and complete detailed projects, without being distracted by immediate concrete experiences.

## Piaget's Studies of Play and Language

Although the major focus of Piaget's early work was on outlining the stages of logical thought, he also studied some other aspects of child development and discussed their theoretical implications. These included the role of play and language in knowledge construction.

## Role of Play in Knowledge Construction

One of Piaget's early areas of study has been extremely influential in research and practice focused on young children—his characterization of the stages of play development, derived primarily from his observations of his own children and of older boys' marble play (1945, 1965). Piaget characterized play development as occurring in three phases and differentiated play from imitation, indicating that play is primarily an assimilation process, whereas imitation is primarily an accommodation process. He believed that children use play to construct their knowledge of the world by trying to relate their new experiences to their existing cognitive schema. By watching children's play, Piaget stated that adults could gain great insight into children's thinking.

In the period from about 6 months to age 3, the most prominent type of play is *practice* play, which involves repeating similar play actions on toys or other objects to master their use, with gradual elaboration of these actions (note the connection to stages 3 to 5 of sensorimotor development). One of the crucial aspects of practice play is that it is not a routine repetition of the same actions over and over. Rather, as actions are mastered, the player continues to change the play, making it more difficult or adding new elements. Thus, practice play differs from the ritual repetition of the same actions that one would see in an autistic child's use of play materials.

By the final sensorimotor stage, *pretense* becomes a major play mode and continues through the ages 4 to 7 period as the predominant mode that can be observed. (Pretense, however, continues through the elementary years in small-scale replica play and in private settings.) Pretense often begins with adult facilitation but it extends into very elaborate social pretense with peers (sociodramatic or fantasy play) through the preschool and early elementary years. Pretense involves many cognitive processes such as role and perspective taking, social comparison, language narration, and social script knowledge. In pretense children create worlds that make sense to them, and adults can learn much about their understandings and misunderstandings by observing their pretense. Children with developmental problems may have difficulty taking appropriate roles and understanding scripts because of the cognitive requirements of pretense.

*Games with rules,* the third type of play Piaget identified, is evident in one-rule games (e.g., social turn taking) at toddler and preschool age, but it becomes a predominant mode of play in the concrete operations period of development. In games with rules the children are in charge of rule making, and the rules change as they negotiate to make the game sensible as well as enjoyable for a range of players with varied skill levels. Much of the time is spent in discussion of the rules, changing them to be "fair," and adapting rules to make the game more fun for the players. Note that games with rules are not the same as "sports" because in sports the rules are rigid and usually adult specified. Thus, they do not provide the same cognitive problem-solving experiences that occur in games with rules, as defined by Piaget.

## Role of Language in Knowledge Construction

Piaget also theorized about the role of language in thought development and believed that language did not drive thought but rather assisted thought to be more elaborated and complex (1926). That is, language is essential for logical and abstract thought but not essential for "thought in action." He studied the language children use during play and characterized this early language as having a large "egocentric" component, focused primarily on the child's own actions and thoughts rather than being an attempt to communicate with others. His research suggested that young children are not always aware of what others are thinking (i.e., do not have a "theory of mind"), and this finding has generated extensive research that helps to explain why many of children's early attempts to communicate may be unsuccessful (e.g., Wellman, 1990). Piaget did think that language was an essential component of logical thought, however, and that its development enabled symbolic representation of ideas to occur, which of course are essential for higher-order thinking. For Piaget, language development has both a nature and a nurture component, and language development is an essential ingredient in the development of mental operations. He saw the transition from the sensorimotor stage to mental representation stages as being signaled by three events: object permanence, language, and pretend play, all of which require the ability to engage in symbolic thought.

## Moral Development as Knowledge Construction

Piaget's theory of moral development was derived after his observations of boys' marble play and from clinical studies of children's responses to moral problem situations (1965). He believed that through peer play in games with rules, children begin to move to higher stages of moral development because they must discuss rules and decide issues of justice (e.g., fair play) to have the game continue. His views on moral development are discussed further in chapter 8.

## Studies of Memory, Problem Solving, and Other Cognitive Processes

Although much of what is remembered and taught about Piagetian theory is drawn from his earlier studies of the structures of thought (i.e., stages of thinking), in his later life, he and his Geneva school colleagues studied more about the functions of thought, focusing on topics such as the development of memory, procedural knowledge, consciousness, and other cognitive processes. For example, they studied how children remembered to serrate a set of rods and found that when they attempted the task again at an older age, they remembered better than they had initially (Piaget, Inhelder, & Sinclair-De Zwart, 1973). Piaget interpreted that to mean that their greater cognitive development enabled them to access the correct form from memory better at an older age. His problem-solving studies investigated the strategies children used at various ages to solve puzzles (Piaget, 1978), and he found evidence that children use their developing thought to design better strategies to control their actions. His study of consciousness asked children to perform tasks and then explain how they did the task (Piaget, 1976). He concluded that children actively reconstruct their conceptions of their own actions as they grow older.

His later theorizing about equilibration attempted to answer the question of how the transition from disequilibrium to coherence occurs (Piaget, 1972b, 1985). He began to revise his stage theory to address some of the "decalage" concerns, rethinking the processes of assimilation and accommodation and noting that "reflective abstraction," in which children take their knowledge to higher levels and reorganize it was an important part of knowledge construction. Structure and functions are both important in his equilibration theory, and abstraction develops from early biological mechanisms, but it is at work at all levels, reorganizing coordinations of actions. Piaget suggested that the stages of thought he had identified could be understood more as short periods of equilibrium, but that the process of knowledge construction was more of a spiral rather than a steplike phenomenon. His work continued until his death at 84; at that time he was on the verge of restructuring some major parts of his theory and beginning to address the problem of the logic of meanings (Piaget & Garcia, 1991). These aspects continue to be studied by his colleagues and students in the Geneva school and by neo-Piagetian researchers.

### Theoretical Influence

There is no question that Piaget's theory has been extremely influential in both Europe and the United States. It has recently also become prominent in China and in other countries throughout the world. His influence was due partly to his emphasis on the nature of children's thinking and its qualitative difference from the thinking of adults, which challenged the ideas drawn from empiricist research and learning theories that were pervasive in the latter part of the 20th century. His methodology of clinical interviews with children has also been influential and has been followed by researchers studying many aspects of development. His discussions of the stages of play and the importance of those stages has also generated much research. Building on his views of the importance of play, a conceptualization of the stages of humor development was created by another researcher (McGhee, 1971). Because the understanding of cognitive incongruity is so important to humor development, by conceptualizing the stages of humor development, McGhee provided a basis for much consequent study of children's humor (e.g., Bergen, 1998). Because Piaget's theory has been very testable, it has stimulated a large body of neo-Piagetian and cognitive science research on theory of mind, logicomathematical development, and play development. Many contemporary theorists, such as Case and Fischer, derived their initial research agenda from his work. His theory continues to generate research, both from those who have adopted or refined many of his ideas (Geneva school colleagues and neo-Piagetians) and those who initially challenged these ideas (information processing and cognitive science researchers). The Piaget Society has continued his theoretical legacy and has promoted extensive research related to Piagetian and neo-Piagetian theory.

Another place where Piaget's theory has been influential is in educational practice, especially in the education of young children. His theory was translated into educational practice by a number of followers. For example, Bruner (1960) suggested "discovery learning" was a method that promoted children's construction of knowledge through interaction with objects and peers, which Piaget recommended. Some of the principles of education derived from Piaget's theoretical views are the following:

- Children must be active participants in their knowledge construction. For young children, concrete experiences that promote physical knowledge and logicomathematical knowledge construction should be provided. These types of knowledge should not be taught as social arbitrary knowledge, because such teaching will promote "verbalizations," not genuine understanding.

- Children's stage of thinking should be assessed, not assumed. Different levels of reasoning are evident in children's "mistakes," and thus teachers should analyze these mistakes to be sure that educational experiences are geared to the children's cognitive stage.

- Equilibration can be initiated by educators through activities that engage students in the need to assimilate and accommodate new information. Higher levels of reasoning are developed by experiences that stimulate thinking.

- The teacher's role is to provide "cognitive conflict" by selecting problems that peers can discuss, and as various children's views are heard and contrasted, this process will facilitate knowledge construction.

Piaget summed up his view of education in this statement, "Every time we teach a child something, we keep him from inventing it himself" (Piaget, 1972c, p. 17).

### Critique of Piaget's Theory

On the whole, Piaget's theory has met many of the requirements of good theory. It has certainly been testable and falsifiable. Piaget and his Geneva school colleagues generated an immense body of work, and they also prompted extensive research from others, especially from empiricists in the United States, who questioned many of the findings. This was partially because the research methods of the Geneva school were not those used by empiricists, and when they replicated Piagetian studies using empiricist methodology, not all his findings were supported. For example, other researchers found that the stages Piaget identified are not as clear cut as his theory implies, and they said there were no clear definitions of the mechanisms that affected the transition from one stage to the next. Modifications of his theory have been proposed based on others' research, and Piaget himself has made modifications; however, many of his basic concepts have shown a robust quality. Experiments replicating stage-related tasks using precise techniques have shown that the general progression he outlined exists, and there do seem to be many aspects of his theory that are still relevant (Case, 1991). The assumption that formal operational reasoning is used in adolescence (or in adulthood) has been challenged and addressed by later theorists (e.g., Labouie-Vief, (1980, 1992); however, Piaget also addressed this question by emphasizing the effects of environmental factors (Piaget, 1972a). Other criticisms of his theory include his lack of emphasis on the relationship of cognition to performance and relatively little attention to social–emotional issues. Researchers on infancy have also questioned his assertions about infants' inability to understand object permanence, and they have conducted studies showing this ability may be evident much earlier than Piaget described (e.g., Gopnik, Meltzoff, & Kuhl, 2001). Their technologically sophisticated techniques for studying infants have resulted in a revision in the age when object permanence is present; however, the idea of an object permanence capability has been accepted.

An early set of cross-cultural studies of Piaget's theory resulted in some support for the presence of generally congruent changes in construction of knowledge across cultures but indicated that the timing of these changes is greatly influenced by cultural factors, and thus decalage is very evident (Dasen, 1977). Because many of Piaget's studies were concerned with logicomathematical knowledge in cultures where other types of knowledge are of more importance, this finding is not surprising. In general, however, Piaget's theory has been judged to be a relatively accurate reflection of children's thought development, even though the rigidity of the stages has not been supported. Although some of the concepts are not simple, it has been internally consistent for the most part. It has provided a useful model on which predictions could be based, and it has resulted in suggestions for numerous educational models used in early education. As is evident from this brief summary, Piaget's theory of cognitive development is multifaceted and complex, and it was still being revised at the end of his life! To understand his entire body of work requires a lifetime of study. (That has been attempted by many of his students!)

## Vygotsky's Genetic/Sociohistorical Theory of Development

The theory of Lev Vygotsky (1934–1986) also did not reach the United States until the latter part of the 20th century, although his theoretical ideas were proposed during the early part of that century (1963, 1967, 1978). This was due both to his death from tuberculosis at an early age and to his work being completed in Russia at the time of the socialist revolution. Vygotsky was a supporter of the revolution, and he articulated a strong sociohistorical theory of human development that was congruent with the orientation of the revolution. He spent some time teaching and working with people with mental disabilities, and these experiences also influenced his theoretical interests. His background included a law degree from Moscow University, but he also studied literature and philosophy and conducted psychological research, receiving a doctorate in psychology from the Moscow Institute of Experimental Psychology based on his writing, rather than on formal course work. He then joined the Institute and taught there until his death. His coworker, Alexander Luria, who was originally oriented toward a psychodynamic view of development, became a strong supporter of Vygotsky's work, and he and other colleagues continued to carry on that work after Vygotsky's death (i.e., the Soviet school). Vygotsky tried to apply the tenets of Marxism to human development problems, and he believed that socialism could eliminate social conflict and exploitation of those with lower-class status. He thought that psychological processes were primarily social in nature and were strongly influenced by the social, historical, and cultural contexts in which children develop. That is, he believed that all human cognition takes place within a matrix of social history, and thus cognition must be considered within this context. Because Vygotsky was so strongly focused on the sociohistorical aspects of development, he was explicit about the role that formal education (the school) has on cognitive development. He was interested in how the school culture can affect children with disabilities as well as those who are developing typically, and he provided many suggestions for fostering higher mental functions in such children. He also hypothesized that because cognition is culturally influenced, if a particular culture has a simplistic language and set of concepts, the thinking processes in that culture may be different from those of a culture with varied and complex verbally defined concepts. Because people become "human" through the internalization of their culture; he saw formal education as essential as a tool of enculturation. That is, school learning was promoted by Vygotsky as an important developmental force.

## Basic Constructs of Vygotsky's Theory

Vygotsky (1978) saw psychological phenomena as being social in two ways: they embody cultural artifacts, and they depend on specific social experiences. Cultural symbols, objects, and language mediate how children organize their mental structures; that is, knowledge is socially constructed (i.e., co-constructed). Children's development is also affected by what the values of the culture communicate as the reasons for behaviors. For example, if people in a culture accept that random factors, such as fate, are what determine events rather than that personal intents and behaviors are the causes of events, their reactions to harmful events will be different. That is, if they believe events are random they might accept their "fate"; if they think events controllable, they may try to change human behaviors or influence the larger society. In regard to the social experiences children encounter from parents, peers, and other adults, Vygotsky indicated that these are major determinants of children's development. Thus, parental interpretations of events influence children's responses to those events in regard to what is worthy of attention and what emotional valence a child attaches to specific experiences.

The "genetic" aspect of his theory refers to his view that biological processes also influence development, but Vygotsky believed this influence varies over the life span. He suggested that two qualitatively different development processes occur, one that is the basic or biologically based process and one that is psychologically/socioculturally based. In infancy biological processes are strong determinants of behavior, but this influence becomes less as social experience comes to dominate. Vygotsky called this experience sociogenesis—the influence of the culture—and believed it is the source of mature thought. Thus, although he agreed with Piaget that knowledge is constructed by children, he stressed that it is constructed within a sociohistorical context; that is, it is *coconstructed.* In contrast to Piaget, who was concerned about universals of thought, Vygotsky stressed culturally mediated thought. He believed human development has been influenced at three levels: (a) phylogenetic, (b) historical, and (c) ontogenetic.

The *phylogenetic* level concerns the development of the human species through evolution. The human species differs from apes by having language, ability to use tools to change environments, and communication over time periods. The *historical* level explains the development of the human species throughout history. Because of language and cultural artifacts, there is a developmental sequence in culture over generations; that is, memory, thought, and other cognitive processes have developed over centuries so that cultures differ in their level and richness. (This seems not too different from the "social Darwinism" popular in Western thought at that time.) The third level, the *ontogenetic,* concerns the development of the individual through childhood/adulthood, and this is the one in which Vygotsky concentrated his research. Each individual's development depends on biological factors (at first) and (subsequently and primarily) on acquiring the culturally mediated signs, symbols, and thought processes of the particular culture. This explains why individual development can be so varied across different cultures. The similar phylogenetic characteristics of the human species combined with the vast differences across cultures in psychological phenomena indicate that biology alone cannot be the determiner of mature human development.

Within the ontogenetic level, Vygotsky looked at a microgenesis level, which is the development of competence at a single task or activity, for which he proposed the concept of the zone of proximal development (ZPD) (1978). He defined the ZPD as the area in which social mediation can assist children to reach new levels of competence. The ZPD is the distance between what tasks children can do independently and their potential competence at those tasks, which can be achieved with adult or peer assistance. Through microgenetic analysis of the child's present abilities to perform an activity without assistance, the "zone" in which adult or peer assistance could help the child reach a higher level of ability can be found, and that is where new knowledge is coconstructed.

Vygotsky's studies and theoretical work primarily focused on this ontogenetic development level. He saw children as actively engaged in constructing their thinking; that is, their action creates their thought. Thus, mental development is the process of internalizing the results of their (primarily social) experiences. Development consists of a progression of dialectical conflicts and resolutions (after Marxist thought), with the resolutions being internalized to form the knowledge base. To understand each child's development, his or her personal experiences within social contexts as well as information about the history of the culture must be known. Vygotsky viewed language and cognition as two complementary processes that interfaced in many ways. From his research on children's block play, he outlined basic stages of problem solving. He also noted developmental stages of language and explained how language and cognitive development are intertwined.

### Stages of Thought and Language Development

Vygotsky (1963) posited four basic stages of thought and language development.

- *Natural/primitive (birth to age 2):* During the first 2 years of life, children's behavior is biologically based, and it is regulated by preverbal thought and preintellectual speech. Thus, both thought and language are present but develop independently, and they are not in a form that has been mediated by the culture. These primitive forms of organization of behavior (subcortical) are transformed as socially mediated experiences occur. There are three functions for verbal expression at this age: emotional release (e.g., crying), social reactions (e.g., laughter at recognition of familiar appearance), and labels for objects and desires (e.g., "milk" or "mommy," paired through interaction with family members).

- *Naive Psychology (ages 2 to 7/8):* During this period children develop a "naive" psychology, and they begin to use the grammar and syntax of their culture. Words begin to have symbolic function. Children ask for labels for objects, vocabulary increases, and language and thought begin to have some basic connections. Language is considered as naive, however, because children still do not understand its function as the regulator of thought. At preschool age, children begin to use running monologues that accompany activities ("private" speech), and "spontaneous" concepts are gained in informal learning settings. Play, especially pretend play role taking, enables children to learn self-regulation and to develop a range of spontaneous concepts (1967). There is a special power in private speech during play and other activities, because, ". . . from obeying the verbal instructions of an adult he [sic] goes on to instruct himself in words, both directly and indirectly; and that for him to say what he plans to do increases his ability to persist and complete an undertaking: that language, in short, performs a regulative function" (Luria & Yudovich, 1971).

Vygotsky believed that the social level of speech was primary (intermental) and the cognitive level was secondary (intramental). He saw conceptual thinking as still at a primitive stage during the preschool–kindergarten period, unmediated by language. In his studies of problem solving using blocks and nonsense words, Vygotsky characterized young children's thinking as being in Stage 1—Unorganized Congeries; that is, objects are grouped based on no shared characteristics or logical relationships. By later preschool and early school age, concept development reaches Stage 2—Complexes: Objects are grouped and organized based on subjective properties that are concrete and factual as opposed to abstract and logical. Language development during this period supports cognitive development in a number of ways, but children are only beginning to use language as a problem-solving tool.

- *Culturally Mediated External Signs (ages 7 to 12/14):* Children begin to use culturally mediated tools (language and other symbols) to aid problem solving. Language is a mediated sign system in which conceptual thinking is transmitted through the use of words/symbols; therefore, language is a crucial tool in understanding how children learn to think. This juncture of thought and speech reflects the development of verbal thought. Once this occurs, concepts can have verbal labels. By school age, culturally mediated signs are needed to encourage children's thought processes. Thus, "reactive" concept formation, which requires the formal learning environment of the school, is needed for children to gain the academic concepts of importance to the culture (Vygotsky, 1994). The mediation of teachers and peers provide scaffolding to bring children to the essential cognitive understandings required by their culture; however, this abstract understanding is derived from the intuitive spontaneous concepts derived from early experiences. Conceptual development reaches Stage 3—Concepts, in which groupings are based on abstract reasoning and logical processing. The ability to analyze and synthesize information is evident, and at this age language becomes a true tool of thought. It is a central cultural tool, restructures the mind, and forms higher-order, self-regulated thought. Ingrowth of language occurs, in which children can manipulate language independently in the form of soundless speech (internal speech) that aids thinking. It is an aid to logical memory that uses symbols to solve problems. Table 6.1 gives examples of this transformation of private speech to inner speech.

- *Ingrowth (age 12 to adult):* By adulthood, thinking is internalized in congruence with the cultural symbols of the individual's society. Early childhood forms of thinking no longer exist in adults. Conceptual thinking is enhanced as language and thought merge. Higher mental functions continue to have social origins, however, and are affected by cultural constraints (Vygotsky, 1978).

## Theoretical Influence

Vygotsky's theory has generated a variety of useful research primarily on practical educational problems related to the role of language in furthering cognitive development, teaching practices using ZPD, and functional assessment of children with special needs. His views were of great influence in the Soviet Union and also in other Communist countries such as China during the mid 20th century. When he and his colleagues began to report differences in thinking levels among groups who had received less formal education (Luria, 1979), which supported his view regarding the importance of formal education for cognitive development, his ideas lost favor in the Soviet Union because this view was seen as a denigration of the proletariat. His colleagues of the Soviet school continued his lines of research after his death, looking at many aspects of socially mediated learning, especially in relation to language (Luria & Yudovich, 1971). Other members of the Soviet school have studied sensation, perception, attention, memory, speech, imagination, and even motor development in preschool children (Zaporozhets & Elkonin, 1971). His work began to be popular in Western countries after World War II when it was translated, and it is presently fostering research on "situated learning" and other aspects of development influenced by sociohistoric factors. Cross-cultural research has been extensive in recent years, and many of these researchers, such as Rogoff (2003), have based their theoretical perspective on Vygotsky's work.

Vygotsky's theory has been influential in education because he stressed the importance of the school in furthering children's cognitive development and pointed out the importance of language for thinking. Other concepts that have been embraced by some educators include his valuing of pretend play as a means of furthering children's ability to self-regulate, emphasis on children's active co-construction of knowledge with peer and adult scaffolding, use of individualized assessments for determining the appropriate "zone" for teaching, and encouragement of "private" speech to aid young children's problem solving. His suggestions for improving assessment and teaching practices for children with disabilities have been especially valued. Because of Vygotsky's emphasis on the role of formal education, his ideas on ways to scaffold learning using the concept of the zone of proximal development and his attention to the education of children with disabilities, Vygotsky's influence has been growing, especially in early education (e.g., Berk & Winsler, 1995). Some of the principles of education derived from his theoretical views are the following:

**Table 6.1**  *Development of Private Speech*

| Category | Description | Examples |
|---|---|---|
| Egocentric communication | remarks directed to another that result in communication failure because they are not adapted to the perspective of the listener | David and Mark are seated next to each other on the rug. David says, "It broke," without explaining what or when. |
| Fantasy play and comments addressed to nonhuman objects | remarks involving role play, talking to objects, and sound effects for objects | Nancy says in a high-pitched voice to no one in particular, "I'll feel better after the doctor gives me a shot." "Ow!" she remarks as she pokes herself with her finger (a pretend needle). |
| | | Jay snaps, "Out of my way" to a chair after he bumps into it. |
| Emotional release and expression | remarks expressing feelings not directed to any particular listener, or remarks having no external stimulus that seem to be attempts to emotionally integrate a past event or thought | Paula looks at the colorful picture on the cover of her new reading book and exclaims to no one in particular. "Wow! Neat!" |
| | | Rachel is sitting at her desk with an anxious look on her face, repeating to herself, "My mom's sick, my mom's sick." |
| Describing one's own activity and self-guidance | remarks about the child's own activity, including descriptions of what the child is doing at the moment and "thinking out loud," or goal-directed plans for action | Carla, while doing a page in her math book, says out loud. "Six." Then, counting on her fingers, she continues, "Seven, eight, nine, ten. It's ten, it's ten. The answer's ten." |
| | | Michael, looking through the dictionary, says to himself, "Now where do I find this?" referring to a word. As he begins to turn the pages, he responds to his own query, "I know, I know, under 'C'." |
| Reading aloud | remarks involving reading written material aloud or sounding out words | Tommy is reading a book, when he begins to sound out a difficult name. "Sher-lock Holm-lock, Sherlock Holme," he repeats, leaving off the initial "s" in his second, more successful attempt. |
| Inaudible muttering | remarks uttered so quietly that they cannot be understood by an observer | Angela mumbles inaudibly to herself as she works on a math problem. |

*Source:* Reprinted from *Development of Private Speech* from L. E. Berk & A. Winsler, *Scaffolding Children's Learning* (Washington, DC: NAEYC, 1995), p. 31. Reprinted with permission from the National Association for the Education of Young Children.

- Formal education is essential for children to develop complex concepts. However, these are gained by children as they interact actively with peers and teachers and co-construct their knowledge through these interactions.

- In early childhood, pretend play is an important activity that helps children learn self-regulation, which is essential for later school success.

- The role of private speech is important to assist in internalizing thought; thus, during the elementary years, children should be allowed to use such private or semiprivate speech as an accompaniment during difficult problem-solving activities.

- Children learn best in their zone of proximal development, which is the distance between their actual developmental level for independent problem solving and their level of potential development possible with adult guidance or with the collaboration of more capable peers.

- Therefore, instead of static testing of children's independent levels of performance, functional microgenetic assessment should be used to determine the ZPD, which can then guide the teacher in scaffolding information to enable children to reach a higher independent level of thought.

- Children with disabilities can be helped to gain higher cognitive levels if teachers use the processes of assessment and scaffolding appropriately. This requires functional assessment and determination of adaptations that will scaffold learning for these children.

### Critique of Vygotsky's Theory

Vygotsky has also provided a testable theory, which has generated both research and practical application. The concepts of the theory are clear, and he has provided a model (ZPD) that has been useful for taking action and making predictions. Although the "germs" of Vygotsky's ideas have been intriguing to many researchers and educators, there are gaps in his theory and unclear concepts, which might have been made more explicit if he had continued his theorizing over many years. For example, although the idea of the ZPD appears to be useful, there is much ambiguity in this concept. It is difficult, even with functional analysis procedures, to predict how developmental difficulties can be ameliorated using his theoretical constructs. His stages of thought and language are outlined very broadly and need further explication, especially in regard to the interface of these developmental strands with various cultural experiences. It is not clear how specific cultural and language-mediated experiences really change the structures and functions of cognition, possibly because of the difficulty of conducting such research. However, within cultural contexts, predictions can be made, and the theory provides a relatively accurate general picture, especially of the role of language in thought development.

Interestingly, although Vygotsky's theory grew directly out of the culture of the socialist state in which he lived, these socialist underpinnings of his approach, such as the use of science to reduce social conflict and exploitation of some societal groups, have received little promotion or understanding by Western psychologists or educators. Perhaps their embrace of his ideas would seem strange to

Vygotsky, and it is at least possible that he would have seen its present use as being "out of context," that is, without sufficient evaluation of the sociohistorical and cultural contexts in which such practices are embedded. Because his theory was "situated" in his own culture, its use without adaptation might be especially problematic. His views may be presently more in line with postmodern theorists who discuss socially constructed cognition in varied cultural contexts. Although Vygotsky's theory became out of favor in the Soviet Union because he and his colleague Luria had pointed out cultural and socioeconomic variations in the society in some of their research, at the present time a number of Russian theorists and researchers are following agendas related to Vygotsky's work. Whether research now being done in other cultural contexts using his theoretical constructs (e.g., Rogoff, 1993, 2003) will find his theory enhanced is a present question of interest.

## Comparing the Theories of Piaget and Vygotsky

Both of these theorists stressed the importance of children's active construction of knowledge and saw their play and language development as being essential in furthering cognitive growth. However, their theoretical explanations differed in a number of ways:

- Piaget focused on cognitive development through knowledge construction as a universal characteristic of humans; Vygotsky stressed the role of the cultural context that makes cognition socially mediated by culturally defined knowledge.

- Piaget saw language as initially egocentric and a separate strand of development from cognition, although essential for representational and logical thought; Vygotsky saw language as initially social and intertwined early not only as an aid to cognitive development but also as a determinant of culturally defined thought.

- Piaget saw play as assimilative and valuable for understanding and expressing children's personal meanings; Vygotsky saw play as a means of organizing thought through verbal mediation, enabling self-regulation to develop.

- Piaget believed that much knowledge can be constructed by the child's direct action on the environment, and adults should not intervene unnecessarily with "arbitrary social knowledge." Vygotsky believed that only early concepts can be gained by direct child action, and thus socially mediated knowledge (through adult/peer scaffolding) is needed for children's knowledge construction.

Many of these distinctions may seem esoteric to the typical student of theory, and in fact, the practices that might arise from the two positions may not appear very different. However, they illustrate underlying differences in theoretical worldviews. For example, the purpose of play in the curriculum would be different, with Piaget advocating its role in physical and logicomathematical knowledge construction and Vygotsky emphasizing its role in self-regulation and "self-talk" to gain higher levels of performance. Similarly, the role of the adult would be slightly different. Piaget's adult would probably be careful not to impose language that would result in "verbalizations" of physical and logicalmathematical knowledge, whereas Vygotsky's teacher would probably assess and scaffold through language to mediate children's construction of knowledge appropriate to the culture. Both of these theories provide many testable hypotheses for further research and practice, which is one of the reasons they have remained prominent, generated research, and been advocated by many educators.

## Other Theories of Language Development

Both Piaget and Vygotsky focused on language as a symbolic function that was integral to higher levels of cognitive development. However, language development itself has been a subject of interest to other theorists. Instead of focusing on language as a facilitator of cognition, these theorists were more interested in the sources from which language developed (biological or environmental) and on investigation of its universal characteristics. They have amassed a large body of research that serves to define the universal characteristics of language. Although their descriptions make clear that there is a close cognitive/language interface, they have focused on describing language characteristics and speculating about biological and environmental influences on its development. During the latter half of the 20th century, linguists and psycholinguists such as Brown and Bellugi (1964), Cazden (1972), Lenneberg (1964), Menyuk (1969), Slobin, (1971), and others have explored the universal characteristics of language and the process of language acquisition.

### Universal Characteristics of Language

Language is a symbolic system that is rule governed and has both a performance (surface structure) and a competence (deep structure) element. The performance element involves both the ability to understand and to produce language, whereas the competence element is the underlying knowledge of language rules. There are rules for sounds (phonological), grammar (syntax and morphology), meaning (semantics), and proper usage (pragmatics) that children must learn to be competent speakers. Each of these systems has rules. Phonological rules govern what sounds can be put together for intelligible speech. These rules differ in different languages. For example, in English, the nonsense word *bluck* can be pronounced easily, whereas the nonsense word *blcku* cannot because it does not follow accepted rules regarding how English sounds can be combined. Syntax and morphology rules define word order in sentences and how plurals, possessives, prefixes, and other aspects of language are arranged. Semantics involves the combinations of these rules into meaningful units of words and sentences. Pragmatics are social rules governing how language can be expressed at various times and places within particular cultures. Although all these rule sets are present in every language, the actual rules vary across languages. Numerous researchers have studied the language acquisition process, and there appears to be a similar sequence of language acquisition common to children in all cultures (Slobin, 1971). There is much controversy, however, over the sources of language development and the processes involved in this development.

### Sources of Language Development

One view of how language develops was provided by B. F. Skinner. In the mid 20th century, Skinner offered a theory of "verbal behavior," which considered language development as just one of many abilities learned through conditioning and imitation. (This was one of the few developmental issues that Skinner attempted to address.) He saw language as governed by reinforcement schedules and other aspects of behaviorist principles. In line with his behaviorist theoretical orientation, Skinner (1945b) posited that verbal behavior was really just a manifestation of classical conditioning (making associations between verbal stimuli, contexts, and responses) and of operant conditioning (reinforcements of verbal attempts). He stated that even the development of language metaphors, abstractions, and concepts could be explained as children's responses to contingent reinforcement. Although this view is relevant for explaining the different languages learned by children in various cultures, it could not account for the many examples of child language that are creations of children, such as saying "foots" to signify two feet, because the child would never have heard this plural style or have been reinforced for saying it. The behaviorists' view of language acquisition as derived from reinforcement of verbal behavior attempts is still of use in helping children with special needs such as autism learn basic language responses (e.g., Lovaas, 2002).

During this same time period, the study of linguistics was prominent, and many linguists were hypothesizing about the sources of language. Lenneberg (1964) hypothesized "that language is a species-specific trait, based on a variety of biologically given mechanisms" (p. 69) and questioned whether it is "possible that language ability—instead of being the consequence of intelligence—is its cause?" (p. 78). A major proponent of a nativist view rather than a behaviorist view was Noam Chomsky, who reacted strongly against the behaviorist explanation and provided a counterargument based on linguistic research. He attacked Skinner's theoretical perspective (1959), arguing that the behaviorist approach could not explain language development because children are not directly reinforced for much of their language expression; they universally generate rules and use structures that are never reinforced or even modeled, and young children in every culture have a similar set of language rules with which they operate. He stated that the unique "generative" aspects of language can only be explained by the presence of an internal mediating force, a language acquisition device (LAD) (1965, 1968). That is, according to Chomsky, the brain is uniquely "wired" in humans for producing language. Chomsky went on to write extensively about linguistic processes from this "nativist" perspective, and he was influential in generating great interest in children's language development. Although his view prevailed at that time, more sophisticated study relating brain activity to language acquisition is presenting a more complex view. However, the nativist view is still supported by some theorists (e.g., Pinker, 1997). Piaget disagreed with Chomsky's view that language was "wired in" because he saw it as developing through both sensorimotor actions and social transmission during the earliest ages. Sinclair (1992) explained that Piaget agreed with Chomsky that underlying principles are important for understanding relationships between language and thought, and that these principles guide thought and language while remaining unconscious. Piaget disagreed with Chomsky's method of studying language acquisition because Piaget's studies were "always grounded in experimental studies or observations of young children" (Sinclair, 1992, p. 221), whereas Chomsky worked backward from adult language samples. Another difference is that Piaget always sought to understand the functional continuity of growth of knowledge, not just the structures. The field of linguistic study has expanded in many directions, and a number of present-day theorists have investigated these issues further. They are discussed in chapter 7.

### Influences of Language Theories

Language theories have lent themselves to a great amount of research, although the research methodology has ranged widely, including intense analysis of individual cases (e.g., Brown & Bellugi, 1964), intervention studies (Luria & Yudovich, 1971), clinical experiments (Sinclair, 1992), and controlled research experiments (Nelson, 1973, 1981). The initial debates over the processes of language development have been informed in recent years by the increasing body of knowledge about brain development. However, many controversies remain on how language and cognition are related and on the most appropriate methods for assisting children with language or learning problems. As language and brain research evidence has increased, it suggests that nature and nurture perspectives may speak to different aspects of language development. For example, the brain does have certain areas (Broca, Wernicke) that seem to be sites where language production and comprehension development are concentrated. Children also generate many sentences that have never been heard or reinforced, and there seems to be a sensitive period for language development. There appears to be a "child syntax" that is common across language environments, with all children going through holophrastic and telegraphic syntax periods. On the other hand, children who live in different language communities do learn the language of that particular community, so there is also an important role for environmental factors in determining the specifics of language acquisition in various cultures. Studies of infant language development, for example, show that infants recognize the phonemes of all languages but gradually learn to recognize only those of the language they hear regularly (Jusczyk, 1995). By 9 to 12 months, their intonation in babbling approximates the language of their language environment. Bates and colleagues (2005; Bates & Elman, 2000) argue that brain plasticity and localization both play a role in language development.

## Summary

A rich body of theory on cognitive and language development was gained during the 20th century. Piaget's views of cognitive development have been especially influential in two ways. First, his theory served to call attention to the fact that cognitive development is occurring from birth and that children's thinking differs from adults and develops throughout the early years of life. Second, because his views were based on observational and clinical studies, he generated a reaction within the empiricist scientific community that resulted in much research to determine which of his views could be empirically validated. Vygotsky's influence has been less extensive but has particularly affected educational practices, especially in early childhood and in special education. Thus, although these theories continue to have controversial aspects, they have been very influential in directing the focus of cognitive and language developmental research and practice. Similarly the controversy over the varied views of language development provided by behaviorist and nativist theories have resulted in intensive and extensive study of language development as a separate area of study. The following case asks for analysis of an educational problem using the lenses of the Piagetian and Vygotskian theoretical views. It also suggests how varied views of language development might influence educational practice.

## Case 6. Teacher Bright and the Math Lessons

Teacher Bright has reviewed the math standards for second grade and wants to be sure that the children in the class have the competencies they need to do well on later proficiency tests. The teacher is focusing on two math tasks for second graders: knowing all the addition and subtraction facts and knowing how to measure with nonstandard units. The teacher has been presenting the math facts in four-set units because he believes they can be learned more efficiently that way. For example, these facts: $4 + 3 = 7$; $3 + 4 = 7$; $7 - 4 = 3$; and $7 - 3 = 4$ can be learned as one set. Teacher Bright has found that most of the children in the class seem to learn them as a set but that Will, Marty, and Suzanne really don't "get" the idea when he shows how they are all part of the same set. They have been trying to memorize each fact separately, which is very inefficient.

Teacher Bright's attempts to have the children learn to measure with standard and nonstandard units are also confusing to about half of the class members. When he gives the students some string and asks them to measure the circumference of pumpkins and then compare that to the ruler and tell how much it is in standard measures, many children give him a blank look, as though they have no idea what he means. When they try to measure a tower using a ruler that is too short for the tower, they don't know how to get the answer. When they use paper clips to measure their desk, most don't understand why that can compare with a ruler measure. Teacher Bright has explained the meaning of "circumference" and "linear measurement" many times. Barbara, one of Teacher Bright's "best" students is especially upset that she is not understanding the measurement problems, even though she can state all the rules for doing the problems.

In an effort to solve the teaching problems, Teacher Bright has gone back and reviewed what he learned about Piaget's studies of preoperational and concrete operational children, and what he knows about Vygotsky's zone of proximal development and his views on the role of language in formal education. The teacher now thinks he may know the reason why some of the children are having difficulty thinking through these tasks. He is also questioning whether the children's language development might be influencing their ability to apply concepts.

What can Teacher Bright learn from Piaget's theory about the cognitive operational abilities that are needed to solve the fact set problem? What might be the cognitive stage of the children who do and don't get the point of the sets?

What would Piaget say about children's conservation of length and ability to coordinate spatial systems that would help Teacher Bright understand why the measurement problems are so hard for many of them?

Would Vygotsky agree that this is an overall developmental stage problem or a "scientific" concept problem? How would he analyze this problem, and what would he suggest as first and later steps in solving it in this formal educational setting?

What insights might be provided by Skinner's, Chomsky's, or other linguistic and psycholinguistic views of language acquisition that might affect the learning of these mathematical concepts?

## Readings

Jean Piaget, *Some Aspects of Operations*, pp. 326–330.

L. S. Vygotsky, *Interaction between Learning and Development*, pp. 331–338.

## Suggested Readings

Chomsky, N. (1968). Future. In N. Chomsky, *Language and mind* (pp. 61–64). New York: Harcourt, Brace, & World.

Luria, A. R., & Yudovich, F. Ia. (1971). The role of speech in the formation of mental processes: An outline of the problem. In A. R. Luria & F. Ia. Yudovich, *Speech and the development of mental processes in the child* (pp. 19–26). Middlesex, England: Penguin. (Original Work Published 1956)

Piaget, J. (1972b). Some aspects of operations. In M. W. Piers (Ed.), *Play and development* (pp. 15–27). New York: Norton.

Piaget, J., & Inhelder, B. (1969). Factors in mental development. In J. Piaget & B. Inhelder, *The psychology of the child* (pp. 152–159). New York: Basic Books.

Vygotsky, L. S. (1978). Interaction between learning and development. In L. S. Vygotsky, *Mind in society: The development of higher psychological processes* (pp. 79–91). Cambridge, MA: Harvard University Press.

"One plus one equals two. Two plus two equals four. Three plus three equals six, and so on and so forth. Well, that's life."

*Source:* © The New Yorker Collection 1987 Al Ross from cartoonbank.com. All rights reserved.

# Further Theoretical Perspectives on Cognitive and Language Development

A s is the case in contemporary personality and social–emotional theorizing, the roots of many present-day cognitive and language theories can be found in the ideas of earlier theorists. Piaget has provided the springboard for a host of neo-Piagetians, some of whom have revised his stages of cognitive development, others who have focused on specific aspects of his theory (e.g., egocentrism), and some who have refuted his theoretical ideas. Vygotsky's ideas have been especially influential in fostering sociohistorical and cross-cultural explanations, and some theorists have incorporated his ideas into other perspectives. Information processing theory is an empiricist approach to studying cognition and language, and aspects of its methodology have been incorporated into the study of many present-day theorists and researchers. According to Robert Kail, the information processing theoretical approach "is now one of the principal approaches to cognitive development" (Kail, 1998, p. 168). He stated that two factors promoted its growth, one of which was the evidence that the research on "verbal behavior," as advocated by behaviorists, although useful in explaining some types of adult cognition, was not a very useful approach for studying children's development. The second influence was the rise of computer technology, which provided a new metaphor for the mind. Kail described the approach as being one that sees the mind as having "mental hardware" that is built in and is similar in concept to the hardware of computers.

Recent advances in brain research and cognitive science have provided elaborations of this perspective.

This chapter discusses the ideas of theorists who have built on Piagetian, Vygotskian, and information processing views of cognition, gives brief overviews of a number of other cognitive science approaches, and discusses recent theoretical perspectives on language development. Although much cognitive study is presently focused on infants and young children, cognitive theorists are also studying these processes in later life. Chapter 10 discusses life span theories of cognition.

## Information Processing Theory and Cognitive Science

In information processing theory, the brain's "mental hardware" is conceptualized as having three components: (a) sensory memory, which holds immediate sensations briefly; (b) working memory, which serves as the mental processing unit; and (c) long-term memory, which is the limitless, permanent storehouse of knowledge. Theorists from this perspective view the process of thinking as using these components to run mental "software." This is what actually allows thought processes to complete tasks. Four steps are hypothesized to occur in thinking: (a) understanding a question/problem, (b) searching memory, (c) comparing memory lists with problem requirements, and (d) responding. Cognitive development in this view consists of becoming able to use more efficient strategies and to gain more working memory capacity, automatic processing ability, and increased speed of processing. Information processing theory is more of a general approach to the study of cognition rather than a comprehensive theory, such as those already discussed. It also differs from rationalist theoretical perspectives because it accepts the basic tenet of behaviorist theory that change is more of a cumulative or additive process rather than resulting in qualitative change, which would be the view of most of the cognitive theorists already discussed. For information processing theorists, change is seen as constant and gradual rather than being abrupt or qualitatively different at new stages. These theorists have typically focused on a few cognitive processes, such as memory, problem solving, and learning of academic information, rather than designing a "grand" theory that attempts to explain many aspects of development.

More recently, brain research is influencing the field of cognitive science because this research indicates that brain development involves the process of synaptogenesis (i.e., making connections among the neurons to form neuronal networks) and pruning (i.e., speeding thinking processes by eliminating unneeded connections). Brain researchers often report evidence of modular activity within the brain; that is, certain brain areas appear to be activated by particular types of experiences (e.g., hearing music or speech, looking at visual schemes). These theorists are beginning to explain cognitive development through the use of computer models that design simulations of neural network formations (i.e., nets). This "connectionist" model is challenging the traditional information processing view that the mind is similar to a digital computer using a symbolic language. Instead, this perspective employs a different theoretical model—a dynamic system of connections (Fodor, 1988; Macdonald, 1995). The connectionist model is particularly of interest to some linguistic theorists (neonativists) and to theorists who focus on infant cognition (Pinker & Prince, 1988).

### Contemporary Knowledge-Seeking Approaches

Due to the overlapping of various theoretical perspectives, contemporary theorists are less easily labeled as using only one of Case's categories of knowledge seeking (as outlined in chapter 1). Case himself has drawn from Piaget's rationalist stance, from information processing empiricism, and from sociohistorical theory in developing his neo-Piagetian theory. Fischer has included perspectives from Piaget and Vygotsky, as well as nonlinear dynamical systems and neuroscience concepts, in his theory of skill growth cycles. Other cognitive science theorists such as Flavell and Wellman have combined methods of empirical science and Piagetian thought to study various aspects of cognitive development such as metacogniton and theory of mind. Rogoff and colleagues have investigated "situated" social and communication development combining Vygotsky's theoretical perspective and empiricism research methods. Information processing theorists such as Kail and Siegler have examined development in specific cognitive areas such as memory and problem solving and have maintained the associationist perspective of cumulative development rather than abrupt stage changes. Cognitive science theorists such as Gopnik have been influenced by ideas of Piaget, Chomsky, and the newer connectionist ideas. Linguistic and psycholinguistic theorists have drawn on empiricist views of information processing theory (e.g., Nelson), sociohistorical perspectives (e.g., Tomasello), and neuropsychological research (e.g., Bates), as well as on traditional linguistic theory. In the past 25 years, there has been an explosion of research and theory related to cognition, language, and their relationship, but none of these theorists is as prominent as some of the theorists already discussed. Only time will tell which of them will carry the most influence in the future; at this time most could be characterized as having proto-theories rather than fully formed theories.

## Case's Neo-Piagetian Theory

Robbie Case (1945–2000) was a professor at Stanford University and later at the University of Toronto, whose untimely death resulted in a loss of a psychologist with great theory-building potential. He has been characterized as "an eager explorer of big questions," and his major interest was in how children's minds develop. He was an avid and precise researcher in testing aspects of Piaget's theory. Although he accepted the central themes of the theory, he had questions about the stages outlined by Piaget and speculated on whether changes in stage were teachable. He did extensive research related to Piagetian stages, particularly in the area of logicomathematical thought, and from these results, he derived a theory that integrated some aspects of information processing theory with Piaget's framework (Case, 1991). Through his analysis of the information processing skills children required to perform a range of cognitive tasks, he found that cognitive development increased the representation of information in domains such as number, space, and social interactions. That is, he stated that children's stage of thinking depends on how much information processing capacity they have. He concluded that humans have "central conceptual structures" and identified the developmental trajectory of these structures. Some of his research was done in collaboration with experienced teachers, and thus, certain of his studies focused on how curriculum innovations designed to improve mathematical learning could affect cognitive development. For example, he led a research team involving teachers and colleagues, who created playful logiomathematical activities to help children at risk for school failure to gain "central conceptual structures" (Griffin, Case, & Siegler, 1994).

### Basic Constructs of Case's Theory

Based on his research findings (1991, 1992), Case revised some of the terminology of Piaget's stage theory and probed the thinking processes that went on within each stage. Although he kept the terminology for the sensorimotor stage, he termed the preoperational stage the *interrelational* (or rational) stage in which children learn to relate phenomena; the concrete operational stage as the *dimensional* stage, in which children learn to categorize with varied dimensions; and the formal operational stage the *vectorial* stage, in which children can predict results of interactions among dimensions. From his extensive research he found that, within each of these stages, there were four similar substages, as follows:

1. Consolidation—This might be considered the "equilibrium" stage, although Case did not use this term. It is represented only with dotted lines on his chart.

2. Unifocal—A new type of structure is assembled but it can only be applied in isolation

3. Bifocal—Two units of the structure can be applied in succession.

4. Elaborated coordination—More structures can be applied simultaneously and integrated into a coherent system (Note: these are the central conceptual structures).

These stages are recursive; that is, the same four substages occur in each major stage. Case stated that the abrupt change of stage that Piaget reported really occurs at the upper bound of each set of substages. This upper bound is determined by the size of working memory and speed of basic operations. Also, individual differences influence what way and how fast structures are built. Therefore, instruction will have different results depending on which processing substage a child is in at the time of instruction and on the child's existing information processing structures. Figure 7.1 shows his conceptual model, which outlines the four stages and the substages within each stage.

### A Multilevel View of Cognitive Development

Case also looked at a wide range of theoretical perspectives on cognitive development and evaluated their relevance in relation to his research findings (1999). He attempted to find a middle ground between the "holistic" theoretical views of rationalist theorists and the "reductionist" views of empiricist theorists, and he also considered individual variation related to sociohistorical views. He described

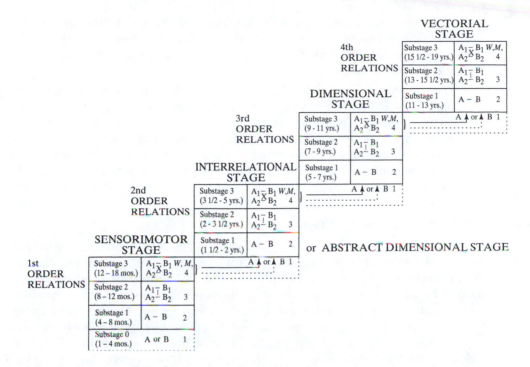

**Figure 7.1**   Model of Cognitive Stage Development

*Source:* Reprinted from *Model of Cognitive Stage Development* from *The Mind and Its Modules: Toward A Multi-Level view of the Development of Human Intelligence* (p. 346), by R. Case, 1992, in R. Case (ed.), *The Mind's Staircase: Exploring the Conceptual Underpinnings of Intellectual Development.* Mahwah, NJ: Lawrence Erlbaum Associates, Inc.

how each theoretical perspective informed understanding of cognitive development, thus giving a multilevel view of the human mind. His view of cognitive development included the following components:

- *Modularity (from neonativist theory):*  There are basic categories of functioning based on the modular structure of the human nervous system. The conceptual theories that children construct reflect this modular structure. Although they are reworked over development, they form the central conceptual structures.

- *Knowledge networks (from neoassociationist/information processing theory):* Central conceptual structures may be represented as semantic networks, which require domain-specific experiences, and the strength of the networks are related to how strongly they are associated. Cognitive strategies are influenced by these networks.

- *Interpretive frames (from sociohistorical theory):* Cultural experiences play a role, which increases with age, in shaping the central conceptual structures. Schooling plays a role by familiarizing children with cultural symbol systems, concepts, and thought conventions. Conceptual structures develop as the culture develops.

- *Executive control structures (from neo-Piagetian theory):* Common developmental constraints are related to executive/working memory systems (partially biologically based). The pattern of cognitive development is hierarchical and recursive.

- *Operational structures (from Piagetian theory):* Construction, differentiation, and coordination of knowledge are essential processes. A generalized intellectual competence involves basic cognitive operations that evolve into systems that can be represented by logical operators (e.g., conservation, reversibility). These are universal in nature and invariant across logicomathematical content. Stage transitions depend on active reflection and resolution of conflicts of thought, and the universal sequence goes from concrete to abstract.

### Theoretical Influence and Critique

Case's theoretical work, because of its basis in rigorous research, is definitely testable and falsifiable. It provides a useful integrative perspective on cognitive development and ties together both empiricist and rationalist perspectives. Although he explained his concepts well, they do not really present a simplified model, although it is an internally consistent and generally economical model that allows clear predictions to be made. At the present time it has not been incorporated into much educational practice, except in the settings in which Case worked with teacher colleagues. However, it provides a strong basis on which other researchers can continue to investigate cognitive development and a useful basis on which educational strategies can build. Its strength is in providing the potential for looking "inside" each stage to determine where the best place for active experiences and instruction might be situated and for using the most important insights from a variety of theoretical perspectives to inform educational practice. His research team studies related to improving mathematics instruction in early grades are especially useful to educators (e.g., Griffin, Case, & Siegler, 1994). His untimely death unfortunately did not allow his own theoretical ideas to be fully developed.

## Fischer's Dynamic Skills Theory

Kurt Fischer (1943–) is a professor at Harvard University and is Director of the Mind, Brain, and Education program at the Harvard Graduate School of Education. He is thus also committed to providing research and theory that will inform education practice. He leads a Dynamic Development Research Group particularly interested in sharing ideas about new cognitive and neuroscientific paradigms that are changing thinking about human development. He has been active in revising Piagetian theory, but he has also drawn from nonlinear dynamical systems (e.g., chaos and complexity theory), neuroscience, and ecological theory to reconceptualize neo-Piagetian cognitive development stages (Fischer, 1980; Fischer & Rose, 1998). He stresses that cognitive development results from an interactive balance between nature and nurture forces (neuroscience/environment) and he discusses how changes in thinking and learning are related to physical changes in the brain.

### Basic Constructs of Fischer's Theory

The cognitive developmental sequence Fischer outlined is expressed in a dynamical systems model of growth cycles with four tiers and 10 levels, each containing four types of mental operations. The system is dominated by growth spurts, reorganizations, and nested, recurring cycles. The recursive aspect is seen in the fourth level in each tier, which is the foundation for the next tier. The four tiers roughly parallel Piagetian stages. However, in relation to ages within the sensorimotor stage Fischer identified two tiers—reflexes and actions; his next tier, called representations, covers the age period from 2 years to midchildhood (both the preoperational and the concrete operational periods), and his final tier, abstractions, roughly parallels formal operations but is developed over a longer age period (throughout adolescence). As Case did, Fischer found that there were three levels of characteristic recursive thinking patterns within each tier, which emerged into the fourth level, with that level being the foundation for the next tier, as follows:

1. **Single set:** Child acts on one set of thinking patterns but not in relation to others (i.e., single reflexes, single actions, single representations, single abstractions).
2. **Mapping:** Child connects one set to another (i.e., connecting each of these to others in the same tier).
3. **Systems:** Child relates sets of actions to form systems of actions (i.e., relating sets that have been mapped to form complex systems).
4. **Systems of systems:** Child connects systems to each other (i.e., this would be the time when a "stage" shift would be seen).

Figure 7.2 shows Fischer's model of growth cycles, with his tiers and recursive levels outlined.

### Constructive Epigenesis as the Means of Development

Fischer called the process of knowledge construction "constructive epigenesis," which stresses the interactions and mutual influence of biological, cognitive, and environmental systems. He related his research to brain research, pointing especially to nested cycles of cortical development that are similar to the nested cycles of cognitive development. His theoretical views, especially in relation to the practice of teaching, give support to the Vygotskian ideas of scaffolding and zones of proximal development because he stressed that most children do not perform at their highest levels of thinking independently but that they can do so with help (Fischer & Rose, 1998). He encouraged teaching to children's lower as well as optimal levels and emphasized the importance of contextual support. His research often involves microgenetic analysis, which was also used by Vygotsky and is being used by researchers from nonlinear dynamical systems perspectives. Fischer indicated that this approach promotes understanding of developmental change at a precise level, which can also be characterized as the learning of specific skills. Microgenetic analysis involves examination of each small step in the

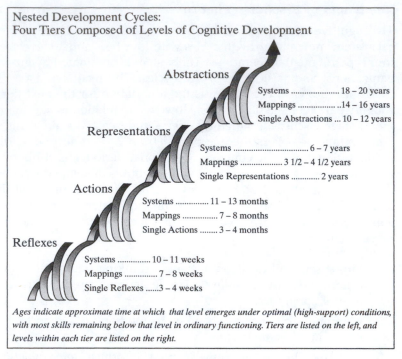

**Figure 7.2**  Model of Growth Cycles
*Source:* Reprinted from *Model of Growth Cycles from Educational Leadership.*
Copyright by K.W. Fischer.

learning process for a particular skill. This type of analysis can inform educational interventions by identifying the steps in the process that particular children have not achieved (Fischer, Bullock, Rotenberg, & Raya, 1993; Fischer & Pipp, 1984; Fischer & Rose, 1999). His approach is often called a "dynamical skills based" model.

### Theoretical Influence and Critique

Fischer has added some ideas to Piagetian theory that are providing a strong impetus for research that focuses on precise levels of developmental analysis. A group of his colleagues are investigating precisely how specific skills may be acquired and what levels within these tiers are involved. This research is extending into areas such as the development of children's reading skill, planning, and emotional–cognitive interfaces. Thus, the theory is very testable and falsifiable, as well as providing a model on which predictions can be based. Fischer's stress on the relation of cognitive development to brain development and his interest in exploring nonlinear dynamical processes to explain his findings are also of potential value, but they do make his model more complex, although it appears to be internally consistent. His theory appears accurate in helping to explain the variability of performance among individuals at relatively similar tiers of development. He also extends precise analysis of cognitive development into the adolescent years. The theory has the potential to be helpful to teachers in similar ways to Vygotsky's theory, but it may go further in identifying the precise changes as development and learning occur. Because Fischer is especially interested in determining the precise tasks that form the development of a skill, as more information is accumulated from microgenetic research, the theory may have practical usefulness in education. Long-term power of the theory, of course, is not known at this time.

## Other Contemporary Perspectives

The list of contemporary theorists and researchers who are investigating aspects of cognitive and language development is extensive. This discussion will draw on some of them who are representative of various theoretical perspectives.

## Theoretical Perspectives Influenced Primarily by Piaget and Vygotsky

In addition to Case and Fischer, Piaget's theoretical concepts have been examined and reexamined by numerous researchers, who have derived revisions or extensions of aspects of the theory. A theorist who was particularly interested in demonstrating mathematically the constructs of Piaget's theory is Juan Pascal-Leone. Two theorists who studied aspects of Piaget's theory and extended them to educational issues are Jerome Bruner and David Elkind. A number of other researchers and theorists studied aspects of Piaget's theory related to young children's theory of mind and infants' development of object permanence. These include John Flavell, Henry Wellman, Alison Gopnik Andrew Meltzoff, and others. Vygotsky's sociohistorical perspective has also influenced present-day theorists such as Barbara Rogoff and others who explore "situated" development.

### Pascal-Leone's Extensions of Piagetian Constructs

Juan Pascal-Leone (1970, 1980) was a student of Piaget and one of the first neo-Piagetians. He attempted to take the stages outlined by Piaget and use mathematical modeling to explain the stage transitions (Pascal-Leone 1970). Thus, he was an influence on Case's method of studying Piagetian stages. He also designed a test to measure these stages and studied the processes of memory development, in particular that of working memory. Although he embraced much of Piagetian thought, his methods followed empiricist designs, primarily in an attempt to demonstrate the transitions outlined in Piagetian constructs. He conceived of dialectical–constructivism, which emphasizes contradictions and synchronizations in individuals and societies (after Riegel, 1976), as well as the structures emphasized in Piagetian theory. Although he investigated some constructs using information processing approaches, he remained a neo-Piagetian. In his later work he has investigated these constructs in relation to neuropsychology (e.g., event-related brain potentials).

### Bruner's Views of Symbolic Development

Jerome Bruner extended Piaget's discussion of the development of symbolic thought by identifying different levels of symbolic thinking: *enactive* representation, which represents past experiences through motor responses; *iconic* representation, which represents these experiences through selective organization of perceptions and images; and *symbolic* representation, which uses language and other abstractions to represent and transform experiences (1960, 1961, 1973). Bruner suggested that all three forms are used throughout life but that young children do not have the ability to represent symbolically until they gain language facility. Once language is achieved, it "moves in the direction of becoming itself free of context and accompanying action. . .[and]. . .directing attention to what is being said rather than to what is being done or seen (Bruner, 1973, p. 701). This enables children to make the transition from "knowing *how* to knowing *that*" (p. 702). He stated that the process of development takes time and that the period of immaturity serves an important purpose (1973). Bruner's view is similar to Vygotsky's assertion that children construct language in the service of thought, and that autonomous thinking begins when children can internalize language (have inner speech) to direct their thinking to higher levels of abstraction. He also saw a very important role for play, especially in parent–child turn taking play, which helps children develop their ability to use communicative turn taking; and he discussed how scaffolding can enable children to learn more complex concepts. He is probably best known, however, for adapting constructivist theory to educational practice by explaining how the Piagetian view of the importance of allowing children to discover concepts can be translated into the educational strategy of "discovery learning" (Bruner, 1960, 1961).

### Elkind's Egocentrism of Adolescence

David Elkind has been instrumental in explaining the implications of Piaget's theory for early childhood education both through his writings and films (1976, 1978). He has also written extensively on the issue of "hurried children" in present society, which he believes creates problems for their natural development (1988). One of Elkind's most frequently cited contributions to Piagetian ideas, however, is his expansion on the concept of egocentrism to the adolescent period. Elkind stated that there is a second period of egocentric thought that also involves a centering on one's own thoughts rather than considering the thoughts of others. He identified "adolescent egocentrism" as having two components. The first is having an imaginary audience (i.e., being "on stage"); because adolescents think their performance is being watched intently by peers, they have difficulty focusing on the actions and needs of others. The second component is having a personal fable (i.e., a unique life story); because adolescents think that their experiences and feelings are unique, this contributes to their belief that they are invulnerable. He believes that this underlies many adolescent risk-taking behaviors. Thus, although Elkind agrees with Piaget that there is an early phase of cognitive egocentrism, he suggested that this type of thinking is evident in a different form during adolescence.

### Flavell's (and Colleagues') Views on Perspective Taking and Theory of Mind

John Flavell is one of many American psychologists who has investigated specific aspects of Piaget's theory over his long academic career. He devised many ingenious studies to look at egocentrism or "perspective taking," memory development, false belief understanding, and metacognition (1977, 1992a, 1992b). Flavell has studied metamemory (ability to understand one's own memory processes), knowledge of false beliefs (ability to know when someone else does not know what we know), and appearance-reality distinctions (ability to distinguish real-appearing objects from real objects) and has concluded that all these abilities are related. Through his studies of perceptual perspectives, he found two levels of visual perspective taking. Level 2 is the understanding that other people have different perspectives, and children at that level can represent that other view (similar to adult abilities.) However, at Level 1 young children (age 3) understand that another person may not see something exactly as they do, but they cannot conceptualize and consciously represent the differences spatially. Thus, they are not egocentric in the sense Piaget claimed, but limited by their representation abilities. On the other hand, in regard to verbal perspective taking, Flavell and his colleagues found that young children do have difficulty communicating clear instructions to others through language. Second graders and eighth graders differ in their ability to give clear directions that take into account that the other person may not have all the knowledge that the speaker has. Also, there seem to be a number of levels of false belief and appearance-reality distinctions. Flavell suggested that there may be a single underlying competency that mediates mastery of all these abilities, and he has emphasized the importance of the development of metacognition (ability to know what we know). His false belief studies provided the foundation for many subsequent studies of "theory of mind." These studies (undertaken by Wellman, 1990, and others) have investigated how children develop their understanding of the thinking of other people who do not have the same information that they have. Studies of how pretend play, which requires role taking, and theory of mind, which requires taking another's perspective, may be connected have also been of current research interest (Lillard, 2001). Both spatial and language abilities are essential in many of these perspective-taking areas. Flavell has based his work primarily on empirical investigations of Piagetian theory, but stated that now he is no longer sure "which ideas about it are Piaget's and which ones are my interpretations or extensions of his. . .like all of Piaget's creatures, I am an incorrigible assimilator" (Flavell, 1992b, p. 107).

## Gopnik's (and Colleagues') Study of Infant/Child Object Permanence and Theory-Building

Allison Gopnik has spent extensive time studying the cognitive processes of infants and young children, primarily with colleagues such as Wellman (1990), Meltzoff (Meltzoff & Moore, 1999), and others (Gopnik, Meltzoff, & Kuhl, 2001; Gopnik & Schulz, 2004; Gopnik & Wellman, 1994). These theorists believe that very young children have more cognitive capabilities than Piagetian and other earlier theories suggest. For example, research from this perspective has indicated that children understand object permanence much earlier that Piaget indicated (Meltzoff & Moore, 1999). The unique experimental designs of this group of researchers have given them evidence they have interpreted to mean that very young children demonstrate "scientific" thinking and test their own "theories" about the world. Because Gopnik's and her colleagues' experiments show that even young children seem to change their theories in response to evidence that conflicts with their earlier ideas, she stated that they are exhibiting behavior similar to that of adult scientists. Thus, she has proposed a "theory theory" as an alternative to the innateness hypothesis outlined by Chomsky (Gopnik, 2003).

Gopnik agrees with Chomsky's idea that young children create representations of the outside world and rules for manipulating those representations (e.g., the language symbol system), and thinks this idea has been an important influence on cognitive science studies of many other cognitive dimensions. She calls this part of Chomsky's theory "cognitive naturalism," which is the idea that knowledge can be understood by scientific investigation of the mind. However, she disputes Chomsky's second major idea, which is that this ability is innate and limited to a small set of representations and rules triggered by the environment, such as semantic and syntax cues. In Gopnik's view, rather than an innate set of representations and rules that can be activated, children have use of the same cognitive devices that adults use in science. Children can develop abstract, coherent systems of causal entities and rules, that is, "theories" to make predictions about evidence, interpret evidence, and confirm or disconfirm theories through their active experimenting in the environment. They construct a theory, but if the evidence does not support it, they then change their theory just as scientists do. She proposed that infants are born with initial innate theories, and they begin revising those theories even in infancy. These intuitive theories of the physical, biological, and psychological worlds become more complex, coherent, and abstract in representing the causal structure of the world. Gopnik is presently tying these ideas to the connectionist method of designing "causal Bayes nets" because she believes that these can provide a more formal account of the inductive inference used in scientific theory-building. Whether the theory theory will gain wide acceptance is not known at this time. It does illustrate, however, how far some theorists have come from William James's idea that infants only know the world as a one of "buzzing confusion."

### Rogoff's (and Colleagues') Cultural Studies of "Situated" Thought

Barbara Rogoff (1950–) is one among many contemporary psychologists who are studying the interactive cultural processes inherent in human development, drawing primarily on the sociohistorical perspective of Vygotsky, but also on ecological and anthropological theory. Rogoff has focused her work on sociocultural aspects of young children's lives, especially in their interactions with parents. In her recent book (2003) she asserted that children's participation in the routine activities of their communities influences how they will develop. She discussed how the similarities and differences in community activities shape children's participation and, thus, their developmental trajectories. With colleagues, Rogoff has investigated how children develop in a number of cultures (e.g., Rogoff & Morelli, 1989; Rogoff & Angelilo, 2002), in particular looking at how adult–child communicative interactions in various cultures affect development. By observing in homes and other informal settings in these cultures, she has described the process through which culturally relevant learning occurs as "guided participation" (1990, 1993). This is usually an informal collaboration of adult and child or peer and child within their everyday activities; that is, the child participates in an "apprenticeship." Learning thus occurs naturally in these contexts and can even occur without direct interaction through the child's observations of everyday activities. In cultures where formal schooling is not the major way of learning, Rogoff said that Vygotsky's view of adult facilitation of the learning of culturally relevant knowledge also operates through parent–child and other social interactions. Whatever is learned is related to what the culture values. For example, in Western culture, children's knowing "readiness skills" such as identifying words is valued, and parent–child interaction might include pointing out boxes in the supermarket that have symbols or words the child might identify, whereas in a tribal culture, perceptual skills related to small changes in the natural environment might be valued, and parent–child interaction might involve such activities. There are subtle ways that more experienced and less experienced participants affect how an activity is structured. The learning occurs through "intersubjectivity," which is promoted by sharing a common activity goal and focus of attention. Rogoff strongly makes the case that the various elements of the "intersubjectivity" interface are so intermingled that they cannot be considered separately; thus, study of developmental processes requires knowledge of the cultural contexts in which such interactions occur (Rogoff, 1997).

## Theoretical Perspectives Influenced Primarily by Information Processing Theory

Although information processing theory has been a strong component of adult studies of various cognitive processes, such as memory, problem solving, and metacognition, it has also been influential in the study of these same processes during early and later childhood.

### Kail's Study of Memory Development

Much of Robert Kail's perspective has centered on information processing theory (Kail & Bisanz, 1992), and his specific focus has been on cognitive activities related to memory development and mental processing speed. Kail has been engaged in a longitudinal study of youth that is examining links between processing speed, working memory, and reasoning. He has found that children have slower processing speeds than adults (Kail, 1991; Kail, Pelligrino, & Carter, 1980) and speed again declines at older ages (Salthouse & Kail, 1983). Memory research conducted by himself and others shows children's memory develops over time (Kail, 1979), primarily in a cumulative fashion. There is evidence that young children do not have all the memory strategies available that are used by older children and adults. For example, in the use of basic mnemonic strategies such as verbal rehearsal, young children of 5 or 6 do not routinely rehearse when asked to recall information, and children of 7 or 8 usually just repeat the words. Older children and adults use elaborated types of rehearsal, modifying their rehearsal to fit the structure of the material to be remembered. Some studies have shown that training in memory strategies helps young children recall but that they may not continue to rehearse if not prompted to do so.

Kail cited other studies of more complex memory tasks such as recall of events from stories, which indicate that older children and adults categorize more dimensions, whereas young children typically use only one dimension and thus cannot remember as well. In regard to remembering more elaborated information, because memory is related to the ability to make inferences and younger children's inferential ability is less well developed, many memory tasks that require inferences are difficult for children. Because elaborated, integrated representations that result from inferences are retained more readily than mnemonic representations, Kail stated that the best predictor of information recall is children's accuracy in answering inferential questions; that is, comprehension and memory develop together. Kail also suggested, however, that there may be some truth to Piaget's view that information stored in memory is restructured as cognitive development occurs (1979). Piaget reported improvements in performance of remembered ordered arrays as children grew older, and replications of Piaget's experiments on cognitive developmental changes in memory task performance are generally consistent with his original work. Other researchers coming from an information processing perspective are studying the development of academic abilities such as the relationship of early phonological awareness to reading (Torgesen, Wagner, & Rashotte, 1994) and counting principles in mathematics (Gelman, Meck, & Merkin 1986). They are interested in identifying the specific understandings that children have that underlie their ability to learn academic subject matter.

### Siegler's Study of Procedural Knowledge and Other Problem-Solving Strategies

Also coming primarily from an information processing perspective, Robert Siegler and colleagues have conducted a series of studies on young children's problem-solving strategy development in areas such as mathematics (1983, 1988). Using a microgenetic method of data collection involving many precise measurements beginning with the child's initial contact with the problem and continuing until the strategies are well learned, Siegler found that young children use a variety of strategies, even after having found one good strategy (2002). He suggested that children use associations (an empiricist term) that include both correct and incorrect strategies. Siegel indicated that children first use the quickest strategy and the one least likely to cause errors; however, their choice may also depend on how strongly they "associate" with a particular ineffective strategy. His studies show that children are capable of self-modifying their behavior and, according to Siegler, these short-term changes in behavior result in developmental change because they increase the number of cognitive associations.

As would be expected from a researcher operating from the information process approach, he sees problem-solving strategy knowledge development as a gradual change process, without abrupt stage shifts. He characterized stage approaches as "simplistic" and asserted that "children's thinking is far more variable than the models suggest" (Siegler, 1997, p. 82). Not only that, he believes that they "inhibit progress in understanding change" (p. 82). Instead he envisions developmental change as a series of overlapping waves that account for the variability of individual and group performance. Siegler explained cognitive development as due to increases in working memory, more knowledge in long-term memory, better ability to monitor understanding, and having more appropriate strategies available to call on. He stressed that microgenetic methods are a "way of meeting the challenges posed by studying change" (p. 85). These densely sampled changes from the time when a process begins to the time that it shows stability can then be used to answer questions about the transition. Researchers using microgenetic methods have found similar results even when their theoretical perspective differed (e.g., neo-Piagetian, Vygotskian, and information processing theorists). One finding is that when children try new strategies, they are usually not proficient at first but have "halting" and varied strategy use. Sometimes changes in strategy follow successes as well as failures, and the strategies used are based on children's existing knowledge. Siegler has also designed computer simulations that mirror the processes used by children, including their ability to self-modify.

## Longitudinal Stability in Cognition

Another empiricist model of an information processing approach to cognitive development is exemplified in the work of a team of researchers led by Marc Bornstein (Bornstein et al., 2006). Using an "infant-controlled habituation-test paradigm" (p. 151), these researchers have investigated young infants' information processing abilities. They presented stimuli and measured infant attention and decrement of attention (habituation) to these stimuli, theorizing that the speed of habituation gives a measure of infant ability to process information (i.e., a measure of their cognition). These researchers followed over 500 infants who were tested with the habituation paradigm, using a variety of additional cognitive and language tests over a 4-year period and also collecting data on a range of other variables such as infant temperament, maternal education, and home environment. They analyzed the numerous measures by using models to determine whether infants' habituation efficiency could predict their performance on later intelligence measures, and they controlled for the effects of temperament, mother's education, and home environment. Figure 7.3 shows their model.

They concluded that habituation efficiency in infancy does predict later cognitive status, at least to a small but significant degree. The information processing theoretical perspective explains these findings as partly related to nervous system functioning but also to variations in infant ability to inhibit attention to familiar or irrelevant stimuli, which frees them to focus attention on new stimuli in the environment and thus increase their cognitive abilities. They can then gain more information, assimilate information more quickly, and store it more efficiently in memory. The researchers stated "Our study shows that very young infants

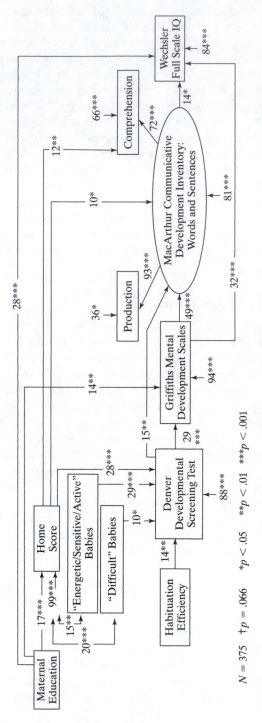

**Figure 7.3  Stability of Cognition Across Early Childhood**

*Source:* Reprinted from *Stability of Cognition Across Early Childhood* from *Stability of Cognition Across Early Childhood: A Development Cascade* (p. 156) by M. H. Bornstein, et al., 2006. *Psychological Science* 17 (2).

$N = 375$   $\dagger p = .066$   $*p < .05$   $**p < .01$   $***p < .001$

Standardized solution for Model 2 based on the completers ($n = 375$). Numbers associated with single headed arrows from one variable in another are standardized path coefficients. Numbers associated with short vertical arrows are error or disturbance terms.

possess an active mental life that they bring to their own development" (Bornstein et al., 2006, p. 157).

## Theoretical Perspectives Influenced by Linguistic and Psycholinguistic Theory

Drawing on the work of earlier linguistic theorists who categorized the basics of language acquisition, researchers have proposed a wide variety of theoretical perspectives on language development in recent years. They include Nelson, Pinker, Tomasello, and Bates, among others. These perspectives are briefly discussed.

### Nelson's View of Early Language and Semantic Knowledge Development

Katherine Nelson has focused much of her work on children's early language development and investigated how it is evidence of their cognitive development. One of her earliest works was an observational study of toddlers' attempts to understand the structure and strategy of language (Nelson, 1973). She has been especially interested in how children gain shared meanings and event knowledge, understand relational terms, and use language narratives to promote script knowledge (Nelson, 1981). In particular, her study of script knowledge has been informative. For example, she found that even at very early ages, young children can generalize cognitive scripts on the basis of one experience with an event, and these generalizations can be influenced by adult comments before, during, and after the event (1981). That is, children do not just remember discrete events but try to "make sense" of the experience by constructing a script or linking the event to an existing script. They have the ability to detect patterns and combine these patterns into higher order events. Nelson concluded, that both general routines and "autobiographical" experiences are narrative constructions and become evident "during the early childhood years (1993). Nelson also stressed that environmental factors play a major role in script formation, however. That is, script knowledge is socially constructed as an interplay between children's capacity for mapping sequences (i.e., making scripts) and their social interactions with parents and other people who provide scaffolds for script building (Nelson et al., 2000; Nelson & Shaw, 2002).

Nelson's longitudinal studies of language development have led her to view children as being "in a dynamic social world of caretakers" (1997, p. 101), which allows them to select the information they need. There is neither only cognitive constructivism or social constructivism but rather a "collaborative constructivism" with social partners directing the child's attention but not determining the child's attention. She commented, "Children are embedded in a social world, thus are part of a system within which cognitive and linguistic development proceeds. Other participants in the system are critical to its development and may exert both positive and negative pressures in different directions" (p. 164). She stressed that longitudinal studies are essential to really understand how change takes place. Prelinguistic knowledge is centered on the events in which the child participates, and it is personal and unique. This event knowledge supports language development because it provides the context in which language can be interpreted. Initially words are understood within these contexts, and then word meanings are expanded as the words are used in other contexts. She also believes that memory begins in relation to event knowledge and is used cognitively to make sense of the world. Nelson stressed that educators must use the process of collaborative constructivism to ensure that every child enters into the "full partnership of language" (p. 114).

## Pinker's View of Language and Mind

Steven Pinker is an experimental psychologist whose work has ranged over many aspects of language and mind relationships. His early work focused on visual cognition, studying human ability to imagine shapes, recognize faces and objects, and direct attention to various areas within a visual field. He developed a theory of how children acquire the vocabulary and grammatical structures of their native language, in particular how the use of verbs shows children's development of language rules. In his extensive study of regular (walk-walked) and irregular (bring-brought) verbs, he described the processes that make language possible, such as accessing words in memory and combining words or parts of words into language rules. He agrees with the view that language is a biological adaptation and has written extensively on this topic. From his linguistic studies, he derived a "computational theory of mind" that links the understanding of the syntax of language to mental computation. He has recently written a number of books directed at general audiences in which he stated that the mind was formed by natural selection as an adaptive problem solving entity (Pinker, 1997). Recently, he has extended this view into many aspects of the concept of human nature (2002). These writings reexamine the nature/nurture debate, and Pinker attacked the "blank slate" (Locke), "noble savage" (Rousseau), and "ghost in the machine" (religious) viewpoints, in favor of an evolutionary perspective. Thus, he has again raised many of the basic questions about human development that have been debated throughout the years. In particular he asserted that spoken language is an instinctive process, "because spoken language has been a feature of human life for tens or hundreds of millennia" (p. 53). Pinker asserted that a basic universal grammar, therefore, underlies all stages of child language (i.e., a continuity assumption). He has also explored, with others, how language development may be explained by "connectionism" (Pinker & Prince, 1988).

## Tomasello's Cultural Constructions of Language

Michael Tomasello has looked at the process of language acquisition from a cultural perspective, and he asserted that human ability to acquire linguistic symbols is related to their ability to identify with other people and "understand them as intentional agents like the self" (1999, p. 7). He believes that, following Vygotsky, there is a cumulative cultural evolution and that is what is responsible for humans' cognitive achievements. When children identify with others, they are able to enter the culture, and their language serves as "especially important symbolic artifacts. . .because they embody the ways that previous generations of human beings in a social group have found it useful to categorize and construe the world for purposes of interpersonal communication" (p. 8). He stated that language frees humans from just seeing perceptual situations; rather, it allows them to make multiple representations of a variety of perceptions. Tomasello discounted both the Skinnerian and Chomskian views of language acquisition; the first, because developmentalists no longer think of children's learning as association-making and isolated but rather integrated with other cognitive and social skills; the second, because there is no need for a posited "universal generative grammar" (2003). Instead, he asserted that there are two sets of skills essential for language acquisition: (a) ability to read intentions (theory of mind), and (b) ability to find patterns (categorization). He thus advocated a "usage-based linguistics," which has its symbolic dimension rather than its grammar as the basis for language acquisition. Competence in a natural language, therefore, consists of mastery of a structured inventory of constructions, which are, of course, related to the specific culture of the child.

### Bates's View of Brain Organization in Language

Elizabeth Bates has studied language disabilities in children who have many types of special needs, and thus her work considers language development from this perspective. From her studies of brain-injured young children and adults (e.g., Bates et al., 1997), she has concluded that there is not an innate predetermined language organization in the brain, although in most adults the left hemisphere is more likely to be dominant. In children with brain injury in the left hemisphere, there is a compensation, and these children "are not aphasic, despite early damage of a sort that often leads to irreversible aphasia when it occurs in an adult" (Bates, 2005, p. 206). She asserted that the "familiar pattern of language localization in adults is the product rather than the cause of development, an end product that emerges out of initial variations in the way that information is processed from one region to another" (p. 206). She said that there can be other "brain plans" for language, due to the "neural plasticity" of the brain, which results in "pluripotentiality," that is, the cortical structure can take on a wide variety of configurations, depending on the environmental input and the timing of that input. She disagreed with Pinker's view of an "instinct," Chomsky's view of a "mental organ," and Fodor's view of an "innate module" (the connectionist view), and called them all versions of the old "phrenology" model of the brain. She also does not accept the behaviorist view of language development. Her depiction of the "phrenological" view that contrasts with her view.

The "emergentist" view, which she proposed, states that language or other domain-specific knowledge can be acquired by a domain-general capacity of the brain. For example, attention, perception, memory, emotion, and motor planning are all required for language acquisition. She stated that "the cognitive machinery that makes us human can be viewed as a new machine constructed out of old parts" (Bates, 2005, p. 231). She outlined a number of mechanisms that she thinks facilitate language development, such as human social organization and reasoning, imitation abilities, excellence in segmenting auditory and visual stimuli, interest in sharing objects, and fascination with joint attention, which are all present in infants within their first year of life. Bates stressed that the plasticity of the brain enables all these abilities to operate in the service of language and thought development. Because language is a system for encoding meaning, it is activated by the same brain regions that are meaningfully activated by the environment. As is evident, Bates's view contrasts to that of some language theorists (e.g., Pinker) but has similarities to that of others (e.g., Tomasello). Needless to say, theoretical perspectives on the relationship of language and cognition continue to be of great interest and controversy.

## Theoretical Influence and Critique

As is evident, theorizing about cognition and language and their interface is of major interest at the present time. Although the underlying viewpoints of the theorists are varied, there is general agreement on the importance of this connection and extensive efforts to test each theoretical view. The strength of most of these perspectives is that they are testable and falsifiable and that most have implications that can be useful to adults who are trying to enhance children's cognitive and language development. Although it is too early to tell, there is sufficient overlap in many of these views that an integrated theory may be developed in the future.

## Trends in Cognitive and Language Development and Themes Useful for Professional Practice

From the many studies of cognition and language development, a set of commonly accepted timelines for the "range of normality" in development of these domains have been identified. Table 7.1 shows these "typical" developmental achievements. Also, although not all the constructs of the theories discussed in chapters 6 and 7 have been validated by extensive evidence, a few general themes can be derived from this set of theories that may be useful for practice. These are provided in Box 7.1.

---

## Summary

The seminal influence of traditional cognitive/language theorists have been extensive in contemporary theoretical and research work. Their influence is seen in the research carried out by contemporary theorists who have attempted to test aspects of the earlier theories or to focus on particular aspects of cognitive/language development using methods influenced by traditional theorists. Cognitive and language relationships continue to be explored, and with the new techniques available from current neuroscience, these relationships may be understood better as research progresses. The theorists discussed here are only a small sample of those who are addressing this rich content area at the present time. In regard to the usefulness of these newer proto-theories, each is providing new insights and giving suggestions for practice that may be important in the future, but it is presently unclear which perspectives will prove to be most fruitful and long lasting. The following case presents a series of questions that these theorists might address differently.

**Table 7.1** Trends in Cognitive and Language Development (Ages Are Approximate)

| | |
|---|---|
| Birth To Age 3 | -Thought is expressed in actions (eye gaze, brain patterns, motor and sensory actions) |
| | -Responds to noise and familiar voices |
| | -Communication through turn-taking behaviors during care and play activities |
| | -Intentional behaviors develop leading to initial understanding of causality and object permanence begin by 6-12 mo. |
| | -Communicates through facial expressions, direction gaze, vocalizations, gestures by 6-12 mo. |
| | -Attempts to control environment through communication by 6-12 mo. |
| | -Understands simple verbal directions if accompanied by cues by 12 mo. |
| | -Uses a few words and imitates rhythm and sounds of native language by 9-12 mo. |
| | -Representational/symbolic thinking begins to be evident through pretense and language by age 1-2 |
| | -Has vocabulary of about 50 words by age 2. |
| | -Uses holophrastic and telegraphic sentences by age 2-3 |
| | -Follows commands, names objects, uses action words by age 2-3 |
| | -About 90% intelligible speech by age 3. |
| Ages 3-6 | -Increased attention and memory by age 3-4 |
| | -Language increases rapidly; private speech occurs by age 3-5 |
| | -Vocabulary of about 2,000 words |
| | -Generates language rules of syntax |
| | -Able to use descriptive words, opposites words, questions by age 4-6 |
| | -Egocentric thought at age 3-4 |
| | -Development of theory of mind by age 4-6 |
| | -Perception of states not transformations |
| | -Language and thought become integrated during this age range. |
| | -Speech intelligible and socially useful by age 4-6 |
| | -Can follow 3-step directions by age 5-6 |
| Ages 6-12 | -Has mastered all vowel and consonant sounds by age 6-7 |
| | -Can tell a story about a picture or event that makes sense by age 6-7 |
| | -Able to think logically about concrete information by age 7-8 |
| | -Can decenter and reverse thinking by age 7-8 |
| | -Can relate accounts of past events by age 8 |
| | -Able to read with ease and write simple compositions by age 8-9 |
| | -Able to carry on an adult-like conversation by age 8-9 |
| | -Develops hierarchical classification by age 7-12 and ability to seriate with transitive inference |
| | -Can follow complex directions by age 8 |
| | -Good control of rate, pitch, and direction of speech by age 8 |
| | -Long term memory, metacognition, and cognitive monitoring improve by age 8-12 |

*(continued)*

**Table 7.1** (*continued*)

| | |
|---|---|
| Ages 12-20 | -Can use hypothetical and deductive reasoning, and propositional thought by age 12-14 |
| | -Increase in decision making abilities |
| | -Social cognition increases and social cognitive monitoring achieved by age 12-14 |
| | -World may be viewed in terms of polarities (good/evil) in this age period |
| | -Vocabulary continues to increase with abstract concepts understood in this age period |
| | -Egocentric thought related to ideas occurs; may result in risk-taking behaviors |
| | -Cognition and emotion interface may prevent logical thought |
| Ages 20-40 | -Can consider diversity of opinions and multiple perceptions |
| | -Selection, entry, adjustment, maintenance of career or other work life achieved |
| | -Problem-solving related to practical issues of child rearing, work, or social life |
| | -Vocabulary and language facility stable unless involved in further education; in that case, continues to develop |
| | -May reason in logical or mythic dimensions |
| | -Wisdom begins to increase |
| | -Achieves highest productivity of creative work |
| Ages 40-60 | -Further understanding of societal organization and complex relationships, and a rethinking of former conclusions may occur |
| | -Episodic memory declines, and depending on health and life circumstances, semantic memory may also decline |
| | -Wisdom may continue to increase |
| | -New learning may occur if life circumstances change |
| | -Language and verbal social skills usually stable during this period |
| Ages 60-80 | -Need to acquire new knowledge may decline due to perception of future as short |
| | -Ability to accumulate information and verbal skills may continue to increase (crystallized intelligence) but abstract reasoning may decline (fluid intelligence) |
| | -Interest in learning more about religion may increase |
| | -Brain plasticity decreases but active thought (problem-solving, new learning) may delay this |
| | -Mental disorders (e.g., Alzheimer's) may begin |
| Ages 80-100 | -Great cognitive variation, some keep mental acuity, others experience mental disorders |

## Case 7. Contempo-Cog School System

The teaching team at the Questions Middleschool in the Contempo-Cog School System is gathered to discuss some curriculum revisions that are to be made in the fourth- through eighth- grade curriculum. The staff has agreed that a "one size fits all" curriculum is not going to enable every child to gain the cognitive and language proficiency that they will need to handle the abstract thinking required in high school. Principal Solver has obtained some funds to bring in a few important guest speakers to the school to give advice about how the curriculum should be revised to foster the highest levels of thinking possible. The speakers

## Box 7.1
## Theoretically-Derived Themes That May Be Useful For Professional Practice

- Cognition develops in relationship to sensorimotor and perceptual actions during the earliest years and, although cognition becomes more abstracted, its roots in action are important.

- Language development appears to have some biological basis, and although the nature of that basis is still debated, the role of experience is also vital, and thus a language-rich environment that builds upon innate predispositions can support full development of language potential.

- Cognitive development also is drawn from a biological base, and even young infants have strategies they use to make sense of their world; these strategies (theories?) assist them in developing more complex cognitive skills as they engage actively with their environment.

- Cognitive and language development are closely intertwined and, although there is debate over the exact nature of the relationship, both are essential for higher levels of thinking.

- Play is important for both cognitive and language development because it provides a way for children to practice and elaborate meaningfully with aspects of both their physical and social environment; their humor development also shows their increasing understanding of incongruity and multiple meanings.

- Cognitive development involves recursive mental processes that are used at each stage (level, tier) to make meaning of experiences. Although functions are similar, structures of the mind differ at younger and older ages.

- Each child will develop cognitive and language abilities that are co-constructed with adults, siblings, and peers; that is, children's development is "situated" in sociohistorical contexts.

- As children's mental processing abilities increase, they will gain more and more information processing capabilities (working and long term memory; problem solving strategies).

are Drs. Case, Fischer, Bruner, and Elkind, each of whom will outline their views of what children's educational needs are during this age period.

What are four questions that the staff might ask the speakers that could inform their teaching practice?

What would the answers of each be to those questions?

Teachers of the Early Thought Preschool-Kindergarten in the Contempo-Cog School System are trying to learn how their part of the whole system may affect how well children in later grades may learn. They can choose one speaker, either Dr. Flavell, Kail, Siegel, Gopnik, Nelson, Bates, Tomasello, or Pinker to speak to them. What is a question they might ask each speaker (different for each) that would help them understand young children's cognition and language development better and thus aid teaching practice?

What would the answers to those questions be?

## Readings

R. Case, *The Origins of Neo-Piagetian Theory*, pp. 339–344.

K. W. Fischer & S. P. Rose, *Growth Cycles of Brain and Mind*, pp. 345–350.

A. Gopnik & L. Schulz, *Mechanisms of Theory Formation in Young Children*, pp. 351–360.

## Suggested Readings

Case, R. (1992). The origins of neo-Piagetian theory. In H. Beilin & P. Pufall (Eds.), *Piaget's theory: Prospects and possibilities* (pp. 63–71). Hillsdale, NJ: Erlbaum.

Fischer, K. W., & Rose, S. P. (1998). Growth cycles of brain and mind. *Educational Leadership*, 56(3), 56–60.

Flavell, J. H. (1992). Perspectives on perspective-taking. In H. Beilin & P. B. Pufall (Eds.), *Piaget's theory: Prospects and possibilities* (pp. 123–135). Hillsdale, NJ: Erlbaum.

Gopnik, A. & Schulz, L. (2004). Mechanisms of theory formation in young children. *Trends in Cognitive Sciences*, 8(8), 371–377.

Kail, R. V. (1979). *The development of memory in children* (pp. 8–18). San Francisco: Freeman.

Nelson, K., & Shaw, L. K. (2002). Developing a socially shared symbolic system. In E. Amsel & J. P. Byrnes (Eds.), *Language, literacy, and cognitive development: The development and consequences of symbolic communication* (pp. 29–36). Mawah, NJ: Erlbaum.

Rogoff, B., & Morelli, G. (1989). Perspectives on children's development from cultural psychology. *American Psychologist*, 44(2), 343–348.

*Source:* Brilliant Enterprises.

# Theories With Major Emphasis on Sociomoral and Gender Role Development

A number of the theorists discussed in the chapters on personality/social/emotional and cognitive/language development also addressed issues of sociomoral and/or gender role development in the course of explaining some aspects of their theories, although they did not create fully formed theories in these domains. Sociomoral development has been defined in three different ways by theorists: (a) as emotional understanding (e.g., demonstrating empathy, guilt and/or shame), (b) as behavioral actions (e.g., honesty, altruism, aggression), and (c) as reasoning (e.g., solving moral dilemmas about justice or caring). Thus, theorists who do address sociomoral development often emphasize different aspects. Gender role development has been explained from many perspectives as well, including those stressing biological/genetic bases, socially reinforced influences, or cognitively constructed concepts. One reason why many theorists addressed these developmental domains at least briefly may be because both sociomoral and gender role development are closely tied to other developmental areas; that is, they are embedded in many actions related to changes in social–emotional and cognitive growth. Freud suggested that the different conflicts faced by males and females during early childhood had moral development implications. Erikson had an underlying morality theme in his later stages, and he included some alternate views of the development of female identity in his discussion of adolescent ego identity development. Piaget outlined stages of moral development based on his study of boys' game play and interviews with young children about moral reasoning. Bandura discussed moral development only briefly as one function of self-efficacy, but he specifically addressed gender issues in self-efficacy development, especially in relation to effects of gender on career choices. Although each of these theorists discussed sociomoral and/or gender role development briefly, only one theorist, Lawrence Kohlberg, developed both a sociomoral and a gender role theory. Kohlberg built on Piagetian theory but focused on extending the study of reasoning to sociomoral and gender-related cognitive dimensions. This chapter will briefly discuss the connections that Freud, Erikson, Piaget, and Bandura have made to sociomoral and to gender role development and then review the major concepts of Kolhberg's theories of sociomoral and gender role development. It concludes with an overview of Gilligan's critique of some of these theoretical views in relation to female development.

## Theoretical Perspectives on Moral Development and Gender Role Development

A number of theorists who were primarily interested in personality and social–emotional development also discussed social–emotional understandings or behavioral aspects of moral development and speculated on gender role development within their theoretical perspective. Because moral development also involves reasoning, theorists focused on cognitive development have considered moral development from that perspective.

### *Freud's Oedipal or Electra Conflict and Development of the Superego*

As discussed in chapter 3, Freud viewed the third stage of development (Phallic) as the time when both gender role and moral development occurred (1938). He said that this is the age period (ages 3 to 5) when children become aware of their sexual characteristics and begin to learn the gender role that their particular society enforces. Gender-related anatomical differences become obvious to boys and girls, and in Freud's view, this promotes an interest in a love relationship with the opposite-sex parent. Because it is not possible to have such an exclusive relationship, a conflict ensues in the child that eventually leads to "appropriate" gender role identification. Freud termed this an *Oedipal* conflict in males (after the Greek tragedy of Oedipus who unknowingly married his mother). The boy desires his mother exclusively (to "marry" her) but of course cannot and may worry that if his father becomes aware of this desire, he may lose his penis (castration anxiety) because he knows that other children (i.e., girls) do not have one. According to Freud, males resolve this conflict by identifying with their father and suppressing the negative emotions aroused by the father's possession of the mother. This results in the creation of the enforcer of morality, the *superego,* which is needed to abide by the behaviors that are demanded by society (but are not what the child desires). That is, the superego becomes the conscience of the child, and it generates the emotions of guilt and shame when the child does not follow moral rules. Freud's view of morality, therefore, fits into the conceptualization of morality as the capacity to have appropriate emotions (i.e., guilt and shame). According to Freud, once the phallic stage is completed, the superego remains as the source of conscience throughout life, and it may be harsh or mild in enforcing moral rules. The superego is also the source of the *ego ideal*, which is the image of self-aspiration, with children initially aspiring to be like the same-sex parents. It contains the seeds of religious belief, self-judgement, and moral censorship. When the ego does not perform as the superego demands, then guilt is strong. This superego "policeman," which is formed during the Oedipal stage, is the source of moral development in Freud's view.

Freud was less clear about female gender role and sociomoral development. His theory of gender identification and superego development did not fit girls' development because they have different sexual characteristics. Freud suggested that girls experience penis envy because they do not have that sexual characteristic and thus feel less worthy. (More recent thinking on the topic has rejected that view, although, because males in Victorian society had many more privileges than females, females might have been realistically envious of the male role!) Freud added to his theory by maintaining that a similar process might occur (the *Electra* conflict), with the girl seeing her mother as a rival for the father's affection, and then coming to terms with the situation and identifying with the mother. Typically, however, females do not have a conflictual relationship with their mothers. Because females do not have the opportunity to resolve this crisis as males do, Freud could not link their superego development to the Oedipal crisis. He suggested that their superego development might be less strong because females tend to be more influenced by feelings and less concerned about justice. This assertion has been criticized by Gilligan (1982), who concluded that his conclusions were really a problem with his theory. Because his theory could not adequately explain female development, she stated that he then reconceptualized the theoretical problem as a problem of female development.

### Erikson's Identity Crises for Males and Females and Growth of Moral/Religious Values

Although Erikson did not discuss early gender or moral development as explicitly as Freud, he initially accepted most of Freud's views. For example, although he stressed the positive aspects of the crises of autonomy and initiative during preschool years, their converse aspects—shame (ages 2 to 3) and guilt (ages 3 to 5)—were described using Freudian terminology. In Erikson's descriptions of crises stages, he did not differentiate male and female gender role development in that early age period; however, he did conduct one study of children's block play in which he reported that males primarily built towers and females, enclosures, which could be explained by their biological differences (Erikson, 1963). The age period in which Erikson primarily addressed gender role differences was adolescence. He focused most of his discussion on males' search for identity, however (1968). His view of female ego identity was that it had a strong biological component, and he also hypothesized that the ego identity crisis might not be as salient for females during adolescence because they are more likely to have concerns about intimacy, rather than identity, at that age. He suggested that once they find their male partner (i.e., gain intimacy), they then gain their identity as an adjunct to their partner's identity. (This view remains a common expectation in many cultures around the world.) Although it is not now as common in Western cultures for women to believe their identity is just part of their husband's identity, it is often the case that being divorced from a "powerful" man may make a women feel less powerful and valued. Erikson's theory of female identity development has also been strongly criticized by feminist theorists, and in his later work, Erikson softened his stance on this issue.

Although he focused most of his discussion of crisis stages on their effect on ego development, Erikson did not really dispute the idea of superego development. Throughout many of the crises stages he discussed, there is a strong moral development base; however, the crises periods are not necessarily made explicit as moral issues. For example, the ability to love others, to care for others, and to have a sense of life integrity are all morality-related themes (related more to care than to justice). Although he generally focused attention on positive social–emotional development, he did identify the alternative (more negative) developmental consequences, such as isolation, stagnation, and despair that could come from not addressing later life stages in a responsible social manner (Erikson, 1984). He also characterized religion as being an important element in positive life consequences, and in later life he focused more on universal moral issues that mark a successful final crisis stage. He indicated that faith was a primary outcome of a positive resolution of the last crisis stage. His writings on the later stage of life, done toward the end of his own life, were collaborations with his wife, Joan Erikson, and they expressed a more egalitarian view.

### Bandura's Views of Gender Roles and Moral Behaviors in Relation to Self-Efficacy

Although he did not develop a complete theory of gender role or moral development, in his early work, Bandura examined the influence of social learning, observation of salient models, and vicarious reinforcement as factors influencing gender role behavior, discussing how parental, peer, and media models may influence the development of gender-appropriate behaviors. Also, his early studies of how antisocial models in the peer group may influence expression of antisocial behaviors had implications for moral development as expressed in moral behavior (1977; Bandura, Ross, & Ross, 1963: Bandura & Walters, 1959). Bandura did not continue this line of investigation extensively; however, many other researchers have conducted studies of the effects of violent television, abusive family models, and peer gangs on moral behavior and of stereotypic gender role models on gender role development. For example, toys with pictures of girls or boys playing with them can influence what toys children of each sex choose, even at preschool age, and aggressive media models may influence behavior during childhood and adolescence (e.g., Carlsson-Paige & Levin, 1987).

In his later work on self-efficacy development (1997), Bandura explained how gender may influence self-efficacy views in a number of areas. For example, women may question their self-efficacy in parenting and their ability to combine a career and family, although this is not usually an issue for men. Females may vary in their perceived self-efficacy about how well they could perform roles typically held by males, and this may account for women's low level of pursuit of careers in science and technical fields, as well as in other occupations dominated by men. These low self-efficacy beliefs about their abilities in those fields may have been supported by their observations of stereotypic behaviors of parents and teachers, media images, and models in the general society. Bandura indicated that perceived low self-efficacy in fields such as mathematics can be a major deterrent to girls' choice of that type of career. Interestingly, young females' self-efficacy in regard to mathematics, science, political involvement, and other typically male-dominated fields is higher when they are young and tends to decrease as they get older.

In regard to moral behavior, he stated, "In the course of socialization, children adopt social and moral standards that serve as guides and deterrents for conduct. The sanctions children apply to themselves keep conduct in line with internal standards. Self-sanctions do not operate unless they are activated, however, and there are many psychological processes by which self-restraints can be disengaged from detrimental conduct" (Bandura, 1997, p. 237). He suggested that because self-efficacy can also be established around antisocial behaviors (e.g., stealing, cheating), moral behavior can go awry in cases where self-efficacy is formed around such behaviors. His general rules for explaining how models are chosen and imitated and his descriptions of later stages of self-efficacy development would also apply to the development of moral behaviors. Bandura's concerns about self-efficacy development, therefore, address some aspects of both gender role development and the development of moral behaviors.

### Piaget's Games with Rules and Heteronomous/Autonomous Moral Development

Piaget studied aspects of moral development during the early part of his professional work, but he was interested in moral reasoning, not behavior or emotions (Piaget, 1965). In his research on moral judgement, Piaget interviewed children about a set of stories that had examples of moral dilemmas that required reasoning about issues of rule breaking, equality, authority, punishment, and reciprocity. For example, some of the stories had unintentional rule breaking with severe consequences, and some had intentional rule breaking without severe consequences. Children were then asked who was most naughty. He concluded that at early ages, children are more likely to think bad consequences rather than bad intentions are evidence of bad behavior. Consistent with his epistemological perspective, he believed that children might initially obey rules adults require of them, but that just behaving in certain ways does not really constitute the development of moral reasoning. That is, these rules may be social arbitrary knowledge and result in "verbalizations," not true moral thought. Thus, he believed that moral reasoning is not gained by interactions with adult authority figures. He defined morality as being able to have moral reasoning ability, not just being able to behave according to rules. He thought that moral reasoning must develop as all reasoning develops—through construction of knowledge—and that this process requires relationships with peers who are equal. When children attempt to resolve cognitive disequilibrium related to issues of fairness and equity (initially in their games-with-rules when they interact with peers), they then progress to higher levels of moral development. After his studies, he concluded that there were three levels of moral judgement: heteronomous, intermediate, and autonomous, as follows.

- *Heteronomous/Moral Realism (ages 5 to 10):* In this stage the child obeys rules handed down by authorities and views the rules as external features that can't be modified. Respect for the rules is derived from the authority figures, and the rules are seen as sacred and unchangeable. This is because there are two cognitive problems: (a) egocentrism—a personal perspective is the only perspective, and moral values are not judged relative to individuals; and (b) realism—rules are regarded as fixed; that is, subjective phenomena is seen as objective (concrete). Moral realism is a function of the cognitive reasoning level of the child, which is egocentric. Acts are judged by their consequences, not by intentions, punishment is evidence of wrongdoing (immanent justice), and duty is defined as obedience to authority. Heteronomous (blind obedience to) rules is preeminent from ages 5 to 7, but by ages 7 to 10, the ability to reason about rules with peers begins.

- *Intermediate (ages 8 to 12, depending on child):* Through interactions with peers, the child gains a sense of autonomy and egalitarianism, and beliefs in immanent justice and punishment begin to change to beliefs in reciprocal punishment that "fits the crime."

- *Autonomous/Moral Cooperation (age 11+):* Rules are not rigid but can be modified through negotiation. They are the products of group arrangements (consensus) and arrived at by cooperative means with reciprocity among equals. Acts are judged by their intentions, not by consequences, and there is the cognitive capacity to differentiate one's own values from those of others. By age 12, autonomous (internalized) rules based on mutual agreement are beginning to be predominant.

In Piaget's study of boys' marble games, he charted the movement through these stages and stated that it is by the process of peer-group interaction that autonomous/moral cooperation develops. In the game play, he saw four successive stages of rule application. The first (age under 2) is purely motor and individual, in which the marbles are used without reference to other children. The second stage (ages 2 to 5) is the egocentric one when children may play together but do not have a common set of rules (e.g., everyone can win). However, rules in general are considered untouchable and sacred if given by adults. Between ages 7 and 8 children reach a stage of incipient cooperation, in which children do try to win, but if asked, they may still give different accounts of the rules. In this stage, however, they begin to regard rules as laws due to mutual consent (at least in game play), and thus they can be altered. Codification of rules occurs about age 11 or 12, when every child has a similar idea of the rules and can negotiate rule changes that will be agreed on and followed by all. Piaget said that when children reach this stage, they are at the autonomous/moral cooperation level. He did not focus any specific study on girls' moral development because his tendency was to think in universals of development. However, Gilligan criticized Piaget's lack of discussion of girls' moral development as a bias that demonstrated his view that *child* development and *male* development were the same (Gilligan, 1982). Chodorow (1974) questioned Piaget's hypothesis that girls may have more "pragmatic" attitudes toward rules and are more tolerant of rule exceptions, resulting in their moral development being not as advanced as that of boys. Later research on girls' game play has pointed out some major differences in their style of play, with different types of rule negotiation, and this seems to be related to the issue of whether justice or caring are most important for moral development, which is discussed later.

## Kohlberg's Theories of Moral Development and Gender Role Identity Development

Although most of the theorists who were interested in either moral development or gender role development did not propose fully developed theories in both of these areas, Kohlberg provided a very complete moral development theory and a relatively strong theoretical perspective on gender role identity.

### Kohlberg's Theory of Moral Development

Lawrence Kohlberg (1927–1987) studied with Piaget, and for his doctoral work, he conducted his famous study of a group of boys' moral reasoning development. He was a professor at Harvard University until he contracted an unusual tropical disease, and he was found dead after he had been reported missing. His death remains a mystery. He is best known for his theory of moral development, which originally involved six stages, although his theory of gender-role development has also been influential. The method used by Kohlberg in his study of moral reasoning development was, following Piaget, to give "moral dilemmas" to the children and then probe their answers to see what reasons they gave for their answer (1970, 1987). Kohlberg was not concerned that they gave a "right" answer; that is, they could say that a person should or should not do something, but the reasons for that action were what he coded to find their level of reasoning. His stages of moral reasoning are based on a coding scheme that evaluated children's interpretations of justice (what is just or fair), as follows.

*Preconventional* (Begins about age 5 and decreases with age):
- Reward and punishment orientation: the moral reason is that the action will have a consequent reward or punishment (e.g., going through a red light—no, because will get a ticket; yes, because will get there faster and no one will see me).
- Naive reciprocity orientation: the moral reason is exchange and retaliation; a "good" act is one that exchanges help or retaliates for hurt (tit for tat; rubbing each other's backs); it is an egoistic orientation (e.g., sharing your sandwich if your friend shares his cake; hitting someone because she hit you).

*Conventional* (Increases to age 13 and stabilizes):
- Good boy/girl orientation: the moral reason is to maintain good relations and approval of others (image); intentions matter but person and role are

combined (e.g., I'm a good girl so I'd never cheat because my family would be hurt; I'm "bad" (clever and tough) so I'd show my friends how to cheat without getting caught).

- Authority and social order maintenance orientation: the moral reason is to obey authority and maintain the social order as it is; intentions matter more than consequences; the moral role extends outside family and friends (e.g., I would give to charity because it is a requirement of belief at my church; I would obey an unjust law because it is the law of the land; I won't help the poor because there is no law that says I must).

*Postconventional* (Increases to age 16/18 to adult):

- Contract and democratic law orientation: the moral reason is to maximize social welfare and fulfill duty as a citizen; if an unjust law exists, it should be changed; there may be conflict between the rights of individual and society; contracts are binding but can be negotiated (e.g., the rights of political prisoners are violated by the new law so I will fight to repeal it—the moral rationale of the ACLU; it is our duty to declare independence if rulers are unfair—the moral rationale of the Declaration of Independence!; we need to support a law that will permit people to choose if they want assisted suicide—the Oregon law).
- Conscience or principle orientation: the moral reason is to meet higher universal human rights or justice; guided by universal moral principles, not the laws of society (e.g., I will go to jail to fight the unjust laws of segregation—M. L. King's moral rationale; I will violate laws in order to save lives—the moral rationale of Germans who concealed Jews in their homes; I will risk my life to save earthquake victims).

Kohlberg had some disagreement with Piaget's views. He did not think respect for authority governed the earliest stage but rather that children perceived reward or punishment as the crucial factor, and he did not think children regarded rules as sacred or that their respect for adults made them respect rules. However, he agreed with Piaget that the higher levels of morality were based on mutual consent and concerns for justice/fairness for all. He strongly felt that knowledge of good exists within children, but it needs to be drawn out through cognitive conflict. His view was that when they discuss moral dilemmas, children can comprehend the reasoning of the stages lower than their own, and they often can comprehend one stage above their own if they hear that reasoning from others. If they can comprehend the higher stage, they usually prefer that reasoning to their own. Thus, creating dissatisfaction about their present knowledge through presenting moral dilemmas can aid moral development. A sample moral dilemma is shown in Box 8.1

Kohlberg's research agenda was continued by his students and research assistants, in particular by Carol Gilligan and Rheta DeVries. Gilligan raised questions regarding his stage conceptualization in regard to females (1982), and DeVries collaborated with Kohlberg to extend the theory to investigate early stages of sociomoral development by analyzing the games of young children and

## Box 8.1
## A Sample Moral Dilemma and Potential Answers

Helen has finished her math work and is in the back of the classroom looking at the books. Tina and Beth are also at the book table but they are not reading. Instead they are rolling a pencil back and forth, at first very quietly across the table, but then they begin throwing it, using their books as a shield so Ms. Walter doesn't see them. Helen observes but tries to concentrate on her book. Then Tina rolls the pencil to Helen and she pushes it back, and the game becomes a three-way throwing contest. After a few minutes Helen gets up and goes back to her desk. At that time Ms. Walters notices Tina and Beth are throwing the pencil and goes to them to reprimand them. She says they will need to stay in for recess as a punishment because throwing things in the classroom is not allowed.

Should Helen tell Ms. Walters that she also threw the pencil? Why or why not?

If answer is Yes, ask these questions:

Why should Helen admit that she threw the pencil?

Did Helen intend to throw the pencil? Does that matter?

Did Helen do it as much as Tina and Beth so should she be punished as much?

If Ms. Walter had not noticed the girls, should Helen have told her what was happening?

Will Tina and Beth be nicer to Helen in the future if she shares the punishment?

If answer is No, ask these questions:

Why should Helen not admit that she threw the pencil?

Is it fair for Tina and Beth to be punished but not Helen?

Should there be a rule about not throwing pencils? Why or why not?

If Helen doesn't admit she threw the pencil, does that make her a bad girl?

What will Tina and Beth think about Helen if she doesn't tell that she participated?

What will Ms. Walters think of Helen if she finds out she threw the pencil?

NOTE: These are sample questions but designed to probe answers of "yes" or "no." The important thing is to advance children's reasoning about moral issues (truth telling, potential to hurt, fairness), not to get them to agree on "yes."

promoting sociomoral values in preschool settings (DeVries, 2001; DeVries & Kohlberg, 1984; Kohlberg & DeVries, 1987). In Kohlberg's later work (1973), he reevaluated the stage progress and confirmed evidence that Stage 5 and Stage 6 reasoning usually does not appear until adulthood, and even then their appearance is partly dependent on adults' levels of education and types of experiences. He even posited a Stage 7 that is more closely allied with Erikson's final life stage. At this stage moral development may involve a "sense of being a part of the whole of life and the adoption of a cosmic, as opposed to a universal humanistic (Stage 6) perspective" (Kohlberg, 1973, p. 203).

Kohlberg was especially interested in designing methods to help children reach higher moral reasoning stages in educational settings (1970). He defined a morally educated person as one who has learned the process of moral deliberation and judgment and tried to operationalize the process of moral reasoning development in a practical way. This is because he wanted schooling to help society realize the principle of justice throughout the world. He designed an educational method using controversial moral dilemmas that were designed to arouse cognitive disagreement among students. He thought a mixture of students who are at different levels of moral development should discuss such dilemmas and that an open Socratic teaching style that encouraged the challenging of others' opinions could be the venue through which stage progress could be made. He tried to establish such "just communities" in which moral reasoning could flourish. He initiated his model in a number of high schools and also developed filmstrips (the media of the time) that teachers could use in elementary schools to facilitate moral reasoning. He strongly believed that this approach was essential for fostering higher levels of moral development. His method (sometimes termed "values education"), however, was very controversial in the educational system because most adults are not comfortable discussing moral dilemmas themselves and did not want their children doing so, especially if the result was a questioning of adult moral decisions or behavior. Kohlberg would view the currently popular "character education" as an extremely low level of moral education because it stresses unquestioning acceptance of adult-initiated moral rules, rather than moral reasoning and growth toward deeper understanding of moral issues. He called such character education approaches the "bag of virtues" approach, which do not lead to true moral development.

### Kohlberg's Theory of Gender Role Development

Kohlberg's gender role theory has received less attention than his moral development theory; however, it is a thought-provoking approach to understanding gender development through a constructivist lens (1966). Kohlberg looked at gender role development as a cognitive process also; that is, one's gender identity is a product of knowledge construction, just as is true of any other concept. He defined the steps in gender role development as follows:

- *Establishing gender identity (ages 1 to 3):* In the first 3 years of life, children learn that they are male or female from the labels given to them and their observations of sex differences. They categorize themselves as a boy or a girl during this period. However, their identity is still fluid; for example, if girls wear slacks, they may think that their identity will change, or if boys observe girls having fun in activities that adults might categorize as "girls' play," they want to engage in those activities (e.g., dressing up in frilly outfits). Most adults teach children their gender category name very early and are pleased when the child can repeat "I'm a boy/girl." They may treat boys and girls differently, say things like, "Boys don't cry" or "Girls shouldn't get dirty," and give gender stereotypic toys to children. All these actions make children cognitively aware of their gender label (identity) at a very early age.

- *Understanding gender constancy (ages 3 to 5):* In the age period from 3 to 5, children begin to understand that their gender is a constant and that there is no way to change to the other sex (they are, of course, unaware of adult sex-change operations!). They know that despite changes in outward appearance (whether they wear pants or dresses), they will remain the same gender. Adults may continue to stress the gender role in various ways, but even if parents want their children to be androgenous (able to do both "boy" and "girl" activities), by this age the peer group begins to enforce gender role behavior also. This is especially true for boys, because the message to boys about not engaging in stereotypically female roles is already very strong. This message comes from parents (especially fathers), other adults, and the media.

* *Adapting to the fact of one's gender class membership (ages 6 to 8/10):* Because gender role development is a cognitive process, by ages 6 to 8, children are very aware of the behaviors that are expected and approved of by members of their gender class. These messages may or may not be given by parents; however, each culture proclaims these messages very strongly through peers, other adults, and in the media of that culture. Thus, children learn that they must construct their gender role to fit the label they have been assigned, and they try to have "cognitive consistency" with that label by acting in ways that fit what members of that class should do. Many parents have been upset when their child, who was raised to have many androgenous interests, suddenly seems to have turned into a stereotypical male or female. For example, a girl may only want to wear dresses even though her mother never does, or a boy may throw away stuffed toys or dolls that he earlier enjoyed because "boys don't play with such toys." Thus, stereotypic (sex typing) behavior is extremely common during this age period. There are also segregated gender groups in play, and when they do play together it is usually "boys chase girls" or "girls against boys" types of games.

Because Kohlberg suggested that gender role identity is a culturally constructed concept, an implication of the theory is that as cultural standards change, the appropriate behaviors that can fit a gender role can expand or contract to fit those changes. For example, in the United States the Title 9 encouragement of girls in high school sports has made engaging in sports at early and later age levels an acceptable fit with a female gender role, but this was not the case in the mid 20th century. The increasing approval of men's ability to be the stay-at-home parent is another example of how what is appropriate within one's gender role may change over time. Although Kohlberg did not extend his gender role development theory past the elementary age period, it is relatively easy to see how it could predict how later environmental influences can result in a wide or narrow range of gender-appropriate roles at various age periods throughout life. Kohlberg did not discount possible biological sex influences; however, the importance of his theoretical perspective is that it explains gender role as a cognitively constructed concept that is open to new constructions as new information is available to individuals of both sexes. The present turmoil over gay/lesbian issues can be partly understood using Kohlberg's cognitive theory of gender-role development. Also, because the culture gives messages that assist in the construction of gender roles, the view of appropriate roles for males and females in various countries or in smaller societies (e.g., religious communities) may differ widely. Presently gender role expectations in many Middle Eastern countries are very different than those in Western societies. Both Middle Eastern and Western viewpoints may change further as their cultures change in the future.

### Theoretical Influence of Kohlberg's and Other Views

All the theories discussed in this chapter have been influential in explaining aspects of moral development. There has been a continuing research interest in exploring the emotions related to morality (empathy, shame, guilt) that Freud and Erikson identified. For example, William Damon (1988) has included these aspects in his description of moral development, and Nancy Eisenberg and colleagues (Eisenberg et al., 1999) have done extensive longitudinal research on empathy, altruism, and other types of what they call "prosocial" development. Bandura's work was especially of interest to theorists who looked at violent models on television (Feschbach, 1974) and effects of peer groups on aggression. Piaget, of course, was the major influence on Kohlberg's work, and Kohlberg generated an entire cohort of researchers. One of Kohlberg's collaborators, Rheta DeVries, has done extensive research and elaboration of his theory, especially in relation to its constructivist implications for education (e.g., DeVries, 2001; DeVries & Kohlberg, 1984; Kohlberg & DeVries, 1987). Later theorists such as Larry Nucci and Elliot Turiel (Nucci & Turiel, 2000) drew on Kohlberg's work in expanding reasoning about rules (personal, social conventional, and moral), as did Damon in his study of children's social world (1977).

In relation to gender role theory, the causes of gender role differences proposed by theorists still include explanations that are primarily biological (Freud, Erikson), social (Bandura), or cognitive (Kohlberg). Most theorists include influences of a number of factors, however, and research on gender role development has been generated by many of these theories. Bandura's influence is seen in studies on types of toys and room decorations in the bedrooms of boys and girls (Rheingold & Cook, 1975) and on preschool teachers' encouragement of gender role stereotypes (Fagot, 1984; Fagot & Leve, 1998). A number of theorists have also built on aspects of Kohlberg's work to develop feminist cognitive versions of gender role theory (e.g., Block, 1979; Bem, 1976, 1981a; Gilligan, 1982).

### Critique of Kohlberg's and Other Theories

Critiques of the theories of the first group of theorists in this chapter apply as they did to the other aspects of their theories; for example, testability of Freud's and Erikson's views is limited, and their bias toward male development issues is noted. Bandura has not really proposed a developed theory, merely given perspectives related to his major interests in social and self-development. Even Piaget directed his attention to moral development for only a brief period, and he addressed gender development only peripherally. In regard to Kohlberg's theory, at the time of its introduction, it created great interest, and because his theory was testable and falsifiable, the task of testing the presence of these stages has been taken on by many researchers throughout the world. From others' research, the stages have been questioned extensively, especially in regard to applicability to females and to people from other cultures. Most prominent of these voices was that of Gilligan (1982), who questioned his scale in regard to its lack of inclusion of moral issues that females are more likely to address. It has also been extensively critiqued on questions of its universality across cultures, and there is lack of evidence that the highest level is usually reached even in Western cultures (i.e., Stage 6 is rare—some say almost nonexistent). The narrow focus on only justice issues has also been a criticism. Research, however, has also shown some support for moral development progress across these stages in many cultures, but in some cultures actual reversals at the higher levels have been found. An extensive review of moral development research, however, indicated that although some aspects of the stages have not been upheld, much of the research has shown that in general the theory has relevance in other cultures (Snarey, 1985). Kohlberg did revise the time periods for achieving the sixth stage and also proposed a seventh stage (Kohlberg, 1973).

His view of how moral development should be promoted in education has also received criticism, partly because his model is difficult to implement (see Power, Higgins, & Kohlberg, 1989). However, it also encountered criticism because it promoted children's discussions of moral dilemmas (allowing the possibility of conclusions that did not fit adult approval), rather than directly teaching "character education." Of course, Kohlberg saw this interest in maintaining children's development at the "respect for authority" stage as hindering their progress to postconventional moral stages. Kohlberg's gender role theory has not received as much attention, and there has been only minimal testing of the theory, although potentially this could be still be investigated more thoroughly. Both of his theoretical perspectives are clear and provide economical and simple models; however, their accuracy has been questioned, and predictions based on the models have been difficult to assess. His theories remain, however, as useful bases for the study of moral and gender role issues.

## Gilligan's Morally "Different Voice"

Carol Gilligan (1936–) was a teaching assistant for Erikson and a research assistant for Kohlberg. After doing her own doctoral research on adult women's moral dilemmas, Gilligan called Freud's, Erikson's, and Piaget's explanations of women's sociomoral development into question because of their masculine bias, and she questioned Kohlberg's theory on two grounds (1978, 1982, 1987, 1999). First, because it was developed through interviews with males from middle and higher socioeconomic levels, generalizing the results to females and people from other income strata was questionable. Second, Kohlberg focused on justice—rights and rules—and considered concerns for justice as the goal of the higher stages, whereas in contrast, Gilligan found that women evaluated their moral dilemmas through another dimension of morality—that of caring and preserving relationships. In her study of women who were contemplating abortions, she found evidence that women often showed thinking that Kohlberg would label Stage 2 or 3. Thus, they would be seen as not reaching the higher stages on Kohlberg's hierarchy. She concluded that women are more inclined to see morality as an issue of caring and relationships rather than of justice and rights. She outlined three stages that seemed to describe female moral development: (a) selfish—concern with self, evident in early childhood; (b) social—concern with others, evident in middle childhood/adolescence; and (c) postconventional/principled—concern with self and others in balanced relationship, evident in (some) adult women. She also studied men thinking about enlisting in the Vietnam War and found these male/female differences. She was appointed to the first gender studies position at Harvard and coordinated the Center on Gender and Education at that institution. She is considered a pioneer in gender studies, particularly in the area of moral development of girls.

### Theoretical Influence and Critique.

Gilligan's own position has been controversial because it posits a "difference feminism," which is in opposition to many feminist theorists who emphasize similarities between men and women, not differences. Her methodology has also been criticized, and some later studies that were more rigorously controlled did not find the differences in moral reasoning that she found. That is, they found that males and females were concerned about both justice (i.e., rights) and caring (i.e, responsibilities). Subsequent research has challenged her theory of female moral development, and it is not particularly influential at the present time. She did call important attention to the fact that many male psychologists did not feel it necessary to study female development but merely generalized from their studies with male subjects. Thus, she performed an important role by addressing the disparity in theoretical perspectives on women's development.

## Summary

The areas of sociomoral and gender role development have been of interest to many theorists whose work was done in earlier generations, and their work has been influential for both research and practical application in the latter part of the 20th century. The major theorist to focus on these two areas was Kohlberg, and he drew on Piagetian theory primarily. Although sociomoral and gender role development continue to be areas of study for some researchers and theorists, there is presently not as strong an emphasis on study and theorizing about sociomoral and gender role development as there is on cognitive and language development. Given their importance and their close connection to cognition and language, that is somewhat surprising. The following case raises questions about how behavior might be interpreted if viewed through the eyes of these theorists for whom moral development was of concern.

## Case 8. Problems in the Middle School

Principal Strong has called together some of the team leaders in her school to discuss what she sees a major breakdown in discipline in the school, especially among the eighth-grade boys. Her team consists of the counselor, assistant principal, school psychologist, nurse, and lead teacher. The principal outlines the problems that she has noted and asks for suggestions as to the reasons for the problems and for strategies for solving the problem. She is especially concerned about a group of boys who last year were considered "good" students who excelled in academic work and in helpfulness to the teacher. This group come from traditional homes with two parents, only one of whom works full time, and they are not lacking in material resources. However, teachers are now reporting that these boys often say they have done homework even when it has not been completed, they taunt and tease girls who used to be their friends, and they think it is funny when one of them succeeds in getting away with something that is against the rules. Their "good" behavior is now sporadic—on some days they uphold that image, and on others they seem to flaunt the rules deliberately. When the teachers confront them about missed homework, they say that the teacher demands are not "fair," that the rules are dumb and should be changed, and that their former friends (girls) are "teacher pets." Some of these boys now seem to be making friends with a different group than those they had last year, and unfortunately, these new friends seem to be not very concerned with schoolwork but mainly interested in sports or just "hanging out." Some of the members of this other group have already been identified as possible candidates for the alternative school program. Last year, the school instituted a Character Education Program, and initially it seemed to be working well, but now when the eighth graders are reminded of the approved character traits, they make fun of those traits. The principal thinks the problem is serious because it is now beginning to affect the girls as well, and even those especially "good" girls are starting to laugh at the boys' out-of-bounds antics and join in the laughter when they create incidents in class. Each of the team members holds a different theoretical view of sociomoral and gender role development. The principal is an advocate of Bandura's perspective; the counselor, a proponent of Kohlberg's view; assistant principal, a Freudian; school psychologist, an Eriksonian; the nurse, a Piagetian; and the teacher a believer in Gilligan's ideas.

First, tell how the team members might explain why the children's behaviors have changed and how their explanations fit (or don't fit) with their views of how sociomoral and gender role development occur.

Then, tell where the points of agreement and disagreement about the problem causes might be between the various team members and the principal.

Then, come up with a plan for helping the eighth graders improve their sociomoral development level and gender role understanding that is congruent with the majority of the team members' views.

Principal Strong's school is in an upper-class suburb. If her school were in a low-income city setting, would the team members have similar or different suggestions?

## Readings

L. K. Kohlberg, *Education for Justice: A Modern Statement of the Platonic View*, pp. 361–365.

L. K. Kohlberg, *A Cognitive–Developmental Analysis of Children's Sex-Role Concepts and Attitudes*, pp. 366–368.

## Suggested Readings

Kohlberg, L. K. (1970). Education for justice: A modern statement of the Platonic view. In N. Sizer & T. Sizer (Eds.), *Five lectures on moral education* (pp. 57–60). Cambridge, MA: Harvard University Press.

Kohlberg, L. K. (1966). A cognitive–developmental analysis of children's sex-role concepts and attitudes. In E. E. Maccoby (Ed.), *The development of sex differences* (pp. 82–83, 164–166). New York: Holt, Rinehart, and Winston.

Gilligan, C. (1987). Characteristics of the feminine voice. In a different voice: Women's conceptions of self and morality. *Harvard Educational Review, 47*(4), 481–517. Reprinted in *Stage theories of cognitive and moral development: Criticisms and applications* (pp. 52–88). Reprint No. 13: Cambridge: Harvard Educational Review.

*"Why does __he__ always get to be the boy?"*

# Further Theoretical Perspectives on Sociomoral and Gender Role Development

Although Kohlberg's Piagetian influenced theory of sociomoral development was very prominent in the latter part of the 20th century, other theorists have continued to elaborate on his ideas, and some have constructed models that expand or contradict aspects of his theory. Kohlberg's theory of gender role development has not been the basis for much elaboration; however, other views of gender development, especially those from feminist perspectives, have been proposed. Freudian views of gender role and moral development are less accepted in the present day, although biologically based arguments, especially for gender role development, have continued to wax and wane over the years. As more information is gained from brain research on possible differences in male and female brain development, the potential biological bases of gender role differences are again gaining attention. Both gender role and moral development from social cognitive perspectives (i.e., Bandura) are still considered relevant by many, especially in relation to the media and other societal models of gender and morality extremes that are evident in present-day culture. This chapter discusses two of the theorists who have made thoughtful elaborations and extensions of Piaget's/Kohlberg's moral development theory, William Damon and Elliot Turiel. It also discusses another strand in present sociomoral development: the development of "prosocial behaviors" such as empathy, perspective taking, and moral judgment, as exemplified in the work of Nancy Eisenberg. The theoretical perspectives on gender role development of feminist theorists such as Sandra Bem and recent speculations about neuropsychological and postmodern explanations for gender role differences in development are also presented in this chapter.

## Damon's Moral Child

William Damon (1944–) is presently at Stanford University, where he directs the Center on Adolescence. His theoretical interests have been focused on sociomoral development of children and adolescents, and he agrees with Piaget and Kohlberg that moral demands are universally applicable (1977, 1988). He used Kohlberg's moral dilemma approach in his research, but with dilemmas that were relevant to children's concerns, such as the fair sharing of toys. He extended Piaget's view of moral development by making it less abstract, by elaborating on the peer and adult influence dimensions, and by applying his findings to real-world situations. He does not think sociomoral development is as uniform as Piaget indicated because he believes it is co-constructed (per Vygotsky) and thus may differ in varied social contexts. He strongly believes, with Kohlberg, however, that a just society will foster mature sociomoral development, which he defines as a combination of moral feeling (emotions), moral judgement (reasoning), and moral conduct (behavior). He also includes the caring/responsibility dimension identified by Gilligan.

Damon's view is that children construct sociomoral knowledge along with logical knowledge and that it is also a developmental process; that is, their understanding changes with age as their modes of social functioning advance. He stated, "Morality is a fundamental, natural, and important part of children's lives from the time of their first relationships" (Damon, 1988, p. 1). The indicators of morality he identified include empathy, shame, guilt, distributive justice, respect for rules and authority, and reciprocity. The dilemmas he used to study justice involved asking children to share unequal numbers of toys and deciding how to distribute bracelets of unequal value to other children. To study obedience to authority he used dilemmas that pitted following parental orders with choosing one's own desired actions. Damon suggested that the process of justice development is facilitated mainly by peer relationships, but that of authority development is facilitated mainly by adults. He found that young children already exhibit moral reasoning in situations they understand. That is, they are concerned about issues of morality and are able to begin distinguishing practical modes (i. e., social conventional practices) from moral modes of action, but their conclusions and actions in regard to moral dilemmas may differ from those of adults because of their level of understanding of the social context and issues.

Practical modes focus on realistic consequences (what is likely to happen), but moral modes focus on how justice is best served or how responsibility is best met. At lower levels of social thinking, children often confuse practical concerns with moral concerns. Damon agreed that at early ages right and wrong are more determined by consequences (punishment orientation), but by primary age children determine consequences by referring to the rightness or wrongness of the act (moral realism). As they advance in age, children differentiate more and more the difference between practical and moral orientations. Damon included internal feelings (empathy, guilt, shame), concerns for justice (distributive justice), obedience to authority (respect for rules), and aspects of caring (reciprocity) in his description of the stages of moral growth, as follows.

*Infancy/early childhood:*
- Empathy: reacting to another's feelings with an emotional response that is similar to the other's feelings. Although beginning in infancy, it further develops through the development of the cognitive ability of perspective (role) taking.
- Shame: feeling of embarrassment when one fails to act in accord with perceived behavioral standards. Arises from parental disgust and disappointment; it is other oriented.
- Guilt: feeling blame for distressing others; initially child confuses causality with contiguity of events but begins to see that personal blame is located in actions by the self that result in harm to others.
- Distributive justice: concern for fair allocation of resources and how to decide the criteria (e.g., need, merit) for distribution; behavior evidence is sharing and turn taking; at first this is exhibited playfully and sporadically. At the earliest ages, however, fairness is confused with personal desire; by ages 6 to 7, fairness means giving equally to all without regard for need (equity).
- Respect for rules and authority: learning to follow the social order; begins with socialization by parents (e.g., their questioning of incorrect behavior and explaining justification for rules; this is called "induction"); influenced by family experiences (authoritarian, authoritative, permissive, harmonious). At age 4 personal desires and obedience are not seen as separate, but by ages 5 to 6 children see authority as an independent force that may oppose child desires but that also must be obeyed. During this age period, rules are primarily seen as immutable and ordained.
- Reciprocity: balancing interests in relationships (giving/taking); reciprocity begins in peer interactions; there is an unbalanced reciprocity in parent/child interactions. By about age 7, children see reciprocity as a factor in obedience, however.

*Middle Childhood:*
- Empathy: includes ability to make an objective assessment of the other's needs while putting themselves in the other's place.
- Shame: less directly linked to parental disapproval; even if a mistake is hidden, there is a feeling of embarrassment.
- Guilt: feelings of responsibility for hurting others' feelings; responsibility for effects of one's actions beyond the immediate situation (longer-term consequences).
- Distributive justice: development of sense of obligation to share resources; internal belief in sharing, although criteria for sharing is still not the same as that of adults. By ages 8 to 9, fairness is not just related to equality (giving equally to all) but other considerations such as merit and need begin to be considered (equity).

- Respect for rules and authority: legitimacy of authority recognized—that it is due not only to adults' power but also to their superior knowledge, experience, and caring. By ages 8 to 9, however, the legitimacy of the authority's experience begins to be considered, and pragmatic issues are distinguished from moral issues in regard to obedience. Rules with peers (or presumably, unrespected adults) are seen as changeable if "unfair."
- Reciprocity: this is a very strong element in friendship relationships and is used to maintain such relationships, evident especially in play negotiations. It requires sense of mutual respect. By ages 8 to 9, there is a sense that obedience to authority includes a consensual relationship quality (i.e., agreeing to follow the authority because it is legitimate).

*Late childhood/adolescence*
- Empathy: generalized ability to have concern for people who live in unfortunate circumstances or endure unusual hardship; if there is an empathetic disfunction, antisocial behavior may result.
- Shame: feelings are further generalized; may feel shame if others in one's group do not live up to standards.
- Guilt: having a social conscience that includes "existential guilt" when noticing contrast between one's own happy circumstances and others' misfortunes.
- Distributive justice: use of principles of equality first but also principles of equity (both need and merit) in allocating resources; concern with distributive justice in society as a whole, not just in own situations.
- Respect for rules and authority: authority is seen as derived from consensus that serves the interests of all; authority is legitimate only when it is good for the subordinate as well as the leader; generalized from family and school to societal rules.
- Reciprocity: generalized to others through role-taking ability; can infer collective perspectives; although exchanges with adults may still be unbalanced, they are approaching a more balanced reciprocity; there is reciprocity in both mutual activity and personal intimacy.

Damon not only studied sociomoral development but also discussed how research can inform parents and other adults about ways to foster moral growth (1988). From his research results, he suggested a number of strategies for fostering moral growth in children, such as promoting empathy and sympathy by directly confronting children's actions that are harmful to others.

Although gender role development was not a major focus of Damon's studies, he has been concerned about gender stereotyping related to what behaviors were permissible for boys and girls and found it followed an interesting sequence (1977, 1994). He found in his studies that young children (ages 4 to 5) thought children of both sexes could engage in most activities, whereas early elementary age children (ages 6 to 7) made much clearer divisions of gender-appropriate behaviors. By ages 8 to 9, children again began to move toward a more open view of gender roles. Damon explained this phenomenon as related to their development of social conventional reasoning, which supports Kohlberg's cognitive view of gender role development. Damon also conducted cross-cultural and longitudinal studies focusing on the way self-understanding develops and found there were two dimensions: self-as-subject and self-as-object, each of which progresses from self-focused to social-context-focused (Damon & Hart, 1988).

As director of the Center on Adolescence, Damon has been especially concerned about enhancing adolescent sociomoral development, and he has promoted "youth charters" for schools and communities that are designed to help them recapture their "moral voice" (1997). Although he speaks about the importance of character, his emphasis is different from the "character education" approach that focuses on a "bag of virtues." Rather, it focuses on helping young people take responsibility and become committed to following the moral goals Damon has identified. Although he is interested in furthering children's moral development, he does not believe that moral behavior is "a set of external standards that adults somehow foist upon an unknowing or unwilling child. Such an assumption distorts our view of the very real and intense moral feelings that children experience on their own accord" (Damon, 1988, p. 2). He is concerned that in our present society, young people are not encountering consistent messages about moral issues, and he advises parents to promote moral development in three ways: (a) encouraging responsibility and performance of service to others; (b) providing a caring, honest, and fair home environment; and (c) evaluating the moral meaning of choices that are made.

### Theoretical Influences and Critique

Damon has presented a clear and research-based theoretical perspective that draws on all three dimensions of sociomoral development: emotions, reasoning, and behavior. Thus, it is testable and potentially falsifiable. The stages he outlined appear to simplify and allow for predictions. He also provided some suggested actions based on these predictions. Whether the model will ultimately be judged as accurate and what his long-lasting theoretical influence will be remains to be seen as further testing of the theory is achieved.

## Turiel's Personal Choices, Social Conventions, and Moral Imperatives

Elliot Turiel (1938–) is presently a professor at the University of California—Berkeley, where he studies the development of social judgments and action, moral reasoning, and concepts of authority and rules in school settings. He and his colleagues have also conducted cross-cultural research on these topics. Turiel's ideas were partially derived from those of Piaget in that he believes social knowledge is mentally constructed, but he asserts that social knowledge of morality and of social conventions differ in important ways. He also has drawn on Kohlberg's ideas but differs from Kohlberg in that he sees moral development as having both justice and caring elements. Some aspects of his theoretical work are also congruent with those of Damon. However, along with colleague Larry Nucci (Turiel, 1983; Nucci & Turiel, 2000), he has been especially interested in gaining in-depth understanding of the knowledge children have of distinctions between personal choices, social conventions, and moral reasoning. He describes moral demands as categorically obligatory requirements for action, regardless of social consensus. They are universally applicable and impersonal. These moral demands can be judged right or wrong without the instruction of others; that is, they develop as children construct knowledge. In contrast, social conventions (what Damon calls practical rules) are arbitrary and related to social organizations. Their purpose is to coordinate the stable interactions of the members of a social system. Social conventions, therefore, are contingent on group membership (i.e., social contexts). Personal choices are preferences of individuals that do not affect morality or convention.

Turiel has clearly described the differences among these three categories (1983). Personal choices are those that have no moral or social consequences; that is, they are open to individual preferences. For example, deciding whether you should buy tomatoes and eggs instead of carrots and milk would be a personal choice, with no social or moral consequences. However, if you belong to a strict vegan club, you should decide not to buy eggs or milk, and if you belong to an organic growers' organization, you should think it wrong to select non–organically grown tomatoes or carrots. These decisions would be based on social conventions that must be followed if you wish to maintain your group membership. Stealing tomatoes, carrots, eggs, or milk rather than buying them, however, would be violating a moral demand. A moral imperative (e.g., not stealing medicine) may be overridden by another moral demand (e.g., saving a life); however, it may not be overridden by a social convention. For example, a social convention for Mafia members might be that members should support the organization goals, but if members are asked to sell stolen or illegal drugs to support the organization, there would be a conflict between a social convention and a moral imperative. This type of conflict is reminiscent of Bandura's (1997) concerns about effects of peer group membership on behaviors of adolescents, which may result in their meeting the social conventions of their group (or gang) by breaking the law or harming others, an act with moral consequences.

According to Turiel, because social conventions are contingent on group membership, they are validated by consensus and are relative to the social context; thus, they can be altered by consensus or by a general change in usage (1978). Social conventions can be considered constitutive systems. They have rules that create or define behavior in particular situations. That is, they are explicit statements about behavior. One of the most likely places to see these in operation with children are in games, because these are a type of constitutive system. The school classroom is another such situation, and many of the rules in the classroom are social conventions rather than moral rules. For example, standing in line without talking may be a social convention of one classroom but not required in another classroom. Social conventions coordinate the stable interactions of those in a particular social system and thus can be changed if the system changes. According to Turiel, children are able to distinguish social conventions from moral considerations at an early age.

Turiel studied children's knowledge of these distinctions by observing children's playground interactions and noting when they discussed transgressions of social conventional and moral rules (1978, 1983). He found that children rarely initiated discussion with peers about social transgressions but they often discussed moral transgression, pointing out the intrinsic consequences. For example, if a child hurt another child, other children would point this out. On the other hand, if a child didn't follow a rule of a game, they were less likely to point it out, and when they did, they would discuss the organizational features rather than the moral consequences. Interestingly, the researchers found that teachers responded almost equally to social conventional and moral transgressions. Most discussions of social transgressions were between teacher and child, although peers also responded to some of these when they were related to peer social interactions. In all contexts studied, however, children responded negatively to transgressions of moral events.

Turiel also gave children examples of transgressions and asked them whether certain transgressions would always be wrong, or if the rule were changed, whether the particular action would then be approved. He presented transgression statements either of a social convention or of a moral demand. For example, one transgression might have been about not following playground rules set by the teacher, such as no writing with chalk on the blacktop part of the playground, and another might have been about an issue of fairness or the hurting of another child. In the social transgression dilemmas, most children agreed that the action would be acceptable if there were no rule prohibiting it, but for the moral transgressions, they asserted that the action would be wrong even if there was no stated rule against that action. Turiel's overall conclusion was that children distinguish moral rules (those that protect human rights and welfare) from social conventions (arbitrary customs such as manners, social rituals, behavior rules) by early elementary age, and they become increasingly sophisticated in distinguishing the difference. They also understand that personal choices may be made without violating social or moral rules. They demonstrate concerns about distributive justice violations as they grow older. By age 5, equality is a concern; by age 6, merit becomes a factor in determining justice; and by age 8, they begin to consider the good of the individual (benevolence). These moral concerns become evident in their strong beliefs that there should be fair distribution of resources, such as sharing and giving fair portions. Table 9.1 shows the age levels when personal, social, and moral actions are judged as acceptable/unacceptable.

Turiel has found that adults often insist on children's conformity to social conventional rules as strongly as they enforce moral rules. Although he does not discuss this in detail, the implication may be that adults do not always help children make the distinctions between universal moral imperatives and the social conventions of their particular societies. In his studies of other cultures, Turiel has found that cultural and religious practices can cause variation in what is considered a moral rule or a social convention. Also, at various historical periods, some social conventions have been treated as though they were moral rules. In a recent book, *The Culture of Morality*, Turiel examines how the realms of personal choice, social convention systems, and universal moral judgements are related (2002). From his work studying various cultures, he concludes that people in lesser positions of power in a social hierarchy (e.g., women, minorities) may work to subvert the social conventions of their society. That is, if social conventions result in unfair treatment of some social groups, they may see those conventions as morally wrong and thus be inclined to subvert these conventions. An example would be if, in a particular culture, women are not allowed to leave an abusive relationship, women might begin to see this convention as transgressing a moral imperative, and they might form a group that would reframe this issue in terms of a violation of human rights. Similarly, a member of a minority group who is enslaved may find it morally correct to escape because the social convention of property rights in that society is not as important as human freedom from slavery.

**Table 9.1**  Personal Choice, Social Convention, and Moral Rules

Number of subjects out of 16 at each grade level sorting actions as "Should be person's business"

| | Grade | | | | |
|---|---|---|---|---|---|
| **Action** | **2** | **5** | **8** | **11** | **College** |
| **Moral** | | | | | |
| Lying[a] | 0 | 0 | — | — | — |
| Stealing | 0 | 0 | 0 | 0 | 0 |
| Hitting | 0 | 0 | 0 | 0 | 0 |
| Selfishness | 0 | 0 | 0 | 0 | 0 |
| Athlete throwing game[b] | — | — | 0 | 0 | 0 |
| Damaging borrowed property[b] | — | — | 0 | 0 | 0 |
| **Social convention** | | | | | |
| Chewing gum in class[a] | 0 | 0 | — | — | — |
| Addressing teacher by first name | 0 | 0 | 0 | 0 | 0 |
| Boy entering girls' bathroom | 0 | 1 | 2 | 3 | 0 |
| Eating lunch with fingers | 5 | 5 | 8 | 8 | 9 |
| Talking without raising hand[b] | — | — | 0 | 0 | 0 |
| Eating in class[b] | — | — | 0 | 0 | 0 |
| **Personal** | | | | | |
| Watching TV on a sunny day[a] | 13 | 16 | — | — | — |
| Keeping correspondence private | 12 | 12 | 13 | 13 | 13 |
| Interacting with forbidden friend | 12 | 13 | 13 | 13 | 13 |
| Boy wearing long hair | 13 | 12 | 15 | 15 | 13 |
| Smoking at home[b] | — | — | 12 | 12 | 12 |
| Refusing to join recreation group[b] | — | — | 12 | 12 | 13 |

*Note:* Eight subjects would be expected to sort an action as "should be person's business" by chance; $p < .05$ or greater when twelve or more subjects sort an action as "should be person's business" using $\chi^2$ goodness-of-fit test.

[a]Actions sorted by subjects in grades 2 and 5 but not grades 8, 11, or college.

[b]Actions sorted by subjects in grades 8, 11, and college, but not grades 2 or 5.

*Source:* Reprinted from *Personal Choice, Social Convention and Moral Rules* from *The Development of Social Knowledge: Morality and Convention,* Tables 4.2, 4.3. Reprinted with the permission of Cambridge University Press.

*(continued)*

**Table 9.1** (*continued*)

Dimensions of social judgments
Number of subjects out of 16 at each grade level sorting actions as "Wrong even in absence of rule"

| Action | Grade | | | | |
| --- | --- | --- | --- | --- | --- |
| | **2** | **5** | **8** | **11** | **College** |
| **Moral** | | | | | |
| Lying[a] | 16 | .16 | — | — | — |
| Stealing | 16 | 15 | 15 | 16 | 16 |
| Hitting | 16 | 16 | 16 | 15 | 16 |
| Selfishness | 16 | 15 | 15 | 14 | 16 |
| Athlete throwing game[b] | — | — | 16 | 15 | 16 |
| Damaging borrowed property[b] | — | — | 16 | 16 | 16 |
| **Social convention** | | | | | |
| Chewing gum in class[a] | 2 | 0 | — | — | — |
| Addressing teacher by first name | 2 | 0 | 0 | 0 | 0 |
| Boy entering girls' bathroom | −1 | 2 | 1 | 0 | 0 |
| Eating lunch with fingers | 0 | 0 | 0 | 0 | 0 |
| Eating in class[b] | — | — | 1 | 1 | 0 |
| Talking without raising hand[b] | — | — | 2 | 1 | 0 |
| **Personal** | | | | | |
| Watching TV on a sunny day[a] | 1 | 0 | — | — | — |
| Keeping correspondence private | 1 | 0 | 0 | 0 | 0 |
| Interacting with forbidden friend | 0 | 0 | 0 | 0 | 0 |
| Boy wearing long hair | 0 | 0 | 0 | 0 | 0 |
| Smoking at home[b] | — | — | 0 | 0 | 0 |
| Refusing to join recreation group[b] | — | — | 0 | 0 | 0 |

*Note:* Eight subjects would be expected to sort an action as "wrong even in absence of rule" by chance; $p < .01$ or greater when fourteen or more subjects sort an action as "wrong even in absence of rule" using $\chi^2$ goodness of fit test.

[a]Actions sorted by subjects in grades 2 and 5, but not grades 8, 11, or college.

[b]Actions sorted by subjects in grades 8, 11, and college, but not grades 2 or 5.

On a less-serious level, Turiel's perspective may also help explain conflicts between parents and children during adolescence, when issues of morality are of great importance to youth. Adolescents may rebel over what they regard as social conventional demands because they frame them as morally wrong. For example, they may believe that their right to free expression (a moral issue) supersedes a "politeness to guests" social convention. Although the complex analysis of sociomoral development proposed by Turiel may need further explication, it does serve to point out how contextual and sociohistorical factors may influence even the most basic of human knowledge constructions—sociomoral development. Further study of Kohlberg's stages of moral development in juxtaposition with study of the social conventions of a society might shed light on how these may influence expressions of higher levels of the stages outlined by Kohlberg.

### Theoretical Influence and Critique

Turiel and his colleagues have presented some interesting theoretical perspectives on sociomoral issues, which are testable and falsifiable. Although not a fully formed theory, this perspective serves to make many aspects of sociomoral behavior seem more understandable, and it provides a framework for studying the development of these three constructs (personal choice, social convention, moral imperative) from early childhood to adulthood. The perspective provides an economical model that seems intuitively accurate and internally consistent on the surface. However, clarification of the distinctions among these three levels, especially in relation to cultural constraints, is in need of intensive study. It does lend itself to some predictions, however, and might make for clearer understanding of the reasoning and behavior of adolescents and disadvantaged groups in particular.

## Eisenberg's Theoretical Perspective on Prosocial Behavior

In contrast to the studies of moral development, which arise primarily from a rationalist world view, the study of prosocial behavior addresses issues of moral development from an empiricist perspective. In an early book by Eisenberg and her mentor (Mussen & Eisenberg-Berg, 1977), they state that at that time (the 1970s) the study of prosocial behavior was just beginning. Prosocial behavior is defined as "voluntary behavior intended to benefit another" (Eisenberg, et al., 2002, p. 1360; Eisenberg, 1986); thus, it is more closely related to the "caring" dimension of moral development than the "justice" dimension. Since that time, Eisenberg and others have studied this developmental domain in great detail, in particular focusing on the development of "caring" behaviors such as empathy (ability to experience another person's distress and/or needs), sympathy (ability to act to assist the distressed person), and perspective taking (ability to cognitively take the role of the other or understand another's situation). Although these researchers saw the theories of Piaget and Kohlberg as providing important information about children's moral reasoning, they thought that these theories dealt with only a part of the question because "their data base consists primarily of children's verbalizations" (Mussen & Eisenberg-Berg, 1977, p. 120). Moreover, they did not believe that these theories tapped "the thoughts, concepts, and judgments about issues such as personal sacrifice and conflicts between one's own needs and those of others" (p. 120). For example, a dilemma that requires one to risk one's self to protect someone else is of a different order that the dilemmas that were presented in these earlier studies. Using a different set of dilemmas, they proposed a set of stages of prosocial development, as follows.

> *Stage 1:* Two types of reasoning (uncorrelated) occur (begins about first grade).
> * Holistic, pragmatic, in which "right" behavior is meeting own needs. Reasons for behavior are help to self, expectations of reciprocity, or helping a friend.

- Needs of others, in which expressions of concern for others' needs are made even if they conflict with own (but no action is taken by child).

*Stage 2:* Approval, interpersonal, stereotyped orientation, in which consideration of others' approval or acceptance defines "good" or "bad" behavior (begins about second grade).

*Stage 3:* Empathetic orientation, in which there is evidence of sympathy, role taking, and guilt or pleasure as consequence of one's own actions (begins about fourth to sixth grade; strongly used by high school age).

*Stage 4:* Transitional: Justifications for helping are weakly stated in terms of values and responsibilities or of rights and justice (begins in adolescence).

*Stage 5:* Strongly internalized: Justifications for helping strongly stated in terms of values and responsibilities or of rights and justice; for example, living up to one's values regarding compassion for the suffering of others (adult stage).

Comparisons of the age levels of prosocial development with the stages of moral reasoning stated by Kohlberg show that prosocial development seems to occur earlier than do values based on justice. A number of studies do show there are correlations between the level of moral judgment and prosocial behaviors (Mussen & Eisenberg-Berg, 1977). However, because empathy requires the ability to discriminate and label the affective states of others, assume the perspective and role of others, and be responsive emotionally to others (Feschbach, 1974), it requires a loss of egocentrism, and thus it increases greatly from about ages 5 to 8, when egocentrism declines. The types of social situations that children who show early empathy have probably experienced include having nurturant parents who are good prosocial models, use reasoning in discipline, and encourage children to accept responsibility. Children more advanced in prosocial behaviors tend to be ones who are self-confident and active and somewhat advanced in moral reasoning, role-taking, and empathy (Mussen & Eisenberg-Berg, 1977).

After charting the basics of prosocial development, Eisenberg went on to study many aspects of prosocial development, and this topic became widely studied by others. One of the findings from many studies is that there are wide individual differences in prosocial behaviors, depending on the situations and settings (e.g., Davis, 1994). Eisenberg has been especially interested in the long-term effects of such development to determine if there is also stability in prosocial behavior. She and colleagues have completed a longitudinal study of individuals from ages 4–5 to adulthood to determine how consistently prosocial dispositions remain (Eisenberg et al., 2001, 2002.) The children's sharing, helping, and comfort offering behaviors in preschool were observed, their donating and helping behaviors were recorded at elementary age, their self-reports of behaviors and cognitions were collected throughout childhood and adolescence, and ratings of prosocial behaviors were obtained from their mothers and friends. The children's spontaneous sharing at preschool age was correlated with later measures of prosocial behavior. The correlation was strongest with measures of sympathy rather than with measures of their personal distress at others' difficulties. Thus, the best predictor of adult sympathy behaviors (actually acting to help someone) appears to be young children's initiation of sharing behaviors with other children. (A behavior preschool teachers spend much effort to encourage!) Eisenberg has concluded that there seems to be a "prosocial personality disposition" that surfaces at an early age, and it is relatively consistent across time. The reasons for this may be due to temperament factors, genetics, and socialization influences. However, presently the results support the view that there are individual differences in prosocial dispositions that appear to be somewhat stable. It is possible that these individual differences become more evident at later ages. Consequently, "As individuals become capable of understanding higher level moral principles and develop sophisticated perspective-taking abilities and a coherent set of values and goals, it is reasonable to expect greater consistency in prosocial responding" (Eisenberg et al., 1999, p. 1370).

### Theoretical Influence and Critique

The study of the prosocial (caring aspect) of moral development has provided an important dimension to the studies of moral development that were undertaken by theorists who were primarily interested in the justice dimension of moral development. Eisenberg's theoretical perspective remains highly testable and falsifiable, and it has generated a great deal of research in recent years. This perspective does not appear to be in competition with that of those who have focused on the justice dimension of moral development; indeed, it offers an enrichment that supports the concerns of Gilligan and others who see the caring dimension of moral development as equally important to the justice dimension. This theoretical perspective needs much more elaboration to be a fully formed theory; however, Eisenberg's longitudinal work is attempting to evaluate its ability to predict later development. As she acknowledged, her developmental hypothesis "merits further attention" (Eisenberg et al., 1999, p. 1370.)

## Theories of Gender Role Development

During the latter part of the 20th century, theories of gender role development were prominent, primarily due to perspectives from feminist theory, which countered long-established "knowledge" about male/female differences. This discussion presents some of the major recent perspectives on gender role development.

### Bem's Gender Schema Theory of Gender Role Development

Although numerous feminist scholars have addressed the cultural and sociohistorical factors that influence gender role development, one of the most influential is Sandra Lipsitz Bem (1944–), who is presently a professor at Cornell University. Bem's major contribution has been in the development of gender schema theory, which grew from her research on psychological androgyny (1976). At the time she began her work, healthy gender role development was seen to be in the adoption of stereotypic behaviors and attitudes that were culturally consistent with one's sex. For example, males were expected to see themselves as strong, independent, and assertive, whereas females were expected to see themselves as weak, dependent, and nurturant. Psychological tests of masculinity and femininity (primarily influenced by Freudian theory) were conceptualized with these two categories as opposites; that is, the tests of gender roles had each set of characteristics as opposite poles of the same scale. Because of this artifact of the tests, it was impossible to score high on both masculine and feminine stereotypic characteristics. Bem, however, believed that many men and women had characteristics of psychological androgyny; that is, they exhibited traits that were judged to be characteristic of both sexes. Bem believed that for healthy functioning in contemporary Western society, having some measure of both sets of traits would be more adaptive. Thus, an androgynous individual would have the best psychological adjustment and flexibility.

Because there were no tests measuring androgyny, Bem devised a new test, The Bem Sex Role Inventory (BSRI), which contains 60 traits—20 stereotypically feminine, 20 sterotypically masculine, and 20 neutral (Bem, 1981b). When the test is scored, an individual can be rated as sex-typed (women feminine; men masculine), sex-reversed (women masculine; men feminine), androgynous (high on both sets of traits), or undifferentiated (low on both.) Bem conducted many studies based on her test results, finding that sex-typed individuals were very restricted in performing non-sex-typed activities, even if they could make money doing so, and that androgynous individuals were most flexible in behavior and thought and thus more adaptive in a range of situations. She believed that psychological androgyny was the healthiest representation of gender role for people of both sexes.

As her theory evolved, however, she reevaluated the psychological androgyny concept, which seemed to reinforce the idea that gender roles were innate, and she felt that even those who incorporated both sets of stereotypes actually were supporting the use of these cultural stereotypes. Thus she decided that gender should not be used as an organizing category at all, beyond the physical description of sex characteristics. Gender schema theory (Bem, 1981a) draws on both Bandura's social cognitive theory and Kohlberg's cognitive theory of gender role development. Bem believes that, in line with Bandura's view, much gender role learning is gained through observing models and from reinforcement and punishment for behaviors judged inappropriate according to stereotypic gender role models. She agrees with Bandura that children actively use that information to organize cognitively their understanding of gender roles and that his constructs of social cognition—attention, retention, performance ability, and motivation—play a part. She also agrees with Kohlberg's view that children categorize themselves (gender identity and constancy) and then recognize behaviors that seem to fit with that category, shunning behaviors that do not fit their gender category. However, she questions why gender has been such a central organizing principle when many other categories could be used to organize behavior.

Because social forces make gender such a prime organizing category, children come to assess attributes differently for each gender, and as they get older, the categories become more rigid. For example, young children may see both sexes as "strong" but at a later age, they apply this characteristic only to boys, even though there is much contradictory evidence. Bem believes that because gender schema theory sees gender roles as learned and dynamically constructed, there is a possibility for changing constructions of gender to be more androgynous. In a more recent study using her BSRI scale, she has investigated the difference between gender schematic and gender aschematic individuals, noting that gender schematic individuals rely on gender schema rather than life experience in determining whether certain actions or characteristics can be judged as attributable to those of the other sex (Bem, 1993). Thus, they create self-fulfilling gender role stereotypes. She advocates efforts to eliminate the cultural associations with male and female gender roles to enable greater individual freedom of expression. The question remains, however, as to why gender is such a powerfully reinforced cultural factor. Other feminist theories have offered a "power and dominance" theory to explain that condition.

## Other Feminist Theoretical Explanations for Gender as an Organizing Social Category

A number of feminist theorists have addressed the question of why gender has remained such a strong organizing category, and they explain it as a function of the socially determined power and dominance position of males, which requires subordination of females to maintain its social power base (Birns & Sternglanz, 1983). This perspective explains why most fathers strongly insist that their sons and daughters exhibit stereotypical gender role behavior in play. It also explains why male peer pressure for conformity to male play stereotypes begins with very young boys (Fagot, 1984). That is, the higher-status group (male) wants to remain higher status and if the lower-status group (female) is allowed to exhibit the same behaviors and characteristics, this will result in a lowering of the higher-status groups' condition. This theory makes sense of the phenomena often seen when males leave a profession if too many females enter it, and boys no longer want to play games that girls begin to play also.

Huston (1983) also addressed family contextual/sociohistorical factors that influence gender role development. She predicted that as men become greater caregivers of young children, the explanations Freud gave of how gender role and moral development occurs differentially in males and females and the views of children about appropriate roles for males and females may also change. For example, when males are the caregivers and females are the out-of-home workers, both sexes may then be seen as powerful in similar ways. Because this would make males more androgynous as well as females being androgynous, young children would have less-differentiated ideas of where power is derived, and perhaps the stereotypical ideas connected to gender would be modulated.

Although the *U.S. Bureau of Labor Statistics 2003 American Time Use Survey* indicated that in homes with two working parents, the mother still performed the vast majority of child-care tasks, a recent study of at-home fathers showed that in these homes both parents play a strong role in child care and that attachment to both parents is strong (Frank, 2005). At-home fathers tended to be somewhat older than at-home mothers and often had some paid work they performed from home. The study suggests that "the at-home-dad family model may serve as the catalyst that moves society beyond some gender-role stereotypes and may play a role in the future of the family as an institution" (Tucker, 2005, p. 13). However, the number of male primary caregivers is still so small that their effect on gender role development is as yet unclear. Recently, however, another developmental issue related to the androgyny of gender roles is receiving increased attention—that of girls who exhibit aggression (Putallaz & Bierman, 2004). Typical views have been that males are "naturally" aggressive, and thus, evidence of female aggression does not meet stereotypic views of gender role development. Eleanor Maccoby, in a new book, looks at female aggression in the context of gender development (2004).

Maccoby, the author of an early exhaustive review of gender role research that countered many stereotypic views of male and female differences (Maccoby & Jacklin, 1975) has also recently addressed the issue of parent/child gender dynamics (Maccoby, 2003). She believes that both child genetic differences and parental stereotypic treatment of each gender are factors in gender role development and suggests that the most promising present approach is in studying this reciprocity. She states, ". . . I want to urge that we do not let ourselves be drawn toward any assumption that when such child effects are strong, parent effects must be weak. Parental behavior is determined by many things other than the child's evocative behavior." (pp. 202–203).

## Brain Development Research as a Theoretical Base for Gender Role Differences

As more information about brain development is being gained from fMRI and other brain scan methods, male and female differences in brain structures and functions are being noted. For example, the role of sex hormones in initial brain development and in the changes in brain structure at puberty are both being investigated by researchers (Achiron, Lipsitz, & Achiron, 2001; Rapaport et al., 1999). Sex differences in the electrical activity of children's brains have been found (Hanlon, Thatcher, & Cline, 1999), and differences in structure in adult brains have been examined (Good, et al., 2001). Functional gender differences (which part of the brain is engaged in language or spatial problem solving) have also been discovered in a number of studies (Phillips, Lowe, Lurita, Dmidizie, & Matthews 2001; Gron, Wunderlich, Spitzer, Tomczak, & Riepe 2000).

As an example of the types of research that are being done, which may influence gender role theory, Baron-Cohen (2003, 2005) discussed findings using brain research methods that indicate male and female brains differ primarily in regard to brain areas activated for "empathy" and for "systemizing." He stated that about 60% of men have "male brains" (systemizing) and 20% have "female brains" (emphathizing). In contrast, 40% of women have "female brains," whereas 20% have "male brains." The other 20% of men and 40% of women have "balanced brains." His work with autistic children led him to believe that they have extreme versions of "male brains." Whether these types of studies will result in firm evidence of male/female brain differences that really affect their gender role identity or behavior is presently unclear; this recent reported evidence of minor or major brain function/structure differences is in need of much further study. However, as evidence of brain differences is clarified, another look at the influence of biological as compared to environmental influences on gender roles will need to be incorporated into theories of development.

### Biological and Environmental Influences on Sexual Orientation and Gender Role Identity

An even more controversial theoretical area is related to how males and females develop their heterosexual, homosexual, or bisexual orientations and how these orientations relate to gender role stereotypic or nonstereotypic identity. Early theories saw nonheterosexual orientations as not "normal," and both psycho-analytic and behaviorist theory recommended treatment to cause a change in ori-entation, which usually was not successful. Research on biological aspects (e.g., genetics, hormones, brain differences) using twin/sibling and male/female com-parisons have indicated that some proportion of orientation may be related to bi-ological factors. However, because these studies have also shown mixed results, a sociobiolgical interactionist theoretical model is now gaining prevalence (Kauth & Kalichman, 1995). These authors state, "Like language, sexual orientation may be a characteristic with a wide biologic range of potentiality" (p. 95). Because so-ciety has had a heterosexual "gender role bias," however, social pressures to con-form to gender role stereotypes to appear heterosexual exist. That is, people often believe that if children conform to clear gender role behaviors (i.e., not showing androgynous behaviors), they are clearly heterosexual. Conversely, they may think that if children have behaviors stereotypically identified as characteristic of the "other" sex, they may not be heterosexual. According to Hardy, ". . . little re-search has been conducted to evaluate the validity of these beliefs" (1995, p. 435). She further stated, "The interplay of gender role development and sexual orien-tation is complex. The limited data suggest several hypotheses that merit further empirical study" (p. 436). Until such study is conducted, the interaction between development of gender role identity and sexual orientation remains unclear, and thus a theory that can provide an accurate model of this development is presently unavailable.

### Theoretical Influence and Critique

The many different theoretical perspectives on gender role development are evi-dence of the controversy that still surrounds this developmental domain. Earlier theories were criticized on the basis that their emphasis on biological factors sup-ported gender role inequalities or made gender role behaviors fixed and narrow. Theories that arose during the late 20th century provided a sociohistorical per-spective that stressed the cognitive, environmental, and cultural forces involved in gender role development. At the present time, there is again a stronger biologi-cal component being hypothesized. Because of the complexity of the issues and the lack of empirically based experimental designs, the testability and falsifiability of these theories is difficult to assess. It is a question whether an economical theory can also appear to be accurate and whether a model can be found that can predict gender role development outcomes because of the heavy sociohistorical influences on such development. Gender role development appears to be an area in which the "situated" factors of culture and historical time period create many variations of expression. However, an internally consistent approach that combines aspects of various theoretical perspectives may be conceptualized in the future, and this could make an important contribution to theory.

## Developmental Trends in Sociomoral and Gender Role Development and Themes Useful for Professional Practice

From the many studies of cognition and language development, a set of commonly accepted timelines for the "range of normality" in development of these domains have been identified. Table 9.2 shows these "typical" developmental achievements. Also, although not all the constructs of the theories discussed in chapters 6 and 7 have been validated by extensive evidence, a few general themes can be derived from this set of theories that may be useful for practice. These are provided in Box 9.1.

**Table 9.2**  Trends in Socio-moral and Gender Role Development (Ages Are Approximate)

| | |
|---|---|
| Birth To Age 3 | -Few differences between males and females at birth beyond anatomical differences |
| | -Essentially a-moral initially, governed only by own internal needs |
| | -Initial evidence of empathy by age 12–18 mo. |
| | -May develop a preference for "boy"or "girl" toys at age 1–2 before gender identity established (may be influenced partially by parental toy provision or interactions) |
| | -Basic gender identity established by age 2–3 |
| | -Same gender play partners reinforced by peers by age 3–4 |
| | -Initial obedience to moral or social convention requirements based on fear of punishment or expectation of rewards |
| | -Shame and guilt for moral/convention transgressions by age 3 |
| | -Imitation of moral/convention behavior by age 3 |
| Ages 3–6 | -Judgments of good and bad behavior based on consequences not intentions |
| | -Use of moral language terms (good, bad) |
| | -Gender constancy established by age 4–5 |
| | -Rivalry with same-sex parent and attachment to opposite-sex parent common in this age period (may affect guilt/shame/conscience) |
| | -Acceptance of stereotypical gender role behaviors and preferences common and reinforced by peers and adults |
| | -Games with rules in play show initial concerns with fairness and empathy |
| | -Distinctions between moral rules and social conventional rules begins |

**Table 9.2** (*continued*)

| | |
|---|---|
| Ages 6–12 | -Moral reasoning based primarily on reciprocity and retaliation |
| | -Gradual change from belief in rules from authorities as unchangeable to understanding of possibility of changing an "unfair" rule by age 12 |
| | -Gradual change from obedience to blanket authority to obedience to expert authority by age 12 |
| | -Clearer distinction between moral and social conventional rules |
| | -Cognitive scheme for gender identity well established |
| | -Differentiation in boys' and girls' behaviors and academic abilities becomes greater (debate as to reasons–biological or social constraints) |
| Ages 12–20 | -Concern for maintaining good relationships and gain approval from others |
| | -Consideration of intentions as well as consequences in judging actions |
| | -Awareness that rules are based on consensus and can be modified by negotiation |
| | -Generally obeys expert authority and social conventions |
| | -Sees moral role as extending outside family and friends |
| | -Puberty changes promote identification with own gender, occurs at ages 9–15, so great variation in this awareness |
| | -Increased conformity to gender role stereotype pressures; major conflicts for non-stereotypic individuals |
| | -Different views of sex/love connections between males and females |
| | -Risk-taking behaviors may increase because moral/social conventional consequences not considered |
| | -May be interest in promoting general social welfare |
| | -Understanding that authority may be unjust; laws exist for social good and may be changed if unjust |
| Ages 20–40 | -Higher levels of moral reasoning may develop (dependent on culture and experiences) |
| | -Concern for promoting moral development and social conventional behavior of younger generation |
| | -Typical male assertiveness and task orientation; female compliance and personal orientation occurs; however, greater variation in gender role identity, assertiveness, task roles, empathy, and other characteristics in different cultural contexts |
| Ages 40–60 | -Moral development continues and often involves rethinking of earlier beliefs and values |
| | -Concern for following personal conscience rather than rules of society may develop |
| | -May make sacrifices to protect moral rightness |
| | -Concern for universal moral principles, not social conventions may be greater |
| | -Females may gain assertiveness and self-confidence; men may gain empathy and other-awareness |
| Ages 60–80 | -Moral development may continue or may be static |
| | -Gender role identity development may change or may be static |
| Ages 80–100 | -May be an integration of moral and identity issues but little is known about this period of life |

## Box 9.1
## Theoretically-Derived Themes That May Be Useful For Professional Practice

- Since socio-moral development includes elements of social, emotional, and cognitive processes, children typically progress through a number of stages or levels. However, many different levels of socio-moral reasoning may be used by the same individuals, depending on their experience and cultural options.
- While the development of higher levels of moral reasoning have usually focused on a "justice" perspective, there is also socio-moral development of a "caring" perspective; although often mentioned in regard to females, both perspectives are evident in the socio- moral development of both genders.
- Play with peers is one of the important ways that children begin to understand moral issues of justice such as fairness of rules. Play with peers also promotes the caring perspective (empathy, sympathy) and can be evident in young children's sharing behaviors.
- Even at early ages, children begin to distinguish between personal choice, social conventions, and moral reasoning and are aware that while the moral issues are universal and immutable; social conventions may change as the norms of the social group change.
- Individuals who lack acceptance into a particular social culture may not accept conformity to the social conventions of that culture, and may even see these conventions as morally unacceptable.
- Gender role development has social, emotional, and cognitive components, and the language of gender is pervasive as an influence on how children see their gender role.
- Cultures vary greatly as to what is permissible in gender role development. While from a developmental perspective, human adaptability and richness of life experience is fostered by both males and females having a wide range of potential behaviors, the value of this perspective varies by culture.
- Neuroscience indicators of brain differences at present do not necessarily imply male/female strengths or weaknesses. They are evidence of the dynamic interaction between biological and environmental forces, however, and eventually may be an explanatory factor in investigation of gender role identity and sexual orientation.

## Summary

Sociomoral and gender role development continue to be of great interest to theorists and probably will continue to be so in the future. In particular, the work of Piaget and Kohlberg has been useful for later theorists such as Damon and Turiel, who have expanded on the developmental aspects of sociomoral development. The caring or prosocial aspects of moral development identified by Gilligan have also been pursued by theorists such as Eisenberg. Recent theoretical views of gender role development have also been affected by earlier theorists, in particular in opposition to tenets of those theorists (e.g., Freud, Erikson) but also in expansion of cognitive aspects (e.g., Kohlberg). The various trends discussed in this chapter address both the questions and the answers concerning these areas of development. As cross-cultural study continues to expand, there may be much more consideration of the messages provided in various cultural contexts that may influence development in these areas and more attention to cohort differences. The following case provides a venue for discussion of theoretical perspectives on sociomoral and gender role development within a contextual/sociohistorical frame.

## Case 9. The Player Family and the Mulah Family

The Player family consists of two boys, Joe (age 10) and George (age 13), and one girl, Linda (age 8). Dad has always been a sports lover, and he has spent a lot of time playing and working with the boys on their sports skills. George has loved sports and is now on the middle school basketball team. Joe doesn't seem to be very interested in sports, and he really prefers playing computer games and being with his friend doing science experiments. He also likes to bake cakes with his mom. Sometimes dad jokes that Linda should have been a boy because she has always been very physically active and sports minded. She begged to be on the Little League Tot squad, is a great swimmer, and now is starting to want to play basketball. Linda also enjoys pretend play and is a great reader, and these are both skills that her parents appreciate. Linda's mom has also encouraged her to help more around the house. Lately Joe has been saying that the other kids tease him when he doesn't want to play ball, and Linda complains that her teacher praises the quiet girls and tells her that she should act more "ladylike." All the children are doing well academically in school at this time, but George seems to be devoting less of his energy toward schoolwork and more toward his peers on the basketball team. Linda's favorite subject is math, and Joe's favorite subject is language arts, especially writing.

The Mulah family has children the same age as those in the Player family: Amahl is 10, Abdul is 12, and Dilek is 8. The boys in this family are on the same sports teams as the Player boys, and their dad is also very active in encouraging their sports development. Amahl, however, is not as good a player as most of the boys on the team, but his father expects him to continue, and he also expects both boys to do very well in their school subjects. All three children are required to be respectful to adults, including teachers. Dilek was a very physically active young child, but now she prefers reading and art activities to outdoor play. She is being taught many home skills by her mother, and she is very conscious of her appearance because modesty is encouraged by her parents. At the parent conference, which was attended by Dilek's father, the teacher indicated that she is doing well academically, especially in math, but that she was very quiet in class. Her father was pleased with the report. Dilek engages in pretend play at home primarily with a girl who lives next door; she does not range far from her home and neighborhood. When he has free time, Amahl spends it writing on the computer or playing video games, whereas Abdul ranges throughout the neighborhood with a group of his friends, usually playing various ball games.

What would Kohlberg and/or Gilligan say is going on cognitively in regard to the children's gender identity?

What would Bem say about the factors that are advancing (or not advancing) the androgynous development of these children? How would she judge Linda's and Dilek's play? All four boys' peer interactions? The teacher's comments about the children? Would the other theorists who have different views of the process of gender role development agree with Bem?

How would Damon describe each of these children's development in regard to empathy, shame, guilt, distributive justice, respect for rules/authority, and reciprocity? Would the same-age children be likely to be at the same or different stages?

How would Turiel judge the demands on these children in regard to their options for personal choices, social convention requirements, and moral rule following? Might he see cultural differences in what behaviors would fit in the each category?

If we were to see these children 5 years later, what would we predict about their academic and sport interests and skills? What would we say about their gender role development? What levels of moral development would they be likely to have? Which theorists would say we could already predict, and which would not think prediction now would be very accurate?

## Readings

E. Turiel, *Development and Opposition to Cultural Practices*, pp. 369–374.

N. Eisenberg, *Empathy and Sympathy; Conclusion*, pp. 375–377.

S. L. Bem, *Toward Utopia: Eradicating Gender Polarization*, pp. 378–380.

## Suggested Readings

Bem, S. L. (1993). *The lenses of gender: Transforming the debate on sexual inequality* (pp. 192–196). New Haven, CT: Yale University Press.

Damon, W. (1988). *The moral child: Nurturing children's natural moral growth* (pp. 13–29). New York: Free Press.

Eisenberg, N. (1986). Empathy and sympathy; Conclusion. *Altruistic emotion, cognition, and behavior* (pp. 30–32, 211–212). Hillsdale, NJ: Erlbaum.

Turiel, E. (2002). *The culture of morality: Social development, context, and conflict* (pp. 104–115). Cambridge: Cambridge University Press.

"*I'm sorry, but I'm morally and politically opposed to hangman.*"

*Source:* © The New Yorker Collection 2004 Danny Shanahan from cartoonbank.com. All rights reserved.

# CHAPTER 10

# Life Span Theories of Cognitive, Sociomoral, Gender Role, and Physical/Motor/Perceptual Development

One of the major areas of life span interest is in examining the trajectory of cognition, not only in regard to its increasing capacities, but also to its potentially decreasing capacities at later life stages. For example, life span theorists such as Schaie and Baltes have studied changes in cognition of individuals who grow up in different historical and cultural contexts, whereas others, such as Labouie-Vief, have focused on expanding Piagetian views of adult cognitive development. Attention to stable or decreasing capacities and to gender role differences in development have been of interest to Neugarten, Huston, and others. Life span theorists have also been very interested in cross-cultural factors such as the influence of family and work differences on adolescent and adult development. Although decreasing abilities would be expected in regard to physical/motor and perceptual development, it is less clear what the sociomoral and gender role developmental trajectory would predict, and changes in language, other than those changes that might be observed in relation to cognitive loss, are not well known. Baltes stated that the life span paradigm sees development as a life-long process that is multidimensional, multidirectional, and open to change at every age (plasticity). Baltes and Schaie point out that "the rate, directionality, and sequentiality of such changes depend not upon the age of the organism, but upon the relative degree of stability in the man-environment [sic] context relevant to a specific behavior class over a given period of time. A life-span perspective also suggests attention to a joint description of the individual and the environment as changing systems" (Baltes & Schaie, 1973, p. 393). Baltes, in particular, has explored wisdom development in later life. Another emphasis in life span development theory has been on the longitudinal course of developmental domains that were initially studied in children. For example, Eisenberg has been interested in longitudinal predictions of stability or change in empathy and sympathy development from childhood to adulthood This chapter addresses some of the particular domains that have been studied through the life span and discusses what directions future life span study might take.

## Life Span Cognitive Theoretical Perspectives

One of the most interesting aspects of life span development is that the theorists often look at development as a whole and note aspects of cognitive, sociomoral, and gender role development as being intertwined. Most life span theorists see cognitive developmental change as being strongly affected by sociohistorical factors, and they often consider sociomoral thought as being more and more tied to cognition at later ages. In addition to Erikson's interest in the social–emotional and sociomoral interface evident at later ages, life span theorists have drawn on a number of theoretical perspectives to study cognition and sociomoral development in later years.

### Schaie's (and Baltes's) View of Cognitive Change over the Life Span

In regard to life span cognitive development, one of the most influential theorists has been K. Warner Schaie, a professor at Pennsylvania State University. In 1956, Schaie began the Seattle Longitudinal Study of cognitive functioning to answer the question of how cognition changes over the life span. The initial study had 500 subjects, ages 21 to 70. Most early studies of cognitive change had used cross-sectional comparisons, comparing groups who were at different ages when their cognition was measured. These studies had shown that older subjects scored lower than younger subjects; that is, that there was an intellectual generation gap. Schaie and his colleague, Baltes, questioned these results because they realized that individuals in each of these cohorts had grown up at different times, and thus they believed that sociohistorical factors might have influenced the performance of the groups. For example, the older groups may have had fewer educational or travel opportunities. Schaie wanted to see whether these decreases reported in cross-sectional studies could be found when cohorts of the same individuals were measured at different periods over their life span. Although cross-sectional comparisons for the cohorts in his study supported this conventional result (cognition scores were lower in later age cohorts), when Schaie analyzed the data by following the changes in individuals longitudinally, he found that there was no strong age-related change in the individuals' cognitive flexibility (ability to shift thinking patterns), and in fact, there was an overall actual increase in visuomotor flexibility (ability to coordinate visual and motor skills in pattern shifting) and in crystalized intelligence (comprehension and reasoning) as the subjects grew older (Schaie, 2005; Baltes & Schaie, 1973). Although he cited some evidence that there may be a "terminal drop" in intelligence immediately before death, in general his longitudinal findings have supported the view that cognitive functioning can be maintained well into old age. As his research has continued over the past half century, Schaie has proposed a cognitive developmental change theoretical perspective, as follows:

- Adolescence is an acquisition period in which knowledge, skills, and information are gained with minimal concern for importance or direct application.
- Young adulthood is an achievement period in which knowledge, skills, and information are used to achieve specific goals, and cognition tends to be focused and intense.
- Middle adulthood is a responsibility period in which cognition is broadened to encompass long-range goals for both the individual and family unit.
- Late adulthood is a reintegration period in which cognition is used to search for meaning in one's life.

Although the purposes of cognition, in Schaie's view, seem to shift in emphasis, his conclusion from his studies is that the changes in cognitive capability are much less extreme than was earlier stated. He believes that looking at sociohistorical and cultural factors in each cohort of subjects is essential in evaluating cognitive change over the life span (Schaie & Willis, 1991).

### Piaget's View of Formal Reasoning in Adulthood

Because there were so many questions raised about Piaget's assertion that the formal operations stage was reached in adolescence, when studies were showing that not all adults reasoned at that level, Piaget wrote his explanation for that *decalage* phenomena (1972a). After explaining the structures of formal thought that should be evident, he discussed the "problems of the passage from adolescent to adult thought" (p. 74). First, he acknowledged that although the sequence of cognitive development was constant, the average age when these stage changes occur "can vary considerably from one social environment to another, or from one country or even regions within a country to another" (p. 75). He suggested three possibilities for this. First, the quality and frequency of intellectual stimulation could differ in various environments, which might result in a slower pace for reaching formal thought. This would not mean that the stage would not be reached because social transmission is not the cause of cognitive stage changes, but it could contribute to the slower pace. His second reason for adults not showing formal operations is that as age increases, the diversification of aptitudes also increases, and individuals might exercise logicomathematical aptitudes differently, which might result in formal thought not being attained as easily by persons with some aptitudes (e.g., drawing) as by those with other aptitudes (e.g., math). Piaget, however, thought that his third reason for not always seeing formal operations in adults is the correct one. He continued to believe that all normal persons reach formal operations at the age of 11 to 15; however, because of different individual aptitudes, their use of these formal structures is not necessarily the same. Depending on an individual's profession or life circumstances, there may be many or few opportunities to use formal logicomathematical reasoning. However, it is likely they use formal reasoning that is appropriate to their own specialty areas. Piaget did not really investigate this hypothesis, however, and it remained for others to try to determine why adults in various cultures, when faced with tasks requiring formal operations, do not always demonstrate formal reasoning.

### *Labouvie-Vief's Life Span Interpretation of Piagetian Theory*

As Piaget himself had pondered, the ability of adults to reason using formal operations (abstract logicomathematical reasoning) and the lack of such reasoning being used by many adults in their life situations has been a major puzzle unexplained by his theory. He posited some possible reasons for that finding; however, a theorist who has focused on this issue is Gisela Labouvie-Vief, presently a professor at Wayne State University. She has been interested in extending Piaget's theory into adulthood by taking into account the context of Western thought in which he devised his theory and trying to explain the developmental changes that might occur over the adult life span in a way that is congruent with Piaget's underlying theoretical view (Labouvie-Vief, 1977, 1980, 1992; Labouie-Vief & Chandler, 1978). Labouvie-Vief's view is that adolescent thought is "overwired" for formal operations (as young children are "overwired" with synaptic connections), whereas adult thought requires the development of some additional "adaptations" related to the demands of life span contexts. She argued that Piaget's theory should not be understood just in terms of the development of logical mental structures but also as construction of knowledge that is increasingly adaptive to the demands of the contexts of life. Labouvie-Vief believes that adult cognitive development can be explained as an example of Piaget's definition of intelligence as an adaptation. That is, these other thinking patterns seen in adults are more adaptive for adult life conditions. She has researched four areas of adult development within this "adaptation" paradigm: adult memory strategies, patterns of text interpretation, emotional reasoning, and changes in sense of self.

In comparing adolescents and middle-age adults on these tasks, Labouvie-Vief has found that adolescents are more likely to use the literal information presented and give logical and abstract answers, whereas the adults are more likely to use "psychological interpretations" that take into account human motivations and intentions. Their answers therefore may reflect "deficits in tasks requiring more objective and formal ways of processing" but "an advantage in ones that specifically require more psychological ones" (1992, p. 215). For example, in memory tasks requiring recall of fables, adults may summarize by focusing on broader issues raised in the fable rather than on the particulars of the story. She thinks that this may often be interpreted as showing a memory decline, although if specifically asked to recall the fable details, the adults can do so; that is just not their preferred way of presenting the recalled information. Labouvie-Vief has proposed a developmental sequence from elementary age to late adulthood, as follows:

- Concrete–presystemic: behavioral actions and psychological states are not yet organized into a coherent abstract system (Piaget's concrete operations period).

- Interpersonal–protosystemic: such actions and states are described in terms of immediate relationships and social networks (transition from Piaget's concrete operations).

- Institutional–intrasystemic: actions and states can be coordinated in coherent abstract systems (Piaget's formal operations period).

- Contextual–intersystemic: actions and states can be reflected on as dialectical tensions between personal desire and institutional constraints (dynamic system of self and actions/external states).

- Dynamic–intersubjective: actions and states are seen in the context of inner psychological mechanisms and viewed from the interpretive perspective of the self (dynamic system of self).

Labouvie-Vief has also addressed the issue of the pervasive themes of Western thought and the tension between logos (rational thought) and mythos (feeling and imaginative). She believes Western society has separated these two, and that cognitive theorists (Piaget and others) stressed the logos sources of knowledge but not the mythos sources. Context-free sources of knowledge (logos) have been valued more than context-sensitive sources (mythos), and there has been a separation of cognition and emotion. Children are in close contact with mythos (e.g., as pretense), they move toward logos during schooling years, and then as aging occurs, there is a move again to the mythos style of thought. Thus, adults do not think less well than adolescents but differently, and Labouvie-Vief's explanations of their successive adaptations in thought support Piaget's own view that life experiences of adults can influence their use of formal operational cognitive processes (Piaget, 1972a). She has noted that there are gender differences in the value and style of thinking from these two sources, with women more likely to use mythos and men to use logos; this may be a result of life experiences, biological factors, or the interaction of the two. She has also addressed the issue of wisdom, which she believes integrates both these types of knowledge (Labouvie-Vief, 1990).

### *Other Theoretical Perspectives on Later Cognitive Development*

In addition to Labouvie-Vief's extensive examination of the later stages of cognition proposed by Piaget, a number of other researchers and theorists have suggested ways that these later stages could be conceptualized. For example, Arlin's research (1975) led her to hypothesize a fifth stage that separated some aspects of fourth-stage formal operational thought into two parts. She renamed Piaget's fourth stage the Problem Solving Stage and added a fifth stage that she termed the Problem Finding Stage. Arlin based her ideas on work of Gruber (1973), who tried to analyze how "creative" thought is generated, because creative thought requires the ability to find problems to solve. (This is reminiscent of Dewey's problem-solving model, in which he said that the first step in good problem solving is "finding the problem.") Even though finding problems appears to be easy, actually it is not, because problems must be found in forms that permit investigation and solution. Arlin's study asked female college students to respond to typical formal operational thought problems (similar to Piaget's tasks). They were also confronted with an array of objects that were not connected to any task and asked to generate questions about the array. The data were coded using categories of Guilford's structure of intellect model (Guilford, 1956; Guilford & Zimmerman, 1956), which moves from units, classes, relations, and systems to transformations and implications levels. Although there was a relationship between the subjects' Piagetian task solutions and their ability to generate questions, their ability to solve problems was a necessary but not a sufficient condition to being able to find problems. That is, 61% of those who could solve the presented problems could not be classified as high problem finders. Arlin suggested that ability to solve relations and systems problems comes earlier than ability to find transformations and implications. Thus, creative levels of thought may take longer to develop, even within formal operational thought processes. Although Fischer described the later stages in his theory somewhat differently, Arlin's data are congruent with his view that higher stages of thinking continue to develop throughout early adulthood.

Another theorist, Robert Sternberg, has discussed adult cognition from an information processing perspective, especially focusing on higher-order reasoning using analogy (1984). Sternberg stated that thinking beyond basic formal operational reasoning can be understood as third-order relational thinking (being able to rate how analogous two analogies are). In a study that asked 8th-grade, 11th grade, and college student subjects to rate how related two analogies were, Sternberg found that the ability to perform third-order analogical reasoning was greater at the later ages, suggesting that across the formal operational years, reasoning ability continues to progress. However, he stated that "it is debatable whether the ability to perform third order reasoning represents a genuine incremental stage beyond those postulated by Piaget (1976). Indeed the whole notion of stages is debatable" (p. 90). He does believe that advanced intellectual functioning can be assessed by problems of third-order reasoning, rather than being assessed by difficulty of vocabulary, spatial visualization, or working memory capacity, which are typical characteristics of problems on adult intellectual tests.

## Theoretical Perspectives on Moral and Wisdom Development at Later Ages

An area of great interest to life span theorists has been that of moral and wisdom development. Kohlberg addressed this question in one of his later writings, and Baltes has focused his later work on this topic. They and others have proposed that wisdom and moral development are closely tied at later ages. As part of the life span emphasis on contextual influences, these theorists have discussed how sociomoral development, and its correlate, wisdom, may be affected by differential later life events.

### Kohlberg's Perspective on the Last Stage of Moral Development

As did Piaget, Kohlberg addressed questions that had arisen about adult moral development and defended his stage theory (1973). He entertained the idea that moral development continues throughout adulthood and that there are different transformations that can only be understood if perceived as emerging from earlier moral thought. He stated that "moral change is clearly a focal point for adult life in a way cognitive change is not" (p. 186). However, advanced cognitive stages are essential for moral stage development, as a "necessary but not sufficient condition" (p. 186). In an earlier study of adult moral stages, he had stated that there was no stage change at later ages, but merely a stabilization of moral stage (Kohlberg & Kramer, 1969). After further research, however, he concluded that Stages 5 and 6 (both postconventional reasoning stages) are not reached until adulthood. Earlier scoring of Stage 6 reasoning in adolescence was really a misclassification of an advanced Stage 4 reasoning stage. He stated that Stages 1 to 4 are essentially tied to cognitive development and do not require exposure to a range of personal experience. Experience leading to later stages of moral development do not require only logical experiences but rather the transfer of logical experiences to social experiences. They involve emotion, which "triggers and accompanies rethinking" (p. 193). Kohlberg contrasted his perspective with that of Erikson, who also saw a greater commitment to moral values in adulthood (i.e., generativity, integrity). He stated that in Erikson's view moral development is a choice of the ego, whereas in his view, moral development is focused on "objective moral principles" (p. 201). Erikson's seventh and eighth stages involve becoming an ethical person. Kohlberg attempted in his hypothesized seventh stage to combine the Eriksonian and his own view of morality. He concluded that the ultimate moral development stage, therefore, is to gain a mature view of the meaning of life. At this point the person should have "the sense of being part of the whole of life and the adoption of a cosmic, as opposed to a universal humanistic (Stage 6) perspective. Kohlberg did not empirically validate his seventh stage; however, it is a point of view that has been shared by philosophers over the centuries.

### Baltes's Perspective on Sociomoral and Wisdom Development

Paul Baltes (1939–2006) was director of the Center of Life Span Psychology at the Max Planck Institute for Human Development at the Free University of Berlin. Baltes is often credited with creating the field of life span psychology, and he has done extensive work on many topics. Baltes's latest focus of research was on the development of wisdom, which has been a topic of interest for philosophers over many centuries (2002). In his search for a "psychological theory of wisdom," he has been investigating both the characteristics of wisdom and its development across the life span. He conceptualized wisdom as "expertise in the meaning and conduct of life" (p. 331). In his list of wisdom characteristics, he included "an explicit interest in achieving a balance between individual and collective interests and a focus on human virtues" (p. 333). The Berlin Wisdom Project has followed a modified version of the Kohlberg moral dilemma model. Subjects are confronted with difficult life problems and tell their views, and these answers are coded by a panel of judges. Some are asked to answer immediately, and others have the opportunity to think about the problem or discuss it with another before answering. His studies do not show that only the old have wisdom; by age 25 many subjects give wise answers, and it appears to be a stable characteristic from about ages 25 to 75. Thus, his empirical evidence does not support a view that wisdom (at least as he defines it) appears only in old age; it does show that it is a stable characteristic not lost until extreme old age. He is in agreement with Kohlberg's later view that moral development continues throughout adulthood and that there are "different transformations" that can only be understood if "perceived as emerging from the earlier formulations" (p. 387).

### Other Neo-Kolbergian Moral Thought Approaches

The study of postconventional moral thought has been of interest to James Rest and colleagues (Rest, Narvacz, Bebeau, & Thoma, 1999). They discussed criticisms of Kohlberg's theory in relation to methodological/theoretical, philosophical, and limited coverage aspects, but they also think some criticisms are unwarranted. They believe that Kohlberg gave an important legacy of a developmental constructivist approach to moral development, but they stated these limitations of the theory: it focused on only one dimension of moral development (justice), the stages were too global and need further intermediate steps identified, it explored "nonintimate" relationships with society rather than the personal side of morality, and therefore the dilemmas don't cover the entire moral domain. Rest and colleagues focused on adult moral thinking and derived their basic approach from Kohlberg, but instead of moral dilemma interviews, they used a "recognition" scale that measures "tacit understanding" with the goal of finding evidence for postconventional thinking. However, they defined postconventional thinking more broadly, as including moral sensitivity, judgment, motivation, and character, and they see it developing as a shift in schemas rather than a clear-cut stage change. That is, higher stages gain in use while lower stages are still in operation. Although they included justice issues (i.e, normative ethics), they also included other aspects of morality. Their work has not supported all of Kohlberg's postconventional ideas, and the validity and reliability of their method of study has also been questioned. One area that Rest et al. deal with that was not a focus of Kohlberg's view is how religion influences moral development.

This was also studied about 25 years ago by Fowler (1981), who examined stages of "faith development." Using an interview approach, Fowler identified six stages of faith development that roughly parallel Kohlberg's stages. The latter stages are "Poetic–Conventional" (teenage and some adults), Individuating–Reflective (usually found in middle and late adulthood), and Paradoxical–Consolidation and Universalizing (two stages that most adults do not reach.) The Individuating–Reflective stage involves adults having an objective understanding of their creeds and a commitment to them, the Paradoxical–Consolidation stage involves recognizing possible fallibilities of one's own faith and accepting those whose beliefs are different from one's own, and the Universalizing stage involves having a global and universal vision that incorporates faith. As present controversies over religion indicate, faith development as a topic of study is gaining renewed interest.

## Theoretical Perspectives on Gender Role and Cross-Cultural Life Course Patterns

Another set of theorists who have drawn on a life span paradigm have been interested in gender role identity changes and cross-cultural influences over the life span. These include earlier and more recent studies of gender role orientations and practices, as well as cross-cultural studies of family and life course patterns.

## Development of Female Role Orientations over the Life Course

In an early study Aletha Huston-Stein and Ann Higgins-Trenk (1978) charted the development of "female role orientations" in the United States over a 30-year period and found that although there were many changes in stereotypes over the period from about 1945 to 1975 (primarily due to feminist influences), in many cases "stereotypes appear to lag well behind reality" (p. 267). The issue of individual variety in life course has continued to be of interest to life span theorists. For example, Jackson and Berkowitz (2005) looked at the "structure of the life course" using data from a National Survey of Families and Households that were collected during 1987–1988. They were particularly interested in noting what kinds of regularity in the adults' life sequence were present for men and women and persons of diverse ethnic backgrounds. Although they found that the majority of the respondents were both working and married, this pattern differed more for women than for men. The "typical" pattern of becoming employed, then marrying, then having children (while continuing to work) was evident in most white and minority group men, whereas the pattern for women was more varied. Fewer women were employed before marriage, and if they were employed, they often left the labor force when they had children. The authors concluded that the life course pattern usually discussed in life span theory courses is really a "male" model. Of course, many of the earlier life course studies focused only on males (e.g., Gould, Levinson).

Jackson and Berkowitz concluded that although the individuality of choice in life span patterns is often stressed in theory, for women, "there is a particular life course pattern that defines the structure of women's lives more than it does men's lives" (2005, p. 86), which is that they leave the job role on the birth of the first child. The pattern is most prevalent for white and Latino women, whereas African-American women are more likely to start families before entering the labor force. They discussed the implications of these different life courses in relation to vulnerabilities, such as limited financial resources, role stress, and adjustments during transition periods and concluded, "Women, and ethnic minorities, who are already economically disadvantaged in society, may find that their role sequencing serves to further exacerbate their status in society . . ." (Jackson & Berkowitz, 2005, p. 86). The analysis of various life course models and the sequencing patterns throughout the life span remains an important data source for life span theory building, but another area of interest is how the individuals in these situations evaluate their satisfaction.

These differences in life course expectations between males and females may also affect their perceptions of equity, and thus this "social convention" of unequal roles may become a moral issue for the individuals whose gender role is perceived as being less equal (per Turiel's hypothesis). Recent studies of depression and decreases in marital satisfaction, adjustment, and quality in Western societies have found that perceptions of the equity in the roles taken do have an effect on these factors (e.g., Pina & Bengtson, 1993). Drawing on "equity theory" Van Willingen and Drentea (2001) examined why both partners may experience less satisfaction in marriage when the norm of equity is not practiced. In the United States, the norm of equity between males and females is greater than in some other societies. Even in the United States, however, household work and family decision-making power is not distributed equally, but whether that is perceived as unfair depends on the gender role ideology, leading to disjuncts between actual inequities and perceptions of inequity (DeMaris & Longmore, 1996). Van Willingen and Drentea, therefore, studied both the perceived equity of partners and the actual equity, in relation to amount of work done in the home by each, and hypothesized that the degree of "social support" would be a mediator of equity. They thought that high levels of actual equity and perceived equity would both be associated with high levels of social support, but that women would have higher perceptions of social support, even if in a higher workload and less-powerful decision-making role. They found that both men and women who performed a greater proportion of household work than their partner reported lower social support levels, which was contrary to earlier studies that showed women would have a different perception; that is, they would be satisfied even when carrying a higher actual workload. They concluded, "Women do not have a higher tolerance for inequality than do men" (Van Willingen & Drentea, 2001, p. 591), even though the society still supports socialization of women for that role. These results were contrary to previous studies in earlier decades among both younger and older women, and the authors suggested that gender-role ideologies have continued to be equalized in U.S. society.

## Family Differences and Life Patterns in Various Societies around the World

Although some variation in life course sequencing and less-stereotypic gender role activities are now seen in present U.S. society, cross-cultural studies done in other parts of the world have not found as much variability of life course patterns or changes in equity roles, especially for women. For example, Fussell (2005) studied Mexican census data from 1970 to 2000 and found that for adults there has been "relatively little change in the timing of life stages and limited change in the statuses that structure each stage" (p. 91). The expected norms of a society have a bearing on these practices and in societies where the norms have changed very little, earlier patterns are still evident.

Recently a number of studies of life patterns and family structure in Western and Eastern Europe have examined changes occuring since the demise of Communist governments (Giele & Holst, 2004; Robila, 2004). Especially in Eastern Europe, there have been major changes in work policies, child-care support, and values, with resulting changes in gender role expectations. For example, Robila described how the changes from Communist systems to free-market systems have affected individuals and families in Eastern Europe, creating fewer job opportunities and greater poverty (at least initially), and she stated, "In general, the deterioration of living conditions affects women more than men, both in private (e.g., increased amount of time women spend on housework and child care) and public spheres. Discrimination against women in the labor market appears in several forms' (p. 4). Although wage discrimination was present under Communist regimes also, there has been a decrease in employment of women in particular in many Eastern European countries. Other changes occurring are increased age of marriage and birth of first child, cohabitation instead of marriage, and thus more out-of-wedlock births. Although long-term trends on adult and child development are not available, according to the life span perspective, these changes will have concomitant effects on developmental domains.

## Views on Life Span Physical/Motor/Perceptual Development

One of the areas of development that has typically been seen as showing "downward development" is that of physical and health decline at later ages. A number of theorists have examined this phenomena, including the last stage of life, the death process.

### Neugarten's View of Later Life Physical and Health Influences

Neugarten has extensively studied the changes that occur in many developmental domains over the life span, but she has been especially interested in how the interaction of environmental factors and physical/motor and health changes may affect later development because there is so much variability in these domains in later adulthood. Although it is true that, overall, developmental change in physical/motor skills after the age of 30 tend toward lowering levels of skill, cultural, socioeconomic, gender, and educational factors greatly influence changes in physical/motor skills in adulthood. Athletes, for example, continue to show excellent physical/motor skills into middle age, although certain physical/motor skills peak earlier than others. On the other hand, lifestyle factors may make some adults more vulnerable to health-related problems (e.g., obesity).

In her studies of middle age and later development, Neugarten (1964, 1968, 1996) found that as the length of the life span increased, the health and physical abilities of many older adults have been maintained into the period once called old age (after age 60). Using data from her studies, she identified old age as now having two periods, with the first being young-old (ages 55 to 75) and the second being old-old (after age 75). The young-old group is still typically physically and psychologically healthy and active, with only about 15% having physical or health problems. The second group, the old-old, are those who may have serious health or physical/motor problems, although even in this group, some are still relatively healthy. Neugarten stressed that the idea of aging has changed and that most of those who retire at age 60 to 65 tend to be in the young-old group, who are "healthy and vigorous" (1996, p. 73). She stated that even in the old-old group, more than a third reported "no limitations due to health"... [and thus] ... "all across adulthood, age has become a poor predictor of ... health, work status, family status, interests, preoccupations and needs" (1996, p. 74). The study of development over the life span of physical/motor and perceptual development at later ages will probably continue to provide new insights into the health and physical abilities of the young-old and old-old.

Changes in basic visual and auditory abilities begin to occur during middle age and show marked deterioration by old age, although there are now many treatments that prolong these abilities, such as cataract removal. In regard to changes in perception, which must rely on sensory input, research reported by Comalli, Wapner, and Werner (1962) showed that the visual perceptual performance of young children and that of the aged are more similar when both are compared to that of young adults. Whether this is due to sensory changes in older adulthood or the loss of ability to differentiate stimuli is not clear. This research result is an example of developmental change rather than developmental progress in perceptual development. From the viewpoint of life span theorists, however, documenting change and variability within contexts is an appropriate focus of their developmental interests.

## End-of-Life Issues

One area of great interest to life span theorists that is also of great interest to neuroscientists, developmental psychobiologists, and genetics researchers is the "problem of aging." Schaie and Willis, in a discussion of the aging process, asked, "Why do people grow old? Why do they die? The answers do not come easily, however. For centuries, scientists have pondered these questions . . ." (Schaie & Willis, 1991, p. 432).

### *Stages of Death*

In the 1960s Elisabeth Kubler-Ross, a psychiatrist, began studying the final stage of life, the death process. She observed and interviewed many persons who were dying from severe illnesses, and she developed a theory of the stages of the dying process (1969). The stages she outlined included the following.

- *Stage 1. Denial and Isolation:* When faced with the prospect of death, most individuals initially react with disbelief and denial that their potential death can be an accurate prediction. They may experience a numbness, a lack of interest in discussing the possibility, and a feeling of isolation from the fact that death may be imminent. This is not unusual and can be an initial coping mechanism. Family and friends may not be able to discuss this situation, and even medical staff may find the person does not raise questions or want to have explanations of conditions that are predicting death.

- *Stage 2. Anger:* When denial can no longer be maintained, a typical reaction is anger and resentment, even envy. Individuals ask why this is happening to them and question the unfairness of the situation. Their anger may be displaced onto family, friends, and medical personnel. This is also a normal reaction because death is not welcome, and when others are not facing death, they are reminders to the person of the prospect of death and thus may be the target of anger.

- *Stage 3. Bargaining:* This stage involves hoping or wishing that some remission of the illness will occur if the person acts in particular ways, tries to be good, or even performs some unusual actions. Bargaining is an attempt to postpone the inevitable end and often has the implication that the person will accept death, "if only" he or she can do certain things first or not have to face certain things. It includes an implicit promise that if these requests are given, then the person will accept death.

- *Stage 4: Depression:* When denial, anger, and bargaining have run their course and the person must come to terms with the fact of imminent death, a sense of great loss is felt. This is usually exacerbated by the many painful treatments or losses of functioning that the person has had to endure. Both past losses—the inability to function as the same person one was—and anticipated losses—the realization that the love and companionship of family and friends will be lost—contribute to depression. This stage is really a realistic acknowledgment of the imminent death situation.

- *Stage 5: Acceptance:* This stage occurs if the death process has been long enough for the other stages to occur. The person has expressed feelings of grief and mourned losses and is usually weak and tired, almost devoid of any feelings. It is not a happy stage but rather an acceptance that the struggle is over. Only the quiet presence of others is needed, not attempts to engage the person in activities of life. The person accepts the situation but is comforted by knowing that medical staff or family and friends are near.

Kubler-Ross's theory of death stages has been especially influential in promoting understanding care of the dying. For example, the hospice movement, which assists persons through the final stages of death, has drawn on this knowledge of the death process. Also, in any situation of great loss these stages are usually seen. For example, those who lose a loved one to death, who face divorce or separation, or even who lose material things (e.g., destruction of home from a hurricane or a theft of a possession) may go through similar, if not as intense, stages.

## Delaying the Aging and Death Process

Some scientists are presently engaged in trying to understand the genetic basis of aging and to examine ways that the aging process can be delayed. For example, they have been locating particular genes that seem to prolong life in yeast and mice and have also been doing genetic studies of human centenarians (Shaw, 2005). They are hypothesizing that genetic interactions with metabolic processes may provide more resilience to disease, and that is why some studies have shown lower-weight individuals may live longer. Although not necessarily increasing the life span, this research may eventually make later life more disease free. Other researchers are investigating whether engaging in certain mental activities such as doing crossword puzzles or playing chess may delay loss of memory and problem-solving skills. Presently this research has not shown clear evidence that mental exercise slows down mental aging; longitudinal research is needed (Salthouse, 2006). Many medical procedures now are creating "robotic" people, at least in a minor way. For example, implanting pacemakers and artificial hearts, conducting hip and other bone replacement surgery, and providing prostheses for amputated limbs are all examples of ways to extend life and quality of life. Some scientists are even predicting a time when nanotechnology and robotic technology will be able to keep people alive for much longer time periods (Kurzwell, 2006).

As more information about aging is discovered at the genetic and neural level, and successful procedures to extend healthy life through technology become available, human development at the behavioral and environmental levels will also be affected (see Gottlieb's model in chapter 12). Thus, developmental psychobiological and nonlinear dynamical systems perspectives appear to be particularly congruent with views of life span researchers because their types of analyses take into account the interactions of systems, from the biological to the historical, incorporating attention to all the system levels. Although life span theorists have considered a range of issues in explaining developmental processes, they have not yet begun in-depth study using the nonlinear dynamical systems perspective with older age populations. These theoretical perspectives may also provide greater understanding of life span development.

### Theoretical Influence and Critique

As the late aging population increases, theoretical interest in the later portion of the age span is likely to continue to expand. Life span development is still a field in its own infancy, and the theoretical base is presently widespread. In coming years, its influence will probably become even greater, and the testing of its explanations for development will become even more extensive. Thus, human development theory may continue to expand its focus on life span change.

## Box 10.1
## Theoretically-Derived Themes That May Be Useful For Professional Practice

- A life span perspective is best understood within the sociohistorical context of individuals. The variations in these experiences promotes variability in life span developmental change.
- Attention to social and emotional development is important throughout life as new experiences are encountered and can result in a richer and fuller life course if developmental support is provided.
- There will be many periods of developmental change, precipitated by biological changes, environmental crisis periods, and nature/nurture interactions that will affect later development depending on how they are resolved; sensitivity to these change periods as typical in the course of development will facilitate successful resolution.
- There will also be a series of cognitive developmental changes (either qualitative or quantitative), precipitated by changes in brain structure and function in interaction with experiences.
- The sequence of thought becomes more abstract at adult age levels, but it may also become more pragmatic as experiences with diverse types of problems occur.
- Socio-moral issues will continue to be faced, and developmental change is to be expected. With age, wisdom, appreciation of the complexities of moral decisions, and gaining identity integrity are possible.
- Gender role issues will also continue to be faced, and developmental change in this domain will continue to be greatly influenced by sociohistorical and cultural contexts.
- Throughout the life span, the human developmental system becomes increasingly self-organized in many ways, but there are always periods of stability and phase shifts, as well as recursive patterns, even at later ages.

## Summary

This chapter has presented a brief overview of life span theoretical work related to cognition, sociomoral, gender, and physical development. Because most life span theory is derived from a sociohistorical perspective, there is particular interest in examining cross-cultural and cross-historical developmental change and/or stability. As global information is shared among theorists, there may be a great expansion of theoretical knowledge about these life span issues in the future.

## Case 10. The Busy Family

The Busy Family has agreed to try therapy because of daughter Tina's (6 years old) school problem. In addition to Tina, the Busy family contains two other children, Bud Jr., who is 14, and baby Andy (10 months old). Mrs. Busy's mother also lives with the family and cares for the children when the parents are working. However, she has been feeling ill lately and has an appointment next week with the doctor. Mr. Busy (Bud) owns a computer company and works long hours. Mrs. Busy (June) is a high school science teacher. She is also an officer in the state science teachers' organization and has just been appointed to the national science magazine board. She will need to attend a meeting in Washington, D.C., in a few weeks. Bud Jr. is doing fairly well in school, although often the parents feel he isn't working up to his capacity. They don't think his middle school teachers are challenging him as much as his elementary teachers did, but at their last conference, Bud's English teacher stated that he needs to be on medication for attention deficit hyperactivity. They were surprised and have not made any decision about this. Bud Jr. also plays on both a soccer and a baseball team. He greatly enjoys these activities, but it means that his mother has to drive him back and forth to games two or three times a week. Baby Andy is presently in transition from crawling to standing; he now can walk briefly when holding on to furniture. He is very attached to his grandmother and cries whenever she leaves him. His parents expect him to begin talking soon because both Bud Jr. and Tina were speaking in complete sentences by age 2. One reason her parents were surprised that Tina's teacher recommended some counseling was because Tina has always been a precocious learner, having talked early and even started to read by kindergarten age. She had a great imagination and often engaged in pretend play. Now that she is in first grade, however, she has become anxious and withdrawn and does not want to go to school. Her school performance has also been affected negatively. Every morning the family is in an uproar because Tina cries and refuses to get dressed for school, and lately her grandmother has had to force her to get on the school bus. At school, Tina acts withdrawn and frightened; she often cries and asks to go home, and when she can't, she says she is sick and doesn't do her work. Tina's teacher is concerned about Tina's behavior disrupting the whole class, as well as preventing Tina from focusing on learning. Another recent event in the family is that Tina's Uncle Joe (June's brother) stopped by to say goodby before he was shipped off to the Iraq war zone. The parents and grandmother say they do not talk much about the war, but naturally they talk about the letters they get from Joe, and they have tried to answer the children's questions about why the war is happening. This uproar around Tina has been especially hard on Grandma because she doesn't have much energy recently. She is not sure whether she is really ill or whether she is just depressed because she is still missing her husband, who died 5 months ago, and is so worried about her son Joe's safety. Bud is especially concerned about Tina's behavior because she seems to be losing ground in her development and learning and has become very clingy with him. He often has to disentangle her from holding on to him when he is ready to leave for work in the morning. Bud and June are both concerned that June's trip to Washington will be hard for Tina to accept. They also think that Bud Jr. and baby Andy are being affected by the daily conflict involving Grandma and Tina (about getting Tina on the bus). Grandma agrees that she is feeling a lot of stress, not only from Tina but also because Andy seems so fussy and she now has to watch him much more carefully because he has begun "traveling" around the house.

The therapy team at Tina's school initially consisted of the school psychologist and the social worker. After the first therapy session with the family, in which the preceding information was divulged, they consulted with four other experts. Each of these experts has hypotheses about why Tina is showing emotional problems, why Bud Jr. is having attention difficulties, and what may be the effects of various family issues on Tina, Bud Jr., baby Andy, the parents, and grandmother. They are meeting to decide what the focus should be at the next therapy sessions.

From the list of theorists studied so far in the text, select six of them (at least one from the personality and social–emotional domain, one from the cognitive and language domain, one from the sociomoral domain, one from the gender role domain, and two from the life span domain).

List the theorists you have chosen and then answer the following questions.

What is one hypothesis that *each* of these theorists might have about some of the family issues?

What are two questions that *each* of them might ask the family to get more information?

How might each of the team members explain the behavior of one (or more) of the family members using concepts from their theoretical perspectives? (Use their theoretical perspectives' terminology.)

What further information might these team members want to gather?

What preliminary suggestions/recommendations might each have for the Busy family?

What issues might each want to ask the family to talk about at the next session?

# Readings

P. B. Baltes, *Wisdom as a Topic of Scientific Discourse about the Good Life*, pp. 381–384.

Bernice L. Neugarten, *Patterns of Aging: Past, Present, and Future*, pp. 385–391.

## Suggested Readings

Baltes, P. B. (2002). Wisdom as a topic of scientific discourse about the good life. In Wisdom: Its structure and function in regulating successful life span development. In C. R. Snyder & S. J. Lopez (Eds.), *Handbook of positive psychology* (pp. 329–332). Oxford, UK: Oxford University Press.

Labouvie-Vief, G. (1990). Retrospect and prospect. In Wisdom as integrated thought: Historical and developmental perspectives. In R. J. Sternberg (Ed.), *Wisdom: Its nature, origins, and development* (pp. 76–79). Cambridge: Cambridge University Press.

Neugarten, B. L. (1996). Patterns of aging. In B. L. Neugarten, *The meanings of age: Selected papers of Bernice L. Neugarten* (pp. 314–323). Chicago: University of Chicago Press.

Piaget, J. (1972a). Intellectual evolution from adolescence to adulthood. *Human Development, 15,* 1–12.

*Source:* © Scott Adams/Dist. by United Features Syndicate, Inc.

# CHAPTER 11

# Theoretical Perspectives from Physical/Motor and Perceptual Development, Neuroscience, and Behavioral Genetics

I n the early part of the 20th century, when the field of child development was identified by American psychologist G. Stanley Hall as a separate and important area worthy of study, an interest in describing the "normal" development of children was generated. Until that time, although some European theorists such as Pestalozzi, Montessori, and Froebel had suggested educational practices to enhance children's development, the study of children's development was not an important focus in the United States. Because there was no body of systematically collected observational or interview data regarding longitudinal developmental changes in children, theoretical explanations for children's development remained limited and vague. Thus, the focus of early 20th-century theorists in the United States was on observing and describing the course of children's "normal" (i.e., typical) development. One of the initial developmental domains that child study researchers observed and described was that of physical/motor development, probably because developmental changes in physical and motor areas were easily observed. During the 1930 to 1950 period, Arnold Gesell and his colleagues conducted longitudinal descriptive studies of many developmental domains, and this work provided much information on children's progress in regard to physical and motor skills, as well as to skills in other domains. One of his contemporaries, Myrtle McGraw, focused on physical/motor development and investigated how specific interventions might further that development and affect development in other domains. In the latter part of the 20th century, interest in studying physical/ motor development waned, perhaps because basic physical/motor developmental change was well charted, but also because of the greater emphasis on other developmental areas, such as cognition and language acquisition.

Processes involved in adult perception were studied extensively during the early 20th century, primarily by the Gestalt psychologists of Europe, but children's perception was not a focus of their study. Building on Gestalt psychology, adult perception was also investigated by a number of researchers in the United States, and theories of perception were proposed. Cognitive theorists such as Piaget and Vygotsky also speculated about the role of perception in cognition. In the mid 20th century, the Gibsons provided a new theoretical view of perception, proposing that perception was not mediated by cognition but could be directly experienced. While James Gibson focused on specific perceptual issues such as visual perception, Eleanor Gibson extensively investigated developmental changes in perception, examining how perceptual development in young children was related to their sensory and motor development.

Other theoretical perspectives that focus on biological aspects of development are ones related to neuroscience issues and to genetic influences on development. These theoretical perspectives are adding to knowledge about the nature/nurture developmental interface. The study of processes involved in the development of physical skills has also gained renewed interest, partly due to the work of Esther Thelen and other nonlinear dynamical systems theorists. This chapter discusses theoretical issues related to physical, motor, and perceptual development and describes the nature/nurture theoretical debates that have shaped the study of these developmental processes. It also discusses theoretical perspectives from neuroscience and behavioral genetics.

## Gesell's Normative/Descriptive Studies and Theory of Development

Preeminent in taking on the early task of understanding children's development was Arnold Gesell (1880–1961). He was an educator, psychologist, and physician (holding both a Ph.D. and an M.D.) who was director of the Yale Clinic of Child Development. He used the laboratory facilities of Yale University to study children by giving them various tasks that would enable him to observe their development in four areas: motor, adaptive (cognitive), language, and personal–social. He initially studied infancy but because of his interest in the longitudinal nature of development, his studies eventually included the study of developmental change through adolescence. During his long tenure at Yale, he involved a number of colleagues in his work, most notably Frances Ilg, who was director of the Guidance Nursery, and Louise Bates Ames, his primary research assistant. Together with his research team, he described the sequences of development through age 16 in all four of the domains he defined. The team also wrote many parenting advice books. The Gesell Institute still provides parenting advice and books on the various age levels, but it is now located at the University of Wisconsin—Stevens Point (gesellinstitute.org).

Gesell's theoretical perspective was a rationalist one, directly opposed to the views of Watson and other empirically oriented theorists, who stressed effects of environment. He emphasized the process of maturation as the major cause of epigenetic changes, using the term *growth* to describe development. Although he was interested in charting the universals of development, he was also conscious of individual variations in developmental growth. For example, in his book outlining preschool development, he stated,

> Growth, therefore, becomes a key concept for the interpretation of individual differences. There are laws of sequence and of maturation which account for the general similarities and basic trends of child development. But . . . each child has a tempo and a style of growth which are as characteristic of individuality as the lineaments of his countenance. (1940, p. 7)

Over the course of many years, Gesell and his colleagues charted typical developmental milestones, designed methods for assessing normative development, and created procedures for diagnosing developmental delays (Ames, 1937; Gesell, 1925, 1940; Gesell & Armatruda, 1947; Ilg & Ames, 1955). Many of the standardized developmental assessment measures currently in use still draw on information collected by Gesell and his colleagues in the mid 20th century. Gesell's fundamental perspective—that the diagnosis of developmental problems must be done within the context of knowledge of typical developmental processes—is still relevant.

Gesell emphasized that the maturational process was regulated by a genetically influenced schedule and that changes in the biological structures of the nervous system are then expressed in behavioral and psychological changes. That is, changes in structures lead to changes in functions. Because of his stress on maturation as the major force in developmental change, he promoted the concept of "readiness." The role of environment was to meet the child's developmental needs when the child was ready to benefit from them. For example, the team studied the maturation of the eye (Gesell & Ilg, 1949) and concluded that it matured at about age 6 or 7. They believed that it was important for children to have mature eyesight before being ready to learn to read. As a result of this emphasis, a number of educational practices were instituted by his followers that stressed delaying school if a child was not "ready" (Ames & Chase, 1974). That is, if a child was judged as "not ready" on a developmental assessment, then it was suggested that the child should be kept out of kindergarten for an extra year to wait for readiness to occur. This is not the view advocated by most theorists and practitioners today. There is still debate about how much emphasis should be placed on formal educational activities during early childhood, however, because the pendulum has swung much further toward initiating reading and mathematical instruction at ages earlier than those Gesell's descriptions of developmental readiness would indicate are appropriate.

Although Gesell's work gives insights into many areas of development, his descriptions of physical and motor skills in particular and his emphasis on using such indicators as evidences of readiness in areas related to school success were especially influential. Therefore, his focus on physical/motor development is emphasized in this chapter. Because of his views concerning the close connections between all areas of development and their relationship to development of humans in general, he saw motor development as related to cognitive and social development as well. For example, Gesell and colleagues detailed the general changes in infants and young children's mobility and gross motor coordination (e.g., sitting, standing, walking, skipping) and in fine motor coordination (e.g, eye–hand coordination, copying squares, circles, diamonds). They charted similar developmental milestones in all four of their domains of development. Although the exact timing is not crucial, for many years these milestones (also available for ages 2 to 15) have provided important information for practitioners who need to assess developmental progress. Gesell suggested that motor skill achievements often are related to similar progress in adaptive, language, and personal–social areas. For example, a gross motor task—being able to skip with alternating feet— and a fine motor task—copying a diamond shape accurately—are two motor skills typically mastered by children of kindergarten age. Surprisingly, these have been fairly accurate indicators of children's readiness for school tasks in other areas of development! Table 11.1 shows aspects of Gesell's study of fine motor development, and Table 11.2 gives an example of his expectations for 60-month overall development.

### General Principles of Physical/Motor Development

Gesell's work resulted in identification of a number of general principles of development, which are discussed by Ames (1989). These principles are still taught in most child development classes today. They are principles of motor developmental direction, reciprocal interweaving, functional asymmetry, individuating maturation, and self-regulatory function.

- *Developmental direction* has three motor growth gradients: cephalocaudal (from the head to outer limb areas); proximal-distal (from trunk to extremities); and ulnar-radial (from palmar to pincer grasp). For example, infants learn to control their head movements earlier than their finger movements or leg movements.

- *Reciprocal interweaving* emphasizes the changing emphases in the course of development, with greater or lesser periods of growth in various parts of the organism. For example, bilateral motor growth alternates with unilateral motor growth.

- *Functional asymmetry* refers to the fact that more mature development may result in asymmetry rather than symmetry. For example, young children use both hands equally and thus an indicator of maturing function is when children's right- or left-hand dominance is established.

- *Individuating maturation* is the process by which more global movements occur before more precise ones. For example, infants use their whole hand to pick up small objects but then they begin to use a pincer movement (thumb and forefinger); other larger movements such as scribbling are usually achieved before precise ones such as fine cutting ability.

**Table 11.1**   Examples of Four- and Five-Year-Old Fine Motor Skills

### 1. Copying Circle

| Age | No. cases | Direction of movement | |
|---|---|---|---|
| | | Clockwise | Counter-clockwise |
| 4 years...................... | 22 | 82% | 18% |
| 5 years...................... | 58 | 48% | 52% |

### 2. Copying Cross

| Age | No. cases | Direction of vertical line | | | Direction of horizontal line | | |
|---|---|---|---|---|---|---|---|
| | | Up | Down | Up and down from horizontal ↑⁚↓ | Right | Left | Left and right from ←⁚→ vertical line |
| 4 years....... | 19 | 16% | 84% | — | 68% | — | 32% |
| 5 years....... | 58 | — | 98% | 2% | 71% | 12% | 17% |

### 3. Copying Square

| Age | No. cases | Direction of vertical lines | | | Direction of horizontal lines | | |
|---|---|---|---|---|---|---|---|
| | | Both up | Both down | One up, one down | Both right | Both left | One right, one left |
| 4 years....... | 10* | 10% | 30% | 60% | 40% | 10% | 50% |
| 5 years....... | 49 | — | 65% | 35% | 43% | 12% | 45% |

\* 21 infants of 4 years attempted to copy the figure but only 10 completed a recognizable square. One child drew a circle counter-clockwise and another drew a base line toward the right and the two sides upward.

### 4. Copying Triangle

| Age | No. cases | Direction of | | | | | Draws rectangle instead of triangle, counter-clockwise | Draws circle instead of triangle, counter-clockwise |
|---|---|---|---|---|---|---|---|---|
| | | Sides | | | Base | | | |
| | | Up | Down | One up, one down | Right | Left | | |
| 4 years....... | 5 | — | 40% | — | 20% | 20% | 40% | 20% |
| 5 years....... | 37 | 5% | 87% | 8% | 60% | 41% | — | — |

### 5. Copying Diamond

| Age | No. cases | Manner of drawing | | | | | | | | |
|---|---|---|---|---|---|---|---|---|---|---|
| 4 years....... | 4 | — | — | — | — | — | 25% | 25% | 25% | 25% |
| 5 years....... | 12 | 8% | 33% | 17% | 25% | 17% | | | | |

*Source:* From Gesell, A. (1940). The first five years of life: The preschool years. New York: Harper and Row (pp. 100–101).

**Table 11.2**  Examples of 60-Month Level Development

**60-Month Level**

| (M) Motor | 48 mos. | 60 mos. | 72 mos. |
|---|---|---|---|
| M-3  SKIPS using feet alternately . . . . . . . . . . . . . . . . . . . . . . . . . . . . . . . . |  |  |  |
| M-10  STANDS on 1 foot more than 8 seconds . . . . . . . . . . . . . . . . . . . . |  |  |  |
| M-11  WALKING BOARDS: 6 cm. board, without stepping off for full length . . . . . . . . . . . . . . . . . . . . . . . . . . . . . . . . . . . . . . . . . |  |  |  |
| M-12  PELLETS: 10 into bottle (20 sec.) . . . . . . . . . . . . . . . . . . . . . . . . . |  | 50 |  |
| **(A) Adaptive** |  |  |  |
| A-6  CUBES: builds 2 steps . . . . . . . . . . . . . . . . . . . . . . . . . . . . . . . . . |  | 61 |  |
| A-17  DRAWING: unmistakable man with body, arms, legs, feet, mouth, nose, eyes . . . . . . . . . . . . . . . . . . . . . . . . . . . . . . . . . . . . . |  |  |  |
| A-21  DRAWING: copies triangle . . . . . . . . . . . . . . . . . . . . . . . . . . . . . | 0 | 40 | 96 |
| A-21  DRAWING: copies rectangle with diagonals (66 mos.) . . . . . . . |  | 48 |  |
| A-18  DRAWING: adds 7 parts incomplete man . . . . . . . . . . . . . . . . . | 10 | 54 |  |
| A-25  DRAWING: correctly places just 1, 2, 3, 4 bubbles . . . . . . . . . . . | 7 | 61 |  |
| A-23  COUNTS: 10 objects correctly . . . . . . . . . . . . . . . . . . . . . . . . . . . | 5 | 72 |  |
| A-23  COUNTS: 12 objects correctly (66 mos.) . . . . . . . . . . . . . . . . . . . |  | 42 | 88 |
| A-32  WEIGHTS: not more than 1 error in 5 block test . . . . . . . . . . . | 15 | 55 |  |
| A-24  Gives correct no. fingers separate hands . . . . . . . . . . . . . . . . . . |  | 66 |  |
| **(L) Language** |  |  |  |
| L-15  NAMES: penny, nickle and dime . . . . . . . . . . . . . . . . . . . . . . . . | 25 | 60 |  |
| L-9  ACTION AGENT: 15 correct . . . . . . . . . . . . . . . . . . . . . . . . . . . . | 33 | 46 |  |
| L-14  NAMES COLORS . . . . . . . . . . . . . . . . . . . . . . . . . . . . . . . . . . . . | 19 | 63 |  |
| L-8  PICTURE: some descriptive comment with enumeration . . . . | 25 | 75 |  |
| L-11  COMPREHENSION QUESTIONS B: 2 correct . . . . . . . . . . . . . | 20 | i |  |
| L-16  3 COMMISSIONS . . . . . . . . . . . . . . . . . . . . . . . . . . . . . . . . . . . . |  |  |  |

*(P-S) Personal-Social*

DRESSING: dresses and undresses without assistance

COMMUNICATION: asks meaning of words

PLAY: dresses up in clothes belonging to grownups

PLAY: can print a few letters (60–66 months)

*Source:* From Gesell, A. (1940). The first five years of life: The preschool years. New York: Harper and Row (pp. 100–101).

- *Self-regulatory fluctuation* in development means that it fluctuates between times of equilibrium and times of disequilibrium. For example, Gesell characterized the ages of 5, 10, and 15 as ones in which equilibrium was most evident, and the age periods in between as showing more "ups and downs." During puberty, for example, growth of some parts of the body, such as hands and feet, occurs before growth in the limbs, making coordination more difficult, and the uneven timing of the appearance of various sex-related characteristics causes numerous changes in body image and affects self-awareness and identity issues. Parents and teachers have found this last principle especially helpful in understanding how a child whose physical (and social–emotional) development seemed so "together" at one age (e.g., age 10) then seems to "lose it" at another (e.g., ages 11 to 13). Fortunately, according to Gesell, adults can expect another period of equilibrium to occur as the maturational process continues in later adolescence.

### Theoretical Influence and Critique

The precision and detail presented by Gesell and his colleagues have long provided the basis for charting developmental trends in various domains, and his descriptions of typical trends in physical/motor development are still referenced today. His methods of collecting descriptive data were testable and falsifiable, and they were done in a systematic manner that provides a wealth of basic information. However, they did not generate much ongoing research and in-depth theorizing on physical/motor or other areas of development, perhaps because his maturational emphasis was so strong that these growth descriptions "left little to do" (Thelen & Adolph, 1992). Because Gesell attributed motor (and other) development to maturational forces, he did not attempt to explain why there were individual differences or what environmental or genetic factors might promote development of specific skills. Thus, his legacy was primarily in the provision of rich developmental descriptions, with little theorizing in regard to explanations of the "whys" of physical/motor development. Gesell and his colleagues wrote many books that influenced parental and educational practice. Because of their maturational emphasis, the advice given was beneficial in keeping parents and educators from pressuring children to achieve physical/motor and other skills before they were ready to do so. However, Gesell's emphasis on maturation also may have prevented the use of planned environmental stimulation that could have furthered readiness. His work was very influential during most of the 20th century because it appeared to be accurate, internally consistent, and economical, and his models of developmental change periods allowed predictions and actions based on the changes he described.

## McGraw's Theory of Physical/Motor Development

Recently, as research techniques have expanded, there has been a recurrence of interest in genetic, neurological, brain structure, experiential, and structure/ function interactions as having potential for explaining physical/motor development. This renewed interest has resulted in the work of Myrtle McGraw being belatedly appreciated. Myrtle McGraw (1899–1988) was a contemporary of Gesell and Watson. She studied physical/motor development of young children in her work at Columbia University. Although McGraw primarily had an epigenetic perspective, through her normative observations, she began to question Gesell's assumption that structure always preceded function (McGraw, 1935). She was interested in how motor development might be affected, not only by the maturational process, but by environmental opportunities. She was also not in agreement with Watson's view that "nurture" was preeminent, however, because she thought Watson's studies, which focused on more mature organisms, did not really speak to the emergent processes of development. Her view was that structure–function interactions might better explain development. She had an ongoing professional relationship with John Dewey whose theories of inquiry informed and were informed by McGraw's research (Dalton, 1996). Dewey believed that the development of problem-solving and judgment abilities were grounded in motor development, and thus he found McGraw's research useful in his theoretical work. There were two major hypotheses McGraw investigated:

1. Whether children's experiences influence how their biological structures develop; that is, are there structure/function interactions?

2. Whether differences in functioning in one structural area (e.g., motor) could influence development of other structures (e.g., cognitive or affective); that is, does systemic interaction occur?

To test her theoretical questions, McGraw engaged in a longitudinal experiment with a pair of twins, providing physical/motor training of one twin beginning at the end of his first month of life and routine care but no specific physical/motor experiences to the other twin. (Although this type of experiment would not be acceptable today, at that time it was not seen as exceptional because learning experiences for infants were not generally advocated.) Johnny, the twin being given motor experiences, was encouraged to move his limbs, crawl, step when held, and engage in other motor activities as he grew older. He was exposed to an incline when he crawled, given roller skates and a tricycle, encouraged to use swimming movements in water, and to lift, build, and climb extensively. Before he was 2 years old, Johnny could climb rapidly, swim, and roller skate, which are abilities well above those typically seen in children of his age. Johnny's skills extended to cognitive skills as well; he had greater ability to assess problem situations; exhibit persistence when facing motor challenges; estimate distances, sizes, and shapes; and make use of tools to solve problems.

McGraw began giving motor activities to Jimmy during the latter part of his second year, and in a much shorter time period he was able to gain most of these skills, although not at the same level of proficiency as Johnny had shown. The experiment ended when they were age 2 but follow-up was done for a number of years. McGraw reported that Johnny continued to show greater facility in motor coordination and actions, whereas Jimmy had greater linguistic skill. (No early training was given on language, but it is possible that Jimmy received more early verbal attention because he was more sedentary.) McGraw stated, "When all activities are considered, it is safe to say that in so far as quality of performance goes, Johnny has consistently exhibited greater motor coordination and an ability to handle his muscles with ease and grace . . . (He) has also shown greater fortitude in performing difficult feats, such as jumping" (McGraw, quoted in Dalton & Bergenn, 1995, pp. 113–114).

Although it seemed clear that Johnny was more accomplished in many ways, when McGraw's results were published in 1944 (she also made a film), her findings were not accepted as evidence that experience could influence structure and function. Because the maturational emphasis was preeminent in child development, primarily due to Gesell's work, interpretation of McGraw's results followed the then-current theoretical view. That is, the fact that Johnny's motor development was stronger was discounted, and more emphasis was placed on the fact that Jimmy was able to learn most of the skills at a later age. The findings were seen as confirmation of a maturational explanation rather than as evidence that experience had affected the structures and functions of the children's motor development. McGraw found that some of the skills taught Johnny at the early age (e.g., tricycle riding) continued to be well demonstrated, but that others (e.g., climbing steep inclines) did not continue at a proficient level. She explained her observations of the stability/instability of motor skills over time as follows:

- Longitudinal stability of early motor interventions depends on fixity (strength of pattern established when intervention is discontinued). More firmly established patterns are more likely to remain.

- Physical changes in body proportions also affect fixity because body proportion changes may make earlier motor patterns difficult to continue. (Thelen's later work confirmed this.)

- Children's greater discrimination, judgment, and other problem-solving skills may make them inhibit expressions of earlier motor behaviors that require greater physical risk taking.

In sum, McGraw concluded that although early intervention can alter typical behavior patterns, long-term permanence reflects the interaction of many developmental systems.

McGraw also stated some general developmental principles from her studies, drawing on the work of the embryologist Coghill (1933), who found that the movement of embryos affected structural development, and the time period when events occurred was critical in embryo development. In regard to children, McGraw concluded the following:

- There are "critical periods" of development that provide an optimum time for particular aspects of development to occur. During this period, the maturity of various systems are most able to interact successfully to create developmental change. (She did not see these periods as the only times when skills could develop, only that at these times the skills were developed more easily.)

- Development is bidirectional and rather than structure influencing function, structure and function interact to influence each other. That is, structural "readiness" can be affected by functional experience.

- The exhibiting of particular behaviors require both the physical ability to perform the behaviors and the attitudes and perceptions that motivate the behavior. That is, systems are interdependent and physical/motor development is affected by and affects cognitive, language, and social–emotional development.

McGraw contributed a chapter to the first edition of *Child Psychology* as did Gesell. In her chapter, she outlined her theoretical views, some of which were contrary to the views of Gesell. Although she was asked to contribute to the second edition of this volume, she declined, and thus her interactive theoretical model was not recognized widely until present-day theorists reevaluated her work (Gottlieb, 1998). They have now rediscovered her theoretical stance and some theorists have been using her work as a basis for building their own theoretical ideas (e.g., Thelen).

### Theoretical Influence and Critique

McGraw initiated a testable and falsifiable approach to theory-building and used both rationalist and empiricist methods in her work. Her views were not very influential, primarily because of the high visibility and influence of Gesell; however, her work has gained recent interest (Gottlieb, 1998). Her predictions were testable, and the creation of interventions to improve children's physical/motor skills has gained support. Her concept of the "critical period" is being partially supported today by brain research (as "sensitive periods"). Although she demonstrated some important principles of nature/nurture interaction, she did not develop her theoretical perspective sufficiently for it to be considered a full theory of development. With the present emphasis on biological and neuropsychological issues in development, however, a number of contemporary theorists are drawing on her early findings as they reanalyze issues in physical/motor development with newer technological tools. In particular, Thelen has drawn on the early findings of McGraw in her dynamical systems theory of motor development. Other theorists from this perspective have also been examining processes involved in physical/motor development. For example, Adolph (1997) observed infants' crawling and walking behavior on inclines and noted changes in accuracy of their judgment about movement in space. She concluded that motor ability is affected by general experiences, body dimensions, proficiency on flat ground, and the specific method of locomotion.

## Gibson's Theory of Perceptual Development

In the late 19th and early 20th centuries, European Gestalt psychologists identified many features of perception in adults, some of which are still taught in psychology courses today. They did not explore perception as a developmental phenomenon, however. Perception has also been an area of interest for many other theorists, but often as one attribute of cognition; this was the view of both Piaget and Vygotsky. That is, perception was seen to be mediated by cognitive action. For example, Piaget studied infant development of form and size constancy and noted that interactions between sensorimotor schemes and perception were responsible for these achievements (Piaget & Inhelder, 1969). He studied perceptual illusions in older children and concluded that those "field" effects discussed by Gestalt psychologists could not explain perceptual development. He then conducted other experiments from which he concluded that the elaboration of a logicomathematical cognitive structure that "goes beyond perception" (p. 49) is required. That is, he believed that mental operations are not directly derived from the perceptual system.

Perception as the major focus of study was investigated by Eleanor Gibson (1910–2002), who spent most of her academic career at Cornell University, although due to "nepotism rules" she did not have a tenured position during most of her career. Her husband (called J. J.) was also at Cornell and was interested in basic perceptual processes. Through intense study of visual perception, he developed a theory that perception is realistically based and determined by the stimulus features of the environment (i.e., the "affordances") (Gibson, 1979). Eleanor Gibson shared this perspective but applied it to developmental issues. The theoretical base for their studies is an ecological one, which takes in features of the environment as explanatory mechanisms. J. J. Gibson's view countered the idea of Gestalt and constructivist theorists who said that perceptions had to be inferred by cognitive processes rather than being directly linked to perceptual structures. The developmental question studied by Eleanor Gibson (1969) was whether infants and young children could directly perceive the elements of their surroundings at an early age or whether a long period of maturation was required. Eleanor Gibson had observed her own children's motor and perceptual development and thought that the processes of perception for children might be similar to those for adults; that is, that the affordances of the environment could be directly perceived without mental inferences. Thus, she conducted experiments to study how children's perceptual skills developed.

She conducted many perceptual experiments during her career but is best known for her experiment with crawling infants using a "visual cliff" (Gibson & Walk, 1960). This was a tablelike structure with a clear glass inset that made the surface appear to be a place where the children would fall off if they continued to crawl in that direction. She found that, contrary to the idea that infants could not distinguish depth perceptually, they refused to cross the area that appeared to be a place where they would fall. Thus, she demonstrated that depth perception is evident by the time children begin to be mobile. Gibson also studied children's perception of surfaces and textures, location of objects in space, perception of directions and events, representations of objects (e.g., pictures and drawings), and perception of symbols, including graphic symbols used in reading.

Gibson (1997) described a number of general propositions regarding perceptual development, including that the environment affords opportunities to use evolved perception and action systems, there is always perception–action reciprocity, behavior is organized in functional segments (i.e., tasks) that are embedded in a stream of behavior (i.e., nested), and that control, prospectivity, and flexibility are the hallmarks of behavior. She defined control as the ability to select the appropriate behavior from one's repertoire of behaviors and stated that this type of behavior can be observed soon after birth. Prospectivity is the "looking ahead" aspect of behavior, that is, the ability to anticipate consequences of actions, whereas flexibility is the ability to choose the segments of behavior appropriate for the task. Perceptual development, therefore, is being able to perceive the affordances in the environment through spontaneous exploratory activity, observe the consequences of such activity, and select means of exploration. Gibson saw perception as contributing to higher-order cognition by providing increased flexibility and problem-solving actions, by discriminating roles for object and self, and by perceiving others as causal agents (i.e., agency). Recently, Gibson stated that human agency, prospectivity, search for order in the world, and flexibility are the major vehicles of development (Gibson & Pick, 2000).

She explained the perceptual process as one of differentiation, in which distinctions are made between objects and events as a result of experiences with the affordances in the environment. In one of her books, she stated, "The trends in perceptual development emerge as the product of both experience with an environment and the maturing powers of an individual. There is no either-or issue" (1969, p. 446). Gibson disagreed with the constructivist idea that perception requires inferences, rather, she said, "Perception is not a matter of matching representation in the head, but one of extracting the invariants in stimulus information. We do not perceive less because we conceive more" (p. 449). She also disagreed with behaviorist and information processing views, stating that the laws of perceptual development ". . .are laws of differentiating and filtering, not laws of association; and laws of the reduction of uncertainty, not laws of external reinforcement" (p. 471). She identified three trends (not stages!) in perceptual development, as follows:

- The trend toward increasing specificity in stimulus discrimination, including the ability to generalize discriminating features to less clear examples, to show less variability in perceptual judgements, and to need less time to make accurate discriminations.

- The trend toward optimization of attention, including the ability to focus actively, to become sustained, systematic, economical, and selective, and to ignore irrelevant information.

- The trend toward increasing economy of information pickup, by gaining minimal sets of distinctive features, detecting invariants, and finding higher-order structures.

Gibson stated, "I am not worried that we do not have all of the answers. Nobody does. The important thing now is to ask the right questions . . ." (Gibson, 1997, p. 42).

### Theoretical Influence and Critique

Gibson provided a testable/falsifiable theory that has been a source of recent studies of perceptual development, especially in infants and young children. As is the case with McGraw, much of Gibson's work was generally overlooked in earlier decades, but her theory of perceptual development is now well recognized, and she gained scientific honors later in life. Gibson was instrumental in demonstrating empirical ways that such perception can be directly explored. According to Miller (2002), Gibson's theory has contributed to "putting the body back into developmental psychology" (p. 362), where it had long been absent. The ecological theory of perceptual development, which Gibson's work exemplified, is now being studied by a number of other researchers. Her colleague, Anne Pick (1997), who has investigated preschool children's systematic categorization of objects based on their affordances, commented, ". . . conceptual learning is grounded in perceptual learning . . ." (p. 366). She added, "From the ecological perspective, perception is not to be contrasted with cognition; it is the most basic kind of cognition" (p. 366).

Presently, infant perception is being studied in detail by numerous researchers. Findings show that 4- to 5-month-olds are able to perceive colors as the same even if lighting conditions change, and they can organize color into categories similar to those adults use (Catherwood, Crassini, & Freiberg, 1989). Their form perception develops during their first year, and by 12 months, they can perceive different forms just by watching a moving light outline them (Skouteris, McKenzie, & Day, 1992). Infants of 9 months perceive the affordances of toys with novel features and try to reproduce those features when shown similar-looking toys (Baldwin, Markman, & Melartin, 1993). Thus, evidence is accumulating that Gibson's view of infant perceptual processes having cognitive properties appears to be accurate.

## Neuroscience Influences on Developmental Theory

Another body of research that is now influencing human development systems theory is that being reported by neuroscientists. The blending of neurological and psychological studies gave rise in the late 20th century to the integrated specialization of neuropsychology. Neuropsychologists have typically been concerned with diagnosing children's learning or behavior problems, using various performance tests, and interpreting the results in terms of their general knowledge of brain structures and functions. However, as more sophisticated techniques for measuring brain activity have been invented, they are now also studying the developmental processes involved in human brain evolution, and this research is suggesting that ". . . the constructionist views of cognitive development pioneered by Piaget and later elaborated by Case (1991) provided plausible steps in constructing models of human cognitive evolution, especially when considered in conjunction with modern understandings of environmental influences on brain development" (Gibson, K. R., 2005, p. 124). Much of the early research has been focused on differences in brains of apes and humans, which involve "degrees of mental construction capacity" (p. 131), rather than totally different types of structures. According to K. R. Gibson, Case's view that "expanded neural information-processing capacities form the basis of expanded mental constructional capacity during the maturation of the human child" (p. 131) is gaining support from neuroscience research evidence. Similarly, Macleod (2005) concluded that Piaget's stress on the importance of sensorimotor activity in infancy has received support from in-depth study of the cerebellum. Although the cerebellum has long been known to govern balance, motor coordination, and motor responses to visual stimuli, its linkages to the higher brain centers has been increasingly evident. Research is even showing that motor aspects of speech production, working memory, and motor planning link the cerebellum with higher cognitive processes (Gibson & Petersen, 1991). Extensive study has also been done regarding plasticity and localization of brain areas related to language development (Bates, 2005). Neuroscientists have provided precise descriptions of the development of the human neurological system during the first years of life (e.g., Chugani, 1999).

Other neuroscientists have investigated whether there are critical periods for both brain development and refinement of particular cognitive skills (Lichtman, 2001); for example, the potential links between increases in brain growth in adolescence with development of scientific reasoning abilities (Kwon & Lawson, 2000). This research may confirm some of Myrtle McGraw's observations of critical/sensitive periods for learning particular skills. Kurt Fischer now draws on brain development theory in his model of developmental change. Fischer compared the cortical growth cycles that have been made evident through brain research to the nested cognitive developmental cycles found in his microgenetic skills research and has proposed a theoretical model that links the cycles of cortical growth to each level of cognitive skill development (Fischer & Rose, 1998).

In addition to neuroscience evidence of brain-cognition links, neuropsychologists have studied brain linkages to social and emotional development. Jaak Panksepp has made links between animal research on brain development in areas related to emotions and human brain development in the emotional domain (1989). For example, he has measured the activity of emotional systems of the brain and charted how the development of higher brain centers affects emotional regulation and self-organization. He has written extensively on how brain emotional systems activity relates to the construction of human social systems (1998a). Panksepp has made a strong case for the importance of play activity (especially rough-and-tumble play) in frontal lobe development in children with attention deficit hyperactivity (1998b) and has also devised interventions for autism based on his studies of brain development (1989). He is especially concerned with "the widespread pathologization of rough-and-tumble play in the American school system" (1998a, p. 320) and pointed out that the pervasive use of psychostimulants to reduce children's activity levels may be harming frontal lobe development in areas related to attention regulation processes; that is, motor activity may be essential for organizing attention. The neuroscience "systems" view of development includes brain development as another part of the person–environment interactive system. Other researchers are also interested in brain system developmental differences, especially for children who have special needs such as autism (e.g., Baron-Cohen, 2003; Carper & Courchesne, 2000), trauma such as sexual abuse or traumatic brain injury (Bremner et al., 1997; Rutter, Chadwick, Schaffer, & Brown, 1980), and learning/reading disabilities (Flowers, Wood, & Naylor, 1991). Many of the studies published in the journal *Developmental Neuropsychology* focus on issues related to the development of special-needs children. Of course, the study of gender role differences related to brain differences has also been of great interest to researchers and theorists (discussed in chapter 9).

Because much brain research has focused on animal brains, human adult brains, and brains of children at developmental risk, information about the typical course of child brain development over the years from birth to adolescence is still somewhat limited. There is, however, a body of research being amassed, and developmental trends are being established (Bergen & Coscia, 2000). For example, researchers have determined that the "building blocks" for brain development are created before birth, with approximately 60% of human genes dedicated to brain development. Only about 25% of the brain's potential developmental is completed at birth, however. The majority of neurons (nerve cells) are present at birth, but most are not connected into networks. The connecting process (synaptogenesis) is rapid during the first year of life, with the sensorimotor areas of the brain being most active during the 2- to 3-month period and the frontal lobe becoming active by 6 to 8 months. Typically, synaptic generation results in a dense set of connections (i.e., "overwired"). The activity pattern of the brain of the 1-year-old child is more similar to that of the adult brain than it is to the activity pattern of the newborn brain. During the first year brain weight increases from about 1 pound at birth to 2 pounds, partly due to the increase in synapses and partly due to the coating of nerve axons with fatty glial cells (myelination) that act to speed neural signals. Because 75% of brain development occurs after birth, the experiences children have during their early years affect the ways their individual brains are structured and the ways they perform.

During the toddler and preschool age periods, the synapses continue to expand and reach about 1,000 trillion—twice the density of the adult brain. The toddler brain is 2½ times as active as the adult brain, and as the glial cells coat the axons, the weight of the brain continues to increase. The structures of the brain that are sensitive to language production (Broca) and comprehension (Wernicke) become active, and language typically develops during this period. Connections among areas of the brain, such as frontal lobe connection to the limbic system, which generates basic emotional responses, result in initial ability to understand emotional meanings. During the age period from 3 to 8, there is extensive growth of frontal lobe networks, and thus, speed of processing, memory, and problem solving increase. The brain is at 90% of its adult weight by age 6, and the frontal lobe of the cortex is at its most dense around age 7. Frontal lobe maturation is evident in children's increased ability to attend and to inhibit impulses. From age 8 through adolescence, the maturation of the frontal lobe continues with pruning being extensive. Myelination of the higher brain centers also continues and is completed in late adolescence. Measures of speed and efficiency of thought, spatial working memory, emotional regulation, planning and problem-solving skills, and metacognition seem to be correlated with brain developmental change. By adolescence there appear to be stable individual differences in brain structures and functions. However, the brain's "plasticity" and resilience continues to provide developmental change throughout the life span as varied experiences occur. Figure 11.1 shows these trends in brain development.

Although the links between brain development research and human development theory are tentative at this time, as more research demonstrating these links with emotional, social, motor, language, and cognitive development are found, the biological and ecological systems are likely to be further integrated. For example, in a review of recent research Kuhn (2006) pointed out that the close connection between brain development and cognition in young children has a parallel in adolescence, when another increase in brain development occurs. Although there is more variability at this second period, evidence points to increases in a range of cognitive processes that parallel this period of brain development.

Segalowitz (1994) sees the field of neuropsychology as potentially contributing greatly to understanding of human development because it may be possible to find the brain correlates of many developmental constructs. He even suggests

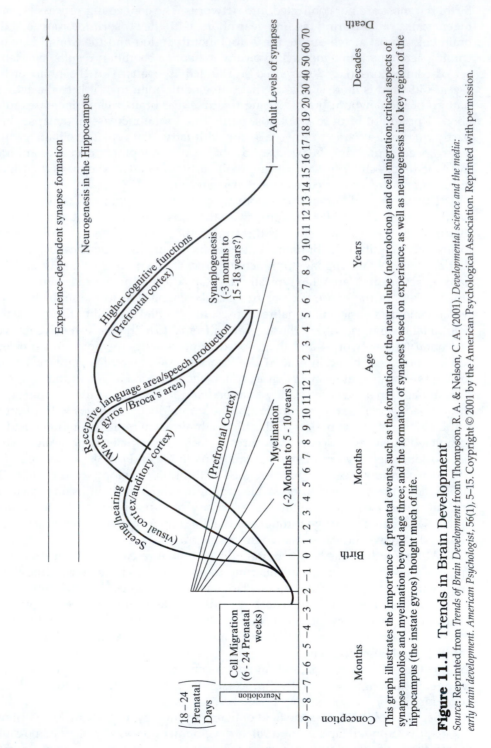

**Figure 11.1  Trends in Brain Development**

*Source:* Reprinted from *Trends of Brain Development* from Thompson, R. A. & Nelson, C. A. (2001). *Developmental science and the media: early brain development. American Psychologist*, 56(1), 5–15. Coypright © 2001 by the American Psychological Association. Reprinted with permission.

This graph illustrates the Importance of prenatal events, such as the formation of the neural lube (neurolotion) and cell migration; critical aspects of synapse mnolios and myelination beyond age three; and the formation of synapses based on experience, as well as neurogenesis in o key region of the hippocampus (the instate gyros) thought much of life.

that brain research might show that Freud's construct of personality development (i.e., id, ego, and superego) "depends on physiological maturation" (p. 74). Thus, he suggested a "grand theory" of development may at last be possible. He stated, "We are at a very important time in the history of developmental psychology because of our new technologies that allow us to make this neurophysiology–psychology mapping. The field of developmental neuropsychology forms the bridge that lead to this new paradigm" (p. 86).

### Theoretical Influence and Critique

The neuroscience perspective is only beginning to influence theories of development, and the major way that this is happening is in reconceptualizing studies of development to include measures of brain activity as part of the analysis. The link between neuropsychologists and developmental theorists is not yet strong, but neuroscience research is beginning to affect study of developmental change. Physical/motor and brain development relationships are the subject of some present-day research; for example, research is showing that animal rough-and-tumble play may affect development of neuronal connections (Siviy, 2002) and that children's active recess play may affect ability to attend to school tasks (Pelligrini & Bjorklund, 1996). Some studies from traditional theoretical perspectives may be replicated with the addition of neurological measures. For example, ERP (event related potentials) are showing differences in brain activity at various ages on some cognitive tasks. Whether this perspective will be a fully developed theory or merely be used to support or discount theoretical ideas of the past is not presently known. However, it may help to answer some of the theoretical debates (e.g., structure or function change) as it is used more in research on human development.

## Plomin's and Scarr's Behavioral Genetics Theoretical Perspective

Another perspective on the interactions among biological and environmental systems comes from behavioral genetics theorists such as Plomin and Scarr, who attempt to account for the amount of influence genetic factors and environmental factors have on development, using methods derived from empiricist research models. At earlier time periods in the study of human development there were distinct perspectives on the amount of influence genetics (nature) had on developmental change as compared to environmental factors (nurture). For example, Francis Galton (1822–1911) extended the evolutionary genetics perspective of Charles Darwin to behavioral traits such as intelligence, and this eugenics movement was popular during the 1920s and 1930s, until the atrocities of the Nazi regime showed the extreme of this viewpoint. Watson's and Skinner's emphasis on environment as the only determining factor of behavior was very influential during the period between 1940 and 1970. With the advent of increasing sophistication in studying genetic factors in humans, which has its basis in the study of molecular genetics and developmental biology initiated by the discovery of the DNA double helix (Watson, 1968; Edleman, 1992), a more sophisticated look at the nature/nurture debate has been evidenced. Neubauer and Neubauer (1996) state, "It becomes plainer by the day that the either/or choice of nature or nurture falls far short in explaining the complexity of human life. The polarization of the debate must be dismantled, and we can consider this alternative: a complementary series of influences where at one end environment fashions certain behavior, and at the other heredity alone molds various traits and disorders—but in between, where most individual features reside, lies the complex interaction of both extremes" (p. 8).

Developmental behavioral genetics researchers such as Robert Plomin (1986, 1989, 1994) and Sandra Scarr (Scarr, 1992; Scarr & McCartney, 1983) have also stated that genetic influences on development must be investigated within the context of environmental system factors, although they define the "system" very differently from theorists such as Bronfenbrenner, whose emphasis is on a wider set of bioecological factors. Both of these theorists have conducted research and reviewed other studies of genetic influences on development, attempting to find the proportion of variance in individuals that is contributed by genes or various environmental influences such as parenting or schooling. These theorists collect a range of variables from longitudinal adoption, kinship, fraternal twin, and identical twin studies to find relationships among these variables at different age levels of the individuals and to compare the amount of variation that can be attributed to genetics and to environment. For example, Plomin (1994) described a multivariate analysis comparing adopted and nonadopted young children's scores on the Bayley (an individual measure) with scores on the HOME (an environmental measure), which reported that correlations are higher for nonadopted children; that is, genetic factors accounted for about a third of the HOME-Bayley correlation at 2 years. The correlation of the HOME with WISC-R scores at age 7 shows an even greater predictive capacity for nonadopted children. He suggested, however, that most studies have used correlations of "passive" variables and suggested that researchers give more attention to children's active role in forming their experiences. He referenced Scarr's work (Scarr & McCartney, 1983) that supports the role of individual child characteristics (derived from genetics) in influencing the environment. These studies look at correlations of child reactive and active variables, and they show that children are "increasingly able to modify, select, and create their environments" (Plomin, 1994, p. 151). Plomin, who is director of the Social, Genetic and Developmental Psychiatry Centre at the Institute of Psychiatry, King's College, London, is presently engaged in an extensive longitudinal study of twins in England to investigate how the genetic/environment relationships over the life span are evidenced.

Scarr (1992) concluded from her research that genes drive experiences and evoke environmental responses; that is, children's innate characteristics affect how much they seek certain experiences and are influenced by such experiences. She believes that with "good enough" parents in an environment that meets the basic needs of the child the genetic influences will be primary. These conclusions were primarily based on the research evidence from the Minnesota Adoption Project, which Scarr conducted with colleague Rich Weinberg (Scarr & Weinberg, 1983). They found that although environmental influence could be seen at early ages, these effects tend to diminish by adolescence when young people create their own environments by their choices of friends and activities, expanding their "non-shared environments." Her studies have also included ones that estimate the relationship between good and poor child care and young children's developmental progress, and her work has been influential in areas of social policy regarding young children's care (Scarr, 1984).

### Theoretical Influence and Critique

Although developmental behavioral genetics theorists are coming from very different theoretical bases than that of rationalist theorists, their view has some congruence with that of Thomas and Chess, who discuss how the "goodness of fit" between children's temperament and parental behaviors influence children's long-term development (Chess & Thomas, 1999). Thomas and Chess, of course, used a research paradigm that arose from a rationalist perspective on development. As genetic research methods become more prominent, there will be many more opportunities to test the theoretical perspective of developmental behavioral genetic theorists and examine how the genetic characteristics of children affect development.

## Summary

The study of physical, motor, and perceptual development was of great interest during the early and mid 20th century, and an extensive body of descriptive data was amassed. Gesell's descriptive research still influences early assessment, although his view of maturation as the primary cause of development has given way to an interactionist view. Both McGraw and Gibson were working at times when women scientists' contributions were often overlooked; however, their work provided some empirical verification of the theoretical issues they studied and has led to much recent research interest. Physical, motor, and perceptual theories have still not received as much attention as theories related to social/emotional, cognitive/language, and sociomoral/gender role development, which have been the focus of most traditional and contemporary theorists. With recent emphasis on microgenetic research, dynamical systems methodology, and the brain research techniques of neuroscience, however, an emphasis on finding relationships among physical, motor, and perceptual development and other developmental areas is likely to be greater in the future.

## Case 3. The Hopeful Family

The Hopeful family has brought their 8-month-old twins, Bart and Bob, to Dr. Gesell and his associate, Dr. McGraw, because they are concerned that Bart is not yet sitting up or crawling, whereas Bob sat up at 6 months and is already pulling himself to stand. Neither Bart or Bob seems to attend to their parents' voices or reach for objects unless the objects are very close. Their older child, Brad, had crawled at 5 months and walked at 10 months, and he had spoken 5 words at 1 year of age. Bart and Bob had been 1½ months premature and weighed only 3½ pounds at birth, and they were also in and out of the hospital for "failure to thrive" for the first 5 months of their life. Bill and Betty Hopeful both work full time, and so Bart and Bob are cared for by Betty's grandmother, who is frail and often ill. (Brad is already in school.) When the doctors examine Bart and Bob, they do not find any obvious sensory or physical/motor anomalies. That is, their hearing and sight seem normal for a 6/7-month-old, reflexes are appropriate, and muscle tone is adequate. They suggest, however, that the twins might benefit by being seen by Dr. Gibson and either Dr. Plomin or Dr. Scarr. At this point, they did not think that brain imaging would be useful.

Based on their theoretical views, what might these doctors say is the status of the twin's development, and what might each think explains that status?

What suggestions might Dr. Gesell and Dr. McGraw give to the Hopefuls, and would their advice be similar?

What other tests might Dr. Gesell's colleague, Dr. Gibson, want to do to find out more about Bart and Bob?

What other information might Dr. Plomin or Dr. Scarr want to have about the children's genetic and environmental situation? Would they judge the parents as "good enough"?

Should Dr. Chugani conduct a neurological evaluation using a bran scan or other tests? What information might this add to what the doctors need to know?

## Readings

E. J. Gibson, From Perception to Inference, pp. 392–394.

Sidney J. Segalowitz, Developmental Psychology and Brain Development: A Historical perspective, pp. 395–401.

## Suggested Readings

Gesell, A. (1940). Understanding the preschool child. In A. Gesell, *The first five years of life* (pp. 3–7). New York: Harper.

Gibson, E. J. (1969). From perception to inference. In E. J. Gibson, *Principles of perceptual learning and development* (pp. 448–450, 471–472). New York: Appleton-Century-Crofts.

Plomin, R. (1989). Environment and genes: Determinants of behavior. *American Psychologist, 44*(2), 105–111.

Segalowitz, S. J. (1994). Developmental psychology and brain development: A historical perspective. In G. Dawson & K. W. Fischer (Eds.) *Human behavior and the developing brain* (pp. 67–73, 75–80). New York: Guilford.

*Source:* © Mike Smith EDT, King Features Syndicate.

# Theoretical Perspectives from Ecological, Bioecological, Developmental Psychobiological, and Nonlinear Dynamical Systems

Many theorists have noted how both the individual and the individual's environment play a role in the course of development, and they have usually discussed these interactions using linear models. One group of theorists has made the nonlinear interactions within the ecological system and the individual person's potential (bioecological) the prime focus of their work. Although their theoretical perspective can be applied to all developmental domains, some have focused more attention on social and cultural influences, and thus their research has primarily investigated social development and behavior within various contexts. The early impetus for "person–environment" systemic analysis came from the work of Kurt Lewin, the founder of the field of social psychology, but it has been elaborated by Urie Bronfenbrenner, who created a model focused on how the embedded ecological systems interact to affect human development. The specific effects of the culture in interaction with the person/environment has also been of particular interest to John Ogbu. As noted in chapter 11, neuroscience is providing a number of insights that are also affecting human development theory, and as neuropsychological study progresses, it is providing evidence about the systemic aspects of developmental change in brain structures and functions from birth to old age. These findings have influenced theoretical perspectives of developmental psychobiology, exemplified by Gilbert Gottlieb's model. Another important influence that has begun to affect recent theories of human development has come from the physical sciences, primarily from theoretical physics. This chapter provides an outline of theoretical perspectives related to ecological, bioecological, developmental psychobiological, and nonlinear dynamical systems as applied to human development. It discusses the theories of Urie Bronfenbrenner, who proposed an ecological/bioecological systems view of development; Gilbert Gottlieb, who proposed a developmental psychobiological systems model; and Esther Thelen, who was a pioneer in application of nonlinear dynamical systems theory to human development problems. Kurt Lewin's early influence on ecological theory and John Ogbu's recent cultural ecological view are also presented.

## Other Theories Affecting Human Development Theory

Many startling new theories of the physical world were proposed and investigated by scientists during the 20th century. The study of the microscopic world— those aspects of the physical world that are not observable to the human eye without technological assistance—has provided much information about the smallest aspects of the universe (e.g., protons, electrons, quarks, muons), resulting in the theory of quantum mechanics, which explains these phenomena, the principles governing their interactions, and the mathematical rules that govern quantum reality (Herbert, 1985). For the most part, these scientists are dealing with linear phenomena, that is, phenomena in which cause and effect can be predicted. However, they have also found some problems that do not lend themselves to linear mathematical models. The scientists who try to predict large-scale environmental phenomena such as weather and disease epidemics are developing a set of understandings of the nonlinear and often chaotic systems they need to explain. Linear predictions are rarely useful in predicting large-scale complex phenomenon (e.g., hurricanes, epidemics); to study such systems scientists use numerous data points from many sources to develop computer-generated models (i.e., mappings). They have discovered that even a small change in input into a chaotic system at one point may result in unexpected impacts at some other points in the system (Gleick, 1987). Other scientists are attempting to understand what happens at "the edge of chaos" when very complex and apparently chaotic systems self-organize. This theoretical perspective, usually called "nonlinear dynamical systems" or "complexity" theory involves trying to understand complex systems such as economics and evolutionary processes that, although they seem chaotic, are really self-organizing (Waldrop, 1992). The important aspect of all this work for human development theory is that there are now many scientists who believe that the phenomena being explained by these models are just examples of how nonlinear dynamical systems operate, and because human beings are similar (e.g., nonlinear dynamic systems), the rules discovered by these scientists might also be applied to problems of human developmental change. Although this is presently just a small part of the human development theoretical landscape, it is possible that more influence will come from these theoretical concepts in the future.

## Lewin's Field Theory

Kurt Lewin (1890–1947) was born in Germany but came to the United States in 1932, subsequently working at Stanford, Cornell, and the University of Iowa. His influence on human development theory was important in a number of ways. First, Lewin stressed that human behavior is the function of both the person and the environment. He designed a formula that expressed the person/environment interaction in symbolic terms, $B = f(P,E)$. The $B$ stands for behavior, which is a function ($f$) of the interaction between the person ($P$) and the environment ($E$) (1931, 1936). He strongly believed it was not possible to explain human behavior without considering both person and environment factors and also their interaction in the field (Deaux & Wrightman, 1988). He developed a model of Force Field Analysis, using diagrams that pictured the conflicting forces affecting behavior issues. Second, his "field theory" advocated that research be done in natural settings, using processes of "action" research. Third, his view that social psychological behavior could be studied in carefully designed empirical research settings created the discipline of social psychology (Ash, 1992). Fourth, much of his research involved the study of group processes, and he greatly influenced the study of cooperative learning and other group process dynamics (Sherman, Schmuck, & Schmuck, 2004). He was not focused on developmental (i.e., change over time) processes, however, but on more immediate behavior change in various environments. Developmental change questions would be taken up later by Bronfenbrenner and other contextual and ecological psychologists.

## Bronfenbrenner's Ecological/Bioecological Theory

Urie Bronfenbrenner (1917–2005) was born in Russia but came to the United States at the age of 6. He was a professor at Cornell University for many years. Bronfenbrenner was greatly influenced by Lewin's assertion that the person is embedded in an ecological field that contains many interacting forces (1979). Bronfenbrenner drew on this perspective to design a bioecological model of human development. He also agreed with Lewin that field research is vital. In his early writing on the basic principles of his theory, he stated that many types of research "involve situations that are unfamiliar, artificial, and short-lived and call for unusual behaviors that are difficult to generalize to other settings. From this perspective, it can be said that much of developmental psychology, as it now exists, *is the science of the strange behavior of children in strange situations with strange adults for the briefest possible periods of time*" (1979, p. 19). Bronfenbrenner's original model, which he called "ecology of human development," had 11 definitions and 4 ecological system levels. He subsequently added another ecological level—the historical one—and renamed the model "bioecological," which stresses consideration of biological systems interaction (1993, 2005). These are Bronfenbrenner's basic definitions from his earlier work, termed the ecology of human development (1979).

> The ecology of human development involves the scientific study of the progressive, mutual accommodation between an active, growing human being and the changing

properties of the immediate settings in which the developing person lives, as this process is affected by relations between these settings, and by the larger contexts in which the settings are embedded. (p. 21)

Human development is the process through which the growing person gains a more extended, differentiated, and valid conception of the ecological environment, and engages in activities of greater complexity in the environment or changes the environment. (p. 27)

The systems in the ecological model outlined by Bronfenbrenner are

1. **Microsystem:** pattern of activities, roles, and interpersonal relations experienced by the developing person in a given (face-to-face) setting, for example, home, child care, playground, school, neighborhood.

2. **Mesosystem:** interrelations among two or more microsystems; for example, interrelation between home and school.

3. **Exosystem:** settings that do not involve the developing person as an active participant, but in which events occur that affect, or are affected by, what happens in the setting containing the developing person; for example, parent's work life (working late) may affect child.

4. **Macrosystem:** consistent settings of the subculture or culture and the belief systems or ideology underlying those consistencies; for example, different socioeconomic or religious factors may perpetuate the setting types or one country's laws or politics may influence the developing person's growth opportunities.

5. **Chronosystem:** historical contexts that affect the settings at any of the other levels; for example, the "baby boomer" generation has had different ecological settings than the "depression" generation (a newer addition to theory—see Bronfenbrenner and Morris, 1998).

Although in the model the various systems appear to be static, in actuality, they are constantly changing and interacting, creating ecological transitions. These ecological transitions occur when there is a change in the developing person's position in the ecological setting as a result of change in role, setting, or both. For example, in the home microsystem, a new baby changes the role and interaction patterns of the parents and older children within that setting and may involve changes in other parts of the microsystem or in the mesosystem, such as in the extended family, the school, or church. If the mother discontinues working, an exosystem change, this may then positively affect child care but negatively affect income. Macrosystem changes may also occur; for example, the parent's loss of income then requires applying for child medical assistance. The chronosystem may also affect the family if war, depression, or other historical change occurs. In the family, one of the parents might be called into active military service if war occurs. All these systemic interactions will affect child health and developmental progress. In contrast to the linear, one cause/one effect method of studying developmental change, research that examines systems in interaction is much more complicated to design.

Because Bronfenbrenner was critical of both existing experimental and naturalistic approaches to research, he discussed how research should be conducted when studying systems. In contrast to the types of research models he had criticized, he suggested that human development research should address the following components:

1. Ecological validity: the extent to which the experienced environment has the properties assumed to be there by the researcher
2. Developmental validity: evidence that the changes observed carry over to other settings and times
3. Planned or natural experiments: ecological experiments should contrast two or more systems while controlling other sources of influence
4. Transforming experiments: ones that systematically alter or restructure existing ecological systems. Analysis must consider the interdependent systems, not just separate systems.

### The Process-Person-Context-Time Model

Bronfenbrenner further developed his theory and added both the chronosystem element and a greater emphasis on the biological person component (Bronfenbrenner & Morris, 1998). This resulted in the PPCT Model, which consists of four elements that interact to affect development. It includes the developmental process (P) of systemic interaction; the person (P) elements of dispositions, resources, and demand characteristics that influence the interactions; the context (C) of nested levels or systems (e.g., micro, meso, exo, macro); and time (T) dimensions such as ontogenetic, family, and historical time. He suggested that research should include all these model elements to provide dynamic explanations for human development. The expansion of the microsystem elements and the addition of the chronosystem provided a more precise but also more dynamic conceptualization of his theory. Bronfenbrenner credits Elder for demonstrating that the model needed consideration of the chronosystem (Bronfenbrenner, 2005).

Figure 12.1 shows one example of how the bioecological system can be conceptualized.

Bronfenbrenner and Morris (1998) stated that development takes place through a "progressively more complex reciprocal interaction" (p. 996) at the person (microsystem, mesosystem) level and at the immediate and remote environment levels (exosystem, macrosystem, chronosystem). Because Bronfenbrenner saw human development as a result of systemic interactions, he was especially concerned about the increasingly chaotic environment of contemporary life (Bronfenbrenner & Evans, 2000). In his last work, he asked, "From the perspective of the bioecological model, what is the prospect for the future development of our species?" (2005, p. 14). His ongoing concern for these broader system elements was initially evidenced in his Russian cross-cultural studies. Also, he was one of the original founders of Head Start, a program designed to affect many ecological levels of children's lives, and his policy work related to families and children continued throughout his life. He believed that it was essential for both scholars and

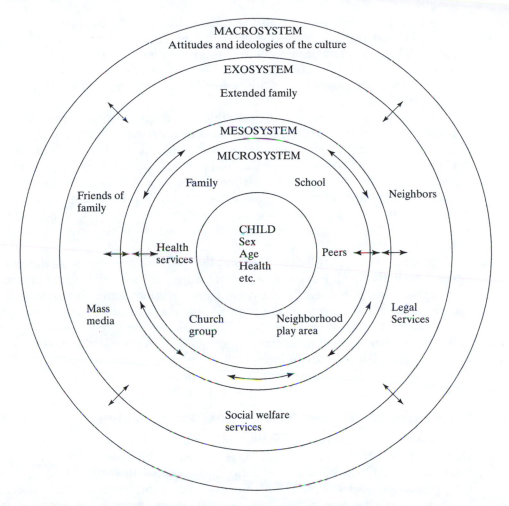

**Figure 12.1** A Conceptualization of a Bioecological System
*Source:* Reprinted from *A Conceptualization of a Bioecological System* from *The Child: Development in a Social Context* (p. 648), by C. B. Kopp & J. B. Krakow (eds.), 1982, Reading, MA: Addison-Wesley. Reprinted by permission.

citizens to promote cultural and policy systems that helped to enhance human development rather than to impede its advancement.

### Theoretical Influence and Critique

Bronfenbrenner's model has been influential in the design of recent research studies, which often now include consideration of a number of ecological and bioecological factors as influences on developmental processes. However, he remained generally unsatisfied with the research approaches that attempted to measure these interactions. For example, he critiqued research that confounds variables at the macrosystem level and suggested that every study include some assessment of the "meaning to the research subjects of key elements of the model to which they are exposed." He also suggested that there should be "a contrast between at least two macrosystems . . . represented . . . by psychological substance" (1993, p. 39). Thus, although the theory is potentially testable, because of its systemic complexity, it is often difficult to falsify or predict from research. The model does serve to simplify a complex perspective but the methodology to test it well is still complex.

Bronfenbrenner's perspective has influenced child assessment practices, especially in relation to young children's assessment. Because children may act differently in various settings, assessment in only one setting may not have developmental validity. For example, a child may use extensive language at home but speak only minimally at school. If the child is not assessed in both settings, the developmental validity of the assessment is suspect. Especially for children with disabilities whose performance may differ greatly in a testing versus an observational setting, ecological assessments are now a more common practice (Bergen & Everington, 1994).

Because of his belief that all levels of the system have effects on children's development, Bronfenbrenner was active in laying out the implications of his theory for policy and practice at the exosystem, macrosystem, and chronosystem levels. He is regarded as one of the world's leading scholars in developmental theory related to human ecology—the field he created. His recent inclusion of the biological within his ecological framework, which renamed it the bioecological theory, extended his work and brought it more clearly into line with neuropsychological and nonlinear dynamical system theoretical trends (2005).

## Ogbu's Cultural Ecological Theoretical Perspective

A prominent and influential contextual/sociohistorical anthropologist, John Ogbu (1939–2003) also contributed insights into developmental change in cultural minority groups in the United States by his discussion of a cultural ecological perspective. Ogbu, a native of Nigeria, was a professor at University of California, Berkeley, until his untimely death while undergoing surgery. From his perspective as a member of an African nation, he examined the "theories of success" of families in low socioeconomic and minority cultures in the United States (1981). His explanation for why such families did not follow "accepted" parenting practices was that in their cultural group there were other behaviors that were valued as helping children to be successful in their environment. That is, their "theories of success" differed from those of the majority culture because they were influenced by the ecological environment (both sociocultural and built environment) in which they lived. He also studied black youth in schools and analyzed why they often did not live up to their academic potential by investigating the many ecological factors that might affect their school performance (1986). He coined the term "acting white" that expressed their fear of being alienated from their own culture if they accepted the majority culture of the school. He also analyzed why various minority groups (ones he termed "voluntary" immigrants such as Asian Americans and ones who were "involuntary" immigrants such as African Americans and Native Americans) had different responses to schooling

(1992, 1994). His most recent book (2003) described how these cultural attitudes were even pervasive for African Americans living in a high socioeconomic area.

### Theoretical Influence and Critique

Ogbu's studies of differential education achievement among minority populations has been influential because they provided an in-depth and extensive description of the varied effects that sociohistorical and cultural ecological factors can have on young people's ability to be successful in school and in society. He demonstrated that this perspective can provide valuable insights into cultural ecological problems and potentially assist in solving some of those problems. However, his work was cut short by his untimely death.

## Gottlieb's Developmental Psychobiological Theoretical Perspectives

When early theorists such as Arnold Gesell and Myrtle McGraw began their work, the emphasis on biological factors influencing development was strong, primarily due to Darwinian evolutionary theory influences. Thus they investigated biological as well as environmental aspects using the research methods available to them at the time (primarily observations of children's behaviors). For example, they observed that the growth and strengthening of infants' arms and their increased visual range enabled them to develop reaching and grasping skills. Their work exemplified the rationalist view of development that includes an element of internal unfolding (epigenesis) in the developmental process but also gave a role to environmental factors. Similarly, Eleanor Gibson found that a particular level of infants' motor skill development (e.g., crawling ability) was closely tied to their cognitive awareness of the appearance of lack of support on the "visual cliff." Infants with crawling ability perceived the apparent depth of the glass covering, whereas those who did not yet have the skill of crawling did not have this awareness. Recent research in neuroscience and neuropsychology have provided stronger support for a systemic view of development, linking biological and psychological aspects more closely, and thus, another look is being taken at biology/psychology interface.

Gilbert Gottlieb (1929–) a professor at the University of North Carolina, Chapel Hill, has studied both avian and human development, and he has attempted to show how recent evidence derived from neuroscience suggests revision in theory regarding epigenetic processes, which rationalist theorists such as Gesell accepted (1992, 2001). Within a developmental psychobiological system framework he suggested that a probabilistic rather than a predictive conception of epigenetic development is more likely. In contrast to the more predetermined unidirectional view of epigenesis that was been more prominent in early theories, Gottlieb proposed a metatheory that sees development as probabilistic, influenced greatly by experience, and featuring systemic reciprocal interactions. He rejected the "outmoded concept that a genetically inspired neural maturation alone leads to the development of innate or instinctive behavior" (2001, p. 1). Thus, he also disagreed with linguists such as Pinker who emphasized that neural maturation governed by genes is the primary cause of complex phenomenon

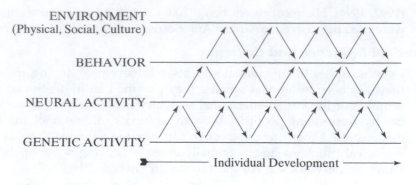

**Figure 12.2**  Bidirectional Influences on Development
*Source:* Reprinted from *A Conceptualization of a Bioecological System* from *Bidirectional Influences on Development from Individual Development and Evolution* (p. 186), by G. Gottlieb, 1992. New York: Oxford University Press.

such as language development. He believes that instead there are "bidirectional experiential coactions in the probabilistic view of epigenesis" (2001, p. 2). Gottlieb has provided a model that demonstrates the different levels of reciprocal interaction that occur during any type of developmental change. They include genetic, neural, behavioral, and environmental activity. The environmental level can also be subdivided into physical, social, and cultural components. Figure 12.2 provides the basics of this reciprocal interaction model, showing that all levels are capable of interacting individually and systemically with all other levels.

Gottlieb stressed that experiences occur at all these levels, and these experiences channel development at all levels, influence thresholds and rates of maturation, and maintain integrity of existing neural or behavioral outcomes. Other important concepts included in his "metatheory" are

- Canalization—the narrowing of responsiveness as a consequence of experience (e.g., pruning of neural synapses; infant loss of responsiveness to the universal range of phonemes by age 1).
- Equifinality—developing organisms with different early conditions can reach the same endpoint, and organisms that start similarly can reach the same endpoint by different routes (e.g., Fischer's skill development theory incorporates equifinality; microgenetic studies are most likely to reveal this).
- Equipotentiality—each cell has the same prospective developmental potential and does not lose this ability even after differentiation (e.g., differentiated cells can be rerouted and fulfill other potentialities; this is evident in the compensatory brain development seen in studies of early brain damage).

Gottlieb indicated that his theoretical view does not provide specifics about developmental processes or domains. However, it does try to give overarching theoretical concepts and to relate epigenetic perspectives to neuroscience research and ecological systems theory.

### Theoretical Influence and Critique

The viewpoint expressed by Gottlieb has provided a basis for a number of present systemic theoretical perspectives, especially for Thelen and other nonlinear dynamical systems theorists. Although Gottlieb has provided a clear, internally consistent, and economical model that appears to be an accurate representation of the neuropsychological interface, it is not an easily tested model. As more research using nonlinear dynamical systems ideas is conducted, its testability and falsifiability will be more easily assessed.

## Nonlinear Dynamical Systems Theory as Developmental Theory

The evidence that this systems perspective is going to be increasingly relevant in influencing human development theory is shown both by the types of research that are being conducted using concepts from this viewpoint and also by the initiation in 1997 of a new journal, *Nonlinear Dynamics, Psychology, and Life Sciences*. In the introduction to the journal, the editor (Guastello, 1997) explained why this new journal was needed and defined the field. He commented,

> Dynamical systems are those whose properties, behaviors, or interrelationships change over time or space . . . that involve attractors, bifurcations, and related concepts explicitly. . . . The output, or behavior, of one subsystem, which may itself display interesting dynamics, becomes the input for another subsystem which imposes a second dynamical process. Thus we have coupled dynamics, or synergetic relationships. With enough synergies, complex adaptive systems in the sense of evolutionary behavior, ecological niches, and ordinary learning emerge. (p. 2)

(Note: Presently the terms *dynamical* and *dynamic* seem to be used interchangeably by many psychological researchers and theorists.)

Complexity theory (often also referred to as "chaos" theory) calls into question the linear explanations typically used in human development theories (e.g., rigid stages, immutable predictions, reductionism) (Gleick, 1987; Waldrop, 1992). Its proponents see all aspects of the universe as having similar characteristics, and thus they assert that principles of complex physical microsystems can be applied to human development systems as well as to environmental systems. This theoretical perspective provides a rich set of metaphors for explaining the dynamical systems of psychological processes. Some of these principles are especially relevant for human developmental change, as follows, each with an example from human development research.

- Self-organizing: systems that may appear chaotic establish patterns of behavior that are complex but ordered; this self-organizing process can be expected to occur but it cannot be predicted precisely. Theorists such as Case and Fischer, who report stages or levels of developmental change in cognition, have also pointed out periods of cognitive disorganization that then appear to become organized as children "construct" their knowledge; individuals differ in the timing of these self-organizing periods.

- Attractors: a system that may appear to be disordered may evolve toward a stable "attracted" state, affected by strong elements. The stages/levels described by Piaget, when children's thinking is organized in a particular way, can be thought of as one type of attractor or stable state.

- Sensitive dependence on initial conditions: a very small input into a system may yield widely disparate results (sometimes called the butterfly effect). Studies of resilient children have often shown that an encounter with one caring adult changed the course of development for a child who was from a "not good enough" environment. Greenspan's advocacy for early intervention with children who have relational problems is another example of this view, as are most early intervention studies.

- Recursion: systems of repeated patterns, action going "back on itself"; this recursive process may result in unanticipated outcomes. In order to move to a higher level of development, children often repeat behavior patterns, and often the patterns become more and more elaborated (e.g., Piaget's practice play, Case's recursive substages).

- Phase shifts: change is observed at the point of a phase shift, which is the point at which the complex of interactions causes qualitative change. A child who is pulling up and holding onto furniture suddenly begins to take walking steps, shifting to an entirely different pattern of locomotion. Thelen has made the multiple factors in the process resulting in the "walking" phase shift explicit.

- Control parameters: boundaries that control patterns of interaction and affect the timing of phase shifts. Control parameters may be invariant over the life of a species (e.g., the restricted range of human arm movement) or may change with age or environmental experiences (e.g., quantity and types of knowledge that an individual can amass varies greatly with life experiences). Life span theory has many evidences of biological and psychological control parameters that come into play as individuals age.

- Fractal: a self-similar pattern may be reproduced at different levels of scale, over and over, resulting in a "nested" perception of development. The language interactions of mother and infant reported by Rogoff are repeated in language interaction patterns at many scale levels in numerous cultures.

- Interdependence: all levels of the system are interrelated and interdependent. Neuroscientists are demonstrating how maturation of neural connections within the brain is related to ability to solve problems, use language, and understand emotional meanings, and these abilities when exercised also interact to strengthen certain neural connections.

- Plasticity: the capacity for system change is always present. Human development has great variability and is open to change throughout the life span, as many of the theorists studying developmental change processes have reported.

- Openness: the system is not closed; it can continue to receive energy from sources outside itself. As encounters with new experiences occur, these enhance social–moral interactions and understandings of social conventions and moral thought; cognition is open to change from other sources of energy.

Quantum mechanics theory has identified a number of other principles, which nonlinear dynamical systems theorists believe have relevance to the study of human development (Herbert, 1985), as follows:

- Measurement of an object or phenomena changes it; there is no such thing as an objective measurement that does not affect what is measured. In observing and measuring human behavior, the event of observation has an effect on what is being observed and measured.

- There is nonlocality rather than locality in the universe; actions at one place can cause effects in other parts. Life span and systems perspectives have many examples of how events that occur far from particular children's face-to-face experience can have profound effects on their development.

- Reality may be a construct of human consciousness. In human development, the question of human consciousness is of extreme interest, and the study of the brain has raised this question to a high level. Thus, physics, neuroscience, neuropsychology, and nonlinear dynamical system theorists, as well as theorists from past eras are joined in searching for the answer to consciousness (e.g., Roser & Gazzaniga, 2004).

Although the idea of studying human development as a nonlinear dynamical system is beginning to appeal to researchers and theorists, only a few developmental psychologists have actually conducted significant work using the principles of this theoretical perspective. This may be partly true because it requires observing and collecting numerous types of precise data (microgenetic) from the same child, as well as sophisticated mathematical computer modeling of these data to map the development of individual cases. Fischer and Rose (1999) cautioned that many "data-driven" and "model-driven" methods have not been adequate to explain these phenomena and suggest "carefully analyzed tasks" and "assessing scale properties across different assessment conditions" are needed to "generate powerful explanations" (p. 197). Coincidentally with the earliest studies of children's development, physical and motor development, the same developmental domain studied by early theorists such as McGraw, was the initial focus of Thelen's research (1984, 1989). She is the most influential theorist who used this perspective and clearly demonstrated its relevance; with her colleague Linda Smith, she conducted some of the earliest definitive studies within this theoretical paradigm.

### Thelen's Theory of Dynamic Human Development Systems

Esther Thelen (1941–2004) was a leading proponent of dynamic systems theory as the key to understanding human development. Although she began her career as a zoologist and had studied wasps and other animal behavior, she turned to the study of infant development, and there she applied many concepts from the ethological and biological science fields. She held a doctorate in biological sciences from the University of Missouri and spent most of her academic career at Indiana University. Her untimely death from cancer cut short her presidency of the Society for Research in Child Development and her work that was providing an integrative way of thinking about this field. Her theoretical ideas, however, have influenced researchers in psychology, kinesiology, cognitive science, computer science, robotics, and neuroscience disciplines. The major area of interest to Thelen and Smith was infant motor development as an example of a nonlinear dynamical system (1994). Thelen drew on the research of another theorist who focused on this field at an earlier time, Myrtle McGraw (Thelen, 1989). Using the lens of nonlinear dynamical systems, the approach of Thelen and Smith differed from traditional ways of studying this development, which they stated were often based on identifying a single cause of behavior. They thought that earlier theorists like McGraw, although she realized there were many factors in a motor movement such as control, strength, and posture, still attributed the achievement of a motor skill to some type of central neural structure. They concluded that a "single-causal model was deficient," because it could not account for the complex nature of motor development. They also stated that a linear model was not appropriate for understanding cognititive development either (Thelen & Smith, 1994, p. 121).

With present-day ability to store and analyze observational data on the computer, Thelen was able to give a much more sophisticated analysis of the complex interaction of factors influencing early motor developmental progress than McGraw could discern. Using the techniques of microgenesis, she minutely measured multiple points of change in the infants' repertoire of actions. For example, an early stable attractor is the infant's kicking pattern, which becomes self-organized over time. Similarly, infant "stepping" movements are present initially, seem to be lost, and then reappear. Thelen found that they were still present if she held infants on a treadmill or had them move in water, and she concluded that one problem infants have is trying to maintain their movements against gravity. Thus, the weight of the child is also a factor because weight bearing is necessary for walking. She concluded that the stepping capability shown in young infants' reflexive behavior, which seems to disappear at a later age, is not really lost but in later infancy it is difficult to reproduce due to greater physical growth in the infant's trunk before leg growth is achieved. Infants can still perform this behavior in water or on a treadmill if supported. In order to walk without assistance, a certain level of physical growth must first be achieved as well as further development of the brain's motor cortex.

By measuring numerous data points and entering them into computer mapping models, she was able to show the peaks, flattenings, and mergings of movement patterns, resulting in an "ontogenetic landscape for locomotion." Figure 12.3 shows a sample of the mapping terrain.

The infant's physical growth dimensions, opportunities for environmental practice, and changes in the neurological structures of the brain all interact dynamically to cause these "phase shifts." Thelen explained these motor developmental processes using many of the principles derived from systems thinking in biology and psychology and from the study of complex and nonlinear systems in physics and mathematics. Her definition of a dynamic(al) system is one that creates changes over time among elements that are interrelated systematically. According to Thelen, the changes she documented are based on these principles of nonlinear dynamical systems, as follows.

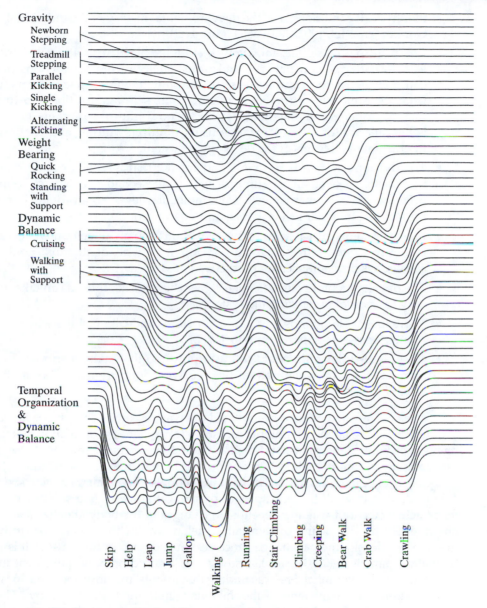

**Figure 12.3** Ontogenetic Landscape for Locomotion
*Source:* Reprinted from *Ontogenetic Landscape for Locomotion* from *A Dynamic Systems Approach to the Development of Cognition and Action* (p. 124), by E. Thelen & L. B. Smith, 1994. Cambridge, MA: MIT Press.

- The basis for novelty in development (ontogenetic change) is not from either genetic or environment instructions but from an integrated relationship among specific stimuli, the total environmental context, the status of anatomical structures and functions, the physiological (biochemical/

biophysical) conditions, and the developmental history of the individual (per Gottlieb's model, 1992, 2001; see Figure 11.2).

- The principle of self-organization is evident; plasticity within constraints lead to patterns, and patterns and order emerge from interactions of the components of the complex system without having explicit instructions from the organism or the environment; thus, self-organization is a fundamental property of living things. There are no "built-in" programs, but there is the capacity for self-organization using multiple, mutual, and continuous interaction of all levels of the developing system.

- The dynamic system is recursive and fractal; that is, it is a nested process that unfolds over many time scales (milleseconds to years). Similar processes occur at many levels, from molecular levels that provide patterns for walking to molar levels that change cognition.

- Linear systems of causality cannot explain human development because causality is multidirectional, fused, and interdependent; thus, nonlinear causality is probabilistic, not predictive.

- The developmental system is open rather than closed; thus, it can take in energy to assist in organizing the system.

- There are stable periods, with attractor states and phase shifts when development moves to a more complex level.

- There is also flexibility and "soft assembly" so that stable periods and dynamic periods may alternate or be recursive; development is not a "hardwired" process.

Thelen's research method exemplified the way research of this type should be conducted, that is, taking of multiple measures (microgenesis) of infant's motor behaviors, physical dimensions, and environmental experiences, entering these data into computer programs, and generating models by which the dynamic interactions of these factors can be explored. Through her models of walking behavior, she was able to demonstrate all the principles of dynamical systems. She showed that infants' achievement of walking depends on changes in the body, the brain, and the environment all interacting dynamically. Thelen was in the process of studying many other developmental change processes, including cognition, using this new theoretical paradigm (2003). Her last study was focused on how movement influenced mental development. She was finding that infants' memory about the location of toys is linked to the movements the child made in trying to locate the toys. Thelen (and colleague Smith) believed that only a dynamic theory can really account for the complexity of human behavior, which enables people to have such a wide variety of thought processes as well as act in so many other dimensions of life. They stated, "The challenge for developmentalists is to understand the developmental origins of this complexity and flexibility. Only dynamics, we believe, is up to the task" (Thelen, 2003, p. 626).

### Theoretical Influence and Critique

Because this is a relatively new idea on the psychological scene, the long-term importance of the nonlinear dynamical systems approach is unclear. Some of its future will depend on Thelen's students, but others are beginning to explore various developmental domains within this theory. Since Thelen's death, it will remain for her colleagues and students to continue research using the nonlinear dynamical systems theory. Developmental domains that are being discussed and studied using nonlinear dynamical systems principles include cognitive processes (Metzger, 1997; Tschacher & Danwalder, 2003); self-development (Marks-Tarlow, 1999); problem solving (Guastello, Hyde, & Odak, 1998); family systems (Koopmans, 1998); temperament (Partridge, 2000), organizational development and educational policy (Levine & Fitzgerald, 1992), and play development (Vanderven, 1998), among others.

There is also an increasing number of writings on the relevance of this theoretical perspective for human development research (e.g., Baron, 2002; Clark, 1997; Metzger, 1997; Richardson, 2000; Van Geert, 2000). In a review of nonlinear dynamical systems theory, Metzger (1997) pointed out work being done at the time of her writing that was beginning to explain relationships between perception and action (Turvey & Carello, 1995) and to explore development of a range of motor skills such as hopping (Roberton, 1993) and reaching (Savelabergh & van der Kamp, 1993). She indicated that study of cognitive processes looked promising but that not much was evident at the time she wrote. However, interest in this approach is growing, even among theorists who initially embraced other theoretical perspectives, such as Gibson and Fischer.

Shortly before her death, in a chapter written for a dynamical systems book, Gibson reiterated her disagreement with the information processing view that perception is a "static representation of an object or a scene" (1997, p. 23), stressing that there is a close connection between perception, action, and cognition. She stated that she wanted perceptual development to be explained without jargon, that builds on her research with infants, and that "deals with the functioning world" (Gibson, 1997, p. 24). She outlined several propositions, including animal–environment reciprocity, perception–action reciprocity, nested units, and flexibility, and she discussed the learning process as linked to human agency.

Fischer and Rose (1999) have also concluded that "nonlinear dynamic analyses of development are blossoming and they promise to produce a remarkable profusion of theoretical and empirical flowers, in the best tradition of Dutch botany" (p. 210). They added, however, that it is difficult to create assessment scales that are precise and valid and noted that unless such scales are developed, it will not be possible to do much meaningful research on the dynamic aspects of development. Whether all domains of development can be investigated using nonlinear dynamical systems theoretical and research models will remain to be seen. Already, however, new methodologies are being attempted to study a range of human dynamical systems problems (Levine & Fitzgerald, 1992). In a commentary on Clark's discussion, Newell (1997) said, "I suspect that Arnold Gesell would have liked to have known about these methodological tools back in the 1930s and 1940s . . . he was clearly interested in characterizing a dynamic geometry of the emergence of movement in infant action and used dynamically relevant terms, such as *stability, gradient, potential,* and so on" (p. 408).

# Trends in Physical/Motor, Perceptual, and Brain Development and Themes Useful for Professional Practice

From the many studies of personality and social/emotional development, a set of commonly accepted timelines for the "range of normality" in development of these domains has been identified. Table 12.1 shows these "typical" developmental achievements. Also, although not all of the constructs of the theories discussed in chapters 11 and 12 have been validated by extensive evidence, a few general themes can be derived from this set of theories that may be useful for practice. These are provided in Box 12.1.

---

**Table 12.1**  Trends in Physical/Motor, Perceptual, and Brain Development (Ages Are Approximate)

| | |
|---|---|
| Birth To Age 3 | -Brains of newborns have all the "building blocks" of neurons but the synaptic connections will develop throughout childhood; thus, the biological/environmental interface will affect brain development at least until late adolescence (and perhaps longer) |
| | -Newborn vision is about 20/400 but by 12 mo. it is similar to adults (20/20) |
| | -Newborn hearing and other senses (e.g., pain, smell, touch) are similar to adults |
| | -Intermodal perception (coordination) begins at about 4 mo. |
| | -Newborns have a range of reflexes, some of which disappear when voluntary movements begin |
| | -Brain growth is rapid and by 12 mo. the brain is more similar to the adult brain than to the newborn brain |
| | -Physical development follows cephalocaudal and proximodistal patterns; thus infants first gain control over their head, shoulders, and trunk before they gain control over their arms and legs |
| | -Perceptual skills of discriminating patterns begin by 4 mo.; discriminate sounds of language at 4-6 mo; sounds of own language primary by age 9-12 mo. |
| | -Gross motor skills develop: head lift at 1 mo.; roll-over at 3-4 mo.; sit at 5-7 mo.; crawl and stand with support at 7-9 mo.; walk with assistance at 9-12 mo.; walk alone at 10-15 mo. |
| | -Fine motor skills develop: take objects to mouth at 4 mo., transfer objects in hands at 5-6 mo.; pull strings to gain objects at 7-8 mo.; show hand preference at 8-10 mo.; hit objects with utensil at 10-11 mo.; pick up small objects with pincer grasp at 11 mo.; put objects in containers at 12 mo. |
| | -Control over body functions (toileting, feeding) by age 2-3 |
| Ages 3-6 | -Growth of 2½ inches and 5-7 pounds each year |
| | -Brain is 9/10 of adult size by age 5 |
| | -Activity level highest of life during this age |
| | -Rudimentary and functional gross motor skills develop: hop, run at age 3; skip, catch ball, hop on one foot at age 4; roller skate and ride bike at age 5-6 |
| | -Rudimentary and functional fine motor skills develop: handedness established by age 4-6; drawing with crayon or pencil by age 3-4; cutting with scissor by age 4-5; tying shoes and buttoning coats by age 6 |
| | -Perceptual/motor skills continue to develop: coordinated movement of objects and body in space; judgment of body movements in small/large spaces by age 4-6 (may initially appear clumsy because large muscles more developed than small muscles) |

**Table 12.1** (*continued*)

| | |
|---|---|
| Ages 6-12 | -Sport-related and other functional motor skills develop (catching small balls, hitting a nail with hammer, building, drawing, playing musical instruments) by age 10-12 are similar to adults |
| | -Growth continues at 2-3 inches a year but is slow and consistent |
| | -Brain development continues with pruning of some dendritic connections, myelination, and faster speed of thought occuring |
| | -Muscle mass and strength increase; legs lengthen and trunks slim (unless obesity occurs) |
| | -Head is smaller proportion of body |
| | -Motor control is smoother and more coordinated but large muscle still superior to small muscle |
| | -Gender differences in motor skill may occur, with boys better at gross motor and girls at fine motor skills (unclear if biological or environmental) |
| Ages 12-20 | -Rapid skeletal and sexual maturation occur |
| | -Brain maturation basically completed during adolescence |
| | -Body image of concern |
| | -Puberty initiates a growth spurt at age 9-14 for girls; 11-18 for boys |
| | -Sexual maturation occurs with physical changes in sexual characteristics |
| | -Menses occurs after initial physical changes and weight gain in girls |
| | -Cardio fitness, stamina, and strength increase |
| Ages 20-40 | -Peak physical performance occurs at age 19-26 |
| | -Peak period of cardio fitness occurs in late 20's |
| | -Motor skills begin to fade in early 30's |
| | -Fatty tissues begins to increase (note that life style and exercise affect these) |
| | -Initial decreases in visual and auditory acuity may occur |
| | -Sexual interest and activity high |
| Ages 40-60 | -Decline in physical development becomes apparent |
| | -Health status may be major concern |
| | -Losses in height, strength in back, legs, tendons may begin |
| | -Increase in weight may occur |
| | -Thinning of skin, hair |
| | -Menopause at about age 50 |
| | -Sexual interest but less frequent |
| | -Cardiovascular fitness can be maintained with exercise |
| Ages 60-80 | -Some neuron loss but dendritic growth continues |
| | -Sensory systems continue to decline but most still functional |
| | -Brain functioning stronger with greater education and use |
| | -More noticeable changes in skin and body height |
| | -Common disorders are arthritis and osteoporosis; other diseases also common |
| Ages 80-100 | -Great variation in health and physical stamina |
| | -Great variation in brain functioning |
| | -Many in this age range are still physically active |

## Box 12.1
## Theoretically-Derived Themes That May Be Useful for Professional Practice

- Because the interactions of many developmental domains are essential for optimum development, attention to physical/motor and perceptual development is important, both for their own value, and as facilitators of other areas of development.

- Perception of the "affordances" in the environment may allow individuals to progressively discriminate relevant information without cognitive mediation.

- The incorporation of information from brain research into human development explanations will assist in supporting or disconfirming present developmental theory

- The bioecological system of individuals must be understood in order to understand their developmental change.

- Human developmental trajectories are probabalistic rather than predictive; the numerous levels of nonlinear dynamical systems may result in small changes having minor or major results and large changes having many, few, or very limited results.

- Because human beings are complex systems, they have the qualities of all such systems; that is, they are self-organizing, open, recursive, flexible, soft assemblied, multidirectional, plastic, and demonstrate both stable periods and phase shifts.

- Play is a medium through which children are free to demonstrate the range of complexity that is characteristic of human dynamical systems.

- Childrearing or educational methods are always in interaction with genetic, neuronal, physical, social, emotional, cognitive, language, socio-moral, and gender role identity dynamics; that is, the dynamical system is relevant in gaining understanding of developmental trajectories.

## Summary

The systems perspectives discussed in this chapter are only in early stages of investigation by human development theorists and researchers. However, they hold potential for explaining human development in more integrated ways than have been done in the past. It remains to be seen how important these theories will be in explaining a range of developmental changes and in providing research that will be useful in supporting their theoretical perspectives. It will also be interesting to see whether they will be important for practitioners who need to solve developmental problems and facilitate positive developmental change for children, adolescents, and adults. The following case focuses on some of these ecological and neuropsychological factors that may affect the development of individuals across the life span.

## Case 12. The Perez Family

The Perez family lives in a low socioeconomic area of a large city. The parents came to the United States as elementary-age children when their family immigrated after sponsorship by a relative (now dead). Mom dropped out of high school at age 16, and although dad graduated from high school, he has only been able to find low-paying and somewhat temporary jobs. He has been working for the past 2 years, however, as a maintenance man in a large apartment complex. Mom has done cleaning in hotels off and on over the years, but is presently not working because she has not recovered well from an automobile accident that still causes her pain. There are three children in the family, Jose (age 14), Benita (age 9), and Rosa (age 2). Both Jose and Benita have been doing well in school so far. Both mom and dad have stressed the importance of school and learning so that the children can get good jobs and maybe even get a college scholarship. However, the parents are not able to provide much homework help and rarely go to school events because they have often worked night shifts. The care of Rosa has been shared by the parents depending on their work schedules. The community where the Perez family lives has few literacy resources—the only library is a 45-minute bus ride away, there are few stores that sell appropriate books or magazines for children, and there are not even many stores with signs to read. The school is also overcrowded and lacks good library and technology resources. The family does have a television set but no computer. Their major social contacts are with the church in their neighborhood. In addition to attending regularly, the children participate in some after-school activity programs at church, and the whole family attends the church social events. When the mother was injured in an accident a few years ago, the church members brought in food and helped care for the children. Rosa is also sometimes cared for by a church member. The family does not have other family members close enough to provide help, although they live in another part of the state.

Mr. Perez just learned that, due to the economic turndown, he will be laid off in about a month. Because he does have minimal health benefits through his employment, he is also worried about those being cut off. The family has never applied for welfare or other government help because they don't feel comfortable interacting with "officials." This is partly due to the experiences of some of their relatives in the country from which they immigrated with their parents years before. Lately, the parents have noticed that Jose doesn't have much to say about school and doesn't bring home much homework. His teacher the year before had said he needed to develop better study skills. Today the attendance officer at the school called to say that Jose had missed 4 days of school this month. The parents are beginning to wonder if he is getting into trouble, although when they confronted him, he denied that. Benita is beginning to ask for "signature" clothes and other items, but so far she has accepted the parents' explanation that these are too expensive to buy. Mrs. Perez is just beginning to notice that Rosa is not talking as much as the other two children did at her age.

How would Bronfenbrenner describe the ecological and bioecological system factors that are positively and negatively affecting the various members of this family? What impact might these systems have on the ability of Jose and Benita and Rosa to finish school? To go to college?

What are the mesosystem interactions (school, church, community with the family) that are positive, and what could be improved?

What influences are the exosystem, macrosystem, and chronosystem having on the family's welfare?

Would Ogbu analyze the issues the family faces differently if they were from an "involuntary immigrant" group rather than a "voluntary immigrant" group?

How would Gottlieb see the bidirectional effects of various systems affecting the family's long-term development?

What variables might Thelen wish to evaluate in determining how the nonlinear dynamical system is affected by the school and sports performance of Jose and Benita? What would she say about Rosa's language development?

## Readings

U. Bronfenbrenner, Development Science in the Discovery Mode; the Bioecological Model of Human Development; Conclusion, pp. 402–403.

E. Thelan, Introduction, pp. 404–411.

## Suggested Readings

Bronfenbrenner, U. (2005). Developmental science in the discovery mode; The bioecological model of human development; Conclusion. In E. Bronfenbrenner *Making human beings human: Bioecological perspectives on human development* (p. 187; 187–188; 195–196). Thousand Oaks, CA: Sage

Thelen, E., & Smith, L. B. (1994). Introduction. In E. Thelen & L. B. Smith, *A dynamic systems approach to the development of cognition and action* (pp. xiii–xxii). Boston: MIT Press.

©ASHLEIGH BRILLIANT 1978.                    POT-SHOTS NO. 1390.

Ashleigh Brilliant

INSIDE EVERY OLDER PERSON,

THERE'S A YOUNGER PERSON,

WONDERING WHAT HAPPENED.

*Source:* © 1987 Ashleigh Brilliant. Reprinted with permission.

# Epilogue: The Future of Human Developmental Theory

The course of human development has always been an area of interest because it is, in many ways, a great mystery. Esther Thelen stated that mystery well:

> Contemporary developmental psychologists are still asking the same question that has intrigued philosophers and scientists since ancient times: How does the human mind, in all its power and imagination, emerge from a squiggly, crying, drooling, creature—the infant? How can people do mathematics, paint pictures, write poetry, play music, create laws, and build cities when we start out so unformed and helpless? Where can these immense talents come from? (2003, p. 17)

The chapters of this book have explained how theorists and researchers from various times and places have attempted to answer these questions. Some of them have selected only one or two developmental questions to try to answer, whereas others have tried to explicate broad theoretical concepts that apply to many developmental domains. Each has been successful, but also unsuccessful, in that the answers to the question of how this human development transformation occurs is only partially and often fuzzily deciphered. Sometimes theories raise as many questions as they answer! In the introduction to this book the overall goal was stated: to help students in education, special education, family studies, social work, counseling, school psychology, developmental psychology, or other disciplines acquire a personally relevant understanding of the theories and to gain a meaningful and deep understanding of theoretical ideas that will be useful for them in the practice of their professional lives. The theoretical domains discussed in this book each have relevance for professional practice.

## Theories of Personality and Social–Emotional Development

The study of personality, social, and emotional development of children and adolescents has been an ongoing interest of theorists who investigated these domains primarily within a rationalist view of knowledge construction. These areas of development have also been of great interest to life span theorists and others who study within a sociohistorical perspective. Some cognitive scientists who draw primarily on empiricist perspectives of knowledge seeking have also looked at issues related to social development, and evidence from genetic behavioral and neuroscience research are finding links between personality and social–emotional behaviors and sensorimotor and cognitive areas of the brain. There is also some initial interest in linking personality, social, and emotional development research and theory related to nonlinear dynamical systems approaches. The issue brought up by Fischer and Rose (1999) about finding assessment scales that can precisely measure aspects of these domains will be an important consideration.

## Theories of Cognitive and Language Development

The theorists who focused on cognition and language have exemplified many worldviews. Of course a strong rationalist presence in this developmental domain has been evident, and the sociohistorical perspective has also proved fruitful in examining issues of cognition and language. Another focus has been found in the information processing theorists who primarily hold an empiricist perspective. The difference between these approaches can be seen in the findings each has had, with some theorists being interested in broad developmental stage change across many cognitive areas, whereas others look at developmental change in specific cognitive areas such as problem solving or memory development. In addition, language development has had contrasting explanations from linguistic and psycholinguistic theorists. Life span theorists have also addressed cognitive change across extensive age periods. More recently, neuropsychological, bioecological, developmental psychobiological, and dynamical systems theorists are beginning to theorize about cognitive and language developmental change, and some theorists are attempting to tie many of these theoretical perspectives together.

## Theories of Sociomoral and Gender Role Development

Because many theories of sociomoral development have been derived from rationalist perspectives, the major theorists who have focused on this domain have identified stages or levels of sociomoral development, but they have all described the content of morality in somewhat different terms. Sociomoral development has also been characterized as influenced by observational learning, and it has been differentiated from personal choice and social conventional behaviors. Although some theorists see gender role development primarily as a cognitive process with a number of stages, there are a wide range of other interpretations concerning how gender role identity is developed. Theorists vary in regard to the developmental goal—well-defined male/female roles or androgynous roles—and on the primary influences—nature or nurture. Many cultural factors also affect these two developmental domains, and life span theorists have seen further development in both these domains at later age levels.

## Theories of Physical/Motor, Perceptual, and Brain Development

Although these are very important domains, theoretical interest in their development has varied across the centuries, with much interest in physical/motor development in the early 20th century and a revived interest in recent years.

Initially maturational causal factors were primary in theories of physical/motor development, but at the present time complex systemic interactions are being explored. Perception has been studied from a number of perspectives and presently ecological theory is prominent, which emphasizes direct rather than indirect (i.e., cognitively mediated) factors. As brain and genetic research become more informative, the linkages among these developmental domains and others will be a major area of theoretical interest.

## Theories of Developmental Systems

System theories do not always focus on particular developmental domains because their assumption is that the principles of these theories will eventually explain development in many domains. Person/environment views see the individual as embedded in the environmental system, and recent views from this perspective stress the influence of the cultural context. The bioecological system has been proposed as a theory encompassing all levels of environmental systemic interaction, and developmental psychobiological perspectives also emphasize the dynamic interaction of all levels, including genetic and neuronal levels as well as those of the person and environment. Nonlinear dynamical systems theory applies to all complex systems, of which human development is one, and this theoretical perspective attempts to verify claims that all complex systems can be explained by similar self-organizing principles.

## The Future of Human Development Theory

As is evidenced by the many congruent and competing theoretical perspectives presented in this book, human development theory is also a complex system with self-organizing features. As new technology becomes accessible to developmental theorists, it may enable theoretical ideas of the past to be empirically verified or discarded to be displaced by other models. Presently, there is a recursive process occurring, in which early perspectives on physical/motor and perceptual development are being reexamined in the light of nonlinear theoretical views, and this reexamination is beginning to extend to other developmental domains. The interaction dimensions of nature and nurture are also being reexamined in the light of neuroscience discoveries, and this debate may be resolved over this next century. A wider view of cultural factors in development is also being taken, in contrast to past assumptions that descriptions of human development within primarily Western worldviews could be applied universally. There is at least some initial questioning of one of these assumptions in particular—that earlier is better (what Piaget once termed "the American question"). Smolucha has pointed with alarm to the movement toward more sophisticated play by preschool age children, perhaps due to media models and cultural pressures (2003), and others have questioned the increased educational policy emphasis on academic learning during preschool.

In a recent discussion of "the role of immaturity" by Bjorklund (1997), he suggested that immaturity in various developmental domains is adaptive for children because it allows the brain to grow over an extended time period, in contrast to the early maturing of other species that do not reach complex developmental levels. Humans have an extended period of playfulness and a slow trajectory of metacognitive development, which result in a great amount of energy expenditure and "unproductive" strategy use. Bjorklund makes the case that this long immaturity can be adaptive because it permits a slow but dense, rich, and elaborative growth of the mind and keeps motivation for learning high. Although this is a perspective not usually taken by contemporary psychologists, educators, and parents, it is an important one to consider in this era of the "hurried child" (Elkind, 1988). In fact, the words of Rousseau, recursively quoted by Bjorklund, are pertinent here:

> Nature wants children to be children before they are men. If we deliberately depart from this order, we shall get premature fruits which are neither ripe nor well flavored and which soon decay. We shall have youthful sages and grown up children. Childhood has ways of seeing, thinking, and feeling, peculiar to itself; nothing can be more foolish than to substitute our ways for them. (quoted by Bjorklund, 1997, p. 153)

As the scientific and technological opportunities for understanding, fostering, and enriching human developmental change processes increase, it may be well to keep in mind the wisdom of other ages, as well as embracing the great potential of the future.

## Creating a Personally Relevant Theoretical Perspective

All the information in this book provides only a starting point for creation of a personally relevant theoretical perspective. Each reader brings to the content a set of genetic, neuronal, personality, social, emotional, physical/motor, perceptual, cognitive, language, sociomoral, and gender role identity qualities that have been in dynamic interaction within themselves and with their environment for many years. They have studied this information, and in the process of studying, critiquing its relevance, questioning its assumptions, selecting among its ideas, discarding or accepting its principles, and assimilating a worldview that is congruent with their own developmental level; by now the creation of a personally relevant theoretical perspective should be possible. Given the basic assumption of this field, however, it is expected that the perspective obtained will continue to develop, changing with experience, and be continually reorganized over their remaining life course.

## Putting a Theoretical Perspective into Practice

The next step in this process is a most important one; that is, gaining some empirical data on the effectiveness of selected theoretical perspectives for solving problems of practice. Whatever the professional field, the personally defined theoretical perspective must be useful; that is the final test. Not only should it be useful in one's profession, however, but it should also provide a guide for one's personal life as well. In the previous chapters, suggestions for practice based on the various perspectives were made. The next step is for readers to incorporate the relevant actions into their personally constructed knowledge of human development theories.

## Summary

This chapter has reviewed some of the numerous theoretical positions and has asked readers to work actively to create their own personally relevant theory of human development that will assist them in their professional work or personal life. The following exercise will give practice in developing and using that personal theoretical perspective to solve problems of professional practice or life course relevance.

## Case 12. The Practitioner's Dilemma

First, describe a human development issue that you are presently encountering in your own life and/or that you are having to address in your professional role.

Then give all the details that you think are relevant to the developmental issue: biological and environmental. Include the other individuals who are part of the system interactions.

Next, make a diagram or other conceptual schema that shows the major relevant factors that should be addressed to improve the developmental outcome for the individuals involved in this issue.

Then review the various theoretical perspectives that have insights, concepts, suggestions, or processes that could be useful to you in addressing this issue.

Next, select one or a combination of these and give an in-depth analysis of the situation using the terminology of the theory or theories.

Finally, determine the action steps that you can take to address the developmental issue. Make a prediction about how likely this action will be to help and in what way it will help. Make a probability estimate of how this developmental change will affect other parts of the system.

Now, try it and evaluate its usefulness! Good luck!

## Reading

David F. Bjorklund, The Role of Immaturity in Human Development, pp. 412–437.

## Suggested Reading

Bjorklund, D. F. (1997). The role of immaturity in human development. *Psychological Bulletin, 122*(2), 153–169.

# Readings

## Freedom to Develop Nature in Education

### Freedom to Develop

From a biological point of view, the concept of liberty in the education of very young children should be understood as a condition most favorable to their physiological and psychological development. A teacher who is urged on by a profound reverence for life, while she is making her interesting observations, should respect the gradual unfolding of a child's life. The life of a child is not an abstraction; it is something that is lived by each one in particular. There is only one real biological manifestation, that of the living individual; and education, that is, the active assistance required for the normal expansion of life, should be directed towards these individuals as they are observed one by one. A child has a body which grows and a mind which develops. Both his physiological and psychic development have a single source, life. We should not corrupt or suffocate his mysterious potentialities but wait for their successive manifestations.

The environment is certainly secondary in the phenomena of life. It can modify, as it can assist or destroy, but it can never create. The source of growth lies within. A child does not grow because he is fed, because he breathes, because he lives in suitable climatic conditions. He grows because his potentialities for life are actualized, because the fertile seed from which life comes is developing according to its natural destiny. An adult eats, breathes, experiences heat and cold, but he does not grow. Puberty does not come because a child laughs or dances, or engages in

*Source:* From Montessori, M. (1972). Freedom to develop; Nature in education. In *The discovery of the child* (6th ed., pp. 61–75). New York: Ballantine.

gymnastic exercises, or eats better than usual, but because of a physiological phenomenon. Life increases, becomes manifest, and perfects the individual, but it is confined within limits and is governed by insuperable laws.

Therefore, when we speak of the freedom of a small child, we do not mean to countenance the external disorderly actions which children left to themselves engage in as a relief from their aimless activity, but we understand by this the freeing of his life from the obstacles which can impede his normal development.

A child is constantly being pushed on by his great mission, that of growing up and becoming a man. Because a child is himself unaware of his mission and of his internal needs, and adults are far from being able to interpret them, many conditions prevail both at home and in school that impede the expansion of his infant life. The freeing of a child consists in removing as far as possible these obstacles through a close and thorough study of the secret needs of early childhood in order to assist it.

Such an objective demands on the part of an adult greater care for, and closer attention to, the true needs of a child; and, practically, it leads to the creation of a suitable environment where a child can pursue a series of interesting objectives and thus channel his random energies into orderly and well-executed actions.

In the gay environment described above, furnished according to the proportions of a child, there are objects which permit the child who uses them to attain a determined goal. There are, for example, simple frames which enable a child to learn how to button, lace, hook, or tie things together. There are also washbasins where a child can wash his hands, brooms with which he can sweep the floor, dusters so that he can clean the furniture, brushes for shining his shoes or cleaning his clothes. All these objects invite a child to do something, to carry out a real task with a practical goal to be obtained. To spread out carpets and roll them up after they have been used, to spread a tablecloth for dinner and to fold it up and replace it carefully after the meal is finished, to set the table completely, to eat correctly, and afterwards to remove the dishes and wash them, placing each object in its proper place in the cupboard, are tasks which not only require increasing skills but also a gradual development of character because of the patience necessary for their execution and the sense of responsibility for their successful accomplishment.

In the Children's Houses these activities which I have just described are called "exercises in practical life" because the children lead a practical life and do ordinary housework with a devotion and accuracy that becomes remarkably calm and dignified.

Besides the various objects which the children are taught to use for their "practical life," there are many others which lend themselves to the gradual development and refinement of a child's intellect. These are, for example, various materials for the education of the senses, for learning the alphabet, numbers, and reading, writing, and arithmetic. These objects are called "materials for development" to distinguish them from those used in practical life.

When we speak of "environment" we include the sum total of objects which a child can freely choose and use as he pleases, that is to say, according to his needs and tendencies. A teacher simply assists him at the beginning to get his bearings among so many different things and teaches him the precise use of each of them, that is to say, she introduces him to the ordered and active life of the environment. But then she leaves him free in the choice and execution of his work. Children as a rule have different desires at any particular moment, and one keeps busy at one thing and another at another without quarreling. In this way they are engaged in an admirable social life full of activity. In peaceful delight the children solve by themselves the various social problems which their free and many-sided activities create from time to time.

An educational influence is diffused throughout the whole environment, and both children and teacher have their roles to play in it.

## Nature in Education

Itard, in his classic work, *Des premiers développements du jeune sauvage d l' Aveyron* (*The First Developments of the Young Savage of Aveyron*), describes in detail the extraordinary drama of an education aimed at dispelling the mental darkness of an idiot and rescuing a child from a state of savagery.

The Savage of Aveyron was an abandoned child that had grown up in purely natural surroundings. The child had been wounded in a woods by assassins, who believed that they had killed him. After he had been cured by natural means, he lived for many years naked and free in the forest. He was finally found by hunters and introduced to civilized life at Paris. Scars on his small body gave evidence of his encounters with wild beasts and of his falls from heights.

The child was found mute and remained so. Pinel diagnosed his mentality as that of an idiot, and he proved to be incapable of assimilating an intellectual training.

And yet scientific education owes its first advances to this boy. Itard, who was interested in philosophy and, as a physician, had specialized in the defects of deaf mutes, undertook the boy's education, using means that had already proved to be partially successful in restoring hearing to people who were almost deaf. He was of the opinion that the defects of the little savage were more the result of his lack of education than of functional disorders. He subscribed to the principle of Helvetius that "a man is nothing without the work of men," and he believed that education could do everything. He was opposed to the principle proclaimed by Rousseau before the French Revolution: "*Tout est bien sortant des mains de l'Auteur des choses, tout dégénère dans les mains de l'homme*," in other words, education is harmful and injurious to man.

Itard's first conclusion was that the little savage proved experimentally through his actions the truth of Helvetius' statement. However, when, with the assistance of Pinel, Itard became convinced that he was dealing with an idiot, his philosophical theories gave way to admirable attempts at education through practical experimentation.

Itard divided the education of this boy into two phases. In the first he sought to bring him within the bounds of ordinary social life. In the second he attempted to educate the mind of the idiot. The boy, who had lived in terrible abandonment, had found his happiness in it. He had become almost a part of the nature which had absorbed him. He took his delight in rain, snow, storms, and boundless vistas, for these had been the object of his vision, his companions, and his love. Civil life means a renunciation of all this, but it brings with it a conquest that facilitates human progress. In the pages of his book Itard has described in vivid terms the efforts he made to bring the little savage to a civilized state. This means that the needs of the child, who was now surrounded with loving care, were multiplied. Itard was a patient worker and keen observer of his pupil's spontaneous acts. His patient work and abnegation, which may be seen in the following description, can be an inspiration to teachers who are preparing themselves to make use of experimental methods in their own teaching:

When for example he was observed in his room, he could be seen weaving back and forth in endless monotony with his eyes always turned towards the window staring out into empty space. If a gust of wind suddenly rose up, or if the sun broke through the clouds and filled the heavens with its light, the boy broke out in laughter as if he were convulsed with joy. At times these periods of joy gave way to a kind of frenzied rage. He twisted his arms, rubbed his eyes with his closed fist, ground his teeth, and threatened anyone who was near him.

One morning the snow was falling heavily. He was still in bed, but waking up he gave a cry of joy, leapt from his bed, ran to the window, and then to the door. Impatiently he went from one to the other, and finally dashed naked out into the garden. There, giving free rein to his joy in sharp cries, he rushed about, rolled in the snow, gathered up large handfuls of it, and ate it with incredible eagerness.

But he did not always show such a lively and boisterous attitude when he was stirred by the great spectacles of nature. At certain times he seemed to experience a kind of calm regret and melancholy. Thus, for example, when the weather was bad and everybody left the garden the little Savage of Aveyron would choose that time to go out. He would go around the garden several times and then sit down on the edge of the fountain.

I have spent whole hours of intense pleasure watching him in that position, noting how his face, which was without expression and twisted into grimaces, would gradually assume an expression of sadness and melancholy, and how his eyes would gaze fixedly at the surface of the water, upon which he would toss from time to time a few dead leaves.

When on a beautiful evening there was a full moon and a silver ray penetrated into his room, he would almost always wake up and go to the window. During a great part of the night he would remain there, motionless, with his head stretched forward, his eyes fixed on the moonlit landscape, immersed in a kind of esthetic contemplation, the silence and stillness of which was only broken at long intervals by a long breath that died away like a sigh of distress.

In other passages of his book, Itard relates how the boy could not walk in a normal fashion, but would only run; and he tells us how he himself used to run after him at first when he was taking him for a walk through the streets of Paris rather than put a violent check on him.

Itard's treatment of the little savage furnishes us with a combination of valuable educational principles that can be generalized and applied to the whole of child education. We may note in particular the gradual and gentle way in which he introduced the boy to the ways of social life, the manner in which he first adapted himself to his pupil rather than wait for the pupil to adapt himself to him, and how he made the new life attractive so that it won the boy with its charm rather than impose it harshly on the child in a way that would have caused him pain and oppression.

I do not believe that there is any writing that offers us so eloquent a contrast between the natural and the social life, and which shows so clearly how the latter is made up of renunciations and restrictions. It is enough to think of how running is reduced to a rhythmical walk, and how a shrill cry is brought down to the modulations of ordinary speech.

At the present time, however, and in the circumstances of modern society, children live very far from nature and have few opportunities of coming into intimate contact with, or having any direct experience of, it.

For a long time it was thought that nature had only a moral influence on the education of a child. Efforts were made to develop a sensible response to the marvels of nature, to flowers, plants, animals, landscapes, winds, and light.

Later an attempt was made to interest a child in nature by giving him little plots of land to till. But the concept of living in nature is still more recent in a child's education. As a matter of fact, a child needs to live naturally and not simply have a knowledge of nature. The most important thing to do is to free the child, if possible, from the ties which keep him isolated in the artificial life of a city. Today child hygiene contributes to the physical education of children by introducing them to the open air in public parks and by leaving them exposed to the sun and water of a beach. Some timid attempts at freeing children from the excessive burdens of city life may be found in the permission given to children to wear simpler and lighter clothes, to go about in sandals or barefooted. Experience has shown that the only means of curing children from tuberculosis and rickets in modern sanitaria is to expose them to nature and to make them sleep in the open air and to live in the sun. When we reflect on this, it should be clear that normal and strong children should not only be able to resist an exposure to nature, but that they would be greatly benefited by it. But there are still too many prejudices in the way. We have readily given up our own freedom and have ended up loving our prison and passing it on to our children. Little by little we have come to look upon nature as being restricted to the growing of flowers or to the care of domestic animals which provide us with food, assist us in our labors, or help in our defense. This has caused our souls to shrink and has filled them with contradictions. We can even confuse the pleasure that we have in seeing animals with that of being near a poor animal destined to die so that it may feed us, or we admire the beauty or the songs of birds imprisoned in little cages with a kind of hazy love of nature. We even think that a tray full of sand from the sea should be a great help to a child. The seashore is often thought to be educational because it has sand like that in a child's box. Imprisoned as we are in such a confused world, it is no wonder that we come to some absurd conclusions.

Actually, nature frightens most people. They fear the air and the sun as if they were mortal enemies. They fear the frost at night as if it were a snake hidden in the grass. They fear the rain as if it were a fire. Civilized man is a kind of contented prisoner, and if now he is warned that he should enjoy nature for his own health, he does so timidly and with his eyes on the alert for any danger. To sleep in the open, to expose oneself to the winds and to the rains, to defy the sun, and to take a dip in the water are all things about which one can talk but which one does not always put into practice.

Who does not run to close a door for fear of a draft? And who does not shut the windows before going to sleep, especially if it is winter or it is raining? Almost everyone believes that it is dangerous and requires a heroic effort to take very long walks in the open country in rain or shine and rely simply on the shelter which nature affords. It is said that one must become accustomed to such efforts, and so no one moves. But how is one to become accustomed to such activities? Perhaps little children should be so conditioned. No. They are the most protected. Even the English, with their enthusiasm for sports, do not want their children to be tried by nature and fatigue. Even when they are quite large, a nurse pushes them in carriages to some shady spot when the weather is good, and she will not let them walk far or act as they please. Where people engage in sports, these become veritable battles among the strongest and most courageous youths, the very ones who are called to arms to fight the enemy.

It would be too soon for us to say: Let the children be free; encourage them; let them run outside when it is raining; let them remove their shoes when they find a puddle of water; and, when the grass of the meadows is damp with dew, let them run on it and trample it with their bare feet; let them rest peacefully when a tree invites them to sleep beneath its shade; let them shout and laugh when the sun wakes them in the morning as it wakes every living creature that divides its day between waking and sleeping. But, instead of this, we anxiously ask ourselves how we can make a child sleep after the sun has risen, and how we can teach him not to take off his shoes or wander over the meadows. Where, as the result of such restraints, a child degenerates, and, becoming irked with his prison, kills insects or small harmless animals, we look on this as something natural and do not notice that his soul has already become estranged from nature. We simply ask our children to adapt themselves to their prison without causing us any trouble.

The strength of even the smallest children is more than we imagine, but it must have a free play in order to reveal itself.

In a city a child will say that he is tired after a brief walk, and this leads us to believe that he lacks strength. But his sluggishness comes from the artificiality of his environment, from ennui, from his awkward clothing, from the pain which his small feet suffer from their leather shoes as they strike the bare pavement of the city streets, and from the enervating example of those who walk about him silent, indifferent, and without a smile. A club which he might join, or attractive clothes which might bring him admiration, are nothing to him. He is on a leash. He is ensnared by laziness and would like to be dragged along.

But when children come into contact with nature, they reveal their strength. Normal children, if they have a strong constitution and are well nourished, can walk for miles even when they are less than two years old. Their tireless little legs will climb long steep slopes in the sunshine. I remember how a child of about six once disappeared for several hours. He had set out to climb a hill, thinking that if he arrived at its summit he would be able to see what lay on the other side. He was not tired, but disillusioned in not having found what he sought. I once knew a couple who had a child barely two years old. Wishing to go to a distant beach they tried to take turns carrying him in their arms, but the attempt was too tiring. The child, however, then enthusiastically made the trip by himself and repeated the excursion

every day. Instead of carrying him in their arms, his parents made the sacrifice of walking more slowly and of halting whenever the child stopped to gather a small flower or saw a patient little donkey grazing in a meadow and sat down, thoughtful and serious, to pass a moment with this humble and privileged creature. Instead of carrying their child, these parents solved their problem by following him. Only poets and little children can feel the fascination of a tiny rivulet of water flowing over pebbles. A child at such a sight will laugh with joy and want to stop to touch it with his hands as if to caress it.

I would suggest that you take up in your arms a child that has not yet begun to walk. On a country road from which may be seen a great and beautiful expanse, hold him in such a way that his back is to the view. Stop there with him! He will turn around and enjoy the beauty of the scene even though he cannot yet stand upright on his own feet and his tongue cannot as yet ask you to pause.

Have you ever seen children standing seriously and sad about the body of a little bird that has fallen from its nest, or watched them run back and forth asking and reporting what has happened with deep concern? Well, these are the children who can soon degenerate to the point where they steal eggs from birds' nests.

Like everything else, a feeling for nature grows with exercise. We certainly do not communicate it by a pedantic description or exhortation made to a listless and bored child shut up within the walls of a room and who has become accustomed to see or hear that cruelty toward animals is just a part of life. But experience strikes home. The death of the first dove killed intentionally by a member of his family is a dark spot in the heart of almost every child. We must cure the unsuspected wounds, the spiritual ills that already afflict these charming children who are the victims of the artificial environment in which they live.

## The Place of Nature in Education

Education in school can fix the attention of a child on special objects which will show exactly how far he has been able to stir up within himself a feeling for nature or will arouse within him latent or lost sentiments. Here, as in every other kind of activity, the function of the school is to supply him with interesting information and motives for action.

A child, who more than anyone else is a spontaneous observer of nature, certainly needs to have at his disposal material upon which he can work.

## Care for Others

Children have an anxious concern for living beings, and the satisfaction of this instinct fills them with delight. It is therefore easy to interest them in taking care of plants and especially of animals. Nothing awakens foresight in a small child, who lives as a rule for the passing moment and without care for the morrow, so much as this. When he knows that animals have need of him, that little plants will dry up if he does not water them, he binds together with a new thread of love today's passing moments with those of the morrow.

One should watch little children when, one morning, after they have for many days placed food and water with loving care near brooding doves, they see the results of their labors. On another day they see a number of dainty chicks that have come from the eggs which a hen has covered with her wings for so long. The children are filled with feelings of tenderness and enthusiasm, and there is born in them a desire to give further help. They collect little bits of straw, threads of old cotton cloth, or wisps of wadding for the birds nesting under the roof or in the trees in the garden. And the chirping that goes on about them tells them thanks.

The metamorphoses of insects and the care which mothers bestow upon their offspring are objects of patient observation on the part of children, and they often give rise to an interest that surprises us. Once a small child was so struck by the changes undergone by tadpoles that he could describe their development, reporting the various phases in the life of a frog like a miniature scientist.

Children are also attracted by plants. One Children's House did not have any land that could be tilled, so flower pots were set out all around a large terrace. The children never forgot to water the plants with a little watering can. One morning I found them all seated in a circle on the floor around a magnificent red rose that had opened up during the night. They were silent and peaceful, completely absorbed in contemplation.

Another time a little girl kept looking down from a terrace in obvious excitement. Her mother and her teachers had seen to it that she had grown up with a love for flowers and gardens, but now she was attracted by something more. "Down there," she told her mother, "there is a garden of things to eat."

It was an orchard, which did not strike the child's mother as being at all remarkable, but which had nevertheless filled her tiny daughter with enthusiasm.

## Prejudices about the Gardens

Our minds are prejudiced even with respect to nature, and we find it very difficult to understand. Our ideas about flowers are too symbolic, and we try to mold a child's reactions to our own instead of following his lead in order to interpret his own real tastes and needs. This is why even in gardens children have been forced to imitate the artificial activities of adults. They find that it takes too long to place a seed in the earth and wait for a little plant to appear; and further the task itself is too small for them. They want to do something big and to bring their activities into immediate contact with the products of nature.

Children indeed love flowers, but they need to do something more than remain among them and contemplate their colored blossoms. They find their greatest pleasure in acting, in knowing, in exploring, even apart from the attraction of external beauty.

## Their Favorite Work

Our experiences have led us to a number of conclusions different from those which I myself once had, and we have been led to these by children who have been left free to make their own choices.

1) The most pleasant work for children is not sowing but reaping, a work, we all know, that is no less exacting than the former. It may even be said that it is the harvest which intensifies an interest in sowing. The more one has reaped, the more he experiences the secret fascination of sowing.

One of the brightest experiences is that of harvesting grain or grapes. The reaping of a field of wheat, the gathering of the grain into sheaves to be bound with bright-colored ribbons, has been most successful and can become the occasion for beautiful farm festivals. The care of the vines, the cleansing of the grapes, and the gathering of the fruit into beautiful baskets can also give rise to various feasts.

Fruit trees provide similar types of work. Even the smallest children like to gather the olives, and they perform a truly useful work in the dilligent search they make for fallen fruit which they put in their baskets. A hunt for strawberries hidden under the leaves of the vines is no less pleasing than looking for fragrant violets.

From these experiments the children derive an interest in the sowing of seeds on a larger scale, as for example, the sowing of a field of wheat with all its various operations. Only an adult can lay out the furrows, but the children can pile up the little heaps of grain to be sown. They can then divide this into little baskets and scatter it along the rows. The growth of so many frail and tender plants gives great pleasure to the eye and to the mind. The uniform quality and the patterns made by the long parallel lines seem to emphasize their growth. Grandeur seems to come from the massing together of single items which are of themselves of little interest. The yellow stalks that toss about in the wind and grow until they are at the height of a child's shoulder entrance the little group waiting for the harvest. Although our small fields were sown for the making of altar breads, we were nevertheless able to conclude that a country life is more suitable for a child than philosophy and the symbolism of flowers.

Little plots of fragrant plants can also have a practical interest. A child's activity then consists in searching for, distinguishing, and gathering the plants with different scents. An exercise in distinguishing things that look alike and in seeking out a scent rather than a flower is exacting and affords the satisfaction of discovery.

Flowers are, of course, also interesting, but gathering them is more unnatural than gathering the fruits of the earth that grow from them. Flowers seem to call insects to themselves rather than men to assist them in carrying out their eternal mission. Actually, children who have been taught how to satisfy their spiritual needs often will sit down near flowers to admire them, but they will soon get up and go in search of something to do since it is their own activity that causes the buds of their charming little personalities to unfold.

## Simplicity

Work for a child must possess some variety within itself. A child does not have to know the reasons for sowing or reaping to have his interest aroused. He will readily undertake very simple actions which have an immediate end or which permit him to use some special effort. He will, for example, gladly pluck weeds from paths or furrows, sweep up dried leaves, or carry away an old branch. In a word, to have a field of activity and occasions for new experiences and difficult enterprises bring satisfaction to the animating spirit which prompts a child to make its way in the world.

We have pictures showing small children walking without fear among cows and in the midst of a flock of sheep, and others showing them sifting earth and carrying it away in wheelbarrows or heaping up big piles of branches from a tree.

Because of the lack of a suitable environment, such works as the care of greenhouses, the preparation of water for aquatic plants, the spreading of nets to protect a pool from insects, and the like, are seldom practicable, but they would not be beyond the strength or will of a child.

## Our Garden

A further conclusion which we reached from observing children in conditions where they could freely manifest their needs was that of limiting the field or garden to their spiritual needs. The opposite conviction, however, is common, namely, that it is good to give children a limitless space. Such an attitude is due to an almost exclusive regard for a child's physical life. The limits seem to be indicated by the swiftness of his feet. Nevertheless, even if, to be specific, we were to take a racetrack as a spatial limit, we would find it to be considerably more restricted than we had thought. Even in a large field, children always run and play in one spot, in a corner or some narrow space. All living beings tend to find a place for themselves and to keep within its boundaries.

This same criterion is also applicable to the psychic life. Its limits must be found in a mean which lies between an excess and an insufficiency of space or anything else. A child does not like one of the so-called "educational playgrounds" since it is too small for him. It is a wretched piece of property not even big enough for himself. A child whose needs are satisfied does not care whether something belongs to him or not. What he wants is precisely a sense of satisfaction. He should be able to watch over as many plants as he can come to know, as many as he can remember, so that he really knows them.

Even for us a garden that has too many plants and too many flowers is a place full of unknowns that are foreign to our consciousness. Our lungs will breathe well there, but the soul is not affected. But neither can a tiny flower bed satisfy us. Its contents are trivial and not sufficient for our needs. They do not satisfy the hunger of the spirit which longs to come into contact with nature. The limits, then, are those which make it our garden, where every plant is dear to us and sensibly helps us to support our inner selves.

The criterion for judging the limits of a child's activities has created a great deal of interest. In many countries attempts have been made to interpret it practically as a garden which corresponds to a child's inner needs. Today, plans for a garden run parallel with those for the building of a Children's House.[1]

---

[1]As the result of further experiments by Dr. Mario Montessori the scientific education of children in nature studies has been further elaborated. It is impossible here to take into account the mass of work and the surprising amount of material that has been suggested solely by the interests and activities of the children themselves. It is enough to note that this includes much with respect to the shape and classification of animals and plants, and this prepares them for further study in physiology. Careful attention has also been given to the preparation of aquaria and plots for the growing of vegetables, which should be present in every school. These means for study have led to a spontaneous and purposeful exploration of nature and to a number of discoveries made by the children themselves. They have satisfied the need which children have to exercise their senses and their powers of motion and have laid the foundations for further far-reaching developments in elementary schools. It provides an answer to the problem of satisfying the interests of older children without forcing them to reluctantly assimilate ideas and terms when their interest in these has already disappeared. A younger child readily and enthusiastically lays the foundations which the older child then uses to satisfy his own higher interests.

# Baby in a Box

## B. F. SKINNER

In that brave new world which science is preparing for the housewife of the future, the young mother has apparently been forgotten. Almost nothing has been done to ease her lot by simplifying and improving the care of babies.

When we decided to have another child, my wife and I felt that it was time to apply a little laborsaving invention and design to the problems of the nursery. We began by going over the disheartening schedule of the young mother, step by step. We asked only one question: Is this practice important for the physical and psychological health of the baby? When it was not, we marked it for elimination. Then the "gadgeteering" began.

The result is an inexpensive apparatus in which our baby daughter has now been living for eleven months. Her remarkable good health and happiness and my wife's welcome leisure have exceeded our most optimistic predictions, and we are convinced that a new deal for both mother and baby is at hand.

We tackled first the problem of warmth. The usual solution is to wrap the baby in half-a-dozen layers of cloth—shirt, nightdress, sheet, blankets. This is never completely successful. The baby is likely to be found steaming in its own fluids or lying cold and uncovered.

Editors' [of Ladies' Home Journal] Note: Occasionally an idea appears so new and challenging, so discussion-provoking, that it seems desirable to publish it at once, without the delay attendant on the testing and experimentation which scientists invariably require before giving approval to a new practice. Such is the following article. Child psychologists and health experts, consulted by the Journal, agree that Baby Skinner is in excellent health, in no way showing harm from her unusual upbringing. The Journal presents the story of how this one baby has been reared, in the belief that mothers everywhere will find it of great interest, will await eagerly the scientists' final verdict.

Source: From B. F. Skinner, "Baby in a Box," Ladies' Home Journal (October 1945). ©1945 Downe Publishing Inc. Reprinted with permission of Ladies' Home Journal.

Schemes to prevent uncovering may be dangerous, and in fact they have sometimes even proved fatal. Clothing and bedding also interfere with normal exercise and growth and keep the baby from taking comfortable postures or changing posture during sleep. They also encourage rashes and sores. Nothing can be said for the system on the score of convenience, because frequent changes and launderings are necessary.

Why not, we thought, dispense with clothing altogether—except for the diaper, which serves another purpose—and warm the space in which the baby lives? This should be a simple technical problem in the modern home. Our solution is a closed compartment about as spacious as a standard crib. The walls are well insulated, and one side, which can be raised like a window, is a large pane of safety glass. The heating is electrical, and special precautions have been taken to insure accurate control.

After a little experimentation we found that our baby, when first home from the hospital, was completely comfortable and relaxed without benefit of clothing at about 86° F. As she grew older, it was possible to lower the temperature by easy stages. Now, at eleven months, we are operating at about 78°, with a relative humidity of 50 per cent.

Raising or lowering the temperature by more than a degree or two will produce a surprising change in the baby's condition and behavior. This response is so sensitive that we wonder how a comfortable temperature is ever reached with clothing and blankets.

The discovery that pleased us most was that crying and fussing could always be stopped by slightly lowering the temperature. During the first three months, it is true, the baby would also cry when wet or hungry, but in that case she would stop when changed or fed. During the past six months she has not cried at all except for a moment or two when injured or sharply distressed—for example, when inoculated. The "lung exercise" which is so often appealed to to reassure the mother of a baby that cries a good deal takes the much pleasanter form of shouts and gurgles.

How much of this sustained cheerfulness is due to the temperature is hard to say, because the baby enjoys many other kinds of comfort. She sleeps in curious postures, not half of which would be possible under securely fastened blankets.

When awake, she exercises almost constantly and often with surprising violence. Her leg, stomach and back muscles are especially active and have become strong and hard. It is necessary to watch this performance for only a few minutes to realize how severely restrained the average baby is, and how much energy must be diverted into the only remaining channel—crying.

A wider range and variety of behavior are also encouraged by the freedom from clothing. For example, our baby acquired an amusing, almost apelike skill in the use of her feet. We have devised a number of toys which are occasionally suspended from the ceiling of the compartment. She often plays with these with her feet alone and with her hands and feet in close cooperation.

One toy is a ring suspended from a modified music box. A note can be played by pulling the ring downward, and a series of rapid jerks will produce Three Blind Mice. At seven months our baby would grasp the ring in her toes, stretch out her leg and play the tune with a rhythmic movement of her foot.

We are not especially interested in developing skills of this sort, but they are valuable for the baby because they arouse and hold her interest. Many babies seem to cry from sheer boredom—their behavior is restrained and they have nothing else to do. In our compartment, the waking hours are invariably active and happy ones.

Freedom from clothes and bedding is especially important for the older baby who plays and falls asleep off and on during the day. Unless the mother is constantly on the alert, it is hard to cover the baby promptly when it falls asleep and to remove and arrange sheets and blankets as soon as it is ready to play. All this is now unnecessary.

Remember that these advantages for the baby do not mean additional labor or attention on the part of the mother. On the contrary, there is an almost unbelievable saving in time and effort. For one thing, there is no bed to be made or changed. The "mattress" is a tightly stretched canvas, which is kept dry by warm air. A single bottom sheet operates like a roller towel. It is stored on a spool outside the compartment at one end and passes into a wire hamper at the other. It is ten yards long and lasts a week. A clean section can be locked into place in a few seconds. The time which is usually spent in changing clothes is also saved. This is especially important in the early months. When we take the baby up for feeding or play, she is wrapped in a small blanket or a simple nightdress. Occasionally she is dressed up "for fun" or for her play period. But that is all. The wrapping blanket, roller sheet and the usual diapers are the only laundry actually required.

Time and labor are also saved because the air which passes through the compartment is thoroughly filtered. The baby's eyes, ears and nostrils remain fresh and clean. A weekly bath is enough, provided the face and diaper region are frequently washed. These little attentions are easy because the compartment is at waist level.

It takes about one and one half hours each day to feed, change and otherwise care for the baby. This includes everything except washing diapers and preparing formula. We are not interested in reducing the time any farther. As a baby grows older, it needs a certain amount of social stimulation. And after all, when unnecessary chores have been eliminated, taking care of a baby is fun.

An unforeseen dividend has been the contribution to the baby's good health. Our pediatrician readily approved the plan before the baby was born, and he has followed the results enthusiastically from month to month. Here are some points on the health score: When the baby was only ten days old, we could place her in the preferred face-down position without danger of smothering, and she has slept that way ever since, with the usual advantages. She has always enjoyed deep and extended sleep, and her feeding and eliminative habits have been extraordinarily regular. She has never had a stomach upset, and she has never missed a daily bowel movement.

The compartment is relatively free of spray and air-borne infection, as well as dust and allergic substances. Although there have been colds in the family, it has been easy to avoid contagion, and the baby has completely escaped. The neighborhood children troop in to see her, but they see her through glass and keep their school-age diseases to themselves. She has never had a diaper rash.

We have also enjoyed the advantages of a fixed daily routine. Child specialists are still not agreed as to whether the mother should watch the baby or the clock, but no one denies that a strict schedule saves time. The mother can plan her day in advance and find time for relaxation or freedom for other activities. The trouble is that a routine acceptable to the baby often conflicts with the schedule of the household. Our compartment helps out here in two ways. Even in crowded living quarters it can be kept free of unwanted lights and sounds. The insulated walls muffle all ordinary noises, and a curtain can be drawn down over the window. The result is that, in the space taken by a standard crib, the baby has in effect a separate room. We are never concerned lest the doorbell, telephone, piano or children at play wake the baby, and we can therefore let her set up any routine she likes.

But a more interesting possibility is that her routine may be changed to suit our convenience.

A good example of this occurred when we dropped her schedule from four to three meals per day. The baby began to wake up in the morning about an hour before we wanted to feed her. This annoying habit, once established, may persist for months. However, by slightly raising the temperature during the night, we were able to postpone her demand for breakfast. The explanation is simple. The evening meal is used by the baby mainly to keep itself warm during the night. How long it lasts will depend in part upon how fast heat is absorbed by the surrounding air.

One advantage not to be overlooked is that the soundproofing also protects the family from the baby! Our intentions in this direction were misunderstood by some of our friends. We were never put to the test, because there was no crying to contend with, but it was never our policy to use the compartment in order to let the baby "cry it out."

Every effort should be made to discover just why a baby cries. But if the condition cannot be remedied, there is no reason why the family, and perhaps the neighborhood as well, must suffer. (Such a compartment, by the way, might persuade many a landlord to drop a "no babies" rule, since other tenants can be completely protected.)

Before the baby was born, when we were still building the apparatus, some of the friends and acquaintances who had heard about what we proposed to do were rather shocked. Mechanical dishwashers, garbage disposers, air cleaners and other laborsaving devices were all very fine, but a mechanical baby tender—that was carrying science too far! However, all the specific objections that were raised against the plan have faded away in the bright light of our results. A very brief acquaintance with the scheme in operation is enough to resolve all doubts. Some of the toughest skeptics have become our most enthusiastic supporters.

One of the commonest objections was that we were going to raise a "softie" who would be unprepared for the real world. But instead of becoming hypersensitive, our baby has acquired a surprisingly serene tolerance for annoyances. She is not bothered by the clothes she wears at playtime, she is not frightened by loud or sudden noises, she is not frustrated by toys out of reach, and she takes a lot of pommeling from her older sister like a good sport. It is possible that she will have to learn to sleep in a noisy room, but adjustments of that sort are always necessary. A tolerance for any annoyance can be built up by administering it in controlled dosages, rather than in the usual accidental way. Certainly there is no reason to annoy the child throughout the whole of its infancy, merely to prepare it for later childhood.

It is not, of course, the favorable conditions to which people object, but the fact that in our compartment they are "artificial." All of them occur naturally in one favorable environment or another, where the same objection should apply but is never raised. It is quite in the spirit of the "world of the future" to make favorable conditions available everywhere through simple mechanical means.

A few critics have objected that they would not like to live in such a compartment themselves—they feel that it would stifle them or give them claustrophobia. The baby obviously does not share in this opinion. The compartment is well ventilated and much more spacious than a Pullman berth, considering the size of the occupant. The baby cannot get out, of course, but that is true of a crib as well. There is less actual restraint in the compartment because the baby is freer to move about. The plain fact is that she is perfectly happy. She has never tried to get out nor resisted being put back in, and that seems to be the final test.

Another early objection was that the baby would be socially starved and robbed of the affection and mother love that she needs. This has simply not been true. The compartment does not ostracize the baby. The large window is no more of a social barrier than the bars of a crib. The baby follows what is going on in the room, smiles at passers-by, plays "peek-a-boo" games, and obviously delights in company. And she is handled, talked to and played with whenever she is changed or fed, and each afternoon during a play period which is becoming longer as she grows older.

The fact is that a baby will probably get more love and affection when it is easily cared for, because the mother is not so likely to feel overworked and resentful of the demands made upon her. She will express her love in a practical way and give the baby genuinely affectionate care.

It is common practice to advise the troubled mother to be patient and tender and to enjoy her baby. And, of course, that is what any baby needs. But it is the exceptional mother who can fill this prescription upon demand, especially if there are other children in the family and she has no help. We need to go one step further and treat the mother with affection also. Simplified child care will give mother love a chance.

A similar complaint was that such an apparatus would encourage neglect. But easier care is sure to be better care. The mother will resist the temptation to put the baby back into a damp bed if she can conjure up a dry one in five seconds. She may very well spend less time with her baby, but babies do not suffer from being left alone, only from the discomforts which arise from being left alone in the ordinary crib.

How long do we intend to keep the baby in the compartment? The baby will answer that in time, but almost certainly until she is two years old, or perhaps three. After the first year, of course, she will spend a fair part of each day in a play pen or out-of-doors. The compartment takes the place of a crib and will get about the same use. Eventually it will serve as sleeping quarters only.

We cannot, of course, guarantee that every baby raised in this way will thrive so successfully. But there is a plausible connection between health and happiness and the surroundings we have provided, and I am quite sure that our success is not an accident. The experiment should, of course, be repeated again and again with different babies and different parents. One case is enough, however, to disprove the flat assertion that it can't be done. At least we have shown that a moderate and inexpensive mechanization of baby care will yield a tremendous saving in time and trouble, without harm to the child and probably to its lasting advantage.

*Professor Skinner's unusual experiment provoked many questions among the Journal staff. Here are many of them, answered by the author himself.* [*Editor,* Ladies Home Journal]

1. *How can the mother hear her baby?*

The apparatus is only partially soundproofed. With the nursery door open we can hear the baby about as clearly as if she were in an ordinary crib with the nursery door closed. If it were desirable to hear very clearly, the window could be left partly open, with the opening covered by a cloth (say, if the child were sick). The soundproofing has enough advantages from the baby's point of view to make it worth while.

2. *Doesn't the discharged sheet have an unpleasant odor?*

Not in our experience. There is no noticeable odor in our nursery. Visitors frequently comment on this fact. The reason seems to be that dry urine does not give off a strong odor. Our practice has been to wipe up any traces of bowel movements before moving the sheet along. In case of bad soiling, the sheet could be moved out far enough to permit dipping the soiled section into a pan of water or the whole sheet could be changed, but this has never been necessary.

3. *Doesn't the canvas mattress acquire an odor?*

Again, not in our experience. The canvas is constantly bathed in warm air, and there is little or no chance for the bacterial action which makes urine smell. The canvas is stretched on a removable frame, and we have a spare to permit cleaning when necessary (every two or three weeks). The canvas could, therefore, be changed in case of vomiting. Or a rubber sheet could be used. (We do use rubber pants at night, to avoid chilling due to evaporation of the wet diaper.)

4. *What happens if the current fails?*

We have an alarm, operated on dry-cell batteries, which goes off if the temperature deviates more than two degrees from the proper setting. This is wholly independent of the power supply and would tell us of trouble long before the baby had experienced any extreme condition.

5. *Don't you believe a baby's daily bath is necessary?*

Artificial stimulation of the skin at bath-time may be necessary when the usual clothing and bedding are used, but not in our apparatus. From the very first the fine condition of our baby's skin attracted attention. The skin is soft, but not moist. It is rubbed gently and naturally throughout the day by the under sheet as she moves about. Much of the patting which is advised at bathtime is to make up for the lack of normal exercise of the skin circulation, which is due to clothing. Since our baby's skin is always exposed to the air, a very lively skin reaction to changes in temperature has developed.

6. *Don't the mother and child both miss daily bathtime fun?*

We have had a lot of fun with our baby—more perhaps than if we had been burdened down with unnecessary chores. We have always played with her when we felt like it, which was often. As for the baby, she has certainly had more than her share of fun. The freedom from clothing and blankets has provided much of it. Her bath is fun, too, though probably not as much as the usual baby's because the contrast is

not so great. The advice of the child specialist to "allow the baby to exercise its legs for a few minutes at bathtime" shows what I mean. Our baby exercises her legs all day long. (My wife insists I say that we do bathe our baby twice a week, though once a week is enough.)

The fact that our baby is not only in perfect physical condition but keenly interested in life and blissfully happy is our final answer to any possible charge of neglect.

## Further Comments (1977)

The word "box" was put in my title by the editors of the *Journal* and it led to endless confusion because I had used another box in the study of operant conditioning. Many of those who had not read the article assumed that I was experimenting on our daughter as if she were a rat or pigeon. Those who read it, however, viewed it quite favorably. Hundreds of people wrote to say that they wanted to raise their babies in the same way. I sent out mimeographed instructions to help those who proposed to build boxes for themselves. My contacts with potential manufacturers were disappointing but eventually an enterprising man, John Gray, organized the Aircrib Corporation and began production on a modest scale. He contributed much of his own time without remuneration, and when he died his son was unable to carry on. Second-hand Aircribs are now in demand.

Our daughter continued to use the Aircrib for sleeping and naps until she was two and a half, and during that time we all profited from it. The long sheet and canvas "mattress" were replaced by a tightly stretched woven plastic, with the texture of linen, which could be washed and dried instantly, and once her bowel-movement pattern was established she slept nude. Urine was collected in a pan beneath the plastic. Predictions that she would be a bed-wetter were not confirmed. She learned to keep dry in her clothing during the day and when she started to sleep in a regular bed she treated it like clothing. Except for one night when we had been traveling and were all rather tired, she has never wet a bed. She proved remarkably resistant to colds and other infections.

Possibly through confusion with the other box, the venture began to be misunderstood. Stories circulated about the dire consequences of raising a baby in any such way. It was said that our daughter had committed suicide, become psychotic, and (more recently), was suing me. The fact is that she is a successful artist living in London with her husband, Dr. Barry Buzan, who teaches in the field of international studies. My older daughter, Dr. Julie Vargas, used an Aircrib with her two daughters, and she and many others have confirmed the results we reported.

The Aircrib has many advantages for both child and parents. For the child it offers greater comfort, safety, freedom of movement, and an opportunity for the earliest possible development of motor and perceptual skills. For the parent it saves labor and gives a sense of security about the baby's well being. There is no danger of being strangled by bedclothes or becoming uncovered on a cold night. It is somewhat more expensive than an ordinary crib, even including mattress, sheets, blankets and laundry, but the resale value is high. It can often save money by saving space. By drawing a curtain over the window at night it can be closed off from the rest of the room, making it possible for a young couple to stay for another year or two in a one-room apartment or to let a baby share a room with an older child.

I do not expect to see Aircribs widely used in the near future. It is not the kind of thing that appeals to American business. It is impossible to convince a Board of Directors that there is a market that justifies tooling up for mass production to keep the price down, and so long as the price remains high a market will not develop.

Nevertheless, the first two or three years are the most important years in a child's life, and I am sure that much more will eventually be done to make them more enjoyable and productive.

B. F. Skinner
*July 1977*

# Rulers, Models, and Nonlinear Dynamics:
# Measurement and Method
# in Developmental Research

Kurl Fischer and Samuel Rose

## Abstract

Nonlinear dynamic systems provide a powerful new framework for analyzing development and other forms of change, but two research approaches have limited research to date. Data-driven approaches have focused on describing specific phenomena, especially actions, and have used dynamic concepts mostly as loose metaphors instead of building explicit models. Model-driven approaches have focused on the rich hypotheses in developmental theory to generate and explore formal models of change processes, mostly involving cognition and language. They have neglected the need for careful research to measure the growth patterns to be explained. The difficulties of doing dynamic research on cognitive, language, and socioemotional development stem in large part from the absence of well constructed scales for assessing behaviors other than actions. Construction of such scales is facilitated by combining scores on carefully analyzed tasks and by assessing scale properties across different assessment conditions, so as to separate growth properties from scale anomalies. With good scales, models and

This paper is dedicated to the memory of the late Samuel Priest Rose. Preparation of this paper was supported by grants from Mr. and Mrs. Frederick P. Rose, NICHD grant #HD32371, and Harvard University. The authors thank Daniel Bullock, June Haltiwanger, Susan Harter, George Potts, Robert Thatcher, Han van der Maas, Paul van Geert, and John Willett for their contributions to the arguments presented here.

Fischer, K. W., & Rose, S. P. (1999). Rulers, models, and nonlinear dynamics: Measurement and method in developmental research. In G. Savelsbergh, H. van der Maas, & P. van Geert (Eds.), *Nonlinear developmental processes* (pp. 197–212). Amsterdam: Royal Netherlands Academy of Arts and Sciences.

data can be used in dynamic interaction to generate powerful explanations of development, as illustrated by models of hierarchical growth and predator-prey relations in cognitive and brain development.

## Introduction

There is a new wave of research and theory on development that promises enormous improvements in the quality of scientific understanding and explanation of how people grow, learn, and change. The approach behind the wave is nonlinear dynamics, which brings with it new concepts, methods, and theoretical tools for explaining more fully the nature of development and other forms of change. This book represents effectively the range and scope of the new, exciting work.

When a new approach bursts onto the scene, it often seems to grow of its own accord, surging forward in specific arenas where new research is easier and moving less energetically in arenas where research is stickier. If nonlinear dynamics is to grow to its full potential in explaining development, scholars need to consider not only the arenas where dynamic research is booming but also those where it is struggling or less mature. The publication of this book on the scope of dynamic developmental research provides a good occasion for assessing the strengths and weaknesses of dynamic work to date. Stepping back to assess the state of the art can help to shape future work, potentially making it richer, more compelling, and more comprehensive, catalyzing the field to take the new approach to its full potential.

Analysis begins with the simple question, What do we want to explain about development and other kinds of change? Children and even adults develop dramatically over many years, providing a natural source of rich observations.

Among all those developments, what kinds of phenomena have researchers focused on, and how well do those choices capture the range of changes that require explanation?

Research on dynamics of development falls primarily into two types, that driven by data on patterns of change and that driven by models of processes of change. Both data-driven research and model-driven research have produced important new knowledge about development. The division of research into these two primary types, however, has also seriously restricted the scope of phenomena under study, producing large gaps in the field. Moving beyond these gaps requires working simultaneously and reciprocally with both data and models in approximately equal parts. It also requires deep analysis of issues of scaling in measures of change—a topic that is vastly neglected in research on development. By bringing together data, models, and scaling, researchers can move beyond the initial, powerful but spotty successes of nonlinear dynamics in explaining development. Perhaps we may even succeed in building a powerful new kind of explanation of change that will transform the field, shifting psychology and related disciplines from the study of dichotomies and other oversimplifications to the description and explanation of some of the richness of human behavior.

## Constructive Dynamics: Phenomena to Be Explained

The promise of nonlinear dynamics is to explain the combination of many influences or components to form human activity, especially processes of development and change in human activity. Virtually all researchers and scholars who use concepts of nonlinear dynamics share an approach that we call *constructive dynamics,* which begins with two central assumptions: First, many influences come together to form the emergent properties of human action and thought. Second, a person is a self-organizing system who regulates these combinations based on feedback from both the immediate world in which the activities are embedded and his or her previous experiences and activities, especially

those immediately preceding the activity to be explained. In other words, a person *constructs activities,* regulating the combination of influences that produce those activities through dynamic processes that centrally involve feedback from the immediate world and prior experience (e.g., Fischer & Bidell, 1997; Gottlieb, 1992; Lerner, 1991).

Constructive dynamics is also constructive in another sense. For many decades concepts from systems theory have been used to criticize work in psychology and related behavioral sciences by pointing out the narrowness and one dimensionality of most social-scientific explanations (Bronfenbrenner, 1979; Sameroff, 1975; Thelen & Fogel, 1989; von Bertalanffy, 1968). However, with classical systems theory few researchers were able to move beyond the criticism to use the concepts constructively to produce better research and theory. In contrast, the new constructive dynamics is generating novel research and theory in many arenas.

The scope of phenomena to be explained by developmental constructive dynamics is vast. The large changes of ontogenesis extend from before birth well into adulthood, if not old age, and include the many aspects of human behavior: action, understanding, thinking, problem-solving, emotion, even consciousness. It is no small task to explain the development of this range of phenomena.

The study of development is blessed with several characteristics that facilitate the application of nonlinear dynamic concepts. First, development involves many instances of systematic change, thus providing orderly phenomena for study. Second, the field of human development has a history of richness in theory, providing fertile sources for ideas about developmental processes that can be used in modeling and research. Witness the work of Freud (1923/1961), Piaget (1983), Vygotsky (1978), and Werner (1948), four of the most influential classical scholars of development. Building upon richly systematic patterns of change and extensive theoretical concepts, researchers may be able to build strong nonlinear dynamic explanations more quickly than in other arenas.

To date, however, most nonlinear dynamic research has focused on analyzing actions, both in development and in human behavior more broadly. Movements of limbs, sense organs (especially eyes), and bodies in space have been the focus of a large proportion of research, as evidenced in the chapters in this book. Much of this research, especially in the study of development, has been data-driven, emphasizing description of specific phenomena involving actions more than construction of models.

## Data-Driven Dynamic Research

Data-driven research centers on identifying and describing specific developmental phenomena that have dynamic properties, such as nonlinear growth and shifting developmental patterns from multiple influences, especially as they apply to actions. Esther Thelen has been an eminent practitioner of this kind of research, and she articulates and defends it in a number of publications, including two books with Linda Smith (Smith & Thelen, 1993; Thelen & Smith, 1994).

In one important series of studies, for example, Thelen and her colleagues demonstrated that a developmental pattern that scholars have attributed to changes in the central nervous system is produced by 'peripheral' changes in the body that had gone unnoticed. The stepping reflex of early infancy disappears because babies' legs grow large in mass and the mass interferes with leg motion and therefore stepping. When an infant who has 'lost' the stepping reflex stands in water, the buoyancy of the water supports the legs and produces a return of the stepping pattern (Thelen & Fisher, 1982). Similarly, when a 7-month-old infant is supported on a treadmill, the movement of the treadmill produces the return of the stepping pattern (Thelen & Ulrich, 1991). With this research, Thelen and her colleagues demonstrated that multiple influences shape growth, not only changes in cognition and brain.

## Beyond Demonstrations to Explanations

Most recent work on dynamics of development has involved such demonstrations of complex or counterintuitive phenomena—complex growth curves, appearances and disappearances of behaviors from unexpected influences, interactions among diverse factors affecting development (Fogel, 1993; Goldfield, 1995; Lewis, 1995; Smith & Thelen, 1993). Dynamic concepts such as attractor, self-organization, and catastrophe have become common parlance in the field, proffered as new metaphors for explaining complex developmental patterns. As a result of such work, more and more people have sat up and taken notice of nonlinear dynamics. However, demonstrations and new global metaphors are not enough. As elegant as such demonstrations are, they only begin the process of building dynamic explanations.

If nonlinear dynamics is to reach its potential in the study of development, we must move from demonstrations to explanations. To be constructive, researchers must build dynamic explanations of developmental patterns, not only showing that multiple factors are relevant to a developing activity, such as stepping, but building explicit models that show how various factors come together to produce the developmental pathways for that activity (stepping and walking). Fortunately, a number of the contributors to this volume have moved to build rigorous dynamic explanations for the demonstrations that they have uncovered, with the goal of combining mathematical models of action processes with careful measurement. To produce real explanations of development of action systems, dynamic analysis requires the combination of explicit models with careful measurement.

## Why So Much Research on Actions?

In research on dynamic development, actions have been the preponderant focus of research, especially actions in infants. The extent of this emphasis is evident in this book, where most of the research involves actions in infants. In contrast, most traditional (nondynamic) developmental research has centered on cognitive or socioemotional development, not actions. Witness the selection of chapters in widely read compendia, such as the *Handbook of Child Psychology* (Damon, 1997), where a whole volume is dedicated to cognitive development, another volume to social development, but only a few scattered chapters emphasize actions. Why is research on action so popular among researchers interested in nonlinear dynamics in contrast to the rest of developmental science?

When developmental patterns are assumed to be complex (nonlinear), a requirement comes to the foreground that is often neglected in traditional research—finely graded measurement. Describing developmental patterns requires the use of powerful rulers to assess behavior. For researchers to detect ups and downs instead of simple linear patterns, a coarse ruler simply will not do.

Unlike most developmental domains, action can be studied with a ready-made ruler of exceptional power—the Cartesian coordinate system for describing locations in space. This system for measuring location in terms of three axes (dimensions) provides researchers with effective rulers for measuring actions with straight-forward precision. Movements can be localized in space and assigned exact numbers in three dimensions, which provide a powerful tool for assessing patterns of action and how they change. No such measurement tools are available for most other kinds of behaviors. The availability of this powerful measurement tool promotes the study of actions by dynamically oriented researchers because it allows them to describe precisely the complex patterns of movement and development that they are searching for.

As important as actions are, people do not simply act. They also talk, think, solve problems, interact with each other, express emotions. Most of the extensive research and rich theory about development involves these other domains, not actions. Dynamical research on development needs to engage these other domains seriously, building on the strengths of past research and theory and constructing tools for careful measurement of cognitive and socioemotional development as well as actions.

## Model-Driven Dynamic Research

Model-driven research differs from data-driven research in a number of ways. Most obviously, it focuses on explicating specific models of growth and development in mathematical terms and testing those models to determine whether they produce the developmental properties that theorists have claimed for them. In addition, its content involves cognitive and language development more than actions, perhaps because the dominant developmental theories (Piaget, Werner, Vygotsky) have emphasized those domains. Among the most distinguished practitioners of this work have been Paul van Geert (1991) and Han van der Maas and Peter Molenaar (1992). The model-driven research has explicated developmental processes with mathematical rigor, giving new life and power to concepts such as equilibration and stage.

# Origins of Human Competence:
# A Cultural-Ecological Perspective

JOHN U. OGBU

*University of California, Berkeley*

Ogbu, John U. *Origins of Human Competence: A Cultural-Ecological Perspective.* CHILD DEVEL-OPMENT, 1981, 52, 413–429. In this essay it is argued that child rearing in the family similar micro settings in the early years of life and subsequent adolescent socialization are geared toward the development of instrumental competencies required for adult economic, political and social roles. These cultural imperatives vary from 1 cultural group to another as do required competencies. In the United States they are different for the white middle class for minority groups like urban ghetto blacks. It follows that the conventional research approach which used white middle-class child-rearing practices and children's competencies as standards is not useful in understanding minority groups' child rearing and competencies. Rather cross-cultural research, a cultural-ecological model is proposed which is not ethnocentric and studies competence in the context of the cultural imperatives in a given population. Cross cultural or intergroup comparison is appropriate if based on data from such contextual studies.

In this paper I am concerned with the problem of developing an appropriate model for cross-cultural research in child rearing and development, particularly for studying minority children in the United States. The paper is divided, into five parts. The first deals with definition of competence and majority-group developmentalists' approach to child rearing and development in a plural society. In the second section I present alternative models, one; currently used by some minority researchers; the other—a cultural-ecological model—being the model I am proposing as appropriate for cross-cultural research. I speculate in the third section on some implications of the cultural-ecological model for research on mi-

nority children. This is followed with some further observations in the fourth section on the relationship between child rearing and schooling among urban ghetto blacks. Here I try to point out; an almost unrecognized feature of ghetto culture, namely, that it is not merely different from white middle-class culture shared by the public schools, but in some important respects appears to be an alternative to mainstream culture. The concluding part of the paper briefly considers the practical implications of the cultural-ecological model.

Let me make it clear from the outset I do not rule out cross-cultural research of minority children or on any other group of children; nor do I rule out cross-cultural comparisons. But I reject the absurdity of searching for a pattern of child rearing and development derived from studying one group (e.g., white middle-class children) in another group (e.g., urban ghetto black children). The first step toward majority-minority or cross-cultural comparison is to study majority child rearing and development qua majority

The writing of this paper was supported by the faculty research fund, University of California, Berkeley, and by NIE grant NIE G 80-0045. An earlier version was presented at colloquia at the University of California, Berkeley; Stanford University; Case-Western Reserve University; and Georgia State College. I am grateful to many colleagues for their helpful comments during the colloquia presentations or as individual readers. Reprints may be obtain from the author, John U. Ogbu, Department of Anthropology, University of California, Berkeley, California 94720.

*Source: Child Development*, 1981, 52, 413–429. ©1981 by the Society for Research in Child Development, Inc.

child rearing and development, and to study minority child rearing and development qua minority child rearing and development. A general theory of child rearing and development should emerge from data derived from mapping out patterns of child rearing and development of different groups (e.g., minorities, majority, social classes, etc.) or societies (Gearing 1976, p. 188) in their respective contexts.

## A Model of Competence in a Pluralistic Society

### *What Is Human Competence?*

"Competence" is increasingly being used to distinguish people who possess certain attributes associated with a white middle-class type of success in school and society, but there is not as yet an accepted definition of the term. Common to most definitions, however, is the notion that competence is the ability to perform a culturally specified task. For example, Ainsworth and Bell (1974, p. 98) define competence in part as the ability to influence environment, and for Inkeles (1968) it is the ability to perform socially valued roles as defined in a given society. Upon a close inspection, "ability" as used in various definitions of competence refers to a set of skills which makes it possible to perform the given task. This is at least the impression one gains from Connolly and Bruner's introduction to *The Growth of Competence* (1974). They state that "in any given society there are sets of skills which are essential for coping with existing realities," and that how individuals function depends on their acquisition of the competencies (i.e., skills) required by these realities. Connolly and Bruner distinguish between specific skills and general skills, with emphasis on the importance of the latter. They give as an example of general skills "middle-class education," or the set of skills associated with technological management. This general skill includes "the capacity for combining information in a fashion that permits one to use flexibility; to go beyond the information given; to draw inferences about things yet to be encountered; and to connect and probe for connection" (p. 4). They call this "operative intelligence—*knowing how* rather than simply *knowing that*"

(p. 3). Competence is, then, a set of functional or instrumental skills. While Connolly and Bruner are primarily concerned with cognitive or intellectual competencies, others focus on linguistic, social-emotional, and practical competencies (White 1973; Williams 1970).

## A Universal Model of Human Development

The dominant research approach, which may be designated as the universal model of human development, makes three fundamental assumptions. The first is that the origins of human competence lie in intrafamilial relationships and parent (or surrogate parent) -child interaction or in early childhood experiences. As Connolly and Bruner (1974) put it, "The general skills, cognitive and emotional, appear to depend on what has properly been called a 'hidden curriculum in the home'" (p. 5). The second assumption is that the nature of human competencies can be adequately studied by focusing on micro-level analyses of the child's early experiences, such as an analysis of the child's experiences within the family and in similar settings. The third assumption is that a child's later school success and perhaps success in adult life depend on the acquisition of white middle-class competencies through white middle-class child-rearing practices.

The work of Burton White and his associates at Harvard illustrates well this approach to the origins of human competence. For about 2 years White and his associates visited the homes of each of 40 children for about 1 hour a week and observed and recorded how the child interacted with its mother and, occasionally, with other people such as the father, older siblings, housekeeper, and peers. From these observations they concluded that "a close social relationship, particularly during the first few months following their first birthday, was a conspicuous feature in the lives of the children who developed best" (White 1979, p. 7). They went on to say that within this parent child interaction it was important for the adult to provide the child with a reasonable amount of safe space and materials to explore, to act as the child's consultant when he needed help and comforting, and to be firm and consistent in discipline. These are some of the maternal behaviors constituting "the core of effective child-rearing" (p. 13). On the child's part it was determined important that he carry out certain social and nonsocial tasks. For example, he should be able to use adults as a resource to learn how to gain people's attention, gain information through vision and steady staring and listen to people speaking to him directly. Effective child rearing combined with appropriate child tasks appeared to correlate with the development of appropriate cognitive, language and social competencies by the age of 3, a development which is hypothesized to ensure their future success in school and probably in society at large.

Using findings from this "naturalistic study, White (1979) designed an experiment in which a group of mothers were taught to rear their children according to the core of effective child-rearing practices, and their children were taught to perform the core of effective child tasks. The results were not entirely as expected. For example, although the child's total social experience correlated with his language development, it did not correlate with his cognitive competence as measured by the Binet test scores. Nevertheless, the researchers concluded that their experiment had established the importance of early childhood experiences not only for cognitive development in general but also for formal schooling. Citing Bronfenbrenner (1974), they stated that "while excellent early development does not guarantee lifelong excellent development, poor progress during the early years seems to be remarkably difficult to overcome" (p. 181). These researchers made three concluding points which are relevant to the present essay. First, they claimed that the origins of competence lie indeed in the hidden curriculum of the home. "After 20 years of research," they said, "we are convinced that much that shapes the final human product takes place [in the home] during the first years of life" (pp. 182, 183). Second, the most important or most essential ingredient in the hidden curriculum of the home is the mother's skills as a teacher. Some children do not develop appropriate competencies for later success in school and society because their par-

ents (i.e., mothers) fail in their child-rearing tasks. Third, the failure of some mothers in this vital task calls for society to intervene in order to train such parents to become good teachers. "We are convinced," they concluded, "that the traditional failure to offer training and assistance to new parents has several harmful consequences. Put simply, people could grow up to become more able and more secure if their first teachers did not have to be 'self-taught' and unsupported" (p. 183).

## Inadequacy of the Universal Model for Cross-cultural Research

The White (1979) studies do not directly address the issue of cross-cultural research. But they started out with the assumption that there are universal "laws" of optimal development. If these laws could be discovered, as they appear to claim to have done with their recent experimental study, then such findings can be used to help groups who do not do as well in school and who are, therefore, in need of compensatory education (White 1979, p. 8). Others are more explicit in pointing out that children from black ghettos and similar "disadvantaged" minorities do not succeed in school and society because they do not have the kind of early childhood experiences described by White et. al. (see Powledge 1967; Stanley 1972, 1973). Connolly and Bruner (1974), for example, believe that ghetto blacks do not have the operative intelligence essential for managing modern technology because of inadequate early childhood experiences. "Research over the last several years has taught us much," they declare. "The slum child, the ghetto, the subculture of defeat do not equip their children with the easy abstract skills of the doctor's, lawyer's, or professor's children" (Connolly & Bruner 1974, p. 5). They point out that the official ideology of despair in these subcultures is produced by generations of unemployment, job discrimination, and the like. Ghetto parents subtly transmit this despair to their children, thus stunting their mental development. The way out of this developmental dilemma is not necessarily to eliminate unemployment and job discrimination (points at which the authors are silent), but to intervene in child-rearing practices, to make "supplementary child-rearing practices available to the parents" (p. 6).

Thus, proponents of the universal model attribute minority children's failure in school to developmental "deficits," and they propose a rehabilitation to correct the deficits and to enhance school success. This deficit perspective is nowhere more fully articulated than in various preschool programs for "disadvantaged children" begun in the 1960s. These programs are based on assumptions that an early acquisition of competencies is critical for later functioning in school and society, that children's experiences with certain types of "curriculum" during the preschool years promote optimal development, and that it is possible to correct the developmental deficits through intervention programs for preschoolers and/or preventive programs directed at parents. The emphasis of a particular program tells us what instrumental competencies are presumed "missing" in minority child rearing and development. For example, we know what competencies are thought to be "missing" when programs are designed to increase parents' knowledge of the core of effective child rearing through lectures, counseling, group discussion, and the like; when programs attempt to train mothers in techniques of cognitive stimulation and social training by showing them how and how much to talk to and play with children; or when programs aim to develop children's cognitive, social-emotional, preacademic skills or a combination of these competencies (Ogbu 1974, pp. 208–211; Rees 1968; White 1973).

It is now generally acknowledged that most of these programs have not been successful in permanently inculcating the competencies assumed to facilitate a white middle-class type of school success (Goldberg 1971; Ogbu 1978). Explanations for their failure have merely encouraged the proponents to stress the need for earlier and earlier intervention, including more emphasis on parent education and parent training. But parent education—increasing parents' knowledge of the core of effective child rearing—has not been particularly successful or effective either. And although parent training seems more effective, its results cannot be generalized because of the selective nature of the participants and because of unresolved methodological problems (White 1973, pp. 245, 257).

I have discussed the inadequacies of the deficit explanations and their attendant remedies elsewhere (Ogbu 1978; Ogbu, Note 1). The point to emphasize here is that the universal model upon which they are derived is not a useful model for cross-cultural study of either the development of human competence or school success. Contrary to the assumptions of the model, there are some nonwhite immigrant groups in the United States who have done relatively well in school even though they were not raised in the way the model suggests or in the manner described to some extent by White (1979) and in various remedial programs (see DeVos 1973; Ogbu 1978; Ogbu, Note 2). Moreover, in the Third World countries some groups do relatively well in Western-type schools even though they do not follow the child-rearing practices advocated in the model. Of particular interest is the fact that "impoverished children" in such societies also tend to do well in school and are not characterized by the same "problems" said to exist among "disadvantaged children" in America (Heyneman 1979; van den Berghe 1980).

The case for the current pattern of intervention rests largely on the belief in the determinism of early childhood events—"that much that shapes the final human product takes place during the first years of life" (White 1979, p. 193). But as far as schooling is concerned, the cross-cultural examples cited above cast serious doubts on the necessity of particular socialization experiences. Not only can children from different child-rearing backgrounds learn well in the same school, but people with different childhood backgrounds can at varying points in their lives acquire the general skills or competencies which, according to Connolly and Bruner (1974), are essential for technological management. Given the opportunity, one does not have to be born and raised in a white middle-class home or receive "supplementary childhood care" to become a doctor, lawyer, or professor in the Western social and economic system.

Furthermore, it will be obvious in my later discussion that the ghetto child's later experiences in the street are probably just as important in shaping his adult instrumental cognitive, linguistic, motivational, socioemotional, and practical competencies as his early childhood experiences in the home. For example, no one who has observed or studied hustlers and pimps in the ghetto will deny that they possess the general skills or operative intelligence—"*knowing how* rather than simply *knowing that*"—which Connolly and Bruner attribute to the white middle class (see Foster 1974, p. 38, Perkins 1975; Milner, Note 3). But hustlers and pimps appear to have acquired their operative intelligence primarily in postchildhood in the street (Perkins 1975; Milner, Note 3). Then, of course, we note that racial barriers have traditionally forced such "intelligent" ghetto people to apply their competencies to the management of activities in a "street economy" rather than in the conventional, corporate economy.

## Alternative Models: Relativistic and Cultural Ecological

All three assumptions underlying the universal model are inappropriate for cross-cultural research, especially for research in black urban life. I propose an alternative model more suitable for cross-cultural studies, a model that does not set up the white middle-class child-rearing practices and competencies as the standard upon which all others are measured. Before doing so, I will briefly indicate other efforts to develop an alternative model for cross-cultural research, which may be designated as a relativistic model.

### The Relativistic Model

By the late 1960s many blacks and other minority-group members rejecting the deficit explanations of school failure began to argue that their people have different cultures whose child-rearing practices promote competencies different from those of the white middle class. If their children failed in school it was probably because the schools' methods of teaching and testing failed to recognize the unique skills of these children (Boykin 1978; Gibson 1978; Ramirez & Castenada 1974; Wright 1970).

Some researchers have made serious efforts to demonstrate that America's minorities have their own cultures. For example, a strong case has been made for the existence of a distinct black culture, with roots in African culture and black experience in the United States (Hannerz 1969; Keil 1977; Lewis 1976; Nobles & Traver 1976; Valentine 1979; Young 1970, 1974; Shack, Note 4). However, there has been very little effort to specify the instrumental competencies unique to black culture except in areas of "expressive life-styles" (e.g., adaptability, social interactional skills, and "styles" in dress, walking, etc.) and language and communication (Abrahams 1972; Hannerz 1969; Keil 1977; Kochman 1972; Labov 1972; Mitchell Kernan 1972; Rainwater 1974; Simons, Note 5). It is largely in the area of language and communication that researchers have gone further to understand unique instrumental competencies of blacks in relation to problems of formal schooling. In general it can be said that researchers have not yet reached the point of clearly delineating the unique competencies of minority groups and how such competencies are acquired.

More germain to the task of this essay is the growing number of studies of competencies outside Western societies (see Cole, Gay, Glick, & Sharp 1971; Dasen 1977; Greenfield 1966). Of particular importance is the suggestion by anthropologists (e.g., LeVine 1967), sociologists (Inkeles 1966, 1968), and cross-cultural psychologists (Berry 1977) that the child-rearing patterns of a population may be influenced by the nature of its instrumental competencies which, in turn, depends on its role repertoire. These researchers agree that competence is defined differently in different populations, and that in each case it is the main task of child rearing to train "infants, children, adolescents (and sometimes adults) so that they can ultimately fulfill the social obligations that their society and culture will place on them" (Inkeles 1966, p. 64). Competencies—cognitive, linguistic, social-emotional, and practical—are cultural requirements which parents and other child-rearing agents are obligated to inculcate in children. Such insights suggest another model—a cultural-ecological model—which studies competencies in the context of real-life situations, thereby avoiding ethnocentrism.

## Cultural-Ecological Perspective

The underlying assumptions of the model we propose are that origins of human competencies—general and specific skills—lie in the nature of culturally defined adult tasks, such as the subsistence tasks of a given population; that insofar as most adults in the population perform their sex-appropriate tasks competently as defined in the culture, it follows that most children in the population grow up as competent men and women; that child-rearing techniques serve only as a mechanism for inculcating and acquiring certain culturally defined instrumental competencies and are, in fact, shaped largely by the nature of those particular instrumental competencies; that child categories and instrumental competencies resulting from child-rearing techniques eventually develop into adaptive adult categories and instrumental competencies in the population; and that minority groups maintaining a kind of symbiotic relationship with a dominant group in a specific environment like the United States tend to evolve alternative rather than merely different instrumental competencies which are characteristic of a spatially distant and non-symbiotic culture. The last assumption has important educational implications which will be explored in the concluding part of the essay.

*Cultural tasks and competence.* —Certain populations possess unique instrumental competencies that meet their societal needs, and they adapt their child-rearing techniques to inculcate these needs. These societal needs may be defined as the cultural tasks which are appropriate for age, sex, and other criteria of distinction. For adults in any population, these culturally defined tasks are to be found in all areas of life, including those pertaining to subsistence, social organization and relations, political organization, and so on. Differences in such cultural tasks are not as readily acknowledged for populations within the United States as they may be for geographically distant ones. But, as we shall argue later, these tasks, particularly subsistence tasks, are in important ways different for the white middle class than for black ghetto residents and similar minorities.

*Child rearing as culturally organized formulas for inculcating competencies.* —An adequate framework for studying child rearing must begin with the acknowledgement that in every relatively stable population or its segment most children grow up to be competent adult men and women. And there appear to be three reasons why this is the case: children are taught more or less the same set of instrumental competencies, they are taught with the same culturally standardized techniques, and the members of the population share the same incentives for teaching the same competencies by the same techniques and to acquire the same competencies. Within this general pattern there are, of course, individual differences due to differences in constitution, "accidents of birth," and, to some extent, individual preferences.

In every relatively stable human population, instrumental competencies have prior existence before individual families which teach these competencies to their offspring through the process of child rearing. Child rearing is thus the process by which parent and other child-rearing agents transmit and by which children acquire the prior existing competencies required by their social, economic, political, and other future adult cultural tasks. The study of the child-rearing process informs us of how the prior existing cognitive, linguistic, social-emotional, and practical competencies are transmitted and acquired; but the study of the range and nature of the cultural tasks requiring these competencies provides us with the knowledge of why a given range and form of such competencies exist at all within the population.

The causal relationship between competencies and child-rearing practices appears to be the reverse of our conventional thinking. Contrary to our usual interpretation of differences in competencies between members of two populations (e.g., white middle class and urban ghetto blacks) as resulting from differences in child-rearing practices, cross-cultural studies would suggest that the nature of the instrumental competencies in a population may determine the techniques parents and parent surrogates employ to raise children and how these children seek to acquire the attributes as they get older (see Aberle 1961; Barry, Child, & Bacon 1959;

Inkeles 1966, 1968; Kohn 1969; LeVine 1967; Maquet 1971; Mead 1939; Miller & Swanson 1958).

Barry et al. (1959) provide a good example of both how subsistence tasks determine personal attributes and how the latter appear to influence child-rearing practices. They first describe the personal attributes valued and rewarded in two types of societies distinguished by levels of subsistence economy, namely, low-food-accumulation societies of hunters and gatherers and high-food-accumulation societies of pastoralists and farmers. The first type of societies rewarded individualism, independence, assertiveness, and risk taking, whereas the second type of societies rewarded conscientious, compliant, responsible, and conservative adult behaviors. Instrumental competencies characteristic of each type of society were congruent with adult subsistence tasks. For example, the authors note that the high-food-accumulation societies of farmers and pastoralists need "responsible adults who can best ensure the continuing welfare of a society with high accumulation economy whose food supply must be protected and developed gradually throughout the year" (p. 62). In such societies people must adhere to a routine designed to maintain high accumulation of food. In contrast, societies with low food accumulation encouraged individual initiative to wrest food daily from nature in order to survive (pp. 62–63). Equally important is the authors' suggestion that these attributes tended to be generalized to the rest of behavior in everyday life (p. 63).

What is the relationship between the instrumental competencies and child-rearing practices of these two types of societies? The authors hypothesized that differences in instrumental competencies would cause the two types of societies to employ different techniques of child rearing: "The kind of adult behavior useful to the society is likely to be taught to some extent to the children, in order to assure the appearance of this behavior at the time it is needed. Hence we predict that the emphasis in childrearing will be toward the development of kinds of behaviors useful for adult economy (p. 53). When they rated 104 societies on several aspects of child-rearing practices, the results generally supported this hypothesis, especially with respect to training in compliance and assertiveness (p. 59).

Another example is Cohen's study (1965); among the Kanuri of Nigeria which shows how the society's rule of behavior for achievement defines social competence and how the latter shapes child-rearing practices. In order to attain higher economic, political, or social status, a Kanuri must show those who have the power to bestow these resources that he is loyal, obedient, and servile. Loyalty, obedience, and servility are therefore not only highly prized in superior-inferior relationships but also generalized to other forms of relationships such as that between parent and child, teacher and student, religious leader and followers. Kanuri parents consciously employ particular techniques to ensure that their children learn to behave properly like clients, that is, that they acquire the instrumental competencies which formed the most important social capital for achieving high status (p. 363).

Some studies in the United States further contribute to our understanding of the linkage between subsistence/cultural tasks and instrumental competencies, and between the latter and child-rearing practices. One such study by Miller and Swanson (1958), indicates that earlier middle-class Americans involved in entrepreneurial subsistence tasks tended to value and stress self-control and self-denial, whereas later generations of the middle class involved in bureaucratic economic tasks tend to value other personal attributes, like the ability to get along with other people and self-confidence. The study shows that there also has been a concomitant change in the child-rearing practices of the middle class because, in contrast to earlier generations, the contemporary middle class trains its children to be accommodating, to express their impulses more spontaneously, and so on (p. 58). Finally, Kohn's study (1969) shows that middle-class bureaucratic and professional jobs are associated with personal attributes of self-direction and the ability to manipulate interpersonal relations, ideas, and symbols. Working-class jobs, on the other hand, are associated with respect for authority and conformity to externally imposed rules. In this study, subjects in the sample from each class employed child-rearing techniques which encouraged their children to develop an adaptive constellation of instrumental competencies. For example, middle-class subjects used reasoning, isolation, appeals to guilt, and the like to elicit appropriate behavior in their children, whereas working-class subjects relied more on physical punishment and other means that enhanced compliance to external rules.

These studies deal mainly with social-emotional competence. In general they show that the cultural tasks—subsistence tasks in our examples—generate adaptive, functional personal attributes or instrumental social-emotional competencies. These qualities are perceived as useful by parents and other child-rearing agents and are taught by appropriate techniques. Berry (1971) suggests why we should more or less expect the nature of instrumental competencies to influence choice of child-rearing practices when he states that "one would not expect to discover a society in which independence and self-reliance are conveyed as goals by a harsh, restrictive method of socialization. Nor, conversely, would one expect to discover a society in which conformity is taught by a method characterized by a stimulation of a child's own interest and of his curiosity" (p. 328). To reiterate, the first reason most children in a given group or society grow up as competent adults is that they are taught more or less the same set of instrumental competences.

The second reason that most children in a relatively stable population grow up as competent adult men and women is that their sex-appropriate instrumental competencies are taught and acquired through culturally standardized techniques. A given population develops its child-rearing practices over a period of time as a set of standardized techniques designed to ensure both that its children survive into adulthood and that they acquire the competencies essential for their adult cultural tasks. This development is based on the people's experiences as a group in dealing with the demands of their physical, social, political, economic, and supernatural environments, that is, the demands of their cultural tasks.

As members of a population learn which strategies are effective and appropriate in exploiting their subsistence resources and which competencies facilitate the use of the strategies, they also learn how best to inculcate these instrumental competencies in their children. The

discovery of child-rearing techniques would initially be characterized by trial and error. But as more effective techniques are found, they become standardized and encoded in the people's customs and are transmitted like other aspects of their culture to subsequent generations. The transmission of standardized knowledge and skills of child rearing and their rationale ensures that parents and other adults in the population will share more or less the same ideas of what children must learn and be—what instrumental competencies they must possess—in order to become competent adults. It also ensures that adults share similar ideas of the techniques and skills with which to help children acquire these functional competencies.

From the perspective of cultural ecology, the child-rearing practices of a population are not an irrational or random set of activities; they form a part of a culturally organized system which evolves through generations of collective experiences in tasks designed to meet environmental demands. The child-rearing practices are a part of a people's cultural knowledge of their adult tasks, of essential competencies, and of the methods of transmitting these competencies to succeeding generations.

Parents and other child-rearing agents are not really independent actors in child-rearing tasks, for two reasons. First, they treat children in the manner constrained by their awareness that their children must develop particular instrumental competencies essential for more or less foreordained social, economic, political, and other culturally standardized knowledge, techniques, and skills of rearing competent children as defined by their society or social group. Individual parents do not invent new ways to raise their children, nor do they invent new competencies to transmit to their children. Except under conditions of rapid social change, both the competencies and the method are culturally sanctioned and more or less preordained.

The third reason most children grow up as competent adults is that people in a given population are motivated to inculcate and to acquire the competencies essential for adult cultural tasks by societal rewards for competence and penalties for incompetence. This phenomenon can be described with the concept of the status-mobility system (LeVine 1967) or "native theory of success." In every population there usually exists a folk theory of how one performs cultural tasks in order to succeed in the status system. That is, how one "makes it," however "making it" is defined, is a shared cultural knowledge. In a population in which status positions or cultural tasks are ranked, "making it" includes both the ability to attain higher status positions or more desirable adult tasks and the ability to perform these tasks successfully. A native theory of success thus includes knowledge of the range of available cultural tasks or status positions, their relative importance or value, the competencies essential for attainment or performance, the strategies for attaining the positions or obtaining the cultural tasks, and the expected penalties and rewards for failures and successes.

A people's theory of success develops out of past experiences with cultural tasks, social rewards, and relative costs. The theory is either reinforced or altered by contemporary experiences, that is, by perceptions and interpretations of available opportunity structures.

As noted earlier, cultural tasks require appropriate instrumental competencies. It follows that those who are successful in performing cultural tasks are likely to be characterized to some degree by appropriate instrumental competencies, qualities, or attributes. Such people become models whose attributes child-rearing agents admire and want to inculcate in children. As children get older and become more aware of the status-mobility system of their society or social group and especially of the competencies for success, they, too, actively seek to acquire the instrumental competencies of the successful members of their population. The images of successful people, living or dead, are culturally buttressed and form a substantial portion of the values guiding parents and other child-rearing agents in their child-rearing tasks and guiding older children in their responses to these efforts (LeVine 1967).

Members of a population do not conceptualize the instrumental competencies which facilitate success in their status-mobility system and do not necessarily explain the relationship between their cultural tasks and instrumental competencies or between the latter and the child-rearing techniques the way social scientists do. Nevertheless, to suggest that natives (be they

white middle-class Americans, black ghetto residents, or African tribesmen) usually have a good knowledge of their status system and of what it takes to make it as behavioral guides is not too far removed from reality.

***The scope of "environment" in human development research.*** —If the way parents and parent surrogates relate to children and the way children respond are influenced by the more or less foreordained social, economic, political, and other cultural tasks by culturally patterned techniques of child rearing and by shared theories of status mobility and child-rearing, then concentration of conventional studies on parent-child relationship in the laboratory, home, or other settings has serious limitations. Some of these limitations have been noted by others from different perspectives (see Bronfenbrenner 1974, 1977, 1979; Inkeles 1966, 1968). Bronfenbrenner (1977, p. 515) for instance, points out that emphasis on rigor by developmental psychologists leads them to design elegant experiments of limited scope and use. "This limitation," he explains, "derives from the fact that many of these experiments involve situations that are unfamiliar, artificial, and short-lived and that call for unusual behaviors that are difficult to generalize to other settings." As an alternative he proposes to study the child in *"the enduring environment in which he lives* or might live if social policies and practices were altered" (1974, p. 2).

From a different perspective, Inkeles (1968, p. 123) points out the shortcoming of researchers' preoccupation with events in the micro setting (e.g., the family) and their inability or unwillingness to examine the impact of social, economic, and political systems—"the imperatives of culture" (Cohen 1971)—under which the child will live and perform as an adult. He notes that those studying child rearing are mostly concerned with personality developmental problems and that this dominant concern leads them to concentrate "on purely intrafamilial and interpersonal aspects of parent-child relations." Even when some researchers introduce social class, occupational differences, ethnicity, and the like as control variables, their investigation still focuses "on the individual parent as the socialization agent." Inkeles then suggests that the study of child rearing should be broadened to include the interests of society and its influences on the child-rearing process. He also suggests that we include how the child learns the content of the significant role he will play as an adult (pp. 123–24).

Cultural ecology provides a framework for broadening our conception of environmental influences on competencies and their acquisition. This framework is derived from the work of anthropologist Julian Steward and his followers. They define cultural ecology as the study of institutionalized and socially transmitted patterns of behavior interdependent with features of the environment (Netting 1968, p. 11; see also Geertz 1962; Goldschmidt 1971). A variant definition more germain to my interest is by Bennett (1969), for whom cultural ecology is the study of how the way a population uses its natural environmental influences and is influenced by its social organization and cultural values and how the relationship between the personal attributes and behaviors of its members and their environment is to be found in the strategies or tasks they have devised for coping with their environmental demands, in the ways of exploiting available resources to attain their subsistence goals and solve recurrent and new problems, as well as in ways of dealing with one another. In this population-environment relationship via cultural tasks, the adaptive, instrumental competencies and behaviors are properties of the total group, not of isolated individuals.

One environmental demand which has a powerful influence on human competence and is faced by all human groups is subsistence, or making a living. For this reason the model I propose deals primarily with the role of subsistence tasks and strategies in the origins of human competence. There are additional reasons for focusing on subsistence demands. First, this is an area where significant cross-cultural studies like those discussed earlier exist, showing its influence on child-rearing practices and outcomes. Furthermore, subsistence quest has dominated man's evolutionary history and has acquired a symbolic significance far beyond the need to satisfy biological drives of hunger; it has become intimately tied to man's quest for status enhancement or self-esteem, especially in modern industrial societies.

While all human populations respond to subsistence demands, they do not all respond alike or with the same set of strategies because they do not occupy the same environment, because their environments do not contain the same resources, and because they have different histories of resource exploitation and of quest for protection. Different populations, therefore, seem to have evolved different strategies more or less appropriate for their given circumstances. And each constellation of subsistence strategies has selected, as it were, from a vast array of practical skills and cognitive, language (communicative), and social-emotional competencies most compatible with it. A given population has usually invested such instrumental competencies with cultural values and stressed them for the upbringing of its children.

Still another reason for focusing on subsistence demands is that the influence of subsistence strategies on personal attributes is just as powerful, even if not direct, in modern industrial societies like the United States as it is in societies of hunter-gatherers and subsistence farmers. In modern industrial societies subsistence strategies largely determine how children are prepared for adult life in the home, community, and school. The linkage between subsistence strategies (i.e., work, job), on the one hand, and instrumental competencies on the other, in the United States is widely recognized by researchers in education and child development (White 1973; Baumrind, Note 6). The direction of causal linkage between participation in American economy and instrumental competencies conventionally stressed is important but quite different from that suggested here. It is often asserted, for instance, that the nature of one's participation in this economy determines not only one's subsistence status but also his or her general status enhancement or self-esteem. As one observer has written (Miller 1971, p. 18), a person's job in the United States is about the most important symbol of his social standing. It is also said that the level of economy at which one participates (e.g., as an unskilled, skilled, or professional worker) is determined primarily by one's instrumental competencies acquired during child rearing or genetically inherited, which subsequently enabled one to acquire formal education appropriate for the attainment of that level of job (Hunt 1969; Jensen 1969; Schultz 1961; Weisbrod 1975). What has not been widely recognized and much less adequately studied is the influence of the nature of one's participation in that economy on his personal attributes. This is the special concern of the cultural-ecological perspective.

### The Cultural-Ecological Model

The cultural-ecological model I propose is represented in figure 1, showing a range of factors that should be considered in order to obtain a more complete and accurate view of the instrumental competencies prevalent in a given population, of their origins, and of their relationship to child rearing.

*Basic concepts.* —The model begins with the concept of effective environment (A), because cultural ecology does not deal with the total physical environment. It deals only with those aspects of it which directly affect subsistence quest and protection from threats to physical survival. Major elements of the effective environment include the population's level of technology and knowledge and nature of available resources. Technology refers to both tools and their uses in subsistence exploitation and protection; knowledge includes people's understanding of the nature of their environment and

the necessary techniques for exploiting its resources (Netting 1968, p. 16). The model posits that a people's effective environment largely shapes their subsistence strategies (B) or modes of resource exploitation. The latter constitute the main cultural tasks in the model and include the range of economic activities available to members of the population.

Available adaptive adult categories (C), or what are usually called adult role models, in the population depend partly on the nature of the subsistence strategies and partly on the native theory of success (D). The adult categories are types of people who in the native view are successful; usually there are native labels for the categories. Each category is not necessarily tied to a particular subsistence strategy. The categories are often distinguished but not too rigidly, by their constellation of instrumental competencies (C). Some instrumental competencies are likely to be shared by many people in the population.

Native theory of success (D) is an important element influencing child-rearing values and practices. As discussed earlier, it is the people's idea of how members of their society or social group get ahead. Its study provides an important clue about what instrumental competencies

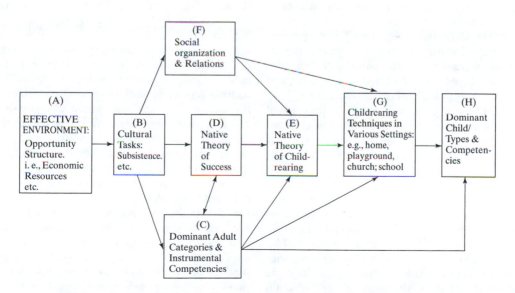

**Figure 1**  A cultural-ecological model of child rearing

people consciously inculcate in children and how they do it, what kinds of adults they want their children to be, and perhaps what kinds of adults older children strive to be.

Child rearing is a future-oriented activity, to a large degree because it prepares children to perform cultural tasks competently as adults (Ogbu 1978, p. 16; see also Aberle & Naegele 1952; Inkeles 1963). To facilitate this there usually is a kind of native theory of child rearing (*E*). People's beliefs about proper ways to raise children are partly based on their notion of how to succeed, their image of successful people in their community, and their organization of child-rearing tasks. The native theory of child rearing does not necessarily correspond to the researcher's or "scientific" model of the same, but it exists to guide adults, in their relationship to children and to rationalize what happens between them and children. From the cultural-ecological perspective an adequate study of child rearing in a given population must probe into the people's conscious model of how children should be raised and the sources of this model (Mayer 1970).

The way people organize their subsistence activities influences how they organize the upbringing of their children. Thus social organization and relations of child rearing (*F*) depends on the organization of and participation in subsistence activities because the latter may affect family or household structure, the type of settings in which children are raised, as well as the personnel or child-rearing agents. Furthermore, the social organization of child rearing is affected by and affects the native theory of child rearing and the actual techniques of child rearing.

Child-rearing techniques (*G*)—the actual process by which adults inculcate and children acquire instrumental competencies for their adult cultural tasks—exist as a part of the culturally organized formulas for upbringing: children are trained by more or less the same standardized techniques which have evolved for transmission of adaptive instrumental competencies functional in adult life. The model posits that actual child-rearing techniques are influenced by the need to produce functional adult categories and to inculcate their competencies; they are also influenced by the native theory of child

rearing and by the social organization of child rearing. Particular forms of techniques may be employed in particular settings, such as home and playground, at particular times and by particular child-rearing agents. These are matters for empirical study. Furthermore, particular child-rearing techniques may depend on the nature of instrumental competencies the child-rearing agents are obligated to inculcate or reinforce.

Ultimately we want to understand the outcomes of child rearing in a given culture. This can be assessed by examining characteristic or dominant attributes of children. The outcomes are labeled in the model as dominant child types and competencies (*H*) and are assumed to be those most likely to develop into dominant adult types and competencies.

## Cross-cultural Research Implications: Ghetto Example

The universal model reviewed earlier focuses on the relationship between child-rearing techniques and child outcomes (boxes *G* and *H* in the ecological model). It interprets developmental outcomes (e.g., dominant child types and competencies) as products of parental teaching skills and knowledge and specific child outcomes. When the universal model is applied comparatively to white middle-class and a minority population, differences in child competencies are not only interpreted narrowly as consequences of parental teaching skills, but also minority parents' teaching skills are termed deficient. The cultural-ecological model requires that we study the transmission and acquisition of competencies in a given population in the context of the demands of the population's cultural tasks, especially its subsistence tasks. Furthermore, it requires that we make no evaluative judgment in terms of good or bad, adequate or inadequate, deficient or not deficient, before we have established that the two populations studied share the same or similar effective environment, employ the same or similar subsistence strategies and/or other cultural tasks, and share the same theories of success and child rearing (Ogbu, in press). Prevailing invidious comparison is not excusable on the ground that researchers are studying the so-called high-risk children or high-risk families (Remy, Note 7) because the results of such studies eventually come to be interpreted by some as typical of minority populations. The challenge is to study first minority child rearing and development qua minority child rearing and development, Navajo child rearing and development qua Navajo child rearing and development, etc. If the researcher lacks the competence, the resources, or the time to study the various forces suggested in the model as shaping child rearing and development in a population, he or she should at least become familiar with the literature describing these forces as a background to the interpretation of his or her research findings.

## Survival Strategies and Schooling: The Problem of Alternative Culture

I suggest that the research model of dominant-group developmentalists reviewed earlier is ethnocentric. Rather than being truly universal, it is merely a pseudouniversal rooted in the beliefs of an ethnocentric population. It is false because it looks at the origins of competence from the wrong end of the relationship between childhood experiences and the competencies essential for functioning in adult life. It decontextualizes competencies from realities of life. As a result, it confuses the process of acquiring and transmitting adaptive, functional, or instrumental competencies with their causes, or origins, which are the reasons for their very presence or absence in a given population.

The consensus among dominant-group developmentalists is that a disproportionate number of ghetto children fail in school because they lack white middle-class types of competencies, including rules of behavior for achievement. And they lack these competencies because ghetto parents lack the capability to raise their children as white middle-class parents raise their own children. In this essay I have argued that ghetto blacks indeed acquire different rules of behavior for achievement and related competencies because such is the requirement for their competence in adult cultural/subsistence tasks

and not merely because ghetto parents lack white middle-class capability in child rearing.

I now add that differences in rules of behavior for achievement and related competencies do not always result in more or less permanent learning handicaps or disproportionate school failure, and that where the latter occurs there are probably additional reasons. For example, differences in rules of behavior for achievement and related competencies may cause initial difficulties in school learning among immigrants to the United States and among Third World peoples adopting Western education. But these people eventually learn successfully either by abandoning or modifying substantially their native competencies and rules of behavior for achievement in favor of those which facilitate school success. They do so for two reasons: first, they tend to perceive school success as providing opportunities to achieve new desirable adult cultural/subsistence tasks; and second, they realize that their native rules of behavior for achievement and related competencies may not provide access to the new desirable adult cultural tasks (Heyneman 1979; van den Berghe 1980; Ogbu, Note 9).

In contrast, ghetto rules of behavior for achievement and related competencies have been developed historically as alternatives to those of the school insofar as the latter represents white middle-class cultural ways whose racial policies and practices prevented generations of blacks from using the same rules of behavior and the same competencies to attain desirable adult tasks open to whites. Under this circumstance ghetto blacks are not oriented toward abandoning or substantially modifying their rules of behavior for achievement and their related instrumental competencies in favor of adopting those of the white middle class. The overall impression one gains from interviewing ghetto blacks, especially males, is that many consider acting white in school and community as unacceptable. People should learn how to deal with white people—how to manipulate white people—and retain their own safety and identity, but not how to behave like white people. This type of "bicultural learning" dates back to a period in black American history when acting white often led to beatings, prison, or death. It is this historical and structural situation which transforms differences in rules of behavior for achievement and in competencies into alternatives that are not easily given up in school setting.

## Conclusion

In this essay I have attempted to make the following points. First, the origins of human competence—specific and general skills—prevalent in a given population lie in the nature of adult cultural tasks. Second, the nature of the instrumental competencies influences child-rearing techniques and outcomes by sharing people's success models, their theories of success and child rearing, and their social organization for child rearing. Third, child-rearing ideas and techniques in a given culture are shared by the home/family and other institutions or settings containing the child in such a way as to make child rearing a kind of culturally organized formula to ensure competence and survival. Fourth, the outcomes of child rearing—the child types and their competencies—appear to be those that eventually develop into adaptive adult types and their competencies. Fifth, minority groups experience a continuing disproportion of school failure mainly when their historical and structural relationship with the dominant groups has led to evolution of alternative competencies. Finally, I have proposed the cultural-ecological model as a framework for studying child-rearing and developmental issues in a way that is not ethnocentric and as a framework broad enough to encompass many important forces often excluded in conventional research.

I have been concerned in this essay primarily with *what is*. But there are policy implications of our analysis with regard to minority children, such as those of the ghetto. First, we think that because instrumental competencies of ghetto children are adaptive alternatives, for example, they are not easily eliminated or modified permanently so long as the originating and supporting conditions (e.g., marginal conventional subsistence resources coupled with availability of attractive street economy) exist or are perceived to exist. That is, efforts to improve ghetto school success which focus primarily on the family and early childhood experiences cannot result in fundamental and enduring changes in ghetto children's characteristic rules of behavior for achievement and related competencies as long as such attributes are functional in ghetto effective environment and can be acquired during the postinfancy period in the street and other settings.

Second, it follows that the most effective way to improve ghetto or minority school success is to increase and improve their conventional economic resources (e.g., provide more and better conventional jobs for youths and adults) to the point where (*a*) significant changes occur in perceptions of opportunity structures in the conventional economy, and (*b*) the street economy and associated survival strategies become less attractive. Finally, until the attractiveness of these alternatives is sufficiently reduced or altogether eliminated, ghetto or minority rules of behavior for achievement and related competencies should be studied systematically and harnessed for teaching and learning in school settings. This cannot be achieved by research focusing on atypical ghetto children and their families—those "at risk." We advocate studying ghetto people and minority people as viable cultural groups. But this should be a transitional strategy and not a permanent approach to social change which is to eliminate all structural barriers.

## Reference Notes

1. Ogbu, J. U. An ecological approach to minority education. Special invited lecture, International Year of the Child, presented at the biennial meeting of the Society for Research in Child Development, San Francisco, 1979.
2. Ogbu, J. U. Education, clientage, and social mobility: caste and social change in the United States and Nigeria. Paper presented at Burg Wartenstein Symposium No. 80: Social inequality: comparative and developmental approaches, Vienna, August 25–September 3 1978.
3. Milner, C. A. Black pimps and their prostitutes. Unpublished doctoral dissertation, University of California, Berkeley, 1970.
4. Shack, W. A. On black American values in white America: some perspectives on the cultural aspects of learning behavior and compensatory education. Paper prepared for the Social Science Re-

search Council: Subcommittee on Values and Compensatory Education 1970–1971.

5. Simons, H. D. Black dialect, reading interference and classroom interaction. Unpublished manuscript, Department of Education, University of California, Berkeley, 1976.

6. Baumrind, D. Subcultural variations in values defining social competence: an outsider's perspective on the black subculture. Unpublished manuscript, Institute of Human Development University of California, Berkeley, 1976.

7. Remy, C. T. The abecedarian approach to social competence: cognitive and linguistic intervention for disadvantaged preschoolers. Paper presented at a workshop on Socialization of Children in a Changing Society, College of Education and Home Economics, University of Cincinnati, April 1979.

8. Hickerson, R. Survival strategies and role models in the ghetto. Unpublished manuscript, Department of Anthropology, University of California, Berkeley, 1980.

9. Ogbu, J. U. Minority school performance as an adaptation. Unpublished manuscript, Department of Anthropology, University of California, Berkeley, 1978.

## References

Aberle, D. F. Culture and socialization. In F. L. K. Hsu (Ed.), *Psychological anthropology.* Evanston, Ill.: Dorsey, 1961.

Aberle, D. F., & Naegele, K. D. Middle-class father's occupational role and attitudes toward children. *American Journal of Orthopsychiatry*, 1952, **22**, 366–378.

Abrahams, R. D. Joking: the training of the man of words in talking broad. In Kochman (Ed.), 1972.

Ainsworth, M. D. S., & Bell, S. M. Mother-infant interaction and the development of competence. In K. Connolly and J. S. Bruner (Eds.), *The growth of competence.* New York: Academic Press, 1974.

Barry, H.; Child, I. L.; & Bacon, M. K. Relation of child-training to subsistence economy. *American Anthropologist*, 1959, **61**, 51–63.

Bennett, J. W. *Northern plainsmen: adaptive strategy and agricultural life.* Arlington Heights, Ill.: AHM, 1969.

Berry, J. W. Ecological and cultural factors in spatial perceptual development. *Canadian journal of behavioral science review*, 1971, 3(4), 324–337.

Berry, J. W. *Human ecology and cognitive style: comparative studies in cultural and psychological adaptations.* New York: Halsted, 1977.

Borkin, A. W. Psychological/behavioral verve in academic/task performance: a pre-theoretical consideration. *Journal of Negro Education*, 1978, **47**, 343–354.

Bronfenbrenner, U. Developmental research and public policy and the ecology of childhood. *Child Development*, 1974, **45**, 1–5.

Bronfenbrenner, U. Toward an experimental ecology of human development. *American Psychologist*, 1977, **32**, 513–531.

Bronfenbrenner, U. *The ecology of human development: experiments by nature and design.* Cambridge, Mass.: Harvard University Press, 1979.

Bullock, P. *Aspirations vs. opportunity: "careers" in the inner city.* Ann Arbor: University of Michigan Press, 1973.

Cohen, R. Some aspects of institutionalized exchange: a Kanuri example. *Cahiers d'etudes Africaine*, 1965, 5(3), 353–369.

Cohen, Y. A. The shaping of men's minds: adaptations to the imperatives of culture. In M. L. Wax, S. Diamond, and F. O. Gearing (Eds.), *Anthropological perspectives on education.* New York: Basic, 1971.

Cole, M.; Gay, J.; Glick, J. A.; & Sharp, D. W. *The cultural context of learning and thinking: an exploration in experimental anthropology.* New York: Basic, 1971.

Connolly, K. J., and Bruner, J. S. Introduction, competence: its nature and nurture. In K. J. Connolly and J. S. Bruner (Eds.), *The growth of competence.* London: Academic Press, 1974.

Dasen, P. (Ed.). *Piagetian psychology: cross-cultural contributions.* New York: Garden, 1977.

DeVos, G. *Socialization for achievement: essays on the cultural psychology of the Japanese.* Berkeley: University of California Press, 1973.

Ellis, H., & Newman, S. N. "Gowster," "ivy-leaguer," "hustler," "conservative," "mack-man," and "continental": a functional analysis of six ghetto roles. In E. B. Leacock (Ed.), *The culture of poverty: a critique.* New York: Simon & Schuster, 1971.

Ferman, L. A.; Kornbluh, J. L.; & Miller, J. A. (Eds.), *Negroes and jobs: a book of readings.* Ann Arbor: University of Michigan Press, 1968.

Foster, H. L. *Ribbin', jivin', and playin' the dozens: the unrecognized dilemma of inner city schools.* Cambridge, Mass.: Ballinger, 1974.

Gearing, F. O. Where we are and where we might go: steps toward a general theory of cultural transmission. In Joan I. Roberts and S. K. Akinsanya (Eds.), *Educational patterns and cultural configurations: the anthropology of education.* New York: McKay, 1976.

Geertz, C. *Agricultural involution: the process of ecological change in Indonesia.* Berkeley: University of California Press, 1962

Gibson M. A. (Ed.). Approaches to multicultural education in the United States: some concepts and assumptions. *Anthropology and Education Quarterly*, 1976, **7**, Special Issue.

Goldberg, M. L. Socio-psychological issues in the education of the disadvantaged. In A. Harry Passow (Ed.), *Urban education in the 1970s*. New York: Teachers College, 1971.

Goldschmidt, W. Introduction: the theory of cultural adaptation. In R. B. Edgerton, *The individual in cultural adaptation: a study of four East African peoples*. Berkeley: University of California Press, 1971.

Greenfield, P. M. On culture and conservation. In J. S. Bruner et al. (Eds.), *Studies in cognitive growth*. New York: Wiley, 1966.

Hannerz, U. *Soulside: inquiries into ghetto culture and community*. New York: Columbia University Press, 1969.

Harrison, B. *Education, training and the urban ghetto*. Baltimore: Johns Hopkins University Press, 1972.

Heyneman, S. P. Why impoverished children do well in Ugandan schools. *Comparative Education*, 1979, **15**(2), 175–185.

Hudson, J. The hustling ethic. In Kochman (Ed.), 1972.

Hunt, N. McV. *The challenge of incompetence and poverty*. Urbana: University of Illinois Press, 1969.

Inkeles, A. Social structure and the socialization of competence. In the Editors, Harvard Educational Review, *Socialization and Schools*. Cambridge, Mass.: Harvard University Press, 1966.

Inkeles, A. Society, social structure and child socialization. In John A. Clausen (Ed.), *Socialization and society*. Boston: Little, Brown, 1968.

Jensen, A. R. How much can we boost I.Q. and scholastic achievement? In the Editors, Harvard Educational Review, *Environment, heredity, and intelligence*. Cambridge, Mass.: Harvard University Press, 1969.

Keil, C. The expressive black male role: the bluesman. In D. Y. Wilkinson and R. L. Taylor, (Eds.), *The black male in America today: perspectives on his status in contemporary society*. Chicago: Nelson-Hall, 1977.

Kochman, T. (Ed.). *Rappin' and stylin' out: communication in urban black America*. Chicago: University of Illinois Press, 1972.

Kohn, M. L. Social class and parent-child relationships: an interpretation. In R. L. Coser (Ed.), *Life cycle and achievement in America*. New York: Harper & Row, 1969.

Labov, W. *Language in the inner city*. Philadelphia: University of Pennsylvania Press, 1972.

Ladner, J. A. Growing up black. In J. H. Williams (Ed.), *Psychology of women: selected writings*. New York: Norton, 1978.

LeVine, R. W. *Dreams and deeds: achievement motivation in Nigeria*. Chicago: University of Chicago Press, 1967.

Lewis, D. K. The black family: socialization and sex roles. *Phylon*, 1976, **36**, 221–237.

Maquet, J. *Power and society in Africa*. New York: World University Library, 1971.

Mayer, P. (Ed.). *Socialization: the approach from social anthropology*. London: Tavistock, 1970.

Mead, M. *From the south seas: studies of adolescence and sex in primitive societies*. New York Morrow, 1939.

Mercer, J. R. *Labeling the mentally retarded* Berkeley: University of California Press, 1973.

Miller, D., & Swanson, G. *The changing American parent*. New York: Wiley, 1958.

Miller, H. P. *Rich man, poor man*. New York: Crowell, 1971.

Mitchell-Kernan, C. Signifying, loud-talking, and marking. In Kochman (Ed.), 1972.

Netting, R. McC. *Hill farmers of Nigeria: cultural ecology of the Jos Plateau*. Seattle: University of Washington Press, 1968.

Newman, D. K. *Protest, politics, and prosperity black Americans and white institutions, 1940–1975*. New York: Pantheon, 1978.

Nobles, W. W., & Traver, S. Black parental. involvement in education: the African connection. In *Child Welfare and Child Development: Alton M. Childs Series*. Atlanta, Ga. Atlanta University School of Social Work 1976.

Ogbu, J. U. *The next generation: an ethnography of education in an urban neighborhood*. New York: Academic Press, 1974.

Ogbu, J. U. *Minority education and caste: the American system in cross-cultural perspective*. New York: Academic Press, 1978.

Ogbu, J. U. Childrearing: a cultural-ecological perspective. In K. Borman (Ed.), *Socialization of children in a changing society*, in press.

Perkins, E. *Home is a dirty street*. Chicago: Third World, 1975.

Powledge, F. *To change a child*. Chicago: Quadrangle, 1967.

Rainwater, L. *Behind ghetto walls: black families in federal slums*. Chicago: Aldine, 1974.

Ramirez, M., & Castenada, A. *Cultural democracy bicognitive development and education*. New York: Academic Press, 1974.

Rees, H. E. *Deprivation and compensatory education: a reconsideration*. Boston: Houghton Mifflin, 1968.

Rist, R. C. Student social class and teacher expectations: the self-fulfilling prophecy in ghetto to schools. *Harvard Educational Review*, 1970, **40**, 411–450.

Schultz, T. W. Investment in human capital. *American Economic Review*, 1961, **5**(1), 1–17.

Schulz, D. A. Variations in the father role in complete families of the Negro lower class. *Social Science Quarterly*, 1968, **49**, 651–659.

Schulz, D. A. Coming up as a boy in the ghetto. In D. Y. Wilkinson and R. L. Taylor (Eds.), *The black male in America*. Chicago: Nelson Hall, 1977.

Scott, J. W. *The black revolts: racial stratification in the U.S.A.* Cambridge, Mass.: Schenkman, 1976.

Silverstein, B., & Krate, R. *Children of the dark ghetto: a developmental psychology.* New York: Praeger, 1975.

Stack, C. B. *All our kin: strategies for survival in black urban community.* New York: Harper & Row, 1974.

Stanley, J. C. (Ed.). *Preschool programs for the disadvantaged: five experimental approaches to early childhood education.* Baltimore: Johns Hopkins University Press, 1972.

Stanley, J. C. (Ed.). *Compensatory education for children ages 2 to 8: recent studies of educational intervention.* Baltimore: Johns Hopkins University Press, 1973.

Valentine, B. *Hustling and other hardwork: life-styles in the ghetto.* New York: Free Press, 1979.

van-den Berghe, P. Review: minority education and caste, by John U. Ogbu. *Comparative Education Review,* 1980, 24, 126–130.

Webster, S. W. *The education of black Americans.* New York: Day, 1974.

Weisbrod, B. A. Education and investment in human capital. In D. M. Levine and M. J. Bane (Eds.), *The "inequality" controversy.* New York: Basic, 1975.

White, B. L. *The origins of human competence: the final report of the Harvard preschool project.* Lexington, Mass.: Heath, 1979.

White, S. H. *Federal programs for young children: review and recommendations.* Vol. 1. *Goals and standards of public programs for children.* Washington, D.C.: Government Printing Office, 1973.

Williams, F. (Ed.). *Language and poverty: perspectives on a theme.* Chicago: Markham, 1970.

Wolfe, T. *Radical chic and mau-mauing the flack catchers.* New York: Strauss & Giroux, 1970.

Wright, N., Jr. (Ed.). *What black educators are saying.* New York: Hawthorn, 1970.

Young, V. H. Family and childhood in a southern negro community. *American Anthropologist,* 1970, 72, 269–288.

Young, V. H. A black American socialization pattern. *American Ethnologist,* 1974, 1(2), 415–431.

# Adolescence

## E. H. ERIKSON

As technological advances put more and more time between early school life and the young person's final access to specialized work, the stage of adolescence becomes an even more marked and conscious period and, as it has always been in some cultures in some periods, almost a way of life between childhood and adulthood. Thus in the later school years young people, beset with the physiological revolution of their genital maturation and the uncertainty of the adult roles ahead, seem much concerned with faddish attempts at establishing an adolescent subculture with what looks like a final rather than a transitory or, in fact, initial identity formation. They are sometimes morbidly, often curiously, preoccupied with what they appear to be in the eyes of others as compared with what they feel they are, and with the question of how to connect the roles and skills cultivated earlier with the ideal prototypes of the day. In their search for a new sense of continuity and sameness, which must now include sexual maturity, some adolescents have to come to grips again with crises of earlier years before they can install lasting idols and ideals as guardians of a final identity. They need, above all, a moratorium for the integration of the identity elements ascribed in the foregoing to the childhood stages: only that now a larger unit, vague in its outline and yet immediate in its demands, replaces the childhood milieu—"society." A review of these elements is also a list of adolescent problems.

If the earliest stage bequeathed to the identity crisis is an important need for trust in oneself and in others, then clearly the adolescent looks most fervently for men and ideas to have *faith* in, which also means men and ideas in whose service it would seem worth while to prove oneself trustworthy. (This will be discussed further in the chapter on fidelity.) At the same time, however, the adolescent fears a foolish, all too trusting commitment, and will, paradoxically, express his need for faith in loud and cynical mistrust.

If the second stage established the necessity of being defined by what one can *will* freely, then the adolescent now looks for an opportunity to decide with free assent on one of the available or unavoidable avenues of duty and service, and at the same time is mortally afraid of being forced into activities in which he would feel exposed to ridicule or self-doubt. This, too, can lead to a paradox, namely, that he would rather act shamelessly in the eyes of his elders, out of free choice, than be forced into activities which would be shameful in his own eyes or in those of his peers.

If an unlimited *imagination* as to what one *might* become is the heritage of the play age, then the adolescent's willingness to put his trust in those peers and leading, or misleading, elders who will give imaginative, if not illusory, scope to his aspirations is only too obvious. By the same token, he objects violently to all "pedantic" limitations on his self-images and will be ready to settle by loud accusation all his guiltiness over the excessiveness of his ambition.

Finally, if the desire to make something work, and to make it work well, is the gain of the school age, then the choice of an occupation assumes a significance beyond the question of remuneration and status. It is for this reason that some adolescents prefer not to work at all for a while rather than be forced into an otherwise promising career which would offer success without the satisfaction of functioning with unique excellence.

In any given period in history, then, that part of youth will have the most affirmatively exciting time of it which finds itself in the wave of a technological, economic, or ideological trend seemingly promising all that youthful vitality could ask for.

Adolescence, therefore, is least "stormy" in that segment of youth which is gifted and well trained in the pursuit of expanding technological trends, and thus able to identify with new

*Source:* Erikson, E. H. (1968). Adolescence. *Identity, youth, and crisis* (pp. 128–135). New York: Norton.

roles of competency and invention and to accept a more implicit ideological outlook. Where this is not given, the adolescent mind becomes a more explicitly ideological one, by which we mean one searching for some inspiring unification of tradition or anticipated techniques, ideas, and ideals. And, indeed, it is the ideological potential of a society which speaks most clearly to the adolescent who is so eager to be affirmed by peers, to be confirmed by teachers, and to be inspired by worth-while "ways of life." On the other hand, should a young person feel that the environment tries to deprive him too radically of all the forms of expression which permit him to develop and integrate the next step, he may resist with the wild strength encountered in animals who are suddenly forced to defend their lives. For, indeed, in the social jungle of human existence there is no feeling of being alive without a sense of identity.

Having come this far, I would like to give one example (and I consider it representative in structure) of the individual way in which a young person, given some leeway, may utilize a traditional way of life for dealing with a remnant of negative identity. I had known Jill before her puberty, when she was rather obese and showed many "oral" traits of voracity and dependency while she also was a tomboy and bitterly envious of her brothers and in rivalry with them. But she was intelligent and always had an air about her (as did her mother) which seemed to promise that things would turn out all right. And, indeed, she straightened out and up, became very attractive, an easy leader in any group, and, to many, a model of young girlhood. As a clinician, I watched and wondered what she would do with that voraciousness and with the rivalry which she had displayed earlier. Could it be that such things are simply absorbed in fortuitous growth?

Then one autumn in her late teens, Jill did not return to college from the ranch out West where she had spent the summer. She had asked her parents to let her stay. Simply out of liberality and confidence, they granted her this moratorium and returned East.

That winter Jill specialized in taking care of newborn colts, and would get up at any time during a winter night to bottle feed the most needy animals. Having apparently acquired a certain satisfaction within herself, as well as astonished recognition from the cowboys, she returned home and reassumed her place. I felt that she had found and hung on to an opportunity to do actively and for others what she had always yearned to have done for her, as she had once demonstrated by overeating: she had learned to feed needy young mouths. But she did so in a context which, in turning passive into active, also turned a former symptom into a social act.

One might say that she turned "maternal" but it was a maternalism such as cowboys must and do display; and, of course, she did it all in jeans. This brought recognition "from man to man" as well as from man to woman, and beyond that the confirmation of her optimism, that is, her feeling that something could be done that felt like her, was useful and worth while, and was in line with an ideological trend where it still made immediate practical sense.

Such self-chosen "therapies" depend, of course, on the leeway given in the right spirit at the right time, and this depends on a great variety of circumstances. I intend to publish similar fragments from the lives of children in greater detail at some future date; let this example stand for the countless observations in everyday life, where the resourcefulness of young people proves itself when the conditions are right.

The estrangement of this stage is *identity confusion*, which will be elaborated in clinical and biographic detail in the next chapter. For the moment, we will accept Biff's formulation in Arthur Miller's *Death of a Salesman:* "I just can't take hold, Mom, I can't take hold of some kind of a life." Where such a dilemma is based on a strong previous doubt of one's ethnic and sexual identity, or where role confusion joins a hopelessness of long standing, delinquent and "borderline" psychotic episodes are not uncommon. Youth after youth, bewildered by the incapacity to assume a role forced on him by the inexorable standardization of American adolescence, runs away in one form or another, dropping out of school, leaving jobs, staying out all night, or withdrawing into bizarre and inaccessible moods. Once "delinquent," his greatest need and often his only salvation is the refusal on the part of older friends, advisers, and judiciary personnel to type him further by pat diagnoses and social judgments which ignore the special dynamic conditions of adolescence. It is here, as we shall see in greater detail, that the concept of identity confusion is of practical clinical value, for if they are diagnosed and treated correctly, seemingly psychotic and criminal incidents do not have the same fatal significance which they may have at other ages.

In general it is the inability to settle on an occupational identity which most disturbs young people. To keep themselves together they temporarily overidentify with the heroes of cliques and crowds to the point of an apparently complete loss of individuality. Yet in this stage not even "falling in love" is entirely, or even primarily, a sexual matter. To a considerable extent adolescent love is an attempt to arrive at a definition of one's identity by projecting one's diffused self-image on another and by seeing it thus reflected and gradually clarified. This is why so much of young love is conversation. On the other hand, clarification can also be sought by destructive means. Young people can become remarkably clannish, intolerant, and cruel in their exclusion of others who are "different," in skin color or cultural background, in tastes and gifts, and often in entirely petty aspects of dress and gesture arbitrarily selected as the signs of an in-grouper or out-grouper. It is important to understand in principle (which does not mean to condone in all of its manifestations) that such intolerance may be, for a while, a necessary defense against a sense of identity loss. This is unavoidable at a time of life when the body changes its proportions radically, when genital puberty floods body and imagination with all manner of impulses, when intimacy with the other sex approaches and is, on occasion, forced on the young person, and when the immediate future confronts one with too many conflicting possibilities and choices. Adolescents not only help one another temporarily through such discomfort by forming cliques and stereotyping themselves, their ideals, and their enemies; they also insistently test each other's capacity for sustaining loyalties in the midst of inevitable conflicts of values.

The readiness for such testing helps to explain (as pointed out in Chapter II) the appeal of sim-

ple and cruel totalitarian doctrines among the youth of such countries and classes as have lost or are losing their group identities—feudal, agrarian, tribal, or national. The democracies are faced with the job of winning these grim youths by convincingly demonstrating to them—by living it—that a democratic identity can be strong and yet tolerant, judicious and still determined. But industrial democracy poses special problems in that it insists on self-made identities ready to grasp many chances and ready to adjust to the changing necessities of booms and busts, of peace and war, of migration and determined sedentary life. Democracy, therefore, must present its adolescents with ideals which can be shared by young people of many backgrounds, and which emphasize autonomy in the form of independence and initiative in the form of constructive work. These promises, however, are not easy to fulfill in increasingly complex and centralized systems of industrial, economic, and political organization, systems which increasingly neglect the "self-made" ideology still flaunted in oratory. This is hard on many young Americans because their whole upbringing has made the development of a self-reliant personality dependent on a certain degree of choice, a sustained hope for an individual chance, and a firm commitment to the freedom of self-realization.

We are speaking here not merely of high privileges and lofty ideals but of psychological necessities. For the social institution which is the guardian of identity *is* what we have called *ideology*. One may see in ideology also the imagery of an aristocracy in its widest possible sense, which connotes that within a defined world image and a given course of history the best people will come to rule and rule will develop the best in people. In order not to become cynically or apathetically lost, young people must somehow be able to convince themselves that those who succeed in their anticipated adult world thereby shoulder the obligation of being best. For it is through their ideology that social systems enter into the fiber of the next generation and attempt to absorb into their lifeblood the rejuvenative power of youth. Adolescence is thus a vital regenerator in the process of social evolution, for youth can offer its loyalties and energies both to the conservation of that which continues to feel true and to the revolutionary correction of that which has lost its regenerative significance.

We can study the identity crisis also in the lives of creative individuals who could resolve it for themselves only by offering to their contemporaries a new model of resolution such as that expressed in works of art or in original deeds, and who furthermore are eager to tell us all about it in diaries, letters, and self-representations. And even as the neuroses of a given period reflect the ever-present inner chaos of man's existence in a new way, the creative crises point to the period's unique solutions.

We will in the next chapter present in greater detail what we have learned of these specialized individual crises. But there is a third manifestation of the remnants of infantilism and adolescence in man: it is the pooling of the individual crises in transitory upheavals amounting to collective "hysterias." Where there are voluble leaders their creative crises and the latent crises of their followers can be at least studied with the help of our assumptions—and of their writings. More elusive are spontaneous group developments not attributable to a leader. And it will, at any rate, not be helpful to call mass irrationalities by clinical names. It would be impossible to diagnose clinically how much hysteria is present in a young nun participating in an epidemic of convulsive spells or how much perverse "sadism" in a young Nazi commanded to participate in massive parades or in mass killings. So we can point only most tentatively to certain similarities between individual crises and group behavior in order to indicate that in a given period of history they are in an obscure contact with each other.

But before we submerge ourselves in the clinical and biographic evidence for what we call identity confusion, we will take a look beyond the identity crisis. The words "beyond identity," of course, could be understood in two ways, both essential for the problem. They could mean that there is more to man's core than identity, that there is in fact in each individual an "I," an observing center of awareness and of volition, which can transcend and must survive the *psychosocial identity* which is our concern in this book. In some ways, as we will see, a sometimes precocious self-transcendence seems to be felt strongly in a transient manner in youth, as if a pure identity had to be kept free from psychosocial encroachment. And yet no man (except a man aflame and dying like Keats, who could speak of identity in words which secured him immediate fame) can transcend himself in youth. We will speak later of the transcendence of identity. In the following "beyond identity" means life after adolescence and the uses of identity and, indeed, the return of some forms of identity crisis in the later stages of the life cycle.

# Jokes and the Unconscious

## Sigmund Freud

The preceding discussion has given us unawares an insight into the evolution or psychogenesis of jokes, which we will now examine more closely. We have made the acquaintance of preliminary stages of jokes, and their development into tendentious jokes will probably uncover fresh relations between the various characteristics of jokes. Before there is such a thing as a joke, there is something that we may describe as 'play' or as 'a jest'.

Play—let us keep to that name—appears in children while they are learning to make use of words and to put thoughts together. This play probably obeys one of the instincts which compel children to practise their capacities (Groos [1899]). In doing so they come across pleasurable effects, which arise from a repetition of what is similar, a rediscovery of what is familiar, similarity of sound, etc., and which are to be explained as unsuspected economies in psychical expenditure.[13] It is not to be wondered at that these pleasurable effects encourage children in the pursuit of play and cause them to continue it without regard for the meaning of words or the coherence of sentences. *Play* with words and thoughts, motivated by certain pleasurable effects of economy, would thus be the first stage of jokes.

This play is brought to an end by the strengthening of a factor that deserves to be described as the critical faculty or reasonableness. The play is now rejected as being meaningless or actually absurd; as a result of criticism it becomes impossible. Now, too, there is no longer

any question of deriving pleasure, except accidentally, from the sources of rediscovery of what is familiar, etc., unless it happens that the growing individual is overtaken by a pleasurable mood which, like the child's cheerfulness, lifts the critical inhibition. Only in such a case does the old game of getting pleasure become possible once more; but the individual does not want to wait for this to happen nor to renounce the pleasure that is familiar to him. He thus looks about for means of making himself independent of the pleasurable mood, and the further development towards jokes is governed by the two endeavours: to avoid criticism and to find a substitute for the mood.

And with this the second preliminary stage of jokes sets in—the *jest*. It is now a question of prolonging the yield of pleasure from play, but at the same time of silencing the objections raised by criticism which would not allow the pleasurable feeling to emerge. There is only one way of reaching this end: the meaningless combination of words or the absurd putting together of thoughts must nevertheless have a meaning. The whole ingenuity of the joke-work is summoned up in order to find words and aggregations of thoughts in which this condition is fulfilled. All the technical methods of jokes are already employed here—in jests; moreover linguistic usage draws no consistent line between a jest and a joke. What distinguishes a jest from a joke is that the meaning of the sentence which escapes criticism need not be valuable or new or even good; it need merely be *permissible* to say the thing in this way, even though it is unusual, unnecessary or useless to say it in this way. In jests what stands in the foreground is the satisfaction of having made possible what was forbidden by criticism.

It is, for instance, simply a jest when Schleiermacher [see p. 37] defines *Eifersucht* [jealousy] as the *Leidenschaft* [passion] which *mit Eifer sucht* [with eagerness seeks] what *Leiden schafft* [causes pain]. It was a jest when Professor Kästner, who taught physics (and made jokes) at

---

[13][The pleasure taken by children in repetition (to which there is a further reference below, p. 281, and on which Freud has already commented in a footnote to *The Interpretation of Dreams* (1900), *Standard Ed.*, 4, 268) is a subject to which Freud recurred much later, in his discussion of his hypothesis of a 'compulsion to repeat' in *Beyond the Pleasure Principle* (1920g), *Standard Ed.*, 18, 35.]

*Source:* Freud, S. (1960). The mechanism of pleasure and the psychogenesis of jokes. In S. Freud, *Jokes and their relation to the unconscious* (pp. 156–169). London: Routledge & Kegan Paul.

Göttingen in the eighteenth[14] century, asked a student named Kriegk, when he was enrolling himself for his lectures, how old he was. 'Thirty years old' was the reply, whereupon Kästner remarked: 'Ah! so I have the honour of meeting the Thirty Years' War [*Krieg*].' (Kleinpaul, 1890.) It was with a jest that the great Rokitansky[15] replied to the question of what were the professions of his four sons: 'Two *heilen* [heal] and two *heulen* [howl]' (two doctors and two singers). The information was correct and therefore not open to criticism; but it added nothing to what might have been expressed in the words in brackets. There can be no mistaking the fact that the answer was given the other form only on account of the pleasure which was produced by the unification and the similar sound of the two words.

I think now at length we see our way clearly. All through our consideration of the techniques of jokes we have been disturbed by the fact that they were not proper to jokes only; and yet the essence of jokes seemed to depend on them, since when they were got rid of by reduction the characteristics and the pleasure of the joke were lost. We now see that what we have described as the techniques of jokes—and we must in a certain sense continue to describe them so—are rather the sources from which jokes provide pleasure, and we feel that there is nothing strange in other procedures drawing from the same sources for the same end. The technique which is characteristic of jokes and peculiar to them, however, consists in their procedure for safeguarding the use of these methods of providing pleasure against the objections raised by criticism which would put an end to the pleasure. There is little that we can say in general about this procedure. The joke-work, as we have already remarked, shows itself in a choice of verbal material and conceptual situations which will allow the old play with words and thoughts to withstand the scrutiny of criticism; and with

that end in view every peculiarity of vocabulary and every combination of thought-sequences must be exploited in the most ingenious possible way. We may be in a position later to characterize the joke-work by a particular property; for the moment it remains unexplained how the selection favourable for jokes can be made. The purpose and function of jokes, however—namely, the protection of sequences of words and thoughts from criticism—can already be seen in jests as their essential feature. Their function consists from the first in lifting internal inhibitions and in making sources of pleasure fertile which have been rendered inaccessible by those inhibitions; and we shall find that they remain loyal to this characteristic throughout their development.

We are also in a position now to assign its correct place to the factor of 'sense in nonsense' (cf. the introduction, p. 8), to which the authorities attribute such great importance as a distinguishing mark of jokes and as an explanation of their pleasurable effect. The two fixed points in what determines the nature of jokes—their purpose of continuing pleasurable play and their effort to protect it from the criticism of reason—immediately explain why an individual joke, though it may seem senseless from one point of view, must appear sensible, or at least allowable, from another. How it does so remains the affair of the joke-work; if it fails to do so, it is simply rejected as 'nonsense'. But there is no necessity for us to derive the pleasurable effect of jokes from the conflict between the feelings which arise (whether directly or along the path of 'bewilderment and enlightenment' [p. 8f.]) from the simultaneous sense and nonsense of jokes. Nor have we any need to enter further into the question of how pleasure could arise from the alternation between 'thinking it senseless' and 'recognizing it as sensible'. The psychogenesis of jokes has taught us that the pleasure in a joke is derived from play with words or from the liberation of nonsense, and that the meaning of the joke is merely intended to protect that pleasure from being done away with by criticism.

In this way the problem of the essential character of jokes is already explained in jests. We may now turn to the further development of

---

[14][In the 1905 edition only, this is misprinted 'sixteenth'.]

[15][Carl Rokitansky (1804–78) was the founder of the Vienna school of pathological anatomy.]

jests, to the point at which they reach their height in tendentious jokes. Jests still give the foremost place to the purpose of giving us enjoyment, and are content if what they say does not appear senseless or completely devoid of substance. If what a jest says possesses substance and value, it turns into a joke. A thought which would deserve out interest even if it were expressed in the most unpretentious form is now clothed in a form which must give us enjoyment on its own account.[16] A combination like this can certainly not, we must suppose, have come about unintentionally; and we must try to discover the intention underlying the construction of the joke. An observation which we made earlier (in passing, as it seemed) will put us on the track. We said above (p. 111) that a good joke makes, as it were, a *total* impression of enjoyment on us, without our being able to decide at once what share of the pleasure arises from its joking form and what share from its apt thought-content. We are constantly making mistakes in this apportionment. Sometimes we over-estimate the goodness of the joke on account of our admiration of the thought it contains; another time, on the contrary, we over-estimate the value of the thought on account of the enjoyment given us by its joking envelope. We do not know what is giving us enjoyment and what we are laughing at. This uncertainty in our judgement, which must be assumed to be a fact, may have provided the motive for the construction of jokes in the proper sense of the word. The thought seeks to wrap itself in a joke because in that way it recommends itself to our attention and can seem more significant and more valuable, but above all because this wrapping bribes our powers of criticism and confuses them. We are inclined to give the *thought* the benefit of what has pleased us in the *form* of the joke; and we are no longer inclined to find anything wrong that has given us enjoyment and so to spoil the source of a pleasure. If the joke has made us laugh, moreover, a disposition most unfavorable for criticism will have been established in us; for in that case something will have forced us into the mood which play has previously sufficed to produce, and for which the joke has tried by every possible means to make itself a substitute. Even though we have earlier asserted that such jokes are to be described as innocent and not yet tendentious, we must not forget that strictly speaking only jests are non-tendentious—that is, serve solely the aim of producing pleasure. Jokes, even if the thought contained in them is non-tendentious and thus only serves theoretical intellectual interests, are in fact never non-tendentious. They pursue the second aim: to promote the thought by augmenting it and guarding it against criticism. Here they are once again expressing their original nature by setting themselves up against an inhibiting and restricting power—which is now the critical judgement.

This, the first use of jokes that goes beyond the production of pleasure, points the way to their further uses. A joke is now seen to be a psychical factor possessed of power: its weight, thrown into one scale or the other, can be decisive. The major purposes and instincts of mental life employ it for their own ends. The originally non-tendentious joke, which began as play, is *secondarily* brought into relation with purposes from which nothing that takes form in the mind can ultimately keep away. We know already what it is able to achieve in the service of the purpose of exposure, and of hostile, cynical and sceptical purposes. In the case of obscene jokes, which are derived from smut, it turns the third person who originally interfered with the sexual situation into an ally, before whom the woman must feel shame, by bribing him with the gift of its yield of pleasure. In the case of aggressive purposes it employs the same method in order

[16]As an example which shows the difference between a jest and a joke proper we may take the excellent joking remark with which a number of the 'Bürger' Ministry in Austria answered a question about the cabinet's solidarity: 'How can we *einstehen* [stand up] for one another if we can't [stand] one another?' Technique use of the same material with slight (contrary) modification. Logical and apposite thought: there can be no solidarity without mutual understanding. The contrary nature of the modification (ein [in]—*aus* [out]) corresponds to the incompatibility asserted in the thought and serves as a representation of it:—[The 'Bürger' (Middle-Class) Ministry took office after the new Austrian constitution was established in 1867, but owing to internal disharmony only lasted for a couple of years. Cf. *The Interpretation of Dreams, Standard Ed.*, 4, 193.]

to turn the hearer, who was indifferent to begin with, into a co-hater or co-despiser, and creates for the enemy a host of opponents where at first there was only one. In the first case it overcomes the inhibitions of shame and respectability by means of the bonus of pleasure which it offers; in the second it upsets the critical judgement which would otherwise have examined the dispute. In the third and fourth cases, in the service of cynical and sceptical purposes, it shatters respect for institutions and truths in which the hearer has believed, on the one hand by reinforcing the argument, but on the other by practising a new species of attack. Where argument tries to draw the hearer's criticism over on to its side, the joke endeavours to push the criticism out of sight. There is no doubt that the joke has chosen the method which is psychologically the more effective.

In this survey of the achievements of tendentious jokes, most prominence has been assumed by—what is more easily seen—the effect of jokes on the person who hears them. More important, however, from the point of view of our understanding, are the functions accomplished by jokes in the mind of the person who makes them or, to put it in the only correct way, the person to whom they occur. We have already proposed [p. 118]—and here we have occasion to repeat the notion—that we should try to study the psychical phenomena of jokes with reference to their distribution between two people. We will make a provisional suggestion that the psychical process provoked by the joke in the hearer is in most cases modelled on that which occurs in its creator. The external obstacle which is to be overcome in the hearer corresponds to an internal inhibition in the maker of the joke. At the least the *expectation* of an external obstacle is present in the latter as an inhibiting idea. In certain cases the internal obstacle which is overcome by the tendentious joke is obvious; in Herr N.'s jokes, for instance, we were able to assume (p. 123) that not only did they make it possible for their hearers to enjoy aggressiveness in the form of insults, but that above all they made it possible for him to produce them. Among the various kinds of internal inhibition or suppression there is one which deserves our special interest, because it is the most far-reaching. It is

given the name of 'repression', and is recognized by its function of preventing the impulses subjected to it, and their derivatives, from becoming conscious. Tendentious jokes, as we shall see, are able to release pleasure even from sources that have undergone repression. If, as has been suggested above, the overcoming of external obstacles can in this way be traced back to the overcoming of internal inhibitions and repressions, we may say that tendentious jokes exhibit the main characteristic of the joke-work—that of liberating pleasure by getting rid of inhibitions—more clearly than any other of the developmental stages of jokes. Either they strengthen the purposes which they serve, by bringing assistance to them from impulses that are kept suppressed, or they put themselves entirely at the service of suppressed purposes.

We may be ready to admit that this is what tendentious jokes achieve; yet we must bear in mind that we do not understand how they are able to put these achievements into effect. Their power lies in the yield of pleasure which they draw from the sources of play upon words and of liberated nonsense; but if we are to judge by the impressions gained from non-tendentious jests, we cannot possibly think the amount of this pleasure great enough to attribute to it the strength to lift deeply-rooted inhibitions and repressions. What we have before us here is in fact no simple effect of force but a more complex situation of release. Instead of setting out the long détour by which I reached an understanding of this situation, I will try to give a short synthetic exposition of it.

Fechner (1897, 1, Chapter V) has put forward a 'principle of aesthetic assistance or intensification', which he has expressed as follows: '*If determinants of pleasure that in themselves produce little effect converge without mutual contradiction, there results a greater, and often a much greater, outcome of pleasure than corresponds to the pleasure-value of the separate determinants—a greater pleasure than could be explained as the sum of the separate effects. Indeed, a convergence of this kind can even lead to a positive resultant of pleasure and the threshold of pleasure may be crossed, where the separate factors are too weak to do so: though they must, in comparison with others, show a perceptible advantage in enjoyableness.*' (Ibid., 51. The italics are Fechner's.)

The topic of jokes does not, I think, give us much opportunity of confirming the correctness of this principle, which can be shown to hold good in many other aesthetic structures. As regards jokes we have learnt something else, which at least fringes upon this principle: namely, that where several pleasure-giving factors operate together we are not able to attribute to each of them the share it has really taken in bringing about the result. (See p. 111.) We can, however, vary the situation that is assumed in the 'principle of assistance' and, as a result of these fresh conditions, arrive at a number of questions which would deserve reply. What happens in general if, in a combination, determinants of pleasure and determinants of unpleasure converge? On what does the outcome depend and what decides whether that outcome is in pleasure or unpleasure?

The case of tendentious jokes is a special one among these possibilities. An impulse or urge is present which seeks to release pleasure from a particular source and, if it were allowed free play, would release it. Besides this, another urge is present which works against this generation of pleasure—inhibits it, that is, or suppresses it. The suppressing current must, as the outcome shows, be a certain amount stronger than the suppressed one, which, however, is not on that account abolished. Now let us suppose that yet another urge makes its appearance which would release pleasure through the same process, though from other sources, and which thus operates in the same sense as the suppressed urge. What can the result be in such a case?

An example will give us our bearings better than this schematic discussion. Let us assume that there is an urge to insult a certain person; but this is so strongly opposed by feelings of propriety or of aesthetic culture that the insult cannot take place. If, for instance, it were able to break through as a result of some change of emotional condition or mood, this breakthrough by the insulting purpose would be felt subsequently with unpleasure. Thus the insult does not take place. Let us now suppose, however, that the possibility is presented of deriving a good joke from the material of the words and thoughts used for the insult—the possibility, that is, of releasing pleasure from other

sources which are not obstructed by the same suppression. This second development of pleasure could, nevertheless, not occur unless the insult were permitted; but as soon as the latter *is* permitted the new release of pleasure is also joined to it. Experience with tendentious jokes shows that in such circumstances the suppressed purpose can, with the assistance of the pleasure from the joke, gain sufficient strength to overcome the inhibition, which would otherwise be stronger than it. The insult takes place, because the joke is thus made possible. But the enjoyment obtained is not only that produced by the joke: it is incomparably greater. It is so much greater than the pleasure from the joke that we must suppose that the hitherto suppressed purpose has succeeded in making its way through, perhaps without any diminution whatever. It is in such circumstances that the tendentious joke is received with the heartiest laughter.[17]

An examination of the determinants of laughing will perhaps lead us to a plainer idea of what happens when a joke affords assistance against suppression. [Cf. p. 178 ff. below.] Even now, however, we can see that the case of tendentious jokes is a special case of the 'principle of assistance'. A possibility of generating pleasure supervenes in a situation in which another possibility of pleasure is obstructed so that, as far as the latter alone is concerned, no pleasure would arise. The result is a generation of pleasure far greater than that offered by the supervening possibility. This has acted, as it were, as an *incentive bonus,* with the assistance of the offer of a small amount of pleasure, a much greater one, which would otherwise have been hard to achieve, has been gained. I have good reason to suspect that this principle corresponds with an arrangement that holds good in many widely separated departments of mental life and it will, I think, be expedient to describe the pleasure that serves to initiate the large release of pleas-

---

[17][Freud had already propounded a parallel theory, to explain the often exaggerated amount of affect experienced in dreams, in Chapter VI of *The Interpretation of Dreams* (1900a), *Standard Ed.,* 5, 478 ff.]

ure as 'fore-pleasure', and the principle as the 'fore-pleasure principle'.[18]

We are now able to state the formula for the mode of operation of tendentious jokes. They put themselves at the service of purposes in order that, by means of using the pleasure from jokes as a fore-pleasure, they may produce new pleasure by lifting suppressions and repressions. If now we survey the course of development of the joke, we may say that from its beginning to its perfecting it remains true to its essential nature. It begins as play, in order to derive pleasure from the free use of words and thoughts. As soon as the strengthening of reasoning puts an end to this play with words as being senseless, and with thoughts as being nonsensical, it changes into a jest, in order that it may retain these sources of pleasure and be able to achieve fresh pleasure from the liberation of nonsense. Next, as a joke proper, but still a non-tendentious one, it gives

its assistance to thoughts and strengthens them against the challenge of critical judgement, a process in which the 'principle of confusion of sources of pleasure' is of use to it. And finally it comes to the help of major purposes which are combating suppression, in order to lift their internal inhibitions by the 'principle of fore-pleasure'. Reason, critical judgement, suppression—these are the forces against which it fights in succession; it holds fast to the original sources of verbal pleasure and, from the stage of the jest onwards, opens new sources of pleasure for itself by lifting inhibitions. The pleasure that it produces, whether it is pleasure in play or pleasure in lifting inhibitions, can invariably be traced back to economy in psychical expenditure, provided that this view does not contradict the essential nature of pleasure and that it proves itself fruitful in other directions.[19]

---

[18]Freud discussed the mechanism of fore-pleasure as it operates in the sexual act at considerable length in Section 1 of the third of his almost contemporary *Three Essays* (1905*d*), *Standard Ed.*, 7, 208 ff. He also pointed out its use in aesthetic creations at the end of his paper on 'Creative Writers and Day-Dreaming' (1908*e*), ibid., 9, 153, as well as in an earlier, posthumously published, paper on 'Psychopathic Characters on the Stage' (1942*a* [1905–6]), ibid., 7, 310, and again in his 'Autobiographical Study' (1925*d*), ibid., 20, 65.

[19]Nonsense jokes, which have not had due attention paid to them in my account, deserve some supplementary consideration.

The importance which our views attach to the factor of 'sense in nonsense' might lead to a demand that every joke must be a nonsense joke. But this is not necessary, because it is only playing with *thoughts* that inevitably leads to nonsense; the other source of pleasure in jokes, playing with *words*, only given that impression occasionally and does not invariably provoke the implied criticism. The twofold root of the pleasure in jokes—from playing with words and playing with thoughts which corresponds to the very important distinction between verbal and conceptual jokes—makes it perceptibly more difficult to arrive at a concise formulation of general statements about jokes. Playing with words produces manifest pleasure as a result of the factors that have been enumerated above (recognition, and so on), and is consequently only to a small degree liable to suppression. Playing with thoughts

cannot have its motive in this kind of pleasure; it meets with very energetic suppression, and the pleasure which it can yield is only pleasure in the lifting of an inhibition. It can accordingly be said that the pleasure in jokes exhibits a core of original pleasure in play and a casing of pleasure in lifting inhibitions.—We naturally do not perceive that our pleasure in a nonsense joke arises from our having succeeded in liberating a piece of nonsense in spite of its suppression; whereas we see directly that playing with words has given us pleasure.—The nonsense that still remains in a conceptual joke acquires secondarily the function of increasing our attention by bewildering us. It serves as a means of intensifying the effect of the joke, but only when it acts obtrusively, so that the bewilderment can hurry ahead of the understanding by a perceptible moment of time. The examples on p. 64 ff. have shown that in addition to this, nonsense in a joke can be used to represent a judgement contained in the thought. But this, too, is not the primary significance of nonsense in jokes.

[*Added* 1912:] A number of productions resembling jokes can be classed alongside of nonsense jokes. There is no appropriate name for them, they might well be described as 'idiocy masquerading as a joke'. There an countless numbers of them, and I will only select two samples:

'A man at the dinner table who was being handed fish dipped his two hands twice in the mayonnaise and then ran them through his hair. When his neighbour looked at him in astonishment, he seemed to notice mistake and apologized: "I'm so sorry, I thought it was spinach." '

Or: ' "Life is a suspension bridge", said one man.—"Why is that?" asked the other.—"How should *I* know?" was the reply.'

These extreme examples have an effect because they rouse the expectation of a joke, so that one tries to find a concealed sense behind the nonsense. But one finds none: they really are nonsense. The pretence makes it possible for a moment to liberate the pleasure in nonsense. These jokes are not entirely without a purpose; they are a 'take-in', and give the person who tells them a certain amount of pleasure in misleading and annoying his heater. The latter then damps down his annoyance by determining to tell them himself later on.

# Theoretical Perspectives

A. BANDURA

People have always striven to control the events that affect their lives. By exerting influence in spheres over which they can command some control, they are better able to realize desired futures and to forestall undesired ones. In primitive times, when people had a limited understanding of the world around them and few ways to alter its workings, they appealed to supernatural agents who were believed to wield control over their lives. People practiced elaborate rituals and codes of conduct in an attempt to gain favor from, or protection against, supernatural powers. Even in contemporary life, when faced with weighty matters of much uncertainty, many people employ superstitious rituals to sway outcomes in their favor. A few instances in which an irrelevant ritual happened to be accompanied by a successful outcome can easily make people believe that the ritual affected the outcome.

The growth of knowledge over the course of human history greatly enhanced people's ability to predict events and to exercise control over them. Belief in supernatural systems of control gave way to conceptions that acknowledged people's power to shape their own destiny. This change in human self-conception and the view of life from supernatural control to personal control ushered in a major shift in causal thinking, and the new enlightenment rapidly expanded the exercise of human power over more and more domains. Human ingenuity and endeavor supplanted conciliating rituals to deities as the way to change the conditions of life. By drawing on their knowledge, people built physical technologies that drastically altered how they lived their daily lives. They developed biological technologies to alter the genetic makeup of animals and plants. They created medical and psychosocial technologies to improve the quality of their

physical and emotional lives. They devised social systems that placed constraints on the types of beliefs and conduct that could be subjected to coercive or punitive institutional control. These entitlements and institutional protections expanded freedom of belief and action.

The striving for control over life circumstances permeates almost everything people do throughout the life course because it provides innumerable personal and social benefits. Uncertainty in important matters is highly unsettling. To the extent that people help to bring about significant outcomes, they are better able to predict them. Predictability fosters adaptive preparedness. The inability to exert influence over things that adversely affect one's life breeds apprehension, apathy, or despair. The ability to secure desired outcomes and to prevent undesired ones, therefore, provides a powerful incentive for the development and exercise of personal control. The more people bring their influence to bear on events in their lives, the more they can shape them to their liking. By selecting and creating environmental supports for what they want to become, they contribute to the direction their lives take. Human functioning is, of course, embedded in social conditions. The environmental supports for valued life paths, therefore, are created both individually and in concert with others. Through collective action, people can improve their lives by modifying the character and practices of their social systems.

The human capacity to exercise control is a mixed blessing. The impact of personal efficacy on the quality of life depends on the purposes to which it is put. For example, the lives of innovators and social reformers driven by unshakable efficacy are not easy ones. They are often the objects of derision, condemnation, and persecution, even though societies eventually benefit from their persevering efforts. Many people who gain recognition and fame shape their lives by overcoming seemingly insurmountable obstacles, only to be catapulted into new social

*Source:* Bandura, A. (1997), Theoretical Perspectives. In *Self-efficacy: The exercise of control* (pp. 1–15), New York: W. H. Freemen.

realities over which they have less control and manage badly. Indeed, the annals of the famous and infamous are strewn with individuals who were both architects and victims of their life courses.

The vastly enhanced human power to transform the environment can have pervasive effects not only on current life but also on future generations. Many technologies that provide current benefits also entail hazards that can take a heavy toll on the environment. Our technical capability to destroy or render uninhabitable much of the planet attests to the growing magnitude of human power. There is much public concern over where some of the technologies we create are leading us. Voracious pursuit of self-interest produces effects that collectively can be harmful to society in the long run. The exercise of social power that places individual interest above the common good creates special interest gridlock that immobilizes efforts to solve the broader problems of society. Without commitment to common purposes that transcend narrow self-interests, the exercise of control can degenerate into personal and factional power conflicts. People must work together if they are to realize the shared destiny they desire and preserve a habitable environment for generations to come. In short, the capacity for human control can be exercised for good or ill.

Because control is central in human lives, many theories about it have been proposed over the years. People's level of motivation, affective states, and actions are based more on what they believe than on what is objectively true. Hence, it is people's belief in their causative capabilities that is the major focus of inquiry. Most theories are couched in terms of an inborn drive for control. Any capability that is widely beneficial—and, thus, highly prevalent—is quickly interpreted as an inborn drive for self-determination or mastery. Theories that contend that striving for personal control is an expression of an innate drive discourage interest in how human efficacy is developed, because people allegedly come fully equipped with it. Instead, such theories dwell heavily on how the drive is socially thwarted and weakened. The fact that virtually all people try to bring at least some influence to bear on some of the things that affect them does

not necessarily indicate the presence of an innate motivator. Nor is control sought as an end in itself. Exercise of control that secures desired outcomes and wards off undesired ones has immense functional value and provides a strong source of incentive motivation. The issue of whether the exercise of control is pushed by an inborn drive or pulled by anticipate benefits will be given considerable attention later.

People make causal contributions to their own psychosocial functioning through mechanisms of personal agency. Among the mechanisms of agency, none is more central or pervasive than beliefs of personal efficacy. Unless people believe they can produce desired effects by their actions, they have little incentive to act. Efficacy belief, therefore, is a major basis of action. People guide their lives by their beliefs of personal efficacy. *Perceived self-efficacy refers to beliefs in one's capabilities to organize and execute the courses of action required to produce given attainments.* The events over which personal influence is exercised vary widely, however. Influence may entail regulating one's own motivation, thought processes, affective states, and actions, or it may involve changing environmental conditions, depending on what one seeks to manage.

People's beliefs in their efficacy have diverse effects. Such beliefs influence the courses of action people choose to pursue, how much effort they put forth in given endeavors, how long they will persevere in the face of obstacles and failures, their resilience to adversity, whether their thought patterns are self-hindering or self-aiding, how much stress and depression they experience in coping with taxing environmental demands, and the level of accomplishments they realize. This chapter examines the nature of human agency and alternative conceptions of personal causation.

## The Nature of Human Agency

People can exercise influence over what they do. Most human behavior, of course, is determined by many interacting factors, and so people are contributors to, rather than the sole determiners of, what happens to them. The power to make things happen should be distinguished from the mechanics of how things are made to happen. For example, in pursuing a particular strategy in an athletic contest, the players do not tell their nervous system to get the motor neurons to move their skeletal musculature in designated patterns. Based on their understanding of what is within the power of humans to do and beliefs about their own capabilities, people try to generate courses of action to suit given purposes without having the foggiest notion of how their choices orchestrate the neurophysiological events subserving the endeavor.

In evaluating the role of intentionality in human agency, one must distinguish between the personal production of action for an intended outcome and the effects that carrying out that course of action actually produce. Agency refers to acts done intentionally. Thus, a person who smashed a set of precariously displayed dishes in a china shop upon being tripped by another shopper would not be considered the agent of the event. Davidson (1971) reminds us, however, that actions intended to serve a certain purpose can cause quite different things to happen. He cites the example of the melancholic Hamlet, who intentionally stabbed the man behind a tapestry who he believed to be the king, only to discover, much to his horror, that he had killed Polonius, the wrong person. The killing of the hidden person was intentional, but the wrong victim was done in. Effects are not the characteristics of agentive acts; they are the consequences of them. Many actions are performed in the belief that they will bring about a desired outcome, but they actually produce outcomes that were neither intended nor wanted. For example, it is not uncommon for people to contribute to their own misery through intentional transgressive acts spawned by gross miscalculation of consequences. Some of the social practices and policies that cause harm were originally designed and implemented with well-meaning intent; their harmful effects were unforeseen. In short, the power to originate actions for given purposes is the key feature of personal agency. Whether the exercise of that agency has beneficial or detrimental effects or produces unintended consequences is another matter.

Beliefs of personal efficacy constitute the key factor of human agency. If people believe they have no power to produce results, they will not attempt to make things happen. In social cognitive theory, a sense of personal efficacy is represented as propositional beliefs. We will see later that these beliefs are embedded in a network of functional relationships with other factors that operate together in the management of different realities. The fact that beliefs are described in the language of mind raises the philosophical issues of ontological reductionism and the plurality of regulatory systems. Mental events are brain activities, not immaterial entities existing apart from neural systems. Were one to perform Bunge's (1980) hypothetical brain transplant, the donor's unique psychic life would undoubtedly accompany the brain to the new host, rather than remain behind with the donor as a mental entity in a separate realm. Physicality does not imply reductionism, however. Thought processes are emergent brain activities that are not ontologically reducible. In his treatise on the paradigmatic shift to cognitivism, Sperry (1993) spells out some of the characteristics of a nondualistic mentalism. Mental states are emergent properties of generating brain processes. Emergent properties differ in novel ways from the elements of which they are created, rather than simply representing increased complexity of the same properties. To use Bunge's (1977) analogy, the emergent properties of water, such as fluidity, viscosity, and transparency, are not simply the aggregate properties of its microcomponents, oxygen and hydrogen.

Thought processes are not only emergent brain activities; they also exert determinative influence. There are many neural systems that subserve human functioning. They operate interactively at different sites and levels to produce coherent experiences out of the multitude of information processing. With regard to this ontological plurality, certain brain structures are specialized for mentation. The thought processes generated by the higher cerebral system are involved in the regulation of visceral, motoric, and other lower level subsystems. For example, a host of microsensory, perceptual, and information processing activities gives rise to a judgment of personal efficacy. Once formed, however, efficacy beliefs regulate aspirations, choice of behavioral courses, mobilization and maintenance of

effort, and affective reactions. The influence between microevents and emergent macroevents
operates both upwardly and downwardly. Thus,
an emergent interactive agency assumes ontological nonreductionism of complex events to simpler ones and plurality of regulatory physical
subsystems that function interconnectedly in a
hierarchically structured system in which higher
neural centers control lower ones.

The fact that cognition is a cerebral occurrence does not mean that the laws expressing
functional relations in psychological theory are
reducible to those in neurophysiological theory.
One must distinguish between how cerebral systems function and the personal and social means
by which they can be orchestrated to produce
courses of action that serve different purposes.
Much of psychology is concerned with discovering principles about how to structure environmental influences and enlist cognitive activities
to promote human adaptation and change. Most
of the subject matter of psychological theory
with regard to psychosocial factors does not
have a counterpart in neurobiological theory
and, therefore, is not derivable from it. These
factors do not appear in neurophysiological theory because many of them involve the construction and organization of events external to the
organism. For example, knowledge of the brain
circuitry involved in learning does not tell one
much about how best to devise conditions of
learning in terms of levels of abstractness, novelty, and challenge; how to provide incentives to
get people to attend to, process, and organize
relevant information; in what modes to present
information; and whether learning is better
achieved independently, cooperatively, or com-
petitively. The optimal conditions must be specified by psychological principles. Nor does understanding how the brain works furnish rules
on how to create efficacious parents, teachers, or
politicians. Although psychological principles
cannot violate the neurophysiological capabilities of the systems that subserve them, the psychological principles need to be pursued in their
own right. Were one to embark on the road to reductionism, the journey would traverse biology
and chemistry and would eventually end in
atomic particles, with neither the intermediate
locales nor the final stop supplying the psychological laws of human behavior.

A major challenge for a physicalistic account
of the mind is to specify the mechanisms through
which the brain creates mental events and explain how these events exert determinative influence. The human mind is generative, creative,
and proactive, not just reactive. Hence, an even
more formidable challenge is to explain how
people come to be producers of thoughts that
may be novel, inventive, or visionary or that take
complete leave of reality, as in flights of fancy.
One can intentionally originate novel coherent
thoughts; for example, visualizing hippopotami
attired in chartreuse tuxedos gracefully navigat-
ing hang gliders over lunar craters. Similarly, one
can conceive of several novel acts and choose to
execute one of them. People bring cognitive productions into being by the intentional exercise of
personal agency. Intentionality and agency raise
the fundamental question of how people actuate
the cerebral processes that characterize the exercise of agency and lead to the realization of particular intentions. This question goes beyond the
cerebral correlates of sensory input and motor
output to the intentional production of cerebral
events in thinking of future courses of action,
evaluating their likely functional value under
differing circumstances, and organizing and
guiding the execution of the chosen options.
Cognitive production, with its purposive, creative, and evaluative properties, defies explanation of novel thoughts in terms of external cueing
of preformed cognitions. In addition to the question of how people bring about thoughts and actions is the intriguing question of how people
generate self-perceiving, self-reflecting, and self-
correcting activities.

Rottschaefer (1985) presents a thoughtful
analysis of human agency operating through intentional and generative cognition as it bears on
the nonintentionalistic views of human behavior
favored by eliminative materialists. People are
agentic operators in their life course not just on-
looking hosts of brain mechanisms orchestrated
by environmental events. The sensory, motor
and cerebral systems are tools people use to accomplish the tasks and goals that give meaning
and direction to their lives (Harré & Gillet, 1994).
Through their intentional acts, people shape the
functional structure of their neurobiological systems. By regulating their own motivation and
the activities they pursue, they produce the ex-

periences that form the neurobiological substrate of symbolic, psychomotor, and other skills. Should people experience any loss or decline in any of their bodily systems, they devise alternative ways of engaging and managing the world around them.

The duality of self as agent and self as object pervades much of the theorizing in the field of personality. The double nature of the self merges in the case of self-influence. In their daily transactions, people analyze the situations that confront them, consider alternative courses of action, judge their abilities to carry them out successfully, and estimate the results the actions are likely to produce. They act on their judgments, later reflect on how well their thoughts have served them in managing the events at hand, and change their thinking and strategies accordingly. People are said to be agents when they act on the environment but objects when they reflect and act on themselves.

Social cognitive theory rejects the dualistic view of the self. Reflecting on one's own functioning entails shifting the perspective of the same agent rather than converting the self from agent to object or reifying different internal agents or selves that regulate one another. It is one and the same person who does the strategic thinking about how to manage the environment and later evaluates the adequacy of his or her knowledge, thinking skills, capabilities, and action strategies. The shift in perspective does not transform the person from an agent to an object,

as the dualist view of the self would lead one to believe. One is just as much an agent when one is reflecting on one's experiences and exerting self-influence as when one is executing courses of action. In social cognitive theory, the self is not split into object and agent; rather, in self-reflection and self-influence, individuals are simultaneously agent and object.

## Human Agency in Triadic Reciprocal Causation

The term *causation* is used in the present context to mean functional dependence between events. In social cognitive theory, human agency operates within an interdependent causal structure involving triadic reciprocal causation (Bandura, 1986a). In this transactional view of self and society, internal personal factors in the form of cognitive, affective, and biological events; behavior; and environmental events all operate as interacting determinants that influence one another bidirectionally (Fig. 1). Reciprocity does not mean that the three sets of interacting determinants are of equal strength. Their relative influence will vary for different activities and under different circumstances. Nor do the mutual influences and their reciprocal effects all spring forth simultaneously as a holistic entity. It takes time for a causal factor to exert its influence. Because of the time lag in the operation of the three sets of factors, it is possible to gain an

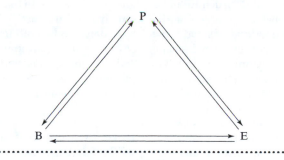

**Figure 1** The relationships between the three major classes of determinants in triadic reciprocal causation. B represents behavior; P the internal personal factors in the form of cognitive, affective, and biological events; and E the external environment. (Bandura, 1986a)

understanding of how different segments of reciprocal causation operate without having to mount a Herculean effort to assess every possible interactant at the same time.

Human adaptation and change are rooted in social systems. Therefore, personal agency operates within a broad network of sociostructural influences. In agentic transactions, people are both producers and products of social systems. Social structures—which are devised to organize, guide, and regulate human affairs in given domains by authorized rules and sanctions—do not arise by immaculate conception; they are created by human activity. Social structures, in turn, impose constraints and provide resources for personal development and everyday functioning. But neither structural constraints nor enabling resources foreordain what individuals become and do in given situations. For the most part, social structures represent authorized social practices carried out by human beings occupying designated roles (Giddens, 1984). As such, they do not compel uniform action. Within the rule structures, there is a lot of personal variation in their interpretation, enforcement, adoption, circumvention, or active opposition (Burns & Dietz, in press). Efficacious people are quick to take advantage of opportunity structures and figure out ways to circumvent institutional constraints or change them by collective action. Conversely, inefficacious people are less apt to exploit the enabling opportunities provided by the social system and are easily discouraged by institutional impediments. It is not a dichotomy between a disembodied social structure and a decontextualized personal agency, but a dynamic interplay between individuals and those who preside over the institutionalized operations of social systems. This interplay involves agentic transactions between institutional functionaries and those who seek to accommodate to or change their practices. Agency is just as integral to institutional functionaries as it is to freelancing individuals. Social cognitive theory thus avoids a dualism between individuals and society and between social structure and personal agency.

Sociostructural theories and psychological theories are often regarded as rival conceptions of human behavior or as representing different levels of causation. This perspective, too, is dualistic. Human behavior cannot be fully understood solely in terms of either social structural factors or psychological factors. A full understanding requires an integrated causal perspective in which social influences operate through self-processes that produce the actions. The self system is not merely a conduit for external influences, as structural reductionists might claim. The self is socially constituted, but, by exercising self-influence, individuals are partial contributors to what they become and do. Moreover, human agency operates generatively and proactively rather than just reactively. Thus, in the theory of triadic reciprocal causation, sociostructural and personal determinants are treated as interacting cofactors within a unified causal structure.

Conceptions of agent causality have been wedded to individual agency. Social cognitive theory adopts a much broader view of agency. People do not live their lives in isolation; they work together to produce results they desire. The growing interdependence of social and economic life further underscores the need to broaden the focus of inquiry beyond the exercise of individual influence to collective action designed to shape the course of events. Social cognitive theory, therefore, extends the analysis of mechanisms of human agency to the exercise of collective agency. People's shared belief in their capabilities to produce effects collectively is a crucial ingredient of collective agency. Collective efficacy is not simply the sum of the efficacy beliefs of individuals. Rather, it is an emergent group-level attribute that is the product of coordinative and interactive dynamics. Later chapters analyze how both individual and collective efficacy beliefs contribute to human adaptation and change. Personal and social change are complementary rather than rival approaches to improving the quality of life.

## Determinism and the Exercise of Self-Influence

The discussion of agent causality raises the fundamental issues of determinism and the freedom to exert some control over one's life. The term *determinism* is used here to signify the production of effects by events rather than in the doctrinal sense meaning that actions are completely determined by a prior sequence of causes independent of the individual. Because most behavior is codetermined by many factors operating interactively, given events produce effects probabilistically rather than inevitably within the reciprocally deterministic system.

Freedom is often considered antithetical to determinism. When viewed from a sociocognitive perspective, there is no incompatibility between freedom and determinism. Freedom is not conceived negatively as exemption from social influences or situational constraints. Rather, it is defined positively as the exercise of self-influence to bring about desired results. This agentic causation relies heavily on cognitive self-regulation. It is achieved through reflective thought, generative use of the knowledge and skills at one's command, and other tools of self-influence, which choice and execution of action require. Self-influences operate deterministically on behavior in the same way external influences do. Given the same environmental conditions, people who have the ability to exercise many options and are adept at regulating their own motivation and behavior will have greater freedom to make things happen than will those who have limited means of personal agency. It is because self-influence operates deterministically on action that some measure of freedom is possible.

The choice of actions from among alternatives is not completely and involuntarily determined by environmental events. Rather, the making of choices is aided by reflective thought, through which self-influence is largely exercised. People exert some influence over what they do by the alternatives they consider; how they foresee and weigh the visualized outcomes, including their own self-evaluative reactions; and how they appraise their abilities to execute the options they consider. To say that thought guides action is an abbreviated statement of convenience rather than a conferral of agency on thought. It is not that individuals generate thoughts that then become the agents of action. The cognitive activities constitute the processes of self-influence that are brought to bear on the courses of action to take. Thus, for example, an individual will behave differently in an efficacious frame of mind than in an inefficacious one. But the individual remains the agent of the thoughts, the effort, and the actions. An elliptical expression should not be misconstrued as a transfer of agency from person to thought.

Agent causation involves the ability to behave differently from what environmental force dictate rather than inevitably yield to them. In enticing and coercive situations, personal agency is expressed in the power to refrain. People construct personal standards that they then use to guide, motivate, and regulate their own behavior (Bandura, 1986a; 1991b). The anticipatory self-respect for actions that correspond to personal standards and self-censure for actions that violate them serve as the regulatory influences. People do things that give them self-satisfaction and a sense of self-worth. They refrain from behaving in ways that violate their personal standards because it will bring self-censure. After self-reactive capabilities are developed, behavior usually produces two sets of consequences—external outcomes and self-evaluative reactions—that can operate as complimentary or opposing influences on behavior. It is not uncommon for individuals to invest their self-worth so strongly in certain convictions that they will submit to prolonged mistreatment rather than accede to what they regard as unjust or immoral. Thomas More, who was beheaded for refusing to compromise his resolute convictions, is a notable example from history. In their everyday lives, people repeatedly confront predicaments in which they forgo expediency and material benefit for self-respect.

Self-influence affects not only choices but the success with which chosen courses of action are executed. Psychological analyses of the mechanisms of personal agency show that people contribute to the attainment of desired futures by enlisting cognitive guides and self-incentives and by selecting and constructing environments to suit their purposes (Bandura, 1986a). The greater their foresight, proficiency, and means of self-influence, all of which are acquirable skills, the more successful they are in achieving what they seek. Because of the capacity for self-influence, people are at least partial architects of their own destinies. It is not the principle of determinism that is in dispute, but whether determinism should be treated as a one-sided or a two-way process. Given the reciprocal interplay between people and their environment, determinism does not imply the fatalistic view that people are only pawns of external forces. Reciprocal causation provides people with opportunities to exercise some control over their destinies as well as setting limits on self-direction.

Arguments against the causal efficacy of thought and other means of self-influence usually invoke a selective regression of causes. In the operant view (Skinner, 1974), people are merely repositories for past stimulus inputs and conduits for external stimulation—they can add nothing to their performance. Through a conceptual sleight of hand, the determinants of human action are regressed to an "initiating cause" located in the environment, thus rendering human thought entirely externally implanted, acausal, and completely redundant. A detailed critique of this conceptual scheme is presented elsewhere (Bandura, 1996). Obviously, thought is partly influenced by experience, but thought is not completely shaped by past stimulus inputs. Operant analyses emphasize how people's judgments and actions are determined by the environment but disregard the fact that the environment itself is partly determined by people's actions. Environments have causes, as do actions. People create, alter, and destroy environments by their actions. The sociocognitive analysis of reciprocal causation does not invite an infinite regression of causes, because individuals originate actions from their experiences and reflective thought rather than merely undergo actions as implants of the past. The emergent creations are not reducible to the environmental inputs. For example, Bach's magnificent masterpieces, which fill sixty volumes of prolific originality, are not reducible to his prior instruction in the mechanics of musical composition, his predecessors' musical works, and the ongoing events in his everyday environment. Since Bach was not endowed with fully orchestrated Brandenburg concertos and hundreds of church cantatas, from which repository did the environmental reinforcers select these artistic creations? Reinforcement cannot select what does not exist in a repertoire. One can, of course, create simple new responses by waiting around for random variations to produce some approximate elements to reward. But given Bach's prolific output, one would have to wait around for

countless lifetimes to shape such artistic creations by selective reinforcement of random variations, if it could ever be achieved at all by this slow, laborious process. Although human ingenuity incorporates some aspects of past experience, it transforms it, adds novel features to it, and thereby creates something that is not just a conglomerate or replica of the past. In short, human behavior is determined, but it is determined partly by the individual rather than solely by the environment. One does not explain a unique musical composition by attributing it to causes in the environment further back in time. The composition is an emergent creation.

The long-standing debate over the issue of freedom was enlivened by Skinner's (1971) contention that, apart from genetic contributions, human behavior is shaped and controlled by environmental contingencies. A major problem with this type of analysis is that it depicts two-way causality between people and environments as one-way control by an autonomous environment. In Skinner's view, freedom is an illusion. It is not that the interdependence of personal and environmental influences is never acknowledged by advocates of this point of view. Indeed, Skinner (1971) has often commented on people's capacity for countercontrol. The notion of countercontrol, however, portrays the environment as the instigator to which individuals can react. In fact, people are foreactive, not simply counteractive. Equivocation by the unidirectionalists created further conceptual ambiguities. Having acknowledged the reality of bidirectional influence, Skinner (1971) negated it by reasserting the preeminent control of behavior by the environment: "A person does not act upon the world, the world acts upon him." The environment thus reappears as an autonomous force that automatically selects, shapes, and controls behavior. Whatever allusions are made to two-way influences, environmental rule clearly emerges as the reigning metaphor in this view of reality.

It is the height of irony when people who exercise the liberties guaranteed by institutions of freedom denigrate freedom as an illusion. Over the course of history, countless people have sacrificed their lives to create and preserve institutions of freedom that prohibit rulers from forcing obedience to unauthorized dictates. Struggles for freedom are aimed at creating institutional safeguards that exempt certain forms of behavior from coercive and punitive control. The less social jurisdiction there is over given spheres of activities, the greater is the causal contribution of self-influence to choice of action in those domains. After protective laws are built into social systems, there are certain things that a society may not do to individuals who choose to challenge conventional values or vested interests, however much it might like to. Legal prohibitions against unauthorized societal control create personal freedoms that are realities, not illusory abstractions. Societies differ in their institutions of freedom and in the number and types of activities that are officially exempted from punitive control. For example, social systems that protect journalists from criminal sanctions for criticizing government officials and their practices are freer than those that allow authoritative power to be used to silence critics or their vehicles of expression. Societies that possess a judiciary independent of other government institutions ensure greater social freedom than those that do not.

When it comes to social change, thoroughgoing environmental determinists become fervent advocates of people's power to change their lives for the better by applying the advocate's psychotechnology. For example, Skinner spent much of the later part of his career promoting, with missionary earnestness, operant technology as the remedy for the world's ills. Even the modest applications of operant conditioning fell short of his claims, let alone providing the panacea for growing worldwide problems. A fervent environmental determinist urging people to change their environment is amusingly self-negating because it contradicts the basic premise of the doctrine of environmentalism. If humans were, in fact, incapable of acting as causal agents, they could describe the changes they were undergoing in response to the dictates of their environment, but they could not select actions based on reasoned plans and foresight of consequences, nor could they intentionally make desired things happen. They can be conduits for environmental forces, but they themselves cannot be creators of programs for environmental change. Boring (1957) provided a thoughtful analysis of the "egocentric predicament" in which advocatory environmental determinists get themselves entangled by regarding themselves as self-directing agents but other folks as being externally determined. The advocates thus exempt themselves from the overriding environmental control that presumably shepherds the rest of the populace. Otherwise, the advocates' own views simply become utterances shaped by their insular environment and, thus, have no special truth value. However, should members of the populace adopt the technology of the advocate, they are suddenly converted into intentional agents who can improve their lives and shape their future.

## Related Views of Personal Efficacy

Self-referent thought plays a paramount role in most contemporary theories of human behavior. Self-conceptions, of course, have many different facets. Although they are all self-referential, not all of the facets are concerned with personal efficacy, and this has been the source of some confusion in the literature. Even theories that explicitly speak to the issue of personal efficacy typically differ in how they view the nature of efficacy beliefs, their origins, the effects they have, their changeability, and the intervening processes through which they affect psychosocial functioning. Theories of the self differ not only in conceptual orientation but also in comprehensiveness. The various theoretical perspectives rarely encompass all the important aspects of efficacy beliefs. Much of the research generated by the various theories is tied to an omnibus measure of perceived control and devoted to a search for its correlates. A full understanding of personal causation requires a comprehensive theory that explains, within a unified conceptual framework, the origins of efficacy beliefs, their structure and function, the processes through which they produce diverse effects, and their modifiability. Self-efficacy theory addresses all these subprocesses at both the individual level and the collective level.

The social cognitive theory of the origin and function of perceived self-efficacy offers certain other analytic and operative advantages. It specifies other aspects of the conglomerate self system. These include, among other things, personal aspirations, outcome expectations, perceived opportunity structures and constraints, and conceptions of personal efficacy. Analysis of how these constituent factors work together and their relative contribution to adaptation and change provides an integrated view of the self (Bandura, 1986a). These sociocognitive determinants are grounded in a large body of empirical evidence about the mechanisms by which they motivate and regulate behavior. The conceptual and empirical linkages of other determinants to perceived self-efficacy deepen understanding of how people guide and shape their own destinies. By embedding the self-efficacy belief system in a unified sociocognitive framework, the theory can integrate diverse bodies of findings in varied spheres of functioning.

The value of a theory is ultimately judged by the power of the methods it yields to effect changes. Self-efficacy theory provides explicit guidelines on how to enable people to exercise some influence over how they live their lives. A theory that can be readily used to enhance human efficacy has much greater social utility than theories that provide correlates of perceived control but have little to say about how to foster desired changes. The following sections review alternative conceptions of personal efficacy, as well as constructs that are sometimes mistakenly grouped with perceived efficacy as if they resembled one another when, in fact, they are concerned with different phenomena.

## Self-Concept

Self-appraisal has often been analyzed in terms of the self-concept (Rogers, 1959; Wylie, 1974). The self-concept is a composite view of oneself that is presumed to be formed through direct experience and evaluations adopted from significant others. Self-concepts are measured by having people rate how well descriptive statements of different attributes apply to themselves. Their role in personal functioning is tested by correlating the composite self-concepts, or disparities between actual and ideal selves, with various indices of adjustment, attitudes, and behavior.

Examining self-referent processes in terms of the self-concept contributes to an understanding of people's attitudes toward themselves and how these attitudes may affect their general outlook on life. There are several features of theories of this type, however, that detract from their power to explain and predict human behavior. For the most part, the theories are concerned with global self-images. Combining diverse attributes into a single index creates confusion about what is actually being measured and how much weight is given to particular attributes in the forced summary judgment. Even if the global self-conception is tied to certain areas of functioning, it does not do justice to the complexity of efficacy beliefs, which vary across different domains of activities, within the same activity domain at different levels of difficulty, and under different circumstances. A composite self-image may yield some weak correlations, but it is not equal to the task of predicting, with any degree of accuracy, the wide variations in behavior that typically occur in a given domain of activity under different conditions. Such theories fail to explain how the same self-concept can spawn different types of behavior. In comparative tests of predictive power, efficacy beliefs are highly predictive of behavior, whereas the effect of self-concept is weaker and equivocal (Pajares & Kranzler, 1995; Pajares & Miller, 1994a, 1995). Self-concept loses most, if not all, of its predictiveness when the influence of perceived efficacy is factored out. Such findings suggest that self-concept largely reflects people's beliefs in their personal efficacy.

## Differentiating Self-Efficacy from Self-Esteem

The concepts of self-esteem and perceived self-efficacy are often used interchangeably as though they represented the same phenomenon. In fact, they refer to entirely different things. Perceived self-efficacy is concerned with judgments of personal capability, whereas self-esteem is concerned with judgments of self-worth. There is no fixed relationship between beliefs about one's capabilities and whether one likes or dislikes oneself. Individuals may judge themselves hopelessly inefficacious in a given activity without suffering any loss of self-esteem whatsoever, because they do not invest their self-worth in that activity. The fact that I acknowledge complete inefficacy in ballroom dancing does not drive me to recurrent bouts of self-devaluation. Conversely, individuals may regard themselves as highly efficacious in an activity but take no pride in performing it well. A skilled forecloser of mortgages of families that have fallen on hard times is unlikely to feel pride for driving them out of their homes proficiently. It is true, however, that people tend to cultivate their capabilities in activities that give them a sense of self-worth. If empirical analyses are confined to activities in which people invest their sense of self-worth, they will inflate correlations between self-efficacy and self-esteem, because the analyses ignore both domains of functioning in which people judge themselves inefficacious but could not care less and those in which they feel highly efficacious but take no pride in performing the activity well because of its socially injurious consequences.

People need much more than high self-esteem to do well in given pursuits. Many achievers are hard on themselves because they adopt standards that are not easily fulfilled, whereas others may enjoy high self-esteem because they do not demand much of themselves or they derive their esteem from sources other than personal accomplishments. Consequently, self-liking does not necessarily beget performance attainments. They are the product of toilsome self-disciplined effort. People need firm confidence in their efficacy to mount and sustain the effort required to succeed. Thus, in ongoing pursuits, perceived personal efficacy predicts the goals people set for themselves and their performance attainments, whereas self-esteem affects neither personal goals nor performance (Mone, Baker & Jeffries, 1995).

The inappropriate equation of self-esteem with perceived self-efficacy has both methodological and conceptual sources. Some of the instruments devised to measure self-esteem include self-appraisals of both personal efficacy and self-worth, thus confounding factors that should be separated (Coopersmith, 1967). Some authors mistakenly regard self-esteem as the generalized form of perceived self-efficacy. For example, Harter (1990) treats judgments of self-worth and personal competence as representing levels of generality within the same phenomenon. Self-worth is said to be global and perceived competence to be domain-specific. Global self-worth is considered to be an emergent superordinate property that is more than the sum of the domain-specific competencies. The assessment of global self-worth is disembodied from particular domains of functioning that contribute in varying degrees to one's sense of self-pride or self-dislike. That is, people are asked how much they like or dislike themselves without any regard to what it is they like or dislike. Measurement of self-worth noncontextually and perceived competence specifically presumably integrates unidimensional and multidimensional perspectives into a hierarchical model of self-evaluation.

As already noted, judgments of self-worth and personal efficacy represent different phenomena, not part-whole relationships within the same phenomenon. Moreover, self-esteem is no less multidimensional than perceived efficacy. People vary in the extent to which they derive a sense of self-worth from their work, their family life, their community and social life, and their recreational pursuits. For example, some students may take pride in their academic accomplishments but devalue themselves in their social facility. Hard-driving executives may value themselves highly in their occupational pursuits but devalue themselves as parents. Domain-linked measures of self-worth reveal the patterning of human self-esteem and the areas of vulnerability to self-disparagement. There is neither conceptual nor empirical justification for construing self-worth globally. Nor is self-esteem the generalized embodiment of specific efficacy beliefs.

There are several sources of self-esteem or self-worthiness (Bandura, 1986a). Self-esteem can stem from self-evaluations based on personal competence or on possession of attributes that are culturally invested with positive or negative value. In self-esteem arising from personal competence, people derive pride from fulfilling their standards of merit. They experience self-satisfaction for a job well done but are displeased with themselves when they fail to measure up to their standards of merit. Personal competencies that provide the means for achieving valued accomplishments afford a genuine basis of self-esteem. This source of self-evaluation enables people to exert some influence over their own self-esteem by developing potentialities that bring self-satisfactions from personal accomplishments.

People often voice evaluations that reflect their likes and dislikes of the attributes possessed by others rather than judging them by their accomplishments. In these instances, the social evaluations are linked to personal attributes and social status rather than to personal competencies. For example, people who are socially relegated to subordinate positions may be disparaged. In conflict-ridden families, parents may deprecate offspring who possess attributes resembling those of a disliked spouse. Social evaluations tend to influence how the recipients come to evaluate their own self-worthiness. Moreover, people are often criticized or deprecated when they fail to live up to the ideals or aspirational standards imposed upon them by others. To the extent that they adopt those onerous standards, most of their accomplishments will bring them nothing but self-devaluation because they fail to measure up. The roles played by personal competence and social evaluation in the development of self-esteem receive support from the studies of Coopersmith (1967). He found that children who exhibited high self-esteem had parents who were accepting, who set explicit attainable standards, and who provided their children with considerable support and latitude to acquire competencies that could serve them well in their pursuits.

Cultural stereotyping is another way in which evaluative social judgments affect a sense of self-worth. People are often cast into valued or devalued groups on the basis of their ethnicity, race, sex, or physical characteristics. They then get treated in terms of the social stereotype rather than on the basis of their actual individuality. In situations that give salience to the stereotype, those stereotyped suffer losses in self-esteem (Steele, 1996). Devaluative societal practices are usually clothed in social justifications that fault the disfavored groups for their maltreatment. Justified devaluation can have more devastating effects on judgments of self-worth than acknowledged antipathy. When

blame is convincingly ascribed to a devalued group, many of its members may eventually come to believe the degrading characterizations of themselves (Hallie, 1971). Discriminatory social practices help to create some of the very failings that serve as justifications for the devaluation. Thus, vindicated inhumanity is more likely to instill self-devaluation in disparaged groups than inhumanity that does not attempt to justify itself. People who possess attributes that are socially disparaged, and who accept the stereotyped negative evaluations of others, will hold themselves in low regard irrespective of their talents.

Because self-esteem has many sources, there is no single remedy for low self-esteem. People who combine limited competencies, exacting standards of self-evaluation, and socially disparaged attributes are the ones most likely to harbor a pervasive sense of worthlessness. These different sources of self-devaluation call for different corrective measures. Self-devaluation rooted in incompetence requires the cultivation of talents for personal accomplishments that bring self-satisfaction. Those who suffer from self-disparagement because they judge themselves harshly against excessively high standards become more self-accepting and self-rewarding after they are helped to adopt more realistic standards of achievement (Jackson, 1972; Rehm, 1982). Self-devaluation resulting from belittling social evaluations requires humane treatment by others that affirms one's self-worth. Self-devaluation stemming from discriminatory disparagement of attributes requires modeling and rewarding a sense of pride in those attributes. Efforts by minorities to instill pride in racial characteristics (for example, "Black is beautiful") illustrate this approach. When self-devaluation arises from multiple sources, multiple corrective measures are needed; for example, fostering pride in one's characteristics but also cultivating competencies that instill a high and resilient sense of personal efficacy for personal accomplishments.

## Effectance Motivation

In seeking motivations for exploratory behavior, White (1959, 1960) postulated an effectance motive. This motive is conceptualized as an intrinsic need to deal effectively with the environment. The production of effects through exploratory activities builds competencies and is said to be satisfying in its own right. The effectance motive presumably develops through cumulative acquisition of knowledge and skills in managing the environment. In these conceptual papers, White argues eloquently for a competence model of human development that is rooted in nonbiologic drives. Behavior is pursued for the feelings of efficacy derived from it. White provides only a general conceptual framework, however, rather than a particularized theory from which testable deductions can be made. How an effectance motive is created by effective transactions with the environment is never spelled out. The impact of failed efforts, which are all too common, receives no mention. Nor is the nature of the intrinsic reward of effective action specified in a way that would be subject to test. Harter (1981) has elaborated White's formulation into a developmental model of intrinsic mastery motivation.

It is difficult to verify the existence of an effectance or mastery motive because the motive is inferred from the very exploratory behavior it supposedly causes. This creates problems of circularity. Without an independent measure of motive strength, one cannot tell whether people explore and manipulate things because they are propelled by a competence motive to do so, or for the satisfactions they derive or anticipate from the activity. There is a marked difference between being driven by an intrinsic effectance motive and being motivated by anticipated outcomes. We will return to this issue in Chapter 6, which presents a conceptualization of intrinsic motivation within the framework of social cognitive theory.

Over the years, theorists have argued about whether it is the push of boredom and apprehension or the pull of novelty that rouses organisms to exploratory action (Berlyne, 1960; Brown, 1953; Harlow, 1953; Mowrer, 1960b). Critics of exploratory drives have been able to explain and to alter some forms of exploratory behavior by the outcomes it produces without recourse to an underlying drive (Fowler, 1971). However, theories concerned solely with external prompts and immediate rewards for action are hard-pressed to explain the directedness and persistence of behavior over extended periods

when immediate situational inducements are weak, absent, or even negative. This type of sustained involvement in activities requires self-regulatory capabilities that operate anticipatorily. Efficacy beliefs play a crucial role in the ongoing self-regulation of motivation, as will be shown later.

The theory of effectance motivation has not been formulated in sufficient detail to permit extensive theoretical comparisons. Nevertheless, effectance theory and social cognitive theory clearly differ over several issues. In the sociocognitive view, choice behavior, effort, and persistence are extensively regulated by beliefs of personal efficacy rather than by an effectance drive. Because efficacy beliefs are defined and measured independently of performance, they provide a basis for predicting the occurrence, generality, and persistence of behavior. In contrast, it is difficult to explain the variability of human behavior in terms of an overall intrinsic motive drive (Bandura, 1991b). People will approach, explore, and try to manage situations within their perceived capabilities, but unless they are externally coerced, they avoid transactions with those aspects of their environment that they perceive exceed their coping abilities.

These alternative views also differ in how they explain the origins of personal efficacy. In effectance theory, the effectance motive develops gradually through prolonged transactions with the environment. The theory thus focuses almost exclusively on exploratory behavior as the source of effectance. In social cognitive theory, efficacy beliefs are developed and altered not only by direct mastery experiences but also by vicarious experience, social evaluations by significant others, and changes in physiological states or how they are construed. These differences in theoretical approach have significant implications for how one goes about creating a strong sense of efficacy.

Beliefs of personal efficacy do not operate as dispositional determinants independent of contextual factors. Some situations require greater self-regulatory skill and more arduous performance than others. Efficacy beliefs will vary accordingly. Thus, for example, the level and strength of personal efficacy in public speaking will differ depending on the subject matter, whether the speech is extemporaneous or from notes, and the evaluative standards of the audiences to be addressed, to mention just a few conditional factors. Therefore, analyses of how efficacy beliefs affect actions rely on microanalytic measures rather than global indices of personality traits or motives of effectance. It is no more informative to speak of self-efficacy in general terms than to speak of nonspecific social behavior.

In effectance theory, affecting the environment arouses feelings of efficacy and pleasure. Although such feelings may arise from performance attainments, attainments do not necessarily enhance perceived self-efficacy. Attainments may raise, lower, or leave unchanged beliefs of personal efficacy, depending on what is made of those attainments. Nor does the successful exercise of personal efficacy necessarily bring pleasure or raise self-esteem. It depends on how attainments measure up against internal standards. If the level of efficacy that is realized falls short of personal standards of merit, the accomplishment may, in fact, leave one with self-discontent. Students with stringent academic standards will not swell with pride upon achieving only modest improvements in academic activities important to them. The pace at which activities are mastered can drastically alter self-evaluative reactions (Simon, 1979a). Accomplishments that surpass earlier ones bring a continued sense of self-satisfaction. But people derive little satisfaction from smaller accomplishments, or even devalue them, after having made larger strides. Early spectacular accomplishments reflecting exemplary proficiency can thus be conducive to later self-dissatisfaction even in the face of continuing personal attainments. Nor will high self-efficaciousness in an activity boost self-satisfaction if the activity happens to be devalued. When competencies are used for inhumane purposes, performers may feel self-efficacious in their triumphs but remain displeased with themselves for the sorrow they have wrought.

The relationship between personal attainments and self-satisfaction is clearly more complex than effectance theory would lead one to believe. A theory of effectance must consider the important role played by personal standards and the cognitive appraisal of attainments in people's affective reactions to their own performances. These are some of the mechanisms that determine whether performance attainments bring pleasure or displeasure. The manner in which internal standards and efficacy beliefs operate as interrelated mechanisms of personal agency and affective self-reactions is addressed in a later chapter.

Effectance motivation is said to come into play only under certain limited conditions (White, 1959), a point that is often overlooked in overextensions of the theory to wide spheres of behavior. The effectance motive is believed to be aroused when the organism is otherwise unoccupied or is only weakly stimulated by organic drives. In the words of White (1960), effectance promotes *spare-time behavior.* In social cognitive theory, efficacy beliefs enter into the regulation of all types of performances, until they become routinized into habitual patterns. Although the theory of effectance motivation lacks verifiable particulars, considerable research disputes its two basic premises: that people are inherently driven to exercise control over their environment and that the achievement of control is inherently self-satisfying (Bandura, 1986a; Rodin, Rennert, & Solomon, 1980). We will return to a more detailed discussion of the issue of inherent motivators shortly.

Yarrow and his associates have recast effectance motivation in a more testable form (Yarrow et al., 1983). They call it mastery motivation and construe it as a striving for competence—which, in turn, is defined as effective action in dealing with the environment. Mastery motivation is manifested in attentiveness, exploratory behavior, and persistence in goal-directed activities. Developmental tests of the nature and correlates of this postulated motive system yield equivocal findings. Behavioral indices of mastery motivation are weakly related to one another and become even more heterogeneous with increasing age of the people tested. A mastery motive that does not hang together presents conceptual problems. The same mastery behavior shows little consistency over even a short time, reflecting surprising instability. Moreover, indices of mastery motivation are not consistently linked to actual competence. The authors, however, place a positive interpretation on this extensive disconnectedness. The mastery motive simply takes on the shape of the empirical findings. The proponents argue that weak relationships between different indices of the same motive serve as evidence that mastery motivation is multifaceted. Increasing heterogeneity indicates that the motive becomes more differentiated with age. Lack of behavioral continuity indicates that the motive undergoes developmental transformation. And the inconsistent linkage between mastery motivation and actual competence is taken as evidence that they create each other interactively, although one would expect reciprocal causation to produce a strong relationship.

A more plausible conclusion to be drawn from the extensive disconnectedness is that striving for competence is not driven by an omnibus mastery motive but rather is motivated by the varied benefits of competent action. What competent functioning is differs across time, milieus, social standards, and domains of activity. Competence requires appropriate learning experiences; it does not emerge spontaneously. Hence, people develop different patterns of competencies and deploy them selectively depending on the match of efficacy beliefs to environmental demands and on anticipated outcomes. A functional analysis of striving for competence can better explain variations in the patterning of human competencies than does one cast in terms of an omnibus mastery motive.

# How Emotional Development Relates to Learning

## Stanley Greenspan, M.D.

People often think that early learning consists of knowing the ABC's, reciting the correct names of objects on picture cards, or performing some other memory exercise. Actually, the process of learning begins through relationships as early as birth, when an infant and mother connect through their own unique form of communication.

Healthy relationships throughout childhood are critical to emotional development, which, in turn, creates a basis for learning in several important areas. These include the ability to communicate and use language, problem solving, and the development of self-esteem. Few would argue that all learning requires the development of these abilities. This means that parents, teachers, and other caregivers play a major role in a child's healthy emotional development and, therefore, in his ability to learn.

In the first four to five years of life, critical ideas or perceptions of life are learned as part of relationships. In these relationships, basic emotional stages are mastered (or not), and these very same milestones become the child's very first cognitive lessons. These combined emotional-cognitive lessons become the basis for all subsequent learning. Therefore, to determine how to help children become capable of formal learning later on, we must pay attention to these early processes or stages.

There are four general stages of early development, each building upon the other, in which children develop emotionally. In turn, mastering these stages enables them to grow socially and cognitively as well. Ultimately, the ability to think—that is, to connect ideas and see relationship—is the result of this four-stage process that makes up the very foundation of learning.

*Source:* Greenspan, S. I. (1990). How emotional development relates to learning. In S. Hanna & S. Wilford, *Floor time: Tuning in to each child* (pp. 1–4), New York: Scholastic.

## Stage One: Engagement

In the first stage of emotional development, ordinarily in the first eight months of life, children are learning to attend and engage. This means simply the ability to share attention with another person. For a baby this would involve little Susie looking in her mother's eyes, focusing on her voice, or examining her mother's changing facial expressions. When shared attention is not developed, babies can become easily distracted or preoccupied.

Together with this capacity for shared attention is the capacity for engaging or relating to another person with some warmth, positive emotion, and expectation of something useful or pleasurable happening in the interaction. We see this in normal development by age three to four months, when a baby eagerly brightens up with a smile, moves her arms and legs to the rhythm of her mother's voice, or vocalizes in response to mommy's and daddy's cadences. The pleasure this provides helps the baby not only develop a sense of security and intimacy, but also to progress in motor development and language acquisition. Her attitude about learning new things is also greatly enhanced. In the absence of trusting, positive expectations, distrust, suspiciousness, or apathy take their place—hardly a foundation for learning.

## Stage Two: Two-Way Communication

Developing a capacity for two-way communication is the second stage that all children need to master, that is, the ability to signal one's own needs and intentions and also comprehend someone else's, and to be able to string these together as part of an interaction. This ability for two-way communication, or intentional communication, is normally learned between 6 and 18 months. For example, five-month-old Eddie reaches out to be picked up and when he is picked up he makes accepting coos and sounds as though he is saying, "That's good. You did just what I wanted you to."

In a more advanced form, eighteen-month-old Sally is stringing together many of what we call "circles of communication"—taking her mother's hand, mother reaching her hand back, and Sally then walking with mother toward the playroom. Here, Sally takes initiative, mother responds, and Sally builds on her mother's response. One circle of communication has been closed. As they walk to the playroom, Sally makes a sound that sounds like "there." Mother responds, "Where?" and Sally points toward the toy chest. Another circle of communication has been closed. As they search for Sally's favorite toys, exchanging grunts, groans, gestures, and the like, many circles of communication are closed, opened, and closed. In normal toddler two-way communication, we will see two and three circles closed in a row, leading up to eventually, at 18 months, as many as 10 or 20 circles being closed in a row.

Two-way communication is, of course, the basis for all language, without which much of learning is impossible. The response an adult gives a child, whose language is just beginning to develop, will play an important role in how confidently a child comprehends and expresses his ideas later on.

When Sally is about to pick up Mother's favorite china bowl, Mother can swoop in silently and pick Sally up (minimal communication). She can use motor, facial, and vocal gestures, as well as words backed up by limits to maximize learning.

Because two-way communication permits information to be shared between two people in a clear, logical manner, it enables a child to figure out important aspects of her social, emotional, and physical world. It is also essential for making assumptions or quick conclusions about whether one is safe or approved of, as well as for holding the kinds of minimal conversations or exchanges of information that are necessary for all learning. For example, based on a few exchanges or gestures, a child can figure out, without words, when she is safe in a group of new people.

## Stage Three: Shared Meanings

A third core process of early development is the ability for learning how to share meanings. This normally occurs between 18 and 36 months, as children learn how to relate their behaviors, sensations, and gestures to the world of ideas. We see this in their use of language when they say, "Give me that," "I am happy," or "I am sad." They are using an idea, as evidenced in their words, to communicate something about what they feel, want, or are going to do.

Children also show their ability to share meanings through ideas in pretend play. Whether the animals are fighting, the dolls are hugging, or there is a tea party, ideas are guiding this play. Through intentional use of language and pretend play, children show that they have reached this level of using ideas. The capacity to share meanings is essential for sharing higher-level information. For example, with ideas, a child can say, "Me mad," or can hug or kiss rather than cling. He can also comprehend the teacher's wishes. When she says, "It's time to go outside!" he knows that it's time to have some fun. With ideas, a child can even master complex concepts like *up and down, hot and cold:* his experiences acquire meaning.

Sharing meanings at a symbolic level is essential for communicating much of the content of what school is all about—from the most basic pleasure of enjoying a story to understanding number and word concepts.

## Stage Four: Emotional Thinking

The fourth process of early childhood development involves emotional thinking. In this stage, children who are three to five years old are organizing ideas or experiences, and learning how to make connections between different ideas. They are learning to organize all the experiences or ideas that have to do with themselves into a sense of self, as well as learning how to organize all the experiences and ideas that have to do with someone else into a picture of another. As part of their ability to organize a sense of who they are, they are also understanding what's inside of themselves and what's outside, what's subjective

# Each Child Is Unique

Our system of caring for and educating children *must* be capable of addressing individual differences and needs, especially during early childhood when so many building blocks are forming for a lifetime. With ingenuity, we can find ways to work within the group situation to see that every child's unique abilities are considered. What follows are some typical child behaviors and ways to approach and respond to each one.

***When a child is frequently clingy:*** We tend to either avoid or give in completely to this kind of behavior. An alternative is to use floor time to establish a new way of relating. You can set limits on the child's intrusiveness by communicating through gestures. You can seek out a child and help her feel close. At the same time, she has to learn a magic word—WAIT. This allows the child to be close by without actually clinging.

***When a child tends to withdraw or become overly passive:*** In this situation, it's important to respect the pace of the child; to take one step at a time, but not to withdraw from him. If the child is reluctant to enter into a group, you can serve as a facilitator in bringing only one other child into the picture first, and gradually another and then another. Be sure to choose a quiet place. If you introduce new ideas slowly, the child will feel more secure as he tries to master his environment. Using this approach during floor time will help the child to become more assertive and take more self-initiative.

***When a child is very aggressive:*** Though difficult to deal with, aggressive behavior can often be transformed by pretend play, during which the child's feelings can be communicated through ideas rather than behavior. At the same time, it's important to use body gestures and tone of voice to set limits. A serious, somewhat stern tone and stance (which gradually gets more serious) is more appropriate (and more effective) than a punitive one. When increasing limits, however, it is important to also increase one's availability for floor time.

***When a child is often inattentive:*** Often, this behavior gets ignored because it doesn't appear to present any serious problems in a group situation. However, children who are frequently inattentive are communicating the need to be focused and engaged. Follow even the most minor signs that indicate a desire and willingness to open a circle of communication. Try to stretch out periods of focusing and relating, and encourage the child to close as many circles of communication as possible. Be sure to build on a child's favored ways of relating during these times (through sounds or movement, looking, etc.)

***When a child is overwhelmed:*** Gradually find out the kinds of things that overwhelm the child (noises, lots of touching, intense emotions, etc.). Offer the child extra security and support when you think he is likely to experience whatever it is that is overwhelming. Learn how to find experiences that help the child feel organized and in control.

or objective; that is, they develop a sense of reality testing. As part of this ability to organize their experiences, they also organize a sense of themselves in terms of mood and self-esteem: Are they a positive person? Optimistic or pessimistic? Negative? Despondent? Thus a picture emerges that is an accumulation of experiences, and these pictures now become more organized.

Children now begin to see themselves in space and time. For example, the sense of time allows them to understand that what they do will have implications for what is going to happen tomorrow. This helps them to have a more mature basis for controlling their impulses. "If I take my nap. I will be able to ride my trike when I wake up."

As part of their sense of space, children in this stage can picture where they are in the world. They know that if they are in school, their mommy is close by and they will see her later in the day. This also helps them to organize their different emotions. They can understand the differences between healthy, constructive assertiveness and destructive aggression, between excitement that's well controlled and excitement that's out of control.

Therefore, this stage of organizing ideas helps children with making connections between different ideas. They can now look for logical connections. Making logical connections is important for abilities like sharing and cooperation. "If I share, others will share with me." Or, "If I'm mean, others will be mean back to me, or I'll get punished, or I won't be liked."

This same ability to connect ideas is also important for understanding why they might feel a certain way. "I was upset today because my mommy was away. . . ." But it is equally important for understanding basic cognitive concepts.

For example, working with puzzles and manipulatives, they learn bigger and smaller, and how to line things up and classify according to shapes and sizes. Virtually all learning—in the early years as well as later on—depends on the ability to connect two or more ideas. The ability to organize thinking and ideas into categories cannot be underestimated.

These four general stages are the foundations of intellectual, emotional, and social functioning in the first four to five years of life and are essential for learning throughout life.

# Children of the Great Depression

## G. H. ELDER

We have followed a group of children from their preadolescent years early in the Depression to their middle-age years, tracing step by step the ways in which deprivation left its mark on relationships and careers, life styles and personalities. The documentation of specific effects has at times entailed a painstaking examination of somewhat fragmentary data on diverse aspects of life experience, often requiring many qualifications. This effort has posed at least as many questions for subsequent inquiry as it has answered.

In this final chapter, we return to main themes in the biographies of individuals and cohorts that experienced the Great Depression. We shall consider, first, the advantages and limitations of the approach here followed as a basis for generalization on the effects of the Depression. It will be well to have in mind our choice of historical time, geographic location, and strategies in carrying out the investigation. Only then can we examine the degree of fit between our findings and the adaptational framework that has guided the analysis. This degree of fit is the focal point of the second part of the chapter. In the third and final section, we shall identify general themes of change since the Depression, using materials that extend well beyond the present study: marriage and family, children's role in the family and community, aspects of work and achievement among the young, and the collective experience of Depression and postwar generations. The relation between social change and the family still represents a largely unexplored territory.

We cannot ignore certain consequences of the Great Depression in other industrial countries that had profound implications for members of the Oakland cohort in World War II. The rise of the Nazi movement is the major example. What do we know about the degree and duration of economic stagnation in the United States relative to conditions in Great Britain, Canada, and Germany? Since this question takes us well beyond the concerns of the present study, it is briefly dealt with in Appendix C.

## The Approach and Other Options

Family adaptations have been viewed in this study as a primary link between economic hardship and the individual—his behavior, personality, and life course. Members of the cohort were born in the early 20s to Caucasian parents in the middle and working classes and spent their childhood and adolescent years in the urban milieus of the San Francisco Bay area. A majority grew up in households which lost heavily in the Depression, including a substantial proportion from the middle class. Economic loss is related to social factors that specify contrasting experiences in the Depression (occupation, education, ethnicity, etc.), but these factors do not identify variations in conditions of life with sufficient accuracy; for example, many of the professional fathers in the Oakland sample lost heavily through unemployment, economic cutbacks, etc. Our approach, then, has been to focus directly on variations in economic hardship (as measured by income loss between 1929 and 1933) among families that were located in the middle and working classes in 1929.

An alternative design might compare the effect of childhood experiences in the Depression and in the postwar era of prosperity. A comparison group would be identified by persons born *after* the economic crisis. One handicap with this type of analysis is that there are many differences between the two childhood eras other than those related to the state of the economy; it would be difficult indeed to disentangle relative deprivation or prosperity from other factors, especially those unique to the epoch. By assessing the effects of economic loss in a single cohort, we have examined the differential effect of the same historical event. The common birthdate means that members of the sample entered the Depres-

*Source:* From Elder, G. (1974). Children of the great depression. In *Children of the Great Depression* (pp. 271–283). Perseus Books Group.

sion and started out life at approximately the same age.

The advantage of confining analysis to a single birth cohort is countered by its limitations for generalization. At least one comparison group which is either older or younger than the Oakland cohort is needed to place life patterns in context and to provide insight on the generality of our findings. From the evidence at hand, we would expect widely varied experiences and outcomes in the Depression across different age groups. Differences in structural constraints and opportunities are known to have varied from year to year in the 30s. Also, age variations can be viewed as a factor in the adaptive potential of the young in situations of socioeconomic change and deprivation. The family dependency of preschool children (circa 1930) would make them more vulnerable than members of the Oakland cohort to the pathogenic effects of economic hardship, while members of an older cohort, with birthdates around 1914, would be under obligation to help struggling parents with family support and would be severely limited in options for employment and advanced education. As one "veteran" put it: "The essence of being in your twenties in the Thirties was that no matter how well tuned up you were, you stayed on the ground. Many of us stayed on the ground, or just above it, for ten years."

In these respects, it is apparent that some risks encountered by older and younger cohorts were generally minimized in the age group of the Oakland children. They were not old enough in the early 1930s to be drawn into full-time roles in family support, and they left home during the incipient stage of war mobilization and economic recovery. The critical phase of intellectual development and social dependency had passed when they entered the 30s; they were old enough to be aware of the crisis besetting their families and the country, and to assume important roles in the household economy. If one were to select an optimum age at which to pass through the Depression decade, it would not differ much from that of the Oakland sample. We must recognize, of course, the undeniable suffering of some of the Oakland parents.

In future research on individuals and families in the Depression, we would favor a cohort which includes the Oakland parents as well as younger adults born during the first decade of

this century. In the present study we could not do justice to the life course of the Oakland parents; the appropriate data were simply not available. The fathers were not interviewed at any point, and the mothers were interviewed only during the first half of the 30s. We could not adequately chart the economic history of families from 1929 to the end of the 30s and into the war years, or trace its impact to household composition and residential patterns, modes of family maintenance, marriage and parent-child relations. With family data of this kind we could at least begin to delineate patterns of economic change in the 30s, the timing and nature of recovery, and their implications for family change.

Knowing what we do about the lives of the Oakland children, there is every reason to expect more profound consequences in the latter stages of the parents' lives. Under what conditions did severe economic hardship lead to disabilities that persisted well beyond the 30s, to a sense of inferiority, a chronic state of poor health, a deep-seated fear of economic insecurity? To some of the Oakland fathers, economic hardships meant despair and helplessness, illness, and alcoholism; and to mothers, emotional distress, humiliation, and a heavy family burden. But their psychology and life pattern in the 40s and 50s, relative to conditions in the Depression, remain a mystery.

This unexamined period is matched by the early life course of the parent generation. To understand why parents responded as they did to crisis situations in the Depression, we would need to know something about their economic and social standards, sex-role values, and preparedness for the adaptive requirements of economic hardships. Inquiry along these lines would take us back to the social history of the grandparent generation, to emigration from Europe, the rural-urban transition, the parents' sociocultural and economic environment during childhood and adolescence.

Relations between the grandparent and parent generations bring into focus the kin network, a sorely neglected aspect of family life in the Depression and more generally in times of crisis. What were the implications of relative isolation from kin for the adaptation of nuclear units to severe economic deprivation? for units with origins in the middle class compared to families of lower status? How did economic aid and kin obligations affect alignments and alienation within the kin system? And what were the social and emotional effects of newly formed three-generation households? Answers to these and related questions bear upon an important theoretical issue: the relative strength and weakness of the nuclear family in adapting to crises in the urban-industrial environment.

Any interpretation of results on the Oakland cohort must take into account its childhood setting and social composition. There is, as we have noted, a fair degree of resemblance between economic change in Oakland and in other large American cities during the 30s, but objective economic indicators cannot be used with confidence to make valid comparative statements of the impact of the Depression and related experiences. Sociopolitical conditions and subjective reality also must be considered. Beyond matters of place, the social characteristics of the sample are sufficient to restrain tendencies to generalize. By and large, neither wealthy nor very poor families (pre-1929) are represented in the sample. Most of the adults are products of the lower-middle and working classes. Throughout the analysis we have given special emphasis to children of the middle class and to the effects of economic loss in their lives, in contrast to the large body of research on children in situations of prolonged, extreme deprivation. The range of social experience among middle- and working-class families offered a broad perspective to our assessment of economic deprivation in the life course. Another important feature of the sample is its ethnic composition. A substantial number of immigrants from Southern Europe and the Scandinavian countries settled in Oakland during the early 1900s and are represented in our sample. The black population of the city is largely a post-Depression phenomenon resulting from the westward movement of Southern blacks to wartime industries.

Two other issues of importance concern the size and representativeness of the sample. Given the option, we would have preferred a larger sample to ensure more stable measurements and greater flexibility in analysis. Nevertheless, the sample is large for long-term studies. Representativeness was subordinated to residential permanence in setting up the longitudinal design.

As a group, however, the Oakland children closely resembled their school classmates on socioeconomic characteristics. All of these considerations, as well as problems distinctive of long-term longitudinal research, have led us to emphasize the suggestive or heuristic aspects of the study. Many additional studies on both similar and different groups—of sharecroppers, farmers, racial minorities, etc.—are needed for an adequate understanding of the human implications of the Depression mosaic.

Limitations are inevitably encountered in the fixed body of data collected before, during, and after the 30s. Retrospective materials are useful in life histories and are often essential to fill the unfortunate number of lacunae, but they are generally a poor substitute for contemporaneous information. No amount of ingenuity can satisfactorily compensate for inadequate statistical information on unemployment among Americans in the 30s, a deficit which also applies to Canada. We have faced similar problems in tracing the effects of economic loss and unemployment in the lives of the Oakland adults. Given our ideal of collecting data to answer preformulated questions, such deficiencies generate some doubt about an investigation which was not envisioned by the original project staff. But if we view the Oakland archive in terms of its potential for this line of approach, *relative* to other options, we can appreciate its resources as a unique opportunity. With this in mind and respect for the archive's limitations, our guideline has been to make the best of what we have.

## Depression Experiences in Personality and the Life Course

Drastic change and adaptive responses provided the focus for our effort to link economic loss among families in the Depression with personality and careers. An extraordinary cultural lag occurred when customary adaptive techniques proved ineffective for coping with urgent problems. Family income in the Oakland sample declined approximately 40 percent between 1929 and 1933, a change which shifted households toward a more labor-intensive economy. More goods and services were produced by family members to meet their own needs. Coupled with this transition were new ways of applying resources and skills to problems, especially through the enlarged family roles of mother and children; adjustments in marital influence and child control; and social strains that developed from the uncertainty, frustration, and adaptive requirements of discordant change and deprivation. These conditions, as proposed linkages between economic loss and the child, were grouped under three general categories: change in the *division of labor,* change in *family relationships,* and *social strains.*

Viewing deprivational situations among the Oakland children in terms of these three conditions, we assumed that their experiences, personality, and life prospects were influenced by environmental changes which accompanied economic loss. This perspective is consistent with the view that children are brought up, intentionally or otherwise, for conditions of life experienced by parents. But the nature of conditions is open to question. Do they represent life situations shaped by the temporary forces of economic depression, or projections onto the future which are based on Depression realities of scarcity and economic insecurity (hence the necessity to maximize forms of economic security), or the anticipation of attractive options in a more abundant life? In the first category we find an array of unintended consequences issuing from family adaptations. Modes of family maintenance—dependence on public assistance, aid from kin and friends, mother's employment, and children's roles in the household economy—constitute responses to family survival requirements in the most basic sense, but they also structured the interactional environment and learning experience of children. We have less evidence of the second type of social condition, which depicts (unconsciously or not) the future in terms of the present (Depression realities), although it does appear in case materials. For example, some Oakland parents encouraged their sons to find economically secure jobs, advice which turned out to be more appropriate for the depressed 30s than for the postwar era of prosperity. Deliberate socialization is consistent with this situation and with the anticipation of a new and more promising world.

Economic loss in the Depression generally produced a disparity between situation and person which called for new adaptations. We assumed that responses to deprivational situations, from autonomous and resilient coping to defensiveness and withdrawal, hinged on adaptive potential involving both personal resources (intellectual skills, etc.) and environmental support within the family; and that children from the middle class ranked higher than those from the working class on the capacity to adapt to change and adversity. Problem-solving resources and support for adaptive responses tend to increase with class position. Middle-class children and parents also rank higher on intellectual resources, and their conceptions of reality are more conducive to effective adaptation in situations of change and uncertainty. In view of these considerations, we expected economic deprivation to influence more adversely the psychological health and life course of children from the working class.

The last factor to be noted in our assessment of economic deprivation in personality and the life course is the circumstance under which Depression experiences are most likely to persist into the adult years. Though few issues have aroused more interest than that of the Depression's legacy, minimal attention has been given to the situations and linkages which affect continuity in the life span. From little more than intuition and self-reflection, hard times during the Depression have been linked to an extraordinary work commitment, a self-conscious desire for security, an inability to partake of pleasure or leisure without guilt feelings. In the realm of child-rearing aspirations, the most popular folk theory asserts that Depression-reared parents strive to endow their offspring with a life free of the hardships and suffering they knew as children; to wit, "We search for affluence with neurotic intensity so that our children will not have to go through what we went through." As soon as we think about conditions leading to such outcomes, we become aware of complexities associated with situational variations in adult life. Are these outcomes more a consequence of adult status, of membership in the upper middle-class, than of early experiences in the Depression? Most informal statements on Depression effects are restricted to this sector of the class structure.

The problem, then, is to specify conditions in the life course which are most likely to favor continuity from the Depression to middle age. Childhood lessons seem most likely to have application to the adult years when situations in each time period are relatively similar. As a general rule, the data supported this hypothesis among men in the Oakland sample; the main effect of deprivation on values occcurred among men who did not achieve higher status than that of their fathers. Status differences among women made little difference in continuities from the Depression since family roles established an overriding bond with the past.

We have briefly identified three general elements in our analysis of the Oakland cohort from 1929 to the mid-60s: proposed *linkages between economic loss and the individual* which structured situations in the 30s (change in the division of labor, change in family relationships, and social strains); variations in *adaptive potential* as a determinant of response to situational change and its psychological impact; and *adult situations*, relative to experiences in the 30s, as a factor in psychological continuity or the enduring effects of the Depression experience. We used modes of adaptive potential and life situations to specify conditions in which family deprivation would be *most* and *least* likely to have certain psychological effects in adulthood. On the assumption that adaptive resources are associated with family status, we expected economic hardship to have less pathogenic consequences for adult health among offspring of middle-class families than among adults from the lower strata. And, as we have noted, adult situations (defined by mobility, etc.) made a difference in the relation between family deprivation and the values of men. The utility and limitations of this general model are most readily seen by tracing relations between economic deprivation, personality, and aspects of the life course. To do so, we have organized our findings in terms of the three linkages, beginning with adaptations in the division of labor.

Economic loss and father's unemployment in the middle and working class were correlated with downward mobility in occupational status, though most deprived families eventually recovered their social position by the early 40s. Unemployment always meant loss of income, but many families, especially in the middle class, received heavy economic losses without joblessness. As the supply of income and savings diminished, families cut back on expenditures, in part by using labor to meet consumption needs, and developed alternative forms of economic maintenance. These options included employment of mother, aid from kin, and dependence on public assistance; reliance on these forms of support was especially prevalent in the working class. Children were most likely to participate in the household economy of deprived families, with girls specializing in domestic tasks and boys in economic roles. Boys sought employment in response to both family and personal needs.

In the area of family relationships, mother's centrality as decision maker and emotional resource is the primary theme among deprived households. Severe economic loss increased the perceived power of mother in family matters within the middle and working class, and diminished father's social prestige, attractiveness, and emotional significance, as perceived by sons and daughters. These conditions weakened father's role as a control figure for the children and the effectiveness of parental control in general, though especially in relation to sons; and encouraged dependence on persons outside the family. More than other children, the sons and daughters of deprived parents sought companionship and counsel among persons outside the home, especially among teachers and friends. Only in the area of occupational choice was the deprived father especially salient to boys, and this finding is restricted to the middle class.

Roles in the deprived household and the matricentric family joined forces in structuring a conducive environment for traditional sex roles and an accelerated movement toward adulthood. Scarcity and labor-intensive adjustments had the effect of lowering adultlike responsibilities toward childhood. Girls were drawn into a household operation which was controlled by mother, whether employed or not, and were oriented toward a domestic future by this experience and constraints on advanced education.

The daughters of deprived parents were most likely to favor domestic activities, adult company, and grown-up status in adolescence, and, if middle-class, to marry earlier than their non-deprived middle-class contemporaries. Family deprivation lessened prospects for education beyond high school. In the middle years of life, a deprived background made a difference in the commitment of women to family life, parenthood, and homemaking in general. Each of these values was linked with family deprivation in the 30s through household responsibilities in a mother-centered household. Family-centered values and a view of life which entails responsibility (e.g., the belief that children mainly change the ways of adults by adding responsibilities) emerged as dominant perspectives in the lives of women who grew up in deprived households.

Family conditions associated with economic loss served to liberate boys from parental controls; oriented them toward adults and adult concerns, including the problem of earning a living; and stressed responsibilities in life. Economic hardships emancipated boys through the autonomy and obligations of work roles, and a household arrangement in which father had less say in family matters than mother. Work roles involved boys from deprived homes in adultlike experiences beyond family boundaries, enlarged their sphere of know-how, and brought greater awareness to matters of economic independence and vocation. These experiences, and the realities of family hardship, accelerated movement toward the adult world. Interest in the company of adults, the desire to be an adult, vocational thinking, and crystallized goals were associated with economic deprivation. In adult life, vocational crystallization tended to minimize the educational disadvantage of family deprivation in worklife and achieved status, regardless of class origin. Value priorities in the deprived group include job security over the potential benefits of occupational risk, responsibility in views of parenthood and children, and satisfactions in the world of family life. However, these values, as well as minimal interest in leisure activity, were related to family deprivation mainly among men who did not advance above their father's status.

It is apparent that many features of child socialization in deprived situations have no clear reference to parental intentions on preparing offspring for the future. Rather they emerged from adaptations to family requirements. Some if not most Depression children were brought up differently from the way in which their parents were raised, but parental intention is much less credible as a source of this difference than structural change and adaptations centering on family needs. In fact, adaptations of this sort may work at cross-purposes in socialization with parental plans or visions for the child. This may have been the case in the domestic upbringing of girls in deprived middle-class homes, and their preference for marriage over advanced education or training. Some unintended consequences of socialization are also illustrated by Farber's study of eighteenth-century Salem. Farber found that "artisan families were responsible for the socialization of persons who were motivated in the extreme for upward social mobility" (1972, p. 201). In this stratum, achievement striving developed out of a way of life that stressed family and kinship as a means of ensuring security of livelihood and status. Such unintended effects on achievement motivation were also evident in the Depression experience, from the incentive value of status loss to pressures to rely on personal resources in getting ahead.

A psychic connection between family deprivation and the Oakland children developed out of social strains and comparisons. Family losses made status or identity uncertain through discordant change on dimensions of family status, among family members (the shift toward female dominance), and between families. Self-consciousness, emotional sensitivity, and emotionality are thought to arise in ambiguous situations, and were found to be correlated with economic deprivation in both social classes, though especially among girls. These emotional states linked conditions of life in deprived families with a relatively early marriage among the daughters of middle-class homes. Family losses increased judgment errors among the Oakland children regarding their status in the eyes of agemates; they believed that they were held in lower esteem than was actually the case. This perception, whether valid or not, was real in its consequences through conflict with self esti-mates; it aroused critical attitudes and sensitivity toward evidence of social elitism and seemed to foster recognition striving among the boys. An-other consistent motivational effect of status change in economic loss is the association be-tween ability and achievement motivation, a re-lation which we interpreted as an index of the degree to which ability is applied or used. In both middle and working classes, achievement motivation was more highly correlated with abil-ity among the offspring of deprived families than among the nondeprived. Lastly, felt hardships in the 30s established a psychological framework or contrast experience which made life appear to be on the upswing between childhood and middle age. Having met difficult times as a child, the off-spring of deprived families were more likely than the nondeprived to feel that life had become more abundant and satisfying.

The final point to be noted on specific relations between economic deprivation and the Oakland cohort concerns adaptive potential in life achieve-ment and health. Middle-class offspring were brighter, more ambitious in goals, and received greater support in problem solving and achieve-ment than the sons and daughters of working-class homes. These differences parallel class vari-ations in the adult status attained by men through education and worklife, and by women through marriage; and they partially account for the more negative effect of economic deprivation among the children of working-class parents. For the most part, however, personal assets in life achievement, which were unrelated to economic loss (intelligence, physical attractiveness of women, etc.), minimized handicaps associated with family situation and limited education.

The implications of class background for adult life are more pronounced in matters of health and well-being. Despite contrary out-comes in the Depression, the overall impact of family deprivation was generally positive among middle-class offspring, with negative outcomes most evident among adults from the working class. Men and women from the de-prived middle class were *more* likely to be judged relatively free of symptoms than the nondeprived, and were also rated higher on ego strength, integration of impulses and strivings, utilization of personal resources, and capacity for growth. They were characterized as more re-silient, more self-confident, and less defensive. On the other hand, most adults of working-class origin showed some impairment, with evidence of psychological health slightly more prevalent in the nondeprived group.

## Summary

Three points summarize the enduring effects of the Depression experience among the Oakland adults: *the paths through which they achieved adult status, as against level of status; adult health and preferences in ways of responding to life's problems; and values.* On the first point, we conclude that family deprivation made life achievement more dependent on effort and accomplishments out-side the educational system. While men from nondeprived families ranked slightly higher on educational attainment, worklife assets and ex-periences counted for more in the deprived group. Likewise, the educational handicap of family deprivation was neutralized by women through their social accomplishments in mar-riage. The favorable career stage of the Oakland cohort in the 30s must be regarded as a key fac-tor in the life accomplishments of adults who grew up in deprived families, when compared to the life course of the non-deprived. Historical research, cited in chapter 7, suggests that the oc-cupational chances of young workers (born in the first decade of the twentieth century) were limited by conditions in the Depression, espe-cially when they had little in the way of formal education and job skills.

On the second main effect, there is evidence that adult health is negatively related to eco-nomic hardships; as was forecast by some ana-lysts in the 30s, though only among the offspring of working-class homes. The opposite relation appears among children of the middle class. The influence of economic hardship was also ex-pressed in sensitivity to economic matters on the domestic scene and in ways of responding to them. Preference for the Democratic party, which is almost entirely limited to the deprived group, can be viewed as a crude index of focal concerns and preferred tactics in national politics.

Lastly, it is clear that economic hardship experienced in the Depression made an enduring contribution to views on "things that matter" in life. The one common value across men and women is the centrality of the family and the importance of children in marriage. Though men from deprived homes did not rank family above work, their priorities and those of women with similar backgrounds exemplify the familistic aura of the postwar years. The parental family in deprived situations did not present an attractive model for emulation, but it socialized girls for a domestic life and projected an adaptive image in difficult times.

Other values which have been attributed to Depression-reared men were linked to economic hardship in the Oakland cohort. Job security is perhaps the best example, though it was seldom given priority among the more able, successful adults. Security concerns emerged among men from deprived homes who were vulnerable to economic fluctuations in the sense that they faced certain limitations in talents and options. Economic hardship made work important, focused attention on getting a job, and presumably inspired hard work, but there is no evidence in our data that work matters more to men from deprived families, relative to other activities, than it does to other men. The valuation of work over family and leisure among highly successful men owes more to their accomplishments than to their background in the Depression.

Economic values from the Depression experience have not received their due in our analysis for lack of appropriate information. This is unfortunate since there is probably a higher ratio of speculation to evidence on this presumed legacy of the 30s than on any other "effect." There is reason to expect economic deprivation to heighten belief in the "power of money," as suggested by the prevalence of monetary rewards in child rearing among families in the lower strata, but we lack evidence at present of a relation between materialistic attitudes and experiences in the 30s. "Depression" rationales for current economic habits in retrospective reports are no substitute for the results of a longitudinal analysis.

By stressing economic deprivation in personality and the life course, we have given little recognition to conditions of life in the nondeprived group and their enduring consequences. The nondeprived have simply represented a comparison group, and yet we might just as well have stressed the effects of economic well-being in the Depression. The findings can in fact be interpreted from this perspective, and we have done so at appropriate points. No comparison yielded more substantial differences in life pattern than the comparison between deprivational groups in the middle class. The relatively nondeprived generally grew up in families headed by fathers who remained employed throughout the 30s; some even improved their earnings and social position. For the most part, household needs did not require employment of the mother or substantial contributions by the children. In most respects, both family situation and opportunities seemed to ensure maximum life chances for these "children of plenty" in an era of generalized privation. And yet from the evidence at hand, this promise does not appear to be fulfilled in their adult lives, at least when compared to the adult experience of children from deprived homes. Beyond the generally acknowledged human costs of economic hardship, especially in the lower strata, the Depression may yield some insights on the social psychology of material abundance, a condition of no small significance in the American experience. Scarcity and abundance are inevitable points of contrast as we move to an overview of central themes from the Depression experience.

# Reflections on the Last Stage—and the First

## ERIK ERIKSON

In wishing to make a contribution to this [work] in honor of Anna Freud, I find my thoughts somewhat dislocated by the fact that Joan Erikson's and my present studies do not concern childhood, but the very last stage of life: old age. To make the most of this I will attempt to restate and to reflect on an overall perspective of human development which promises to reveal some affinities between the end and the beginning of human life. Such a perspective becomes possible in our day when scientific, clinical, and public interest has, over several decades, shown special interest in a series of life stages. There was the Mid-Century White House Conference which was—no doubt in partial response to discoveries of psychoanalysis—dedicated to "a healthy personality for every child." There were the '60s when problems of identity so widely suggested themselves in the dramatic public behavior as well as in the psychopathology of youth and thus called for our psychosocial and historical considerations. And then, indeed, middle and early adulthood were discovered. Thus, the stages of life were highlighted by a historical relativity both in the ways in which they were experienced and in the methods used to conceptualize them at different times by observers of varying ages and interests. Indeed, historical changes have recently mobilized a general, and somewhat alarmed, awareness of the rapidly changing conditions of old age and an intense interest in the special nature of this last stage. Together, these factors will never again permit us to treat masses of survivors as an accidental embarrassment: old age must eventually find a meaningful place in the economic and cultural order—meaningful to the old and to the occupants of all other age groups, beginning with childhood. But this permits us to look at the facts observed and the theories developed and discussed with the new

hope that we may all learn to view infancy and childhood as the "natural" foundation of a truly desirable long life. This also means —and has meant for quite a while now—that we can no longer base our developmental perspectives preponderantly on clinical reconstructions of the past, on a search for regressions to and fixations on ever earlier stages and their conflicts and disbalances. Even our clinical orientation can only gain systematically from the additional study at each stage of life of the potentials for developmental recovery and genuine growth—and this up to the very last stage. There, even "elderlies" (and not only "elders"), rather than sporting a new childishness, may fulfill some of the promises of childhood like those which seem to be contained in such sayings as the biblical "Unless you turn and become like children. . . ." And some of these oldest all-human sayings may gain new meaning in our time when history reveals so shockingly what some (and primarily masculine) values of adulthood have contributed to the chances of a self-destruction of our species.

The timeless sayings of the past also serve to remind us that it is difficult to make any meaningful observations of the developmental details of human life without implying more or less conscious, large-scale configurations which back in Freud's time were still recognized and appreciated without much apology as part of a worker's *Weltanschauung*—that is, his or her way of viewing the design of the world and of human life within it. To begin with a prominent example: if the basic scheme is that of "developmental lines" (A. Freud, 1965), the outline of their details will clarify a firm direction in the linear growth of capacities from "lower" to "higher" stages of development. This naturally reflects the ethos of maturation implicit in the theories of psychosexuality and of the ego: and so the list ranges "from dependency to emotional self-reliance," "from egocentricity to peer relationships," or simply "from dependence to independence" and from "irrational to rational." This scheme has, of course, led to a wealth of observations.

*Source:* From Erikson, E. H. (1984). Reflections on the last stage—and the first. *Psychoanalytic Study of the Child,* 29. Copyright 1984 by Albert J. Solnit; Ruth S. Eissler, and Peter B. Neubauer.

Joan Erikson and I, in turn, have been trying to make explicit an "epigenetic" scheme of psychosocial development—epigenesis being a term first used in embryology. In our vocabulary (E. H. and J. M. Erikson, 1950), the overall term "life *cycle*" forces on our configurations a rounding out of the whole course of life which relates the last stage to the first both in the course of individual lives and in that of generations. We have, somewhat simplistically, designed a chart of stages which (some readers surely saw it coming) I must "once more" briefly present in order to clarify the epigenetic connection between old age and infancy. However, I employ such repetitiousness with ever fewer apologies, because we have learned over the years how difficult it is even for highly trained individuals to keep in mind the logic of a contextual conceptualization of developmental matters. And it is such contextuality which keeps a theory together and helps to make the observations based on it "comprehensible" in Einstein's sense, although they remain forever relative to the position of a single view within the viewpoints of its time and place.

So here is the chart of psychosocial stages. In its horizontals, we designate the stages of life, and this from the bottom up, in consonance with the image of growth and development: Infancy and Early Childhood, the Play Age and the School Age, Adolescence and Young Adulthood, Adulthood and Old Age. Along the diagonal we designate the basic *psychosocial crises*, each of which dominates one stage, beginning in the lower left corner with Basic Trust vs. Basic Mistrust and ending with Integrity vs. Despair in the upper right corner. As can never be said too often, each stage is dominated both by a syntonic and a dystonic quality—that is: Mistrust as well as Trust and Despair as well as Integrity are essential developments, constituting together a "crisis" only in the sense that the syntonic should systematically outweigh or at least balance (but never dismiss) the dystonic. So the diagonal is not an "achievement" scale meant to show what we totally "overcome"—such a simplification comes all too easily in our optimistic culture—the dystonic part of each conflict. But, of course, the final balance of all stages of development must leave the syntonic elements dominant in order to secure a *basic strength* emerging from

each overall crisis: at the beginning, it is Hope, and, at the end, what we are calling Wisdom.

Following the diagonal one step upward from the lower left corner we find the second psychosocial crisis to be that of Autonomy vs. Shame and Doubt, from which the strength Will emerges. Every diagonal step, however, leaves some as yet empty squares beneath, beside, and above it. Beneath Will and beside Hope we must assume some early development in which the crisis of Will is anticipated, while to the left of the Will crisis and thus contemporaneously with it, there must be a Hope already experienced enough to take conflicts of Will into account. Thus begins a vertical development along which Hope can be renewed and mature at every further stage—all the way up to the last stage where we will call it Faith. Indeed, by that time, the individual will have joined the generational cycle and will (with the crisis of Generativity vs. Stagnation) have begun to transmit some forms of faith to coming generations. All these stage-wise connections, on study, prove to be overriding necessities, as they provide the developmental impetus stage for stage in the dominant conflicts of life. In sum, this means that while each basic conflict dominates a particular stage along the diagonal, each has been there in some rudimentary form below the diagonal; and each, once having fully developed during its own dominant stage, will continue (above the diagonal) to mature further during all the subsequent stages and under the dominance of each stage-appropriate crisis.

These, then, are some of the epigenetic principles as applied to psychosocial development. But such development is, of course, systematically intertwined throughout not only with physical growth but also with the *psychosexual stages* which obey corresponding laws. This we will not pursue in this presentation. But it is obvious that in the beginning Hope must be truly "fed" with the libido verified in oral-sensory enjoyment, while in the second stage, the training of Will is invigorated by the experience of anal-muscular mastery. Correspondingly, it must be clear that the psychosexual stages, in turn, could not be fully actual without the contemporaneous maturation of the psychosocial strengths.

In our review, this leads us to the question of the psychosexual status of the last two stages of life—adulthood and old age. For both, I have

**Table 1**

| | 1 | 2 | 3 | 4 | 5 | 6 | 7 | 8 |
|---|---|---|---|---|---|---|---|---|
| Old Age | Integrity vs. Despair. WISDOM | | | | | | | |
| Adulthood | | Generativity vs. Stagnation. CARE | | | | | | |
| Young Adulthood | | | Intimacy vs. Isolation. LOVE | | | | | |
| Adolescence | | | | Identity vs. Confusion. FIDELITY | | | | |
| School Age | | | | | Industry vs. Inferiority. COMPETENCE | | | |
| Play Age | | | | | | Initiative vs. Guilt. PURPOSE | | |
| Early Childhood | | | | | | | Autonomy vs. Shame, Doubt. WILL | |
| Infancy | | | | | | | | Basic Trust vs. Basic Mistrust. HOPE |

found it necessary as well as plausible to suggest a maturation beyond a mere fulfillment of *genitality*. For adulthood to which we ascribe the psychosocial crisis of Generativity vs. Stagnation (which vitalizes procreativity and productivity as well as creativity) I have claimed (exploring once more the full meaning of the Oedipus saga) a *procreative libido* without the satisfaction or sublimation of which, in fact, genitality could not really mature (Erikson, 1980). For presenile old age, in turn, I have claimed a psychosexual stage which keeps a *generalized sensuality* alive even as strictly genital expression weakens.

And so, in returning to the psychosocial stages, we must now account for two of our somewhat grandiose designations of old-age strengths, namely, Integrity (if "vs. Despair") and Wisdom. In comparison with these terms, the designation of Hope in the first stage makes sense enough: for how can one start living without a lot of ready trust, and how to stay alive without some healthy mistrust? On the other hand (and in the other corner), despair certainly seems to be an almost too fitting dystonic "sense" for one who faces a general reduction of capacities as well as the very end of life. But the demand to develop Integrity and Wisdom in old age seems to be somewhat unfair, especially when made by middle-aged theorists—as, indeed, we then were. And we must ask: do the demands that "Integrity" suggests still hold when old age is represented by a fast-increasing, and only reasonably well-preserved group of mere long-lived "elderlies"?

So back to the chart and to the length and width of its four corners: how do they connect with each other? For the upper left corner, we have found a convincing syntonic term and concept: Faith. And here we can at last illustrate an experiential similarity in the chart's uppermost right and lowest left corners. Faith has been given cosmic worldwide contexts by religions and ideologies which offered to true believers some sense of immortality in the form of some unification with a unique historical or cosmic power which in its personalized form we may call an *Ultimate Other*. We can certainly find an experiential basis for such hope in the infant's meeting with the *maternal personage* faced "eye

to eye" as what we may call the *Primal Other*. This basic visual mutuality as experienced at life's beginning and matured up through the stages may well continue to enliven in mature age the vision offered by more or less metaphysical vistas and vedas and of the countenances of prophets and great leaders in faiths and in ideologies, which (alas) confirm hopefulness as the most basic of all human strengths. The relation of (lower left corner) Hope and (upper left) Faith, then, contains a first example of an experiential similarity, namely, that of a mutual "meeting" with an all-important Other—which appears in some form on each stage of life, beginning with the maternal, but soon also the paternal Other confirmed by visual and, indeed, various sensual experiences of rich mutuality.

It is, in this context, an ironical fact, that psychoanalysis has come to attach to this very Other the cold term "Object," which originally meant, of course, the aim of libidinal energy. By the end of life (this Primal Other having become an Ultimate Other), such deeply experienced faith is richly realized not only in religion, but also in mythology and in the arts; and it is confirmed by the detailed rituals and ritualizations which mark the beginning and the end of life in varying cultures—ritualizations that, in our time, must find new ways of expressing an all-human sense of existence and an anticipation of dying. For all this, I assume, the overall term Wisdom may still serve.

The experience of the Other, of course, appears in various forms and with varying certainty throughout life: and here we can refer to the literary evidence of Freud's friendship to [Wilhelm] Fliess. Freud called him, indeed, "der Andere," meaning the Other; and it is very clear that, for a time, they used each other in exchanges of wisdom well beyond professional conversation (Erikson, 1955). Thus, throughout development, a series of "others" will be encountered beginning with the fraternal and sororal others who are first and most ambivalently shared in childhood. Later, when identity is better defined, friends and comrades emerge. And then there is that territorial Other, the "Neighbor," who occupies his own (but often, alas, too close) territory. When he becomes the inimical Other, he can turn into a totally estranged Other, almost a member of another species: and, indeed, I have come to call this process pseudospeciation, a development of truly mandatory importance as human survival comes to depend on the inventive cultivation of shared neighborhoods.

This finally brings us to another basic experience for which we, I think, lack the right word. To truly meet others with whom to share a "We," one must have a sense of "I." In fact, one must have it before one can have the now much advertised "self." Freud obviously was concerned with this, for he at times wrote of an "*Ich*," the English counterpart of which quite transparently is "I," although translation habitually turns it into "ego." This must be emphasized in these reflections because a sense of "I" becomes a most sensitive matter again in old age, as an individual's uniqueness gradually and often suddenly seems to have lost any leeway for further variations such as those which seemed to open themselves with each previous stage. Now non-Being must be faced "as is." But radically limited choices can make time appear forfeited and space depleted quite generally; while (to again follow the psychosocial strengths from left to right) the power of Will is weakened; Initiative and Purpose become uncertain; meaningful work is rare; and Identity restricted to what one has been. And if we follow the line to the adult stages and their bequest of Love (the fulfillment of a sense of "You") and of Care (which holds the generations together), we face that great inequality of fate which can limit the chances in old age of continued intimacy and of generative (and even "grand-generative") relationships. The resulting compulsive preoccupation with the repetition of meaningful memories, however, rather than being only symptomatic of mere helpless regression, may well represent a "regression in the service of development" in Peter Blos's (1980) term: for, in fact, there are now new age-specific conflicts for the sake of which the old person's sense of "I" must become free.

For these conflicts I can for the moment find only existential terms in contrast to strictly psychoanalytic ones. There is, on the border of Being and Not-Being, a sense of Dread in Kierkegaard's meaning, which is not explained by our present theories concerning anxiety; there is a sense of Evil which no classical sense

of guilt necessarily covers; and there is, as we have just pointed out, a sense, or a lack of sense, of "I" or Existential Identity which our identity theories cannot fathom: these are all problems of Being, the open or disguised presence of which we must learn to discern in the everyday involvements of old people.

If we now have begun to connect (in an admittedly sweeping way) the first stage with the last, and both with a major collective institution—here belief systems—we could now assign major institutional trends to all the succeeding stages. To give just one more example—for I really promised only to clarify what I can in the relation of the last stage and the first—the basic need for Autonomy remains related throughout life to the universal human institution of the Law, which defines the leeway and the limits of individual Will, and with its punishments assigns Self-Doubt and Shame to transgressors— all of which, of course, influence the way in which right and wrong are taught to children in a given culture.

Epigenetically speaking, then, we can say that all the later age-specific developments are grounded or rooted in (and in fact dependent on) the strengths developed in infancy, childhood, and adolescence. And if the sense of autonomy "naturally" suffers grievously in old age, as the leeway of independence is constricted, there can also mature an active acceptance of appropriate limitations and a "wise" choice of involvements in vital engagements of a kind not possible earlier in life—and possibly (this we must find out) of potential value to a society of the future. Finally, just because I have been so active in outlining the development of Identity in adolescence, I may repeat that (a few squares to the right) the new and final sense of existential identity can convey a certain freedom from the despair associated with unlived or mislived—or, indeed, overdone—identity potentials.

So we return to what we claimed to be the dominant syntonic trait in the last stage, namely, Integrity. This in its simplest meaning is, of course, a sense of coherence and wholeness which is no doubt at risk under such terminal conditions of a loss of linkages in somatic, psychic, and social organization. What is demanded here could be simply called "Integrality," a readiness to "Keep things together," the best wording of which I owe to a little boy who had asked his mother what was going to happen when he died. "Your soul will go to heaven," she said, "and your body into the ground." "Mommy," he said, "if you don't mind, I'd like to keep my stuff together." Throughout life, then, we must allow for a human being's potential capacity under favorable conditions to let the integrative experience of earlier stages come to fruition; and so our chart allows along the right-most vertical, from infancy up, the gradual maturation of a quality of being, for which integrity does seem to be the right word.

Our anchor point in earliest childhood, however, remains the newborn's and the infant's developmental readiness for *mutuality*, which today is being demonstrated in all detail by the best workers in the area of child development and pediatrics: by which we mean the surprising power of potential unfolding born with this vulnerable creature, if only it is met in its readiness for energizing as well as instructive interplay, as it and its caretakers (literally) face each other. Only when such potentialities are studied exhaustively can clinical observers know what potentials are endangered in early situations at risk or where mutuality was, in fact, broken in misdevelopment.

We have circumscribed a lifetime, then. But the mere mention of mutuality will remind us of what is missing in this presentation, namely, a detailed discussion of Young Adulthood and its crisis of Intimacy and Isolation which is decisive in mobilizing the lifelong power of Love; and of Adulthood itself with its crisis of Generativity vs. Stagnation, which brings to maturation the adult strength of Care—and its demands for generational mutuality. This second-to-the-last stage on our diagonal bequeaths to the last what we called a grand-generative aspect of old age: a general grandparenthood, then, which must demand a useful and mutual place in the life of children, offering to the growing as well as to the old individuals an energizing as well as disciplined interaction according to the mores of technology and culture. As we reveal the potentials of early interplay, perhaps we will at last recognize what, in spite of such historical and cultural relativities, is invariantly human—that is, true for the whole human species and thus part of an indivisible specieshood which mankind can no longer afford to ignore.

## References

Blos, P. (1980). The life cycle as indicated by the nature of the transference in the psychoanalysis of children. *Int. J. Psychoanal.*, 61: 146–151.

Erikson, E. H. (1955). Freud's 'The Origins of Psycho-Analysis.' *Int. J. Psychoanal.*, 36: 1–15.

——— (1980). On the generational cycle. *Int. J. Psychoanal.*, 61: 213–223.

——— (1982). *The Life Cycle Completed.* New York: Norton.

——— & Erikson, J. M. (1950). Growth and crisis of the "healthy personality." In *Symposium on the Healthy Personality*, ed. M. J. E. Senn. New York: Josiah Macy, Jr. Foundation, pp. 91–146.

Freud, A. (1965). Normality and pathology in childhood, *W.*, 6.

Freud, S. (1954). *The Origins of Psychoanalysis.* New York: Basic Books.

# Some Aspects of Operations

## JEAN PIAGET

In the context of this paper an operation is an action which is internalized and is reversible; that is, it can take place in either direction. It is characteristic for an operation to be part of a total structure. We cannot conceive of a single operation in isolation; rather, each operation is an integral part of a whole, which in turn consists of many operations. For example, the structure of classification consists of many operations of logical classes (grouping of items with common characteristics) or the structure of seriation consists of the operations of putting things into an ascending or descending order. What, then, is a structure? A structure is a system with a set of laws that apply to the system as a whole and not only to its elements. For instance, within the structure of the series of whole numbers there are laws of groups which apply, there are other laws of lattices which apply. Both the laws of group and the laws of lattice apply to the whole system and not just to any isolated number of any isolated element within the system. These laws, moreover, are not static laws, they are laws of transformation. A given structure is characterized by the type of transformation which its laws represent. To give, once again, an example: If, in the series of whole numbers, we add seven plus five, we get twelve. Seven and five are both prime numbers. Twelve, on the other hand, is divisible by two, three, four, and six, so we have, in a real sense, performed a transformation.

A second characteristic of structures is that they are self-regulating; there is a sort of closure. When we apply the laws of transformation to any element of the series of whole numbers, we get another element of the same series. It's a system that is closed in itself and, moreover, we don't have to go outside the system for such laws. The whole system and the functioning of the laws within the system can go on indefinitely without any external elements. An example: A structure is

not observable. For this reason many empiricists don't like the notion of structure. They simply don't believe in it. But although it cannot be observed, it is nonetheless a psychological reality. A structure is the sum total of what a child's mind can do. But a child, or indeed an adult, is not aware of the structures that underlie his intellectual work. If an adult knows and applies logic or mathematics, he won't be able to describe to himself the structures that enable him to function intellectually as he does. Even so, the structures exist. As we observe not other people's behavior, but their thought processes, we can see the laws which characterize intellectual structures. Also, we can witness the appearance of new psychological realities when a structure solidifies. For instance, at the moment of solidification, one element brings along the other elements of the structure, so that there is a feeling of intellectual necessity, in fact, inevitability. Let me give you an example: We have experimented with seriation of sticks of different lengths. We give the child a series of ten sticks differing in about a centimeter in length and ask him to put them in order from the shortest to the longest. Young children respond to this request by putting couples of sticks together: a small one and a big one, a small one and a big one. Some children manage triplets. But that is all they are able to do. Somewhat later on, they will be able to make a real series but they do it by trial and error. They will put down a random number of sticks, and they will correct them until they look right. But eventually, at the age of seven or eight, children go about seriation very systematically. They'll find the smallest stick and then place the smallest of all the sticks that remain next to it; then find the smallest of the remaining ones and place it again until the whole series is constructed. In this way, a child builds his structure without any error and at the same time he is coordinating his actions. One stick, he knows, is bigger than all those that have preceded it, and smaller than all those that remain. He knows this because of the systematic way in which he has built his structure. Here, then, we have the con-

*Source:* Piaget, J. (1972). Some aspects of operations. In M. W. Piets (Ed.), *Play and development* (pp. 15–27). New York: Norton.

cept of reversibility: If the stick on one end of the series of sticks of unequal lengths is the longest of them all, then the stick on the other end must be the shortest. A seven-year-old learns this all in one action, simply by virtue of the internal relations involved in the structure.

Now what is this structure? In this instance of seriation which we just mentioned, the structure is a system of asymmetric relationships. We mean by this the following: If stick number one is longer than stick number two, then stick number two cannot possibly be longer than stick number one. The structure is transitive. I would like to look at this aspect of transitivity. If the ability to order things systematically is a real structure, then the child should be capable of carrying out other relationships of transitivity at the same time that he is capable of ordering sticks of different lengths.

We examined this proposition and presented a child with two sticks, stick A being longer than stick B. The child noted which one was longer. Then we hid A, the longer one, under the table and gave the child a third stick, C, which was shorter than the middle-sized one, B, which at this point was clearly visible. We then asked him to compare the two visible sticks with the third hidden one. Young children at the stage where they are making couples in the seriation would say that they couldn't tell whether this one was shorter or longer than the other one, because they hadn't seen them together. But a group of seven- or eight-year-old youngsters, the age when children are able to build seriation systematically, will say, "Well, of course, stick C is shorter than stick A; it just goes without saying."

It is clear, then, that at seven or eight, children experience a feeling of necessity apropos of transitive relationships. They don't have to see the two sticks together; they just know that C must be shorter than A if A is larger than B and B is larger than C. This seems to verify to me the psychological existence of a structure even though structures as such are not observable. What we can observe, however, is a child's behavior in relation to things in his environment, and from this we can infer structure.

My coworkers and I have studied the nature and development of operations for many years. For the past several years, however, we have been working on other problems, of which two experiments in the area of memory shall be discussed here. The first one is based on the above seriation of little sticks of increasing size. In this case, the young children with whom we worked did not construct the order themselves, but were shown a system already made—a system of sticks getting bigger and bigger and bigger. A week later we asked these children what they remembered of it. It turned out that they remembered the experiment in accordance with the stage in which they would have been, had they been asked to construct it themselves. Some of them claimed that a week before we had shown them couples of sticks: a big one, a little one, a big one, a little one, and so on. Others maintained that we had shown them triplets: a big one, a middle-sized one, a small one, a big one, a middle-sized one, a small one, and so on. The striking thing was that the children remembered not what they had perceived, but their own interpretation of the precept. They interpreted the experiment on their own level of assimilation. There is another aspect to this experiment which is even more striking. Six months later, 70 per cent of the same age group of children had a better recollection of what we had shown them than they did a week after the initial demonstration. They had not seen this display in the meantime; instead, we met with them again six months later and asked them if they recalled what we had shown them a long time ago, and 70 per cent of them had progressed in the following manner: Those that had remembered the sticks in couples now remembered triplets.

The memory, then, is a retention of how one has interpreted things at the time of encounter, but it becomes more realistic as the intellectual interpretation improves. Perhaps there is a clue in this for a student preparing for exams. If he starts preparing himself six months before, his memory may have gotten better by the time he has to take the exam.

In another experiment concerning memory, we showed some young children three glass containers, two with water and one empty. Container A had blue water, container B had red water, and C was used as an intermediary so that we could change the red water into glass A and the blue water into glass B. When we questioned these children who had, as yet, no notion of transitivity, as to what they remembered about this little procedure, they didn't recall the use of container C at all. They described what we did in the following manner: "You took this glass (A) and that glass (B) and you poured them into each other, and that changed the red in one of them and the blue in the other." They even started to do it themselves and we had to stop them so that they wouldn't pour their water all over the table. Not being as yet in possession of the structure involved, they totally ignored its existence in this particular experiment. The interesting thing here is that even when we were not interested in operations proper but were looking specifically at memory, we ran into more evidence for the existence of operations. The same happened when we studied the problems of causality. We were, for instance, looking at children's ideas on how movement is transmitted. We had a number of balls in a trough, marked A through H. We let ball A run down the trough to hit the others and all of them stayed still except, of course, for H, which moved off the end of the row. Children who have acquired the notion of transitivity explain this by saying that something moved across this row of little balls from A to H and that it was H where the movement continued. But at an earlier age, they have ideas like this: Ball A came down the trough and then went around behind them and scooted out the other end. So here, when looking at cause-and-effect relations, we run again into the question of the operational level of children. There is, however, one phenomenon of general validity in the development of operations, a phenomenon which I have called decallage: It is the fact that the same operations sometimes appear in the same child at different times, according to the specific content to which they are applied. Thus, children who already have the notion of transitivity of length nonetheless fail to understand the transitivity of weight. We did the following experiment with children who already could solve the problem of transitivity of length: We had two brass cylinders, A and B, of the same size and the same weight. We also had a leaden ball C, which all the children believed to be heavier than either A or B. Then we would ask them to compare B and C on the scale. They

would weigh the items and find that C weighed the same as B. That was a big surprise to them, but they believed it. Then we repeated the original question and they would assert again that A and B weighed the same, and that B and C weighed the same. When, however, we asked them, "What about A and C? Aren't they the same weight?" They said, "Oh, no." They wouldn't accept it. "Maybe once (as if by chance) C might weigh the same as A," they conjectured, "but not twice." This sort of thinking goes on until about the age of nine and is analogous to the findings of the Binet-Simon test which consists of ordering five boxes of the same volume but of different weights. That, too, is understood at about nine or ten, but not at an earlier age.

Here is yet another example: According to the law of conservation of matter, the amount of plasticene in a given ball remains constant even if you change its shape. Children of seven or eight years will agree that this is so, but they will not believe until they are nine or ten that two balls weigh the same, even though their shapes differ. The question is *why?* Why do the same operations in the selfsame child occur two or three years apart, if and when they are applied to a different content? The fact is that these operations are concrete. By this we mean that the child understands them only with regard to specific objects. He does not hypothesize, and some objects seem to defy logic more than others. Length, for instance, is a very simple, easily understood characteristic, but not weight. Weight is hard to understand. Young children will say, for instance, that an object dangling from a string high up in the air must be light; and if it hangs down very low, they conclude that it must be heavy.

If one object is resting on another and extends over the edge, they'll say that the part of the object that is resting weighs, but the part that is hanging doesn't weigh. So weight has its own dynamic properties and is much more difficult to put into a logical or operational structure than, say length. A number of authors who criticize my notion of stages forget that there is this quite well documented phenomenon of decallage, which testifies to their existence. One might wonder if it's possible to develop a theory of decallage. I hope so. I think that our work on causality may lead us in that direction. The essential thing, it seems to me, is the nature of the object—the resistance of the object to which the operations are applied.

In the development of operations the subject follows more or less regular laws of development, but not the objects. They vary greatly in being accessible to logic. I would just like to point out that there is a very similar problem in physics, the problem of understanding friction. There is no general theory of friction and each case is explained in its own terms. And the physicist finds it equally as difficult to explain friction as we do explaining decallage.

I would like to turn now to some questions regarding the origin of operations, since they are formed by what I call reflexive abstraction. Simple abstraction leads to finding out properties of objects themselves. If, for instance, we pick up a couple of objects and hold them in our hands and weigh them and find that one is heavier than the other, that is something we have learned about specific objects. It is a qualitative thing about the object. Reflexive abstraction, on the other hand, does not stem from observing objects, but derives from actions—our own actions. I would like to give an example that a friend of mine told me and to which he attributes his career as a mathematician. When he was a small boy, he was counting some stones and he counted them from left to right and found there were ten. Then he counted them from right to left and, lo and behold, there were ten again. Then he put them in a circle, and finding ten once again, he was very, very excited. He found, essentially, that the sum is independent of the order. This is a discovery. It is a reflexive abstraction stemming from his own actions. The order was not in the stones themselves. It was his actions that gave the stones their orderly arrangement. The sum wasn't in the stones either; there was no sum until he came and put the stones in one-to-one correspondence with the number system. What he found, then, was that his action of ordering the stones and his other action of adding them up were independent of one another, and a different ordering action did not lead to a different sum. Reflexive abstraction is a general practice in mathematics. New findings

in mathematics are produced by carrying out operations on other operations. Similarly, children develop as they apply psychological operations to other operations. Numerical multiplication, for instance, is simply a series of additions (another kind of operation): Three added to three added to three many times. A further example that develops much later in a child's life is proportionality.* There we have an equality of two relations which themselves depend upon numerical multiplication. And then, even later than that, there is the notion of distributivity, which in turn presupposes the notion of proportions. It's an operation carried out on another operation, namely proportionality. Distributivity may look simple. It may look as if any child who knows how to add and multiply and who understands adding and multiplying could understand the distributive law. But this is not so; distributivity is understood very late in development. We have a couple of experiments in this area, one from the realm of physics. We have an elastic band with some marks on it. We show it to the child and ask him to predict where those marks will be when we stretch the band. Until eleven or twelve years of age, children understand this to be a question of addition. They don't understand that when the elastic is stretched over its whole length, the marks will be distributed differently and that the problem is one of a distributive relationship. They just think that something is going to be added somewhere when the elastic is stretched, so they are unable to predict where the marks will be. Some people might point out that what we are talking about is a physical difficulty and not an operational one. To check that, we set up an other experiment. In that one we had two glasses, each about one-third full of water, and another empty glass. We poured the water from the first two into the third one. Then we doubled the amount of water

---

*In a different context, Piaget described an experiment about proportionality involving two kinds of disks, a large number of which—say ten—were marked X and a small number of which—say three—were marked O. The disks were placed in a container and children were asked to reach into the container and to predict how many O disks and X disks they would have picked up.

in the third one and asked children to predict where it would be in the first two glasses when we poured it back into them. It is not until eleven or twelve years of age that children are able to predict that there will now be twice as much in glass 1 and 2 because there was twice as much in the third glass. They were able to state that there would be "a little more," but the proportional understanding of distributivity was not at their disposal.

It is the idea of reflexive abstraction which helps us to see development as a series of regulatory thought processes, not only as the necessary result of either heredity or experience. I have two colleagues on whom I've been calling in my work, one of them named Berlin, who is a neobehaviorist and sees me as a neobehaviorist also. The other one, named Belling, is a maturationist and sees me as a maturationist also. To Berlin, then, intellectual knowledge comes from contacts with the external world, whereas Belling thinks that it is all a question of maturation of the nervous system. The truth is that I am neither a maturationist nor a neobehaviorist. I am an interactionist. What interests me is the creation of new thoughts that are not preformed, not predetermined by nervous system maturation nor predetermined by encounters with the environment, but are constructed within the individual himself, constructed internally through the process of reflexive abstraction and constructed externally through the process of experience. There is, in other words, a third hypothesis possible, in addition to the behaviorist's and the maturationist's. It is not maturation per se or the environment in and of itself which brings about intellectual development. Rather, it is education which makes reflexive abstraction possible. This goes for intellectual processes in general and in particular for language. Language has a logic of its own and implicit operations.

I would like, at this juncture, to describe some experimental work which was done by Hermine St. Clair in our laboratories in Geneva. She took two groups of children, one of "conservers" (children who understand the principle of conservation of a given volume or weight) and the other of "nonconservers." She found that there were significant systematic differences

in the way they used language in certain areas. For instance, the "nonconservers" used what linguists call scalers. They would describe things in terms of being big and little and fat. Whereas the "conservers" used what linguists call vectors or comparatives; for instance, "this pencil is bigger than that one, but it's thinner than," and so on. So there clearly was here a demonstrable and tight connection between linguistic level and operational level. Then she went on to do some work with the first group, the "nonconservers," to train them to use language that was similar to the language of the "conservers." She trained them in the use of comparatives and the other characteristics of the more highly developed language, thinking that perhaps the more sophisticated language would lead to a higher level of operational thinking in these children. When she retested them, however, she found that they used the more sophisticated language but there was almost no difference in their operational thinking. Words did not change their thought processes, although 10 per cent of them did make a small cognitive progress with the help of vocabulary. These children, however, were probably in an interstage and ready for the next cognitive step anyway. Language, then, does not seem to be the way to develop intelligence in children.

By way of concluding, I would like to speak a few words on the pedagogical applications of what I've been telling you today. I'm not an educator, I have no advice to give. Education is an area of its own and educators must find the appropriate methods, but what I've found in my research seems to me to speak in favor of an active methodology in teaching. Children should be able to do their own experimenting and their own research. Teachers, of course, can guide them by providing appropriate materials, but the essential thing is that in order for a child to understand something, he must construct it himself, he must re-invent it. Every time we teach a child something, we keep him from inventing it himself. On the other hand, that which we allow him to discover by himself will remain with him visibly, as it did in the case of my mathematician friend, for all the rest of his life.

# Interaction between Learning and Development

## L. S. VYGOTSKY

The problems encountered in the psychological analysis of teaching cannot be correctly resolved or even formulated without addressing the relation between learning and development in school-age children. Yet it is the most unclear of all the basic issues on which the application of child development theories to educational processes depends. Needless to say, the lack of theoretical clarity does not mean that the issue is removed altogether from current research efforts into learning; not one study can avoid this central theoretical issue. But the relation between learning and development remains methodologically unclear because concrete research studies have embodied theoretically vague, critically unevaluated, and sometimes internally contradictory postulates, premises, and peculiar solutions to the problem of this fundamental relationship; and these, of course, result in a variety of errors.

Essentially, all current conceptions of the relation between development and learning in children can be reduced to three major theoretical positions.

The first centers on the assumption that processes of child development are independent of learning. Learning is considered a purely external process that is not actively involved in development. It merely utilizes the achievements of development rather than providing an impetus for modifying its course.

In experimental investigations of the development of thinking in school children, it has been assumed that processes such as deduction and understanding, evolution of notions about the world, interpretation of physical causality, and mastery of logical forms of thought and abstract logic all occur by themselves, without any influence from school learning. An example of

such a theory is Piaget's extremely complex and interesting theoretical principles, which also shape the experimental methodology he employs. The questions Piaget uses in the course of his "clinical conversations" with children clearly illustrate his approach. When a five-year-old is asked "why doesn't the sun fall?" it is assumed that the child has neither a ready answer for such a question nor the general capabilities for generating one. The point of asking questions that are so far beyond the reach of the child's intellectual skills is to eliminate the influence of previous experience and knowledge. The experimenter seeks to obtain the tendencies of children's thinking in "pure" form, entirely independent of learning.

Similarly, the classics of psychological literature, such as the works by Binet and others, assume that development is always a prerequisite for learning and that if a child's mental functions (intellectual operations) have not matured to the extent that he is capable of learning a particular subject, then no instruction will prove useful. They especially feared premature instruction, the teaching of a subject before the child was ready for it. All effort was concentrated on finding the lower threshold of learning ability, the age at which a particular kind of learning first becomes possible.

Because this approach is based on the premise that learning trails behind development, that development always outruns learning, it precludes the notion that learning may play a role in the course of the development or maturation of those functions activated in the course of learning. Development or maturation is viewed as a precondition of learning but never the result of it. To summarize this position: Learning forms a superstructure over development, leaving the latter essentially unaltered.

The second major theoretical position is that learning *is* development. This identity is the essence of a group of theories that are quite diverse in origin.

*Source:* Vygotsky, L. S. (1978). Interaction between learning and development. In L. S. Vygotsky, *Mind in Society: the development of higher psychological processes* (pp. 79–91). Cambridge MA: Harvard University Press.

One such theory is based on the concept of reflex, an essentially old notion that has been extensively revived recently. Whether reading, writing, or arithmetic is being considered, development is viewed as the mastery of conditioned reflexes; that is, the process of learning is completely and inseparably blended with the process of development. This notion was elaborated by James, who reduced the learning process to habit formation and identified the learning process with development.

Reflex theories have at least one thing in common with theories such as Piaget's: in both, development is conceived of as the elaboration and substitution of innate responses. As James expressed it, "Education, in short, cannot be better described than by calling it the organization of acquired habits of conduct and tendencies to behavior." Development itself is reduced primarily to the accumulation of all possible responses. Any acquired response is considered either a more complex form of or a substitute for the innate response.

But despite the similarity between the first and second theoretical positions, there is a major difference in their assumptions about the temporal relationship between learning and developmental processes. Theorists who hold the first view assert that developmental cycles precede learning cycles; maturation precedes learning and instruction must lag behind mental growth. For the second group of theorists, both processes occur simultaneously; learning and development coincide at all points in the same way that two identical geometrical figures coincide when superimposed.

The third theoretical position on the relation between learning and development attempts to overcome the extremes of the other two by simply combining them. A clear example of this approach is Koffka's theory, in which development is based on two inherently different but related processes, each of which influences the other. On the one hand is maturation, which depends directly on the development of the nervous system; on the other hand is learning, which itself is also a developmental process.

Three aspects of this theory are new. First, as we already noted, is the combination of two seemingly opposite viewpoints, each of which has been encountered separately in the history of science. The very fact that these two viewpoints can be combined into one theory indicates that they are not opposing and mutually exclusive but have something essential in common. Also new is the idea that the two processes that make up development are mutually dependent and interactive. Of course, the nature of the interaction is left virtually unexplored in Koffka's work, which is limited solely to very general remarks regarding the relation between these two processes. It is clear that for Koffka the process of maturation prepares and makes possible a specific process of learning. The learning process then stimulates and pushes forward the maturation process. The third and most important new aspect of this theory is the expanded role it ascribes to learning in child development. This emphasis leads us directly to an old pedagogical problem, that of formal discipline and the problem of transfer.

Pedagogical movements that have emphasized formal discipline and urged the teaching of classical languages, ancient civilizations, and mathematics have assumed that regardless of the irrelevance of these particular subjects for daily living, they were of the greatest value for the pupil's mental development. A variety of studies have called into question the soundness of this idea. It has been shown that learning in one area has very little influence on overall development. For example, reflex theorists Woodworth and Thorndike found that adults who, after special exercises, had achieved considerable success in determining the length of short lines, had made virtually no progress in their ability to determine the length of long lines. These same adults were successfully trained to estimate the size of a given two-dimensional figure, but this training did not make them successful in estimating the size of a series of other two-dimensional figures of various sizes and shapes.

According to Thorndike, theoreticians in psychology and education believe that every particular response acquisition directly enhances overall ability in equal measure. Teachers believed and acted on the basis of the theory that the mind is a complex of abilities—powers of observation, attention, memory, thinking, and so forth—and that any improvement in any specific ability results in a general improvement in all abilities. According to this theory, if the student increased the attention he paid to Latin grammar, he would increase his abilities to focus attention on any task. The words "accuracy," "quick-wittedness" "ability to reason," "memory," "power of observation," "attention," "concentration," and so forth are said to denote actual fundamental capabilities that vary in accordance with the material with which they operate; these basic abilities are substantially modified by studying particular subjects, and they retain these modifications when they turn to other areas. Therefore, if someone learns to do any single thing well, he will also be able to do other entirely unrelated things well as a result of some secret connection. It is assumed that mental capabilities function independently of the material with which they operate, and that the development of one ability entails the development of others.

Thorndike himself opposed this point of view. Through a variety of studies he showed that particular forms of activity, such as spelling, are dependent on the mastery of specific skills and material necessary for the performance of that particular task. The development of one particular capability seldom means the development of others. Thorndike argued that specialization of abilities is even greater than superficial observation may indicate. For example, if, out of a hundred individuals we choose ten who display the ability to detect spelling errors or to measure lengths, it is unlikely that these ten will display better abilities regarding, for example, the estimation of the weight of objects. In the same way, speed and accuracy in adding numbers are entirely unrelated to speed and accuracy in being able to think up antonyms.

This research shows that the mind is not a complex network of *general* capabilities such as observation, attention, memory, judgment, and so forth, but a set of specific capabilities, each of which is, to some extent, independent of the others and is developed independently. Learning is more than the acquisition of the ability to think; it is the acquisition of many specialized abilities for thinking about a variety of things. Learning does not alter our overall ability to focus attention but rather develops various abilities to focus attention on a variety of things. According to this view, special training affects overall development only when its elements, material, and processes are similar across specific domains; habit governs us. This leads to the conclusion that because each activity depends on the material with which it operates, the development of consciousness is the development of a set of particular, independent capabilities or of a set of particular habits. Improvement of one function of consciousness or one aspect of its activity can affect the development of another only to the extent that there are elements common to both functions or activities.

Developmental theorists such as Koffka and the Gestalt School—who hold to the third theoretical position outlined earlier—oppose Thorndike's point of view. They assert that the influence of learning is never specific. From their study of structural principles, they argue that the learning process can never be reduced simply to the formation of skills but embodies an intellectual order that makes it possible to transfer general principles discovered in solving one task to a variety of other tasks. From this point of view, the child, while learning a particular operation, acquires the ability to create structures of a certain type, regardless of the diverse materials with which she is working and regardless of the particular elements involved. Thus, Koffka does not conceive of learning as limited to a process of habit and skill acquisition. The relationship he posits between learning and development is not that of an identity but of a more complex relationship. According to Thorndike, learning and development coincide at all points, but for Koffka, development is always a larger set than learning. Schematically, the relationship between the two processes could be depicted by two concentric circles, the smaller symbolizing the learning process and the larger the developmental process evoked by learning.

Once a child has learned to perform an operation, he thus assimilates some structural principle whose sphere of application is other than just the operations of the type on whose basis the principle was assimilated. Consequently, in making one step in learning, a child makes two steps in development, that is, learning and development do not coincide. This concept is the essential aspect of the third group of theories we have discussed.

## Zone Of Proximal Development: A New Approach

Although we reject all three theoretical positions discussed above, analyzing them leads us to a more adequate view of the relation between learning and development. The question to be framed in arriving at a solution to this problem is complex. It consists of two separate issues: first, the general relation between learning and development; and second, the specific features of this relationship when children reach school age.

That children's learning begins long before they attend school is the starting point of this discussion. Any learning a child encounters in school always has a previous history. For example, children begin to study arithmetic in school, but long beforehand they have had some experience with quantity—they have had to deal with operations of division, addition, subtraction, and determination of size. Consequently, children have their own preschool arithmetic, which only myopic psychologists could ignore.

It goes without saying that learning as it occurs in the preschool years differs markedly from school learning, which is concerned with the assimilation of the fundamentals of scientific knowledge. But even when, in the period of her first questions, a child assimilates the names of objects in her environment, she is learning. Indeed, can it be doubted that children learn speech from adults; or that, through asking questions and giving answers, children acquire a variety of information; or that, through imitating adults and through being instructed about how to act, children develop an entire repository of skills? Learning and development are interrelated from the child's very first day of life.

Koffka, attempting to clarify the laws of child learning and their relation to mental development, concentrates his attention on the simplest learning processes, those that occur in the preschool years. His error is that, while seeing a similarity between preschool and school learning, he fails to discern the difference—he does not see the specifically new elements that school learning introduces. He and others assume that the difference between preschool and school learning consists of non-systematic learning in one case and systematic learning in the other.

But "systematicness" is not the only issue; there is also the fact that school learning introduces something fundamentally new into the child's development. In order to elaborate the dimensions of school learning, we will describe a new and exceptionally important concept without which the issue cannot be resolved: the zone of proximal development.

A well known and empirically established fact is that learning should be matched in some manner with the child's developmental level. For example, it has been established that the teaching of reading, writing, and arithmetic should be initiated at a specific age level. Only recently, however, has attention been directed to the fact that we cannot limit ourselves merely to determining developmental levels if we wish to discover the actual relations of the developmental process to learning capabilities. We must determine at least two developmental levels.

The first level can be called the *actual developmental level,* that is, the level of development of a child's mental functions that has been established as a result of certain already *completed* developmental cycles. When we determine a child's mental age by using tests, we are almost always dealing with the actual developmental level. In studies of children's mental development it is generally assumed that only those things that children can do on their own are indicative of mental abilities. We give children a battery of tests or a variety of tasks of varying degrees of difficulty, and we judge the extent of their mental development on the basis of how they solve them and at what level of difficulty. On the other hand, if we offer leading questions or show how the problem is to be solved and the child then solves it, or if the teacher initiates the solution and the child completes it or solves it in collaboration with other children—in short, if the child barely misses an independent solution of the problem—the solution is not regarded as indicative of his mental development. This "truth" was familiar and reinforced by common sense. Over a decade even the profoundest thinkers never questioned the assumption; they never entertained the notion that what children can do with the assistance of others might be in some sense even more indicative of their mental development than what they can do alone.

Let us take a simple example. Suppose I investigate two children upon entrance into school, both of whom are ten years old chronologically and eight years old in terms of mental development. Can I say that they are the same age mentally? Of course. What does this mean? It means that they can independently deal with tasks up to the degree of difficulty that has been standardized for the eight-year-old level. If I stop at this point, people would imagine that the subsequent course of mental development and of school learning for these children will be the same, because it depends on their intellect. Of course, there may be other factors, for example, if one child was sick for half a year while the other was never absent from school; but generally speaking, the fate of these children should be the same. Now imagine that I do not terminate my study at this point, but only begin it. These children seem to be capable of handling problems up to an eight-year-old's level, but not beyond that. Suppose that I show them various ways of dealing with the problem. Different experimenters might employ different modes of demonstration in different cases: some might run through an entire demonstration and ask the children to repeat it, others might initiate the solution and ask the child to finish it, or offer leading questions. In short, in some way or another I propose that the children solve the problem with my assistance. Under these circumstances it turns out that the first child can deal with problems up to a twelve-year-old's level, the second up to a nine-year-old's. Now, are these children mentally the same?

When it was first shown that the capability of children with equal levels of mental development to learn under a teacher's guidance varied to a high degree, it became apparent that those children were not mentally the same age and that the subsequent course of their learning would obviously be different. This difference between twelve and eight, or between nine and eight, is what we call *the zone of proximal development. It is the distance between the actual developmental level as determined by independent problem solving and the level of potential development as determined through problem solving under adult guidance or in collaboration with more capable peers.*

If we naively ask what the actual developmental level is, or, to put it more simply, what more independent problem solving reveals, the most common answer would be that a child's actual developmental level defines functions that have already matured, that is, the end products of development. If a child can do such-and-such independently, it means that the functions for such-and-such have matured in her. What, then, is defined by the zone of proximal development, as determined through problems that children cannot solve independently but only with assistance? The zone of proximal development defines those functions that have not yet matured but are in the process of maturation, functions that will mature tomorrow but are currently in an embryonic state. These functions could be termed the "buds" or "flowers" of development rather than the "fruits" of development. The actual developmental level characterizes mental development retrospectively, while the zone of proximal development characterizes mental development prospectively.

The zone of proximal development furnishes psychologists and educators with a tool through which the internal course of development can be understood. By using this method we can take account of not only the cycles and maturation processes that have already been completed but also those processes that are currently in a state of formation, that are just beginning to mature and develop. Thus, the zone of proximal development permits us to delineate the child's immediate future and his dynamic developmental state, allowing not only for what already has been achieved developmentally but also for what is in the course of maturing. The two children in our example displayed the same mental age from the viewpoint of developmental cycles already completed, but the developmental dynamics of the two were entirely different. The state of a child's mental development can be determined only by clarifying its two levels: the actual developmental level and the zone of proximal development.

I will discuss one study of preschool children to demonstrate that what is in the zone of proximal development today will be the actual developmental level tomorrow—that is, what a child can do with assistance today she will be able to do by herself tomorrow.

The American researcher Dorothea McCarthy showed that among children between the ages of three and five there are two groups of functions: those the children already possess, and those they can perform under guidance, in groups, and in collaboration with one another but which they have not mastered independently. McCarthy's study demonstrated that this second group of functions is at the actual developmental level of five-to-seven-year-olds. What her subjects could do only under guidance, in collaboration, and in groups at the age of three-to-five years they could do independently when they reached the age of five-to-seven years. Thus, if we were to determine only mental age—that is, only functions that have matured—we would have but a summary of completed development, while if we determine the maturing functions, we can predict what will happen to these children between five and seven, provided the same developmental conditions are maintained. The zone of proximal development can become a powerful concept in developmental research, one that can markedly enhance the effectiveness and utility of the application of diagnostics of mental development to educational problems.

A full understanding of the concept of the zone of proximal development must result in reevaluation of the role of imitation in learning. An unshakable tenet of classical psychology is that only the independent activity of children, not their imitative activity, indicates their level of mental development. This view is expressed in all current testing systems. In evaluating mental development, consideration is given to only those solutions to test problems which the child reaches without the assistance of others, without demonstrations, and without leading questions. Imitation and learning are thought of as purely mechanical processes. But recently psychologists have shown that a person can imitate only that which is within her developmental level. For example, if a child is having difficulty with a problem in arithmetic and the teacher solves it on the blackboard, the child may grasp the solution in an instant. But if the teacher were to solve a problem in higher mathematics, the child

would not be able to understand the solution no matter how many times she imitated it.

Animal psychologists, and in particular Köhler, have dealt with this question of imitation quite well. Köhler's experiments sought to determine whether primates are capable of graphic thought. The principal question was whether primates solved problems independently or whether they merely imitated solutions they had seen performed earlier, for example, watching other animals or humans use sticks and other tools and then imitating them. Köhler's special experiments, designed to determine what primates could imitate, reveal that primates can use imitation to solve only those problems that are of the same degree of difficulty as those they can solve alone. However, Köhler failed to take account of an important fact, namely, that primates cannot be taught (in the human sense of the word) through imitation, nor can their intellect be developed, because they have no zone of proximal development. A primate can learn a great deal through training by using its mechanical and mental skills, but it cannot be made more intelligent, that is, it cannot be taught to solve a variety of more advanced problems independently. For this reason animals are incapable of learning in the human sense of the term; *human learning presupposes a specific social nature and a process by which children grow into the intellectual life of those around them.*

Children can imitate a variety of actions that go well beyond the limits of their own capabilities. Using imitation, children are capable of doing much more in collective activity or under the guidance of adults. This fact, which seems to be of little significance in itself, is of fundamental importance in that it demands a radical alteration of the entire doctrine concerning the relation between learning and development in children. One direct consequence is a change in conclusions that may be drawn from diagnostic tests of development.

Formerly, it was believed that by using tests, we determine the mental development level with which education should reckon and whose limits it should not exceed. This procedure oriented learning toward yesterday's development, toward developmental stages already completed. The error of this view was discovered earlier in practice than in theory. It is demonstrated most clearly in the teaching of mentally retarded children. Studies have established that mentally retarded children are not very capable of abstract thinking. From this the pedagogy of the special school drew the seemingly correct conclusion that all teaching of such children should be based on the use of concrete, look-and-do methods. And yet a considerable amount of experience with this method resulted in profound disillusionment. It turned out that a teaching system based solely on concreteness—one that eliminated from teaching everything associated with abstract thinking—not only failed to help retarded children overcome their innate handicaps but also reinforced their handicaps by accustoming children exclusively to concrete thinking and thus suppressing the rudiments of any abstract thought that such children still have. Precisely because retarded children, when left to themselves, will never achieve well-elaborated forms of abstract thought, the school should make every effort to push them in that direction and to develop in them what is intrinsically lacking in their own development. In the current practices of special schools for retarded children, we can observe a beneficial shift away from this concept of concreteness, one that restores look-and-do methods to their proper role. Concreteness is now seen as necessary and unavoidable only as a stepping stone for developing abstract thinking—as a means, not as an end in itself.

Similarly, in normal children, learning which is oriented toward developmental levels that have already been reached is ineffective from the viewpoint of a child's overall development. It does not aim for a new stage of the developmental process but rather lags behind this process. Thus, the notion of a zone of proximal development enables us to propound a new formula, namely that the only "good learning" is that which is in advance of development.

The acquisition of language can provide a paradigm for the entire problem of the relation between learning and development. Language arises initially as a means of communication between the child and the people in his environment. Only subsequently, upon conversion to internal speech, does it come to organize the child's thought, that is, become an internal mental function. Piaget and others have shown that reasoning occurs in a children's group as an argument intended to prove one's own point of view before it occurs as an internal activity whose distinctive features is that the child begins to perceive and check the basis of his thoughts. Such observations prompted Piaget to conclude that communication produces the need for checking and confirming thoughts, a process that is characteristic of adult thought. In the same way that internal speech and reflective thought arise from the interactions between the child and persons in her environment, these interactions provide the source of development of a child's voluntary behavior. Piaget has shown that cooperation provides the basis for the development of a child's moral judgment. Earlier research established that a child first becomes able to subordinate her behavior to rules in group play and only later does voluntary self-regulation of behavior arise as an internal function.

These individual examples illustrate a general developmental law for the higher mental functions that we feel can be applied in its entirety to children's learning processes. We propose that an essential feature of learning is that it creates the zone of proximal development; that is, learning awakens a variety of internal developmental processes that are able to operate only when the child is interacting with people in his environment and in cooperation with his peers. Once these processes are internalized, they become part of the child's independent developmental achievement.

From this point of view, learning is not development; however, properly organized learning results in mental development and sets in motion a variety of developmental processes that would be impossible apart from learning. Thus, learning is a necessary and universal aspect of the process of developing culturally organized, specifically human, psychological functions.

To summarize, the most essential feature of our hypothesis is the notion that developmental processes do not coincide with learning processes. Rather, the developmental process lags behind the learning process; this sequence then results in zones of proximal development.

Our analysis alters the traditional view that at the moment a child assimilates the meaning of a word, or masters an operation such as addition or written language, her developmental processes are basically completed. In fact, they have only just begun at that moment. The major consequence of analyzing the educational process in this manner is to show that the initial mastery of, for example, the four arithmetic operations provides the basis for the subsequent development of a variety of highly complex internal processes in children's thinking.

Our hypothesis establishes the unity but not the identity of learning processes and internal developmental processes. It presupposes that the one is converted into the other. Therefore, it becomes an important concern of psychological research to show how external knowledge and abilities in children become internalized.

Any investigation explores some sphere of reality. An aim of the psychological analysis of development is to describe the internal relations of the intellectual processes awakened by school learning. In this respect, such analysis will be directed inward and is analogous to the use of x-rays. If successful, it should reveal to the teacher how developmental processes stimulated by the course of school learning are carried through inside the head of each individual child. The revelation of this internal, subterranean developmental network of school subjects is a task of primary importance for psychological and educational analysis.

A second essential feature of our hypothesis is the notion that, although learning is directly related to the course of child development, the two are never accomplished in equal measure or in parallel. Development in children never follows school learning the way a shadow follows the object that casts it. In actuality, there are highly complex dynamic relations between developmental and learning processes that cannot be encompassed by an unchanging hypothetical formulation.

Each school subject has its own specific relation to the course of child development, a relation that varies as the child goes from one stage to another. This leads us directly to a reexamination of the problem of formal discipline, that is, to the significance of each particular subject from the viewpoint of overall mental development. Clearly, the problem cannot be solved by using any one formula; extensive and highly diverse concrete research based on the concept of the zone of proximal development is necessary to resolve the issue.

# The Origins of Neo-Piagetian Theory

## R. Case

Although Piaget continued to modify his theoretical system well into the 1970s and 1980s (Beilin, 1983; Chapman, 1988), the framework that constituted the starting point for most neo-Piagetian investigators was the classic one, which was completed during the mid 1960s, and which was summarized by Piaget at that time (Piaget, 1970). According to this theory, infants and children can most profitably be viewed as a young scientists, who construct ever more powerful theories of the world, as a result of applying structures of ever increasing generality and power. These structures, in turn, can most profitably be construed as systems of logical operations, which remain invariant in the face of considerable differences in surface content and cultural milieu, and which can be modeled using symbolic logic.

While empirical experience, social experience, and maturation were all acknowledged by Piaget to play some role in influencing children's construction of these structures, by far the most important role was assigned to "logico-mathematical experience" (Piaget, 1964). That is to say, by far the most important role was assigned to the universal experience of operating on the world, and then reflecting on one's own operations. It was presumed that this reflexive activity was the underlying motor of cognitive development, and that the primary criteria it brought to bear on children's thought were rational ones, such as the search for coherence, consistency, and breadth of application. It was as a result of this sort of reflexive activity, and the dynamic internal process from which it stemmed, that children's logical structures were presumed to be reworked periodically, into systems of increasing consistency and power.

Piaget's theory had a number of important strengths, which were acknowledged by inves-

tigators in a wide variety of fields. Because the theory placed such a strong emphasis on rational structures and processes, however, it was also subjected to strong criticism. This was especially true in North America, where the prevailing epistemology placed a far stronger emphasis on empirical or sociocultural factors. The epistemology that underpinned Piaget's theory has been contrasted with that of his critics along a number of dimensions (Beilin, 1983, 1989, this volume; Chapman, 1988; Overton, 1984, 1990a). From the present perspective, however, the most important features of this epistemology were (a) its explicit rejection of the classic empiricist position on knowledge and its acquisition, and (b) its tentative and rather selective endorsement of the dialectical position on knowledge and its acquisition. Each of these features led to a clash with mainstream psychology—the former with psychology as practiced in the Anglo–American community, and the latter with psychology as practiced in the Soviet community. Since neo-Piagetian theory was born in direct response to these two clashes, it is important to examine the epistemological issues that were at stake.

According to the classic *empiricist* epistemology, the process of knowledge acquisition is one in which the sensory organs first detect stimuli in the external world, and the mind then detects the customary patterns or "conjunctions" in these stimuli (Hume, 1955). North American psychologists who were influenced by this view tended to believe that children's knowledge had its origins in a growing familiarity with their external world, and the regularities that this world contains. The process of development was thus seen as a continuous one, in which children construct rules of ever increasing generality for representing and dealing with the regularities in their environment (Gibson, 1969; Klahr & Wallace, 1976; Siegler, 1978). The knowledge possessed by scientists was viewed in a similar fashion: namely, as a body of facts and laws whose origins lie in careful observation of empirical

*Source:* Case, R. (1992). The origins of neo-Piagetian theory. In H. Beilin & P. Pufall (Eds.), *Piaget's theory: Prospects and possibilities* (pp. 63–71). Hillsdale, NJ: Erlbaum.

phenomena, followed by a process in which causal hypotheses are articulated and subjected to rigorous empirical scrutiny (Brainerd, 1978).

To those who endorsed this view of knowledge and its acquisition, or who were influenced by it, Piaget's theory of intellectual development appeared seriously flawed. The major substantive problems that were cited were as follows: (a) the theory postulates a psychological system that operates in an monolithic fashion, under the guidance of a set of an ill-defined "logical structures" and processes; (b) the theory assigns external, empirical observations and influences a relatively unimportant role in the formation and alteration of these structures and processes. Not only are these suggestions at variance with empiricist epistemology, they appear to be at variance with empirical data on children's development as well. Many tasks that are supposedly tests of the same underlying logical structure do not even correlate with each other (Pinard & Laurendeau, 1969). In addition, children's absolute level of performance on such tasks varies widely from one situation to the next—so widely in fact, that certain properties that are supposed to be characteristic of one stage of development (e.g., decentration during the period of concrete operations) may actually be observed at the previous stage, a good 6 years earlier. Finally, training studies have shown that it is relatively easy to influence children's understanding of logical principles, by exposing them to appropriately simplified forms of empirical experience (Beilin, 1971a, 1971b; Gelman, 1969).

For those whose epistemology had its origins in the sociohistoric tradition, the problems with Piaget's theory were different, but equally serious. According to the sociohistoric view, knowledge and thought evolve in a social and historical context, and cannot be understood without reference to the nature and dynamic tensions that are inherent in that context. Psychologists who have been influenced by this position see the origin of children's knowledge as lying in their culture, and the intellectual and linguistic tools that their culture has evolved for coping with its environment (Bruner, 1966, 1989; Cole & Bruner, 1971; Lave, 1988; McDermott, 1990; Vy-

gotsky, 1962). While Piaget was always quick to acknowledge the importance of social factors in development, and while his model of equilibration was inherently dialectical, the fact remains that the central constructs in his system were defined in universal terms, and were seen as conforming with rational principles rather than social or linguistic ones.

When viewed from the sociohistoric perspective, then, Piaget's portrait of the young child appeared too universal, and too focused on the subject, rather than the cultural and linguistic institutions in which the subject's life is embedded. The methods that Piaget employed likewise appeared too uncritical with regard to their cultural and linguistic biases. Finally, once again, the theory did not appear to square with the available data. These data suggested (a) that different cultures pass Piagetian tasks at different ages, and reach different terminal levels (Dasen, 1972); (b) that children's response to Piagetian tasks within a culture varies widely as a function of such factors as language (Bruner, 1966; Cole & Scribner, 1974; Olson, 1986a, 1986b) and formal schooling (Cole, Gay, Glick, & Sharp, 1971; Greenfield, 1966); and (c) that the structures of Western thought themselves appear to have evolved in major ways over the last 500 years, and to be in a continued state of evolution (Keating, 1980; Olson, 1986a, 1986b).

The problems pointed out by scholars in the empiricist and sociohistoric traditions were not the only ones that influenced the direction of neo-Piagetian thought. Even among those scholars who accepted most of Piaget's underlying (rationalist) assumptions about knowledge and its acquisition, there was dissatisfaction with certain aspects of his theory. Of particular concern were (a) The absence of a sufficiently detailed treatment of stage transition: that is, the central mechanism by which children replace early forms of logical structures with more powerful ones (Pascual–Leone, 1969); (b) The absence of any treatment of "performance" factors: that is, factors which affect children's ability to apply particular structures in particular contexts (Overton, 1990b; Pascual–Leone, 1969); and (c) The absence of any account of individual differences in the developmental process (Pascual–Leone, 1969). The common theme running through this last set of criticisms was that Piaget's theory was incomplete. To present a more complete picture, it was argued, a more detailed account would have to be provided of the processes on which the structure of children's thought was dependent.[1]

Neo-Piagetian theory was born in response to these three general categories of criticism, that is, the criticisms raised by empiricist, socio-historic, and rationalist scholars (Pascual–Leone, 1969). What neo-Piagetian theorists attempted to do was to *preserve* those aspects of Piagetian theory that gave it its breadth, coherence, and explanatory power, to *develop* those aspects of the theory that made it seem too static, vague, or difficult to operationalize, and to *alter* those aspects of the theory that assumed a child whose development was relatively insensitive to its physical environment, or who derived only modest intellectual benefits from its cultural and linguistic heritage.

As the neo-Piagetian movement gained sway, different neo-Piagetian theorists made different decisions regarding which elements of Piaget's theory to retain, which to develop, and which to alter, in order to accomplish the foregoing objectives (see Biggs & Collis, 1982; Case, 1978, 1985; Demetriou & Efklides, 1988; Fischer, 1980; Fischer & Ferrar, in press; Halford, 1982, 1988; Mounoud, 1986; Pascual–Leone, 1970, 1988a). They also differed in which of the foregoing objectives they saw as most central. Nevertheless, there was a good deal of commonality in the general directions they pursued. Thus, after 20 years of further writing and research, it now seems possible to specify a set of core propositions on which neo-Piagetian theorists are generally agreed, and to examine the solution that these propositions imply to the problems just described.

[1] Unlike the previous critique, this last critique was one with which Piaget was in substantial agreement, and which he spent the last 15 years of his life working on himself (Beilin, 1989; Chapman, 1988).

## Core Postulates of Neo-Piagetian Theory

### Postulates Retained from the Classic Piagetian System

The following traditional Piagetian postulates are ones that were retained by most neo-Piagetian theorists, in developing new or revised systems of their own.

***A1. Children Assimilate Experience to Existing Cognitive Structures.*** Children do not simply "observe" the world around them and note its regularities. Rather, they actively assimilate this world to their existing cognitive structures.

***A2. Children Create Their Own Cognitive Structures.*** Children's cognitive structures are not merely a product of their empirical experience. They are also a product of their own attempts to organize that experience in a coherent fashion.

***A3. Children Pass Through a Universal Sequence of Structural Levels.*** Three or four general levels of cognitive structure can be identified in children's intellectual development. While different neo-Piagetian theorists labeled and analyzed these structures somewhat differently, they all agreed that there is a preliminary stage in which sensorimotor structures predominate, followed by two or three further stages in which children's intellectual structures become increasingly symbolic and abstract.

***A4. Earlier Structures Are Included in Later Ones.*** The increasingly abstract structures of later stages build on, and yet transforms, those of earlier stages. Thus, for example, the higher-order conservation concepts that are possessed by elementary school children, although they are qualitatively different from those possessed by infants (Mounoud & Bower, 1974; Starkey, Spelke, & Gelman, 1983), are not unrelated to them. Rather, they are based on these concepts, and constitute a higher-order "reworking" of them.

***A5. Characteristic Ages for the Acquisition of Different Structures May Be Identified.*** A characteristic age range may be identified for the acquisition of structures at any of the major levels specified by the theory, providing that children have been exposed to what might be termed an "optimal environment."

## Postulates That Extend the Classic Piagetian System

The following postulates are ones that were not just retained, but refined and extended, by neo-Piagetian theorists.

*B1. Development and Learning Must be Distinguished.* Like Baldwin (1894) before him, Piaget made a distinction between development, which was said to involve a transformation or "accommodation" of a child's existing structural framework, and learning, which was said to involve the assimilation of new content to an existing structural framework (although some more minor accommodation of the framework may be necessary for this to take place). Virtually all neo-Piagetian theorists maintained some sort of distinction of this sort, and sought to explicate the processes which underlie each form of change. Thus, for example, Fischer (1980) distinguished the process of "intercoordination," which is subject to very strong developmental constraints and which can lead to a major change in children's level of cognitive functioning, from processes such as differentiation, refocusing, and chaining, which do not appear to be subject to such strong developmental constraints, and which lead instead to a greater degree of elaboration or complexity *within* an existing structural level.

Pascual–Leone (1969, 1988a), who is generally regarded as the founder of the neo-Piagetian movement, focused on the different way in which attention is involved in these two general classes of transformation. When engaged in major structural reorganization, Pascual–Leone suggested that children must actively inhibit the application of a current logical structure (L). At the same time, they must assemble a new structure, by bringing a new set of schemes to full activation and coordinating them, via mental effort (M). He called this attention-driven learning Logical or LM learning, and asserted that it is strongly dependent on development. In the second type of structural change, which does not involve this sort of focused mental effort, Pas-

cual–Leone assumed that children merely need to apply an existing logical structure repeatedly to a variety of situations, and that this repeated activation itself will cause the existing structure to differentiate, and to incorporate new "cues" (C) in its releasing components. He called this second process LC-learning, and associated it with learning rather than development.

In the context of my own system (Case, 1985), a distinction was made between processes such as problem solving and exploration on the one hand, and processes such as consolidation and automatization on the other. The former sort of processes were presumed to lead to the formation of new cognitive structures, as existing schemes are coordinated into new patterns, via an attentionally mediated and often socially directed set of mental steps. The second set of processes were presumed to lead to the formation of stronger associations or cues among existing structural units, with the result that they can be activated more automatically. Finally it was suggested that—in order for development to take place smoothly—both sets of processes must always be at work. That is to say, the initial change in children's structures that takes place during stage transition, as a result of independent or socially facilitated exploration and problem solving, must necessarily be followed by a process in which the new structure is consolidated and automated via repeated application. Otherwise, further developmental progress is unlikely to take place.

To the reader who is unfamiliar with neo-Piagetian theory, the foregoing descriptions may appear somewhat dense. Only three points need be recognized, however, at this juncture: (a) most neo-Piagetian theories contain distinctions that derive from Piaget's original contrast between development and learning; (b) the various proposals, while different, are nonetheless compatible with each other (see also Halford, 1982; Mounoud, 1986); and (c) most of the proposals utilize the reformulated distinction they propose as a springboard from which to launch a more detailed account of the stage transition process.

*B2. Developmental Restructuring Is Not System-Wide in Nature.* A second neo-Piagetian notion that involves an extension of the classic Piagetian position is actually one on which Piaget's position evolved over the years. In his best-known work, which was done in his middle years, Piaget spoke of the processes of structural transformation as though they operated on the entire system of structures in the child's repertoire (the "structure of the whole"). In his later work, however, he suggested that such processes operate on one particular class or subgroup of structures at a time (Piaget, 1985). It is this latter position that has been adopted by neo-Piagetian theorists. Thus, whether they characterize the process of development as one that entails the intercoordination of lower-level skills (Fischer, 1980), attentionally driven (LM) learning (Pascual–Leone, 1988a), or problem solving and exploration (Case, 1985), most neo-Piagetian theorists are quite explicit in asserting that the process which drives these activities operates on a small subset of schemas at a time, not on the child's entire structural repertoire. As will be indicated in the next section, they have also provided specific examples that are worked out in considerable detail, as to how these processes might actually unfold in particular physical and social contexts.

**B3. A Cyclical Recapitulation of Structural Sequences May Be Identified.** A third notion of Piaget's that neo-Piagetian theorists extended was the idea that there is a cyclical recursion through substages at each general stage or level of development. Once again, although this notion does exist within the classic Piagetian system (where it goes by the name of "vertical displacement" or "vertical décalage"), it is relatively undeveloped. In the context of several neo-Piagetian theories, however, the notion has been considerably strengthened, and stated in a much more stringent form. The suggestion is that there is a progression through exactly the same *number* of structural steps at each major stage, and that these steps are traversed in exactly the same *sequence* (Biggs & Collis, 1982; Case, 1978, 1985; Fischer, 1980; Mounoud, 1986).[2]

---

[2] Pascual–Leone has made no commitment to this proposition; however, he has suggested that, if true, the proposition is not inconsistent with his system (Pascual–Leone, 1986).

## Postulates That Alter the Classic Piagetian System

The final group of neo-Piagetian postulates are ones that required a genuine alteration, rather than simply an extension, of the classic Piagetian system.

*C1. Cognitive Structures Must be Redefined.* In most neo-Piagetian systems, children's cognitive structures are not defined in terms that involve symbolic logic. Rather, they are defined in terms of their form, complexity, and level of hierarchical integration. This apparently simple shift in conceptualization has a number of far-reaching consequences. One consequence is that the formal structures of Western science and mathematics (e.g., those structures that involve the partitioning of the world into variables, which are then systematically manipulated and controlled), can be seen as cultural inventions, not as universals. Another implication is that other structures, such as those involved in the visual arts or in social analysis, can be seen as playing a role in children's development that is just as important as that played by structures of a logical and mathematical nature. A third consequence is that sociocultural processes and institutions can be seen as playing a vital role in promoting children's development, particularly at higher stages. Finally, a fourth consequence is that adult thought in other cultures can be seen as different from, yet every bit as sophisticated as, that which is exhibited in the West.

*C2. There Is a Shifting Upper Limit on the Complexity of Children's Cognitive Structures.* There is a potential contradiction between two of the groups of postulates that have been mentioned so far: namely, those dealing with generality and those dealing with cultural, contextual, or individual specificity. On the one hand, the new forms of structural analysis that were proposed are more broadly applicable than Piaget's, and thus more general. They also yield similar age norms to those that Piaget proposed, across an even wider range of domains. On the other hand, the processes of structural transformation are held to apply more locally, and thus to be capable of yielding considerable unevenness or "displacement" in children's measured level of development. How can development simultaneously be seen as more general *and* more specific than Piaget's system implies? Stated differently, if the processes of structural transformation are of genuinely local applicability, why is there any typical age of acquisition across different sorts of cognitive structure at all?

In answer to this question, neo-Piagetian theorists have proposed a distinction between general processes which *constrain* and/or *potentiate* development, and more specific processes that operate *within* these general constraints and potentials. Although the processes of structural transformation are held to operate quite locally, and thus to give rise to considerable variation in measured developmental level, they are also presumed to be constrained by a shifting upper limit in the level at which children can function. This general constraint is seen as restricting the amount of variation that is observed in many situations, by introducing a rather literal "ceiling effect." A "floor" effect is often presumed as well, due to the fact that certain aspects of children's experience are universal (e.g., exposure to some form of caretaker, to some form of language, to some form of motor opportunity, and to some form of cultural training).

### C3. Maturation Plays a Strong Role in Determining the Upper Limit on Working Memory.
A third postulate held in common among most neo-Piagetian theorists is that there are specifiable biological factors that regulate the gradual shift in this upper limit. Although different theorists talk about these biological factors in different ways, their proposals are once again compatible, and quite unified in the overall view that they provide (see, for example, Case, 1985, chap. 17; in press-b; Fischer, 1987; Mounoud, 1986; Pascual–Leone, 1974, 1989a).

### C4. The Attentional System Plays a Strong Role in Determining This Upper Limit.
Following the lead of Pascual–Leone (1969), and to a lesser extent McLaughlin (1963)[3] most neo-

Piagetian theorists have assumed that the child's attentional capacity, or "working memory" is one of the major constraining factors on children's developing cognition: That is, attention is one of the major factors that is subject to this sort of biological influence.

### C5. Individual Differences Must Be Considered Before a Full Picture of Development Is Possible.
A final proposition to which most (though perhaps not all) neo-Piagetian theorists ascribe is that individual differences play a critical role in determining the particular use to which children put their working memory, and the particular developmental pathways that their thinking follows (Case, 1992; Demetriou & Efklides, 1988; Fischer & Knight, in press; Lautrey, DeRibaupierre, & Rieben, 1987; Pascual–Leone, 1969, 1974).

Beyond the foregoing sets of propositions, different neo-Piagetian theories have diverged considerably, in accordance with the theoretical predilections of their developers. All neo-Piagetian theorists have included at least some further element from Piaget's system in their own theories, and imported other elements from elsewhere. However, the particular elements that they have retained and imported have varied widely. A detailed presentation of these differences is beyond the scope of this chapter. However, just to give a flavor of their nature, it is perhaps worthwhile to mention that certain neo-Piagetian theorists have attempted to preserve and elaborate on Piaget's notions of conflict and equilibration (Pascual–Leone, 1988a), while others have emphasized the search for consistency and reflexive abstraction (Halford, 1988; Halford & Wilson, 1980), and still others have emphasized the notions of differentiation and coordination (Case, 1988b; Fischer & Ferrar, in press). Taking off from these different points in the classic Piagetian system, then, each of the theorists cited here has worked out a detailed set of propositions concerning the nature of children's cognitive structures at different ages, and the way in which these structures are transformed, as children move from one stage or level in their development to the next.

---

[3] McLaughlin's (1963) work appears to have had the greatest influence on Halford, who used the STM values proposed by McLaughlin in his own work.

# Growth Cycles of Brain and Mind

### Kurt W. Fischer and Samuel P. Rose

Changes in thinking and learning relate to physical changes in the brain. The repeating patterns of these changes suggest common growth cycles in behavior and in the brain—a cyclical property that explains the remarkable human capacity for plasticity.

Recent research and theory in cognitive neuroscience have produced insights into how the development of the brain, especially the cerebral cortex, relates to thinking and learning (Fischer & Rose, 1996; Thatcher, 1994). These insights have important implications for educational practice and policy (Case, 1993; Fischer & Bidell, 1997). Prior conceptions typically treated development as a sequence of stages, like the steps of a ladder, but current work replaces that overly simple notion with the rich biological concept of a recurring growth cycle: Both behavior and the brain change in repeating patterns that seem to involve common growth cycles (Case, 1991; Fischer, 1980).

These growth cycles repeat several times between birth and 30 years of age. Each recurrence produces a new capacity for thinking and learning that appears to be grounded in an expanded, reorganized neural network. Humans have a new opportunity for relearning skills and reshaping networks that they missed learning in earlier cycles. This cyclical property seems to explain the remarkable human capacity for plasticity, including recovery from damaging environments and neural injuries, especially when later development occurs in a benevolent, nurturing environment (Diamond & Hopson, 1998).

On the side of thinking and learning, the cyclical changes in capacity are not evident in everything that children or adolescents do because most of their acting, thinking, and learning do not push the limit of their capacities. Each new round of the cycle, called a developmental

level, is most evident in a person's optimal level, the most complex skill or understanding that he or she can produce. Usually a person produces this optimal level only with strong contextual support, like that from a teacher, a tutor, or a text. Without such support, most thinking and learning occur at lower levels, not at the optimal level.

## Cycles of Cognitive Development and "Stages"

A prerequisite for understanding our argument is to purge the classical conception of development, which treats thinking and learning as a progression through a series of stages that form steps in a developmental ladder. Instead, in the dynamic skills framework, development is much more variable and flexible and shows complex, dynamic patterns of change with many of the properties described by mathematical theories of complexity, chaos, and catastrophe (van der Maas & Molenaar, 1992; van Geert, in press).

A useful metaphor for some of the dynamic properties is a developmental web, with thinking and learning changing in parallel along multiple strands or domains, as reflected in such concepts as Gardner's (1993) multiple intelligences. A child develops a set of spatial skills and a separate set of musical skills, as illustrated by the strands on the left and right, respectively, of the web in Figure 1. When a new developmental level emerges, optimal performance along most strands shows discontinuous change, reflected in growth spurts and reorganizations, which are marked by changes in direction, forks, and intersections of the strands in

*Source:* Fischer, K. W., & Rose, S. P. (1998). Growth cycles of brain and mind. *Educational Leadership*, 56 (3), 56–60.

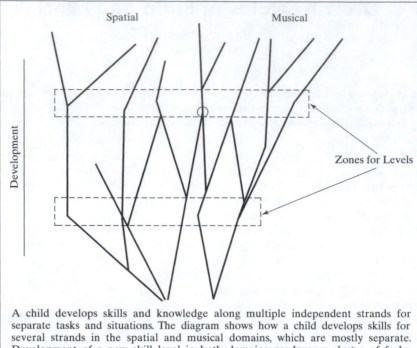

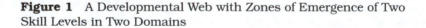

A child develops skills and knowledge along multiple independent strands for separate tasks and situations. The diagram shows how a child develops skills for several strands in the spatial and musical domains, which are mostly separate. Development of a new skill level in both domains produces a cluster of forks, intersections, and changes in direction across most strands, as indicated by the gray boxes for two successive levels. Skills relating the spatial and music domains intersect at one point (marked by a small circle) when the child begins to learn musical notation, which requires an integration of spatial and musical skills.

**Figure 1**   A Developmental Web with Zones of Emergence of Two Skill Levels in Two Domains

the web. These changes do not occur all at once, but they are distributed across a specific age period or zone marked by the boxes in Figure 1. With the emergence of each level, a child can build a new, more complex kind of skill or understanding in diverse domains.

Each new level produces a cluster of spurts in optimal skill and understanding across many domains in a particular age period, a cognitive surge analogous to the spurts in height that children periodically show. Unlike height, however, cognitive spurts are evident only under optimal support conditions, not across the entire array of children's behaviors. A good teacher will bring

them out in the classroom, but they will typically not be evident when a child is working or playing alone or without support.

Development involves a long series of new levels, each constructed independently in parallel for each strand or domain. The first ones develop in the child shortly after birth, and they continue to emerge until he or she reaches approximately 30 years of age. These spurts in capacity seem to be grounded in two recurring growth cycles. The shorter-term cycle involves constructing successive *levels* of skill or understanding, moving from single units, to mappings relating a few units, to systems relating multiple units, and finally to the formation of a new kind of unit that reorganizes and simplifies systems. This reorganization and simplification in turn is nested in a longer-term cycle, moving through four different forms of action and thought called *tiers* (reflexes, actions, concrete representations, and abstractions) (Case, 1991; Fischer, 1980). Both cycles seem to be based in the growth of neural networks, involving a combination of changes in connections among regions of the cortex and changes in brain activity in particular regions.

A metaphor that illustrates the nature of the long-term cycle of tiers is the construction of a cube or other solid figure in four levels, as shown in Figure 2. To build a cube, we first com-bine single points to form lines. We combine lines to form squares, then squares to form cubes. The cube in turn is a new building block that begins the process again, as we combine cubes to form lines, and so forth. The shorter-term cycle occurs within each level.

If we focus on only the leading edge of change—the zone of emergence for each optimal level—we can summarize the development of skill capacities and neural networks as shown in Figure 3. The four forms of action and thought (tiers) are on the left of the figure, and the skill levels for each tier are on the right. Capacities to build reflex skills (species-specific actions and perceptual patterns) emerge in the first dozen weeks of life and eventually produce the first sensorimotor actions (grasping, looking, walking, eating, and the like).

Capacities for building more complex senso-rimotor actions emerge between 3 months and 2 years and eventually create the first concrete representations (for example, forming sentences, symbolizing specific people as independent agents, naming categories of emotions, counting numbers). Optimal levels for representational capacities develop during childhood, between 2 and 12 years. Eventually a child understands his or her first abstractions (such as literary and mathematical concepts: personality and motivational characteristics: concepts of society, law, and philosophy). Optimal abstraction capacities appear between 10 and 25 years of age and produce the capacity to build principles relating multiple abstractions (such as evolution by natural selection, reflective judgment, the Golden Rule). The right part of the diagram shows the second cycle of specific skill levels and their approximate ages of emergence.

## Nested Cycles of Cortical Development

In the last few years, new discoveries about brain functioning have led to the first evidence of recurring cortical growth cycles. Especially exciting are the striking parallels of these cortical cycles with the cognitive-developmental cycles for levels and tiers. Previously, scientists did

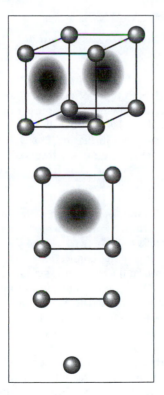

**Figure 2** Cycle of Four Levels Forming a New Unit of Action and Thought

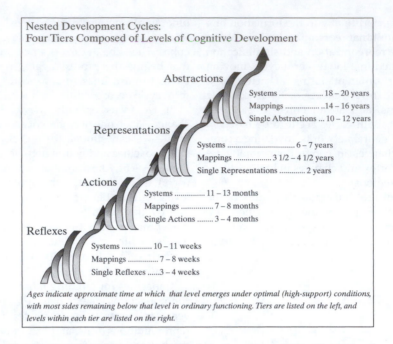

**Figure 3**   Nested Developmental Cycles: Four Tiers Composed
of Levels of Cognitive Development

not have access to enough data on the development of brain functioning to support any specific analysis of cortical growth cycles. The recent discoveries have provided strong sources for analyzing patterns of change in cortical activity and connection. Studies in three countries have found similar cyclical patterns of cortical change with age in childhood and adolescence (Bell, in press: Fischer & Rose, 1996; Matousek & Petersén, 1973; Somsen, van't Klooster, van der Molen, van Leeuwen, & Licht, 1997; Thatcher, 1994).

First the amount of energy in the electroencephalogram (EEG), which indicates electrical activity in the cortex, shows systematic spurts that closely parallel the spurts observed in optimal levels for cognitive development. In addition, connections among cortical regions, which are measured by EEG coherence (the correlations of wave patterns between regions), demonstrate qualitative shifts at the same age periods. The ages for these two kinds of brain changes are remarkably similar to those listed in Figure 3 for cognitive levels.

Second, both types of measures—energy and connection—show not only spurts but also specific growth cycles that parallel the two cognitive cycles shown in Figures 2 and 3: one cycle for the development of new forms of action and thought and a second cycle for the development of specific skill levels (Fischer & Bidell, 1997). Figure 4 shows the cycle for the development of skill levels and is based on data for growth spurts in cortical connections reported by Robert Thatcher (1994).

Spurts in cortical connections move systematically around the cortex in a similar pattern for each skill level, presumably reflecting changes in neural networks. The jagged lines indicate cortical locations that show the largest growth in connections, and the arrows specify the sequence in which growth moves around the cortex. Spurts in the growth of connections begin with front to back connections in both hemispheres and then shift to involve mostly right hemisphere connections. Within the right hemisphere, they gradually move from long distance connections to more local connections. Then

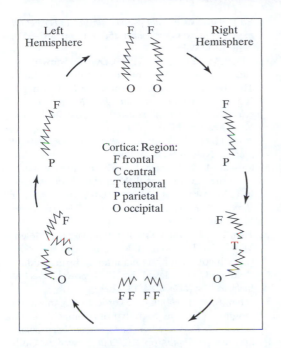

Cortica: Region:
F frontal
C central
T temporal
P parietal
O occipital

**Figure 4** A Cycle of Growth of Cortical Connections for Each Level of Network Formation and Skill Development

they shift to the left hemisphere, where they move gradually from local to long distance connections. When the spurts reach front to back in the left hemisphere (and simultaneously in the right), the process starts over again for the next level.

The cycle in Figure 4 repeats for every level, and three occurrences of this cycle are nested in the longer-term cycle for each tier. That is, in Figure 3, the cycle of connections occurs for every loop in the shaded spiral arrows.

## Variation in Levels, not Consistent Stages

Unfortunately, we can easily misconstrue this new cycles framework for understanding development and learning as a model of stages. Chil-

dren and adults do not develop in stages, although optimal levels of skill do show relatively sudden spurts and reorganizations. People vary enormously in the skill levels they use every day, only occasionally functioning at their optimal level, as teachers see with their students. Full development of each new level emerges gradually over a long period. Even under optimal conditions in a single domain, such as spatial reasoning, the concurrent zone spans time. There is no sudden transformation, no instant change at, say, 10 years of age to understanding abstract concepts about space. Instead, children show a cluster of changes over several years, such as 10 to 12 years for optimal level with spatial concepts. Across several domains, such as spatial and musical concepts, the age span is even longer.

In ordinary functioning without optimal support, students vary greatly in their skill levels. They typically perform at lower levels, because in everyday life, support for optimal skills seldom exists. Educators need to teach to ordinary functioning, not only to optimal levels, because students need to use what they learn in the many situations where there is no optimal support. To sustain a high skill level without support, a student requires extensive practice and experience. Even intelligent adults have to work for long periods to master new abstract concepts in unfamiliar domains, for example, when teachers extend their knowledge to non-Euclidian space, new musical styles, or the mechanisms of neural networks. Capturing the educational implications of growth cycles requires analyzing the full range of variation in levels of skill and understanding, not focusing primarily on optimal levels or growth spurts (Bidell & Fischer, 1992).

## Implications for Educators

These findings and concepts have important implications for the development of thinking and learning.

1. Cognitive growth and brain growth both show remarkable resilience and plasticity when children live and learn in adequate environments. The cyclical nature of cortical growth and

optimal cognitive development seems to foster these characteristics of resilience and plasticity.

2. Brain development involves a recurring growth cycle of neural networks and learning, in which a child not only learns skills and concepts once, but also relearns and reworks them anew at each successive optimal level.

3. Children (and adults) function at multiple levels of skill and understanding, even for a single topic or domain. Their concepts and skills vary across a wide range of levels, and normal functioning is usually not at optimal level.

4. An individual's level of skill and understanding depends pervasively on contextual support for high-level functioning. Effective teaching and, at later ages, effective textual presentation powerfully support high-level functioning. Removing the support leads to a natural, rapid drop in the level of understanding.

5. Educators need to focus on teaching children at lower, as well as at optimal, levels because independent learning and thinking usually occur at lower levels, with optimal functioning limited to supportive situations.

## References

Bell, M. A. (in press). The ontogeny of the EEG during infancy and childhood: Implications for cognitive development. In B. Garreau (Ed.), *Neuroimaging in child psychiatric disorders*. Paris: Springer-Verlag.

Bidell, T. R., & Fischer, K. W. (1992). Cognitive development in educational contexts: Implications of skill theory. In A. Demetriou, M. Shayer, & A. Efklides (Eds.), *Neo-Piagetian theories of cognitive development: Implications and applications for education* (pp. 9–30). London: Routledge & Kegan Paul.

Case, R. (Ed.) (1991). *The mind's staircase: Exploring the conceptual underpinnings of children's thought and knowledge*. Hillsdale, NJ: Eribaum.

Case, R. (1993). Theories of learning and theories of development. Special issue: Learning and development. *Educational Psychologist, 28*(3), 219–233.

Diamond, M., & Hopson, J. (1998). *Magic trees of the mind: How to nurture your child's intelligence, creativity, and healthy emotions from birth through adolescence*. New York: Dutton.

Fischer, K. W. (1980). A theory of cognitive development: The control and construction of hierarchies of skills. *Psychological Review, 87*, 477–531.

Fischer, K. W., & Bidell, T. R. (1997). Dynamic development of psychological structures in action and thought. In R. M. Lerner (Ed.) & W. Damon (Series Ed.), *Handbook of child psychology: Vol 1. Theoretical models of human development* (5th ed., pp. 467–561), New York: Wiley.

Fischer, K. W., & Rose, S. P. (1996). Dynamic growth cycles of brain and cognitive development. In R. Thatcher, G. R. Lyon, J. Rumsey, & N. Krasnegor (Eds.), *Developmental neuroimaging: Mapping the development of brain and behavior* (pp. 263–279). New York: Academic Press.

Gardner, H. (1993). *Multiple intelligences: The theory in practice*. New York: Basic Books.

Matousek, M., & Petersén, I. (1973). Frequency analysis of the EEG in normal children and adolescents. In P. Kellaway & I. Petersén (Eds.), *Automation of clinical electroencephalography* (pp. 75–102). New York: Raven Press.

Somsen, R. J. M., van't Klooster, B. J., van der Molen, M. W., van Leeuwen, H. M. P., & Licht, R. (1997). Growth spurts in brain maturation during middle childhood as indexed by EEG power spectra. *Biological Psychology, 44*, 187–209.

Thatcher, R. W. (1994). Cyclic cortical reorganization: Origins of human cognitive development. In G. Dawson & K. W. Fischer (Eds.), *Human behavior and the developing brain* (pp. 232–266). New York: Guilford Press.

van der Maas, H., & Molenaar, P. (1992). A catastrophe-theoretical approach to cognitive development. *Psychological Review, 99*, 395–417.

van Geert, P. (in press). A dynamic systems model of basic developmental mechanisms: Piaget. Vygotsky, and beyond. *Psychological Review.*

*Authors' note:* Preparation of this article was supported by grants from Mr. and Mrs. Frederick P. Rose, the Harvard University Graduate School of Education, and NICHD grant HD32371. The authors thank Thomas Bidell, Daniel Bullock, Robbie Case, Donna Coch, Jane Haltiwanger, Robert Thatcher, and Paul van Geert for their contributions to the arguments presented here.

**Kurt W. Fischer** is Professor and Director of the Cognitive Development Laboratory at Harvard University Graduate School of Education, Larsen Hall 703, Appian Way, Cambridge, MA 02138-3752 (e-mail: kurt_fischer@harvard.edu). The late **Samuel P. Rose** taught child development at the University of Colorado at Denver.

# Mechanisms of Theory Formation in Young Children

ALISON GOPNIK AND LAURA SCHULZ

*Department of Psychology, University of California
at Berkeley, Berkeley, CA, 94720, USA*

Research suggests that by the age of five, children have extensive causal knowledge, in the form of intuitive theories. The crucial question for developmental cognitive science is *how* young children are able to learn causal structure from evidence. Recently, researchers in computer science and statistics have developed representations (causal Bayes nets) and learning algorithms to infer causal structure from evidence. Here we explore evidence suggesting that infants and children have the prerequisites for making causal inferences consistent with causal Bayes net learning algorithms. Specifically, we look at infants and children's ability to learn from evidence in the form of conditional probabilities, interventions and combinations of the two.

Over the past 30 years we have discovered an enormous amount about what children know and when they know it. In particular, young children, and even infants, seem to have intuitive theories of the physical, biological and psychological world (for recent reviews see [1–3]). These theories, like scientific theories, are complex, coherent, abstract representations of the causal structure of the world. Even the youngest preschoolers can use these intuitive theories to make causal predictions, provide causal explanations, and reason about causation counterfactually [4–7]. Moreover, both studies of natural variation in relevant experiences, and explicit training studies, demonstrate that children's intuitive theories change in response to evidence [8–11].

But the real question for developmental cognitive science is not so much what children know and when they know it, but how children's theories develop and change and why

*Source:* Mechanisms of theory formation in young children (pp. 371–377), by A. Gopnik and L. Schulz, 2004, *Trends in Cognitive Sciences* 8 (8). Copyright © 2004 by Elsevier, Ltd.

children's theories converge towards accurate descriptions of the world. It is all very well to suggest that children's learning mechanisms are analogous to scientific theory-formation. However, what we would really like is a more precise specification of the mechanisms that underlie learning in both scientists and children.

One such candidate learning mechanism has recently attracted considerable interest within the fields of computer science, philosophy and psychology. The causal Bayes net account of causal knowledge and learning provides computational learning procedures that allow abstract, coherent, structured representations to be derived from patterns of evidence, given certain assumptions [12–15]. One advantage of this formal learning account is that it specifies, with some precision, the kinds of abilities that must be in place in order for learning to occur. We will give an overview of the causal Bayes net formalism and then outline recent research regarding two foundational types of abilities that would support causal learning within this formal account. Some aspects of these abilities have already been investigated empirically, but we will also point to crucial questions that have yet to be explored.

## Causal Bayes nets

Causal directed graphical models, or causal Bayes nets, have been developed in the philosophy of science and statistical literature over the last 15 years [12–15]. The models provide a formal account of a kind of inductive inference that is particularly important in scientific theory-formation. Scientists infer causal structure by observing the patterns of conditional probability among events (as in statistical analysis) by examining the consequences of interventions (as in experiments) or, usually, by combining the two

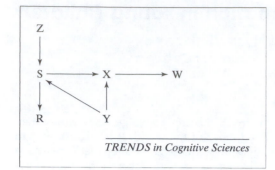

**Figure 1** A causal Bayes net, R, S, W, X, Y, Z represent variables and the arrows represent causal relations between those variables.

types of evidence. Causal Bayes nets provide a mathematical account of these inferences and so a kind of inductive causal logic.

Causal relations are represented by directed acyclic graphs. The graphs consist of variables, representing types of events or states of the world, and directed edges (arrows) representing the causal relations between those variables (see Figure 1). The structure of a causal graph constrains the probability of the variables in that graph. In particular, it constrains the CONDITIONAL INDEPENDENCIES among those variables (see Glossary). These constraints can be captured by a single formal assumption: the CAUSAL MARKOV ASSUMPTION. The causal Markov assumption specifies that, given a particular causal structure, only some patterns of conditional independence will occur among the variables. Therefore, we can use knowledge of the causal graph to predict the patterns of conditional probability.

## Glossary

### Assumptions

**The causal Markov assumption:** For any variable $X$ in a causal graph, $X$ is independent of all other variables in the graph (except for its own direct and indirect effects) conditional on its own direct causes.

**The faithfulness assumption:** In the joint distribution on the variables in the graph, all conditional independencies are consequences of the Markov assumption applied to the graph.

**The intervention assumption:** A variable $I$ is an intervention on a variable $X$ in a causal graph if and only if: (1) $I$ is exogenous (that is, is not caused by any other variables in the graph); (2) directly fixes the value of $X$ to $x$; and (3) does not affect the values of any other variables in the graph except through its influence on $X$.

### Definitions of independence and conditional independence

**Conditional independence:** Two variables are independent in probability conditional on some third variable $Z$ if and only if $P(x, y|z) = P(x|z)*P(y|z)$. That is for every value $x$, $y$, and $z$ of $X$, $Y$ and $Z$ the probability of $x$ and $y$ given $z$ equals the probability of $x$ given $z$ multiplied by the probability of $y$ given $z$.

**Unconditional independence:** Two variables $X$ and $Y$ are unconditionally independent in probability if and only if for every value $x$ of $X$ and $y$ of $Y$ the probability of $x$ and $y$ occurring together equals the unconditional probability of $x$ multiplied by the unconditional probability of $y$. That is $P(x$ and $y) = P(x)*P(y)$.

The constraints also allow us to determine what will happen when we intervene from outside to change the value of a particular variable. When two variables are genuinely related in a causal way then, holding other variables constant, intervening to change the value of one variable should change the value of the other. Indeed, philosophers have recently argued that this is just what it means for two variables to be causally related [16,17]. If we assume a particular formal definition of intervention (the INTERVENTION ASSUMPTION), we can use causal Bayes nets to predict the effects of interventions on a causal structure. A central aspect of causal Bayes nets, indeed the thing that makes them causal, is that they allow us to freely go back and forth from evidence derived from observations to inferences about interventions and vice-versa.

We can also use the formalism to work backwards and learn the causal graph from patterns of conditional probability and intervention. This type of learning requires a third assumption: the FAITHFULNESS ASSUMPTION. Given the faithfulness assumption, it is possible to infer complex causal structure from patterns of conditional dependence and independence and intervention. In some cases, it is also possible to accurately infer the existence and even the structure of new unobserved variables that are common causes of the observed variables [18,19]. Computationally tractable learning algorithms have been designed to accomplish these tasks and have been extensively applied in a range of disciplines [e.g., 20,21].

Recently, several investigators have suggested that adults' causal knowledge might involve implicit forms of Bayes nets representations and learning algorithms [22–27]. However, adults have extensive experience and often, explicit tuition in causal inference. If young children could use versions of Bayes nets assumptions and computations they would have a powerful tool for making causal inferences. They might, at least in principle, use such methods to uncover the kind of causal structure involved in everyday intuitive theories. [28,29] However, learning of the sort represented by the causal Bayes net formalism requires: (i) the ability to learn from conditional probabilities, (ii) the ability to learn from interventions, and (iii) the ability to combine these two types of learning. Is there any evidence that young children have these prerequisite abilities?

## Learning from conditional probabilities

The basic data for Bayes net inferences are judgments about the conditional independence of variables, judgments that require computing the conditional probabilities of values of those variables. There has recently been a great deal of work suggesting that, given non-causal data, such probabilities are computed spontaneously even by infants [30]. One such finding showed that eight-month-old infants could calculate the conditional probabilities of linguistic syllables in an artificial language [31]. Since then the experiments have been replicated with non-linguistic tones [32], with simultaneous visual stimuli [33], and with temporal sequences of visual stimuli [34]. These findings suggest that conditional probability information is available to infants and may be translated into more abstract representations.

There are still, however, many unanswered questions. Previous experiments have pitted conditional probabilities of 1 against those of less than one (usually 0.33), and shown that infants

can distinguish these levels of probability. We do not know if infants can discriminate among finer degrees of conditional probability. Moreover, we do not know if infants can calculate CONDITIONAL DEPENDENCE and INDEPENDENCE, that is, whether they can tell that one stimulus is dependent on another only conditional on some other stimulus (a kind of conditional conditional probability). Finally, we do not know whether infants' ability to track the conditional probability of non-causal stimuli in these domains extends to an ability to track the conditional probability of candidate causes and effects. However, studies answering these questions should be feasible with the existing techniques.

We do know more about conditional probability judgments in young children. Clearly, young children cannot explicitly and consciously relate conditional probability to causation. However, we can show children novel causal relations among novel types of events, for example, by presenting them with a newly-invented machine. We give children information about the conditional probabilities of those events and see what causal conclusions they draw.

Two-and-a-half-year-olds can discriminate conditional independence and dependence, that is, conditional conditional probabilities, even with controls for frequency, and can use that information to make judgments about causation [35]. In these experiments children saw various combinations of objects placed on a machine, which did or did not light up. The children were told that 'blickets make the machine go' and were asked to identify which objects were blickets. For example, children saw the sequence of events depicted in Figure 2a, and the control sequence depicted in Figure 2b. In Figure 2a the effect $E$ (the detector lighting up) is correlated with both object A and object B. However, $E$ is independent in probability of B conditional on A, but $E$ remains dependent on A conditional on B. In Figure 2b each block activates the detector the same number of times as in Figure 2a but the conditional independence patterns are the same for A and B. Children consistently choose A rather than B as the blicket, in the first condition, and choose equally between the two blocks in the second condition. Assuming that the causal

(a) One-cause condition

Object A activates the detector by itself    Object B does not activate the detector by itself    Both objects activate the detector (demonstrated twice)    Children are asked if each one is a blicket

(b) Two-cause condition

Object A activates the detector by itself (demonstrated three times)    Object B does not activate the detector by itself (demonstrated once)    Object B activates the detector by itself (demonstrated twice)    Children are asked if each one is a blicket

(c) Inference condition

Both objects activate the detector    Object A does not activate the detector by itself    Children are asked if each is a blicket

(d) Backward blocking condition

Both objects activate the detector    Object A activates the detector by itself    Children are asked if each is a blicket

*TRENDS in Cognitive Sciences*

**Figure 2**  Screening-off and backwards blocking. In the screening-off procedure [35], children are presented with two conditions: (a) In the one-cause condition, only object A causes the machine to go; (b) In the control two-cause condition, both A and B cause the machine to go. In the backwards-blocking procedure [36], there are also two conditions: (c) In the inference condition only B makes the machine go; (d) In backwards blocking, A makes the machine go, and B may or may not make the machine go. (See text for results.)

relations are deterministic, generative and non-interactive, a Bayes net account would generate a similar conclusion.

Moreover, in similar experiments, four-year-old children used principles of Bayesian inference to combine prior probability information with information about the conditional probability of events. [36]. For example, suppose children see the sequence of events in Figures 2c and 2d. On a Bayes net account, the causal structure of 2c is clear: A does not cause the effect and B does, and the children also say this. However, the causal structure of 2d is ambiguous, it could be that A and B both make the detector go, but it is also possible that only A does. Indeed, children give both types of responses. However, we can increase the prior probability of the 'A only' structure by telling the children beforehand that almost none of the blocks are blickets. Children who are told that blickets are rare are more likely to choose the 'A only' structure—that is to say that A is a blicket but B is not.

Four-year-olds can also perform even more complex kinds of reasoning about conditional dependencies, and they do so in many domains, biological and psychological as well as physical. In one experiment children were shown a monkey puppet and various combinations of flowers in a vase (see Figure 3). They were told that some flowers made the monkey sneeze and others didn't. Then they were shown the following sequence of events: Flowers A and B together made monkey sneeze. Flowers A and C together made monkey sneeze. Flowers B and C together did not make monkey sneeze. Children correctly concluded that A would make the monkey sneeze by itself, but B and C would not [37]. In a frequency control condition, in which

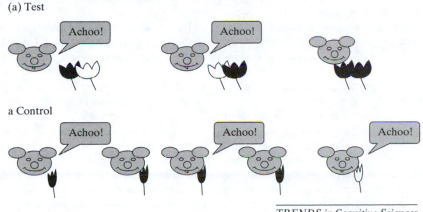

(a) Test

a Control

*TRENDS in Cognitive Sciences*

**Figure 3** Screening-off in a biological task [37]. (a) Test condition: children see that the red and yellow flowers together make Monkey sneeze and that the blue and yellow flowers together make Monkey sneeze, but that the red and blue flowers together do not make Monkey sneeze. (b) Control condition: children see identical frequency information but each flower is presented singly; the red and blue flower each make Monkey sneeze half the time; the yellow flower makes Monkey sneeze all the time. In each condition, children are asked which flower makes the Monkey sneeze. Children correctly choose the yellow flower in the test condition but choose at chance in the frequency control condition.

flowers B and C made monkey sneeze half the time and flower C all the time, children chose each of the three flowers equally often.

## Learning from interventions

Conditional probability is one basic type of evidence for causation. The other basic type of evidence involves understanding interventions and their consequences. The technical definition of the INTERVENTION ASSUMPTION might look formidable but it actually maps well onto our everyday intuitions about intentional goal-directed human actions. We assume that such actions are the result of our freely willed mental intentions, and so unaffected by the variables they act on (Clause 1). Clause 2 is basic to understanding goal-directed action. When actions are genuinely goal-directed we can tell whether our actions are effective: that is whether they determine the state of the variables we act upon, and we modify the actions if they are not. Clause 3 is essential to understanding means–ends relations. When we act on means to gain an end we assume that our actions influenced other variables (our ends) through, and only through, the influence on the acted-upon variable (the means).

Moreover, we assume that these features of our own interventions are shared by the interventions of others. This is an important assumption because it greatly increases our opportunities for learning about causal structure—we learn not only from our own actions but also from the actions of others.

Several features of this understanding of intervention appear to be in place at a very early age. In terms of Clause 2, infants seem to 'parse' sequences of human actions into meaningful goal-directed units [38,39]. By around seven months of age, infants understand at least some particular goals of human action and understand that goal-directed actions should be understood differently than interactions between objects [40–42]. For instance, if infants see a hand reach several times towards a particular object and the location of the object is changed, infants look longer when the hand reaches to a new object in the familiar location (i.e. the goal changes) than the familiar object in a novel location (i.e.

the path changes). When a stick, rather than a hand, contacts the object, infants react only to the change in path. By one year, infants seem to understand even more complex facts about means–ends relations, relevant to Clause 3. For example, 12–14 month-olds recognize that actors understand means–ends relations and may take different alternative routes to obtain an end [43,44].

In terms of Clause 1, by 18 months, infants will 'read through' failed actions to infer the underlying intention of the actor [45]. When 18-month-olds see another person try and fail to pull apart an object for example, they will immediately pull apart the object themselves—something they will not do if they see a machine perform a similar action on the object. By two years, children explicitly and spontaneously explain goal-directed actions as the result of internally generated mental states, desires or intentions, that are designed to alter the world in particular ways [7].

Infants also generalize from their own interventions to those of others and vice-versa. For example, you can train three-month-old infants to reach for objects by giving them Velcro mittens that allow them to manipulate objects they would not otherwise be able to grasp [46]. Infants who received such training generalized from their own interventions and were more likely to understand the directed reaches of others. Conversely, the extensive literature on early imitation shows that nine-month-old infants who see another person perform a novel intervention (i.e. an experimenter touching the top of a box with his head to make the box light up) will adopt that intervention themselves—the babies will put their own heads on the box [47].

## Learning from combinations of conditional probabilities and interventions

We have seen that infants and young children seem to conceive of their own and others interventions in a distinctive way that might support causal learning. The crucial aspect of causal Bayes nets, however, is that intervention and conditional probability information can be coherently combined and inferences can go in both directions. Animals have at least some forms of the ability to infer conditional probabilities, and even conditional independencies, among events—as in the phenomenon of blocking in classical conditioning [48]. They also have at least some ability to infer causal relations between their interventions and the events that follow them, as in operant conditioning and trial and error learning. However, there is, at best, only very limited and fragile evidence of non-human animals' ability to combine these two types of learning in a genuinely causal way [49,50]. Why is it that when Pavlov's dogs associate the bell with food, they don't just spontaneously ring the bell when they are hungry? The animals seem able to associate the bell ringing with food, and if they are given an opportunity to act on the bell and that action leads to food, they can replicate that action. Moreover, there may be some transfer from operant to classical conditioning. However, the animals do not seem to go directly from learning novel conditional independencies to designing a correct novel intervention. Moreover, surprisingly primates show only a very limited and fragile ability to learn by directly imitating the interventions of others, an ability that is robustly present in one-year-old humans [50].

By contrast, very young children solve causal problems in a way that suggests just this coordination of observation and action. Preschool children, for instance, can use contingencies, including patterns of conditional independence, to design novel interventions to solve causal problems. Three-year-olds in the blicket detector experiments use information about conditional independence to produce appropriate interventions (such as taking a particular object off the detector to make it turn off) that they have never seen or produced before. [35–37].

Even more dramatically, four-year-olds used patterns of conditional dependence to craft new interventions that required them to cross domain boundaries, and overturn earlier knowledge [37]. For example, children were asked beforehand whether you could make a machine light up by flicking a switch or by saying 'Machine, please go'. All of the children said that flicking the switch would work but talking to the machine

would not. Then the children saw that the effect was unconditionally dependent on saying 'Machine, please go', but was independent of the switch conditional on the spoken request. When children were then asked to make the machine stop 75% said 'Machine, please stop'.

Most crucially, however, four-year-olds can also combine patterns of conditional dependence and intervention to infer causal structure and do so in a way that recognizes the special character of intervention. This kind of inference is naturally done by Bayes nets and is not a feature of other accounts of causal reasoning such as associationist [51,52] or causal power [53] accounts. Children can use such combinations of information to identify causal direction (Does X cause Y or does Y cause X?) and even to infer the existence of unobserved variables. They can even do so when the relations between the events are probabilistic rather than deterministic [29].

For example, four-year-olds were shown a 'puppet machine' in which two stylized puppets moved simultaneously. They were told that some puppets *almost* always, but not always, made others go. In one condition they saw the experimenter intervene to move puppet X, and puppet Y also moved simultaneously on five of six trials. On one trial the experimenter moved X and Y did not move. In the other condition children simply observed the puppets move together simultaneously five times, but on one trial the experimenter intervened to move X and Y did not move. The children accurately concluded that X made Y move in the first case, whereas Y made X move in the second [29].

## Conclusion

Although much more research is necessary (e.g. see Box 1), it seems that infants and young children can detect patterns of conditional probability, understand the nature of their own and others interventions, and to at least some extent, integrate conditional probability and intervention information spontaneously and without reinforcement.

Each of these abilities, by itself, provides a powerful foundation for learning of several kinds, not just causal learning. Significantly, for

# Questions for future research

### Questions about conditional probability

- Can children distinguish only conditional probabilities of 1 and <1 or can they make finer distinctions? Are judgments of conditional independence possible in infancy?
- How do children get from frequency information to judgments of conditional probability? How do they deal with the problem of small sample sizes?

### Questions about intervention

- Do children treat only human actions as interventions or can they recognize 'natural experiments'?
- Do children understand that actions must fulfill the criteria of the Intervention Assumption to count as interventions? Do they discount 'bad' interventions?

### Questions about causal structure

- Can children use patterns of evidence to discriminate more complex causal structures (e.g. causal chains versus common causes versus common effects)? Can they use them to determine parameterizations of a graph (e.g. the strength of causal links, and whether they are deterministic, generative, inhibitory or interactive)?
- Can children use patterns of evidence to determine unobserved as well as observed causal structure, to discover new variables, or split or merge existing variables?
- How do children integrate spatial and temporal information with information about conditional probability and intervention?

example, in at least one experiment infants treated the units that emerged from statistical auditory regularities as English words, that is, as genuinely linguistic representations that could be combined with others in a rule-governed way [54]. Infants might similarly use conditional probabilities of visual stimuli to segregate scenes into object representations, which can then be combined in a rule-governed way [55]. Furthermore, understanding and imitating the interventions of others, not only in simple action imitation but in more complex cases such as taking on the goals of others, provides infants with powerful tools for learning social behavior [47].

Recent work on the causal Bayes net formalism, however, suggests that combining these two types of learning provides particularly powerful tools for learning causal structure, of the kind encoded in intuitive theories, and provides a formal account of how this might be done. Elements of such learning appear to be in place in infancy, and these elements are clearly used to learn causal relations by early childhood.

## Acknowledgements

This research was supported by NSF grant DLS0132487. We thank Clark Glymour and Thomas Richardson for helpful comments.

## References

Gopnik, A. and Meltzoff, A.N. (1997) *Words, Thoughts and Theories*, MIT Press

Gelman, S.A. and Raman, L. (2002) Folk biology as a window onto cognitive development. *Hum. Dev.* 45, 61–68

Flavell, J.H. (1999) Cognitive development: children's knowledge about the mind. *Annu. Rev. Psychol.* 50, 21–45

Harris, P.L. *et al.* (1996) Children's use of counterfactual thinking in causal reasoning. *Cognition* 61, 233–259

Hickling, A.K. and Wellman, H.M. (2001) The emergence of children's causal explanations and theories: evidence from everyday conversation. *Dev. Psychol.* 37, 668–683

Sobel, D.M. (2004) Exploring the coherence of young children's explanatory abilities: evidence from generating counterfactuals. *Br. J. Dev. Psychol.* 22, 37–58

Wellman, H.M. *et al.* (1997) Young children's psychological, physical, and biological explanations. In *The Emergence Of Core Domains Of Thought: Children's Reasoning About Physical, Psychological, And Biological Phenomena. (New Directions for Child Development, No. 75)* (Wellman, H.M. and Inagaki, K., eds), pp. 7–25, Jossey-Bass/Pfeiffer

Slaughter, V. and Gopnik, A. (1996) Conceptual coherence in the child's theory of mind: Training children to understand belief. *Child Dev.* 67, 2967–2988

Slaughter, V. *et al.* (1999) Constructing a coherent theory: children's biological understanding of life and death. In *Children's Understanding Of Biology And Health* (Siegal, M. Peterson, C. *et. al.*, eds), pp. 71–96, Cambridge University Press

Slaughter, V. and Lyons, M. (2003) Learning about life and death in early childhood. *Cogn. Psychol.* 46, 1–30

Ross, N. *et al.* (2003) Cultural and experimental differences in the development of folkbiological induction. *Cogn. Dev.* 18, 25–47

Glymour, C. and Cooper, G. (1999) *Computation, Causation, and Discovery*, AAAI/MIT Press

Pearl, J. (1988) *Probabilistic Reasoning in Intelligent Systems*, Morgan Kaufmann

Pearl, J. (2000) *Causality*, Oxford University Press

Spirtes, P. *et al.* (1993) *Causation, Prediction, and Search (Springer Lecture Notes in Statistic)*, Springer-Verlag

Hausman, D.M. and Woodward, J. (1999) Independence, invariance and the causal Markov condition. *Br. J. Philos. Sci.* 50, 521–583

Woodward, J. (2003) *Making Things Happen: A Theory of Causal Explanation*, Oxford University Press

Silva, R. *et al.* (2003) Learning measurement models for unobserved variables. In *Proceedings of the 18th Conference on Uncertainty in Artificial Intelligence*, AAAI Press

Richardson, T. and Spirtes, P. (2003) Causal inference via ancestral graph models. In *Highly Structured Stochastic Systems* (Green, P. *et al.*, eds), Oxford University Press

Ramsey, J. *et al.* (2002) Automated remote sensing with near-infra-red reflectance spectra: carbonate recognition. *Data Mining and Knowledge Discovery* 6, 277–293

Shipley, B. (2000) *Cause and Correlation in Biology*, Oxford University Press

Glymour, C. (2001) *The Mind's Arrows: Bayes Nets and Graphical Causal Models in Psychology*, MIT Press

Glymour, C. (2003) Learning, prediction and causal Bayes nets. *Trends Cogn. Sci.* 7, 43–48

Glymour, C. and Cheng, P. (1999) Causal mechanism and probability: a normative approach. In *Rational Models of Cognition* (Oaksford, K. and Chater, N., eds), pp. 295–313, Oxford University Press

Rehder, B. and Hastie, R. (2001) Causal knowledge and categories: the effects of causal beliefs on categorization, induction, and similarity. *J. Exp. Psychol. Gen.* 130, 323–360

Steyvers, M. *et al.* (2003) Inferring causal networks from observations and interventions. *Cogn. Sci.* 27, 453–489

Waldmann, M.R. and Hagmayer, Y. (2001) Estimating causal strength: the role of structural knowledge and processing effort. *Cognition* 1, 27–58

Gopnik, A. and Glymour, C. (2002) Causal maps and Bayes nets: a cognitive and computational account of theory-formation. In *The Cognitive Basis of Science* (Carruthers, P. *et al.*, eds), pp. 117–132, Cambridge University Press

Gopnik, A. *et al.* (2004) A theory of causal learning in children: causal maps and Bayes nets. *Psychol. Rev.* 111, 3–32

Aslin, R.N. *et al.* (1998) Computation of conditional probability statistics by 8-month-old infants. *Psychol. Sci.* 9, 321–324

Saffran, J.R. *et al.* (1996) Statistical learning by 8-month old infants. *Science* 274, 1926–1928

Saffran, J.R. *et al.* (1999) Statistical learning of tone sequences by human infants and adults. *Cognition* 70, 27–52

Fiser, J. and Aslin, R.N. (2002) Statistical learning of new visual feature combinations by infants. *Proc. Natl. Acad. Sci. U. S. A.* 99, 15822–15826

Kirkham, N.Z. *et al.* (2002) Visual statistical learning in infancy: evidence of a domain general learning mechanism. *Cognition* 83, B35–B42

Gopnik, A. *et al.* (2001) Causal learning mechanisms in very young children: two-, three-, and four-year-olds infer causal relations from patterns of variation and covariation. *Dev. Psychol.* 37, 620–629

Sobel, D.M. *et al.* (2004) Children's causal inferences from indirect evidence: backwards blocking and Bayesian reasoning in preschoolers. *Cogn. Sci.* 28, 3

Schulz, L. and Gopnik, A. (2004) Causal learning across domains. *Dev. Psychol.* 40, 162–176

Baldwin, D.A. and Baird, J.A. (2001) Discerning intentions in dynamic human action. *Trends Cogn. Sci.* 5, 171–178

Baldwin, D.A. *et al.* (1999) Infants parse dynamic action. *Child Dev.* 72, 708–717

Woodward, A.L. (1998) Infants selectively encode the goal object of an actor's reach. *Cognition* 69, 1–34

Woodward, A. and Sommerville, J.A. (2000) Twelve-month-old infants interpret action in context. *Psychol. Sci.* 11, 73–77

Phillips, A. *et al.* (2002) Infants' ability to connect gaze and emotional expression to intentional action. *Cognition* 85, 53–78

Gergely, G. *et al.* (2002) Rational imitation in preverbal infants. *Nature* 415, 755

Gergely, G. *et al.* (1995) Taking the intentional stance at 12 months of age. *Cognition* 56, 165–193

Meltzoff, A.N. (1995) Understanding the intentions of others: reenactment of intended acts by 18-month-old children. *Dev. Psychol.* 31, 838–850

Woodward, A.L. *et al.* (2001) How infants make sense of intentional action. In *Intentions and Intentionality: Foundations of Social Cognition* (Malle, B. *et al.*, eds), pp. 149–169, MIT Press

Meltzoff, A.N. and Prinz, W., (eds). (2002). Cambridge University Press

Rescorla, R.A. and Wagner, A.R. (1972) A theory of Pavlovian conditioning: variations in the effectiveness of reinforcement and nonreinforcement. In *Classical Conditioning II: Current Theory and Research* (Black, A.H. and Prokasy, W.F., eds), pp. 64–99, Appleton-Century-Crofts

Povinelli, D. (2000) *Folk Physics for Apes: The Chimpanzee's Theory of How the World Works*, Oxford University Press

Tomasello, M. and Call, J. (1997) *Primate Cognition*, Oxford University Press

Shanks, D.R. and Dickinson, A. (1987) Associative accounts of causality judgment. In *The Psychology of Learning and Motivation: Advances in Research and Theory* (Vol. 21) (Bower, G.H., ed), pp. 229–261, Academic Press

Shanks, D.R. (1985) Forward and backward blocking in human contingency judgement. *Q.J. Exp. Psychol. B* 37, 1–21

Cheng, P.W. (1997) From covariation to causation: a causal power theory. *Psychol. Rev.* 104, 367–405

Saffran, J. (2001) Words in a sea of sounds: the output of infant statistical learning. *Cognition* 81, 149–169

Fiser, J. and Aslin, R.N. (2001) Unsupervised statistical learning of higher-order spatial structures from visual scenes. *Psychol. Sci.* 12, 499–504

# Education for Justice: A Modern Statement of the Platonic View

LAWRENCE KOHLBERG

When I called this essay a Platonic view I hoped it implied a paradox that was more than cute. It is surely a paradox that a modern psychologist should claim as his most relevant source not Freud, Skinner, or Piaget but the ancient believer in the ideal form of the good. Yet as I have tried to trace the stages of development of morality and to use these stages as the basis of a moral education program, I have realized more and more that its implication was the reassertion of the Platonic faith in the power of the rational good.

It is usually supposed that psychology contributes to moral education by telling us appropriate *methods* of moral teaching and learning. A Skinnerian will speak of proper schedules of reinforcement in moral learning, a Freudian will speak of the importance of the balance of parental love and firmness which will promote superego-identification, and so on. When Skinnerians or Freudians speak on the topic of moral education, then, they start by answering yes to Meno's question "Is virtue something that can be taught?" and go on to tell us how. In *Walden Two*, Skinner not only tells us that virtue comes by practice and reinforcement but designs an ideal republic which educates all of its children to be virtuous in this way.

My own response to these questions was more modest. When confronted by a group of parents who asked me "How can we help make our children virtuous?" I had to answer, as Socrates, "You must think I am very fortunate to know how virtue is acquired. The fact is that far from knowing whether it can be taught, I have no idea what virtue really is." Like most psychologists, I knew that science could teach me nothing as to what virtue is. Science could speak

about causal relations, about the relations of means to ends, but it could not speak about ends or values themselves. If I could not define virtue or the ends of moral education, could I really offer advice as to the means by which virtue should be taught? Could it really be argued that the means for teaching obedience to authority are the same as the means for teaching freedom of moral opinion, that the means for teaching altruism are the same as the means for teaching competitive striving, that the making of a good storm trooper involves the same procedures as the making of a philosopher-king?

It appears, then, that we must either be totally silent about moral education or speak to the nature of virtue. In this essay, I shall throw away my graduate school wisdom about the distinction of fact and value and elaborate a view of the nature of virtue like that of Socrates and Plato. Let me summarize some of the elements of this Platonic view.

First, virtue is ultimately one, not many, and it is always the same ideal form regardless of climate or culture.

Second, the name of this ideal form is justice.

Third, not only is the good one, but virtue is knowledge of the good. He who knows the good chooses the good.

Fourth, the kind of knowledge of the good which is virtue is philosophical knowledge or intuition of the ideal form of the good, not correct opinion or acceptance of conventional beliefs.

Fifth, the good can then be taught, but its teachers must in a certain sense be philosopher-kings.

Sixth, the reason the good can be taught is because we know it all along dimly or at a low level and its teaching is more a calling out than an instruction.

Seventh, the reason we think the good cannot be taught is because the same good is known differently at different levels and direct instruction cannot take place across levels.

*Source:* Kohlberg, L. K. (1970). Education for justice: A modern statement of the Platonic view. In N. Sizer & T. Sizer (Eds.), *Five lectures on moral education* (pp. 57–60). Cambridge, MA: Harvard University Press.

Eighth, then the teaching of virtue is the asking of questions and the pointing of the way, not the giving of answers. Moral education is the leading of men upward, not the putting into the mind of knowledge that was not there before.

I will spend little time on my disagreements with Plato, except to point out that I conceive justice as equality instead of Plato's hierarchy. I should note, however, that I have earlier discussed my views within John Dewey's framework. In speaking of a Platonic view, I am not discarding my basic Deweyism, but I am challenging a brand of common sense first enunciated by Aristotle, with which Dewey partly agrees. According to Aristotle's *Ethics*, "virtue is of two kinds, intellectual and moral. While intellectual virtue owes its birth and growth to teaching, moral virtue comes about as a result of habit. The moral virtues we get by first exercising them; we become just by doing just acts, temperate by doing temperate acts, brave by doing brave acts."

Aristotle then is claiming that there are two spheres, the moral and the intellectual, and that learning by doing is the only real method in the moral sphere. Dewey, of course, does not distinguish the intellectual from the moral and objects to lists of virtues and vices in either area. Nevertheless, Deweyite thinking has lent itself to the Boy Scout approach to moral education which has dominated American practices in this field and which has its most direct affinities with Aristotle's views.

American educational psychology, like Aristotle, divides the personality up into cognitive abilities, passions or motives, and traits of character. Moral character, then, consists of a bag of virtues and vices. One of the earliest major American studies of moral character, that of Hartshorne and May, was conducted in the late twenties. Their bag of virtues included honesty, service, and self-control. A more recent major study by Havighurst and Taba added responsibility, friendliness, and moral courage to the Hartshorne and May bag. Aristotle's original bag included temperance, liberality, pride, good temper, truthfulness, and justice. The Boy Scout bag is well known, a Scout should be honest, loyal, reverent, clean, brave.

Given a bag of virtues, it is evident how we build character. Children should be exhorted to practice these virtues, should be told that happiness, fortune, and good repute will follow in their wake; adults around them should be living examples of these virtues; and children should be given daily opportunities to practice them. Daily chores will build responsibility; the opportunity to give to the Red Cross will build service or altruism, etc.

Let us start at the beginning, then. The objection of the psychologist to the bag of virtues is that there are no such things. Virtues and vices are labels by which people award praise or blame to others, but the ways people use praise and blame toward others are not the ways in which they think when making moral decisions themselves. You or I may not find a Hell's Angel truly honest, but he may find himself so. Hartshorne and May found this out to their dismay forty years ago by their monumental experimental studies of children's cheating and stealing. In brief, they and others since have found:

1. You can't divide the world into honest and dishonest people. Almost everyone cheats some of the time; cheating is distributed in bell-curve fashion around a level of moderate cheating.

2. If a person cheats in one situation, it doesn't mean he will or won't in another. There is very little correlation between situational cheating tests. In other words, it is not a character trait of dishonesty which makes a child cheat in a given situation. If it were, you could predict he would cheat in a second situation if he did in the first.

3. People's verbal moral values about honesty have nothing to do with how they act. People who cheat express as much or more moral disapproval of cheating as those who don't cheat.

The fact that there are no traits of character corresponding to the virtues and vices of conventional language should comfort us. Those who would try to capture for themselves the bag of virtues prescribed by the culture find themselves in the plight described by the theme song of the show, "You're a Good Man, Charlie Brown."

You're a good man, Charlie Brown. You have humility, nobility and a sense of honor that is very rare indeed. You are kind to all the animals and every little bird. With a heart of gold, you believe what you're told, every single solitary word. You bravely face adversity; you're cheerful through the day; you're thoughtful, brave and courteous. You're a good man, Charlie Brown. You're a prince, and a prince could be a king. With a heart such as yours you could open any door—if only you weren't so wishy-washy.*

If, like Charlie Brown, we define our moral aims in terms of virtues and vices, we are defining them in terms of the praise and blame of others and are caught in the pull of being all things to all men and end up being wishy-washy. The attraction of the bag of virtues approach to moral education is that it encourages the assumption that everyone can be a moral educator. It assumes that any adult of middle-class respectability or virtue knows what virtue is and is qualified to teach it by dint of being adult and respectable. We all have to make these assumptions as parents, but perhaps they are not sound. Socrates asked "whether good men have known how to hand on to someone else the goodness that was in themselves" and goes on to cite one virtuous Greek leader after another who had nonvirtuous sons. Shortly, I will describe what I believe to be a valid measure of moral maturity. When this measure was given to a group of middle-class men in their twenties and also to their fathers, we found almost no correlation between the two. The morally mature father was no more likely to have a morally mature son than was a father low on moral development. So numbers now support Socrates' bitter observation that good fathers don't have good sons or don't qualify as teachers of virtue.

*Lyrics from the title song "You're a Good Man, Charlie Brown," from the musical play "You're a Good Man, Charlie Brown," words and music by Clark Gesner © 1965 and 1967 by Jeremy Music Inc. and reprinted by permission.

In the context of the school, the foolishness of assuming that any teacher is qualified to be a moral educator becomes evident if we ask "Would this assumption make sense if we were to think of moral education as something carried on between one adult and another?" A good third-grade teacher of the new math and a good math teacher of graduate students operate under much the same set of assumptions. How many moralizing schoolteachers, however, would wish to make the claim that Protagoras made to young graduate students, that "I am rather better than anyone else at helping a man to acquire a good and noble character, worthy of the fee I charge."

If we think of moral education as something carried on at the adult level, we recognize that the effective moral educator is something of a revolutionary rather than an instiller of virtues. Protagoras could safely collect his fees for improving character because he meant by moral education the teaching of the rhetorical skills for getting ahead. When Socrates really engaged in adult moral education, however, he was brought up on trial for corrupting the Athenian youth.

Perhaps there is still nothing more dangerous than the serious teaching of virtue. Socrates was condemned to death, because, as he said in the *Apology*:

> I do nothing but go about persuading you all, old and young alike, not to take thought for your person or property, but for the improvement of the soul. I tell you virtue is not given by money, but that from virtue comes money, and every other good of man, public as well as private. This is my teaching, and if this is the doctrine which corrupts the youth, my doctrines are mischievous indeed. Therefore, Men of Athens, either acquit me or not; but whichever you do, understand that I shall never alter my ways not even if I have to die many times.

I stress the revolutionary nature of moral education partly because at this time it is comforting to reach back into history and recall that it is not only America that kills its moral educators. Martin Luther King joins a long list of men who had the arrogance not only to teach justice but to live it in such a way that other men felt uncomfortable about their own goodness, their own justice. In the last weeks, one has frequently heard the question, "Why King, not Carmichael or Brown?" It is not the man who preaches power and hate who gets assassinated. He is not a threat; he is like the worst in others. It is the man who is too good for other men to take, who questions the basis on which men erect their paltry sense of goodness, who dies.

Martin Luther King and Socrates as examples of moral educators suggest that while the bag of virtues encapsulated the need for moral improvement in the child, a genuine concern about the growth of justice in the child implies a similar concern for the growth of justice in the society. This is the implicit basis of Kozol's challenging the moral authority of a passive teacher in a ghetto school. I do not mean to imply by this that true moral education is a matter of political indoctrination of the young in the name of reform. Rather, I am arguing that the only constitutionally legitimate form of moral education in the schools is the teaching of justice and that the teaching of justice in the schools requires just schools. It has been argued by Ball that the Supreme Court's Schemp decision calls for the restraint of public school efforts at moral education since such education is equivalent to the state propagation of religion, conceived as any articulated value system.

The problems as to the legitimacy of moral education in the public schools disappear, however, if the proper content of moral education is recognized to be the values of justice which themselves prohibit the imposition of beliefs of one group upon another. The requirement implied by the Bill of Rights that the schools recognize the equal rights of individuals in matters of belief or values does not mean that the schools are not to be "value-oriented." Recognition of equal rights does not imply value neutrality, i.e., the view that all value systems are equally sound. Because we respect the individual rights of members of particular groups in our society, it is sometimes believed that we must consider their values as valid as our own. Because we must respect the rights of an Eichmann, how-

ever, we need not treat his values as equal to that of the values of liberty and justice.

Public education is committed not only to maintenance of the rights of individuals but to the transmission of the values of respect for individual rights. The school is no more committed to value neutrality than is the government or the law. The school, like the government, is an institution with a basic function of maintaining and transmitting some, but not all, of the consensual values of society. The most fundamental values of a society are termed moral, and the major moral values in our society are the values of justice. According to any interpretation of the Constitution, the rationale for government is the preservation of the rights of individuals, i.e., of justice. The public school is as much committed to the maintenance of justice as is the court. Desegregation of the schools is not only a passive recognition of the equal rights of citizens to access to a public facility, like a swimming pool, but an active recognition of the responsibility of the school for "moral education," i.e., for transmission of the values of justice on which our society is founded. From our point of view, then, moral education may legitimately involve certain elements of social reform if they bear directly on the central values of justice on which the public schools are based.

The delicate balance between social reform and moral education is clarified by the example of Martin Luther King if you recognize that King was a moral leader, a moral educator of adults, not because he was a spokesman for the welfare of the Negroes, not because he was against violence, not because he was a minister of religion, but because, as he said, he was a drum major for justice. His words and deeds were primarily designed to induce America to respond to racial problems in terms of a sense of justice, and any particular action he took had value for this reason and not just because of the concrete political end it might achieve.

I have used King as an example of a moral educator to indicate that the difference between the political reformer and the moral educator is not a difference in the content of their concern. Civil rights is as much a matter of morality as is honesty in financial matters. The distinctive feature of moral education as against ordinary political action is in the relation of means and ends. A black power politician using unjust means in the name of civil rights is clearly not in the enterprise of teaching justice anymore than is the policeman in the enterprise of teaching honesty when he shoots down rioters. In King's case, however, acts of civil disobedience flowed directly from a sense of principles of justice and thus were moral leadership, not just propaganda or protest.

Let me recapitulate our argument so far. We have criticized the bag of virtues concept of moral education on the grounds first that there were no such things and second, if they were, they couldn't be taught or at least we didn't know how or who could teach them. Like Socrates, we claimed that ordinary people certainly didn't know how to do it, and yet there were no expert teachers of virtue as there were for the other arts. Rather than turning to nihilism, we pointed to an effective example of a moral educator at the adult social level, Martin Luther King. Since we could not define moral virtue at the individual level we tried it at the social level and found it to be justice and claimed that the central moral value of the school, like that of the society, was justice. Justice in turn is a matter of equal and universal human rights. We pointed to the cloud of virtue-labels attributed to King and pointed out that only one meant anything. Justice was not just one more fine-sounding word in a eulogy, it was the essence of King's moral leadership.

My hope is to have stirred some feelings about the seriousness and the reality of that big word, that Platonic form, justice, because men like King were willing to die for it. I suppose there may have been men willing to die for honesty, responsibility, and the rest of the bag of virtues, but, if so, we have no empathy with them. I am going to argue now, like Plato, that virtue is not many, but one, and its name is justice. Let me point out first that justice is not a character trait in the usual sense. You cannot make up behavior tests of justice, as Hartshorne

and May did for honesty, service, and self-control. One cannot conceive of a little set of behavior tests that would indicate that Martin Luther King or Socrates were high on a trait of justice. The reason for this is that justice is not a concrete rule of action, such as lies behind virtues like honesty.

To be honest means don't cheat, don't steal, don't lie. Justice is not a rule or a set of rules, it is a moral principle. By a moral principle we mean a mode of choosing which is universal, a rule of choosing which we want all people to adopt always in all situations. We know it is all right to be dishonest and steal to save a life because it is just, because a man's right to life comes before another man's right to property. We know it is sometimes right to kill, because it is sometimes just. The Germans who tried to kill Hitler were doing right because respect for the equal values of lives demands that we kill someone murdering others in order to save their lives. There are exceptions to rules, then, but no exception to principles. A moral obligation is an obligation to respect the right or claim of another person. A moral principle is a principle for resolving competing claims, you versus me, you versus a third person. There is only one principled basis for resolving claims: justice or equality. Treat every man's claim impartially regardless of the man. A moral principle is not only a rule of action but a reason for action. As a reason for action, justice is called respect for persons.

Because morally mature men are governed by the principle of justice rather than by a set of rules, there are not many moral virtues but one. Let us restate the argument in Plato's terms. Plato's argument is that what makes a virtuous action virtuous is that it is guided by knowledge of the good. A courageous action based on ignorance of danger is not courageous; a just act based on ignorance of justice is not just, etc. If virtuous action is action based on knowledge of the good, then virtue is one, because knowledge of the good is one. We have already claimed that knowledge of the good is one because the good is justice.

# A Cognitive-Developmental Analysis of Children's Sex-Role Concepts and Attitudes

LAWRENCE KOHLBERG
*University of Chicago*

Even if one does not accept the Freudian saga of the libido, one can hardly question the psychoanalytic assumption that sexuality constitutes the most significant area of interaction between biological givens and cultural values in human emotional life. If biological instincts are important in any area of man's social life, they are certainly most important in the sexual domain. Therefore it is in this area that we will most likely discover the nature of the interaction between biological and cultural patternings.

Oddly enough, our approach to the problems of sexual development starts directly with neither biology nor culture, but with cognition. In this chapter we shall elaborate and document a theory which assumes that basic sexual attitudes are not patterned directly by either biological instincts or arbitrary cultural norms, but by the child's cognitive organization of his social world along sex-role dimensions. Recent research evidence suggests that there are important "natural" components involved in the patterning of children's sex-role attitudes, since many aspects of sex-role attitudes appear to be universal across cultures and family structures, and to originate relatively early in the child's development. This patterning of sex-role attitudes is essentially "cognitive" in that it is rooted in the child's concepts of physical things—the bodies of himself and of others—concepts which he relates in turn to a social order that makes functional use of sex categories in quite culturally universal ways. It is not the child's biological instincts, but rather his cognitive organization of social-role concepts around universal physical

dimensions, which accounts for the existence of universals in sex-role attitudes.

Our theory, then, is cognitive in that it stresses the active nature of the child's thought as he organizes his role perceptions and role learnings around his basic conceptions of his body and his world. We shall stress (as does Mischel in this volume) the importance of the observational learning of social roles, i.e., learning that results from observation of the behavior of others rather than learning that results from reinforcement of one's own responses. We shall point out that this learning is cognitive in the sense that it is selective and internally organized by relational schemata rather than directly reflecting associations of events in the outer world. In regard to sex-role, these schemata that bind events together include concepts of the body, the physical and social world, and general categories of relationship (causality, substantiality, quantity, time, space, logical identity, and inclusion).

While we are talking about cognitive organization, and universals common to all children in sexual cognitions, we must take into account the fact that basic modes of cognitive organization change with age. As Piaget and his followers have documented in depth and detail, the child's basic cognitive organization of the physical world undergoes radical transformations with age development. So, too, do the child's conceptions of his social world. We shall review research findings which suggest that not only do young children's sex-role attitudes have universal aspects, but also that these attitudes change radically with age development. These age changes do not seem to be the result of age-graded sex-role socialization, but rather to be "natural" changes resulting from general trends of cognitive-social development. There is little reason to accept Freud's (1905) and Gesell and Ilg's (1943) view that these age changes are directly related to the maturation of the body or of body instincts. Instead, we shall

*Source:* Kohlberg, L. K. (1966). A cognitive–developmental analysis of children's sex-role concepts and attitudes. In E. E. Maccoby (Ed.), the development of sex differences (pp. 82–83, 164–166). New York: Holt, Rinehart, and Winston.

review evidence suggesting that these trends are the result of general experience-linked changes in modes of cognition. Sex-role concepts and attitudes change with age in universal ways because of universal age changes in basic modes of cognitive organization. Increasing evidence from studies in the Piaget tradition suggests culturally universal developmental shifts in conceptualizations of physical objects. Because children's sex-role concepts are essentially defined in universal physical, or body terms, these concepts, too, undergo universal developmental changes. As an example, recent research indicates that children develop a conception of themselves as having an unchangeable sexual identity at the same age and through the same processes that they develop conceptions of the invariable identity of physical objects.

In summary, then, the parent-child correlations for boys' sex-role attitudes seem to indicate that family climates can either facilitate or impede "natural" developmental trends. For girls, this interpretation is less satisfactory; but the complexity of the findings for girls, and the fact that they have not been replicated, makes it difficult for one to come up with an obvious alternative interpretation. Regardless of ultimate findings on parent-child sex-role correlates, the specificity of the correlations already established indicates that very generalized reinforcement and identification mechanisms do not in themselves provide an adequate explanation for the development of sex-role attitudes in children. These correlations become intelligible only when we interpret them in terms of the common or "natural" sex-role concepts, values, and identifications of children of a given age and sex. The development of these concepts and values, however, can be explained in terms of the basic cognitive-developmental trends and processes documented earlier in this chapter:

1. Gender identity or self-categorization as boy or girl is the basic organizer of sex-role attitudes.

2. This gender identity results from a basic physical reality judgment made relatively early in the child's development.

3. While this cognitive judgment is crystallizing into a conception of a constant, or categorical, gender identity during the years two to seven, the child's sex-role and body concepts may be influenced by certain environmental variables, with significant consequences for current and later sex-role attitudes.

4. Basic self-categorizations determine basic valuings. Masculine-feminine values develop out of the need to value things that are consistent with or like the self.

5. Basic universal sex-role stereotypes develop early in young children. These stereotypes arise from the child's conceptions of body differences, conceptions that are supported by visible differences in the sex assignment of social roles.

6. These basic sex-role stereotypes, then, lead to the development of masculine-feminine values in children. Although in general these stereotypes award superior prestige-competence values to the male role, they also award a number of superior value attributes to the female role. As awareness of these prestige values and stereotypes develops in the years four to eight, there is a tendency for both sexes to attribute greater power and prestige to the male role. However, the greater relative prestige of the adult male role does not imply an absence or decline of absolute prestige, or positive value, of the female role, a prestige that is sufficient to channel the girls' competence strivings into feminine role values.

7. After masculine-feminine values are acquired, the child tends to identify with like-sex figures, in particular the like-sex parent. Desire to be masculine leads to the desire to imitate a masculine model, which leads to a deeper emotional attachment to the model.

8. While identification with a like-sex person, and the formation of sex-role values in general, may be facilitated and consolidated by appropriate parental behavior, this process seems to take place without the presence of a same-sex parent, and under a variety of child-rearing conditions. It would appear that the clearest influences of parental practices are negative, not positive; i.e., certain parent attitudes may create specific anxieties and conflicts inhibiting the development of appropriate sex-role attitudes, but it is not at all clear whether certain parent attitudes can create appropriate sex-role attitudes.

9. To a large extent, the foregoing trends follow a regular course of development, which is largely determined by cognitive (rather than physiological-chronological) maturity. These trends are the result of the child's cognitive-developmental organization of a social world in which sex roles are related to body concepts and to basic social functions in relatively universal ways.

10. On the motivational side, these developmental trends can be interpreted as the product of general motives to structure, and adapt oneself to, physical-social reality, and to preserve a stable and positive self-image.

# Development and Opposition to Cultural Practices

E. TURIEL

In Chapter 4, I recounted events from Mernissi's (1994) recollection of life in the harem of Morocco and contemporary events in Iran. The resistance, subterfuge, and subversion described indicate that people do not simply accept cultural practices, societal norms, or social arrangements (in the sense of hierarchical orderings). I used these examples to illustrate that people's lives in culture involve more than it would seem from the idea that development entails an increasing conformity to societal standards. These are examples of how people, even in contexts of strongly sanctioned practices and arrangements, make moral judgments about the existing social system that include opposition to it. The oppositions in those cases included judgments about injustices and unmet rights, as well as assertions of areas of personal jurisdiction and choice. As examples, listening to music and dancing, and chewing gum, are not activities usually thought to constitute fundamental rights or civil liberties. For many, these are taken for granted as personal choices causing no harm. In cases where they are forbidden or limited, however, listening to music and dancing became symbolic of resistance to what were perceived to be unfair restrictions—as was the case for chewing gum in the view of Mernissi's mother.

These examples are, in many respects, in line with the propositions put forth by Piaget and Kohlberg. They are examples illustrating that people do scrutinize their social world; that is, they make judgments about social relationships. The examples indicate that social development, as held by Piaget, is not due to a unidirectional cause from the community to the individual. The activities suggest that the women of the harem and people in Iran participate in the elaboration

of norms, and are not willing to accept them ready-made. They even participate in efforts at transforming social norms and societal ways. In addition, the examples illustrate that there is a multiplicity of interactions of different types, as Piaget maintained. The women in the harem had multiple ways of interacting with the men (and the system), and they were not always in opposition to them. The examples show, moreover, that children have a variety of types of interactions with adults. In the harem, they sometimes received different and conflicting messages from fathers and mothers. In Iran, children received different messages from parents and religious or governmental leaders, as well as different messages from different religious or governmental leaders. Children must ponder and interpret the variety of communications they receive and what is more often than not a perplexing social world with its share of conflicts.

In certain respects, however, the examples from Morocco and Iran are not in line with the formulations of Piaget and Kohlberg. In Kohlberg's formulation, it is only at the highest stages of moral development that people understand moral concepts in ways that they can scrutinize, critique, resist, or attempt to change the practices, laws, or arrangements of their society. The idea of a prior-to-society perspective, which is not formed until the highest stages, is that the individual is able to make judgments allowing evaluations of existing societal arrangements. The stages prior to the postconventional level supposedly involve ways of thinking in which conventions, rules, laws, authority, and social order define the moral. At those stages, therefore, there is a concordance between people's moral thinking and the cultural or societal ways. Individual and society are not in conflict. Insofar as there is conflict in earlier stages (the preconventional), it is due to thinking based on avoidance of sanctions and fulfillment of personal needs and desires. At these stages, morality is not distinguished from sanctions or personal ends.

*Source:* Turiel, E. (2002). Development and opposition to cultural practices. In E. Turiel, The Culture of Morality: Social Development, Context, and Conflict (pp. 13–29). New York: Free Press.

The examples from Morocco and Iran suggest that resistance, critique, and attempts to change certain social practices are not tied to ways of making moral judgments characterized as developmentally advanced ways of thinking. In those situations, many people of varying ages engaged in hidden, subversive activities, as well as open defiance. My interpretation, based on research findings discussed in this and subsequent chapters, is that, at different ages, people make moral judgments that can include recognition of unfair or unjust practices and arrangements. For children and young adolescents, this is likely to occur with regard to practices in the family and school and among peers. For older adolescents and adults, it occurs also with regard to cultural practices, societal arrangements, and the political system. From childhood to adulthood, people's moral judgments can lead them to support aspects of societal arrangements and be critical of other aspects. Furthermore, nonmoral judgments regarding personal jurisdiction and choice appear to have been involved in the Moroccan and Iranian events. Activities like listening to music and dancing are often judged to be part of a domain that involves a personal sphere of action (Nucci, 1996). Judgments about the personal domain often are coordinated with moral judgments about fairness and rights in the types of hidden or defiant activities seen in the harem and in Iran.

My interpretation of the events in the harem and in Iran contrasts with the types of developmental progressions proposed by Piaget and Kohlberg. In their respective developmental sequences, moral judgments become increasingly differentiated or distinguished from personal considerations (as in the shift from stages 1 and 2 to 3 and 4 in Kohlberg's sequence) and conventions, rules, and authority (as in the shift from heteronomy to autonomy in Piaget or from stages 3 and 4 to 5 and 6 in Kohlberg). My contrasting interpretation is based on the proposition, supported by extensive research, that children begin to make distinctively moral judgments of welfare, justice, and rights that differ from their judgments about personal spheres of action, as well as judgments about the conventions of social systems.

## Distinctions in Judgments: The Moral and Conventional

One set of studies, conducted in the United States and Korea, has shown that young children's moral judgments are not formed by respect for authority and that they have nuanced understandings of the roles and jurisdiction of adults and peers in such positions within social systems (Braine, et al., 1991; Damon, 1977; Kim, 1998; Kim & Turiel, 1996; Laupa, 1991, 1994; Laupa & Turiel, 1986, 1993; Tisak, 1986; Tisak et al., 2000). This body of research directly examined different facets of children's understandings of authority, consistently finding that children do not regard adults as the only sources of legitimate authority; they do not regard adults in positions of authority as all-knowing or their dictates and rules as synonymous with the good or right; and they do not believe, when justice is in conflict with authority, that authority is right and justice is wrong.

In evaluating commands from persons in authority, children do grant legitimacy to peers, as well as adults, in positions of authority (such as in a school) and they do not necessarily grant greater legitimacy to the commands of an adult authority over those of a peer authority. Children do take seriously the type of act commanded and will consider an authority's command wrong if they judge the act wrong. Children also place boundaries on an authority's jurisdiction within social institutions or contexts. These features of children's judgments were revealed through research that examined how they evaluate different types of acts commanded by individuals of different ages (peers or adults) and in different positions in the social institution (i.e., a school). It has been found consistently that with regard to acts like stealing or inflicting physical harm, children as young as 5 or 6 years of age judged by the nature of the actions rather than by what is commanded by persons in authority in schools (Kim, 1998; Kim & Turiel, 1996; Laupa & Turiel, 1986). For instance, whether or not they hold positions of authority, commands from peers or adults that children stop fighting were judged legitimate. In addition, commands from peers (with or without positions of authority in a school) that children stop fighting were judged more legitimate than conflicting commands from adult authority, such as a teacher, that children be allowed to continue fighting. By contrast, children do give priority to adult authority over children or other adults who are not in positions of authority when it comes to other types of actions, such as turn-taking and interpretations of game rules. These types of findings were similar in studies with children from Korea, where supposedly there is much reverence for adult authority, and in studies with children from the United States, where supposedly reverence for adults is not as strongly felt. Studies in the United States also showed that children do not accept the legitimacy of a parent's directives to engage in acts like stealing and inflicting harm (Damon, 1977; Laupa, Turiel, & Cowan, 1995).

The context of authority commands includes their status as authorities, their position in a social institution, and the actions involved. The same person in authority commanding one type of act makes for a different "object of judgment" from the same person in authority commanding another type of act. These objects of judgment or total contexts differ because people bring to bear on the situations different domains of judgment, including their moral judgments of welfare, justice, and rights, as well as judgments about the conventions of social systems. The application by even young children of domains of reasoning to authority and rules can be illustrated with an example of interview responses given by a 5-year-old boy. The boy's responses come from a study in which children from 5 to 11 years of age were presented with hypothetical stories of preschools in which certain actions are permitted. In one story, children are allowed to be without clothes on warm days (a conventional issue). In a second story children are allowed to hit each other (a moral issue). Prior to the presentation of these hypothetical stories, the children had judged both acts as wrong. The first interview excerpt begins with the boy's responses to the question of whether it is all right for a school to allow hitting, and the second, with his responses as to whether it is all right to allow children to remove their clothes (the excerpts come from Turiel, 1983, p. 62):

No, it is not okay. (WHY NOT?) Because that is like making other people unhappy. You can hurt them that way. It hurts other people, hurting is not good. (MARK GOES TO PARK SCHOOL. TODAY IN SCHOOL HE WANTS TO SWING BUT HE FINDS THAT ALL THE SWINGS ARE BEING USED BY OTHER CHILDREN. SO HE DECIDES TO HIT ONE OF THE CHILDREN AND TAKE THE SWING. IS IT OKAY FOR MARK TO DO THAT?) No. Because he is hurting someone else.

Yes, because that is the rule. (WHY CAN THEY HAVE THAT RULE?) If that's what the boss wants to do, he can do that. (HOW COME?) Because he's the boss, he is in charge of the school. (BOB GOES TO GROVE SCHOOL. THIS IS A WARM DAY AT GROVE SCHOOL. HE HAS BEEN RUNNING IN THE PLAY AREA OUTSIDE AND HE IS HOT SO HE DECIDES TO TAKE OFF HIS CLOTHES. IS IT OKAY FOR BOB TO DO THAT?) Yes, if he wants to, he can, because it is the rule.

For this child, all rules are not alike and the type of act involved is evaluated in relation to the jurisdiction of a person in authority. With regard to removing one's clothes, the justification of the act and the school policy are based on rules and authority. Although the principal is the "boss and in charge" of the school, it matters in one case but not in the other. This boy's responses provide an example of the general findings of the study (Weston & Turiel, 1980). The majority of children at all the ages responded in similar fashion, distinguishing between moral and conventional issues regarding rules and authority.

Drawing distinctions between domains is important not only to an understanding of the different paths of thought in children's development, but also to an understanding of morality itself. Many of the confusions about society and morality that I have considered may, indeed, stem from a failure to draw boundaries between the moral and nonmoral. Too often, too much is grouped into the moral in ways that do not correspond to how people, starting in childhood, think about welfare, justice, and rights. Moral judgments defined this way need to be distinguished from judgments about social organization and the conventions that further the coordination of social interactions within social systems. Conventions are shared behaviors (uniformities, rules) whose meanings are defined by the social system in which they are embedded. Therefore, the validity of conventions lies in their links to existing social systems. Morality, too, applies to social systems, but contrasts with convention in that it is not determined by existing uniformities. As delineated by moral philosophers, moral prescriptions are not specific to a given society; they are not legitimated by agreement; and they are impartial in the sense that they are not determined by personal preferences or individual inclinations (Dworkin, 1977; Gewirth, 1978; Habermas, 1990a, 1990b; Rawls, 1971, 2001).

The responses of the 5-year-old boy just presented, which reflected a distinction in his thinking, came from one of our early studies that examined how children and adolescents make judgments in the moral and conventional domains. The 5-year-old's responses well illustrate some of the ways young children distinguish between morality and convention. I wish to stress, however, that the evidence regarding the domain distinctions in childhood and adolescence is solid and quite extensive. Over a period of more than twenty years, nearly 100 studies have been conducted that support the proposition that children make judgments that differ in accord with the moral and conventional domains. The studies cover a range of issues, and they used a variety of methods. In the context of related issues, I do consider in this book many of the studies. But this is not the place to provide a review of the research. Several reviews are available in the literature (see Killen, McGlothin, & Lee-Kim, in press; Nucci, 2001; Smetana, 1995b; Tisak, 1995; Turiel, 1983, 1998a, 1998b). These reviews provide details of the research findings, which yield, in my estimation, extremely strong evidence in support of the proposition that starting at a young age, children's moral judgments are distinct from their judgments about social conventions. Studies that have tested possible alternative interpretations of the initial findings (Miller & Bersoff, 1988; Tisak & Turiel, 1984, 1988) also support this proposition. The majority

of the studies were conducted in the United States, but a substantial number, obtaining similar results, were done in non-Western countries, including India (Bersoff & Miller, 1993; Madden, 1992; Miller & Bersoff, 1992), Korea (Song, Smetana, & Kim, 1987), Indonesia (Carey & Ford, 1983), Nigeria (Hollos, Leis, & Turiel, 1986), and Zambia (Zimba, 1987).

On the assumption that the evidence is very well grounded, my aim here is to provide an outline of the central features of the research and thinking within the domains. One of the ways of studying children's thinking has been to present them with a series of social acts or transgressions classified in accord with the distinctions among the domains. Thus, moral actions pertained to physical harm (e.g., hitting others, pushing them down), psychological harm (e.g., teasing, name calling, hurting feelings), and fairness or justice (e.g., failing to share, stealing, destroying others' property). These acts were depicted as intentional and resulting in negative consequences to others. By contrast, conventional issues pertained to uniformities or regulations serving functions of social coordination (e.g., pertaining to modes of dress, forms of address, table manners, forms of greeting). Two dimensions of thought, in particular, have been examined with regard to domains. One pertains to the criteria for domains (referred to as *criterion judgments*); the second pertains to the ways individuals reason about courses of action (referred to as *justifications*). Assessments of criterion judgments have included questions as to whether the actions would be right or wrong in the absence of a rule or law, if the act would be all right if permitted by a person in authority (e.g., a teacher in a school context), whether an act would be all right if there were general agreement as to its acceptability, and whether the act would be all right if it were accepted in another group or culture.

The results of the studies show that children's moral judgments are based, initially, primarily on concepts of harm or welfare and subsequently on concepts of justice and rights, as well. Children and adolescents judge moral obligations not as contingent on rules or authority and as applicable across social contexts. Moral transgressions, such as hitting or stealing, are not judged by the existence of rules, the directives of authorities, or commonly accepted practices (e.g., the act is wrong even if it were acceptable practice in a culture). Rather, rules pertaining to moral issues are judged as unalterable by agreement, and such acts would be considered wrong even if there were no rules governing them. Instead of rules and authority, moral judgments are grounded in concepts of avoiding harm, protecting people's welfare, and ensuring fairness. At the same time, children do develop understandings of the conventions, including rules and authority, of social organizations (e.g., the conventional rules in the organization of a classroom or school; conventions pertaining to matters like dress or forms of address). In contrast with moral issues, conventions are judged to be contingent on rules and authority, and as particular to groups and institutional contexts. Justifications for judgments about conventional issues are based on understandings of social organization, including the role of authority, custom, and efficiency in coordinating social interactions.

That children form judgments in the different domains does not mean that emotion plays an unimportant role in moral and social development. As already stated, Piaget theorized that emotions like sympathy and empathy contribute to the process. Indeed, young children do show reactions of sympathy and empathy when witnessing distress in others (Eisenberg & Fabes, 1991; Hoffman, 1991; Lennon & Eisenberg, 1987). Such emotions are related to children's judgments about harm. Furthermore, there is research indicating that different emotions are associated with moral and conventional events (Arsenio, 1988; Arsenio & Ford, 1985; Arsenio & Fleiss, 1996). As an example, in one study (Arsenio, 1988) children from 5 to 12 years of age were presented with descriptions of several different types of acts, and asked which emotions would be experienced by different participants (actors, recipients, and observers). For events entailing positive moral actions, such as helping and sharing, children generally attributed positive emotions, like happiness, to the actors. For conventional transgressions, children attributed neutral or somewhat negative emotions (sadness, anger) to the participants. In the case of moral transgressions entailing one person victimizing another, such as by stealing a toy, children attributed very negative emotions to the recipients and observers, and attributed somewhat positive emotions to the perpetrators of the acts. In

addition, children can use information about emotional responses to infer the types of experiences that would lead to such reactions.

Similar results were obtained in a study which also assessed children's reasons as to why people in the events would experience the emotions attributed to them (Arsenio & Fleiss, 1996). These reasons, too, varied by domain of event and role of participants. With regard to conventional transgressions, children thought that negative emotions would be felt by those in authority who tend not to want rules violated. The negative emotions expected of victims of moral transgressions were thought to occur because of the harm, loss, or injury resulting from the acts. For people who transgress, however, it was thought that the material gains obtained by them would result in some feelings of happiness. Older children tend to attribute mixed emotions to transgressions, expecting that, in addition to positive emotions for a desired outcome, they would experience negative feelings as a consequence of the effects of their acts on others. Since the moral transgressions were evaluated as wrong by the children, it would appear that their attributions of positive emotional outcomes to victimizers do not determine their moral judgments about the acts. Instead, with regard to moral evaluations, the victims' reactions seem to be what is taken into account. It would also appear that older children are able not only to give priority to the victim in their moral judgments but also to understand that a victim's reactions can feed back upon an actor (the victimizer) and produce in that person a mixture of positive and negative reactions. (For more extensive discussion, including of similar findings in a study conducted in Korea, see Arsenio and Lover, 1995.)

Emotional attachments and attributions are particularly strong in people's religious lives. Religious rules, maxims, and authorities are deeply felt. Even so, it is not necessarily the case that people with strong religious commitments judge moral issues by religious dictates. Nor is it the case that religious people do not understand the conventional features of religion. Although it is sometimes thought that religious doctrines determine the moral course for religiously committed persons, our research has shown that more involved processes are at work. A set of studies

(Nucci, 1985, 1991; Nucci & Turiel, 1993) looked at judgments about morality and religious precepts among children and adolescents from devout religious groups. The groups in the research were Amish-Mennonites, Dutch Reform Calvinists, and two Jewish groups, conservative and orthodox. The judgments of members of these groups were studied with regard to moral rules pertaining to stealing, hitting, slander, and property damage and to nonmoral rules connected to the authority and rituals of the religion such as day of worship, women's or men's head covering, circumcision, and keeping kosher.

Although the nonmoral religious practices are strictly maintained by these groups, most judged that those rules should be dependent on the religious context. The nonmoral religious rules were judged to be relative to one's religious group and contingent on God's word. Thus, it was thought that religious rules were not applicable to people of other religions, and that members of their own religion would not be obligated to follow the rules if there were nothing in the Bible about them. Judgments about the moral rules entailed a different kind of connection to religion. It was thought that members outside one's religion were also obligated to follow those rules, and evaluations of the moral acts were not judged to be dependent on God's word. Acts like hitting others or stealing would be wrong even if there were nothing in the Bible or if God had not said anything about these acts—because of harm or injustice. As an 11-year-old boy (a conservative Jew) put it when asked if it would be all right for Jewish people to steal if it were written in the Torah that they should: "Even if God says it, we know he can't mean it, because we know it is a very bad thing to steal . . . maybe it's test, but we just know he can't mean it." When questioned on why God would not mean it, he said, "because we think of God as very good—absolutely perfect person" (taken from Nucci, 1991, p. 32).

The boy evaluated religious dictates in conjunction with an evaluation of the act, and did not solely presume that religion determines the good. Similarly, the Dutch Reform Calvinists in the research, who have a strong belief in the compelling nature of God's commands, generally thought that a command from God would not make it right—and that God would not give such a command. As an example, a 15-year-old female reasoned that God would not give such a command "because it is the right thing to do, and He's perfect, and if He's stealing He can't be perfect" (Nucci, 1985, pp. 168–169). These responses and the data more generally indicate that the relation between religion and morality entails an interweaving between moral judgments and what is given and should exist in religious precepts. Moral criteria of welfare, justice, and rights are applied to religion to at least the same extent as religious doctrine is seen to establish the good. Practices of importance to the religion, but of conventional type, are judged differently in that they are seen as binding only to members of the religion and contingent on rules and authority within the religious system.

# Empathy and Sympathy

## N. Eisenberg

## Definition of Empathy

Over the years, empathy has been defined in several different ways. In the past, researchers often described empathy as social insight (Dymond, 1949), or as the cognitive ability to comprehend the affective (and sometimes cognitive) status of another (Borke, 1971, 1973; Deutsch & Madle, 1975; Hogan, 1969). However, more recently, the ability to understand another's cognitive state has been labeled by developmentalists as "cognitive role taking," whereas the ability to discern and interpret another's affective responses has been called "affective role taking" (Ford, 1979; Shantz, 1975; Underwood & Moore, 1982).

In recent work, empathy has been defined in two different but related ways. Some writers have viewed empathy as the vicarious feeling of another's emotional state, e.g., as the vicarious matching of emotional responses (Feshbach & Roe, 1968; Stotland, 1969). Hoffman (1982a) describes this response as: "a vicarious affective response that is more appropriate to someone else's situation than to one's own [p. 281]." On the other hand, Batson and Coke (1981) have defined empathy as concern or compassion for another's welfare, for example, as "an emotional response elicited by and congruent with the perceived welfare of another [p. 169]." In some operationalizations of empathy, elements of both emotional matching and sympathy are included (e.g., Bryant, 1982; Davis, 1983a; Mehrabian & Epstein, 1972), that is, empathy is considered a vicarious response that is not inconsistent with the perceived welfare of another, and often involves sympathetic concern.

It is my view that there are at least three types of emotional reactions that frequently have been

Source: Eisenberg, N. (1986). Empathy and Sympathy; Conclusion. In N. Eisenberg, *Altruistic emotion, cognition, and behavior* (pp. 30–32, 211–212). Hillsdale, NJ: Erlbaum.

labeled as "empathy," and that these three reactions should be differentiated. In some instances, the individual merely reflects the emotion of the other. In this situation, the individual feels the same emotion as the other, and is neither highly self-concerned nor other-directed in orientation. I would suggest that this type of emotional orientation be labeled as "empathy" or "emotional contagion," and that pure empathic responding occurs most frequently among very young children.

In other situations, the individual responds to another's emotion with an emotion that is not identical to the other's emotion, but is congruent with the other's emotional state and his or her welfare. An example of this reaction would be when an individual feels concern for another who is distressed or sad. This type of reaction frequently has been labeled as "sympathy" (e.g., Wispe, 1984) or "sympathetic distress" (Hoffman, 1984b). This type of emotional responding should be especially likely to motivate altruistic behavior.

The third type of reaction that often has been mislabeled as empathy is a negative, self-oriented concern in reaction to another's emotional state. For example, an individual may feel worried or anxious rather than sympathetic in response to another's distress. As for sympathy, there is not necessarily an exact match between the emotion of the observer and the other. However, unlike sympathy, the response is self-oriented rather than other-oriented. Batson (Batson & Coke, 1981) has labeled such a self-oriented reaction as "personal distress."

Empathy (as defined above) is a relatively noncognitive response, one that might occur in very young children who do not clearly differentiate between one's own distress and that of another. Moreover, children and adults may initially respond to emotion-eliciting events involving others with an empathic response which, via cognitive processing, becomes either personal distress (if the focus is on the self) or sympathy (if the focus is upon another). For persons aged 1–2 years or older who can differentiate between their own and others' distresses (Radke-Yarrow, Zahn-Waxler, & Chapman, 1983), it is likely that initial vicarious emotion will be appraised or interpreted by the empathizer (cf. Giblin, 1981). This is not to say that empathizing necessarily occurs prior to sympathizing or personal distress; an individual's cognitive assessment in a situation could lead directly to feelings of personal distress or sympathy.

Because empathy, sympathy, and personal distress are very different reactions, most likely with different antecedents and consequences, differentiation of these reactions when possible would undoubtedly result in both increased conceptual clarity and more comprehensible empirical findings. In this book, I will use the terms "empathy," "sympathy," and "personal distress" as defined above when possible. However, many theorists and researchers have not distinguished among these terms; thus, when reviewing their research and conceptualizations, it often is impossible to determine whether they were referring to or assessing empathy, sympathy, or personal distress. Moreover, in some situations it is difficult to distinguish among the three types of responses. Consequently, I will often use the word "empathy" to refer to undifferentiated emotional responsiveness that could be sympathy, empathy, or personal distress.

## Conclusion

Altruistic behavior, like most social behaviors, is complex and multiply determined. Moreover, its significance to the actor can vary, and is difficult to ascertain. In this book, the cognitive and emotional bases for altruism were examined, as were developmental changes in individuals' conceptions regarding the nature of altruism and other prosocial acts. Moreover, models for conceptualizing the manner in which cognitive and affective factors interact with other factors in influencing prosocial development (reasoning and behavior) were presented.

As is often the case when dealing with a complex social behavior, the research and models presented throughout this book raise more questions than they answer. Some of the thorniest questions concern the ways in which cognition

and emotion interact, and the causal nature of such interactions. For example, it is unclear whether the cognitive components of moral personal goals are firmly established prior to the development of the tendency to self-reinforce for actions consistent with a given moral value (or self-punish for behavior inconsistent with the value), or if children first learn from socializers to self-reinforce behaviors consistent with a value and only later internalize the relevant value. Similarly, the degree to which cognitive processing (e.g., related to the source of the other's need or the subjective expected utility of a potential prosocial behavior) precedes versus follows sympathetic or empathic responding and reflexive helping in a crisis needs clarification.

Another question of considerable importance concerns the degree to which altruistic moral judgment is limited by developmental factors. To what extent is the individual's level of moral judgment (and, consequently, motives for assisting) a direct function of level of socio-cognitive capabilities versus situational factors and nonmoral values and needs? To what degree do individuals feel a press to reason at the highest level they are capable of holding (as hypothesized by cognitive developmentalists)? What factors affect the directionality of the relation between moral judgment and behavior?

Throughout this book, we hope we have suggested not only questions and issues that need to be examined, and directions in which to move. For example, with regard to the altruistic emotions, it is clear that our thinking must be more differentiated than has generally been the case. Sympathy, empathy, and feelings of personal distress must be differentiated conceptually and empirically; moreover, we need to move from asking *if* there is a relation between empathy and altruism to asking *when*, on a conceptual basis, can a relation between sympathy (or empathy or personal distress) and altruism (or other types of prosocial behaviors) be expected. A similar approach is needed when defining socio-cognitive skills (such as role taking) and examining their role in altruism. Furthermore, we must take seriously the notion of social scripts and the automatic quality of behavior in some situations, as well as the internal conflicts that can arise from the activating of several, often conflicting, values, norms, needs, and preferences in a single situation.

Obviously, there is much to be done. In all likelihood, we will never fully understand the interplay of factors that affect the probability of altruistic behavior, and the role that development plays in the process. Nonetheless, the quest to understand the positive side of human nature is not only an exciting one, but one that could enhance the quality of life for all.

# Toward Utopia: Eradicating Gender Polarization

## S. BEM

Up to this point, I have tried to lay the ground-work for a feminist consensus on gender policy by reframing the debate around the androcentrism of social institutions. Now, however, I want to move beyond androcentrism to gender polarization and advocate a vision of utopia in which gender polarization, like androcentrism, has been so completely dismantled that—except in narrowly biological contexts like reproduction—the distinction between male and female no longer organizes either the culture or the psyche. This particular utopia is controversial because it challenges the fundamental belief in the differing psychological and sexual nature of males and females, and it is also inconsistent with what is arguably the dominant voice in contemporary American feminist thought—the woman-centered voice, discussed earlier.

Gender polarization is the organizing of social life around the male-female distinction, the forging of a cultural connection between sex and virtually every other aspect of human experience, including modes of dress, social roles, and even ways of expressing emotion and experiencing sexual desire. Accordingly, to dismantle gender polarization requires severing all these culturally constructed connections and cutting back the male-female distinction to a narrow—if critically important—relevance having primarily to do with the biology of reproduction. With complete gender depolarization, the biology of sex would become "a minimal presence" in human social life (Connell, 1987, p. 289). In other words, the totality of human experience would no longer be divided into cultural categories on the basis of gender, so people of different sexes would no longer be culturally identified with different clothes, different social roles, different personalities, or different sexual and affectional

partners any more than people with different-colored eyes or different-sized feet are now.

This absence of gender-based scripts should not be taken to mean that males and females would merely be freer to be masculine, feminine, or androgynous, heterosexual, homosexual, or bisexual, than they are now. Rather, the distinction between male and female would no longer be the dimension around which the culture is organized, which means, in turn, that the very concepts of masculinity, femininity, and androgyny, heterosexuality, homosexuality, and bisexuality, would be as absent from the cultural consciousness as the concepts of a "hetero-eye-colored" eroticism, a "homo-eye-colored" eroticism, and a "bi-eye-colored" eroticism are now.

Although feminists as a whole may not yet have committed themselves to eradicating gender polarization, two separate critiques of gender polarization underlie my own commitment to eradicating it from both the culture and the psyche. The first derives from a broad humanistic concern with the way that gender polarization prevents men and women alike from developing their full potential as human beings, the second from a specifically feminist concern with the foundation that gender polarization provides for androcentrism.

According to the humanistic critique, which was popular among androgyny theorists like myself during the late 1960s and early 1970s, the division of human experience into the masculine and the feminine restricts human potential in at least three related ways.

First, gender polarization homogenizes women and men, rather than allowing either the diversity that naturally exists within each sex or the overlap that naturally exists between the two sexes to flower in social and psychological life. Besides being inconsistent with the diversity of human nature, this homogenization is inconsistent with the American value of freedom to transcend the arbitrary boundaries of ascribed characteristics like sex, race, and caste.

*Source:* Bem, S. L. (1993). Toward Utopia: Eradicating gender polarization. In S. L. Bem, the lenses of gender: Transforming the debate on sexual inequality (pp. 192–196). New Haven, CT: Yale University Press.

Second, gender polarization dichotomizes not only people but also ways of relating to the world into masculine and feminine types, thereby leaving undefined and unconceptualized not only the androgynous kinds of people who were once the focus of so much feminist attention but also the androgynous ways of relating to the world that so often seem to capture the essence of the human condition. Take, for example, the gender-polarizing dichotomy between male autonomy and female connectedness. Although all human beings everywhere are simultaneously and inextricably separate and autonomous selves, as well as fully interconnected and interdependent members of a human community, no concept in a gender-polarizing culture reflects this two-sided fact about the human condition. Take, for another example, the gender-polarizing dichotomy between male rationality and female emotionality. Although the human psyche is simultaneously and inextricably both rational and emotional, once again, no concept in a gender-polarizing culture reflects this fact.

Finally, gender polarization so dramatically expands the meaning of what it is to be male or female that a paradoxical cultural concept is thereby created: the idea of being a "real" man or woman, as opposed to a merely biological man or woman. This paradoxical concept, in turn, makes both men and women vulnerable to the feeling that their maleness or femaleness cannot be taken for granted but must instead be worked at, accomplished, and protected from loss through misbehavior. The culture has developed no comparable concept of a "real" human being, which is why people have no comparable sense of insecurity about whether they are walking or playing or eating or thinking or having sex in a way that is adequately human; they simply go about the business of doing whatever they have each been biologically enabled to do.

The essence of the humanistic objection to gender polarization is thus that it turns men and women into gender caricatures and thereby denies them the fullest measure of their human possibilities. In contrast, the essence of the specifically feminist objection to gender polarization is that it aids and abets the social reproduction of male power by providing the funda-mental division between masculine and feminine upon which androcentrism is built. This antifeminist aspect of gender polarization manifests itself at three levels: the institutional, the psychological, and the ideological.

At the institutional level, gender polarization aids and abets the social reproduction of male power by dichotomizing the social world into the masculine domain of paid employment and the feminine domain of home and childcare, thereby sustaining a gender-based division of labor and obscuring the need for any institutional mechanisms—like paid childcare—that would enable any one individual to easily participate in both domains. Such coordinating mechanisms will continue to be seen as unnecessary as long as gender polarization ensures that different people—that is, men and women—do different things; and the absence of such coordinating mechanisms will continue to promote sexual hierarchy by denying women access to economic and political power.

At the psychological level, gender polarization aids and abets the social reproduction of male power by dichotomizing identity and personality into masculine and feminine categories, thereby providing a concept of *psychological* masculinity and femininity to which the culture can readily assimilate its androcentric conceptions of power and powerlessness. This unholy alliance of androcentrism and gender polarization predisposes men to construct identities around dominance and women to construct identities around deference; it also enables those who deviate from these mutually exclusive identities to be defined, by both the culture and themselves, as pathological.

And finally, at the ideological level, gender polarization aids and abets the social reproduction of male power by prompting the cultural discourse to misrepresent even the most blatant examples of sexual inequality as nothing more or less than sexual difference. Put somewhat differently, gender polarization enables religion, science, law, the media, and so on, to rationalize the sexual status quo in a way that automatically renders the lens of androcentrism invisible. The sexual status quo is not made to seem rational by gender polarization alone, of course; the lens of biological essentialism further rationalizes the sexual status quo by defining difference itself as biologically natural.

In addition to the humanist and feminist arguments against gender polarization, there is an overarching moral argument that fuses the antihumanist and antifeminist aspects of gender polarization. The essence of this moral argument is that by polarizing human values and human experiences into the masculine and the feminine, gender polarization not only helps to keep the culture in the grip of males themselves; it also keeps the culture in the grip of highly polarized masculine values. The moral problem here is that these highly polarized masculine values so emphasize making war over keeping the peace, taking risks over giving care, and even mastering nature over harmonizing with nature that when allowed to dominate societal and even global decision making, they create the danger that humans will destroy not just each other in massive numbers but the planet.

The one good thing about the thoroughness with which gender polarization is embedded in androcentric institutions is that institutional changes designed to eradicate androcentrism will necessarily challenge gender polarization as well. Consider the suggestion made earlier, for example, that society provide institutional ways to coordinate work and family. In addition to challenging androcentrism, this institutional change would begin to break down the boundary between the masculine world of paid employment and the feminine world of home and childcare; it would also begin to challenge the polarization of identity and personality by giving women experience with power and status, and men experience with nurturance and service to others. Although other kinds of institutional changes would deal more directly with gender polarization, my own view is that—apart from the critical issue of ending all forms of discrimination against lesbians, gay men, and bisexuals—the most effective way to begin dismantling gender polarization is to dismantle androcentrism.

Ultimately, gender depolarization would require even more than the *social* revolution involved in rearranging social institutions and reframing cultural discourses. Gender depolarization would also require a *psychological* revolution in our most personal sense of who and what we are as males and females, a profound alteration in our feelings about the meaning of our biological sex and its relation to our psyche and our sexuality.

Simply put, this psychological revolution would have us all begin to view the biological fact of being male or female in much the same way that we now view the biological fact of being *human*. Rather than seeing our sex as so authentically who we are that it needs to be elaborated, or so tenuous that it needs to be bolstered, or so limiting that it needs to be traded in for another model, we would instead view our sex as so completely given by nature, so capable of exerting its influence automatically, and so limited in its sphere of influence to those domains where it really does matter biologically, that it could be safely tucked away in the backs of our minds and left to its own devices. In other words, biological sex would no longer be at the core of individual identity and sexuality.

# Wisdom as a Topic of Scientific Discourse About the Good Life

## P. B. Baltes

Wisdom has been discussed and studied in philosophy and religion for thousands of years (for an overview, see Assmann, 1994; Kekes, 1995; Rice, 1958). More recently, scholars from other disciplines such as cultural anthropology, political science, education, and psychology also have shown interest in wisdom. Indeed, one can argue that wisdom is becoming a center of trans-disciplinary discourse (e.g., Agazzi, 1991; Arlin, 1990; Assmann, 1994; Baltes, 1993; Lehrer, Lum, Slichta, & Smith, 1996; Maxwell, 1984; Nichols, 1996; Nozick, 1993; Oelmüller, 1989; Smith & Baltes, 1990; Staudinger & Baltes; 1996b; Sternberg, 1990; Welsch, 1995).

In defining and studying wisdom from a psychological point of view, we attempt to pay careful attention to what philosophers offer regarding the nature of the structure and function of wisdom. Without such attention, we would lose the special strength that the concept of wisdom holds for specifying the content and form of the primary virtues and behaviors that individuals aspire to as they attempt to regulate their lives toward an "universal canon of a good life."

To prevent a possible misunderstanding, we acknowledge the scientific limits of our work on wisdom. Specifically, any empirical manifestation of wisdom falls short of the theoretical aspiration. In this spirit, we do not maintain that a psychological theory will ever capture wisdom in its full-blown cultural complexity. Our hope, however, is that this intermarriage of philosophy and psychology results in lines of psychological inquiry where virtues, values, and the mind can meet in a new and productive collaboration. We believe that this may be possible because, at a high level of analysis, the concept of wisdom appears to be culturally universal. To illustrate, Table 1 summarizes characteristics that in our historical studies of wisdom we have found in Asian, African, and Western traditions (Baltes, 1993; Baltes & Smith, 1990; Baltes & Staudinger, 2000).

## Psychological Theories of Wisdom: From Implicit to Explicit Theories

Because of its enormous cultural and historical heritage, a psychological definition and operationalization of wisdom is extremely difficult. This could be why many wisdom researchers

**Table 1**   General Criteria Derived from an Analysis of Cultural-Historical and Philosophical Accounts of Wisdom

Wisdom addresses important and difficult questions and strategies about the conduct and meaning of life.

Wisdom includes knowledge about the limits of knowledge and the uncertainties of the world.

Wisdom represents a truly superior level of knowledge, judgment, and advice.

Wisdom constitutes knowledge with extraordinary scope, depth, measure, and balance.

Wisdom involves a perfect synergy of mind and character, that is, an orchestration of knowledge and virtues.

Wisdom represents knowledge used for the good or well-being of oneself and that of others.

Wisdom, though difficult to achieve and to specify, is easily recognized when manifested.

*Source:* Baltes, P. B. Wisdom as a topic of scientific discourse about the good life. In wisdom: Its structure and function in regulating successful life span development. In C. R. Snyder & S. J. Lopez (Eds.), *Handbook of positive psychology* (pp. 329–332). Oxford, UK: Oxford University Press.

have restricted their research efforts to lay-persons' implicit theories of wisdom and wise persons (Clayton & Birren, 1980; Holliday & Chandler, 1986; Kramer, 2000; Sowarka, 1989; Staudinger, Sowarka, Maciel, & Baltes, 1997; Sternberg, 1985, 1990). Empirical research based on explicit theories of wisdom-related behavior is relatively rare.

### Implicit Theories

With implicit theories, we mean the beliefs or mental representations that people have about wisdom and the characteristics of wise persons. In studies on implicit beliefs about wisdom and wise persons, one finds quite a high degree of overlap in the core aspects of wisdom, even though authors have focused on slightly different aspects and named their components differently.

All conceptions include cognitive as well as social, motivational, and emotional components (e.g., Birren & Fisher, 1990; Kramer, 2000). The cognitive components usually include strong intellectual abilities, rich knowledge and experience in matters of the human condition, and an ability to apply one's theoretical knowledge practically. A second basic component refers to reflective judgment that is based on knowledge about the world and the self, an openness for new experiences, and the ability to learn from mistakes. Socioemotional components generally include good social skills, such as sensitivity and concern for others and the ability to give good

advice. A fourth motivational component refers to the good intentions that usually are associated with wisdom. That is, wisdom aims at solutions that optimize the benefit of others and oneself.

Sternberg's (1998) effort at specifying a comprehensive theory of wisdom is in the tradition of these implicit lines of inquiry. In his theory, consisting so far of a coordinated set of characterizations rather than empirical work, Sternberg emphasizes the role of "balance." Specifically, wisdom is conceptualized as the application of tacit knowledge toward the achievement of a common good achieved through a balance among multiple interests, including one's own interests and those of others.

A factor-analytic study conducted by Staudinger, Sowarka, et al. (1997) illustrates the implicit theories tradition of wisdom. One hundred and two participants rated 131 attributes regarding the degree to which each represents the notion of an ideally wise person. The attributes were selected from past work on implicit theories and work generated by the Berlin Wisdom Paradigm (see subsequently). As shown in Table 2 a four-dimensional structure of an ideally wise person was obtained. Consistent with past research, these dimensions refer to (a) exceptional knowledge concerning the acquisition of wisdom; (b) exceptional knowledge concerning its application; (c) exceptional knowledge about contextual and temporal variations of life; and (d) person-related competencies.

---

**Table 2**   Implicit Beliefs about Wise People: Four Dimensions

Factor 1   Exceptional knowledge about wisdom acquisition
- comprehends the nature of human existence
- tries to learn from his or her own mistakes

Factor 2   Exceptional knowledge about use of wisdom
- knows when to give/withhold advice
- is a person whose advice one would solicit for life problems

Factor 3   Exceptional knowledge about context of life
- knows that life priorities may change during the life course
- knows about possible conflicts among different life domains

Factor 4   Exceptional personality and social functioning
- is a good listener
- is a very humane person

## Explicit Theories

The second cluster of wisdom theories represents explicit psychological theories (Baltes & Smith, 1990; Baltes & Staudinger, 1993; Pasupathi & Baltes, in press; Sternberg, 1990). They are meant to focus on cognitive and behavioral expressions of wisdom and the processes involved in the joining of cognition with behavior. One main objective of such theories is to develop theoretical models of wisdom that allow for empirical inquiry—by means of quantitative operationalization of wisdom-related thought and behavior—as well as for the derivation of hypotheses that can be tested empirically (e.g., about predictors of behavioral expressions of wisdom).

To date, the theoretical and empirical work on explicit psychological conceptions of wisdom can be divided roughly into three groups: (a) the conceptualization of wisdom as a personal characteristic or a personality disposition (e.g., Erikson, 1959; McAdams & de St. Aubin, 1998); (b) the conceptualization of wisdom in the neo-Piagetian tradition of postformal and dialectical thinking (e.g., Alexander & Langer, 1990; Kramer, 1986, 2000; Labouvie-Vief, 1990; Peng & Nisbett, 1999); and (c) the conceptualization of wisdom as an expert system dealing with the meaning and conduct of life, as advocated in the Berlin Wisdom Paradigm (e.g., Baltes & Smith, 1990; Dittmann-Kohli & Baltes, 1990; Staudinger & Baltes, 1994). The latter is the focus of the remainder of this chapter.

## The Berlin Wisdom Project: Wisdom as Expertise in the Fundamental Pragmatics of Life

In this section, we shall describe the conception of wisdom upon which the Berlin Wisdom Project is based. Thereafter, we will discuss some general considerations concerning the development of wisdom across the life span.

### The Content Domain of Wisdom

Proceeding from the notion that wisdom involves some form of excellence (see Table 24.1), the Berlin Wisdom Project conceptualizes wisdom as an expertise in the meaning and conduct of life. Our conceptualization of wisdom as expertise signals that we expect most people not to be wise. What we expect, however, is that the behavioral expressions we observe in individuals can be ordered on a "wisdom scale." In general, wisdom is foremost a cultural product deposited in books of wisdom rather than in individuals.

The contents to which this expertise of wisdom refers are the "fundamental pragmatics of life," that is, knowledge about the essence of the human condition and the ways and means of planning, managing, and understanding a good life (cf. Baltes & Smith, 1990; Baltes & Staudinger, 1993, 2000). Examples of the fundamental pragmatics of life include knowledge and skills about the conditions, variability, ontogenetic changes, and historicity of human development; insight into obligations and goals in life; knowledge and skills about the social and situational influences on human life; as well as knowledge and skills about the finitude of life and the inherent limits of human knowledge.

As these examples reveal, the contents to which wisdom refers are markedly different from those of other domains that have been reported in the traditional expertise literature (Ericsson & Smith, 1991). Most research on expertise has focused on domains where well-defined problems can be used to systematically study experts' and laypersons' knowledge systems (e.g., physics or chess). In the domain of the fundamental pragmatics of life, contrariwise, problems are almost by definition illdefined, and no clear-cut "optimal" solutions exist (see also Arlin, 1990). Nevertheless, we assume that wisdom has a clear conceptual core and that its manifestations can be evaluated. As our empirical studies show, most people, after some training, are able to reach high levels of consensus in their evaluation of wisdom-related products.

### Antecedents of Wisdom

Our concept of wisdom as expertise and the linkage of this concept to life span theory (Baltes, 1987, 1997) suggest an ensemble of three broad domains of antecedents or determining factors—each comprising internal and external factors and processes—to be influential in the development of wisdom at the level of individuals. Before describing these three domains in detail, we need to discuss five more general considerations concerning the ontogenesis of wisdom.

First, as is typical for the development of expertise, we assume that wisdom is acquired through an extended and intense process of learning and practice. This clearly requires a high degree of motivation to strive for excellence, as well as a social-cultural and personal environment that is supportive of the search for wisdom. Second, wisdom is a complex and multifaceted phenomenon; therefore, for wisdom to emerge, a variety of experiential factors and processes on micro- and macro-levels are required to interact and collaborate. Third, given that wisdom involves the orchestration of cognitive, personal, social, interpersonal, and spiritual factors, its antecedents are diverse in nature. Fourth, because developmental tasks and adaptive challenges change across life, and the human condition is inherently a life-course phenomenon, we expect wisdom to reach its peak relatively late in adult life. Fifth, we believe that, as with other fields of expertise, the guidance of mentors, as well as the experience and mastery of critical life experiences, are conducive to individual manifestations of wisdom.

We now turn to the three domains of ontogenetic conditions and processes that influence the development of wisdom, namely, facilitative experiential contexts, expertise-relevant factors, and person-related factors (for a graphical representation of our developmental model, see Baltes & Staudinger, 2000, Figure 1, p. 121). In our developmental model, *facilitative experiential contexts* for the development of wisdom include chronological age, education, parenthood, professions that require individuals to strengthen their skills in social-emotional intelligence, familiarity with books such as autobiographical novels, or the historical period, which varies along dimensions of salience and facilitation in matters of the human condition. A second domain that is central to the development of wisdom refers to *expertise-relevant factors* such as experience in life matters, organized tutelage, the availability of mentorship in dealing with life problems, and motivational factors such as a general interest in aspects of human life or a motivation to strive for excellence. Finally, we consider *person-related factors* such as basic cognitive processes, aspects of intelligence, creativity, flexible cognitive styles, and personality dispositions such as openness to experience or ego strength.

These three domains of ontogenetic influences are interrelated, and we believe that, in the sense of equifinality (Kruglanski, 1996), different combinations of the domains may lead to similar outcomes. Thus, there is no single "optimal" pathway, but rather several different ways to acquire wisdom. Nevertheless, it is assumed that there is a productive collaboration among the relevant factors. For example, external factors like the presence of mentors or the experience and mastery of critical life experiences are certainly conducive to the development of wisdom. For these factors to be influential, however, preconditions such as being highly motivated to live in a "good" way and a requisite level of cognitive efficacy probably are necessary. The notion that wisdom requires the presence of several intra- and interindividual factors that need to interact in certain ways underlines that wisdom refers to qualities that can be acquired only by very few people.

# Patterns of Aging: Past, Present, and Future

BERNICE L. NEUGARTEN

The topic of aging and longevity has become an "in" thing in the mind of the American public. The mass media have discovered it, as witnessed by the recent cover story in *Newsweek,* the article "Is Senility Inevitable?" in *Saturday Review,* the article in *National Geographic* about remote villages in Ecuador and the Soviet Union where persons are said to live to the advanced ages of 125 and 130, and by a rash of newspaper headlines such as "Scientists Seek the Key to Longevity."

This "discovery" by the mass media stems from the fact that a few biologists are predicting that we stand on the brink of a scientific breakthrough that will add from twenty-five to thirty years to the average life-span. Understandably enough, these claims have caught the attention of the science editors and reporters.

Aging is neither an "in" nor an "out" topic, but one that has always been here and is here to stay. Interest in aging constitutes the wave of the future as far as social scientists, social workers, and medical practitioners are concerned. The reason is obvious. Since the turn of the century, the total United States population has increased nearly threefold; but the number of persons aged 65 and over has increased almost sevenfold. In 1970, there were about 20 million older people in the United States; by the year 2000, there will be over 28 million. The latter figure is based on persons already alive and on projection of present death rates. Because it takes no account of possible medical advances or breakthroughs in biology, it is a conservative estimate.

The growing number of aged persons is not in itself a social problem if a social problem is defined as a state of affairs which needs correction. Few persons would seriously maintain that

*Source:* Based on the Sidney A. and Julie P. Teller Lecture presented at the School of Social Service Administration, University of Chicago, May 2, 1973. Reprinted by permission from *Social Service Review* 47, no. 4 (December 1973): 571–80; ©1973 by The University of Chicago; all rights reserved.

it is wrong to have many older people in the population or that remedial steps should be taken to pare down their numbers. On the contrary, nations prize longevity and count it an accomplishment, not a failure, that increasing numbers of men and women live to old age. The problem is the lack of preparation for the "sudden" appearance of large numbers of older people and the lag in adapting social institutions to their needs.

To be more exact, the social problems are of two types. First, a certain proportion of older people suffer from poverty, illness, and social isolation. These people, whom we call the needy aged, create acute problems in the field of social welfare. Second, broader problems arise from the need of all individuals in the society to adjust to the new rhythms of life that result from increased longevity. All members of society must adapt to new social phenomena such as multigenerational families, retirement communities, and leisure as a way of life. The second set of social problems, as much as the first, leads to the innumerable questions of social policy that arise as the whole society accommodates itself to the new age distribution.

How should society meet the needs of older people? How does their increasing presence affect other groups in the society? What new relationships are being generated between young and old? More and more people are asking these questions in their professional as well as their private lives. For example, biological and social scientists have evolved a new science, gerontology; the Gerontological Society, created in 1940, now has a membership of some twenty-two hundred scientists and professional workers; and there are now some fifty-five gerontological societies and organizations in different countries belonging to the International Gerontological Association. The medical profession is arguing over the creation of a new specialty, geriatrics. While the move toward developing new specialties is regarded by many physicians as a step backward rather than forward, nevertheless the first professor of geriatrics in an American university was appointed in 1973. Social workers are experimenting with new types of services for older clients; adult educators are seeking ways of serving the older as well as the younger adult; recreational workers are trying new programs for older people; a few law schools are turning attention to the special legal problems that arise. Business corporations are concerned with the nagging questions of arbitrary or flexible retirement, the vesting of pension funds, and ways of preparing middle-aged workers for the adjustments they will make after retirement. Commissions, committees, and public agencies are proliferating at local, state, and national levels to cope with problems of older people.

All this is leading to a different climate of awareness and to changing images of old age as one looks to the recent past, the present, and the future.

## The Past

Negative stereotypes of old age were strongly entrenched in a society that prided itself on being youth oriented, future oriented, and oriented toward doing rather than being. Old people were usually regarded either as poor, isolated, sick, unhappy, desolate, and destitute—the "old age, it's a pity" perspective—or, on the contrary, as powerful, rigid, and reactionary. The first of these inaccurate images, usually inadvertently repeated through the mass media, probably originated from social workers, physicians, and psychiatrists who served the disadvantaged, the poor, and the physically and mentally ill—the needy aged.

In that climate—and, of course, it has not entirely disappeared—most people saw aging as alien to the self, and they tended to deny or repress the associated feelings of distaste and anxiety. In a society in which the frequency of death among the young had been drastically reduced by the conquest of infectious disease, and in which death had become increasingly associated only with old age, these pervasive attitudes, irrational and unconscious though they may have been, served also to maintain a psychological distance between young and old.

There was also the fact—and it is still true, although rapidly changing—that, in comparison with other age groups, the aged were economically and socially disadvantaged. They included a disproportionate number of foreign-born, unskilled men, who had come to the United States without much formal education, who had worked most of their lives at low-paying jobs, who had accumulated no savings through their lifetimes, and who were living in relative poverty after a life of hard work.

To reiterate, the image of old age was, from many different perspectives, a negative one.

## The Present

Images are now changing in the direction of reality; and reality means diversity. Older people are coming to be recognized for what they are: namely, a very heterogeneous group. With 10 percent of our population now over sixty-five years old, and with nearly half that group now great-grandparents, a very large number of young people are interacting with older members of their own families. With people now becoming grandparents between the ages of forty and fifty, and with more than one-half of all women in that age group in the labor market, young children see their grandmothers going to work every day and their mothers staying at home with them. We are beginning to delineate a "young-old" population and to see it as different from the "old-old."

The image of the old man in the rocking chair is now matched by the white-haired man on the golf course. Even television images are beginning to change. "Maude" is a forceful, liberal, middle-aged woman; "A Touch of Grace" portrays an elderly widow being courted by an elderly man, with both persons portrayed sympathetically; "Sanford and Son" are a black father and his adult son who have a close and mutually supportive relationship in which the old father emerges as the wiser and more astute.

A different example of the changing images of aging appears in a newspaper picture a few months ago. Captioned "Happy Pappy," it showed Strom Thurmond, the sixty-nine-year-old senator from South Carolina, with his young wife, their eighteen-month-old daughter, and their newborn son. Only six years earlier, in contrast, a newspaper report of the marriage of Supreme Court Justice Douglas to a twenty-three-year-old coed had included some very venomous comments. Five members of the House of Representatives had introduced resolutions calling on the House Judiciary Committee to investigate the moral character of Douglas; one said he should be impeached. If the newspaper account of Justice Douglas's marriage appeared today, it would probably take a much less hostile form, judging at least from the story about Senator Thurmond.

There are other social forces at work which change the images and status of the aged. The so-called youth culture seems to be recognizing new affinities with older people. That culture forgoes instrumentality—work, achievement, production, competition—for expressivity. "Being" rather than "doing," it values reflection, relatedness, and freedom to express one's authentic self. Some young people regard these qualities as characteristic of older people, and they find allies in the old. Some young people perceive the old as alienated from the dominant culture and from the "establishment," although, of course, there is no evidence that a higher proportion of the old than of the young or middle-aged are in truth alienated.

It is possible, also, that sizable segments of the young are seeking to strengthen their ethnic identifications and turn to their grandparents for reaffirmation of ethnic cultural values.

## Findings of Social Scientists

The findings of social researchers are contributing to the changing images of aging. For example, studies of large and representative samples of older people have shown that they are not isolated from other family members. While most older people prefer to live in their own households, they live near children or relatives and see other family members regularly. Overall, a higher proportion of old people who are sick live with their families than do those who are well. Old persons, contrary to the stereotype, are not dumped into mental hospitals or nursing homes or homes for the aged by cruel and indifferent children. Furthermore, older persons are not necessarily lonely or desolate if they live alone.

Few older persons ever show overt signs of mental deterioration or senility. Only a small proportion ever become mentally ill; for those who do, psychological and psychiatric treatment is by no means futile.

Retirement is neither good nor bad; some men and women want to keep on working, but more and more choose to retire early, as soon as they have enough income to live without working. The newest studies show that there is an increasing alienation from work and that increasing proportions of the population seem to value leisure more than work. Retired persons do not grow sick from idleness or from feelings of worthlessness. Three-fourths of the persons questioned in a recent national sample reported they were satisfied or very satisfied with their lives since retirement, a finding that is in line with earlier surveys. Most persons over sixty-five years old think of themselves as being in good health and act accordingly. On the average, after a short period of readjustment after retirement, men do not fail to establish meaningful patterns of activity.

Although there are some signs of increased age segregation, as in the retirement communities that have multiplied in the United States, this trend involves only a small proportion of older persons, and they constitute a self-selected group who appear to be exercising a larger rather than a smaller degree of freedom in choosing where to live. Furthermore, what studies are available indicate that in such communities, where the density of older people is relatively high, social interaction has increased. On the whole, it cannot be said that urban industrial societies preclude the social integration of the old.

In a series of studies of individuals between the ages of fifty and eighty carried out over a period of years at the University of Chicago, great diversity was found in the social and psychological patterns associated with successful aging. Various kinds of data were gathered on several hundred persons, all living "normal" lives in the community, including information on types of social interaction, role performance, investment in various roles and life-styles, degree of satisfaction with life—past and present—and personality type. It was found that as they grew older some persons sloughed off various role responsibilities with relative comfort and remained highly content with life. Others showed a drop in social role performance (e.g., as worker, friend, neighbor, or community participant), accompanied by a drop in life satisfaction. Still others, who had long shown low levels of activity accompanied by high satisfaction, changed relatively little as they aged.

For instance, in one group of seventy- to eighty-year-olds, eight different patterns of aging were empirically derived. They included the Reorganizers, Focused, Disengaged, Holding-on, Constricted, Succorance-seeking, Apathetic, and Disorganized. It appeared, furthermore, that the patterns reflected long-standing life-styles; within broad limits—given no major biological accidents or major social upheavals—an individual's pattern of aging was predictable from his way of life in middle age. In other words, aging is not a leveler of individual differences—until, perhaps, at the very end of life.

If there is no single social role pattern for the aged in 1970, the diversity is likely to become even greater in the future. With better health, more education, and more financial resources, older men and women will exercise—or at least will wish to exercise—greater freedom to choose the life-styles that suit them.

All this is not to deny the fact that, at the very end of life, there will continue to be a shorter or longer period of dependency, and that increased numbers of the very old will need care, either in their own homes or in special institutional settings. For persons who are terminally ill or incapacitated, it will be idle, in the future as in the present, to speak of meaningful social roles or of increased options in life-styles. For the advanced aged, the problems for the society will continue to be those of providing maximum social supports, the highest possible levels of care and comfort, the assurance of dignified death, and an increasing element of choice for the individual himself or for members of his family regarding how and when his life shall end.

## Questions for the Future

In looking to the future, rather than focus upon the diversities among individual older people,

one might well look at the society as an age-differentiated system and at relationships among age groups. In this context, questions about the prolongation of life can be reconsidered.

Generational conflict and relationships among age groups fluctuate according to historical, political, and economic factors. Under fortunate circumstances, an equilibrium is created whereby all age groups receive an appropriate share of the goods of the society and an appropriate place for their different values and world views. Under other circumstances, conflict may increase, as when the old, through some presumed historical failure, become "de-authorized" in the eyes of the young or when the young become overly advantaged in the eyes of the old. Whatever the forces of social change, the quality of life for all members of society and the social cohesion among age groups are influenced by the relative numbers of young, middle-aged, and old present at any given time.

If, indeed, the life-span is to be further extended, resulting in a dramatic increase in the numbers of the old, will industrialized societies be more ready for them than before and better prepared to meet their needs? Will the status of the aged become better or worse?

The answers are by no means clear. For one thing, generational conflicts may be increasing. If so, will they involve, on the one hand, the young and society at large and, on the other hand, the old and society at large? Is a new age divisiveness appearing and are there new antagonisms that can be called "ageism"? Is the world entering a period of social change in which, like earlier struggles for political and economic rights, there is now also a struggle for age rights? If so, will the struggle be joined not only by the young but also by the old who might otherwise become its victims?

Such questions have no easy answers, for the underlying social dynamics are complex. In the United States, for example, resentments against delinquency, student activism, the drug culture, and the counterculture often become uncritically fused into hostility toward the young as an age group. At the same time, there have been new attempts to integrate the young, as witnessed by the recent lowering of the voting age from twenty-one to eighteen. And there are the dramatic instances, such as the election of a youthful mayor or youth-controlled city councils of Berkeley or Madison, in which traditional age values were swept aside by other political considerations.

Anger toward the old may also be on the rise. In some instances, because a growing proportion of power positions in the judiciary, legislative, business, and professional arenas are occupied by older people, and because of seniority privileges among workers, the young and middle-aged become resentful. In other instances, as the number of the retired increases, the economic burden is perceived as falling more and more upon the middle-aged taxpayer.

These issues are not merely academic, as illustrated in recent journalistic accounts:

An editorial, syndicated in many metropolitan newspapers and occasioned by the 20 percent rise in social security benefits, was headlined, "Budget Story: Bonanza for Elderly." It said, "America's public resources are increasingly being mortgaged for the use of a single group within our country, the elderly." It went on to distort the situation by saying, "One-fourth of total federal spending is earmarked for only one-tenth of the population . . . clearly this trend cannot continue for long without causing a bitter political struggle between the generations."

Another example is an article that appeared two years ago in the *New Republic*. The author advocated that all persons lose the vote at retirement or age seventy, whichever was earlier. Reviewing changes that had occurred in his native California, he said: "We face a serious constitutional crisis—California faces civil war—if we continue to allow the old an unlimited franchise. There are simply too many senile voters and their number is growing."[10]

However, older people are becoming more vocal and more active in the political process. As they become accustomed to the politics of confrontation they see around them, they are beginning to voice their demands. For instance, appeals to "senior power" came into prominence in 1971 at the White House Conference on Aging. There are more frequent accounts of groups of older people picketing and protesting over such local issues as reduced bus fares or better housing projects. Whether such incidents remain isolated and insignificant or whether an activist politics of old age is developing in the

United States is still a debatable question, but it would be a mistake to assume that what characterized the political position of older people in the past decades will be equally characteristic in the future.

Another factor to be considered is the creation of advocacy groups. The American Association for Retired Persons, which makes its appeal primarily to middle-class older persons, claims a membership of 3.5 million. The National Council of Senior Citizens, oriented primarily toward blue-collar groups, claims a membership of some 3 million. The Grey Panthers, smaller but more militant, is now organizing nationwide.

Given the complexity of such trends, we presently lack good indexes for assessing the degree of social cohesion among age groups. As we develop so-called intangible social indicators (e.g., of levels of life satisfaction or levels of alienation), social scientists might well build indexes relating to expectations and attitudes of various age groups toward each other and monitor those attitudes in assessing the social health of the nation.

Some observers take an optimistic and others a pessimistic view of the progress thus far achieved in equalizing the needs of various age groups. All in all, it is probably fair to say that, in at least the affluent societies of the world, the status of the aged has begun to show marked improvement during the past few decades. The question is whether such gains as have been achieved can be continued in the face of a dramatic extension of the life-span.

Two general strategies for lengthening the life-span are being pursued: the first is the continuing effort to conquer major diseases. It has been variously estimated that, if the problems of cancer and cardiovascular diseases are solved, life expectancy at age 65 will be increased five to ten years, thus redistributing deaths so that they will come more often at the end of the natural life-span, at about age eighty to ninety.

The second strategy involves altering intrinsic biological processes, which are presumed to underlie aging and which seem to proceed independent of disease processes. That is, the genetic and biochemical secrets of aging should be discovered, and then the biological clock that is presumably programmed into the human species could be altered. This second approach is directed at control of the rate of aging rather than control of disease. A few biologists claim that such a breakthrough will occur within the next twenty years and that it will result in an extension of the natural life-span itself, so that men will have not an additional ten, but an additional twenty-five years of life.

If the natural life-span were to be increased in the relatively short period of a few decades, the effects upon society might well be revolutionary. It is an unhappy fact that few social scientists, and even fewer biological scientists, have given serious thought to the social implications, although speculative essays and fictional accounts by journalists have begun to appear alongside more familiar forms of science fiction.

One writer has published a social satire describing a society in which people when they reach the age of fifty are automatically segregated from others, even from their own children, then painlessly put to death when they reach sixty-five. Another has described the solution in opposite terms in a society in which the old are in control, and the few young who are allowed to be born seek ways to accelerate their own aging in order to take their places in the society of elders. These parodies are examples of ageism carried to the extreme: in the first instance ageism is directed against the old; in the second, against the young.

There have been few serious attempts to extrapolate from available data in pondering such questions as these: Can an increased life-span be achieved without keeping marginally functioning individuals alive for extended periods? Would a major increase in the proportion of the aged so aggravate the problem of health, medical care, income, and housing that the old would be worse off than now? What would be the major deleterious and the major beneficial effects of a prolonged life-span upon the rest of society? Given present economic and governmental institutions, can even the affluent societies support greatly enlarged numbers of retired persons? Can income be divorced from work rapidly enough to balance off inequities among age groups? Will free time be truly free— that is, will it be desired by most individuals? Can it be supported by adequate income and by

a reasonable level of good health? Will it be socially honored—that is, will the work ethic change rapidly enough into a leisure ethic? Or, if the employable age were to be extended, would the effects be deleterious upon both young and old? Could spectacular unemployment be avoided in either or both groups? Could technological obsolescence be overcome in the old? Could our educational systems be transformed rapidly enough into opportunity systems for self-fulfillment for the middle-aged and old as well as for the young? Will our social and humanistic and ethical values accommodate to a drastically altered age distribution? What will be the effects upon successive groups of young, and what will be the eventual effects upon their old age?

Lest we be overwhelmed by unanswerable questions, it should be said that, in contrast with those biologists whose statements make newspaper headlines, most biologists take a more conservative view of the future and believe that dramatically lengthened life-spans are still far off.

But whether or not a breakthrough is imminent, we are nevertheless already witnessing transformations in the age distribution of the society, in which the number of older people is rapidly increasing. And we can be quite sure that medical advances will continue to prolong life, even if we are far from solving the biochemical or genetic secrets of aging. Many gerontologists believe that if average life expectancy is increased by only five more years—to say nothing of twenty-five years—the effects upon our present economic and welfare institutions will be profound.

Man's desire for longevity can now be whetted by the findings of social scientists, such as those already mentioned. If—as now appears true—the institutional arrangements of industrialized societies do not inevitably lead to the social isolation of the old, if—as also appears true—man does not lose his ability to learn as he grows old, and if there is no universal set of personality changes that lead inevitably to disengagement from society, then the old person stands to benefit as much from social advances as does the young person.

What, then, will be the new social and ethical pressures for prolonging life? What will be the risks of a prolonged life-span, not only to older people themselves, but to the society as a whole? How can these risks be weighed against the benefits? How can social values be weighed against economic values, and how can a new priority of social values be effected?

These are questions that will inevitably preoccupy us more and more over the next decades. In pursuing our research programs and our action programs and in working out broad-scale social solutions, the social scientist will join with the biological scientist, the policy maker, the jurist, the ethicist, and the social worker. We will need, as never before, the insights and the experience and the social philosophy of the profession of social work.

## Notes

1. Steward, Douglas J. "The Lesson of California: Disfranchise the Old." *New Republic* (August 29, 1970).

# From Perception to Inference

## E. J. GIBSON

It is often asserted that the young child is stimulus bound, enslaved by the surrounding milieu, dependent on the present sensory information, and that perceptual development is a process of liberation from the constraints of stimulation. Another way of putting this has been to say that he is misled by perceptual factors and must make inferences. A related statement is that cognitive development consists in "going beyond the information given" (Bruner, 1957).

One cannot doubt that the child's conceptual life expands as he matures and gains experience. Concepts and generalized rules can have a guiding and directing effect on perception, just as labels and verbal instructions can have. I have discussed this in chapters 7 and 8. Labels or instructions can direct attention to distinctive parts of a display, and concepts, especially rule-like ones, can help to reveal structure not easily or automatically detected perceptually. But this is not to say that perception is left behind in favor of inference as we grow up, nor is it even to say that perception develops by making use of inference.

What is wrong with saying that the young child is stimulus bound, and that cognitive development is a liberation from these bonds by the operations of intelligence? This is Piaget's opinion. One must admit its popularity and its persuasiveness, for a neonate's attention does seem to be captured by a few kinds of events in its environment. But the developmental change is not one of doing without stimulus information; it is one of seeking stimulus information in a directed, systematic fashion. Does perception mislead us, whereas conception and generalization lead to truth and reality? Concepts and generalizations can sometimes themselves mislead us; we speak of biased observation. It is then not perception that is misleading. We are misled by

the failure to grasp the invariants in the stimulus flux. When the invariants occur over a temporal sequence of transformations, as in an event like the pouring of water from one container to another, they may or may not be detected. A still shot of a filled container at one moment of stimulation can be misleading, like a single frame from a motion picture, for invariants occur that can be discovered only over variation and transformation.

Does the child need more information in stimulation, or more redundancy in stimulation, than adults do because his concepts are immature? One kind of evidence cited for this conclusion is drawn from experiments with incomplete figures (Gollin, 1960, 1961). Children can fill in the figures and recognize them better as age increases. To quote Wohlwill, "Compared to the adult the young child requires more redundancy in a pattern to perceive it correctly; thus both incomplete and very complex patterns will be difficult for him (1960, p. 281)." They may be more difficult but not, I suggest, because "the younger child requires a greater amount of surplus information." He cannot handle more information than an adult, and is far less adept at seeing and using redundancy in stimulation when it is present. Distinctive features of objects do have to be learned, however, and an increased knowledge of them would be expected to aid in recognizing incomplete pictures.

Bruner, also, has claimed that "less redundancy is needed as we grow older" (Bruner, Olver, Greenfield, et al., 1966, p. 23), using again the evidence from recognition of incomplete pictures. The reasoning is that perception is based on representations, on a constructed model of reality against which the input is tested. As this model grows richer, he suggests, the child uses it to fill in details that are not given in stimulation.

As the reader knows by now, I disagree with this interpretation of perception and perceptual development. Perception is not a process of matching to a representation in the head, but one of extracting the in-variants in stimulus in-

*Source:* Gibson, E. J. (1969). From perception to inference. In E. J. Gibson, *Principles of perceptual learning* (pp. 448–450, 471–472). New York: Appleton-Century-Crofts.

formation. Constraints in stimulation can be useful, and adaptive development depends on more effective pickup of this information rather than less dependence upon it. Although our concepts increase in number, richness, and complexity as we grow older, it does not follow that our percepts become more and more reflections of our concepts. We do not perceive less because we conceive more. If we did, it would be maladaptive for getting information about what is going on in the world around us.

## Stages or Transitions?

The manifestations of change over time are a fascinating problem for the dramatist, the archaeologist, and the biologist alike. Shakespeare celebrated the seven ages of man, wondering how the mewling infant could possibly be identified with the whining schoolboy, the lover, and the "lean and slippered plantaloon." Yet, dramatic as these contrasts are, there is some identity over the ages of man. Are these different stages arbitrarily chosen from a sequence that really proceeds in continuous fashion, or are there times in the sequence when the transition is abrupt and a quite new organization follows? Biologically, there is no clear-cut answer to this question. One can point to the insects where there is a metamorphosis in development, with a radical shift in structure and manner of adapting to the environment, but one can also point to cases of continuous growth where the transformation is spectacular only if it is speeded up, as if in a time-lapse motion picture that emphasizes the change.

This chapter is concerned with trends. But the identifying of psychological trends is difficult. Does a trend imply a gradual transition in a kind of behavior, maintaining identity while exhibiting progress toward some biological adaptation? If so, how do we describe the changed behavior and still recognize the identity? Or does a trend imply not gradual transitions but stages of behavior, with abrupt changes in organization comparable to metamorphosis in insects?

Human growth, after birth, does not display metamorphosis. The closest thing to it is the speeded-up change at adolescence, and perhaps the heightened responsiveness occurring at so-called critical periods during infancy. We are aware of the great docility of the human organism, and the extent to which its behavior can be shaped by programmed schedules of training. The contribution of the environment is so great that the appearance of stages might result from the program that the culture has provided for the child's education.

I want to look for trends in development, but I am very dubious about stages. Instead of the child study psychologists of fifty years ago, who thought of the child as almost a distinct species, or even the more recent experimental child psychologists, let us try to be developmental psychologists. Let us examine developmental studies of perceptual activity, hoping to discover generalizations that will reveal the laws of behavior and its adaptation to ongoing events. We look for a progressive sequence which spans the activity from birth to maturity.

It is a hazardous undertaking, but I am going to propose, and summarize evidence for, certain trends in perceptual development. To repeat, trends do not imply stages in each of which a radically new process emerges, nor do they imply maturation in which a new direction exclusive of learning is created.

## Epilogue

I have set forth as positively as I can the nature of perceptual learning, first what is learned, and then what I believe to be some of its laws. They are laws of differentiation and filtering, not laws of association; and laws of the reduction of uncertainty, not laws of external reinforcement. Finally, I have described the developmental trends in perceptual functioning—progressive specificity, optimization of attention, and progressive economy information pickup. Now I must admit how much remains unanswered. We do not know how the distinctive features are discovered. We do not know how attention functions to filter out the irrelevant and preserve the critical information. I think we are still a pretty long way from knowing.

It cheers one up a bit, however, to know that mysteries remain even in the older sciences, to judge from this paragraph by the Nobel-prize-winning physicist Feynman:

The biggest mystery of physics is where the laws are known, but we don't know exactly what's going on. We don't know the strategy in the middle game. We know castling, or how the different pieces move, and we know a little bit about the end game, but nothing in the middle.

We get reports from the experimentalists, the watchers of the chess game, and we try to analyze the information. We may even suggest a new experiment. But we're still waiting and hoping for the big strategy. Then maybe we'll really understand how wonderful is nature.[1]

So goes the psychology of perception and its development. We know something about the laws, and what experiments we can be doing to improve our knowledge of them, but the "strategy in the middle" leaves us a great deal to think about.

[1] *New York Times Magazine*, October 8, 1967.

# Developmental Psychology and Brain Development: A Historical Perspective

### SIDNEY J. SEGALOWITZ

> *. . . the laws of brain-action are at bottom mechanical laws—we do not in the least explain the* nature *of thought by affirming this dependence. . . . The authors who most unconditionally affirm the dependence of our thoughts on our brain to be a fact are often the loudest to insist that the fact is inexplicable, and that the intimate essence of consciousness can never be rationally accounted for by any material cause. It will doubtless take several generations of psychologists to test the hypothesis of dependence with anything like minuteness.*
>
> —James (1892, pp. 6–7)

## Introduction

Developmental psychology has had an ambivalent partnership with the neurosciences. Although they coexist in the same university departments, the same textbooks, and even occasionally the same undergraduate courses, the marriage has been one filled with sudden flirtations followed by the disillusionment of long-term incompatibility. Developmentalists who are not themselves physiologically oriented have accepted the notion that understanding the brain can have some clinical utility; that it can impress the general public, because the medical sciences are always headline-worthy topics; and that it has some place in textbooks claiming to be complete. But in this chapter, I argue that, to date, there is little in classic developmental theories that really owes much *specifically* to an understanding of the brain and its developmental growth pattern. This, of course, has not stopped correlative brain mechanisms from being used after the fact to bolster the context for certain psychological constructs. However, developmental neuroscience has progressed enough recently that we are now in an era when the field of developmental neuropsychology—the disci-

*Source:* Segalowitz, S.J. (1994). Developmental psychology and brain development: A historical perspective. In G. Dawson & K.W. Fischer (Eds.), Human behavior and the developing brain (pp. 67–73, 75–80). New York: Guilford.

pline that relates brain growth to behavior in a developmental context—can be usefully informative to developmental psychology and can drive developmental theory.

We have been at this threshold before, and we may wonder what happened to the promising integration of developmental psychology and brain maturation that seemed ready to flourish in the 1920s and 1930s. In this review, I trace some of the reasons during the last century for developmental psychology's historical difficulty in embracing the issue of brain maturation; why it is currently changing; and how we can look for a fruitful blending of the two fields in the future. My review focuses on historical trends and is necessarily brief in reviewing empirical literature that is covered extensively elsewhere in this volume.

## What is a Neuropsychology of Development?

Psychology in the modern era has always been based on the notion that the brain is the organ of the mind, and psychologists have often made reference to reputed neurological mechanisms. For the purposes of this chapter, I define a "neuropsychology of development" as more than a specification of possible brain correlates of developmental constructs; this we could refer to as a "physiology of development." Physiological reductionist positions were very popular at the beginning of this century—for example, Burbank's (1909) Lamarckian treatment of child development and deCrinis's (1932) histological explanation of development (the latter is described further below). Such physiological description is neither necessary nor sufficient for developmental psychology, even if the facts involved are correct. Suppose we have a psychological theory that says that function *A* leads ontogenetically into function *B*. Being able to suggest brain correlates for *A* and *B* has great merits, but it does not by itself advance developmental theory. This can only be done if there is information about those brain correlates that can be used to inform the developmental theory, such as the relationship between the physiological substrates of *A* and *B*. Physiological correlates in themselves are fascinating, may be useful clinically, and are prerequisites to constructing theories that in the end will bring psychological and neurological development together. However, physiology on its own has never been prerequisite to developmental theory, since sometimes the psychological and neurological facts match on levels and sometimes they do not. For example, although Freud was a neurologist by training, he did not insist that psychological development from id to ego to superego had to involve physical maturation of specific brain areas, although he presumably would have been delighted to be able to specify some.

In discussing neuropsychological development, we cannot avoid discussing the notion of maturation–a concept that has bothered developmental psychologists because of its reductionist implications, but one that is nonetheless essential. In this chapter, by "brain maturation" I mean the physical growth of the brain in terms of general processes (e.g., dendritic expansion, myelination) and in terms of regional development (e.g., subcortical centers, various parts of the cortex), whether these processes and development are influenced by psychological experiences or are independent of them. For a neuropsychology of development to be useful, we must be able to talk of regional structural and functional development in order to account for the development of specific systems (such as language, social behavior, perception mechanisms, and executive control functions). However, I assume that the reader appreciates that such brain growth is not independent of nutritional and experiential factors (Changeux & Dehaene, 1989; Gottlieb, 1976, 1983, 1992; Greenough & Black, 1992).

In this chapter, I focus primarily on "grand" theories of psychological development, and quickly review some current trends that seem to be leading to a new, somewhat eclectic integration of psychology and developmental neurophysiology. Many of the other chapters in this book are devoted to explaining the details of these current trends, and the sheer number of them places us at a very exciting time in the development of our interdisciplinary field.

## A Brief Synopsis of the First Half-Century (1895–1946)

### Freud and Baldwin

We are approaching the centenary of the publication of two important books, each of which represents an attempt to integrate some aspects of brain physiology and function into central concepts in developmental psychology and psychology in general. Freud (1895/1966) sketched a quasi-cell-assembly model of the brain mechanisms corresponding to processes central to his psychodynamic approach, including the underpinnings of cathexis and identification (Pribram & Gill, 1976). This exercise was ambitious, but represented the common notion of the time that the nervous system acts to reduce stimulation and that development over time consists only of a quantitative increase in synaptic connectivity (Holt, 1965). There was little place in Freud's framework either for an overall inhibitory mechanism that may help focus attention on internal cognitive processes (Macmillan, 1992), or for qualitative changes in brain function as a result of maturation.

Baldwin (1894/1925) also speculated on the relationship between brain function and child development, with a keen appreciation for the complexity of the central nervous system and the near impossibility of ever really accounting for the current issues in consciousness within a brain model. Both Baldwin and Freud were acutely aware of the need for progress in neuroscience before they could speak about these issues with confidence—a recurrent theme with other major developmentalists who followed them.

Freud and Baldwin, and later Piaget, had a great interest in the phylogenesis of the brain, but surprisingly little interest in its ontogenesis. This might have been so because biological science was just coming through two tremendous intellectual revolutions: Darwin's (1859/1901) theory of evolution firmly removed the assumption that biological structures are permanently fixed for all time; and the rediscovery of Gregor Mendel's notion of genetic material fixed at conception placed this fluidity in phylogenesis and not ontogenesis (see Moore, 1972). Thus, Baldwin argued that brain structures do not change with growth, but rather represent fundamental processing components from birth:

> [A] psychology which holds that we have a "speech faculty," an original mental endowment which is incapable of further reduction, may appeal to the latest physiological research and find organic confirmation, at least as far as a determination of its cerebral apparatus is concerned; but such support for the position is wanting when we return to the brain of the infant. Not only do we fail to find the series of centres into which the organic basis of speech has been divided, but even those of them which we do find have not taken up the function, either alone or together, which they perform when speech is actually realized. In other words, the primary object of each of the various centres involved is not speech, but some other simpler function; and speech arises by development from a union of these separate functions. (Baldwin, 1895/1925, pp. 6–7)

It is interesting to note the basic similarity of this position to a contemporary one on hemispheric specialization (Witelson, 1977, 1987).

### Carmichael and Gesell

During the 1920s and 1930s, Carmichael (1926, 1927, 1928, 1946), Gesell (1929), and their students began to write about how the physiological maturation of the brain must be held accountable for some of the development of skills during childhood. Carmichael and Kuo's basic animal work expressed an appreciation for maturation in the growth of motor function, but the question remained as to whether this could be extrapolated to mental functions. Gesell in fact sought what we would see as a modern integration, recognizing the paucity of the nature-nurture division:

> If we manage to envisage maturation as an active physiological process, we overcome the rather stilted antithesis of the nature-versus-nurture problem. Galton tells us that in his day the very term *heredity* was strange. With the advent of Mendelism the term took on popularity and became oversimplified. Individual unit characters of inheritance were too specifically identified with discrete chromosome particles, and heredity came to be regarded too mechanically as a fixed mode of transmission. Geneticists now emphasize the fact that these particles are chemicals which interact with each other and with many other factors to produce the organism. And if we but knew the bio-chemistry and biophysics of the interactions we should be mak-ing much less earnest use of such words as *heredity, environment*, and *maturation*. (Gesell, 1933, p. 209)

However, while feeling confident that developmental psychology must embrace an integration of brain maturation with experience, he did express concern about anyone's ability to document such an integration:

> The role of maturation in the higher spheres of intellectual and moral life is, on the basis of present knowledge, difficult to determine. On theoretical grounds some may even question whether the concept of maturation can be applied to these higher and more rarefied fields of behavior accessible to introspection but not to photography. *Nevertheless, if there is a general physiology of growth which governs the entire development of the individual, we may well believe that maturation maintains a role in the higher orders of thought and feeling.* (Gesell, 1933, pp. 223–224; emphasis added)

## *Piaget*

While Gesell remained firmly committed to a neurodevelopmental approach, Piaget took an alternate route. He appreciated the theoretical implications and complexities of the phylogenesis of the brain, and also, as he indicated later, realized that he did not have enough information about brain development and brain function to be able to articulate the role of brain maturation in child development (Piaget & Inhelder, 1966/1969). He recognized that a truly developmental theory of neuropsychology would be needed, but he seemed to have no vision of how such a theory might look (as compared to McGraw, 1946 [see below], who had such a vision but did not have a developmental theory into which to place her observations). Piaget tried to apply the principles of biological functioning in phylogeny and ontogeny to philosophical constructs such as epistemology (MacNamara, 1976), while rejecting any further involvement of physiological constructs in mental development. He maintained that such constructs are inherently nondevelopmental, and that they represent "vitalism, apriorism and Gestalt: habit deriving from intelligence, habit unrelated to intelligence and habit explained, like intelligence and perception, by structurings whose laws remain independent of development" (Piaget, 1947/1966, p. 88). Piaget's view of any attempt to introduce brain factors would necessarily include only fixed characteristics. One example of this is the argument that the child's sense of speed is a basic construct inherent in the structure of the retina (Piaget, 1970).

His attempt to reconcile evolutionary biology with his notion of genetic epistemology (the ontogenetic "evolution" of mind) was truly valiant (Piaget, 1947/1966). However, it still resulted in no notion of brain development, save for the idea that experience leads to further neuronal connections—a position that he, like Baldwin before him, immediately recognized as nothing more than pure associationism. This position "is scarcely upheld any longer in its pure associationist form, except for some authors, *of predominantly physiological interests,* who think they can reduce intelligence to a system of 'conditioned' responses" (Piaget, 1947/1960 p. 16; emphasis added).

## *The Integration That Slipped Away*

At this point, Myrtle McGraw (1946) presented an intriguing review of the issue of maturation in child development. She argued strongly for true integration of brain growth and experience, as Carmichael and Gesell had done before her, with her own data focusing again on motor development. However, she also knew that differential cortical maturation must be necessary for some type of understanding in development theory, and quoted an intriguing paper by deCrinis (1932) on this issue. deCrinis had mapped out histologically those cortical areas (in human or where dendritic growth matured earlier versus later, using a technique that he claimed would reflect functional maturation and not just physical growth. This supported the earlier speculation derived from the growth of myelin that functional development is first found in sensory and motor areas, and last in what we now consider to be multimodal intertiary areas of integrative functions (Segalowitz, 1992). What is interesting is that we would recognize his pattern as fitting not only the mapping sequence of primary sensorimotor cortex to unimodal association areas to heteromodal cortex (Mesulam, 1985), but also our current conception of stages in cognitive development. Unfortunately, deCrinis

## Incorporating The Construct of Brain Development into Developmental Theory

Most schools of developmental psychology that have flourished over the past 50 years have ignored a link with brain maturation not only implicitly but also explicitly, and have supported this inattention with the following sorts of arguments. Although it may be the case that the brain matures to some extent during the psychologically impressionable early years, these changes are limited in two ways: (1) Such changes are universal and of a general sort, so that while one individual may generally be more mature than others, there are no specific interactions in brain development that could account for interesting variations among children as they grow; and (2) such changes are so gradual and so small, compared to the dramatic environmental changes children live through in early childhood, that there is little to suggest that most of the variance involved in growth could be attributable to the maturation of the brain, even including dramatic developmental milestones such as the acquisition of language. Thus, Skinner (1957) could confidently discuss language acquisition as just another learned behavior. Dollard and Miller (1950) could deal with socialization, including the metacognitive structures for mature social behavior, as simply a product of a reinforcement schedule. And Piaget, of course, could describe how a child constructs higher and higher levels of cognition through assimilation and accommodation. In all these cases, the focus was on universal aspects of development—on how the broad strokes of development are the same across children, and individual differences are primarily nuisance factors. The dramatic increase in perceptions of the importance of individual differences in development, aided greatly by physiological approaches, supersedes these theoretical frameworks.

The status that individual differences have in growth and behavior rests on the constructs that theorists permit. If a theorist does not permit any constructs that reflect differences among people, the strength of that theory in accounting for individual differences is necessarily weak. However, in the approaches already considered, we find a variety of constructs for variability. For example, Gesell's maturational approach permits differences in the rate of growth (Gesell & Amatruda, 1941). This monolithic variable cannot account for qualitative differences among children, such as how some become more verbal, some more shy, or some more athletic. Yet, to the extent that there are general developmental structures, one could at least support a developmental psychology that includes differing rates of global maturation.

Similarly, Piaget's approach acknowledges differential rates of maturation, whether during the earlier sensorimotor period or the later operational periods. His approach, also resting on universal stages, could naturally incorporate an individual growth rate construct. However, the real engine of cognitive development for him is exposure to cognitive conflict (disequilibrium),

with individual differences in the rate of growth resulting from differing experiential backgrounds (Piaget, 1972). From a neuropsychological perspective, this leads to an interesting debate as to whether the Piagetian constructivist approach has subtly captured the *results* of some interaction between brain growth and experience (Segalowitz & Hiscock, 1992), or has rather described the forces *driving* those changes (Keating, 1990).

Behaviorist theory has its own constructs for dealing with individual variation: differences in reinforcement schedules, and differential stimulus-stimulus pairing. This is not the place to explore the adequacy of these notions, but one does wonder about the exceptional cases where early talent develops in the absence of social support or even normal intellectual functioning, such as cases of children who have a level of linguistic sophistication completely at odds with their general intellectual level (Obler & Fein, 1988).

A neuropsychological approach is partly compatible with all of these traditional developmental theories, with the proviso that we recognize the mind-brain isomorphism. Any mental differences must be reflected in some way by variation in brain structure and activity. Psychological development involves brain changes, just as differences across people must involve variations in brain structure and function (Bunge, 1980).

## The Last 25 Years

### Lenneberg's Biological Foundations of Language

We can trace much of the current interest among developmental psychologists in the maturation of the brain to Eric Lenneberg's book *Biological Foundations of Language*, published in 1967. Hemispheric specialization had already aroused general interest with the popularizing work of the California group investigating commissurotomy patients (e.g., Gazzaniga, 1970; Sperry, 1968). Lenneberg's breakthrough was a melding of developmental issues with brain maturation. He proposed that the hitherto unending debate over why there seems to be a critical period for second-language (and presumably first-language) acquisition was missing a critical variable. The issue for him was not whether learning styles of children differ at various ages, but whether the left hemisphere of the brain is still adaptable enough to acquire language in adulthood, and whether adaptability decreases as brain tissue becomes specialized for cognitive functions. Within 10 years of the publication of his seminal book, there was a rush of activity concerning the role of brain lateralization in children's mental growth, much of it showing that some basic assumptions in Lenneberg's model were wrong despite their widespread acceptance at the time. Hemispheric specialization has turned out not to be a gradual developmental process that is only mature by puberty; rather, it is present in many guises throughout infancy (Segalowitz & Berge, in press; Segalowitz & Gruber, 1977). Similarly, it turns out that functional specialization does not entail a lessening of functional plasticity (Kinsbourne & Hiscock, 1977; see Huttenlocher, Chapter 4, this volume).

The lasting effect of *Biological Foundations of Language* was an appreciation that there is a biological context for human mental functions, even complex ones. This was important because Chomsky (1965) had convinced many people of the notion of a "language acquisition device" of unspecified nature that somehow catapults a child into language learning, without any specification of what such a device may be. However, it was implicitly accepted at the time that a description of the biological correlates of this sort of mental functioning would be an adequate basis for postulating the existence of this construct.

Lenneberg's (1967) description of the biological basis for language was readable; it was addressed to psychologists; and it was promising as a model for a new developmental framework that was inaccessible from traditional, behaviorally oriented approaches. In historical terms, *Biological Foundations of Language* was a critical catalyst that eventually broke through some very powerful, even political, forces in developmental psychology that resisted any brain construct (described below).

An irony here is that the appreciation that the brain has specific mechanisms for language (or for any other mental function) does not necessarily lead to any alteration of our conception of that mental function, except to confirm its existence. That is, our notion of how that function is structured need not change solely because of its having a biological correlate (James, 1892). Historically, however, this new approach did lead to two new appreciations. First, we expect some individual differences in mental function to take particular forms and not others, solely because of biological differences among people. Second, the brain may be seen to provide constraints on development that purely behavioral models cannot predict. The first factor concerning individual differences is historically the stronger in drawing developmental psychologists to neurophysiology, but it is the second issue that keeps them there.

## Individual Differences

I have argued elsewhere (Segalowitz & Bryden, 1983; Segalowitz, 1987) that we must come to grips with the notion that everyone's brain does not appear to be organized in the same way. This sounds like a truism of a trivial sort, and some of the implications are indeed trivial. Our measures of brain organization, especially those behavioral tasks designed to reflect hemispheric functional asymmetries (e.g., dichotic listening, visual half-field presentation), are known to have poor test-retest reliability and cross-test validation on occasion (Segalowitz, 1986), although some electrophysiological measures are more promising (Segalowitz & Barnes, 1993; Tomarken, Davidson, Wheeler, & Kenney, 1992). These difficulties have been traced to several sources (Segalowitz and Bryden, 1983): the measurement devices' having poor psychometric properties (Chapman & Chapman, 1988); the devices' being sensitive to the subject's attentional set, level of arousal, or mood; and other factors that are truly based on differences in the functional organization of the cortex. Some of the differences across measures may also stem from their reflecting different constructs of hemispheric specialization (Segalowitz & Berge, in press).

Once we accept the notion of individual variation—say, in cerebral specialization for language—

it is not a long leap to try to conclude that some of these differences are responsible for individual differences in language or cognitive functioning (Glass, 1987). For example, Semrud-Clikeman, Hynd, Novey, and Eliopoulous (1990) provide evidence that individual differences in reading skill are related to specific anatomical brain asymmetries in children. Similarly, anatomical asymmetries are related to the ability to recover from language disability brought on by a stroke. The average right-hander has more posterior tissue in the left hemisphere than in the right, but severe aphasics with relatively greater tissue on the right side are more likely to recover their language functions. This suggests that even in adults the right hemisphere is capable of taking on new functions after trauma to the left hemisphere, and that the extent of this recovery is dependent to some degree on the distribution of tissue in the brain (Pieniadz, Naeser, Koff, & Levine, 1983; cf. Burke, Yeo, Delaney, & Conner, 1993).

Although there is evidence that experience can shape neural networks, there is no general model for experience affecting the left-right distribution of hemispheric specialization, although it certainly can influence which process becomes active in a particular context. Among examples of this are the recent findings of Dawson, Panagiotides, Klinger, and Hill (1992), who report a reversed asymmetry of frontal activation in infants of depressed mothers, which presumably could be attributed to different affective processes being active (see Dawson, Chapter 11, this volume). The countercases illustrating how environmental influences can affect hemispheric specialization that are usually quoted stem from dramatically altered early experience—such as extreme neglect and abuse, where brain damage cannot be ruled out (Curtiss, 1977); and congenital deafness, where the use of sign language is related to lessened right-hemisphere dominance for spatial skills when measured in certain ways (Neville, 1977). From the point of view of normal subjects, however, such physiological factors are purely chance events, not related to early psychological environment (see Mills, Coffey, & Neville, Chapter 13, this volume).

## Accounting for Gradual or Epigenetic Change

One of the continual controversies that developmentalists face is the question of the extent to which skill development is attributable to training, education, and rearing. Constructivist perspectives such as Piaget's have made the question more complicated by emphasizing the general reasoning skills underlying concrete problem solving. For example, a child's performance on problems of the Tower of Hanoi sort (moving a size-ordered set of rings from one post to another post one at a time, without ever placing a larger one on a smaller one) can improve somewhat because of very specific facts learned about the task at hand, but most would agree that improvements in the development of general problem-solving strategies and in working memory capacity are more important factors (Shallice, 1988).

However, in an attempt to account for gradual improvement in memory during the childhood years, cognitivists have relied almost exclusively on notions of improved strategies for remembering, such as the clustering of information or development of mnemonic strategies for self-cueing (Brown, Bransford, Ferrara, & Campione, 1983; Gelman, 1978). The notion that brain maturation plays a role in supporting or promoting the development of such strategies is hardly discussed, although the circumstantial evidence is substantial (Diamond, 1990b; Goldman-Rakic, 1987; Howard & Polich, 1985).

We are now in the midst of an important historical period in developmental theory. For the first time, epigenetic change in cognitive structures can be attributed to maturation of a specific cortical structure. Frontal lobe maturation has been linked to the appearance of specific cognitive constructs (see Bell & Fox, Chapter 10, this volume; Diamond, 1990a; Diamond et al., Chapter 12, this volume; Segalowitz & Rose-Krasnor, 1992); this provides us with a truly maturational construct accounting for the timing of certain cognitive developments, and perhaps for their existence.

# Developmental Science in the Discovery Mode

## U. Bronfenbenner

How is this domain defined? Human development is the scientific study of the conditions and processes shaping the biopsychological characteristics of human beings through the life course and across successive generations.

Here the principal aim is not the customary one of verifying hypotheses already formulated. It is a more extended process involving a series of progressively more differentiated formulations, with the results at each successive step setting the stage for the next round. The corresponding research designs, therefore, must be primarily generative rather than confirming versus disconfirming. Thus, the procedure is not the usual one of testing for statistical significance. Rather, the research designs must provide a framework for carrying out an equally essential prior stage of the scientific process: that of developing hypotheses of sufficient explanatory power and precision to warrant being subjected to empirical test. In short, we are dealing with science in the *discovery* mode rather than in the *verification* mode.

At the same time, as in any scientific endeavor, it is essential that the successive formulations and the corresponding research designs be made explicit. It is necessary to have a systematic conceptual framework within which evolving formulations and designs can be classified and ordered in terms of their stage of scientific development in the discovery process (Bronfenbrenner & Morris, 1998).

### The Bioecological Model of Human Development

The characteristics of the person appear twice in the bioecological model: first as one of the four

principal elements—process, person, concept, and time (PPCT)— influencing the form, power, content, and direction of the proximal processes; and then again as the "developmental outcome"— that is, a quality of the developing person that emerges at a later point in time as the result of the mutually influencing effects of the four principal elements of the bioecological model. In sum, the characteristics of the person function both as an indirect producer and as a product of development.

How does the bioecological model fare when analyzed in a PPCT framework? Which elements are present, and how are they presumed to relate to each other? Two studies conducted some years ago, when analyzed in PPCT terms, come close to meeting the requirements of this theoretical model and its corresponding research design.

### Conclusion

America has yet to confront the reality that the growing chaos in the lives of our children, youth, and families pervades too many of the principal settings in which we live our daily lives: our homes, health care systems, child care arrangements, peer groups, schools, neighborhoods, workplaces, and means of transportation and communication among all of them.

These are the settings in which our society has concentrated fragmented resources and efforts to reverse the mounting developmental disarray. Even though the United States experienced an economic upswing in the late 1990s, the sparse bits of recent demographic data give little indication of a true and lasting turnaround. The rising trend of chaos and its consequences also extend to other spheres of our society.

Not long ago, one of our nation's leading corporate executives gave a major lecture at Cornell's Graduate School of Management. His title was "Growing Chaos in America's Corporate Enterprises." He said that no sooner is a new

*Source:* Bronfenbrenner, U. (2005). Developmental science in the discovery mode; The bioecological model of human development; Conclusion. In E. Bronfenbrenner, *Making Human beings human: Bioecological Perspectives on human development* (pp. 187; 187–188; 195–196). Thousand Oaks, CA: Sage.

production policy implemented after weeks of planning and testing than an order comes down from above "to scrap the whole thing" because the policy has been changed.

Transforming experiments have been carried out in the United States, but their developmental effects have never been investigated systematically. Perhaps one of the most successful was the G.I. Bill, which gave educational and housing benefits and hope to a whole generation of World War II veterans and their families. The same deserved legacy was not bestowed on their comrades-in-arms in the wars that followed.

A second example is Head Start. But from what I know both from looking at its budgets and its mounting bureaucratic controls and from personal experience as an external member of a Head Start Parents' Policy Committee, the prospects for the future are hardly rosy. Head Start parents are today drawing on their own meager resources to continue some of the programs that are needed most, and they take time off from jobs (when they have them) to help fellow families in emergencies because of illness or the desperate need for childcare.

Such heroic acts are signals to the rest of American society. They sound a call for a transforming experiment in strengthening parenthood, one that can draw on the deepest sources of our national strength. As yet, this call is not being heard, either by our scientists or by our citizens. We do not heed the immortal words of John Donne: "Do not ask for whom the bell tolls; it tolls for thee."

# Introduction

E. Thelen

L. B. Smith

People lead lives of both thought and action. One of the enduring puzzles of human existence is how we acquire physical and mental activities of such great complexity from our simple origins as a single cell. How do we come to understand the world so we can act within it? How do we construct a social and physical reality? Where do our rich mental lives of metaphor, fantasy, and invention come from? At the same time, what enables our brains to control our limbs and body segments to perform intricate and skilled actions? For thousands of years, philosophers and other scholars of the mind have recognized that clues to these profound questions may be found in the developing child.

Like so many before us—Baldwin, Darwin, Gesell, Piaget, Werner—we approach the mystery of human development with the conviction that the acquisition of mental life is continuous with all biological growth of form and function. Because humans can perform so many special activities, it is easy to think of our ontogeny as special. What we argue in this book is that while the endpoints of human development are complex and unique, the processes by which we reach those endpoints are the same as those that govern development in even simple organisms, and to some degree, even in complex, nonliving systems.

Thus, in our approach to fundamental questions of mental life, we invoke principles of great generality. These are principles of nonlinear dynamic systems, and they concern problems of emergent order and complexity: how structure and patterns arise from the cooperation of many individual parts. Nonlinear systems principles originated in physics, chemistry, and mathemat-

ics. Although a few visionary biologists have recognized the relevance of nonlinear dynamics to the study of biological systems (e.g., von Bertalanffy, 1968; Waddington, 1977), only within the last few years have these principles been rigorously and formally applied (e.g., Glass and Mackey, 1988; Kelso, Mandell, and Shlesinger, 1988). Such principles describe systems of diverse material substrates that live in many different time scales. We believe these principles are especially powerful in integrating organic ontogeny at every level from morphology to behavior. We devote the first section of the book to describing principles of dynamic systems and to reinterpreting behavioral and developmental data in dynamic terms.

But even the most potent general principles are insufficient; developmentalists also need to understand process and mechanism at the level of the phenomena of real life. What are the organic and environmental factors that engender change? How can we begin to untangle the complex web of causality when real infants live and develop in a world filled with people, things, and events in continuous interaction? A major task of this book, therefore, is to instantiate dynamic principles into the realm of process and mechanism. We seek to demonstrate that these general principles *do* capture both the essence of ontogeny and its local details and variations, and indeed can offer new and powerful explanations of experimental data from infants and children.

We are especially dedicated to showing that behavior and development are dynamic at many levels of explanation, in particular, that phenomena described at the level of behavior are congruent with what is known about the brain and how it works. We are not seeking reductionist explanations, but harmonious ones. Neuroanatomy and physiology support all behavior, although, as we argue later, they are not logically causal. Thus, we will ground our thinking

*Source:* Thelen, E., & Smith, L. B. (1994). Introduction. In E. Thelen & L. B. Smith, A dynamic systems approach to the development of cognition and action (pp. xiii–xxii). Boston: MIT Press.

about process and mechanism in a developmental theory of the brain.

## What Development Looks Like: The View from Above

What does it mean to say that an organism "develops"? We seek here to find commonalities across all development, from the first cleavage of the fertilized egg, through the earliest somatic and morphological differentiation, the complex processes of neurogenesis and emerging physiological competences, and their ultimate expression in behavior throughout the life span. What unites these diverse processes that occur over time? We look at ontogeny first with our lowest level of magnification.

Over the broad sweep of time, the most global quality of developing organisms is that they go from being small and simple to being bigger and more complex. By complexity, we mean simply an increase in the number of different parts and activities, and the relations among them. Development is linear and quantitative, as growth is always incremental. At the same time, development is also nonlinear and qualitative, since complexity invokes new forms and abilities.

There is a remarkable *orderliness* to this process. Within any species, development normally proceeds with inexorable regularity and even inevitability. We can describe quite precisely the behavioral and physiological repertoire of the human newborn and predict with great certainty that all intact humans will walk, speak the language of their culture, form social relationships, reach reproductive maturity, and engage in certain mental operations. We can circumscribe the ages and sequences of these events, and many others, with significant reliability. Our everyday language reflects this orderliness when we speak of "stages of child (or adult) development," "developmental milestones or timetables," and even the "ticking of the biological clock."

The sweep of development is more than just orderly, it is *progressive* or directional. The changes, both qualitative and quantitative, are not reversible. Once a new structure emerges, or a growth level is attained, or a behavior performed, the organism does not revert back to earlier forms. Certain functions may decline in old age or with disease, but the developmental process does not become undone; the organism does not look like an immature form. Although certain behaviors may appear childlike, age or brain damage does not create an immature organism.

Across all species, the direction of development leads toward increasing nutritional independence from the parent animal and the attainment of reproductive maturity. Seeking food and mates requires an accurate match between those properties in the environment necessary for the realization of those goals and the perceptual and motor apparatus of the animal. Development progresses toward such an adaptive match.

The orderly, progressive, incremental, and directional qualities of development in the broadest sweep give rise to the impression of a *teleological* process, one guided by design. How can organisms move so surely toward the goal of adaptive, adult functioning in so determined a fashion without a plan? Where is the guidebook for this inevitable change from simple to more complex? It seems like this destiny must be written, somewhere, somehow, as instructions to be read as ontogeny proceeds.

Developmentalists have devoted considerable effort to uncovering the grand ontogenetic plan. The classic "nature-nurture" controversy, a standard in every textbook, is a reflection of the quest for understanding where development *comes from*. At one extreme, the developmental ground plan is seen as residing entirely within the organism, as a set of genetic blueprints, which contains all the information needed for the final adult form and which needs only to be "read" sequentially over time. At the other extreme, the organism is viewed as containing none of the information for its final destiny, but as absorbing structure and complexity from the order in the environment through experience with the environment.

Surprisingly, several current approaches to development continue to side with either a version of genetic determinism or bald environmentalism. However, most developmentalists at least pay lip service to the view that development is a function of the *interaction* between genetically determined processes and input from the environment. Interactionism and transactionalism are everyone's comfortable buzzwords, and the proffered "solution" to the nature-nurture dichotomy.

There are several reasons why the commonly accepted interactionist position is inadequate to explain the grand sweep of developmental progress. First and foremost is the serious logical impasse created by seeking the developmental plan in *any* preexisting agency, a point most recently made by Oyama (1985) in compelling detail. Remember that the premier developmental question is how organic form is created—the emergence of *novelty and complexity* in structure and function. Invoking any prior plan *within* the organism leads to infinite regress. For example, we ask where does the structure of the mind come from? If it comes from the structure of the central nervous system (CNS), where is that encoded? If the structure of the nervous system is entirely encoded in the genes, how does a sequential one-dimensional chemical code lead to an elaborated, three-dimensional and functionally specific structure? Where are the *rules* that govern this transition from code to organism? Thus, we have to postulate yet *another* set of instructions, and so on. In essence, genetic determinism just sidesteps the question of origins and dumps the problem onto the laps of the evolutionists, who must account for behavioral novelty. If we propose, in contrast, that the structure of the mind comes from information or knowledge from the world, how is that information evaluated? By what criteria does the organism know what is "good"? What is to be paid attention to and be assimilated into the mental repertoire? Again, this requires another level of representations of the final developmental product.

The dilemma of where the information for the adult resides does not disappear with interactionism. Interactionist positions, as presently formulated, only combine *two* logically untenable views, without any notion of how their combination resolves the fundamental regressive nature of both of them. Information is *both* within the organism *and* "out there" and combines in some unspecified way. The genes alone cannot specify the end-state of the developmental process, as they play out in a continuous, and essential, supporting matrix of the cell, tissue, organism, and environment. Extragenetic factors are themselves also insufficient specifiers of the egg-into-adult transformation. Interactionist positions do not make it clear how combining two imperfect codes creates the complete blueprint. If genes and environment "combine," we must specify how their interactions over time create new forms and new behaviors.

Maturationism, environmentalism, and interactionism are imperfect developmental theories because they essentially *prescribe* the adult form before it develops. These views take no account of *process*, of how new form and function are realized over time. Development is not the specification of the outcome—the product—but is the route by which the organism moves from an earlier state to a more mature state. By assuming prescription or teleology, we simply finesse process since the outcome is encapsulated in the plan.

The view from above, therefore, lends itself to explanations that provide a source of order and information for ontogenetic innovations. But conventional theories are logically unsatisfactory, as they provide no principled account of what moves the system forward. Conventional approaches are also deficient because they also fail to account for developmental processes at a closer level of observation.

## What Development Looks Like: The View from Below

The grand sweep of development seems neatly rule-driven. In detail, however, development is messy. As we turn up the magnification of our microscope, we see that our visions of linearity, uniformity, inevitable sequencing, and even irreversibility break down. What looks like a cohesive, orchestrated process from afar takes on the flavor of a more exploratory, opportunistic, syncretic, and function-driven process in its instantiation. In succeeding chapters, we provide many concrete examples of the messy, fluid, context-sensitive nature of behavioral development.

First, development appears to be modular and heterochronic. That is, not all of the structures and functions of the animal develop apace or as a unified whole. We observe enormous species differences in the relative maturity of component structures and functions at birth, presumably in response to selective pressures. Although many species are born altricial or precocial in both sensory and motor capabilities (horses vs. rats), the newborns of other species are a mixed bag. Humans, for example, have precocial sensory functions, but altricial motor abilities at birth. Anokhin (1964) pointed out that the developmental process can be remarkably responsive to ecological demands on the young; even single neural tracts can be selectively accelerated to provide necessary function. There are equally striking disparities in the relative rates of growth and change of perceptual, motor, cognitive, and social elements within the species. That is, each component may have its own characteristic developmental trajectory, exhibiting times of accelerated change, times of slow, linear increment, and times of quiescence. The paradox is that the organism moves along as an adapted, integrated whole as the component structures and processes change in fits and starts.

Most remarkably, when we experimentally dissect an ontogenetic phenomenon, we often discover that elements of a seemingly integrated behavioral performance can be detected long in advance of the fully functional behavior. That is, under special conditions, the organism may demonstrate *precocial* abilities in one domain. Other elements appear to mature more slowly and can never be isolated from mature performance. One striking example of precocial abilities from the animal literature is weaning in rat pups. Rat pups do not normally eat and drink independently for about 3 weeks after birth. However, Hall and Bryan (1980) demonstrated that even newborn rat pups will ingest liquid or semisolid food from the floor of a test chamber when the temperature of the chamber is sufficiently warm. Why should such components be available but "waiting in the wings"? What, then, drives the organism to new levels of performance? How do these cryptic precursors become manifest?

The boundaries of progressive stages are equally blurred by seeming regressions in performance and losses of previously well-established behaviors. Some of these losses appear species-wide, as in the universal decline of suckling behaviors in mammals, and may be adaptive solutions to ontogenetic changes in life demands. Other losses are more immediately context-bound and short-term, especially when new abilities are first emerging.

Thus, although orderly and switch-like from afar, developmental change is more tentative and fluid from close up. In immature animals, performance seems to be variable and easily disrupted. When we observe behavioral development under stable and uniform conditions, it looks itself stable and uniform. If we only ask one set of questions, we elicit a restricted set of answers. Only when we introduce instabilities, novelty, and variability into the context do we elicit and test the range of response capabilities of the animal. Under challenges of variability, we often discover a flexibility of solutions not apparent under more restricted conditions.

At the close-up range, therefore, the rules seem not to hold. What determines the behavioral performance seems less like the grand plan or timetable than the immediacy of the situation or the task at hand. Our efforts to organize developmental phenomena into lawful relations appear stymied by the phenomena themselves.

## Goals for a Developmental Theory

What, then, do we require of a developmental theory that spans levels, domains, and species? In table 1, we list six goals we believe are essential, and we elaborate them further below. The primary thrust of development is the generation of novel structure and behavior. A developmental explanation must do better than assuming it was all there to begin with. So the first need is for a principled understanding of where novelty comes from. This explanation must encompass two, seemingly paradoxical, levels. At low magnification, events seem planful. Development proceeds with clocklike qualities, measuring off events in time with global precision and regularity. Likewise, the process seems to have global teleology; it is goal-directed and common to all intact individuals. At closer range, however, we

**Table 1**   Goals for a Developmental Theory

1. To understand the origins of novelty.

2. To reconcile global regularities with local variability, complexity, and context-specificity.

3. To integrate developmental data at many levels of explanation.

4. To provide a biologically plausible yet nonreductionist account of the development of behavior.

5. To understand how local processes lead to global outcomes.

6. To establish a theoretical basis for generating and interpreting empirical research.

must explain diversity, flexibility, and asynchrony: how to account for the mobility of behavior units and the ability of even young organisms to reorganize their behavior around context and task.

It is our basic assumption that the end-state of the organism is not instantiated at the beginning of the journey toward maturity. Thus, our principles must explain how global developmental trajectories can arise from diverse, heterogeneous, mobile, and dynamic local effects. We will argue that these variable, fluid, task-sensitive local effects are not just noise in a grand developmental plan, but are *the processes that engender developmental change.* Indeed, it is the very nature of such local complexity to produce behavior with global simplicity. We have as a recurring theme, therefore, the necessity for compatibility among time scales. As developing organisms perceive and act in daily life, there must be continuity between these activities and changes over a long time scale.

At the same time, we seek a biologically valid, but nonreductionist, account of the development of behavior. At first glance, this may seem a contradiction in terms. When developmental psychologists invoke the "biological bases" of behavior, they usually mean the neurophysiological, hormonal, or genetic aspects of human functioning: behavior is assumed to be "based" on these more fundamental processes. No one would question that the nervous system, the hormonal system, and the genes are essential contributors to human behavior. It is, however, a serious error to partition the contributors to development into those that somehow reside within the organism as biological, genetic, innate, and therefore primary, and those outside

the organism, which may include the everyday features of the physical and social environment, as only supportive and nonbiological.

We hope to show at many levels that no one element alone has causal primacy or forms the basis for behavior. The ontogenetic niche, as West and King (1987) have named the normal and expected environment, determines developmental outcome as surely as the "wetware" within the bounds of the organism itself. A language environment for a developing human is as biological as a left hemisphere. The boundaries between what is "innate" and what is "acquired" become so blurred as to be, at the very least, uninteresting, compared to the powerful questions of developmental process.

Thus, here we turn the reductionist-dichotomous paradigm on its head to ask how behavior arises from a multitude of underlying contributing elements. It is not so much how the whole can be understood as a function of the pieces, but how the pieces can come together to produce the whole. At the same time that we reject a simple reductionist view of organic development, we also believe strongly, like others before us, that cognitive growth is an extension of adaptive ontogeny in general. This means that while cognition may not be understood solely in terms of neural structures, accounts of cognitive change must be entirely harmonious with what is known about the structure and function of the nervous system and its development.

Our commitment to a biologically consistent theory means that we categorically reject machine analogies of cognition and development. For several decades, the preeminent metaphor for understanding human cognition has been the digital computer. The brain may well share certain operations with a digital computer, but it is different from a machine on the most fundamental thermodynamic level, as we detail in succeeding chapters. A developmental theory must be appropriate to the organism it serves; thus, we deliberately eschew the machine vocabulary of processing devices, programs, storage units, schemata, modules, or wiring diagrams. We substitute, instead, a vocabulary suited to a fluid, organic system, with certain thermodynamic properties.

We propose here a radical departure from current cognitive theory. Although behavior and development appear structured, there are no structures. Although behavior and development appear rule-driven, there are no rules. There is complexity. There is a multiple, parallel, and continuously dynamic interplay of perception and action, and a system that, by its thermodynamic nature, seeks certain stable solutions. These solutions emerge from relations, not from design. When the elements of such complex systems cooperate, they give rise to behavior with a unitary character, and thus to the illusion of structure. But the order is always executory, rather than rule-driven, allowing for the enormous sensitivity and flexibility of behavior to organize and regroup around task and context.

By this view, cognition—mental life—and action—the life of the limbs—are like the emergent structure of other natural phenomena. For example, in certain meteorological contexts, clouds form into thunderheads that have a particular shape, internal complexity, and behavior. There is a clear order and directionality to the way thunderheads emerge over time. Likewise, in the establishment of ecological communities in the colonization of an island or in the growth of a secondary forest, the types and abundance of various plants and animals follow a well-defined sequence leading to the climax ecosystem. Again, there is order, direction, and structure just as there is in development. But there is no design written anywhere in a cloud or a program in the genes of any particular species that determines the final community structure. There is no set of instructions that causes a cloud or a group of plants and animals to change form in a particular way. There are only a number of complex physical and biological systems interacting

over time, such that the precise nature of their interactions leads inevitably to a thunderhead or to a forest. We suggest that action and cognition are also emergent and not designed.

Our dynamic approach shares many similarities with the "general systems" principles of von Bertalanffy (1968), Laszlo (1972), and others, and the organismic view of development associated with the eminent biologists Waddington (1966, 1977) and Weiss (1969). Systems and organismic accounts have long been a powerful "root metaphor" in developmental psychology (Reese and Overton, 1970; see, e.g., Brent, 1978, 1984; Bronfenbrenner, 1979; Fogel, 1993; Gesell, 1946; Gottlieb, 1991a, b; Horowitz, 1987; Kitchener, 1982; Lerner, 1978; Overton, 1975; Piaget, 1971; Sameroff, 1983; Werner, 1957; Wolff, 1987). Systems notions appear and reappear in developmental accounts because they provide a logically compelling formulation for the complexities of developmental change. Developmental data from many content domains are interpretable only with systems principles which stress wholeness, self-organization, nonlinearity, developmental buffering or equifinality, and hierarchical levels of organization.

Unfortunately, there is a major gap between the post hoc invocation of systems principles and their translation into *empirical studies of developmental process* (Thelen, 1989). This is especially true in accounts of cognitive development. Piaget, for example, offers *equilibration* as the fundamental process of acquiring new structures (Chapman, 1988). Piaget adapted his formulations of equilibration deliberately from the embryologist Waddington (Haroutunian, 1983), and the root metaphor is both organic and systemic. Nonetheless, in the enormous corpus of research and theory inspired by Piaget, there is little discussion or investigation of the process itself. Instead, focus has been on the nature of the structural outcome. Left unanswered by researchers are questions such as: What is equilibration? Why and how does the organism seek a stable relationship with its environment? What moves the organism to seek new levels of problem solving?

In our dynamic account, we embrace systems principles and the organic metaphor. But we strive to expand these ideas into more detailed and useful models of major developmental phenomena. To do this, we follow current trends in biology. In the recent past, the biological study of the whole organism has been overshadowed by the remarkable and compelling advances made by reductionist paradigms in genetics and molecular biology. The tide is turning now with the emerging study of complex systems rooted in powerful mathematical and physical principles. Such principles have allowed the synthetic behavior of biological systems at more macro levels to be modeled in an elegant and formal manner (see, e.g., Baltes, 1987; Fogel, 1993; Gleick, 1987; Haken, 1977; Kelso, Mandell, and Shlesinger, 1988). We, in turn, base our model of developmental change on a semiformal adaptation of the dynamic principles which are proving so insightful for understanding the behavior of systems at many levels of organization. We hope, in this way, to give substance and generality to ideas which have been historically attractive to developmentalists.

We hope to give substance to theorizing about systems in development by outlining and demonstrating concrete and realizable empirical instantiations of these principles. We attempt to translate systems principles into programs of research. Developmentalists may believe in nonlinearity, emergent properties, and multiple causality, but many conventional experimental methods and analyses are ill-suited to detect such phenomena. We believe that commitment to holistic thinking will require adopting some new and unconventional empirical strategies, as well as using and interpreting our conventional strategies in new ways.

The second way we go beyond description and structural constructs is to suggest a *neurologically plausible* mechanism of the ontogeny of cognition and action that is entirely harmonious with general dynamic principles. To do this we invoke the selectionist theory of Gerald M. Edelman (1987, 1988, 1992), an inclusive and elegant account that encompasses embryology, neuroembryology, and behavior. Edelman's *theory of neuronal group selection* fits our basic requirement for a plausible account of ontogeny: that there be no homunculus in the brain or in the genes directing the process. We must emphasize here, as we do later in the book, that this is

not a reductionist retreat. Rather, we believe it adds to the power of a dynamic explanation to demonstrate dynamic principles at work at several levels of analysis. That is, events at the behavioral level are mirrored and supported by neural and morphological dynamics. And equally important, we believe, Edelman's account provides remarkable, enduring insight into our concern for time scales, or how local processes build into the global outcome.

Readers will also recognize that our developmental account is both inspired by and consistent with tenets of ecological psychology, especially the work of Eleanor J. Gibson (1969, 1988). In particular, we invoke Gibson's beliefs that the world contains information and that the goal of development is to discover relevant information in order to make a functional match between what the environment affords and what the actor can and wants to do. We share her beliefs in the primacy of perception and action as the basis for cognition, and in the fundamental role of exploration. We will show how experiments conducted from a Gibsonian perspective are congruent with, and amplify, dynamic principles. Finally, we recognize that our developmental account is also compatible with the school of developmental theorists who trace their heritage to Vygotsky (e.g., Cole, 1985; Luria, 1976; Rogoff, 1982; Vygotksy, 1978, 1986; Wertsch, 1985) and who emphasize the contextual, historical, and cultural origins of human thought. Indeed, as we suggest in the final chapter, a dynamic account provides a biological rationale for contextualism and offers a potential reconciliation and integration of processes at both macro- and microlevels of analysis.

The heart of our enterprise, therefore, is to demonstrate that these principles *explain developmental data* in ways that are both logically satisfying and useful, and plausible at many levels of analysis. We emphasize from the start that our search for more powerful explanatory principles for development has been primarily datadriven. Both of us faced a decade's research that we could not interpret using available models. The data were intriguing and perplexing, but we clearly needed new ways to make sense of them. We each soon realized that the puzzles in our own data sets were not unique, but mirrored the larger issues for developmental study as a whole.

Unquestionably, the largest corpus of theory-driven developmental data lies in the domain of cognition. Literally thousands of papers have been published on the milestone events of early mental life, such as the acquisition of symbolic reasoning and language. Because cognitive processes are both extraordinarily complex and usually opaque—i.e., only by indirect means can they be measured—they present the greatest theoretical challenge. Action theory, the concerns of perception and movement, proceeds with more observables and is more directly amenable to dynamic analysis. Thus, we begin with the development of locomotion. Locomotor development illustrates both the nature of the theoretical challenge and the application of the principles to a developmental problem that is more transparent and more accessible. Understand that we do not wish, by this organization, to characterize action as "mere" motor development or to assign primacy to either movement or cognition. Indeed, we will spend considerable effort building an argument for the inextricable causal web of perception, action, and cognition.

# The Role of Immaturity in Human Development

DAVID F. BJORKLUND

*Florida Atlantic University*

The possibility that infants' and young children's immature behaviors and cognitions are sometimes adaptive is explored and interpreted in terms of evolutionary theory. It is argued that developmental immaturity had an adaptive role in evolution and continues to have an adaptive role in human development. The role of developmental retardation in human evolution is discussed, followed by an examination of the relation between humans' extended childhood and brain plasticity. Behavioral neoteny, as exemplified by play, is examined, as are some potentially adaptive aspects of infants' perception and cognition that limit the amount of information they can process. Aspects of immature cognition during early childhood that may have some contemporaneous adaptive value are also discussed. It is proposed that viewing immaturity as sometimes adaptive to the developing child alters how children and their development are viewed.

*Nature wants children to be children before they are men. If we deliberately depart from this order, we shall get premature fruits which are neither ripe nor well flavored and which soon decay. We shall have youthful sages and grown up children. Childhood has ways of seeing, thinking, and feeling, peculiar to itself; nothing can be more foolish than to substitute our ways for them.*

—Jean Jacques Rousseau

People understandably tend to see development as being progressive: from immature and inefficient structures and functions to mature and efficient ones. Early, immature forms are seen as "unfinished" and incomplete versions of the adult; the child is a "work in progress." From this viewpoint, immaturity is a necessary evil, something that people must get through on their way to adulthood, where the "real show of humanity emerges on stage" (L. Thomas, 1993, p. 175). This is not an unreasonable view. A prolonged period of youth is necessary for humans. Humans, more than any other species, must survive by their wits; human communities are more complex and diverse than those of any other species, and this requires that they have not only a flexible intelligence to learn the conventions of their societies but also a long time to learn them. But the species's physical and cognitive development need not progress synchronously. Their prolonged bodily development could in theory be accompanied by rapid cognitive and social development. This would result in a physically dependent child who has the intellectual and social wherewithal to master the ways of the world.

The conclusion that development is progressive seems obvious from the way theorists traditionally view development—from immaturity to

*Source:* Bjorklund, D. F. (1997). The role of immaturity in human development. *Psychological Bulletin, 122* (2), 153–169.

Portions of this article were presented at the German Psychological Conference (Developmental Psychology Group). Leipzig, Germany, in September 1995, and at the Conference on Human Development, Birmingham, Alabama, in March, 1996. This article was supported by National Science Foundation Grant SBR-9422177.

I would like to thank Barbara Bjorklund, Thomas Coyle, Rhonda Douglas, Cynthia Park, Kristina Rosenblum. Holly Stewart, and Robin Vallacher for comments on earlier versions of this article.

Correspondence concerning this article should be addressed to David F. Bjorklund, Department of Psychology, Florida Atlantic University, 777 Glades Road, Boca Raton, Florida 33431. Electronic mail may be sent via Internet to bjorkldf@fau.edu.

maturity—with the adult as the product that "counts." But there are other ways to view development. For example, insects metamorphose: from caterpillar to butterfly (larva to adult or imago). The caterpillar has an integrity of its own; it often leads a complex and sometimes more active life than the sexually mature butterfly. Entomologists cannot view the caterpillar merely as an immature form of the butterfly but must view the caterpillar as an animal with its own organization and requirements that are adapted to its present environment, not to an environment it will live in as a butterfly. A butterfly is the inevitable product of a caterpillar, but the two are qualitatively distinct; the caterpillar is not just an immature version of the butterfly.

Mammals, of course, do not metamorphose. Yet, looking at the young—at infants and children as having an integrity of their own, as organisms with abilities specially adapted to the particular physical, social, and cognitive demands of their environment—provides a different picture of immaturity. Seen from this vantage, immaturity is not a necessary evil but possibly may play an adaptive role in a child's life and development. Some aspects of childhood are not specific preparations for adulthood. Rather, they are designed by evolution to adapt the child to its current environment but not necessarily to a future one. This is a very different view from the one implicitly assumed by most contemporary child developmental psychologists. Early accomplishments, and particularly early trauma, are seen to set the stage for later development. This is surely an accurate interpretation for many behaviors and characteristics, but believing that all psychological development progresses in such a way can be misleading and can distort one's view of ontogeny.

My colleagues and I have examined the argument for the adaptive nature of immaturity for cognition in general (Bjorklund & Green, 1992) and language and language remediation specifically (Bjorklund & Schwartz, 1996). We have argued that the immature child has a cognitive integrity of his or her own and that young children's thinking should not be viewed solely from the perspective of what it is not and how close it is to what it will become; rather, theorists should ask what functions it might afford the

child at that particular time in development. Although a similar point of view has reflected the canonical perspective of developmental psychobiologists (whose subjects are mainly infrahuman mammals and birds) since at least the early 1980s (e.g., Oppenheim, 1981; Spear, 1984; Turkewitz & Kenny, 1982), it is a novel perspective for cognitive developmentalists focusing on humans. I broaden our previous perspective in this article, arguing that developmental immaturity had an adaptive role in human phylogeny and that it continues to have an adaptive role in human cognitive and social ontogeny.

Consistent with the perspective of contemporary developmental psychobiologists, the theory implicitly underlying this review is Darwin's. A number of social and cognitive developmental psychologists have recently recognized the significance of evolutionary theory to develop an understanding of normal human ontogeny (e.g., Bjorklund, 1997; Fernald, 1992; Geary, 1995; Siegler, 1996), although this perspective is not without controversy (e.g., Morss, 1990). With respect to the adaptive nature of developmental immaturity, I argue that some immature forms and behaviors may have been selected in evolution for either their immediate or eventual survival values. Of course, many aspects of immaturity, if not most, are maladaptive to the young organism and reflect necessary trade-offs for other contemporary or future adaptive functions. But immaturity should not immediately be associated with ineffectiveness. Rather, one should question whether some particular aspect of immaturity may afford the young organism some temporary advantage.

For instance, it has long been recognized that adaptations may be limited to a particular time in development, infancy, for example, facilitating the young organism's chances of surviving to adulthood and eventually reproducing (e.g., Tooby & Cosmides, 1992). This is reflected by the concept of *ontogenetic adaptations*—neurobehavioral characteristics of young animals that serve specific adaptive functions for the developing animal. These are not simply incomplete versions of adult characteristics but have specific roles in survival during infancy or youth and disappear when they are no longer necessary. Oppenheim (1981) went as far as to suggest that "even the absence of adult capabilities may be developmentally adaptive . . . [and] should be considered in any comprehensive theory of ontogeny" (p. 92). Oppenheim discussed specializations of embryos that served to keep them alive but that disappear or are discarded once they serve their purpose, such as the yolk sac, embryonic excretory mechanisms, and hatching behaviors in embryonic birds.

Postnatal behaviors are also candidates for ontogenetic adaptations, including reflexes such as suckling and less well-defined behaviors such as play (Oppenheim, 1981). Some aspects of human infants' cognitions may also serve a specific, short-term function rather than prepare the child for later accomplishments. For example, the imitation of facial expressions by newborns (e.g., Meltzoff & Moore, 1977, 1983) has been considered by some to be an example of an ontogenetic adaptation (Bjorklund, 1987). In about half of the experiments investigating neonatal imitation in humans (see Anisfeld, 1991), newborns are found to imitate adult facial gestures (usually tongue protrusion), although imitation of facial expressions decreases to chance levels by about 2 months (e.g., Abravanel & Sigafoos, 1984; Fontaine, 1984; S. W. Jacobson, 1979). This pattern, and that tongue protrusions can be elicited by other stimuli such as a red pen looming at an infant's face (S. W. Jacobson, 1979), led some theorists to propose that the imitation seen during the first 2 months of life is qualitatively different from and unrelated to that observed in later infancy. Rather than serving to acquire new behaviors, which seems to be the primary function of imitation in later infancy and childhood, several theorists have speculated that neonatal imitation has a very different and specific function for the neonate. For example, S. W. Jacobson suggested that imitation of facial gestures is functional during nursing, Legerstee (1991) proposed that it serves as a form of prelinguistic communication, and Bjorklund (1987) suggested that it facilitates mother–infant social interaction at a time when infants cannot intentionally direct their gaze and control their head movements in response to social stimulation. Support for these latter interpretations was provided by Heimann (1989), who reported significant correlations between degree of neonatal imitation and later quality of mother–infant interaction at 3 months.

Thus, early imitation appears to have a specific adaptive function for the infant (i.e., to facilitate communication and social interaction) that is presumably different from the function that imitation serves in the older infant and child (but see Meltzoff & Moore, 1992, for a different interpretation).

Also central to contemporary evolutionary psychology is the idea that adaptive behavior was selected, not for survival in modern culture, but rather in the environment of evolutionary adaptiveness, stretching back far into the Pleistocene Age. Thus, a behavioral characteristic that may have been adaptive for our ancestors may or may not continue to have adaptive value for contemporary humans. For example, our penchant for sweet and fatty foods, which signal a high-caloric meal, was surely adaptive for our nomadic ancestors. Such a penchant is less adaptive today and in fact is often maladaptive in societies where availability of high-caloric food is not a problem (Nesse & Williams, 1994). Also, remember that not all contemporary behaviors or forms were selected in evolution. Some are merely the by-products of other adaptations or the necessary consequences of physical growth. However, these behaviors and forms, although perhaps not selected in human evolution, were at least not sufficiently detrimental to human ontogeny to result in extinction. That is, their impact on evolution may have been neutral, in that they were not positively selected for but merely did not interfere with reproductive potential. An appreciation of evolutionary theory is not necessary for appreciating the potentially adaptive function of developmental immaturity, but it provides an overarching framework that, I believe, ties together well the research findings from diverse literatures.

In the sections below, I first examine the role of developmental retardation in human evolution, followed by a discussion of the consequences of humans' prolonged period of youth and brain growth on behavioral plasticity and flexibility. I then examine the possibility that sensory and cognitive systems that limit the quantity of information an infant receives may facilitate sensory development, learning, and language acquisition. I then examine two aspects of cognitive immaturity—egocentricity and poor metacognition—that may have some adaptive advantages together with their obvious maladaptive ones. I conclude by proposing that a view of ontogenetic immaturity as more than a handicap that needs to be overcome provides theorists with a different and important view of children, their development, and their education.

## The Role of Retardation in Human Evolution

A simple, and now discredited, idea about evolution that was popular among biologists in the 19th century is the seductive idea of progress. Evolution was seen as leading ever upward and onward, with *Homo sapiens* as being the ineluctable conclusion—the "Great Chain of Being." Evolution was seen as purposive and always leading to increased complexity. This was captured by the principle of orthogenesis. *Orthogenesis* is based on the assumption that an inherent perfecting force in all of organic life makes evolution directional and always moving "forward." More "advanced" species, such as humans, relative to less advanced species, such as chimpanzees (or, more properly, the human apelike ancestors), evolved by the addition of something to the adult stages of their ancestors. So, for example, humans evolved "more" brain.

This idea was reflected in Haeckel's famous biogenetic law (see Gottlieb, 1992; Gould, 1977; and Mayr, 1982, for historical reviews). The biogenetic law is captured by the phrase, "ontogeny recapitulates phylogeny," meaning that the development of the individual (ontogenetic development) goes through, or repeats, the same sequences as the evolutionary development of the species (phylogenetic development) and that modifications to a species are in the form of additions or accelerations to the adult stage. (Variations of recapitulation theory found their way into psychology through the work of G. Stanley Hall [1904], the first child development theorist of modern psychology. Hall proposed that postnatal ontogenetic development goes through the same behavioral–psychological stages as did the species in phylogenetic time. Hall's ideas were widely regarded, but his recapitulation theory met debilitating criticism based on both logical arguments [e.g., Thorndike, 1913] and embryological data [e.g., Davidson, 1914].)

## Neoteny

Contemporary evolutionary theorists no longer see evolution as progressive in the sense of developing toward ever-increasing levels of complexity (see Gould, 1989); nor is the biogenetic law taken seriously. Many aspects of evolution can be seen as additions or accelerations of a developmental trend but certainly not all and perhaps not even most. In many cases, important evolutionary changes are brought about by retardation of development, not by acceleration. This is reflected by the concept of *neoteny*, which means literally "holding youth" or the retention of embryonic or juvenile characteristics by a retardation of development. Neoteny is an example of the process of *heterochrony*—genetic-based differences in developmental timing. de Beer (1958) proposed that changes in the timing of ontogeny are the driving force of evolution, and many evolutionary biologists over the course of this century have concurred. For example, Thomson (1988) stated that heterochrony can "readily lead to qualitative shifts" (p. 131) in the morphology of a species. More specific to the retardation of development, Wesson (1991) has suggested that neoteny seems to be a good strategy for evolutionary innovation, permitting "a new beginning and relatively rapid change as the organism backs up evolutionarily to get a better start" (p. 205). Many other theorists over the course of the century have concurred with and extended de Beer's perspective, believing that humans' retarded rate of development contributed significantly to the human species's morphological and behavioral characteristics (e.g., Bolk, 1926; Garstang, 1922; Gould, 1977; Groves, 1989; Montagu, 1989; Wesson, 1991; Wilson, 1980). Groves, for example, has done a careful analysis of the characteristics of hominid skeletons, from *Australopithecines* through *Homo sapiens*, and concluded that the line that eventually lead to modern humans did so by becoming increasingly neotenous.

Theorists of human evolution, such as Bolk (1926), Gould (1977), and Montagu (1962, 1989), have listed a number of physical and functional neotenous features of humans. These include the shape of the head and face, a late eruption of teeth, the size and orientation of the pelvis, a delicate (or gracile) skeleton, and a nonopposable big toe, among others. Although one could speculate on the potential adaptive value of the maintenance of immature facial features, for example, other neotenous characteristics have seemingly played a central role in human evolution. For example, the angle at which the human spine connects to the skull permits *bipedality* (locomoting on two feet). The first great step to humanness was the upright stance, achieved 4.5 to 5.0 million years ago by *Australopithecines.* Bipedality freed the hands, which was possibly important for using tools and carrying things; it changed the structure of the pelvis, making birth more difficult by requiring that infants be born prematurely so that more brain development could occur postnatally; it changed the structure of the neck and the supralaryngeal airway, resulting in the ability to make sounds and contributing, perhaps, to the evolution of spoken language.

Bipedality requires a change in the angle at which the spine connects with the skull. The opening in the skull where the spine connects to the skull is referred to as the *foramen magnum.* In all embryonic mammals, the foramen magnum is located at the bottom of the skull, so that the spine enters the skull at a right angle to the top of the skull and parallel to the plane of the face. During prenatal development, the location of the foramen magnum shifts toward the back of the skull, so that in most species of mammals the spine is essentially parallel to the top of the skull and perpendicular to the plane of the face. However, in humans, the position of the foramen magnum does not change appreciably beyond this embryonic stage. Development is retarded, so that at birth and into adulthood the sharp angle of the spine to the skull is maintained. That is, the foramen magnum maintains its embryonic position, with the result being that the skull sits atop the spine, thus permitting one to look forward while standing upright. Because the foramen magnum shifts toward the back of the skull in other mammals, forward sight is more easily accomplished when the animal is on all four feet. Thus, bipedality results from retention of an embryonic characteristic—development is retarded, setting the stage for major evolutionary change (see Gould, 1977; and Montagu, 1989).

Although bipedality is clearly a characteristic central to the definition of human, perhaps the species's most outstanding trait is intelligence. Here, people have clearly developed beyond their evolutionary ancestors rather than having development retarded to some earlier embryonic or infantile state (Byrne, 1995). When one is looking at mammals as a group, human brains are far larger than expected for their body size (Jerison, 1973). This increased brain size in humans is selective, with some areas of the brain having evolved at a faster pace than others, most notably the neocortex, the area of the brain most centrally involved in higher cognitive activities (see Eccles, 1989).

This enlargement of the brain was achieved, in part, however, by maintaining the rapid rate of prenatal brain growth into postnatal life. The rate of prenatal brain development is remarkably similar for all primates, including humans (see Bonner, 1988). The brain develops rapidly in comparison with the overall size of the body. Brain growth slows down quickly after birth for chimpanzees, macaque monkeys, and other primates but not for humans. The pace of human brain development begun prenatally continues through the second year of postnatal life (see Gould, 1977). By 6 months, the human brain weighs 50% of what it will in adulthood; at 2 years, about 75%; at 5 years, 90%; and at 10 years, 95% (Tanner, 1978). In contrast, total body weight is about 20% of eventual adult weight at 2 years and only 50% at 10 years. So the brain, which grows rapidly before birth, continues its rapid development postnatally by retaining the rate of growth characteristic of the prenatal period.

The retention of the embryonic growth rate for the brain into the first 2 years of postnatal life is necessitated in part by some physical limitations of women. If a species is going to have a big brain in relation to its body, it will also, of course, have a big skull. But the skull that houses a 2-year-old human brain is far too large to pass through the birth canal of a woman. The evolutionary pressures that resulted in an enlarged brain required that gestation be relatively short. If humans were as well developed bodily at birth as their simian cousins, their heads would never fit through the birth canal, which is limited in width because of the constraints of bipedality. The result is a physically immature infant, motorically and perceptually far behind the sophistication of other primate infants but with a brain that will continue to grow and eventually be able to process language and think symbolically.

## The Slow Rate of Growing Up: Consequence to Human Evolution

One of the most important neotenous aspects of human development is a human's prolonged period of immaturity and dependency; this has important implications for how people live as a species. Compared with other primates, humans take a disproportionate amount of time to reach reproductive maturity. The closer a species's common ancestor is with *Homo sapiens*, the longer the period of immaturity: in lemurs approximately 2 years, in macaques approximately 4 years, in chimps approximately 8 years, and in humans approximately 15 years (Poirier & Smith, 1974).

Slow growth clearly has its disadvantages, mainly, the likelihood that an individual may die before reproducing. However, there are more obvious advantages to humans' extended immaturity. Although *Homo sapiens* have seemingly evolved many domain-specific "programs" for dealing with specific problems and with other members of the species (what Cosmides & Tooby, 1987, refer to as *Darwinian algorithms*), humans, more than any other species, depend on learning and behavioral flexibility for their success. The complexities of human societies are enormous and highly variable, and it takes an extended childhood to acquire all that must be learned to succeed. Because brain growth continues well into adolescence, neuronal connections are created and modified long after they have become fixed in other species (M. Jacobson, 1969). The result is a more "flexible" brain (in terms of what neural connections can be made), which means more flexible thinking and behavior. Additionally, an extended youth provides the opportunity to practice complex adult roles, which, because of their cultural variability and complexity, cannot be hard wired into the brain.

One argument for the importance of delayed development to human evolution centers around the foundation of the human family and social structures (e.g., Gould, 1977; Wesson, 1991). The human infant is totally dependent at birth and will remain dependent on adults for well over 1 decade. Pair bonding and some division of labor (both within and between family members) may be a necessary adaptation to the pressures presented by the slow growth of offspring, increasing the likelihood that children would survive to sexual maturity. The long period of dependency also means that the man's genetic success could not be measured just by how many women he inseminated or by how many children he sired. His inclusive fitness would depend on how many of his offspring reached sexual maturity, thus assuring him of becoming a grandfather. To increase the odds of this happening, his help in the rearing of his children would be needed.[1]

A prolonged maturation rate may have contributed to some phylogenetic changes in the human species over the past 4 or 5 million years, but their extended physical immaturity also has a contemporary impact on development. Perhaps

[1] Mithen (1996) has recently speculated that the slow brain growth of ancient *Homo sapiens* was necessary to produce the cognitive architecture of modern humans. Consistent with contemporary assumptions of evolutionary psychology (e.g., Tooby & Cosmides, 1992), he proposed that the hominid brain was modular, with separate components for social, technical (i.e., tool use), and natural history intelligence, *Cognitive fluidity,* which Mithen claimed characterizes the modern mind, requires communication among the various modules (and general intelligence); he proposed that this requires an extended childhood to accomplish. To support his claim, Mithen pointed to evidence that brain development in Neanderthals, based on a discrepancy between rate of dental and cranial development (Akazawa, Muhesen, Dodo, Kondo, & Mizouguchi, 1995; Zollikofer, Ponce de León, Martin, & Stucki, 1995; Stringer, Dean, & Martin, 1990; but see Trinkaus & Tompkins, 1990, for an alternative interpretation), was much faster than in modern humans. Based on archeological evidence, Mithen proposed that Neanderthals demonstrated minimal cognitive fluidity and that it was only because of a prolongation of childhood that the architecture of the modern brain could develop.

the most important aspect of prolonged growth for humans today is related to the *plasticity*, or modifiability, of the brain and the consequences that has on one's behavior. The human brain continues to gain weight well into the third decade of life. The process of *myelination*—the insulation of neurons to yield faster signal transmission with less interference—is a slow one in human brain development, with the associative areas of the neocortex not being fully myelinized until adulthood (Yakovlev & Lecours, 1967). This slow growth provides humans with the flexibility to make many changes within their lifetimes.

Earlier in this century, it was believed that children who suffered severe deprivation for much more than their first year of life were destined to a life of mental retardation and psychopathology. Both human and animal work clearly shows that this is not true (Clark & Hanisee, 1982; Skeels, 1966; Snomi & Harlow. 1972). Babies suffering from malnutrition and reared in stultifying institutions or war-torn lands do show signs of their abuse and neglect. They have learned to be unresponsive to social attention and to shut out a hostile world. But a person's slow development can be kind to such deprived and abused children. Given proper stimulation, children can learn new ways of responding. Young brains are not like tape recorders; they do not record everything for posterity. Young brains, because of their immaturity, can be rewired, resulting in enhanced plasticity of cognition and behavior. Were children born with more mature brains, or if development proceeded more rapidly than it does, the mental, social, and emotional flexibility of young children would be lost. This behavioral and cognitive flexibility is perhaps the human species's greatest adaptive advantage, and it is afforded by the prolonged period of mental (and thus brain) inefficiency.

## Behavioral Neoteny

Although humans' slow rate of brain growth may be the proximal cause for the plasticity and flexibility of human cognition, it is accompanied by an extended period of physical and behavioral development. Several theorists have written of behavioral neoteny as the extended juvenile character of human behavior (Cairns, 1976; Lorenz, 1971; Mason, 1968a, 1968b). Cairns (1976) and Mason (1968a) have postulated, for example, that important aspects of human social behavior such as attachment are influenced by behavioral neoteny (see also Cairns, Gariepy, & Hood, 1990; and Montagu, 1989), and, according to Lorenz, such juvenile characteristics as curiosity are responsible for human's behavioral flexibility.

### Behavioral Neoteny and Flexibility

With respect to behavioral flexibility, Mason (1968a, 1968b) argued that neoteny is a general primate characteristic, both in terms of physical development—as was discussed briefly previously—and in terms of behavior. Mason noted that the prolongation of infancy is greater in chimpanzees than monkeys and greater yet in humans. This extension of infancy and its physical dependence is accompanied by weaker and less persistence of primitive infantile responses (e.g., reflexive grasp, rooting, and oral grasping) and a "loosening" of behavioral organization. As a result, Mason (1968a) stated,

> developmental stages are less sharply delimited in humans than in other primates. Sensitive periods in development are more difficult to establish, there is less likelihood that the withholding of any specific experience will result in developmental arrest, and there is a much stronger tendency for behavior to reflect a blending or intermingling of different developmental stages, different response patterns, and different motivational systems. (p. 101)

Making similar arguments, Cairns (1976) pointed out that both the instability of individual differences and the high malleability of social behavior over infancy, which are found in all social mammals, are extended in human children and may be due to neoteny. Thus, the behavioral plasticity that characterizes the human species may be due, in large part, to an extended period of immaturity. From this perspective, prolonged infancy and childhood not only provide more time to learn but also when accompanied by a reduced reliance on "instinctive" behaviors may in fact require a greater need for learning.

As all historical sciences, evolutionary theory suffers from the inability to test empirically some of its hypotheses. One cannot turn back the clock and manipulate some factors to determine the phylogenetic outcomes. However, experimental evidence does exist, demonstrating the effects of changes in developmental timing on social behavior across several generations. For example, in a series of experiments, Cairns and his colleagues (Cairns et al., 1990; Cairns, MacCombie, & Hood, 1983) observed that aggressive behavior in mice, measured by latency to attack, increased with age and experience. Mice were selectively bred for latency to attack; one line was selected for high aggression, and another line was selected for low aggression. Cairns and his colleagues noted that later generations of low-aggressive animals exhibited a gradual reduction in asymptotic levels of aggression compared with the foundational generation. More specifically, later generations of low-aggressive animals did not display the typical age-related increases in aggression observed in the first generation. Cairns et al. (1990) described this pattern as an example of neoteny, "the progressively longer persistence of 'immature' features in the ontogeny of descendent generations" (p. 59). Thus, changes in the timing of ontogeny (here, prolonged retardation) affected the social behavior of individuals and, over several generations, altered the average value of this behavior in the genetic line. Results such as these make more plausible the hypothesis that variations in developmental timing (heterochrony) can influence the behavioral development of a species (e.g., Cairns et al., 1990; Gottlieb, 1987, 1992).

## Play

Play, which is found in many animals, is extended into adulthood in humans and can be rightfully considered an example of behavioral neoteny (Lorenz, 1971). Many theorists believe that it is primarily through play that children's cognition develops (e.g., Dansky, 1980; Piaget,

1962), and it can be viewed as a vehicle by which neoteny affects development.

There is no doubt of the widespread occurrence of play during the immature stages of many animals. Like the extended period of youth and, in fact, correlated with it, play is most frequently found in species that are behaviorally flexible and particularly in neotenized organisms (Beckoff, 1972; Poirier & Smith, 1974; Vandenberg, 1981). In an early review of animals' play, Groos (1976) stated that "animals can not be said to play because they are young and frolicsome, *but rather they have a period of youth in order to play*" (p. 75).

The benefits of play are numerous. For example, play provides the juvenile animal with, among other things, the opportunity to develop motor skills, practice mastery of social behaviors, and learn by experimenting in a situation of minimum consequences (Bruner, 1972; Dolhinow & Bishop, 1970). Play, like genetic mutations, provides a source of creativity that may eventually help produce cultural diversity by discovering new ways to solve old problems (Oppenheim, 1981; Vandenberg, 1981); because of the youthful tendency toward play and curiosity in animals, it is likely that new innovations will be introduced by the young rather than the adult. This was demonstrated in the acquisition of the skill of potato washing in Japanese macaque monkeys (Kawai, 1965). A monkey troop was living in the wild but was observed and fed by Japanese scientists. The monkeys were given sweet potatoes, which were often sandy. One juvenile monkey "learned" to wash potatoes in sea water before eating them. Other juveniles subsequently learned, and then so did some adult females; this innovation was then passed on to infants as part of the culture. Few adult males ever learned this, however. Admittedly, it is unlikely that important cultural innovations will be made through the play of human children. Nevertheless, the discoveries children make through play may serve as the basis of later innovations or true creativity, which become important later in life.

Play is observed in the adults of many mammals, although usually in the context of courtship or parent-child interaction (Fagen, 1981). There is no other species that demonstrates curiosity and play into adulthood to the extent that *Homo sapiens* do. This orientation toward play caused the historian Huizinga (1950) to refer to humans as *Homo ludens*, "playful man." Novelty and the unknown are typically avoided in adult animals, with the notable exception of humans. In fact, what academics do for a living is often termed as *playing* with ideas. Intellectual curiosity, or play, is a hallmark of the human species and likely a necessary component to invention.

## Immaturity as a Form of Protection From Overstimulation

Humans' slow brain development not only permits an extension of behavioral plasticity but may also protect the young organism from overstimulation. Turkewitz and Kenny (1982) proposed that, similar to the arguments cited earlier made by Oppenheim (1981), the immaturity of sensory and motor systems may play adaptive roles early in development. The limited motor capacities of *altricial* animals (i.e., those who are physically immature and helpless at birth and need substantial parental care) prevents them from wandering far from their mother, thus enhancing their chances of survival. Of greater interest, however, was their proposal that sensory limitations of many young animals are adaptive because they serve to reduce the amount of information infants have to deal with, which facilitates their constructing a simplified and comprehensible world. In the next section, this proposal is assessed by examining the consequences of stimulation in excess of a species's norms on the subsequent perception and learning of young animals. It is followed by a section examining the consequences of early learning experiences on later learning by infant animals and humans. In the third section, I discuss the possibility that limitations of young children's working memory may make the process of language acquisition easier. Most of the research I present in the next two sections was conducted with animals. Although one must be cautious in generalizing research findings across species, infancy is a time when such comparisons are most apt to be informative, and I believe that, given the similarities of perceptual development across a wide range of species (see Gottlieb, 1971), mechanisms found to underlie the development of infrahuman animals can gainfully inform the psychologist interested in human development, especially considering the dearth of evidence from testing human participants.

## Adaptive Value of Immature Sensory Systems

Turkewitz and Kenny (1982) proposed that early maturing senses may not develop properly if other senses were "competing" with them for neurons and that limited sensory functioning reduces sensory input and serves to decrease competition between developing senses. From this perspective, immature sensory systems are not handicaps that must be overcome but are adaptive and necessary for proper sensory development and sensory learning.

Evidence in support of Turkewitz and Kenny's (1982) proposal has been reported for a number of species, with most research conducted with precocial birds (i.e., ducks and bobwhite quail), in which—as with all vertebrates—hearing develops before vision (Gottlieb, 1971). Like other precocial birds, ducks and bobwhite quails show a preference for the maternal species call, which is important in attachment. Working with quails, Lickliter and his colleagues (Lickliter, 1990, 1993; Lickliter & Hellewell, 1992; Lickliter & Lewkowitz, 1995) used a procedure to provide quails with visual exposure while still in the egg. The procedure involved cutting a hole in the egg near the head and providing patterned light 2 to 3 days prior to hatching. In one series of experiments (Lickliter, 1990), quail chicks were placed in the middle of a round tub 1 or 2 days after hatching. The maternal call of a quail was played from a speaker on one side of the tub and the maternal call of a chicken was played from a speaker on the opposite side. Quail chicks in the control group (egg opened and no premature visual experience) showed the species-typical pattern: Most approached the speaker emitting the maternal bobwhite quail call (29 of 32 animals). However, most of the experimental animals showed no preference (25 of 44 animals), and some (14 of 44 animals) even preferred the call of the chicken. Similar results of interference of early visual exposure on later approach behavior have been found with ducks (Gottlieb. Tomlinson, & Radell, 1989). Other research has shown that specific types of auditory stimulation can interfere with subsequent visual development in bobwhite quails (McBride & Lickliter, 1994) and that extra visual stimulation can interfere with olfaction in rats (Kenny & Turkewitz, 1986). The extension of the idea that limited sensory abilities might be adaptive in altricial mammals was made explicitly by Spear (1984) in reference to neonatal rats, which are functionally deaf and blind: "If this animal could be made to see and hear, it seems at least as likely that severely maladaptive behavior would result due to distraction from the more conventional events (e.g., odors) upon which its survival depends" (p. 335).

It should be noted that, in the Lickliter (1990) study, the prehatching visual stimulation did result in the acceleration of visual development in the chicks. However, this acceleration was at the expense of the development of the auditory system, which seriously hindered species-typical attachment behavior. It is also worth noting that attenuated prehatching stimulation results in a slowing of sensory systems (Lickliter & Lewkowitz, 1995). In general, developmental changes in sensory systems appear to be timed to correspond to species-typical experiences. When an animal receives stimulation that varies substantially from the species-typical pattern, postnatal sensory development is impaired. Because the auditory system develops before hatching, there is the opportunity for some prenatal learning to occur. For example, quail and duck chicks recognize the call of their mothers versus the calls of other female birds shortly after hatching (e.g., Gottlieb, 1988). Lickliter and Hellewell (1992) assessed the effects of extra-pre-hatching stimulation on such auditory learning. Quail embryos heard a specific maternal call, some with and some without additional visual stimulation, while still in the egg (Experiment 4A). Twenty-four hours after hatching, the quail chicks were put in a choice situation, where they heard the previous, familiar maternal call versus the maternal call of another bobwhite quail (a *novel* call). Preference for the fa-

miliar maternal call was the key dependent measure. Replicating their earlier findings (e.g., Lickliter & Hellewell, 1992, Experiment 1A). Lickliter and Hellewell reported that the bobwhite quail chicks exposed only to the maternal call showed a significant preference for that call. In contrast, the chicks that received the additional visual stimulation showed no such preference, making no distinction between the familiar and novel calls. That is, extra visual stimulation interfered with auditory learning. These findings are consistent with the position that the species-typical pattern, in which one system receives stimulation and develops before another, is adaptive. Hastened development in one system can interfere with development in a second system.

The findings of Lickliter and Hellewell (1992) are consistent with Turkewitz and Kenny's (1982) proposal that the differential rates of maturation of sensory systems minimize intersensory competition. Accelerating development of a late developing system interferes with the development of the normally early developing system. A related hypothesis is that intersensory interference can occur even when a fully developed sensory system (e.g., the vestibular system), which should not be competing for neurons with an immature system, receives extra stimulation. That is, stimulation that exceeds the species-typical range can interfere with development, regardless of whether the stimulated system is fully developed or still immature.

This possibility was investigated in a series of auditory-learning experiments by Radell and Gottlieb (1992). As in the Lickliter and Hellewell (1992) experiments, mallard duck embryos heard a specific maternal call. Some prehatchlings also received extra levels of vestibular, proprioceptive, and tactile stimulation, delivered by placing eggs on a rocking waterbed. Four to 8 hr after hatching, the ducklings were put in a choice situation where they heard simultaneously the familiar and novel maternal duck calls. When low and species-typical levels of motion were experienced (Experiment 4), no differences in choice behavior were observed between the control (no motion) and experimental animals. However, when the waterbed motion was substantially greater than would normally be experienced by the duck embryos, significant differences between control and experimental animals were found. Whereas 91% of the ducklings in the no-motion condition approached the familiar maternal call (Experiment 1), only 42% of the ducklings in the high-motion condition did so (Experiment 2A). Thus, it appears as if stimulation in excess of the species-typical range in any sense modality can interfere with ontogeny of a still-developing sense. These findings, although suggesting a modification of the Turkewitz and Kenny (1982) hypothesis, are consistent with the idea that slow developing and immature systems provide opportunities for earlier developing systems to develop properly. What these data indicate, however, is that the type of excessive sensory stimulation that can interfere with development extends beyond that associated with still-developing systems.

I know of no experiments comparable with those performed on precocial birds that assess the effects of excessive levels of stimulation on perceptual development in human infants. However, experiments in the early days of infant-perception research indicate that infants' preference for visual complexity increases with age, with younger infants preferring to look at less complex stimuli (usually stimuli with less contour) than do older infants (e.g., Greenberg & O'Donnell, 1972; Hershenson, Munsinger, & Kessen, 1965; H. Thomas, 1965), suggesting that there is an optimal level of perceptual stimulation for infants that increases with age. Also an equally venerable literature indicates that enriched visual, tactile, kinesthetic, or all of the above stimulations for premature or low-birthweight infants (Scarr-Salapatek & Williams, 1973; Solkoff, Yaffee, Weintraub, & Blase, 1969; J. L. White & LaBarba, 1976) or for orphanage-reared infants (B. L. White & Held, 1966) results in enhanced perceptual, physical, or intellectual development. There is every reason to believe that providing human infants with a perceptually varied and stimulating environment positively fosters development. However, animal research informs theorists that stimulation should be within the species-typical range and that stimulation that exceeds this range early in development may have unintended maladaptive consequences.

## Consequences of Early Learning on Later Learning

The findings of Lickliter and Hellewell (1992) and of Gottlieb and his colleagues (Gottlieb et al., 1989; Radell & Gottlieb, 1992) indicate that extra-pre-natal stimulation in one sensory system (vision or vestibular) can adversely affect later learning in another system. Related to this issue is the question of whether an early learning experience in infancy can interfere with later learning. Relatively little research focused directly on this question, although relevant research does exist for at least three species, rats, monkeys, and humans.

Using rat pups, Rudy, Vogt, and Hyson (1984) reported a classical conditioning study in which animals were trained to make mouthing activity (which was initially elicited by the unconditioned stimulus of a 10% sucrose solution) to auditory stimuli (e.g., a 2,000 Hz, 9 dB tone SPL). Conditioning began when the pups were 10, 12, or 14 days old, and testing continued until they were 16 days old. Despite the greater experience on the conditioning task, performance on Days 14 and 15 was worse for the animals that began training at 10 days old than for those that began training at 12 days old. Moreover, these pups never performed better than the pups who began training at 14 days old, leading Rudy et al. to conclude that the early training had a detrimental effect on the pups' ability to benefit from later training.

Spear and Hyatt (1993) discussed the results of two unpublished studies from their laboratory on conditioning in infant rats that similarly show impairment of later learning as a result of earlier learning experiences. In one study, rat pups that were given active avoidance training at 15 days old took more trials to reach the criterion on the same task at 75 days old than rats that were exposed to the tasks for the first time at 75 days old (p. 188). In a second study cited by Spear and Hyatt (an unpublished dissertation by N. Lariviere, 1990), rat pups, beginning as early as 12 days old, were exposed to some or all of the components of a classical conditioning task involving lights, tones, or both. Pups were given a criterion test at postnatal Days 17 and 18—the earliest time that conditioning with flashing lights paired with foot shock is usually observed. Spear and Hyatt reported that animals that had previously been exposed to the conditioned and the unconditioned stimuli demonstrated substantially impaired conditioning on Days 17 and 18. They concluded that "apparently, if experience with an episode to be learned later is given too early in life, learning of that episode in later ontogeny is impaired" (p. 189).

Similar evidence of a detrimental effect of early learning on later learning was provided by Harlow (1959), who studied object-discrimination learning in rhesus monkeys. Infant monkeys were given single discrimination tasks (e.g. triangle vs. circle) with three-dimensional stimuli that varied on multiple dimensions, such as color, form, size, and material. They were given 25 trials per day, 5 days per week for 4 weeks. Testing began when animals were either 60, 90, 120, 150, or 366 days old. Beginning at 120 days

old (or later), these monkeys were given new sets of more complicated learning-set problems, using the same set of stimuli as on single-discrimination problems. Monkeys were tested on 4 problems per day, 5 days per week, 6 trials per problem, for a total of between 400 and 600 problems. Performance on these problems, beginning at 120 days old, is shown in Figure 1 as a function of the age at which the monkeys began training.

Performance of the two youngest groups of monkeys never strayed far from chance levels (50%), despite the fact that they were 10 and 11 months old at the conclusion of training. From 260 days old and onward, these early trained monkey's performance was inferior to that of the other groups with less experience but matched for age. This suggests that early training was detrimental to later learning for these young monkeys. Harlow (1959) concluded that

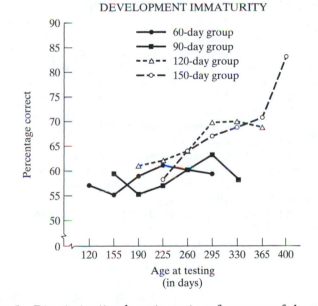

**DEVELOPMENT IMMATURITY**

**Figure 1** Discrimination learning set performance of rhesus monkeys as a function of age at which testing began. Adapted from Figure 14 of "The Development of Learning in Rhesus Monkey," by H. F. Harlow, 1959, *American Scientist*, December, p. 474. Copyright 1959 by *American Scientist*. Adapted with permission.

there is a tendency to think of learning or training as intrinsically good and necessarily valuable to the organism. It is entirely possible, however, that training can either be helpful or harmful, depending upon the nature of the training and the organism's stage of development. (p. 472)

Research with human infants pertinent to this question was conducted by Papousek and initially reported in the late 1960s (see Papousek, 1977; and Sameroff, 1971). Infants were conditioned to turn their heads in response to auditory stimuli—turn one way to the sound of a bell and the other way to the sound of a buzzer. Training began either at birth, Day 31, or Day 44. The older infants had had some training on simpler discrimination tasks, whereas this complex learning task was the first experience for the newborns.

The younger the children started the training, the more trials it took them to attain criterion ($M$ no. of trials to reach the criterion: newborns = 814; 31-day-olds = 278; 44-day-olds = 224). This makes sense if age of maturation is the critical factor. But note that, whereas the difference between the 31- and 44-day-old infants is consistent with such a maturation hypothesis, the data from the newborns are not. They required many more trials than would be predicted based on age (i.e., maturation) alone. This is made clear when one examines the age at which infants reached the criterion ($M$ age in days at which infants reached the criterion: newborns = 128; 31-day-olds = 71; 44-day-olds = 72). Infants who began training at birth took nearly twice as long to master the discrimination-learning problem as infants who began at 31 and 44 days old. Because infants apparently had a variety of testing experiences between the time of their first and final exposures on this task and because control groups that did not experience retroactive interference were not tested, one must be cautious when interpreting these results (C. Rovee-Collier, personal communication, September 30, 1996). But these data are suggestive of the possibility that not all learning experiences are necessarily good for infants—sometimes, learning experiences are not only useless for infants who lack the requisite cognitive abilities but some-

times may actually be detrimental to later learning and development.

Despite the long history of research in infant learning, there appear to be few other studies designed to assess the consequences of early learning experiences on later learning. The only other relevant study I am aware of was performed by Little, Lipsitt, and Rovee-Collier (1984).[2] In this study, separate groups of 10-, 20-, and 30-day-old infants were subjected to classical eyelid conditioning procedures and then tested again with the same procedures 10 days later. For infants whose initial testing was at 20 days old, there was a savings effect: Their performance 10 days later was greater than that of 30-day-old infants tested for the first time. There was no such savings effect 10 days later for infants whose initial testing began at 10 days old, but there was also no decrement in performance, as might be expected given the findings of Papousek (1977).

There is a paucity of research on the topic of the effects of early learning experience on later learning. There is no question that infants begin learning at birth and before (e.g., DeCasper & Spence, 1986), and I find it unlikely that learning experiences early in life will have long-term negative consequences. However, the meager evidence suggests that some specific learning experiences can adversely affect later specific learning experiences (e.g., Harlow, 1959; Papousek, 1977) and that there may be no benefit in terms of savings to begin a learning task very early in infancy (Little et al., 1984). This is clearly an area in which further research on well-trodden topics is warranted.

## Language Acquisition: When Less Is More

From a phylogenetic perspective, language is clearly an "addition." If the great apes are any indication of what human's common ancestors may have been like, they were not language users. No other primate engages in anything that even closely resembles human language in their natural habitat; although enculturated

---

[2]I wish to thank Carolyn Rovee-Collier for pointing out this study to me.

chimpanzees can presumably learn several hundred words and a limited syntax, they seem unable to advance beyond the language competence of an average 2-year-old human child (Savage-Rumbaugh et al., 1993). From this perspective, language would not seem to be a good candidate to look for adaptive immaturity. Yet, much as an immature nervous system reduces the amount of stimulation the infant receives and thus facilitates the development of the various sensory systems, so too might certain immature characteristics of children's information-processing abilities set the stage for the rapid process of first- and second-language acquisition observed in young children.

Most scholars of language development have adhered to the idea that there is a critical or sensitive period for the acquisition of a first and second language (e.g., Hurford, 1990; Lenneberg, 1967; Locke, 1993; Newport, 1991). There are at least four sources of evidence for this assertion (see Locke, 1993): (a) People who were socially deprived or isolated during infancy and early childhood typically demonstrate only a tenuous mastery of language (e.g., Curtiss, 1977). (b) eventual proficiency of a second language is greater the younger one is when exposed to that language (e.g., Johnson & Newport, 1989), (c) the eventual proficiency of sign language by deaf people—their first language—is greater the younger one is when exposed to that language (e.g., Newport, 1990), and (d) recovery of language function from brain damage is greater when the damage occurs earlier rather than later (e.g., Witelson, 1987). From this and other evidence, it appears that, as the brain matures, it loses its plasticity to acquire language.

There has been some interesting speculation that young children's fantastic language-acquisition ability may be accompanied by a set of immature cognitive skills. Recall the research with ducks and bobwhite quails indicating that sensory immaturity in one system was associated with enhanced development in another system (e.g., Lickliter, 1990). A similar relation may exist between young children's limited information-processing skills and language acquisition.

Newport (1991) has developed a model of language acquisition based on what she calls the "less is more" hypothesis. Her proposal is that

cognitive limitations reduce competition, thus simplifying the language corpus the infant and young child must process and making it easier to learn language. With success and time, maturationally paced abilities gradually increase, as does language learning. Young children in the early stages of language learning start out slowly—actually more slowly than do adults learning a second language. They perceive and store only component parts of complex stimuli. They start with single morphemes (usually a single syllable) and gradually increase complexity and the number of units they can control. They are able to extract only limited pieces of the speech stream. But this results in a simplified corpus that actually makes the job of analyzing language easier. Adults, in contrast, start out learning a second language faster than children; they are more competent initially, producing more complex words and sentences. They more readily perceive and remember the whole complex stimulus. But this advantage is short lived. Adults extract more of the input but are then faced with a more difficult problem of analyzing everything all at once.

Newport (1991) conducted a computer simulation, varying the amount of information that would be processed in the computer's "working memory" at one time. A restricted input filter (i.e., limited working-memory store) yielded (a) some loss of data for morphology learning, thus making learning initially more difficult; (b) greater loss of data at the whole-word level than the morphology level; and (c) an improvement in the signal-to-noise ratio, such that there is greater loss of data from accidental co-occurrences than from systematic co-occurrences of form and meaning. Overall, a restricted filter (i.e., limited working memory) was more successful at acquiring morphology than was a less restricted filter or no filter at all. The latter "entertained" too many alternatives and could not uniquely determine which was the better one.

A similar interpretation has been derived from experiments with connectionist networks by Elman (1994). Elman used a specific type of connectionist network called a *simple recurrent network* (Elman, 1990). In his simulation, Elman (1994) provided the network with sentences involving subject—verb agreement for number and the potential for multiple relative clause embeddings. The network had to "learn" both local and long-distance subject–verb agreement (e.g., "The zebras who the lion chases find the hiding place"). In this example, there is local agreement between *lion* and *chase*. However, the agreement between *zebras* and *find* is long distance, dependent on the hierarchical structure of the sentence.

Initial attempts, in which the entire corpus was presented to the network in a random order, failed to yield evidence of language acquisition. The network did not learn correct long-distance subject–verb agreement (i.e., the wrong form of the verb was selected by the network). Following these initial failures, Elman (1994) simplified the corpus that the network received, beginning with only simple sentences and gradually increasing the percentage of complex sentences presented to the network. Under these conditions, the network was correct in its selecting grammatically correct forms of verbs (i.e., verbs that agree with the appropriate subjects) for all of the different sentence types. In a subsequent simulation, Elman varied the network's memory for words, beginning with a limited memory of three to four words and increasing memory at subsequent stages in the simulation. Now when the entire corpus, including both simple and complex sentences, was presented to the network, learning occurred, much as it did in the earlier simulation (i.e., when sentence complexity increased in stages). In both situations, limitations in what the network could process, determined either by the simplicity of the sentences presented or the limitation of how much the network could keep in its memory at any one time, produced language learning. Elman used the metaphor, "the importance of starting small," to describe his findings and suggested the critical period for language acquisition reflects the developmental delay of certain abilities rather than the loss of some language-specific capacities. Thus, young children's limited working-memory capacity restricts how much language information can be processed. This simplifies what is analyzed, making the task of language acquisition easier.

## Adaptive Value of Cognitive Immaturity

Immature sensory systems or limited working-memory capacity are proposed to be adaptive because they reduce the amount of stimulation an organism receives, thus making the process of sensory or language development easier. Other aspects of immaturity, rather than fostering the development of specific systems by simplifying input, may provide some immediate benefits to the organism, although these benefits may be coupled with some handicaps.

Certain aspects of young children's cognitive functioning can be seen in this light. The cognitive limitations of preschool children are well documented. This theme was central in Piaget's theory, as reflected by his description of the stimulus-bound, egocentric, and intuitive preoperational child in contrast to the decentered, nonegocentric, and logical concrete-operational child. One need not be a Piagetian or an advocate of any stage theory to believe in the immaturity of preschool thought. The 5- to 7-year shift (e.g., S. H. White, 1965; 4- to 7-year shift. Nelson, in press; or the 3.5- to 4.0-year shift, Pemer, 1991) has been noted by a variety of theorists, who have provided a variety of explanations to account for the mental deficiencies of preschool children.

Such cognitive immaturity, although real, may reflect deficiencies only in relation to the cognition of older children. Some aspects of young children's immature cognition may have an adaptive role for them at that particular time in development. It is deficient in terms of what it is to become, but it may be quite efficient in terms of what problems it helps the child to solve at this particular point in development.

In a previous article, Bjorklund and Green (1992) introduced the possibility that some aspects of young children's immature cognition—especially egocentricity and poor metacognition—could, under some circumstances, be adaptive. It was not argued then, nor is it argued here, that such immature characteristics were always adaptive; in fact, it seems obvious that an overly self-centered perspective and the state of being out of touch with one's cognitive abilities is generally maladaptive. However, these detriments to good cognition may have associated with them some occasional benefits. In other words, looking only at the negative side of young children's limitations provides an incomplete and overly pessimistic picture of these children's cognitive functioning. In this section. I review briefly the findings that led Bjorklund and Green to their earlier interpretation; and 1 present new data and theory to bolster the position that young children's immature cognition can have some positive consequences.

### Egocentricity

It is well established that people of all ages tend to remember more information when they relate the target information specifically to themselves at time of encoding, later at retrieval, or both (e.g., Kail & Levine, 1976; Lord, 1980; Nadelman, 1974; Pratkanis & Greenwald, 1985). One implication of self-referencing memory experiments is that young children's egocentric tendencies may bias them to encode events in terms of themselves more so than older children would, thus enhancing their retention (see Mood, 1979).

More recent research in source monitoring similarly has suggested that young children's bias toward self-referencing may contribute to enhanced cognition rather than as solely a detriment to thought. *Source monitoring* refers to people's ability to ascertain the origins of some information. In one type of source monitoring, people must determine whether they themselves had performed an action or if they had observed someone else perform it. In a series of experiments, Foley, Ratner, and their colleagues (Foley & Ratner, 1996; Foley, Ratner, & Passalacqua, 1993) asked 4-, 6-, and 8-year-old children to make a collage with an adult. Children were later unexpectedly asked to tell the experimenter who had put each of the objects on the collage, themselves or the adult. What Foley, Ratner, and their colleagues were interested in was attribution errors: To what extent would children falsely attribute an action (putting objects on the collage) of their own to an adult ("You did it" false attribution) versus falsely attribute an action done by an adult to themselves ("I did it" false attribution)?

Six- and 8-year-old children were no more likely to make "I did it" false attributions as "You did it" false attributions (Foley et al., 1993). In contrast, 4-year-olds were consistently more likely to attribute an action performed by an adult to themselves ("I did it") than the reverse (Foley & Ratner, 1996, in press; Foley et al., 1993; Ratner & Foley, 1997). Young children's pattern of responding can be attributed to an egocentric perspective (i.e., when in doubt, take personal credit for an action). Foley, Ratner, and their colleagues suggested that this bias may result in better learning of the actions of others, in part because misattributing the actions of another to oneself may result in children linking the actions to a common source (themselves), thus producing a more integrated and easily retrievable event memory. According to Foley and Ratner (1996),

> if the bias we report is a reflection of children's more frequent anticipations or subsequent re-creations of the actions of another person, increasing confusion between self and others, actions themselves may be better understood and better remembered when these anticipations occur. Thus, children who actually display a pronounced source monitoring bias may subsequently perform quite well on their own after guided participation in a similar joint activity. Thus, taking the other "into'" the self may be an important mechanism for promoting children's learning and remembering. (pp. 19–20)

Ratner and Foley (1997) have recently collected data to test this hypothesis. Five-year-old children were asked to place six pieces of furniture in the rooms of a doll house (cf. Freund, 1990). One group did this in collaboration with an adult, alternating turns with the adult. For children in the no-collaboration group, half of the items had already been placed in the house by the adult before the child entered the room and the adult asked the child to place the remaining items in the rooms. When the children were later asked questions about who had placed each item in each room, those in the collaboration group made significantly more "I did it" attribution errors than those in the no-collaboration group. Moreover, when the children were later given the furniture and asked to place each piece in the room where they had been placed before, those in the collaboration group were correct more often and also made more planning-explanatory statements while recategorizing than did those in the no-collaboration condition. Thus, as Ratner and Foley predicted, collaboration led to both more self-attribution errors and better learning than did no collaboration. Although other interpretations are possible (e.g., a greater depth of processing for children in the collaboration group from watching the adults place items), this is consistent with the claim made here; that is, in some circumstances, an egocentric bias can have a positive effect on learning.

The results of these experiments should not be interpreted as reflecting that egocentricism in young children is not sometimes a hindrance to good cognition. It is an expression of an immature cognitive system and may hamper more "mature" thought in many situations. Social responding is especially hampered by an egocentric attitude, and children must overcome their generally self-centered perspective if they are to interact comfortably in the adult world. However, the findings of the various studies cited above do indicate that a focus on only the detrimental aspects of young children's egocentricism without considerating the possible adaptive functions yields an incomplete picture of children's development.

## Metacognition

Another area in which young children's immature cognition may sometimes be a blessing in disguise is metacognition, particularly as it relates to how competent children see themselves. *Metacognition* refers to the knowledge people have about the workings of their own minds— their mental weak and strong points, skills they posses, and ability to evaluate and monitor their own problem solving. For most forms of cognition, one can think of a corresponding form of metacognition. The developmental relation between cognition and metacognition is a bidirectional one, with changes in one factor influenc-

ing changes in the other (see Schneider, 1985). Although both cognition and metacognition within a domain typically improve with age, the relation between the two is not always strong (e.g., Cavanaugh & Borkowski, 1980). However, that good metacognition is usually associated with good cognition is illustrated by studies with school-aged children that show a positive correlation between metacognition and intelligence (e.g., Schneider, Körkel, & Weinert, 1987). That is, as one would expect, school-aged children with good metacognition are, on average, brighter than school-aged children with poor metacognition.

*Prediction-performance relations.* One aspect of metacognition that is particularly relevant for my purpose is the relation between children's predictions of their abilities and their actual performance. On the other side of the coin is posttask evaluation (*postdiction*), how well children think they have performed some task. Prediction and postdiction are important factors in both cognitive and social development. Bandura (1989) has concluded that the confidence people have in their competence in a particular domain influences what tasks they choose to perform and how long they persist at those tasks. Thus, a child's degree of confidence influences which tasks he or she attempts and how long he or she persists at a task before quitting. This, in turn, determines to a significant extent what is learned.

There is abundant evidence that preschool and early school-aged children overestimate their own abilities on a broad range of cognitive tasks (e.g., Bjorklund, Gaultney, & Green, 1993; Schneider, 1991; Stipek & Mac Iver, 1989; Yussen & Levy, 1975), and in general think they are "smarter" than others think they are (e.g., Stipek, 1981, 1984; Stipek & Hoffman, 1980; Stipek, Roberts, & Sanborn, 1984). Stipek (1981, 1984) reported that young children's assessments of their school-related abilities are quite high. Most children in the first grade and before think of themselves as being "one of the smartest kids in my class." It is only at the second and third grades that children begin to have a more realistic estimate of their academic standing. Beginning about this time, children's assessments of their school abilities are consistent with the assessments of their teachers and peers. Stipek (1984) has stated that children's tendencies to overestimate their skills may provide them with basic confidence in their own competence. Rather than trying to make young children's judgments of their abilities more accurate, she believes that theorists should "try harder to design educational environments which maintain their optimism and eagerness" (p. 53).

There seems to be no single reason for young children's overly optimistic bias in their abilities. When given specific feedback, preschool children can make more accurate assessments of their abilities (e.g., Clifford, 1978; Stipek & Daniels, 1988), and they are able to make accurate assessments of other children's abilities, arguing that they have the cognitive competence to make accurate predictions. Young children seem to have different, more lenient criteria for evaluating success and failure for themselves than for others (e.g., Schneider, 1991; Stipek, 1981), do not differentiate effort from ability (e.g., Harter & Pile, 1984), and may have a difficult time distinguishing their wishes (how they wish to perform) from their actual expectations (e.g., Stipek, 1984).

Regardless of the reasons for young children's inaccurate predictions of their performance, such overestimation of one's ability would seem to be a detriment to skilled performance. As noted earlier, in school-aged children, IQ and metacognition are usually positively related (e.g., Schneider et al., 1987). Nonetheless, Bjorklund and Green (1992) have argued that being out of touch with one's physical and mental abilities has benefits for young children, those who are at the low end of the physical- and mental-ability scales. When children have poor metacognitive skills, they believe that they are capable of more than they really are. This encourages exploration of new territories and reduces fear of failure in young learners. This was demonstrated in a study of *meta-imitation* (the knowledge of one's own imitative abilities; Bjorklund et al., 1993). In the study, 5-year-old children who were more accurate in predicting and postdicting their imitative abilities (i.e., who overestimated less) had higher IQs than did the less accurate children. In contrast, 3- and 4-year-old children with higher IQs were those who

most overestimated their imitative abilities (see Figure 2; because almost all children overestimated, lower scores represent less overestimation [and thus greater accuracy] and higher scores represent more overestimation [and thus greater inaccuracy]).

Bjorklund et al.'s (1993) interpretation of these results was that immature metacognition allows young children to imitate a broad range of behaviors without the knowledge that their attempts are inadequate. Without this negative feedback, bright young children continue to try their hand at many behaviors, thus permitting them to practice and improve their skills at a time when trial-and-error learning is so important. As their motor skills improve, so do their metacognitive skills, which later in development are associated with more advanced thinking abilities.

Seligman (1991) has proposed that children's overly positive view of their abilities, and of the world in general, is not something limited to upper-middle-class children who can afford to be optimistic about the future but is characteristic of the species and was selected in evolution:

> The child carries the seed of the future, and nature's primary interest in children is that they reach puberty safely and produce the next generation of children. Nature has buffered our children not only physically— prepubescent children have the lowest death rate from all causes—but psychologically as well, by endowing them with hope, abundant and irrational. (p. 126)

*Metacognition and strategy development.* Another area in which children's poor metacognition may occasionally provide some benefit is strategy development. Typically, children's metacognitive knowledge about strategy use and task performance is positively related, although such positive relations are not always found and are often constrained by context (see Bjorklund & Douglas, 1997; Schneider & Bjorklund, in press; and Schneider & Pressley, 1997).

Recent research has shown that, when children use strategies, they sometimes do not experience substantial benefits in task performance compared with their performance when not

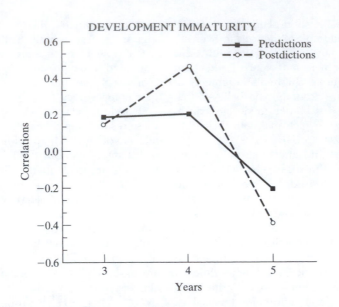

**Figure 2**  Correlation between IQ scores and prediction and postdiction imitation scores by age (note that negative correlations imply that children with higher IQs overestimated less, i.e., were more accurate, than did children with lower IQs). Data from Bjorklund, Green, and Gaultney (1993).

using a strategy or to that of older children who are comparably strategic. Miller (1990, 1994) has identified this pattern as a *utilization deficiency*. It has been investigated most frequently in the area of memory development; although it is a relatively recent discovery, partial or strong evidence of utilization deficiencies has been found in over 90% of developmental studies involving spontaneous strategy implementation (see Miller & Seier, 1994) and in more than half of memory training studies (see Bjorklund, Miller, Coyle, & Slawinski, in press) published over the past 20 years. Utilization deficiencies are not limited to the use of memory strategies but have been found for strategies of selective attention (e.g., Miller, Haynes, DeMarie-Dreblow, & Woody-Ramsey, 1986), reading (e.g., Gaultney, 1995), and analogical reasoning (e.g., Muir-Broaddus, 1995), among others (see Bjorklund & Coyle, 1995; Miller, 1994; and Miller & Seier, 1994, for reviews). It is precisely when children demonstrate utilization deficiencies that poor

metacognition may facilitate rather than hinder performance.

In a series of experiments from our laboratory, my colleagues and I assessed utilization deficiencies in children between Ages 6 and 13 for the memory strategy of organization (grouping and recalling sets of categorically related items together). Children were given different sets of categorized items over a series of trials. A utilization deficiency is defined as occurring when measures of strategy use increase significantly between consecutive trials in the absence of a corresponding increase in recall (Bjorklund, Coyle, & Gaultney, 1992; Bjorklund, Schneider, Cassel, & Ashley, 1994; Coyle & Bjorklund, 1996). Utilization deficiencies were rarely observed for the youngest children (6-year-olds), most of whom were not yet using strategies, or for the oldest children (13-year-olds), most of whom were using strategies effectively. Utilization deficiencies were observed, however, in about ⅓ of the 7- to 9-year-old children tested, both for spontaneous strategy use (Bjorklund et al., 1992; Coyle & Bjorklund, 1996) and for generalization of a trained strategy (Bjorklund et al., 1994).

Why should children use an effort-consuming strategy to guide their behavior when it has no positive impact on their task performance? One speculation is that utilization deficiencies may be related to children's poor metacognition and a belief that problem solving requires hard work (Bjorklund & Coyle, 1995; Bjorklund et al., in press). Perhaps children believe that performance may be enhanced by using a systematic approach to a problem, but they do not have the metacognitive knowledge to realize that this approach does not (as yet) yield benefits. Children may know, from informal instructions by adults or their own spontaneous problem solving, that doing something or thinking about how to solve a problem is in general more advantageous than doing nothing or not thinking about a problem. If this is the case, children may adopt a strategic approach to a problem when one is discovered, leading eventually to the efficient use of that and other strategies. This is similar to the argument made by Wellman (1988) in describing preschool children's use of *faulty strategies*—effortful, goal-directed activities that do not help performance. Discussing preschoolers' possible motivations for using faulty strategies, Wellman (1988) asserted that "young children may simply come to prefer a strategic or intelligent approach to problem solving, regardless of immediate payoffs . . . [and that] . . . faulty approaches are generated by coherent but mistaken notions of what will work" (p. 26).

Siegler (1996) has speculated that utilization deficiencies may play an important role in children's adaptive strategy choices. In discussing the phenomenon of utilization deficiencies, he stated that

the cognitive system may operate as if it knew the law of practice. With practice, any new procedure is likely to become faster, easier, and more accurate. If a new approach is even approximately as useful as an established one, it makes sense from a long-term perspective to use the new procedure, because substantial im-

provement in its effectiveness is more likely. (p. 141)

Although I know of no evidence that utilization deficiencies result in long-term strategic benefits, there is evidence that a utilization deficiency may lead to more effective strategy use relatively quickly. In the experiment by Bjorklund et al. (1992), 44% of the third-grade children who were classified as utilizationally deficient demonstrated increases in recall on subsequent trials. That is, for these children, the utilization deficiency was short lived, with children eventually experiencing the benefit of strategy use. Microgenetic and short-term longitudinal studies will be necessary to evaluate the long-term benefits of utilization deficiencies on children's cognition.

Thus, young children's poor metacognition may provide them an advantage (cf. Bjorklund et al., 1993); a child with better metacognitive skills may realize quickly that the extra effort being put into the task is not resulting in improved performance and thus resort to a nonstrategic approach. In contrast, by being out of touch with the relationship between strategy use and task performance, utilizationally deficient children may persist in using a strategy until it becomes sufficiently efficient to result in improved task performance. In this case, children's immature cognition is adaptive, leading to eventual (though not immediate) benefits.

## Concluding Remarks

In this article, I have attempted to place the concept of developmental immaturity in the perspective of evolutionary theory and to demonstrate how the concept can be applied to achieve a better understanding of human development. The principal premise of this article is that developmental immaturity can sometimes be adaptive and has been selected in evolution for the survival value it afforded the young organism. Some, but not all, aspects of developmental immaturity may still be adaptive to modern humans. When one considers the nature of the physical world in which a child at any particular age lives and the tasks he or she must master, some immature qualities may afford more advantages than disadvantages. I do not wish to imply, however, that all aspects of developmental immaturity are adaptive. Many aspects of a prolonged youth may be necessary correlates of other adaptive changes and may themselves have no adaptive function. In fact, they may be maladaptive, just not so maladaptive as to cause extinction.

In proposing that psychologists and educators view children's immature behavior and forms for their possible advantages, I do not intend this perspective as praise for immaturity or to suggest that children's immature thinking and behavior should be extended. Although it is tempting to take a romanticized view of childhood—as a time of carefree play and innocence—I am not arguing for the artificial prolongation of youth by "babying" children. Adults of a society must see to it that children grow up to be independent and responsible people. Prolongation of immaturity is deleterious, and maturity is still the goal of development. Instead, I suggested that there may be some adaptive functions for immaturity that co-exist with the maladaptive ones—at least at certain times in development.

This view of development provides a strikingly different perspective than the one traditionally taken by contemporary psychologists, educators, and parents. How we view development affects how we see children develop. It influences what questions we ask about development, how we educate children, and our perspective toward remediation. The current perspective should not turn any major theory of development on its head, but it should provide a new respect for the immature cognitions and behaviors of infants and young children.

## References

Abravanel, E., & Sigafoos, A. D. (1984). Explaining the presence of imitation during early infancy. *Child Development, 55,* 381–392.

Akazawa, T., Muhesen, S., Dodo, Y., Kondo, O., & Mizouguchi, Y. (1995, October 19). Neanderthal infant burial. *Nature, 377,* 585–586.

Anisfeld, M. (1991). Neonatal imitation: A review. *Developmental Review, 11,* 60–97.

Bandura, A. (1989). Human agency in social cognitive theory. *American Psychologist, 44,* 1175–1184.

Beckoff, M. (1972). The development of social interaction, play, and metacommunication in mammals: An ethological perspective. *Quarterly Review of Biology, 47,* 412–434.

Bjorklund, D. F. (1987). A note on neonatal imitation. *Developmental Review, 7,* 86–92.

Bjorklund, D. F. (1997). In search of a metatheory for cognitive development (or Piaget is dead and I don't feel so good myself). *Child Development, 68,* 142–146.

Bjorklund, D. F., & Coyle, T. R. (1995). Utilization deficiencies in the development of memory strategies. In F. E. Weinert & W. Schneider (Eds.), *Memory performance and competencies: Issues in growth and development* (pp. 161–180). Hillsdale, NJ: Erlbaum.

Bjorklund, D. F., Coyle, T. R., & Gaultney, J. F. (1992). Developmental differences in the acquisition and maintenance of an organizational strategy: Evidence for the utilization deficiency hypothesis. *Journal of Experimental Child Psychology, 54,* 434–448.

Bjorklund, D. F., & Douglas, R. N. (1997). The development of memory strategies. In N. Cowan (Ed.), *The development of memory in childhood* (pp. 201–246). London: London University College Press.

Bjorklund, D. F., Gaultney, J. F., & Green, B. L. (1993). "I watch, therefore I can do": The development of meta-imitation over the preschool years and the advantage of optimism in one's imitative skills. In R. Pasnak & M. L. Howe (Eds.), *Emerging themes in cognitive development* (Vol. 1, pp. 79–102). New York: Springer-Verlag.

Bjorklund, D. F., & Green, B. L. (1992). The adaptive nature of cognitive immaturity. *American Psychologist, 47,* 46–54.

Bjorklund, D. F., Miller, P. H., Coyle, T. R., & Slawinski, J. L. (in press). Instructing children to use memory strategies: Evidence of utilization deficiencies in memory training studies. *Developmental Review.*

Bjorklund, D. F., Schneider, W., Cassel, W. S., & Ashley, E. (1994). Training and extension of a memory strategy as a function of knowledge base and IQ: Evidence for utilization deficiencies in the acquisition of an organizational strategy. *Child Development, 65,* 951–965.

Bjorklund, D. F., & Schwartz, R. (1996). The adaptive nature of developmental immaturity: Implications for language acquisition and language disabilities. In M. Smith & J. Damico (Eds.), *Childhood language disorders* (pp. 17–40). New York: Thieme Medical.

Bolk, L. (1926). On the problem of anthropogenesis. *Proceedings of the Royal Academy of Amsterdam, 29,* 465–475.

Bonner, J. T. (1988). *The evolution of complexity by means of natural selection*. Princeton, NJ: Princeton University Press.

Bruner, J. S. (1972). The nature and uses of immaturity. *American Psychologist, 27,* 687–708.

Byrne, R. (1995). *The thinking ape: Evolutionary origins of intelligence*. Oxford, England: Oxford University Press.

Cairns, R. B. (1976). The ontogeny and phylogeny of social interactions. In M. E. Hahn & E. C. Simmel (Eds.), *Communicative behavior and evolution* (pp. 115–139). New York: Academic Press.

Cairns, R. B., Gariepy, J.-L., & Hood, K. E. (1990). Development, microevolution, and social behavior. *Psychological Review, 97,* 49–65.

Cairns, R. B., MacCombie, D. J., & Hood, K. E. (1983). A developmental–genetic analysis of aggressive behavior in mice: I. Behavioral outcomes. *Journal of Comparative Psychology, 97,* 69–89.

Cavanaugh, J. C., & Borkowski, J. G. (1980). Searching for metamemory–memory connections: A developmental study. *Developmental Psychology, 16,* 441–453.

Clark, E. A., & Hanisee, J. (1982). Intellectual and adaptive performance of Asian children in adoptive American settings. *Developmental Psychology, 18,* 595–599.

Clifford, M. M. (1978). The effects of quantitative feedback on children's expectations of success. *British Journal of Educational Psychology, 48,* 220–226.

Cosmides, L., & Tooby, J. (1987). From evolution to behavior: Evolutionary psychology as the missing link. In J. Dupre (Ed.), *The latest on the best essays on evolution and optimality* (pp. 277–306). Cambridge, MA: MIT Press.

Coyle, T. R., & Bjorklund, D. F. (1996). The development of strategic memory: A modified microgenetic assessment of utilization deficiencies. *Cognitive Development, 11,* 295–314.

Curtiss, S. (1977). *Genie: A psycholinguistic study of a modern day "wild child."* New York: Academic Press.

Dansky, J. L. (1980). Make-believe: A mediator of the relationship between play and associative fluency. *Child Development, 51,* 576–579.

Davidson, P. E. (1914). *The recapitulation theory and human infancy*. New York: Teachers College.

DeCasper, A. J., & Spence, M. J. (1986). Prenatal maternal speech influences newborns' perception of speech sounds. *Infant Behavior and Development, 9,* 133–150.

de Beer, G. (1958). *Embryos and ancestors* (3rd ed.). Oxford, England: Clarendon Press.

Dolhinow, P. J., & Bishop, N. H. (1970). The development of motor skills and social relationships

among primates through play. In J. P. Hill (Ed.), *Minnesota Symposia on Child Psychology* (pp. 180–198). Minneapolis: University of Minnesota Press.

Eccles, J. C. (1989). *Evolution of the brain: Creation of the self*. New York: Routledge.

Elman, J. (1990). Finding structure in time. *Cognitive Science, 14,* 179–211.

Elman, J. (1994). Implicit learning in neural networks: The importance of starting small. In C. Umilta & M. Moscovitch (Eds.), *Attention and performance XV: Conscious and nonconscious information processing* (pp. 861–888). Cambridge, MA: MIT Press.

Fagen, R. (1981). *Animal play behavior*. New York: Oxford University Press.

Fernald, A. (1992). Human maternal vocalizations to infants as biologically relevant signals: An evolutionary perspective. In J. H. Barkow, L. Cosmides, & J. Tooby (Eds.), *The adapted mind: Evolutionary psychology and the generation of culture* (pp. 391–428). New York: Oxford University Press.

Foley, M. A., & Ratner, H. H. (1996). *Children's anticipations in memory for collaboration: A way of learning from others*. Manuscript submitted for publication.

Foley, M. A., & Ratner, H. H. (in press). Biases in children's memory for collaborative exchanges. In D. Herrmann, M. K. Johnson, C. McEvoy, C. Hertzog, & P. Hertel (Eds.), *Basic and applied memory: Research on practical aspects of memory*. Mahwah, NJ: Erlbaum.

Foley, M. A., Ratner, H. H., & Passalacqua, C. (1993). Appropriating the actions of another: Implications for children's memory and learning. *Cognitive Development, 8,* 373–401.

Fontaine, R. (1984). Imitative skill between birth and six months. *Infant Behavior and Development, 7,* 323–333.

Freund, L. S. (1990). Maternal regulation of children's problem-solving behavior and its impact on children's performance. *Child Development, 61,* 113–126.

Garstang, W. (1922). The theory of recapitulation: A critical restatement of the biogenetic law. *Journal of the Linnean Society of London Zoology, 35,* 81–101.

Gaultney, J. F. (1995). The effect of prior knowledge and metacognition on the acquisition of a reading comprehension strategy. *Journal of Experimental Child Psychology, 59,* 142–163.

Geary, D. C. (1995). Reflections of evolution and culture in children's cognition: Implications for mathematical development and instruction. *American Psychologist, 50,* 24–37.

Gottlieb, G. (1971). Ontogenesis of sensory function in birds and mammals. In E. Tobach, L. R. Aronson,

& E. Shaw (Eds.), *The biopsychology of development* (pp. 67–128). New York: Academic Press.

Gottlieb, G. (1987). The developmental basis of evolutionary change. *Journal of Comparative Psychology, 101,* 262–271.

Gottlieb, G. (1988). Development of species identification in ducklings: XV. Individual auditory recognition. *Developmental Psychobiology, 21,* 509–522.

Gottlieb, G. (1992). *Individual development and evolution: The genesis of novel behavior.* New York: Oxford University Press.

Gottlieb, G., Tomlinson, W. T., & Radell, P. L. (1989). Developmental intersensory interference: Premature visual experience suppresses auditory learning in ducklings. *Infant Behavior and Development, 12,* 1–12.

Gould, S. J. (1977). *Ontogeny and phylogeny.* Cambridge, MA: Harvard University Press.

Gould, S. J. (1989). *Wonderful life: The Burgess Shale and the nature of history.* New York: Norton.

Greenberg, D. J., & O'Donnell, W. J. (1972). Infancy and the optimal level of stimulation. *Child Development, 43,* 639–645.

Groos, K. (1976). The value of play for practice and self-realization. In J. S. Bruner, A. Jolly, & K. Sylva (Eds.), *Play—Its role in development and evolution* (pp. 65–83). New York: Basic Books.

Groves, C. P. (1989). *A theory of human and primate evolution.* Oxford, England: Clarendon Press.

Hall, G. S. (1904). *Adolescence: Its psychology and its relation to physiology, anthropology, sociology, sex, crime, religion, and education* (Vols. 1–2). New York: Appleton.

Harlow, H. F. (1959, December). The development of learning in the Rhesus monkey. *American Scientist,* 459–479.

Harter, S., & Pike, R. (1984). The pictorial scale of perceived competence and social acceptance for young children. *Child Development, 55,* 1969–1982.

Heimann, M. (1989). Neonatal imitation gaze aversion and mother–infant interaction. *Infant Behavior and Development, 12,* 495–505.

Hershenson, M., Munsinger, H., & Kessen, W. (1965, February 5). Preference for shapes of intermediate variability in the newborn human. *Science, 147,* 630–631.

Huizinga, J. (1950). *Homo ludens: A study of the play element in culture.* Boston: Beacon Press.

Hurford, J. R. (1990). The evolution of the critical period for language acquisition. *Cognition, 40,* 150–201.

Jacobson, M. (1969, February 7). Development of specific neuronal connections. *Science, 163,* 543–547.

Jacobson, S. W. (1979). Matching behavior in the young infant. *Child Development, 50,* 425–420.

Jerison, H. J. (1973). *Evolution of the brain and intelligence.* New York: Academic Press.

Johnson, J. S., & Newport, E. L. (1989). Critical period effects in second language learning: The influence of instructional state on the acquisition of English as a second language. *Cognitive Psychology, 21,* 60–99.

Kail, R. V., & Levine, L. E. (1976). Encoding processes and sex-role preferences. *Journal of Experimental Child Psychology, 21,* 256–263.

Kawai, M. (1965). Newly acquired pre-cultural behavior of a natural troop of Japanese monkeys. *Primates, 6,* 1–30.

Kenny, P., & Turkewitz, G. (1986). Effects of unusually early visual stimulation on the development of homing behavior in the rat pup. *Developmental Psychobiology, 19,* 57–66.

Legerstee, M. (1991). The role of person and object in eliciting early imitation. *Journal of Experimental Child Psychology, 51,* 423–433.

Lenneberg, E. H. (1967). *Biological foundations of language.* New York: Wiley.

Lickliter, R. (1990). Premature visual stimulation accelerates intersensory functioning in bobwhite quail neonates. *Developmental Psychobiology, 23,* 15–27.

Lickliter, R. (1993). Timing and the development of perimatal perceptual organization. In G. Turkewitz & D. A. Devenny (Eds.), *Developmental time and timing* (pp. 105–123). Hillsdale, NJ: Erlbaum.

Lickliter, R., & Hellewell, T. B. (1992). Contextual determinants of auditory learning in bobwhite quail embryos and hatchlings. *Developmental Psychobiology, 25,* 17–24.

Lickliter, R., & Lewkowitz, D. J. (1995). Intersensory experience and early perceptual development: Attenuated prenatal sensory stimulation affects postnatal auditory and visual responsiveness in bobwhite quail chicks (*Colinus virginianus*). *Developmental Psychology, 31,* 609–618.

Little, A. H., Lipsitt, L. P., & Rovee-Collier, C. (1984). Classical conditioning and retention of infant's eyelid response: Effects of age and interstimulus interval. *Journal of Experimental Child Psychology, 37,* 512–524.

Locke, J. L. (1993). *The child's path to spoken language.* Cambridge, MA: Harvard University Press.

Lord, C. G. (1980). Schemas and images as memory aids: Two modes of processing social information. *Journal of Personality and Social Psychology, 38,* 257–269.

Lorenz, K. (1971). *Studies in animal and human behavior.* Cambridge, MA: Harvard University Press.

Mason, W. A. (1968a). Early social deprivation in the nonhuman primates: Implications for human behavior. In D. C. Glass (Ed.), *Environmental influ-*

*ence* (pp. 70–101). New York: Rockerfeller University Press and Russell Sage Foundation.

Mason, W. A. (1968b). Scope and potential of primate research. In J. H. Masserman (Ed.), *Science and psychoanalysis. Vol. 12: Animal and human* (pp. 101–118). New York: Grune & Stratton.

Mayr, E. (1982). *The growth of biological thought: Diversity, evolution, and inheritance.* Cambridge, MA: Belknap Press.

McBride, T., & Lickliter, R. (1994). Specific postnatal auditory stimulation interferes with species-typical responsiveness to maternal visual cues in bobwhite quail chicks. *Journal of Comparative Psychology, 107,* 320–327.

Meltzoff, A. N., & Moore, M. K. (1977, October 7). Imitation of facial and manual gestures by human neonates. *Science, 198,* 75–78.

Meltzoff, A. N., & Moore, M. K. (1983). Newborns imitate adult facial gestures. *Child Development, 54,* 702–709.

Meltzoff, A. N., & Moore, M. K. (1992). Early imitation within a functional framework: The importance of person identity, movement, and development. *Infant Behavior and Development, 15,* 479–505.

Miller, P. H. (1990). The development of strategies of selective attention. In D. F. Bjorklund (Ed.), *Children's strategies: Contemporary views of cognitive development* (pp. 157–184). Hillsdale, NJ: Erlbaum.

Miller, P. H. (1994). Individual differences in children's strategic behavior: Utilization deficiencies. *Learning and Individual Differences, 6,* 285–307.

Miller, P. H., Haynes, V. F., DeMarie-Dreblow, D., & Woody-Ramsey, J. (1986). Children's strategies for gathering information in three tasks. *Child Development, 57,* 1429–1439.

Miller, P. H., & Seier, W. L. (1994). Strategy utilization deficiencies in children: When, where, and why. In H. W. Reese (Ed.), *Advances in child development and behavior* (Vol. 25, pp. 107–156). New York: Academic Press.

Mithen, S. (1996). *The prehistory of the mind: The cognitive origins of art, religion and science.* London: Thames & Hudson.

Montagu, A. (1989). *Growing young* (2nd ed.). Grandy, MA: Bergin & Garvey.

Montagu, M. F. A. (1962). Time, morphology, and neoteny in the evolution of man. In M. F. A. Montagu (Ed.), *Culture and the evolution of man* (pp. 324–342). New York: Oxford University Press.

Mood, D. W. (1979). Sentence comprehension in preschool children: Testing an adaptive egocentrism hypothesis. *Child Development, 50,* 247–250.

Morss, J. R. (1990). *The biologising of childhood: Developmental psychology and the Darwinian myth.* Hillsdale, NJ: Erlbaum.

Muir-Broaddus, J. E. (1995). Gifted underachievers: Insights from the characteristics of strategic functioning associated with giftedness and achievement. *Learning and Individual Differences, 7,* 189–206.

Nadelman, L. (1974). Sex identity in American children: Memory, knowledge, and preference tests. *Developmental Psychology, 10,* 413–417.

Nelson, K. (in press). Memory development from 4 to 7 years. In A. Sameroff & M. Haith (Eds.), *Reason and responsibility: The passage through childhood.* Chicago, IL: University of Chicago Press.

Nesse, R. M., & Williams, G. C. (1994). *Why we get sick: The new science of Darwinian medicine.* New York: Times Books.

Newport, E. L. (1990). Maturational constraints on language learning. *Cognitive Science, 14,* 11–28.

Newport, E. L. (1991). Constraining concepts of the critical period for language. In S. Carey & R. Gelman (Eds.), *The epigenesis of mind: Essays on biology and cognition* (pp. 111–130). Hillsdale, NJ: Erlbaum.

Oppenheim, R. W. (1981). Ontogenetic adaptations and retrogressive processes in the development of the nervous system and behavior. In K. J. Connolly & H. F. R. Prechtl (Eds.), *Maturation and development: Biological and psychological perspectives* (pp. 73–108). Philadelphia: International Medical.

Papousek, H. (1977). Entwicklung der lernfähigkeit im säuglingsalter [The development of learning ability in infancy]. In G. Nissen (Ed.), *Intelligenz, lernen, und lernstörungen [Intelligence, learning, and learning disabilities]* (pp. 75–93). Berlin: Springer-Verlag.

Perner, J. (1991). *Understanding the representational mind.* Cambridge, MA: MIT Press.

Piaget, J. (1962). *Play, dreams, and imitation in childhood.* New York: Norton.

Poirier, F. E., & Smith, E. O. (1974). Socializing functions of primate play. *American Zoologist, 14,* 275–287.

Pratkanis, A. R., & Greenwald, A. B. (1985). How shall the self be conceived? *Journal for the Theory of Social Behavior, 15,* 311–328.

Radell, P. L., & Gottlieb, G. (1992). Development of intersensory interference: Augmented prenatal sensory experience interferes with auditory learning in duck embryos. *Developmental Psychology, 28,* 795–803.

Ratner, H. H., & Foley, M. A. (1997, April). *Children's collaborative learning: Reconstructions of the other in the self.* Paper presented at the meeting of the Society for Research in Child Development, Washington, DC.

Rudy, J. W., Vogt, M. B., & Hyson, R. L. (1984). A developmental analysis of the rat's learned reactions to gustatory and auditory stimulation. In R. Kail & N. E. Spear (Eds.), *Memory development: Comparative perspectives* (pp. 181–208). Hillsdale, NJ: Erlbaum.

Sameroff, A. J. (1971). Can conditioned responses be established in the newborn infant: 1971? *Developmental Psychology, 5,* 1–12.

Savage-Rumbaugh, E. S., Murphy, J., Sevcik, R. A., Brakke, K. E., Williams, S. L., & Rumbaugh, D. M. (1993). Language comprehension in ape and child. *Monograph of the Society for Research in Child Psychology, 58* (Serial No. 233).

Scarr-Salapatek, S., & Williams, M. L. (1973). The effects of early stimulation on low-birth-weight infants. *Child Development, 44,* 94–101.

Schneider, W. (1985). Developmental trends in the metamemory–memory behavior relationship: An integrative review. In D. L. Forrest-Pressley, G. E. MacKinnon, & T. G. Waller (Eds.). *Cognition, metacognition, and human performance* (Vol. 1, pp. 57–109). New York: Academic Press.

Schneider, W. (1991, April). *Performance prediction in young children: Effects of skill, metacognition, and wishful thinking.* Paper presented at the meeting of the Society for Research in Child Development, Seattle, WA.

Schneider, W., & Bjorklund, D. F. (in press). Memory. In B. Damon (Series Ed.), D. Kuhn, & R. S. Siegler (Vol. Eds.). *Handbook of child psychology, Vol 2: Cognitive, language, and perceptual development.* New York: Wiley.

Schneider, W., Körkel, J., & Weinert, F. E. (1987). The effects of intelligence, self-concept, and attributional style on metamemory and memory behaviour. *International Journal of Behavioural Development, 10,* 281–299.

Schneider, W., & Pressley, M. (1997). *Memory development between 2 and 20* (2nd ed.). Mahwah, NJ: Erlbaum.

Seligman, M. E. P. (1991). *Learned optimism: How to change your mind and your life.* New York: Pocket Books.

Siegler, R. S. (1996). *Emerging minds: The process of change in children's thinking.* New York: Oxford University Press.

Skeels, H. M. (1966). Adult status of children with contrasting early life experiences. *Monograph of the Society for Research in Child Development, 31* (Serial No. 105).

Solkoff, N., Yoffee, S., Weintraub, D., & Blase, B. (1969). Effects of handling on the subsequent development of preterm infants. *Developmental Psychology, 1,* 765–768.

Spear, N. E. (1984). Ecologically determined dispositions control the ontogeny of learning and memory. In R. Kail & N. E. Spear (Eds.), *Memory development: Comparative perspectives* (pp. 325–358). Hillsdale, NJ: Erlbaum.

Spear, N. E., & Hyatt, L. (1993). How the timing of experience can affect the ontogeny of learning. In G. Turkewitz & D. A. Devenny (Eds.), *Developmental time and timing* (pp. 167–209). Hillsdale, NJ: Erlbaum.

Stipek, D. J. (1981). Children's perceptions of their own and their classmates' ability. *Journal of Educational Psychology, 73,* 404–410.

Stipek, D. (1984). Young children's performance expectations: Logical analysis or wishful thinking? In J. G. Nicholls (Ed.), *Advances in motivation and achievement. Vol. 3: The development of achievement motivation* (pp. 33–56). Greenwich, CT: JAI Press.

Stipek, D., & Daniels, D. (1988). Declining perceptions of competence: A consequence of changes in the child or the educational environment? *Journal of Educational Psychology, 80,* 352–356.

Stipek, D., & Hoffman, J. (1980). Development of children's performance-related judgments. *Child Development, 51,* 912–914.

Stipek, D., & Mac Iver, D. (1989). Developmental change in children's assessment of intellectual competence. *Child Development, 60.* 521–538.

Stipek, D., Roberts, & Sanborn, M. (1984). Preschool-age children's performance expectations for themselves and another child as a function of the incentive value of success and the salience of past performance. *Child Development, 55,* 1983–1989.

Stringer, C. B., Dean, M. C., & Martin, R. D. (1990). A comparative study of cranial and dental development within recent British samples among Neanderthals. In C. J. DeRousseau (Ed.), *Primate life history and evolution* (pp. 115–152). New York: Wiley–Liss.

Suomi, S., & Harlow, H. (1972). Social rehabilitation of isolate-reared monkeys. *Developmental Psychology, 6,* 487–496.

Tanner, J. M. (1978). *Fetus into man: Physical growth from conception to maturity.* Cambridge, MA: Harvard University Press.

Thomas, H. (1965). Visual fixation responses of infants to stimuli of varying complexity. *Child Development, 36,* 629–638.

Thomas, L. (1993). *The fragile species.* New York: Scribner.

Thomson, K. W. (1988). *Morphogenesis and evolution.* New York: Oxford University Press.

Thorndike, E. L. (1913). *Educational psychology: Vol. 1. The original nature of man.* New York: Teachers College.

Tooby, J., & Cosmides, L. (1992). The psychological foundations of culture. In J. H. Barkow, L. Cosmides, & J. Tooby (Eds.), *The adapted mind: Evolutionary psychology and the generation of culture* (pp. 19–136). New York: Oxford University Press.

Trinkaus, E., & Tompkins, R. L. (1990). The Neanderthal life cycle: The possibility, probability and perceptibility of contrasts with recent humans. In C. J. DeRousseau (Ed.), *Primate life history and evolution* (pp. 153–180). New York: Wiley–Liss.

Turkewitz, G., & Kenny, P. (1982). Limitations on input as a basis for neural organization and perceptual development: A preliminary theoretical statement. *Developmental Psychobiology, 15*, 357–368.

Vandenberg, B. (1981). Play: Dormant issues and new perspectives. *Human Development, 24*, 357–365.

Wellman, H. M. (1988). The early development of memory strategies. In F. E. Weinert & M. Perlmutter (Eds.), *Memory development: Universal changes and individual differences* (pp. 3–29). Hillsdale, NJ: Erlbaum.

Wesson, R. (1991). *Beyond natural selection.* Cambridge, MA: MIT Press.

White, B. L., & Held, R. (1966). Plasticity of sensorimotor development. In J. F. Rosenblith & W. Allinsmith (Eds.), *The causes of behavior* (2nd ed., pp. 60–70). Boston: Allyn & Bacon.

White, J. L., & LaBarba, R. C. (1976). The effects of tactile and kinesthetic stimulation on neonatal development in the preterm infant. *Developmental Psychobiology, 9*, 569–577

White, S. H. (1965). Evidence for a hierarchical arrangement of learning processes. In L. P. Lipsitt & C. C. Spiker (Eds.), *Advances in child development and behavior* (Vol. 2, pp. 167–220). New York: Academic Press.

Wilson, P. J. (1980). *Man, the promising primate: The conditions of human evolution.* New Haven, CT: Yale University Press.

Witelson, S. F. (1987). Neurobiological aspects of language in children. *Child Development, 58*, 653–688.

Yakovlev, P. I., & Lecours, A. R. (1967). The myelenogenetic cycles of regional maturation of the brain. In A. Minkowski (Ed.), *Regional development of the brain in early life* (pp. 3–70). Oxford, England: Blackwell.

Yussen, S., & Levy, V. (1975). Developmental changes in predicting one's own span of short-term memory. *Journal of Experimental Child Psychology, 19*, 502–508.

Zollikofer, C. P. E., Ponce de León, M. S., Martin, R. D., & Stucki, P. (1995, May 25). Neanderthal computer skulls. *Nature, 375*, 283–285.

# References

Achiron, R., Lipsitz, S., & Achiron, A. (2001). Sex related differences in the development of the human fetal corpus collosum: In utero ultrasonographic study. *Prenatal Diagnosis, 21,* 116–120.

Adler, A. (1927). *The practice and theory of individual psychology* (P. Radin, Trans.). New York: Harcourt, Brace & Co.

Adolph, K. (1997). Learning in the development of infant locomotion. *Monographs of the Society for Research in Child Development, 62*(3, Serial No. 351).

Ainsworth, M. D. S. (1979). Infant-mother attachment. *American Psychologist, 34,* 932–937.

Ainsworth, M. D. S., & Bowlby, J. (1991). An ethological approach to personality development. *American Psychologist, 46,* 333–341.

Ames, L. B. (1937). The sequential patterning of prone progression in the human infant. *Genetic Psychology Monograph, 19,* 409–460.

Ames, L. B. (1989). *Arnold Gesell—Themes of his work.* New York: Human Sciences Press.

Ames, L. B., & Chase, J. A. (1974). *Don't push your preschooler.* New York: Harper & Row.

Anderson, C. A., & Bushman, B. J. (2001). Effects of violent video games on aggressive behavior, aggressive cognition, aggressive affect, physiological arousal, and prosocial behavior: A meta-analytic review of the scientific literature. *Psychological Science, 12,* 353–359.

Aristotle. (1962). *Nicomachean ethics* (M. Ostwald, Trans.). Indianapolis: Bobbs-Merrill.

Arlin, P. K. (1975). Cognitive development in adulthood: A fifth stage? *Developmental Psychology, 11*(5), 602–606.

Ash, M. G. (1992). Cultural contexts and scientific change in psychology: Kurt Lewin in Iowa. *American Psychologist,* 198–207.

Ausubel, D. P., Sullivan, E. V., & Ives, S. W. (1980). *Theory and problems of child development* (3rd ed.). New York: Grune & Stratton.

Baldwin, A. L. (1968). *Theories of child development.* New York: Wiley

Baldwin, D. A., Markman, E. M., & Melartin, R. J. (1993). Infants' ability to draw inferences about nonobvious object properties: Evidence from exploratory play. *Child Development, 64,* 711–728.

Baldwin, J. M. (1897). *Social and ethical interpretations in mental development.* New York: Macmillan.

Baltes, P. B. (1978). *Life-span development and behavior, Vol. 1.* New York: Academic Press.

Baltes, P. B. (1999). Theoretical propositions of life-span developmental psychology: On the dynamics between growth and decline. In R. M. Lerner & J. V. Lerner (Eds.), *Theoretical foundations and biological bases of development in adolescence* (pp. 37–52). New York: Garland.

Baltes, P. B. (2002). Wisdom: Its structure and function in regulating successful life span development. In C. R. Snyder & S. J. Lopez (Eds.), *Handbook of positive psychology* (pp. 327–350). Oxford, UK: Oxford University Press.

Baltes, P. B., Reese, H. W., & Nesselroade, J. R. (1977). *Life-span developmental psychology: Introduction to research methods.* Monterey, CA: Brooks/Cole.

Baltes, P. B., & Schaie, K. W. (1973). On life-span developmental research paradigms: Retrospects and prospects. In P. B. Baltes & K. W. Schaie (Eds.), *Life-span developmental psychology: Personality and socialization* (pp. 365–395). New York: Academic Press.

Bandura, A. (1977). *Social learning theory.* Englewood Cliffs, NJ: Prentice Hall.

Bandura, A. (1986). *Social foundations of thought and action: A social cognitive theory.* Englewood Cliffs, NJ: Prentice Hall.

Bandura, A. (1997). *Self-efficacy: The exercise of control.* New York: W. H. Freeman.

Bandura, A., Ross, D., & Ross, S. A. (1963). Imitation of film-mediated aggressive models. *Journal of Abnormal and Social Psychogy, 66,* 3–9, 11.

Bandura, A., & Walters, R. H. (1959). *Adolescent aggression: A study of the influence of child-training practices and family interrelation.* New York: Ronald Press.

Bandura, A., & Walters, R. H. (1963). *Social learning and personality development.* New York: Holt, Rinehart, & Winston

Baron, R. M. (2002). Exchange and development: A dynamical, complex systems perspective. *New Directions for Child and Adolescent Development, 95* (53–71). New York: Wiley.

Baron-Cohen, S. (2003). *The essential difference: Men, women, and the extreme male brain.* New York: Basic Books.

Baron-Cohen, S. (2005). The essential difference: The male and female brain. *Phi Kappa Phi Forum, 85*(1), 23–26.

Bates, E. (2005). Plasticity, localization, and language development. In S. T. Parker, J. Langer, & C. Milbrath (Eds.), *Biology and knowledge revisited: From neurogenesis to psychogenesis* (pp. 205–254). Mahwah, NJ: Erlbaum.

Bates, E., & Elman, J. (2000). The ontogeny and phylogeny of language: A neural network perspective. In S. T. Parker, J. Langer, & M. L. McKinney (Eds.), *Biology, brains, and behavior: The evolution of human development* (pp. 89–130). Sante Fe, NM: School of American Research Press; Oxford, UK: James Currey, Ltd.

Bates, E., Thal, D., Trauner, D., Fenson, J., Aram, D., Eisele, J., & Nass, R. (1997). From first words to grammar in children with focal brain injury. *Developmental Neuropsychology, 13,* 447–476.

Belsky, J., & Cassidy, J. (1994). Attachment: Theory and evidence. In M. Rutter & D. F. Hay (Eds.), *Development through life: A handbook for clinicians* (pp. 373–402). London: Blackwell Scientific Publications.

Bem, S. L. (1976). Probing the promise of androgyny. In A. Kaplan & J. F. Bean (Eds.), *Readings toward a psychology of androgyny* (pp. 47–68). Boston: Little, Brown.

Bem, S. L. (1981a). Gender schema theory: A cognitive account of sex typing. *Psychological Review, 88,* 354–364.

Bem, S. L. (1981b). *Bem Sex Role Inventory: Professional manual.* Palo Alto, CA: Consulting Psychologists Press.

Bem, S. L. (1993). *The lenses of gender: Transforming the debate on sexual inequality.* New Haven, CT: Yale University Press.

Bergen, D. (1998). Development of children's humor. In W. Ruch (Ed.), *Measurement approaches to the sense of humor* (pp. 329–360). Berlin: Mouton deGruyter.

Bergen, D., & Coscia, J. (2000). *Brain research and childhood education.* Olney, MD: ACEI.

Bergen, D., & Everington, C. (1994). Assessment perspectives for young children with severe disabilities or environmental trauma. In D. Bergen, *Assessment methods for infants and toddlers: Transdisciplinary team perspectives* (pp. 216–233, 270–271). New York: Teachers College Press.

Bergen, D., Reid, R., & Torelli, L. (2001). *Educating and caring for very young children: The infant/toddler curriculum.* New York: Teachers College Press.

Berk, L. E., & Winsler, A. (1995). *Scaffolding children's learning: Vygotsky and early childhood education.* Washington, DC: National Association for the Education of Young Children.

Bernays, E. (1923). *Crystalizing public opinion.* New York: Boni and Liveright.

Bierhalter, G. (1993). Helmholtz's mechanical foundation of thermodynamics. In D. Cahan (Ed.), *Hermann von Helmholtz and the foundations of nineteenth century science* (pp. 432–458). Berkeley. University of California Press.

Bijou, S. W. (1964). An empirical concept of reinforcement and a functional analysis of child behavior. *Journal of Genetic Psychology, 104,* 215–223.

Bijou, S. W. and others (1971). *The exceptional child: Conditional learning and teaching ideas.* New York: MSS Information Corporation.

Bijou, S. W., & Baer, D. M. (1978). *Behavior analysis of child development.* Englewood Cliffs, NJ: Prentice Hall.

Birns, B., & Sternglanz, S. H. (1983). Sex-role socialization: Looking back and looking ahead. In M. B. Liss (Ed.), *Social and cognitive skills: Sex roles and children's play* (pp. 235–251). New York: Academic Press.

Bjorklund, D. F. (1997). The role of immaturity in human development. *Psychological Bulletin, 122*(2), 153–169.

Block, J. H. (1979). Another look at sex differentiation in the socialization behavior of mothers and fathers. In J. Sherman & F. L. Demmark (Eds.), *Psychology of women: Future directions of research* (pp. 29–85). New York: Psychological Dimensions.

Bornstein, M. H., Hahn, C.-S., Bell, C., Haynes, O. M., Slater, A., Golding, J., et al. (2006). Stability in cognition across early childhood: A developmental cascade. *Psychological Science, 17*(2), 151–158.

Bowlby, J. (1944). Forty-four juvenile thieves: Their characters and home life. *International Journal of Psychoanalysis, 25,* 19–52, 107–127.

Bowlby, J. (1982). Attachment and loss: Retrospect and prospect. *Journal of the American Orthopsychiatric Society,* 664–677.

Bowlby, J. (1988). *A secure base: Clinical applications of attachment theory.* London: Routledge.

Bowlby, J. (1989). The role of attachment in personality development and psychopathology. In S. I. Greenspan & G. H. Pollock (Eds.), *The course of life: Vol. 1. Infancy* (pp. 229–270). Madison, CT: International Universities Press

Bowlby, J., & Ainsworth, M. (1965). *Child care and the growth of love* (2nd ed.). Middlesex, UK: Penguin Books, Ltd.

Brazelton, T. B. (1974). *Toddlers and parents: A declaration of independence.* New York: Delacorte Press.

Bremner, J. D., Randall, P., Vermetten, E., Staib, L., Bronen, R. A., Mazure, C. et al. (1997). Magnetic resonance imaging-based measurement of hippocampal volume in posttraumatic stress disorder related to childhood physical and sexual abuse: A preliminary report. *Biological Psychiatry, 41*(1), 23–32.

Bretherton, I., & Waters, E. (1985). *Growing points of attachment: Theory and research.* Chicago: University of Chicago Press.

Bronfenbrenner, U. (1979). *The ecology of human development.* Cambridge, MA: Harvard University Press.

Bronfenbrenner, U. (1993). The ecology of cognitive development: Research models and fugitive findings. In R. H. Wozniak & K. W. Fischer (Eds.), *Development in contexts: Acting and thinking in specific environments* (pp. 3–44). Hillsdale, NJ: Erlbaum.

Bronfenbrenner, U. (2005). *Making human beings human: Bioecological perspectives on human development.* Thousand Oaks, CA: Sage.

Bronfenbrenner, U., & Evans, G. W. (2000). Developmental science in the 21st century: Emerging theoretical models, research designs, and empirical findings. *Social Development, 9*(1), 115–125.

Bronfenbrenner, U., & Morris, P. A. (1998). The ecology of developmental process. In W. Damon (Series Ed.) & R. M. Lerner (Vol. Ed.), *Handbook of child psychology: Vol. 1. Theoretical models of human development* (5th ed, pp. 993–1028). New York: Wiley.

Brown, R., & Bellugi, U. (1964). Three processes in the child's acquisition of syntax. In. E. Lenneberg (Ed.), *New directions in the study of language.* Cambridge, MA: MIT Press.

Bruner, J. S. (1960). *The process of education.* New York: Vintage.

Bruner, J. S. (1961). The act of discovery. *Harvard Educational Review, 31*(1), 21–32.

Bruner, J. S. (1973) *Beyond the information given: Studies in the psychology of knowing.* New York: Norton.

Burton, G. M. (1986). Values education in Chinese Primary Schools. *Childhood Education, 35,* 250–255.

Carey, W. B., & McDevitt, S. C. (1978). Revision of the Infant Temperament Questionnaire. *Pediatrics, 61*(5), 735–738.

Carey, W. B., & McDevitt, S. C. (1994). *Prevention and early intervention: Individual differences as risk factors for the mental health of children.* New York: Brunner/Mazel.

Carlsson-Paige, N., & Levin, D. E. (1987). *The war play dilemma: Balancing needs and values in the early childhood classroom.* New York: Teachers College Press.

Carper, R. A., & Courchesne, E. (2000). Inverse correlation between frontal lobe and cerebellum sizes in children with autism. *Brain, 123,* 836–844.

Case, R. (Ed.). (1991). *The mind's staircase: Exploring the conceptual underpinnings of children's thought and knowledge.* Hillsdale, NJ: Erlbaum.

Case, R. (1992). NeoPiagetian theories of intellectual development. In H. Beilin & P. Pufall (Eds.), *Piaget's theory: Prospects and possibilities* (pp. 61–104). Hillsdale, NJ: Erlbaum.

Case, R. (1999). Conceptual development in the child and in the field: A personal view of the Piagetian legacy. In E. K. Scholnick, K. Nelson, S. A. Gelman, & P. H. Miller (Eds.), *Piaget's legacy* (pp. 23–51). Mahwah, NJ: Erlbaum.

Cassidy, J., & Shaver, P. R. (1999). *Handbook of attachment: Theory, research, and clinical applications.* New York: Guilford Press.

Catan, L. (1986). The dynamic display of process: Historical development and contemporary uses of the microgenetic method. *Human Development, 29,* 252–263.

Catherwood, D., Crassini, B., & Freiberg, K. (1989). Infant response to stimuli of similar hue and dissimilar shape: Tracing the origins of the categorization of objects by hue. *Child Development, 60,* 752–762.

Cazden, C. B. (1972). *Child language and education.* New York: Holt, Rinehart, & Winston.

Chan, W. (Trans.). (1963). K'ung Fu-Tzu (Confucius) The great learning. In W. Chan, *A source book on Chinese philosophy.* Princeton, NJ: Princeton University Press.

Charles, D. C. (1970). Historical antecedents of life-span developmental psychology. In L. R. Goulet & P. B. Baltes (Eds.), *Life-span developmental psychology: Research and theory* (pp. 24–53). New York: Academic Press.

Chess, S., & Thomas, A. (1990). Temperament and its functional significance. In S. Greenspan & G. Pollock (Eds.), *The course of life (Vol. II,* pp. 163–228.) Madison, CT: International Universities Press.

Chess, S., & Thomas, A. (1999). *Goodness of fit: Clinical applications from infancy thorough adult life.* Philadelphia: Brunner/Mazel.

Chess, S., Thomas, A., & Birch, H. G. (1972). *Your child is a person: A psychological approach to parenthood without guilt.* New York: Viking.

Chodorow, N. (1974). Family structure and feminine personality. In M. Z. Rosaldo & L. Lamphere (Eds.), *Woman, culture, and society* (pp. 43–66). Stanford, CA: Stanford University Press.

Chomsky, N. (1959). A review of B. F. Skinner's "Verbal Behavior." *Language, 35,* 44–47.

Chomsky, N. (1965). *Aspects of the theory of syntax.* Cambridge, MA: MIT Press.

Chomsky, N. (1968). *Language and mind.* New York: Harcourt, Brace, & World.

Chomsky, N. (2000). *New horizons in the study of language and mind.* New York: Cambridge University Press.

Chugani, H. T. (1999). PET scanning studies of human brain development and plasticity. *Developmental Neuropsychology, 16*(3), 379–381.

Clark, J. (1997). Dynamical systems perspective on the development of complex adaptive skill. In C. Dent-Read & P. Zukow-Goldring (Eds.), *Evolving explanations of development: Ecological approaches to organism-environment systems* (pp. 383–406). Washington, DC: American Psychological Association.

Coates, D. L. (1999). The cultural and culturing aspects of romantic experience in adolescence. In W. Furman, B. B. Brown, & C. Feiring (Eds.), *The development of romantic relationships in adolescence* (pp. 330–363). Cambridge, UK: Cambridge University Press.

Coghill, G. E. (1933). The neuroembryonic study of behavior: Principles, perspectives, and aims. *Science,78,* 131–138.

Coles, C. (2004). Humanoid robots: Functional and fun. *The Futurist, 38*(1), 12–13.

Collins, N., & Read, N. (1990). Adult attachment, working models, and relationship quality in dating couples. *Journal of Personality and Social Psychology, 58,* 644–663.

Collins, W. A., & Sroufe, I. A. (1999). Capacity for intimate relationships: A developmental construction. In W. Furman, B. B. Brown, & C. Feiring (Eds.), *The development of romantic relationships in adolescence* (pp. 125–147). Cambridge, UK: Cambridge University Press.

Comalli, P. E., Wapner, S., & Werner, H. (1962). Interference effects of Stroop color-word test in childhood, adulthood, and aging. *Journal of Genetic Psychology, 100,* 47–53.

Comenius, J. A. (1907). *Didactica magna.* London: A. & C. Black. (Original work published 1632).

Comenius, J. A. (1967). *Orbis pictus.* London, Oxford University Press. (Original work published 1657).

Cooley, C. H. (1902). *Human nature and the social order.* New York: Scribner.

Coopersmith, S. (1967). *The antecedents of self-esteem.* San Francisco: Freeman.

Coplan, R. J., Bowker, A., & Cooper, S. M. (2003). Parenting daily hassles, child temperament, and social adjustment in preschool. *Early Childhood Research Quarterly, 18*(30), 376–395.

Corbetta, D., & Thelen, E. (1994). Shifting patterns of interlimb coordination in infants' reaching: A case study. In S. Swinnen, H. Heuer, J. Massion, & P. Casaer,

(Eds.), *Interlimb coordination: Neural, dynamical, and cognitive constraints* (pp. 413–441). New York: Academic Press.

Dalton, T. C. (1996, Winter). Reconstructing John Dewey's unusual collaboration with Myrtle McGraw in the 1930's. *SRCD Newsletter,* 1–3, 8–10.

Dalton, T. C., & Bergenn, V. W. (Eds.) (1995). *Beyond heredity and environment: Myrtle McGraw and the maturation controversy.* Boulder, CO: Westview.

Damon, W. (1977). *The social world of the child.* San Francisco: Jossey-Bass.

Damon, W. (1988). *The moral child: Nurturing children's natural moral growth.* New York: Free Press.

Damon, W. (1994). *Childhood gender segregation: Causes and consequences.* San Francisco: Jossey-Bass.

Damon, W. (1997). *The youth charter: How communities can work together to raise standards for all children.* New York: Free Press.

Damon, W., & Hart, D. (1988). *Self-understanding in childhood and adolescence.* Cambridge: Cambridge University Press.

Dasen, P. (1977). *Piagetian psychology: Cross-cultural contributions.* New York: Gardner Press.

Davis, M. H. (1994). *Empathy: A social psychological approach.* Madison, WI: Brown and Benchmark.

Davis, S. F., & Palladino, J. J. (2003). *Psychology* (4th ed.). Upper Saddle River, NJ: Pearson/Prentice Hall.

Deaux, L., & Wrightman, J. S. (1988). *Social psychology.* Pacific Grove, CA: Brooks/Cole.

DeGangi, G. A., Breinbauer, C., Roosevelt, J. D., Porges, S., & Greenspan, S. (2000). Prediction of childhood problems at three years in children experiencing disorders of regulation during infancy. *Infant Mental Health Journal, 21*(3), 156–175.

DeMaris, A., & Longmore, M. A. (1996). Ideology, power, and equity: Testing competing explanations for the perception of fairness in household labor. *Social Forces, 74,* 1043–1071.

Deissner R., & Tiegs, J. (2001). *Notable selections in human development* (2nd ed.). Guilford, CT: McGraw-Hill.

deVries, M. (1984). Temperament and infant mortality among the Masai of East Africa. *American Journal of Psychiatry, 141,* 1189–1194.

DeVries, R. (2001). Constructivist education in preschool and elementary school: The sociomoral atmosphere as the first educational goal. In S. L. Golbeck (Ed.), *Psychological perspectives on early childhood education: Reframing dilemmas in research and practice* (pp. 153–180). Mahwah, NJ: Erlbaum.

DeVries, R., & Kohlberg, L. (1984). *Programs of early education: The constructivist view.* New York: Longman.

Dewey, J. (1997). *How we think.* Toronto: Dover. (Original Work Published 1910).

Dewey, J. (1916). *Democracy and education.* New York: Macmillan.

Doyle, A. B. (2000). *Attachment to parents and adjustment in adolescence: Literature review and policy implications.* Ottawa: Childhood and Youth Division, Health Canada.

Dweck, C. S. (1975). The role of expectancies and attributions in the alleviation of learned helplessness. *Journal of Personality and Social Psychology, 31,* 647–685.

Edleman, G. M. (1992).*Bright air, brilliant fire: On the matter of mind.* New York: Basic Books.

Eisenberg, N., Guthrie, I. K., Murphy, B. C., Shepard, S. A., Cumberland, A., & Carlo, G. (1999). Consistency and development of prosocial dispositions: A longitudinal study. *Child Development, 70*(6), 1360–1372.

Eisenberg, N. (1986). *Altruistic emotion, cognition, and behavior.* Hillsdale, NJ: Erlbaum.

Eisenberg, N., Guthrie, I. K., Cumberland, A., Murphy, B. C., Shepard, S. A., Zhou, Q., & Carlo, G. (2002). Prosocial development in early adulthood: A longitudinal study. *Journal of Personality and Social Psychology, 82*(6), 993–1006.

Eisenberg, N., Zhou, Q., & Koller, S. (2001). Brazilian adolescents' prosocial moral judgment and behavior: Relations to sympathy, perspective taking, gender-role orientation, and demographic characteristics. *Child Development, 72*(2), 518–534.

Eiss, H. (1994). *Images of the child.* Bowling Green, OH: Bowling Green State University Press.

Elder, G. (1974). *Children of the great depression.* Chicago: University of Chicago Press.

Elder, G. (1980). Adolescence in historical perspective. In J. Adelson (Ed.), *Handbook of adolescent psychology* (pp. 3–46). New York: Wiley.

Elder, G. (1994). Time, human agency, and social change: Perspectives on the life course. *Social Psychology Quarterly, 57*(1), 4–15.

Elder, G. (1999). The life course as developmental theory. In R. M. Lerner & J. V. Lerner (Eds.), *Theoretical foundations and biological bases of development in adolescence* (pp. 71–83). New York: Garland.

Elder, G., & Rockwell, R. C. (1979). The life-course and human development: An ecological perspective. *International Journal of Behavioral Development, 2,* 1–21.

Elkind, D. (1976). *Child development and education: A Piagetian perspective.* New York: Oxford University Press.

Elkind, D. (1978). *The child's reality: Three developmental themes.* Hillsdale, NJ: Erlbaum.

Elkind, D. (1988). *The hurried child: Growing up too fast too soon.* Reading, MA: Addison-Wesley.

Erikson, E. H. (1958). *Young man Luther: A study in psychoanalysis and history.* New York: Norton.

Erikson, E. H. (1963). *Childhood and society* (2nd ed.). New York: Norton.

Erikson, E. H. (1968). *Identity, youth, and crisis.* New York: Norton.

Erikson, E. H. (1969). *Ghandi's truth on the origins of militant nonviolence.* New York: Norton.

Erikson, E. H. (1972). Play and actuality. In M. W. Piers (Ed.), *Play and development* (pp. 127–163). New York: Norton.

Erikson, E. H. (1977). *Toys and reason.* Toronto: G. J. McLeod Limited.

Erikson, E. H. (1984). Reflections on the last stage—and the first. *Psychoanalytic Study of the Child, 39,* 155–165.

Fagot, B. (1984). Teacher and peer reactions to boys' and girls' play styles. *Sex Roles, 11,* 691–702.

Fagot, B., & Leve, L. D. (1998). Gender identity and play. In D. P. Fromberg & D. Bergen (Eds.), *Play from birth to twelve and beyond: Contexts, perspectives, and meanings* (pp. 187–192). New York: Garland.

Farver, K. M. (1993). Cultural differences in scaffolding pretend play: A comparison of American and Mexican mother–child and sibling–child pairs. In K. MacDonald (Ed.), *Parent–child play: Descriptions and implications* (pp. 349–366). Albany: State University of New York.

Feschbach, N. D. (1974). The relationship of child-rearing factors to children's aggression, empathy, and related positive and negative social behaviors. In J. de Witt & W. W. Hartup (Eds.), *Determinants and origins of aggressive behavior* (pp. 427–436). The Hague: Mouton.

Fischer, K. W. (1980). A theory of cognitive development: The control and construction of hierarchies of skills. *Psychological Review, 6*(87), 477–531.

Fischer, K. W., Bullock, D. H., Rotenberg, E. J., & Raya, P. (1993). The dynamics of competence: How context contributes directly to skill. In R. H. Wozniak & K. W. Fischer (Eds.), *Development in contexts: Acting and thinking in specific environments* (pp. 93–117). Hillsdale, NJ: Erlbaum.

Fischer, K. W., & Pipp, S. L. (1984). Processes of cognitive development: Optimal level and skill acquisition. In R. J. Sternberg (Ed.), *Mechanisms of cognitive development* (pp. 45–80). New York: Freeman.

Fischer, K. W., & Rose, S. P. (1998). Growth cycles of brain and mind. *Educational Leadership, 56*(3), 56–60.

Fischer, K. W., & Rose, S. P. (1999). Rulers, models, and nonlinear dynamics: Measurement and method in developmental research. In G. Savelsbergh, H. vander Maas, & P. van Geart (Eds.), *Nonlinear developmental processes* (pp. 197–212). Amsterdam: Royal Netherlands Academy of Arts and Sciences.

Flavell, J. H. (1977). Metacognitive aspects of problem-solving. In J. B. Resnick (Ed.), *The nature of intelligence* (pp. 231–235). Hillsdale, NJ: Erlbaum.

Flavell, J. H. (1992a). Cognitive development: Past, present, and future. *Developmental Psychology, 28*(6), 998–1005.

Flavell, J. H. (1992b) Perspectives on perspective-taking. In H. Beilin & P. B. Pufall (Eds.), *Piaget's theory: Prospects and possibilities* (pp. 107–139). Hillsdale, NJ: Erlbaum.

Flowers, D. L., Wood, F. B., & Naylor, C. E. (1991). Regional cerebral blood flow correlates of language processes in reading disability. *Archives of Neurology, 48,* 637–643.

Fodor, J. (1988). *Psychosemantics.* Cambridge, MA: MIT Press.

Fowler, J. W. (1981). *Stages of faith: The psychology of human development and the quest for meaning.* San Francisco: Harper Collins.

Fraiberg, S. (1968). *The magic years: Understanding and handling the problems of early childhood.* London: Methuen.

Frank, R. (2005). Research on at-home dads. Retrieved from http://slowlane.com/research/laymen-research.html

Froebel, F. (1887). *The education of man.* New York: Appleton-Century.

Freud, A. (1946). *The ego and the mechanisms of defence* (C. Baines, Trans.). New York: International Universities Press.

Freud, A. (1989). Child analysis as the study of mental growth (normal and abnormal). In S. I. Greenspan & G. H. Pollock (Eds.), *The course of life: Vol. 1. Infancy* (pp. 1–14.) Madison, CT: International Universities Press.

Freud, A., & Burlingham, D. T. (1943). *War and children.* New York: Medical War Books.

Freud, S. (1936). *The ego and the mechanisms of defense.* New York: International Universities Press.

Freud, S. (1938). *The basic writings of Sigmund Freud* (A. A. Brill, Trans.). New York: Random House.

Freud, S. (1960). *Jokes and their relation to the unconscious.* London: Routledge & Kegan Paul.

Freud, S. (1962). *The ego and the id* (J. Riviere, Trans.). New York: Norton.

Friedlander, P. (1973). *Plato* (H. Meyerhoff, Trans.). Vols. 1-3. Bollingen Series 5a. Princeton, NJ: Princeton University Press.

Fussell, E. (2005). Measuring the early adult life course in Mexico: An application of the entropy index. In R. Macmillan (Ed.), *The structure of the life course: Standardized? Individualized? Differentiated? (Advances in life course research, Vol. 9)* (pp. 90–122). London: Elsevier.

Gelman, R., Meck, E., & Merkin, S. (1986). Young children's numerical competence. *Cognitive Development, 1,* 1–29.

Gesell, A. (1925). *The mental growth of the preschool child: A psychological outline of normal development from birth to the sixth year.* New York: Macmillan.

Gesell, A. (1940). *The first five years of life.* New York: Harper.

Gesell, A. (1949). *Gesell developmental schedules.* New York: The Psychological Corporation.

Gesell, A., & Amatruda, C. S. (1947). *Developmental diagnosis: Normal and abnormal child development, clinical methods and pediatric applications.* New York: Hoeber.

Gesell, A., & Ilg, F. L. (with Ames, L. B., Learned, J., & Bullis, G. E.). (1949). *Child development.* New York: Harper & Row.

Gesell, A., Ilg, F. L, & Ames, L. B. (1956). *Youth: The years from ten to sixteen.* New York: Harper.

Gibson, E. J. (1969). *Principles of perceptual learning and development.* New York: Appleton-Century-Crofts.

Gibson, E. J. (1997). An ecological psychologist's prolegomena for perceptual development: A functional approach. In C. Dent-Read & P. Zukow-Goldring (Eds.),

*Evolving explanations of development: Ecological approaches to organism-environment systems* (pp. 23–54). Washington, DC: American Psychological Association.

Gibson, E. J., & Pick, A. D. (2000). *An ecological approach to perceptual learning and development.* New York: Oxford University Press.

Gibson, E. J., & Walk, R. D. (1960). The "visual cliff." *Scientific American, 202,* 64–71.

Gibson, J. J. (1979). *The ecological approach to visual perception.* Boston: Houghton Mifflin.

Gibson, K. R. (2005). Human brain evolution. In S. T. Parker, J. Langer, & C. Milbrath (Eds.), *Biology and knowledge revisited: From neurogenesis to psychgenesis* (pp. 123–143). Mahwah, NJ: Erlbaum.

Gibson, K. R., & Petersen, A. (1991). *Brain maturation and cognitive development: Comparative and cross-cultural perspectives.* Hawthorne, NY: Aldine de Gruyter.

Giele, J. Z., & Holst, E. (Eds.). (2004). *Changing life patterns in Western industrial societies.* Amsterdam: Elsevier.

Gilligan, C. (1978). In a different voice: Women's conceptions of self and morality. *Harvard Educational Review, 47*(4), 481–517. Reprinted in *Stage theories of cognitive and moral development: Criticisms and applications* (pp. 52–88). Reprint No. 13: Cambridge: Harvard Educational Review.

Gilligan, C. (1982). *In a different voice: Psychological theory and women's development.* Boston: Harvard University Press.

Gilligan, C. (1987). A different voice in moral decisions. In D. L. Eck & D. Jain (Eds.), *Speaking of faith: Global perspectives on women, religion and social change* (pp. 236–245). Philadelphia: New Society.

Gilligan, C. (1999). New maps of development: New visions of maturity. In R. M. Lerner & J. V. Lerner (Eds.), *Theoretical foundations and biological bases of development in adolescence* (pp. 121–134). New York: Garland.

Gleick, J. (1987). *Chaos: Making a new science.* New York: Penguin.

Goerner, S. (1994). *Chaos and the evolving ecological universe.* Langhorne, PA: Gordon and Breach.

Goldberg, S., Muir, R., & Kerr, J. (Eds.). (1995). *Attachment theory: Social, developmental, and clinical perspectives.* Hillsdale, NJ: Analytic Press.

Goldhaber, D. E. (2000). *Theories of human development: Integrative perspectives.* Mountain View, CA: Mayfield.

Gonzalez-Mena, J. (2005). *Diversity in early care and education: Honoring differences* (4th ed.). New York: Anchor.

Good, C. D., Johnsrude, I., Ashburner, J., Henson, R. N. A., Friston, K. J., & Frackowiak, R. S. J. (2001). Cerebral assymmetry and the effects of sex and handedness on brain structure: A voxel-based morphometric analysis of 455 normal adult human brains. *NeuroImage, 14*(3), 685–700.

Gopnik, A. (2003). The theory as an alternative to the innateness hypothesis. In N. Hornstein & L. Antony (Eds.), *Chomsky and his critics.* (pp. 238–254). New York: Blackwell Publishing.

Gopnik, A., Meltzoff, A. N., & Kuhl, P. K. (2001). *The scientist in the crib.* New York: Harper Collins.

Gopnik, A. & Schulz, L. (2004). Mechanisms of theory formation in young children. *Trends in Cognitive Sciences, 8*(8), 371–377.

Gopnik, A., & Wellman, H. M. (1994). The theory theory. In L. A. Hirschfeld & S. A. Gelman (Eds.), *Mapping the mind: Domain specificity in cognition and culture* (pp. 257–293). New York: Cambridge University Press.

Gottlieb, G. (1992). *Individual development and evolution: The genesis of novel behavior.* New York: Oxford University Press.

Gottlieb, G. (1998). Myrtle McGraw's unrecognized conceptual contribution to developmental psychology. *Developmental Review, 18,* 437–448.

Gottlieb, G. (2001). The relevance of developmental-psychobiological metatherory to developmental neuropsychology. *Developmental Neuropsychology, 19*(1), 1–9.

Gould, R. L. (1975). Adult life stages: Growth toward self-tolerance. *Psychology Today, 74,* 76–78.

Gould, R. L. (1978). *Transformations: Growth and change in adult life.* New York: Simon and Schuster.

Goulet, L. R., & Baltes, P. B. (1970). *Life-span developmental psychology: Research and theory.* New York: Academic Press.

Graber, J. A., Britto, P. R., & Brooks-Gunn, J. (1999). What's love got to do with it? Adolescents' and young adults' beliefs about sexual and romantic relationships. In W. Furman, B. B. Brown, & C. Feiring (Eds.), *The development of romantic relationships in adolescence* (pp. 364–398). Cambridge, UK: Cambridge University Press.

Gray, J. R. (2004). Integration of emotion and cognitive control. *Current Directions in Psychological Science, 13*(2), 46–48.

Greenspan, S. I. (1989). The development of the ego: Insights from clinical work with infants and young children. In S. I. Greenspan & G. H. Pollock (Eds.), *The course of life: Vol. 1. Infancy* (pp. 85–164). Madison, CT: International Universities Press.

Greenspan, S. I. (1990). How emotional development relates to learning. In S. Hanna & S. Wilford. *Floor time: Tuning in to each child* (pp 1–4). New York: Scholastic.

Greenspan, S. I. (1992). *Infancy and early childhood: The practice of clinical assessment and intervention with emotional and developmental challenges.* Madison, CT: International Universities Press.

Greenspan, S. I., & Benderly, B. L. (1997). *The growth of the mind: And the endangered origins of intelligence.* Reading, MA: Addison-Wesley.

Greenspan, S. I., & Breslau-Lewis, N. (1999). *Building healthy minds: The six experiences that create intelligence and emotional growth in babies and young children.* Cambridge, MA: Perseus.

Greenspan, S. I., & Greenspan, N. T. (1985). *First feelings: Milestones in the emotional development of the child.* New York: Viking.

Griffin, S. A., Case, R., & Siegler, R. S. (1994). Rightstart: Providing the central conceptual prerequisites for first formal learning of arithmetic to students at risk for school failure. In K. McGilly (Ed.), *Classroom lessons: Integrating cognitivie theory and classroom practice* (pp. 24–49). Cambridge, MA: MIT Press.

Groffmann, K. J. (1970). Life span developmental psychology in Europe: Past and present. In L. R. Goulet & P. B. Baltes (Eds.), *Life-span developmental psychology: Research and theory* (pp. 54–68). New York: Academic Press.

Gron, G., Wunderlich, A., Spitzer, M., Tomczak, R., & Riepe, M. (2000). Brain activation during human navigation: Gender different neural networks as substrate of performance. *Nature Neuroscience, 3*(4), 404–408.

Gruber, A. (1973). *Foster home care in Massachusetts: A study of foster children, their biological and foster parents.* Boston: Commonwealth of Massachusetts, Governors' Commission on Adoption and Foster Care.

Guastello, S. J. (1997). Science evolves: An introduction to nonlinear dynamics, psychology, and life sciences. *Nonlinear Dynamics, Psychology, and Life Sciences, 1*(1), 1–6.

Guastello, S. J., Hyde, T., & Odak, M. (1998). Symbolic dynamic patterns of verbal exchange in a creative problem solving group. *Nonlinear Dynamics, Psychology, and Life Sciences, 2*(1), 35–58.

Guilford, J. P. (1956). *The nature of human intelligence.* New York: McGraw-Hill.

Guilford, J. P., & Zimmerman, W. S. (1956). Fourteen dimensions of temperament. Washington: *Monograph of the American Psychological Association, 70*(10), 1–26.

Gump, L. S., Baker, R. C., & Roll, S. (2000). Cultural and gender differences in moral judgment: A study of Mexican Americans and Anglo-Americans, *Hispanic Journal of Behavioral Sciences, 22*(1), 78–93.

Hall, C. S., & Lindzey, G. (1957). *Theories of personality.* New York: Wiley (2nd ed, 1970).

Hall, G. S. (1920). *Youth.* New York: Appleton-Century.

Hall, G. S. (1923). *Life and confessions of a psychologist.* New York: D. Appleton.

Hall, G. S. (1924). *Adolescence: Its psychology and its relations to physiology, anthropology, sociology, sex, crime, religion and education.* New York: D. Appleton.

Hanlon, H. Thatcher, R., & Cline, M. (1999). Gender differences in the development of EEG coherence in normal children. *Developmental Neuropsychology, 16*(3), 479–506.

Hanna, S., Wilford, S., Benham, H., & Carter, J. (1990). *Floor time: Tuning in to each child. A professional development program guide.* New York: Scholastic.

Hardy, M. S. (1995). The development of gender roles: Societal influences. In L. Diamant & R. D. McAnulty (Eds.), *The psychology of sexual orientation, behavior, and identity: A handbook* (pp.425–443). Westport, CT: Greenwood.

Harter, S. (1983). Developmental perspectives on the self-system. In P. H. Musson (Series Ed.) & E. M. Heterington (Vol Ed.), *Handbook of child psychology: Vol 4. Socialization, personality, and social development* (4th ed., pp. 275–386). New York: Wiley.

Harter, S. (1985). *Manual for the self-perception profile for children.* Denver, CO: University of Denver.

Heider, F. (1958). *The psychology of interpersonal relations.* New York: Wiley.

Herbert, N. (1985) *Quantum reality: Beyond the new physics.* New York: Random House.

Hetherington, E. M., & Blechman, E. A. (Eds.). (1996). *Stress, coping, and resiliency in children and families.* Mahwah, NJ: Erlbaum.

Hinde, R. A. (1982). *Ethology, its nature and relation with other sciences.* New York: Oxford University Press.

Horney, K. (1937). *The neurotic personality of our time.* New York: Norton.

Huston, A. C. (1983). Sex-typing. In E. M. Hetherington (Ed.) & P. H. Mussen (Series Ed.). *Handbook of child psychology: Vol. 4. Socialization, personality, and social development* (pp. 387–468). New York: Wiley.

Huston-Stein, A., & Higgins-Trenk, A. (1978). Development of females from childhood through adulthood: Career and feminine role orientations. In P. Baltes (Ed.), *Life-span development and behavior* (Vol. 1, pp. 358–297). New York: Academic Press.

Ilg, F. L., & Ames, L. B. (1955). *Child behavior.* New York: Harper.

Jackson, P. B., & Berkowitz, A. (2005). The structure of the life course: Gender and racioethnic variation in the occurrence and sequencing of role transitions. In R. Macmillan (Ed.), *The structure of the life course: Standardized? Individualized? Differentiated? (Advances in life course research, Vol. 9)* (pp. 55–90). London: Elsevier.

James, W. (1982). *Psychology: the briefer course.* New York: Holt, Rinehart & Winston.

Jung, C. G. (1917). *Collected papers on analytical psychology* (2nd ed.) (C. E. Long, Trans.). New York: Moffat, Yard.

Jusczyk, P. W. (1995). Language acquisition: Speech sounds and phonological development. In J. L. Miller & P. D. Eimas (Eds.), *Handbook of perception and cognition: Vol. II. Speech, language and communication.* San Diego: Academic Press.

Kail, R. V. (1979). *The development of memory in children.* San Francisco: Freeman.

Kail, R. V. (1998). *Children and their development.* Upper Saddle, NJ: Prentice Hall.

Kail, R. V. (1991). Processing speed declines exponentially with age during childhood and adolescence. *Developmental Psychology, 27,* 259–266.

Kail, R. V., & Bisanz, J. (1992). The information processing perspective on cognitive development in childhood and adolescence. In R. J. Sternberg & C. A. Berg (Eds.), *Intellectual development* (pp. 229–260). New York: Cambridge University Press.

Kail, R. V., Pellegrino, J., & Carter, P. (1980). Developmental change in mental rotation. Journal of Experimental Child Psychology 29, 102–116

Kasen, S., Vaughan, R. D., & Walter, H. J. (1992). Self-efficacy for AIDS prevention behaviors among tenth grade students. *Heath Education Quarterly, 19,* 187–202.

Kauth, M. R., & Kalichman, S. C. (1995). Sexual orientation and development: An interactive approach. In L. Diamant & R. D. McAnulty (Eds.), *The psychology of sexual orientation, behavior, and identity: A handbook* (pp. 81–103). Westport, CT: Greenwood.

Kendler, H. H., & Kendler, T. S. (1962). Vertical and horizontal procedures in problem solving. *Psychological Review, 60*, 1–16.

Klein, M. (1949). *The psychoanalysis of children.* London: Hogarth.

Kohlberg, L. K. (1966). A cognitive–developmental analysis of children's sex-role concepts and attitudes. In E. E. Maccoby (Ed.), *The development of sex differences* (pp. 82–172). New York: Holt, Rinehart, and Winston.

Kohlberg, L. (1970). Education for justice: A modern statement of the Platonic view. In N. Sizer & T. Sizer, (Eds.), *Five lectures on moral education.* Cambridge, MA: Harvard University Press.

Kohlberg, L. (1973). Continuities in childhood and adult moral development revisited. In P. B. Baltes & K. W. Schaie (Eds.), *Life-span developmental psychology: Personality and socialization* (pp. 180–207). New York: Academic Press.

Kohlberg, L. (1987). *The philosophy of moral development: Moral stages and the idea of justice.* San Francisco: Harper & Row.

Kohlberg, L., & DeVries, R. (1987). *Child psychology and childhood education: A cognitive-developmental view.* New York: Longman.

Kohlberg, L., & Kramer, R. (1969). Continuities and discontinuities in childhood and adult moral development. *Human Development, 12*, 93–120.

Koopmans, M. (1998). Chaos theory and the problem of change in family systems. *Nonlinear Dynamics, Psychology, and Life Sciences, 2*(2), 133–148.

Kosko, B. (1993). *Fuzzy thinking.* New York: Hyperion.

Kubler-Ross, E. (1969). *On death and dying.* New York: Collier.

Kuhl, P. K., Conboy, B. T., Padden, D., Nelson, T., & Pruitt, J. (2005). Early speech perception and later language development: Implications for the "critical period." *Language Learning and Development, 1*(3 & 4), 237–264.

Kuhn, D. (2006). Do cognitive changes accompany developments in the adolescent brain? *Perspectives on Psychological Science, 1*(1), 59–67.

Kurzwell, R. (2006). The future of human-machine intelligence. *The Futurist, 40*(2), 39–40, 42–46.

Kwon, Y., & Lawson, A. E. (2000). Linking brain growth with the development of scientific reasoning ability and conceptual change during adolescence. *Journal of Research in Science Teaching, 37*(1), 44–62.

Labouvie-Vief, G. (1977), Adult cognitive development: In search of alternative interpretations. *Merrill-Palmer Quarterly, 33*, 227–263.

Labouie-Vief, G. (1980). Beyond formal operations: Uses and limits of pure logic in life span development. *Human Development, 23*, 141–161.

Labouvie-Vief, G. (1990). Wisdom as integrated thought: Historical and developmental perspectives. In R. J. Sternberg (Ed.), *Wisdom: Its nature, origins, and development.* Cambridge: Cambridge University Press.

Labouvie-Vief, G. (1992). A neo-Piagetian perspective on adult cognitive development. In R. J. Sternberg & C. A. Berg (Eds.), *Intellectual development* (pp. 197–228). New York: Cambridge University Press.

Labouvie-Vief, G., & Chandler, M. J. (1978). Cognitive development and life-span developmental theory: Idealistic versus contextual perspectives. In P. Baltes (Ed.), *Life-span development and behavior* (Vol. 1, pp. 182–211). New York: Academic Press.

Lang, F. R. (2004). The filial task in mid-life: Ambivalence and the quality of adult children's relationships with their older parents. In K. Pillemer & K. Luscher (Eds.), *Intergenerational ambivalences: New perspectives on parent–child relations in later life* (pp. 183–206). Amsterdam: Elsevier.

Lenneberg, E. H. (1964). A biological perspective of language. In E. H. Lenneberg (Ed.), *New directions in the study of language.* Cambridge, MA: MIT Press.

Lerner, R. M., & Ryff, C. D. (1978). Implementing the life-span view: Attachment. In P. B. Baltes (Ed.), *Life-span development and behavior* (Vol. 1, pp. 1–44). New York: Academic Press.

Levine, R. L., & Fitzgerald, H. E. (1992). *Analysis of dynamic psychological systems: Methods and applications* (Vol. 2). New York: Plenum Press.

Levinson, D. J. (1986). A conception of adult development. *American Psychologist, 41,* 3–8, 13.

Lewin, K. (1931). Environmental forces in child behavior and development. In C. Murchison (Ed.), *A handbook of child psychology* (pp. 94–127). Worcester, MA: Clark University Press.

Lewin, K. (1936). *Principles of topological psychology.* New York: McGraw-Hill.

Lichtman, J. W. (2001). Developmental neurobiology overview: Synapses, circuits, and plasticity. In D. B. Bailey, J. T. Bruer, F. J. Symons, & J. W. Lichtman (Eds.), *Critical thinking about critical periods* (pp. 27–44). Baltimore: Paul Brookes.

Lillard, A. (2001). Explaining the connection: Pretend play and theory of mind. In S. Reifel (Ed.), *Theory in context and out: Vol 3. Play and culture studies* (pp.173–178). Westport, CT: Ablex.

Lo, L. N. K. (1987). Mao Zedong's developmental theories and their influence on contemprorary Chinese education. *The Chinese University Education Journal, 15*(2), 26–38.

Locke, J. (1910). Some thoughts concerning education. In C. W. Eliot (Ed.), *English philosophers,* Vol. 37. New York: Villier. (Original work published 1693).

Lovaas, O. I. (2002). *Teaching individuals with developmental delays: Basic intervention techniques.* Austin, TX: Pro-Ed.

Luria, A. R. (1979).*The making of mind: A personal account of Soviet psychology.* Cambridge, MA: Harvard University Press.

Luria, A. R., & Yudovich, F. Ia. (1971). *Speech and the development of mental processes in the child.* Middlesex, UK: Penguin.

Maccoby, E. (2003). The gender of child and parent as factors in family dynamics. In A. C. Crouter & A. Booth (Eds.), *Children's influence on family dynamics: The neglected side of family relationships* (pp. 191–206). Mahwah, NJ: Erlbaum.

Maccoby, E. (2004). Aggression in the context of gender development. In M. Putallaz & K. L. Bierman (Eds.), *Aggression, antisocial behavior, and violence among girls: A developmental perspective* (pp. 3–22). New York: Guilford.

Maccoby, E., & Jacklin, C. (1975). *The psychology of sex differences.* Stanford, CA: Stanford University Press.

Macdonald, C. (Ed.). (1995). *Connectionism: Debates on psychological explanation.* Oxford, UK: Blackwell.

Macleod, C. E. (2005). Cerebellar anatomy and function: From the corporeal to the cognitive. In S. T. Parker, J. Langer, & C. Milbrath (Eds.), *Biology and knowledge revisited: From neurogenesis to psychogenesis* (pp. 145–177). Mahwah, NJ: Erlbaum.

Main, M., & Goldwyn, R. (1984). Predicting rejection of her infant from mothers' representation of her own experience. *Child Abuse and Neglect, 8,* 203–217.

Main, M., & Solomon, J. (1990). Procedures for identifying infants disorganized/disoriented during the Ainsworth strange situation. In M. Greenberg, D. Cicchetti, & E. Cummings (Eds.), *Attachment in the preschool years: Theory, research, ad intervention* (pp. 121–160). Chicago: University of Chicago Press.

Maio, G. R., Fincham, F. D., Regalia, C., & Paleari, F. G. (2004). Ambivalence and attachment in family relationships. In K. Pillemer & K. Luscher (Eds.), *Intergenerational ambivalences: New perspectives on parent-child relations in later life* (pp. 285–312). Amsterdam: Elsevier.

Mann, H. (1868). *Annual reports on education.* Boston: H. B. Fuller.

Marcia, J. E. (1966). Development and validation of ego-identity stages. *Journal of Personality and Social Psychology, 3,* 551–558.

Marger, M. N., & Obermiller, P. J. (1982, April). *Urban Appalachian and Canadian Maritime Migrants: A comparative study of emergent ethnicity.* Paper presented at the Annual Meeting of the Southern Sociological Society, Memphis.

Marks-Tarlow, T. (1999). The self as a dynamical system. *Nonlinear Dynamics, Psychology, and Life Sciences, 3*(4), 311–345.

Martin, R. M. (1998). Approaches to the sense of humor: A historical review. In W. Ruch (Ed.), *The sense of humor: Explorations of a personality characteristic* (pp. 15–62). Berlin: Mouton de Gruyter.

McAdoo, H. P. (1999). Stress absorbing systems in black families. In R. M. Lerner & J. V. Lerner (Eds.), *Adolescence: Development, diversity, and context* (pp. 61–82). New York: Garland.

McGhee, P. (1971). Cognitive development and children's comprehension of humor. *Child Development, 42,* 123–138.

McGraw, M. B. (1935). *Growth: A study of Johnny and Jimmy.* New York: Appleton-Century-Crofts.

Meltzoff, A. N., & Moore, M. K. (1994). Imitation, memory, and the representation of Persons Infant Behavior and Development 17, 83–99.

Meltzoff, A. N., & Moore, M. K. (1999). A new foundation for cognitive development in infancy: The birth of the representational infant. In E. K. Scholnick, K. Nelson, S. A. Gelman, & P. H. Miller (Eds.), *Piaget's legacy* (pp. 53–78). Mahwah, NJ: Erlbaum.

Menyuk, P. (1969). *Sentences children use.* Cambridge, MA: MIT Press.

Metzger, M. A. (1997). Applications of nonlinear dynamical systems theory in developmental psychology: Motor and cognitive development. *Nonlinear Dynamics, Psychology, and Life Sciences, 1*(1), 55–68.

Miller, P. H. (2002). *Theories of developmental psychology* (4th ed.). New York: Worth.

Montessori, M. (1965). *Dr. Montessori's own handbook.* New York: Schocken. (Original work published 1914).

Montessori, M. (1972). *The discovery of the child* (6th ed.). (M. J. Costelloe, Trans.). New York: Ballentine.

Morris, S. R. (1998). No learning by coercion: Paidia and Paideia in Platonic Philosophy. In D. P. Fromberg & D. Bergen (Eds.), *Play from birth to twelve and beyond: Contexts, perspectives and meanings* (pp. 109–118). New York: Garland.

Mortimer, J. T., Oesterle, S., & Kruger, H. (2005). Age norms, institutional structures, and the timing of markers of transition to adulthood. In R. Macmillan (Ed.), *The structure of the life course: Standardized? Individualized? Differentiated? (Advances in life course research, Vol. 9)* (pp. 175–203). London: Elsevier.

Mussen, P., & Eisenberg-Berg, N. (1977). *Roots of caring, sharing, and helping: The development of prosocial behavior in children.* San Francisco: W. H. Freeman.

Nachmanovich, S. (1990). *Free play.* Los Angeles: Tarcher.

Nelson, K. (1973). Structure and strategy in learning to talk. *Society for Research in Child Development Monographs, 38,*(1-2 Serial No. 149).

Nelson, K. (1993). The psychological & social origins of autobiographical memory. *Psychological Science,* 4(1) 7–14

Nelson, K. (1981). Social cognition in a script framework. In J. H. Flavell & L. Ross (Eds.), *Social-cognitive development: Frontiers and possible futures* (pp. 97–118). New York: Cambridge University Press.

Nelson, K. (1997). Cognitive Change as collobarative construction. In E. Amsel & K. A. Renninger (Eds.), Change & Development: Issue of Theory Method, & Application (pp. 99–115). Mahwah, NJ: Erlbaum.

Nelson, K., Henseler, S., & Plesa, D. (2000). Entering a community of minds: "Theory of mind" from a feminist standpoint. In P. H. Miller & E. K. Scholnick (Eds.), *Toward a feminist developmental psychology* (pp. 1–61). London: Routledge.

Nelson, K., & Shaw, L. K. (2002). Developing a socially shared symbolic system. In E. Amsel & J. P. Byrnes (Eds.), *Language, literacy, and cognitive development: The development and consequences of symbolic communication* (pp. 27–57). Mahwah, NJ: Erlbaum.

Neubauer, P. B., & Neubauer, A. (1996). *Nature's thumbprint: The new genetics of personality.* New York: Columbia University Press.

Neugarten, B. L. (1964). *Personality in middle and late life: Empirical studies.* New York: Atherton Press.

Neugarten, B. L. (Ed.). (1968). *Middle age and aging: A reader in social psychology.* Chicago: University of Chicago Press.

Neugarten, B. L. (1996). *The meanings of age: Selected papers of Bernice L. Neugarten.* Chicago: University of Chicago Press.

Neugarten, B. L. (1973). Sociological perspectives on the life cycle. In P. B. Baltes & K. W. Schaie (Eds.), *Life-span developmental psychology: Personality and socialization* (pp. 53–71). New York: Academic Press.

Newell, K. M. (1997). Comment on Clark. In C. Dent-Read & P. Zukow-Goldring (Eds.), *Evolving explanations of development: Ecological approaches to organism-environment systems* (pp. 407–412). Washington, DC: American Psychological Association.

Nucci, L. P., & Turiel, E. (2000). The moral and the personal: Sources of social conflicts. In L. P. Nucci, G. B. Saxe, & E. Turiel (Eds.), *Culture, thought and development* (pp. 115–140). Mahwah, NJ: Erlbaum.

Ogbu, J. U. (1981). Origins of human competence: A cultural–ecological perspective. *Child Development, 52,* 413–429.

Ogbu, J. U. (1986). The consequences of the American caste system. In U. Neisser (Ed.), *The school achievement of minority children: New perspectives* (pp. 19–56). Hillsdale, NJ: Erlbaum.

Ogbu, J. U. (1992). Understanding cultural diversity and learning. *Educational Researcher, 21*(8), 5–14.

Ogbu, J. U. (1994). From cultural differences to differences in cultural frame of reference. In P. M. Greenfield & R. R. Cocking (Eds.), *Cross-cultural roots of minority child development* (pp. 365–392). Hillsdale, NJ: Erlbaum.

Ogbu, J. U. (2003). *Black American students in an affluent suburb: A study of academic disengagement.* Mawah, NJ: Erlbaum

Pajeres, F. (2002). *Overview of social cognitive theory of self-efficacy.* Retreived March 10, 2005, from http://www.emory.edu/EDUCATION/mfp/eff.html

Panksepp, J. (1989). The neurobiology of emotions: Of animal brains and human feelings. In T. Manstead & H. Wagner (Eds.), *Handbook of psychophysiology* (pp. 5–26). Chichester, UK: Wiley.

Panksepp, J. (1998a). *Affective neuroscience: The foundations of human and animal emotions.* New York: Oxford University Press.

Panksepp, J. (1998b). Attention deficit hyperactivity disorders, psychostimulants, and intolerance of childhood playfulness: A tragedy in the making? *Current Directions in Psychological Science, 7*(3), 91–98.

Partridge, T. (2000), Temperament development modeled as a nonlinear complex adaptive system. *Nonlinear Dynamics, Psychology, and Life Sciences, 4*(4), 339–357.

Pascual-Leone, J. (1970). A mathematical model for the transition rule in Piaget's developmental stages. *Acta Psychologica, 32,* 301–345.

Pascual-Leone, J. (1980). Constructive problems for constructive theories: The current relevance of Piaget's work and a critique of information-processing simulation psychology. In R. Kluwe & H. Spade (Eds.), *Development models of thinking* (pp. 263–296). New York: Academic Press.

Pascual-Leone, J. (2000). Reflections on working memory: Are the two models complementary? *Journal of Experimental Child Psychology, 77,* 138–154.

Paul, R., & Elder, L. (2003). *How to study and learn a discipline: Using critical thinking concepts and tools.* Dillon Beach, CA: The Foundation for Critical Thinking.

Pelligrini, A., & Bjorklund, D. G. (1996). The place of recess in school: Issues in the role of recess in children's education and development. *Journal of Research in Childhood Education, 11*(1), 5–13.

Pepper, S. C. (1945). *World hypotheses, a study in evidence.* Los Angeles: University of California Press

Pestalozzi, J. H. (1894). *How Gertrude teaches her children* (L. E. Holland & F. E. Turner, Trans.). London: Swan Sonnenschein.

Phillips, M., Lowe, M., Lurito, J. T., Dmidizic, M., & Matthews, V. (2001). Temporal lobe activation demonstrates sex-based differences during passive listening. *Radiology, 220,* 202–207.

Piaget, J. (1924). *Judgment and reasoning in the child.* London: Routledge & Kegan Paul.

Piaget, J. (1926). *The language and thought of the child.* New York: Harcourt Brace.

Piaget, J. (1936) *Origins of intelligence in the child.* London: Routledge & Kegan Paul.

Piaget, J. (1945). *Play, dreams and imitation in childhood.* London: Heinemann.

Piaget, J. (1954). *The construction of reality in the child.* New York: Basic Books

Piaget J. (1965). *The moral judgement of the child.* New York: Norton

Piaget, J. (1968). *Six psychological studies* (A. Tenzer, Trans.). New York: Random House.

Piaget, J. (1969). *The child's conception of time.* London: Routledge.

Piaget, J. (1972a). Intellectual evolution from adolescence to adulthood. *Human Development, 15,* 1–12.

Piaget, J. (1972b). *Psychology and epistemology: Towards a theory of knowledge.* Hammondsworth, England: Penguin.

Piaget, J. (1972c). Some aspects of operations. In M. W. Piers (Ed.), *Play and development* (pp. 15–27). New York: Norton.

Piaget, J. (1976). *The grasp of consciousness* (S. Wedgwood, Trans.). Cambridge, MA: Harvard University Press.

Piaget, J. (1978). *Success and understanding* (A. J. Pomerans, Trans.). Cambridge, MA: Harvard University Press.

Piaget, J. (1985). *The equilibration of cognitive structures.* Chicago: University of Chicago Press.

Piaget, J., & Garcia, R. (1991). *Toward a logic of meanings.* Hillsdale, NJ: Erlbaum.

Piaget, J., & Inhelder, B. (1969). *The psychology of the child.* New York: Basic Books.

Piaget, J., Inhelder, B., & Sinclair-De Zwart, H. (1973). *Memory and intelligence* (A. J. Pomerans, Trans.). New York: Basic Books.

Pick, A. (1997). Perceptual learning, categorizing, and cognitive development. In C. Dent-Read & P. Zukow-Goldring (Eds.), *Evolving explanations of development:*

*Ecological approaches to organism-environment systems* (pp. 335–370). Washington, DC: American Psychological Association.

Pina, D. L., & Bengston, V. I. (1993). The division of household labor and wives' happiness: Ideology, employment, and perceptions of social support. *Journal of Marriage and the Family, 55,* 901–912.

Pinker, S. (1997). Evolutionary biology and the evolution of language. In A. B. Scheibel & J. W. Schopf (Eds.), *The origin and evolution of intelligence* (pp. 137–160). Boston: Jones & Bartlett.

Pinker, S. (2002). *The blank slate: The modern denial of human nature.* New York: Viking.

Pinker, S., & Prince, A. (1988). On language and connectionism: Analysis of a parallel distributed processing model of language acquisition. *Cognition, 23,* 73–193.

Plomin, R. (1986). *Development, genetics, and psychology.* Hillsdale, NJ: Erlbaum.

Plomin, R. (1989). Environment and genes: Determinants of behavior. *American Psychologist, 44*(2), 105–111.

Plomin, R. (1994). *Genetics and experience: The interplay between nature and nurture* (Vol. 6). Thousand Oaks, CA: Sage.

Power, F. C., Higgins, A., & Kohlberg, L. (1989). *Lawrence Kohlberg's approach to moral education.* New York: Columbia University Press.

Putallaz, M. & Bierman, K. L. (2004). *Agression, antisocial behavior, and violence among girls: A developmental perspective.* New York: Guilford Press.

Ransbury, M. K. (1991). Friedrich Froebel 1782–1982: A reexamination of Froebel's principles of childhood learning. In J. D. Quisenberry, E. A. Eddowes, & S. L. Robinson (Eds.), *Readings from Childhood Education* (Vol. 2.) Wheaton, MD: ACEI.

Rapaport, J. L., Giedd, J. N., Blumenthal, J., Hamburger, S., Jeffries, N., Fernandez, T., et al., (1999). Progressive cortical change during adolescence in childhood-onset schizophrenia: A longitudinal magnetic resonance imaging study. *Archives of General Psychiatry, 56*(7), 649–654.

Rest, J., Narvacz, D., Bebeau, M. J., & Thoma, S. J. (1999). *Postconventional moral thinking: A neo-Kohlbergian approach.* Mahwah, NJ: Erlbaum.

Rheingold, H. L., & Cook, K. V. (1975). The contents of boys' and girls' rooms as an index of parents' behavior. *Child Development, 46,* 459–463.

Richardson, K. (2000). *Developmental psychology: How nature and nurture interact.* Mahwah, NJ: Erlbaum.

Riegel, L. F. (1976). The dialectics of human development. *American Psychologist, 31,* 689–698.

Roazen, P. (1975). *Freud and his followers.* New York: Alfred Knopf.

Roberton, M. A. (1993). New ways to think about old questions. In L. Smith & E. Thelen (Eds.), *A dynamic systems approach to development: Applications* (pp. 95–117). Cambridge: MIT.

Robertson, J., & Robertson, J. (1953). *A two-year-old goes to hospital.* London: Tavistock Clinic.

Robila, M. (Ed.). (2004). *Families in Eastern Europe*. Amsterdam: Elsevier.

Rogoff, B. (1990). *Apprenticeship in thinking: Cognitive development in social context*. New York: Oxford University Press.

Rogoff, B. (1993). Children's guided participation and participatory appropriation in sociocultural activity. In R. H. Wozniak & K. W. Fischer (Eds.), *Development in contexts: Acting and thinking in specific environments* (pp. 121–154.) Hillsdale, NJ: Erlbaum.

Rogoff, B. (1997). Evaluating development in the process of participation: Theory, methods, and practice building on each other. In E. Amsel & K. A. Renniger (Eds.), *Change and development: Issues of theory, method and application* (pp. 265–285). Mahwah, NJ: Erlbaum.

Rogoff, B. (2003). *The cultural nature of human development*. New York: Oxford University Press.

Rogoff, B., & Angelillo C. (2002). Investigating the coordinated functioning of multifaceted cultural practices in human development. *Human Development, 45,* 211–225.

Rogoff, B., & Morelli, G. (1989). Perspectives on children's development from cultural psychology. *American Psychologist, 44*(2), 343–348.

Roopnarine, J. L., Hooper, F. H., Ahmeduzzaman, M., & Pollack, B. (1993). In K. MacDonald (Ed.), *Parent–child play: Descriptions and implications* (pp. 287–304). Albany: State University of New York.

Roser, M., & Gazzaniga, M. S. (2004). Automatic brains—interpretive minds. *Current Directions in Psychological Science, 13*(2), 56–59.

Rousseau, J. J. (1911). *Emile*. New York: E. P. Dutton. (original work published 1762).

Rovee-Collier, C. (1997). The development of infant memory. *Current Directions in Psychological Science, 8*(3), 80–85.

Rutter, M., Chadwick, O., Schaffer, D., & Brown, C. (1980). A prospective study of children with head injuries: Descriptions and methods. *Psychological Medicine, 10,* 633–645.

Ryff, C. D. (1995). Psychological well-being in adult life. *Current Directions in Psychological Science, 4,* 99–104.

Salthouse, T. A. (2006). Mental exercise and mental aging: Evaluating the validity of the "use it or lose it" hypothesis. *Perspectives on Psychological Science, 1*(1), 68–87.

Salthouse, T. A., & Kail, R. (1981). Memory development throughout the lifespan: The role of processing rate. In P. B. Baltes & O. G. Brin (Eds), *Lifespan Development and Behavior* (Vol 5) New York: Academic Press.

Savelabergh, G. J. P., & van der Kamp, J. (1993). The coordination of infant's reaching, grasping, catching and posture: A natural physical approach. In G. J. P. Savelabergh (Ed.), *The development of coordination in infancy* (pp. 289–358). Amsterdam: Elsevier.

Scarr, S. (1984). *Mother care other care*. New York: Basic Books.

Scarr, S. (1992). Developmental theories for the 1990's: Developmental and individual differences. *Child Development, 63*, 1–19.

Scarr, S., & McCartney, K. (1983). How people make their own environments: A theory of geneotype-environmental effects. *Child Development, 54*(2), 424–435.

Scarr, S., & Weinberg, R. A. (1983). The Minnesota Adoption Studies: Genetic differences and malleability. *Child Development, 54*(2), 260–268.

Schaie, K. W. (2005). *Developmental influences on adult intelligence: The Seattle longitudinal study.* New York: Oxford University Press.

Schaie, K. W., & Willis, S. L. (1991). *Adult development and aging* (3rd ed). New York: HarperCollins.

Schunk, D. H. (1987). Peer models and children's behavioral change. *Review of Educational Research, 57*, 149–174.

Segalowitz, S. J. (1994). Developmental psychology and brain development: A historical perspective. In G. Dawson & K. W. Fischer (Eds.), *Human behavior and the developing brain.* New York: Guilford.

Shaw, J. (2005). The aging enigma: Scientists probe the genetic basis of longevity. *Harvard Magazine, 108*(1), 46–53, 91.

Sherman, L., Schmuck, R. A., & Schmuck, P. A. (2004, September). *Kurt Lewin's contribution to the theory and practice of education in the United States: The importance of cooperative learning.* Symposium presentation at the International Conference on Kurt Lewin: Contribution to Contemporary Psychology, Moglino, Poland.

Siegler, R. (1983). Information processing approaches to development. In P. H. Mussen (Ed.), *Handbook of child psychology* (4th ed., Vol. 1, pp. 129–213). New York: Wiley.

Siegler, R. (1988). Individual differences in strategy choices: Good students, not-so-good students, and perfectionists. *Child Development, 59*, 832–851.

Siegler, R. (1997). Concepts and methods for studying cognitive change. In E. Amsel & K. A. Renninger (Eds.), *Change and development: Issues of theory, method, and application* (pp. 77–97). Mahwah, NJ: Erlbaum.

Siegler, R. (2002). Microgenetic studies of self-explanations. In N. Granott & J. Parziale (Eds.), *Microdevelopment: Transition processes in development and learning* (pp. 31–58). New York: Cambridge University Press.

Sinclair, H. (1992). Changing perspectives on child language acquisition. In H. Beilin & P. B. Pufall (Eds.), *Piaget's theory: Prospects and possibilities* (pp. 211–288). Hillsdale, NJ: Erlbaum.

Siviy, S. M. (2002). Neurobiological substrates of play behavior: Glimpses into the structure and function of mammalian playfulness. In M. Bekoff & J. Byers (Eds.), *Animal play: Evolutionary, comparative, and ecological perspectives.* New York: Cambridge University Press.

Skinner, B. F. (1945a, October). *Baby in a box.* Ladies' Home Journal, 98–104.

Skinner, B. F. (1945b). *Verbal behavior.* New York: Appleton-Century-Crofts.

Skinner, B. F. (1974). *About behaviorism.* New York: Knopf.

Skouteris, H., McKenzie, B. E., & Day, R. H. (1992). Integration of sequential information for shape perception by infants: A developmental study. *Child Development, 63,* 1164–1176.

Slobin, D. L. (1971). *Psycholinguistics.* Glenview, IL: Scott, Foresman.

Smolucha, F. (2003). The teening of preschool play. Contemporary perspectives on play in early childhood education. In O. N. Saracho & B. Spodek (Eds.), *Contemporary Perspectives in Early Childhood Education* (pp. 153–170). Greenwich, CT: Information Age Publishing.

Snarey, J. R. (1985). Cross-cultural universality of social–moral development: A critical review of Kohlbergian research. *Psychological Bulletin, 97*(2), 202–232.

Spiegel, A. (2005, March). Freud's nephew and the origins of public relations [Radio series episode]. In *Morning Edition.* Washington, DC: National Public Radio.

Spodek, B. (1989). Chinese kindergarten education and its reform.*Early Childhood Research Quarterly, 4,* 31–50.

Spodek, B., & Saracho, O. N. (1998). The challenge of educational play. In D. Bergen (Ed.), *Play as a medium for learning and development* (pp. 9–22). Portsmouth, NH: Heinemann.

Stein, R. (1991). *Psychoanalytic theories of affect.* New York: Praeger.

Sternberg, R. J. (1984). Higher order reasoning in postformal operational thought. In M. L. Commons, F. A. Richards, & C. Armon (Eds.), *Beyond formal operations: Late adolescent and adult cognitive development* (pp. 74–91). New York: Praeger.

Stevenson, H. W., Lee, S. Y., & Stigler, J. (1981, Summer). The reemergence of child development in the Peoples Republic of China. *Newsletter of the Society for Research in Child Development,* 1–5.

Swinnen, S., Heuer, H., Massion, J., & Casaer, P. (1994). *Interlimb coordination.* New York: Academic Press.

Thelen, E. (1984). Learning to walk: Ecological demands and phylogenetic constratints. In L. P. Lipsett & C. Rovee-Collier (Eds.), *Advances in infancy research* (Vol. 3, pp. ). Norwood, NJ: Ablex.

Thelen, E. (1989). The rediscovery of motor learning: Learning new things from an old field. *Developmental Psychology, 25*(6), 946–950.

Thelen, E. (2003). Grounded in the world: Developmental origins of the embodied mind. In W. Tschacher & J. P. Danwalder (Eds.), *The dynamical systems approach to cognition: Concepts and empirical paradigms based on self-organization, embodiment, and coordination dynamics. Studies of nonlinear phenomena in life science* (Vol. 10, pp. 17–44). London: World Scientific.

Thelen, E., & Adolph, K. E. (1992). Arnold Gesell: The paradox of nature and nurture. *Developmental Psychology, 28*(3), 368–380.

Thelen, E., & Smith, L. B. (1994). *A dynamic systems approach to the development of cognition and action.* Boston: MIT Press.

Thomas, A., Chess, S., Birch, H. G., Hertzig, M. E., & Korn, S. (1963). *Behavioral individuality in early childhood.* New York: New York University Press.

Thomas, A., Chess, S., & Birch, H. G. (1970). The origin of personality. *Scientific American, 223*, 102, 104–109.

Thomas, R. M. (2005). *Comparing theories of child development.* Belmont, CA: Thomson/Wadsworth.

Thorndike, E. L. (1914). *Educational psychology* (Vol. 3). New York: Teachers College Press.

Thornton, S. P. (2005). Sigmund Freud. In J. Fieser & B. Dowden (Eds.), The Internet Encyclopedia of Philosophy. Retrieved from http://www.iep.utm.edu/f/freud

Torgesen, J. K., Wagner, R. K., & Rashotle, CA. (1994). Longitudinal studies of phonological processing and reading. Journal of Learning Disabilities, 27(5), 276–286

Tomasello, M. (1999). *The cultural origins of human cognition.* Cambridge, MA: Harvard University Press.

Tomasello, M. (2003). *Constructing a language: A usage-based theory of language acquisition.* Cambridge, MA: Harvard University Press.

Tschacher, W., & Danwalder, J. P. (Eds.). (2003). *The dynamical systems approach to cognition: Concepts and empirical paradigms based on self-organization, embodiment, and coordination dynamics. Studies of nonlinear phenomena in life science, Vol. 10.* London: World Scientific.

Tucker, P. (2005). Stay-at-home dads. *The Futurist, 39*(5), 12–13.

Turiel, E. (1978). Social regulations and domains of social structure. In W. Damon (Ed.), *New directions in child development: Social cognition* (No. 1, pp. 45–74). San Francisco: Jossey-Bass.

Turiel, E. (1983). *The development of social knowledge.* Cambridge: Cambridge University Press.

Turiel, E. (2002). *The culture of morality: Social development, context, and conflict.* Cambridge: Cambridge University Press.

Turvey, M. T., & Carello, C. (1995). Some dynamical themes in perception and action. In R. E. Port & T. vanGelder (Eds.), *Mind as motion* (pp. 373–401). Cambridge: MIT Press.

U. S. Bureau of Labor Statistics. (2003). *American time use survey.* Retrieved from http://www.bis.gov/tus/home.htm

Valliant, G. E. (1977). *Adaptation to life.* Boston: Little, Brown.

Valliant, G. E. (2002). *Aging well: Surprising guideposts to a happier life from the landmark Harvard study of adult development.* Boston: Little, Brown.

Vanderven, K. (1998) Play, proteus, and paradox: Education for a chaotic and supersymmetric world. In D. P. Fromberg & D. Bergen (Eds.), *Play from birth to twelve and beyond: Contexts, perspectives, and meanings* (pp. 119–132). New York: Garland.

Van Geert, P. (1997). Variability and fluctuation: A dynamic view. In E. Amsel & K. A. Renninger (Eds.), *Change and development: Issues of theory, method, and application* (pp. 193–212). Mahwah, NJ: Erlbaum.

Van Geert, P. (2000). The dynamics of general developmental mechanisms: From Piaget and Vygotsky to dynamic systems models. *Current Directions in Psychological Science, 9,* 64–88.

Van Willigen, M., & Drentea, P. (2001). Benefits of equitable relationships: The impact of sense of fairness, household division of labor, and decision making power on perceived social support. *Sex Roles, 44*(9/10), 571–597.

Vygotsky, L. S. (1963). *Thought and language.* Cambridge, MA: MIT Press.

Vygotsky, L. S. (1967). Play and its role in the mental development of the child. *Soviet Psychology 5,* 6–18.

Vygotsky, L. S. (1978). *Mind in society: The development of higher psychological processes.* Cambridge, MA: Harvard University Press.

Vygotsky, L. S. (1994). The development of academic concepts in school aged children. In R. van der Veer & J. Allsiner (Eds.), *The Vygotsky reader* (T. Prout & R. van der Veer, Trans.). London: Blackwell.

Waldrop, M. M. (1992).*Complexity.* New York: Simon & Schuster.

Wang, A., & Ren, G. (2004). Zhongmei liangguo ertong ziwogainian de bijiaoyanjiu [A comparative study of self-concept of Chinese and American school age children]. *Zhongguo Xinji Weisheng Zazhi [Chinese Mental Health Journal], 18,* 204–296.

Watson, J. B. (1914). *Behavior: An introduction to comparative psychology.* New York: Holt, Rhinhart, & Winston.

Watson, J. D. (1968). *The double helix.* New York: New American Library.

Wellman, H. M. (1990). *The child's theory of mind.* Cambridge, MA: MIT.

Werner, E. E. (1992). The children of Kauai: Resiliency and recovery in adolescence and adulthood. *Journal of Adolescent Health, 13,* 262–268.

Werner, H. (1957). *Comparative psychology of mental development.* New York: International Universities Press.

Whiting, B., & Edwards, C. P. (1973). A cross-cultural analysis of sex differences in the behavior of children aged three through 11. *The Journal of Social Psychology, 91,* 171–188.

Wilson, M. N. (1989). Child development in the context of the black extended family. *American Psychologist, 44*(2), 380–385.

Zaporozhets, A. V., & Elkonin, D. B. (Eds.). (1971). *The psychology of preschool children.* Cambridge, MA: MIT Press.

# Author Index

# Subject Index